Honour in African History

This is the first published account of the role played by ideas of honour in African history from the fourteenth century to the present day. It argues that appreciation of these ideas is essential to an understanding of past and present African behaviour. Before European conquest, many African men cultivated heroic honour, others admired the civic virtues of the patriarchal householder, and women honoured one another for industry, endurance, and devotion to their families. These values both conflicted and blended with Islamic and Christian teachings. Colonial conquest fragmented heroic cultures, but inherited ideas of honour found new expression in regimental loyalty, respectability, professionalism, working-class masculinity, the changing gender relationships of the colonial order, and the nationalist movements that overthrew the old order. Today, the same inherited notions obstruct democracy, inspire resistance to tyranny, and motivate the defence of dignity in the face of AIDS.

JOHN ILIFFE is Professor of African History at Cambridge University and a Fellow of St. John's College. He is the author of many books, including *The African Poor: A History* (Cambridge, 1987) and *Africans: The History of a Continent* (Cambridge, 1995). *The African Poor* was awarded the Herskovits Prize of the African Studies Association of the United States.

African Studies Series   *107*

(continued after the index)

Honour in African History

John Iliffe
Cambridge University

CAMBRIDGE
UNIVERSITY PRESS

PUBLISHED BY THE PRESS SYNDICATE OF THE UNIVERSITY OF CAMBRIDGE
The Pitt Building, Trumpington Street, Cambridge, United Kingdom

CAMBRIDGE UNIVERSITY PRESS
The Edinburgh Building, Cambridge CB2 2RU, UK
40 West 20th Street, New York, NY 10011-4211, USA
477 Williamstown Road, Port Melbourne, VIC 3207, Australia
Ruiz de Alarcón 13, 28014 Madrid, Spain
Dock House, The Waterfront, Cape Town 8001, South Africa

http://www.cambridge.org

© John Iliffe 2005

First published 2005

Printed in the United States of America

Typeface Times 10/13 pt.   *System* LATEX 2_ε [TB]

A catalog record for this book is available from the British Library.

Library of Congress Cataloging in Publication Data

Iliffe, John.
   Honour in African history / John Iliffe.
      p. cm. – (African studies series ; 107)
   Includes bibliographical references and index.
   ISBN 0-521-83785-5 – ISBN 0-521-54685-0 (pbk.)
   1. Honor – Africa – History.   I. Title.   II. Series.
DT21.I44   2004
303.3′72′096–dc22   2004045687

ISBN 0 521 83785 5 hardback
ISBN 0 521 54685 0 paperback

FOR
JOHN LONSDALE
COLLEAGUE, FRIEND,
AND SCHOLAR

Contents

PART TWO: FRAGMENTATION AND MUTATION

Maps

Illustrations

Preface

This book draws on forty years of research and study during which I have incurred more debts of gratitude than I can list, but I am especially grateful to Cedric Barnes, Shane Doyle, Sarah Irons, Bill Noblett, John Rowe, Michael Twaddle, and the staff of the Cape Archives Depot, Cape Town.

The book is dedicated to John Lonsdale, with whom I have worked closely for almost the whole of my career. How much I have learned from him will appear from the text. How much I owe him for his unfailing enthusiasm and consideration will, I hope, appear from this dedication.

Abbreviations

ANC	African National Congress (of South Africa)
BIFAN	*Bulletin de l'Institut Français [Fondamental] de l'Afrique Noire*
CA	Cape Archives Depot, Cape Town
CAB	Cabinet [records in PRO]
CEA	*Cahiers d'Etudes Africaines*
CFA	Communauté Financière Africaine
CMS	Church Missionary Society [records in Birmingham University Library]
CO	Colonial Office [records in PRO]
CPP	Convention Peoples' Party (Ghana)
CS	Chief/Colonial Secretary
CSSH	*Comparative Studies in Society and History*
CUL	Cambridge University Library
CWM	Council for World Mission [records in SOAS Library]
DO	Dominions Office [records in PRO]
FO	Foreign Office [records in PRO]
FOCP	Foreign Office Confidential Print
ICU	Industrial and Commercial Workers Union (of South Africa)
IJAHS	*International Journal of African Historical Studies*
JACS	*Journal of African Cultural Studies*
JAH	*Journal of African History*
JES	*Journal of Ethiopian Studies*
JHSN	*Journal of the Historical Society of Nigeria*
JMAS	*Journal of Modern African Studies*
JSAS	*Journal of Southern African Studies*
KAR	King's African Rifles

KNA	Kenya National Archives
MMS	Methodist Missionary Society [records in SOAS Library]
MNA	Malawi National Archives
NS	New Series
OAU	Organisation of African Unity
PDG	Parti Démocratique de Guinée
PP	Parliamentary Papers
PRO	Public Record Office, London
RAL	*Research in African Literatures*
RH	Rhodes House, Oxford
RKA	Reichskolonialamt [records in Bundesarchiv, Berlin]
SAHJ	*South African Historical Journal*
SAIRR	South African Institute of Race Relations
S of S	Secretary of State
SOAS	School of Oriental and African Studies, London
TANU	Tanganyika African National Union [records at party headquarters]
TNA	Tanzania National Archives, Dar es Salaam
TRC	Truth and Reconciliation Commission (South Africa)
UNA	Uganda National Archives
UP	Unofficial Papers
UPC	Union des Populations de Cameroun
WAFF	West African Frontier Force
WFA	White Fathers Archives, Rome
WO	War Office [records in PRO]
ZNA	Zimbabwe National Archives

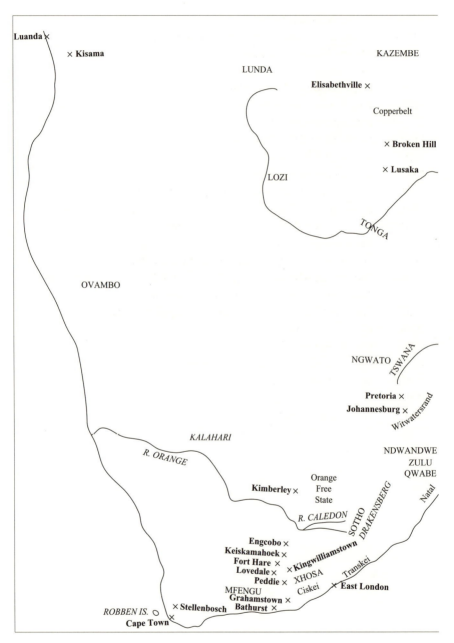

Map 1. Southern Africa

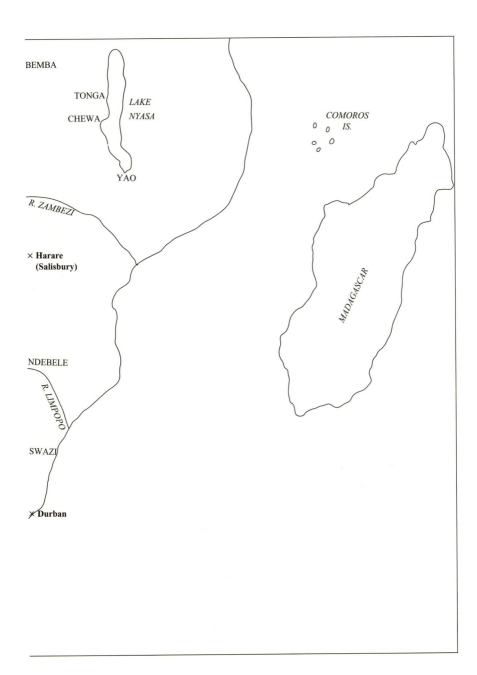

BEMBA

TONGA   *LAKE*

CHEWA   *NYASA*

     YAO

R. ZAMBEZI

× **Harare
(Salisbury)**

NDEBELE

R. LIMPOPO

SWAZI

×**Durban**

*COMOROS
IS.*

MADAGASCAR

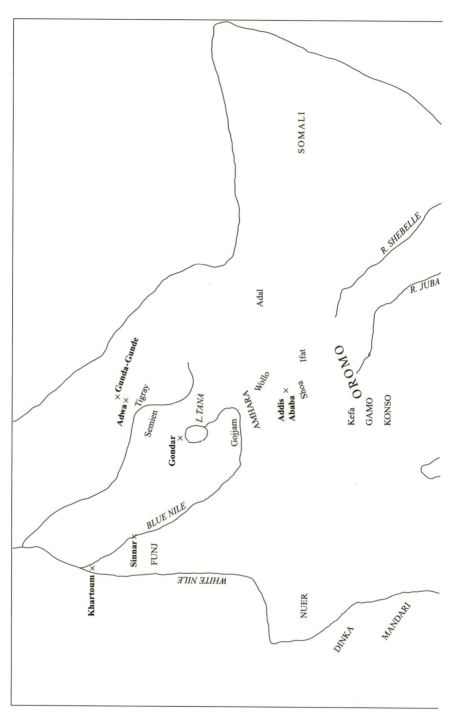

xviii

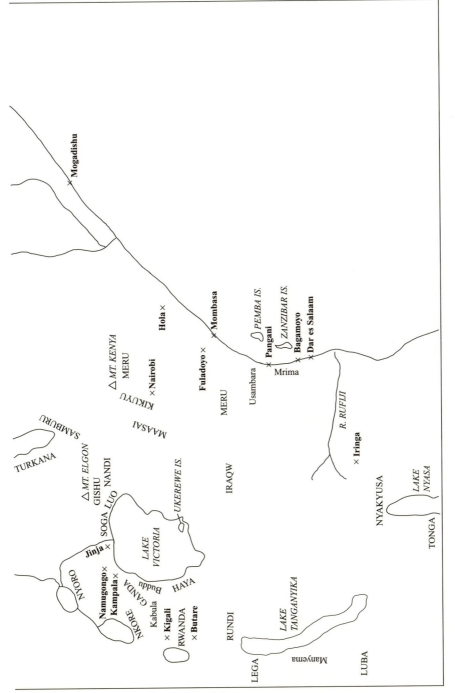

Map 2. Eastern Africa

xix

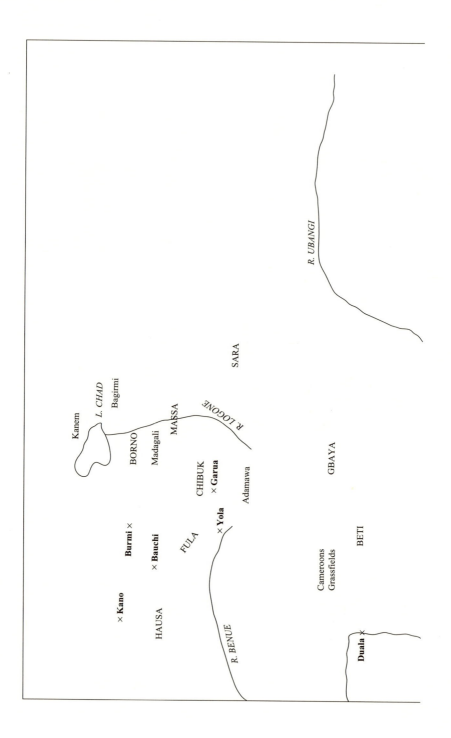

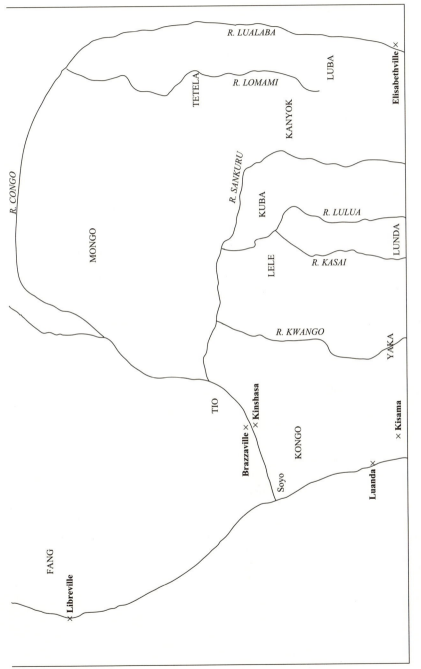

Map 3. West-Central Africa

xxi

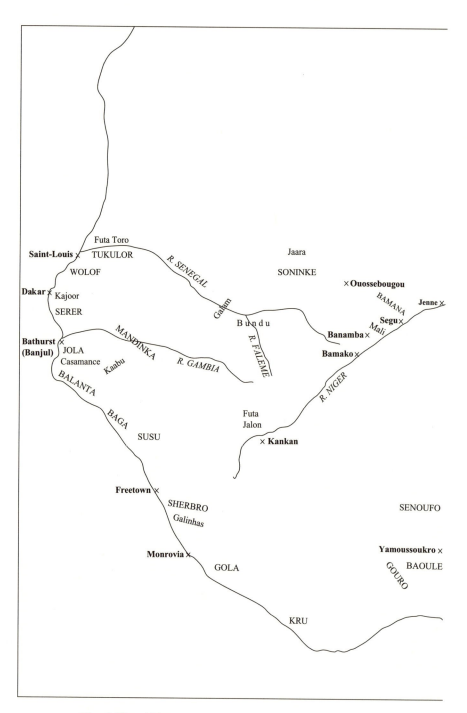

Map 4. West Africa

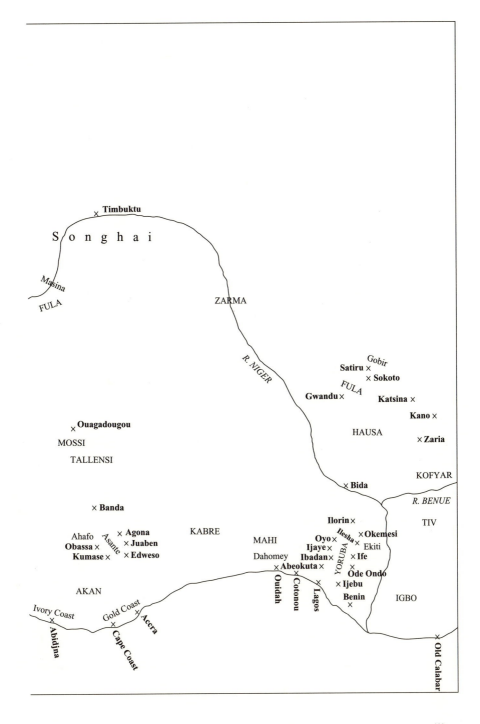

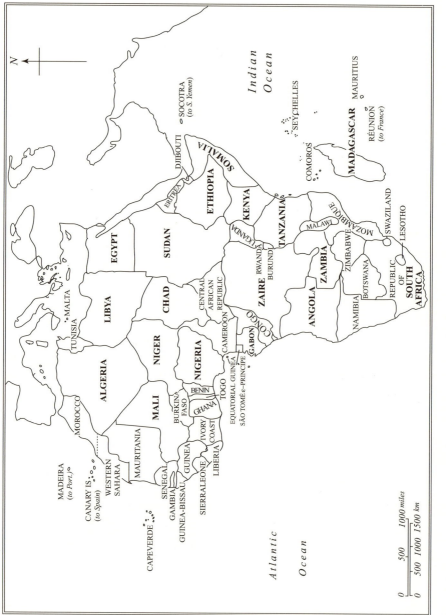

Map 5. Independent African states. *Source*: Adapted from Roland Oliver, *The African experience* (London, 1991), p. 233.

1 The Comparative History of Honour

The central argument of this book is that understanding African behaviour, in the past and the present, must take account of changing notions of honour, which historians and others have neglected.[1] Until the coming of world religions, honour was the chief ideological motivation of African behaviour. It remained a powerful motivation even for those who accepted world religions.

This conviction first arose while I was teaching the history of precolonial Africa, especially when trying to understand the late nineteenth-century civil wars that accompanied the arrival of Christianity in the Buganda kingdom on the northern shore of Lake Victoria. The Christians' behaviour seemed inexplicable, for they endured without resistance a terrible persecution, while quarrelling furiously among themselves and taking obvious pleasure in their enemies' sufferings. A specialist, Michael Twaddle, suggested that one way to understand them might be to study heroic behaviour in ancient Greece as described in Moses Finley's *The world of Odysseus*.[2] He was largely right. Buganda's Christians practised a heroic honour with many similarities to that dramatised in *The Iliad*, where members of a male warrior elite competed for individual reputation, chiefly by physical combat according to recognised procedures that imposed little moral restraint on violence and egotism. At its extreme, in Finley's words, 'everything pivoted on a single element of honour and virtue: strength, bravery, physical courage, prowess. Conversely, there was no weakness, no unheroic trait, but one, and that was cowardice and the

---

[1] The book is confined to sub-Saharan Africa, excluding Moors, Tuareg, and northern Sudanese but including Ethiopians, Funj, and southern Sudanese.

[2] M. I. Finley, *The world of Odysseus* (2nd edn, London, 1977). For Michael Twaddle's own account, see his *Kakungulu and the creation of Uganda, 1868–1928* (London, 1993), esp. pp. 18, 66, 81, 103–4, 112, 301.

1

consequent failure to pursue heroic goals.'[3] Buganda's heroes displayed greater concern for loyalty to chief and king than those of *The Iliad*, while real heroes, of course, pursued additional routes to honour, perhaps by generosity, gifts of leadership, or arts of peace, but the repeated demonstration of martial prowess in the pursuit of individual preeminence remained indispensable. Heroic cultures of this type, with many variations, have been described in regions as diverse as early medieval Europe, Aztec Mexico, pre-Tokugawa Japan, early South India, and Melanesia.[4] This book will suggest that many African peoples observed similar heroic practices, often into the early twentieth century, but they have seldom been studied. The most important work on the subject in sub-Saharan Africa, Boubakar Ly's doctoral thesis on the sociology of honour among the Wolof and Tukulor peoples of Senegal, has never been published and lacks the chronological framework to make it easy to use historically, while his plea, in an article, that 'reflections of the same type may be made by other Africans on their own societies' has gone unheard.[5] Although there have been some recent anthropological studies, only Catherine Ver Eecke's on the Fula and Karin Barber's on the Yoruba have adequate historical dimensions.[6]

Nevertheless, there is an extensive literature about honour in Africa, but it concerns North Africa as part of a broad Mediterranean culture area extending perhaps further eastwards into the Islamic world. These anthropological studies of Mediterranean honour took the Sahara as their southern border.[7]

---

[3] Finley, *World*, p. 28.

[4] H. Munro Chadwick, *The heroic age* (reprinted, Cambridge, 1967); Inga Clendinnen, 'The cost of courage in Aztec society,' *Past and Present*, 107 (1985), 44–89; Eiko Ikegami, *The taming of the samurai: honorific individualism and the making of modern Japan* (Cambridge, Mass., 1995), parts 2 and 3; K. Kailasapathy, *Tamil heroic poetry* (Oxford, 1968); C. R. Hallpike, *Bloodshed and vengeance in the Papuan mountains: the generation of conflict in Tanade society* (Oxford, 1977), pp. 251–3.

[5] Boubakar Ly, 'L'honneur et les valeurs morales dans les sociétés ouolof et toucouleur du Sénégal,' Thèse pour le Doctorat de Troisième Cycle de Sociologie, Université de Paris (Faculté des Lettres et Sciences Humaines), 2 vols., 1966; idem, 'L'honneur dans les sociétés ouolof et toucouleur du Sénégal,' *Présence Africaine*, 61 (1967), 39, n32.

[6] Catherine Ver Eecke, 'Pulaaku: Adamawa Fulbe identity and its transformations,' PhD thesis, University of Pennsylvania, 1988; Karin Barber, *I could speak until tomorrow: oriki, women, and the past in a Yoruba town* (Edinburgh, 1991). For other recent anthropological studies, see Paul Spencer, *The Samburu: a study of gerontocracy in a nomadic tribe* (London, 1965), pp. 103–12; Marc J. Swartz, *The way the world is: cultural processes and social relations among the Mombasa Swahili* (Berkeley, 1991); Pascal Bacuez, 'Honneur et pudeur dans la société swahili de Zanzibar,' *Journal des Africanistes*, 67, 2 (1997), 25–48.

[7] Two major collections were J. G. Peristiany (ed.), *Honour and shame: the values of Mediterranean society* (London, 1965), and J. G. Peristiany and Julian Pitt-Rivers (eds.), *Honor and grace in anthropology* (Cambridge, 1992). See also Charles Lindholm, *Generosity and jealousy: the Swat Pukhtun of northern Pakistan* (New York, 1982).

They described small-scale, rural societies, often antagonistic to distant state institutions, in which honour was not the prize of a warrior elite but the concern of any family and individual competing for respect by displaying qualities of manhood and womanhood. Manliness demanded capacity to sustain and defend a household, to maintain personal autonomy, to avenge insult or violence, and perhaps to demonstrate hospitality, integrity, wit, and style.[8] Female honour was seen in the literature chiefly from a male perspective as the preservation of virginity before marriage and chastity within it.[9] The centrality of sexual shame to honour codes has also been stressed for the early modern European states that cultivated the duel.[10] It has fostered the view that extreme concern for female chastity is an essential characteristic of a true honour culture, which perhaps partly explains why study of the subject stopped at the Sahara. Yet chastity was less important, although significant, in other honour cultures such as Japan.[11] Moreover, some anthropologists have thought it exaggerated in Mediterranean studies,[12] and feminist scholars, in particular, have stressed the need to replace male views of female honour by studies of what women honoured in themselves and one another.[13] This book will try to obey the feminist injunction; although chastity was an important component of female honour in many African societies, women appear commonly to have given greatest weight to fertility, endurance, and active support of children and household.

If it is true that honour cultures with strong heroic elements survived in many African societies until colonial rule, then it is important to discover what happened to them during the twentieth century and whether they continue to shape contemporary behaviour. It may be asked, for example, whether the intense concern with appearances characteristic of honour cultures[14] has remained a feature of African social and political life, whether, as the Senegalese historian

---

[8] See, for example, Raymond Jamous, *Honneur et baraka: les structures sociales traditionnelles dans le Rif* (Cambridge, 1981); Michael Herzfeld, *The poetics of manhood: contest and identity in a Cretan mountain village* (Princeton, 1985).

[9] For example, Julian Pitt-Rivers, 'Honor,' in *International encyclopaedia of the social sciences* (New York, 1968), vol. 6, pp. 505–6; David D. Gilmore, 'Introduction: the shame of dishonor,' in his *Honor and shame and the unity of the Mediterranean* (Washington, D.C., 1987), pp. 2–21.

[10] Donald R. Larson, *The honor plays of Lope de Vega* (Cambridge, Mass., 1977), esp. pp. 17–22; Elizabeth A. Foyster, *Manhood in early modern England: honour, sex and marriage* (London, 1999).

[11] Ikegami, *Taming*, pp. 244–6; Mariko Asano-Tamanoi, 'Shame, family, and state in Catalonia and Japan,' in Gilmore, *Honor*, pp. 104–20.

[12] J. Davis, *People of the Mediterranean: an essay in comparative social anthropology* (London, 1977), pp. 77, 98.

[13] Unni Wikan, 'Shame and honour: a contestable pair,' *Man*, NS, 19 (1984), 635–52; Alison Lever, 'Honor as a red herring,' *Critique of Anthropology*, 6, 3 (Winter 1986), 83, 86, 94, 101–2.

[14] Kenneth S. Greenberg, *Honor and slavery* (Princeton, 1996), ch. 1.

Cheikh Anta Diop put it, 'Every African is an unconscious aristocrat'.[15] Relations between genders and generations require consideration, as does corruption, whose roots in other continents have often been traced to premodern value systems.[16] One especially important question is whether legacies from honour cultures are important obstacles to democracy, as they were, although for different reasons, in interwar Japan. Equally important and easier to demonstrate is how surviving notions of honour have influenced African responses to the AIDS epidemic, often in self-destructive ways.

These lines of thought suggest that honour is a linking theme running through much of African history. This book is a set of variations on that theme. But honour is notoriously the 'most elusive of social concepts', an 'alluring, even seductive' word that can become vacuous unless clearly defined.[17] At the same time, the definition must be broad enough to embrace Homeric heroes, Mediterranean villagers, German duellists, and Japanese *samurai*. The most useful definition, because it is stripped of cultural specificity and designed for cross-cultural comparison, is Frank Henderson Stewart's minimalist characterisation of honour as 'a right to respect'.[18] As a right – like, say, a right to privacy – honour exists both subjectively and objectively. It exists subjectively in the sense that individuals believe they are entitled to respect. But it exists objectively only if others treat them with respect and if the individuals can if necessary enforce respect. Most or all people believe that they have a right to respect as individuals, but they can enjoy and confer it only as members of groups. The groups determine the criteria of honour, but any society is likely to contain several such groups with different criteria, so that honour is a contested category.

Stewart's analysis raises three other points necessary to the present argument. First, he distinguishes between vertical honour, a right to special respect enjoyed by those of superior rank, and horizontal honour, a right to be respected by one's equals.[19] While high-status groups in stratified societies generally try to enforce their right to respect and deny that of others, their view cannot be taken as that of the society as a whole – although the mistake is often made – because the denial is not necessarily accepted by the inferiors, who, in addition, may enjoy honour through the respect of their equals (and inferiors, if any). Although it is true that a claim to honour that cannot be enforced is vanity, so that courage

---

[15] Quoted in Ly, 'L'honneur et les valeurs,' vol. 2, p. 500.

[16] Natalie Zemon Davis, *The gift in sixteenth-century France* (Oxford, 2000).

[17] Orlando Patterson, *Slavery and social death: a comparative study* (Cambridge, Mass., 1982), p. 80; Wikan, 'Shame,' p. 635.

[18] Frank Henderson Stewart, *Honor* (Chicago, 1994), p. 21. The following paragraphs are based chiefly on this book.

[19] Ibid., pp. 54–63.

is the *sine qua non* of honour,[20] nevertheless even slaves may have means to enforce such claims, not only on other slaves but sometimes, in practice, on their masters.[21]

Second, the enjoyment of horizontal honour depends on behaviour approved by the group and can therefore in principle be lost absolutely by gross violation of its code, as happened when a Mediterranean woman was murdered by her kinsmen for sexual misconduct or an officer lost his commission by refusing to fight a duel. Stewart accepted this, especially where notions of honour were highly codified, but he suggested that in the real world things might be less clear-cut.[22] Others have argued more strongly that in practice honour was commonly a right that could be enjoyed in greater or lesser degree.[23] The question is important to this book because one of the most sensitive studies of honour in sub-Saharan Africa, Paul Spencer's account of the Samburu pastoralists of Kenya in the late 1950s, distinguished between honour, which all defended, and prestige, a supplementary value for which some competed.[24] If this were generally true, much of the behaviour described in this book as competition for honour would properly relate rather to prestige. However, there is reason to doubt the general truth of the distinction. Even the Samburu did not make it in their own language, having no word for honour as Spencer defined it.[25] Accounts of honour elsewhere have often stressed its competitive character. 'The world of Odysseus', for example, 'was fiercely competitive, as each hero strove to outdo the others,' and students of Mediterranean honour often stressed its competitive character: 'a constant struggle to gain a precarious and transitory advantage over each other.'[26] No other evidence from sub-Saharan Africa has been found to suggest a sharp distinction between honour and prestige, although, of course, certain actions were always more honourable or dishonourable than others.

A third point arising from Stewart's analysis is that in both Europe and China the primary criterion of honour shifted over time from rank and behaviour to moral character, from what a person had or did to what a person was. This accompanied a reconciliation between the demands of honour and those of

---

[20] Julian Pitt-Rivers, 'Honour and social status,' in Peristiany, *Honour and shame*, p. 22; Pitt-Rivers, 'Honor,' p. 505.

[21] Bertram Wyatt-Brown, *The shaping of Southern culture: honor, grace, and war, 1760s–1890s* (Chapel Hill, 2001), pp. 3, 303; this volume, p. 123.

[22] Stewart, *Honor*, pp. 123–5.

[23] Wikan, 'Shame,' pp. 644, 648.

[24] Spencer, *Samburu*, p. 107.

[25] Ibid., p. 103.

[26] Finley, *World*, p. 118; Herzfeld, *Poetics*, p. 11.

virtue (as taught by religion) and law (as enforced by the state).[27] Elements of such a shift will be seen to have occurred in certain parts of Africa, perhaps especially under Muslim influence.

The first half of this book analyses the role of honour in precolonial Africa in the terms suggested by Stewart's definition. It begins with the heroic, pre-Islamic code of the aristocratic horsemen of the West African savanna, dramatised in epic literature but challenged, defeated, absorbed, and transmuted during the nineteenth century by Islam. In Ethiopia, by contrast, heroic honour was challenged by Christianity from an earlier date, but there the contest created a heroic Christianity more than a Christian heroism. The West African cavalry ethos began also to penetrate the Yoruba world of rank and civil honour in southern Nigeria, but this was more radically militarised during the nineteenth century by civil war and firearms. The state rather than the horse became the fount of honour not only in Yorubaland but in the pre-Islamic, infantry-dominated kingdoms of West and Central Africa, where, during the eighteenth and nineteenth centuries, vertical honour was predominant and soldierly duty to the state began to supplant heroic egotism. Yet Africa's many stateless peoples also pursued honour, balancing the heroic notions of young men against the more sedate code of mature householders. Heroic and householder honour probably coexisted in most regions, but they are especially well documented in nineteenth-century southern Africa, where the warrior ethos of Zulu and related peoples contrasted with the mundane claims to respect displayed in the earliest court records. That honour thus existed at all social levels emerges yet more clearly from the experience of slaves. On the eve of colonial rule, the Great Lakes region of East Africa witnessed a unique fusion of heroic traditions and imported Christianity, indicating that accommodation to honour cultures was the key to successful innovation in precolonial Africa.

The second part of the book considers what Boubakar Ly called 'the crisis of honour' created by colonial conquest.[28] Military defeat destroyed the coherence of honour cultures, despite tenacious resistance by their adherents. As colonial rule became entrenched, heroic honour fragmented. It was not transformed en bloc, as had happened in Japan where the Tokugawa period (c.1600–1868) had tamed the *samurai* into servants of the state,[29] for Africa's colonial regimes lacked the legitimacy, the power, and the time to achieve that. Instead, elements of the fragmented tradition were incorporated into new ethics: the military codes of colonial armies, the ideals of respectability and professionalism, notions of

---

[27] Stewart, *Honor*, chs. 3 and 7; Hsien Chin Hu, 'The Chinese concepts of "face",' *American Anthropologist*, NS, 46 (1944), 45.

[28] Ly, 'L'honneur dans les sociétés,' p. 62.

[29] See Ikegami, *Taming*, parts 4–7.

gender, and the masculinities of miners and townsmen. Yet because the taming of African honour was incomplete, elements also survived to find expression in nationalism and armed liberation movements, in postcolonial politics and responses to AIDS.

The limited historical sources available in Africa often make it difficult to pursue these elusive issues. There were no written codes of honour. The earliest sources in many parts of the continent are boasts, praise poems, or epics. Early Muslim writings display the interaction between heroic honour and Muslim virtue. In Ethiopia the chronicles of kings and hagiographies of saints provide a continuous source from the fourteenth century. The Swahili literature of the East African coast is available from at least the eighteenth century. After 1500 European travellers' accounts multiply, to be supplemented by commercial and political documents from the western and southern coasts and then in the nineteenth century by mission sources and the first colonial legal records. The sources for the colonial period are more extensive, even overwhelming; the most useful are autobiographies, military and court records, compilations of customary law, investigations of corruption, anthropological studies, and novels.

This scarcity of sources is an important obstacle to the historical study of honour in Africa, but it has not been the main obstacle in writing this book. The chief problem has been an inability to read almost all the sources in African languages. As Boubakar Ly insisted, any satisfactory study of honour must begin by analysing the vocabulary used to discuss it.[30] Historians of honour in other continents have frequently centred their work on the changing meanings of words.[31] Similar studies in Africa over the full range of Ethiopian, Swahili, or Hausa sources could be immensely rewarding, but those with the necessary linguistic skills must undertake them. Only the most tentative suggestions about the language of honour can be made here, generally on the evidence of dictionaries. Almost equally valuable for the history of honour are legal records, especially defamation cases in which plaintiffs defended their reputations. Kirsten McKenzie has shown their value in her study of honour and respectability among white people in the early nineteenth-century Cape Colony.[32] Following her example, one body of legal records concerning Africans in the Eastern Cape during the later nineteenth century has been used in this book, but many records await study.

---

[30] Ly, 'L'honneur et les valeurs,' vol. 1, p. 15.

[31] Bichr Farès, *L'honneur chez les Arabes avant l'Islam: étude de sociologie* (Paris, 1932); Hsien, 'Chinese concepts'; Charles Barber, *The theme of honour's tongue: a study of social attitudes in the English drama from Shakespeare to Dryden* (Göteborg, 1985).

[32] Kirsten Elizabeth McKenzie, 'Gender and honour in middle-class Cape Town: the making of colonial identities 1828–1850,' DPhil thesis, University of Oxford, 1997.

Some who read this book may be surprised, even affronted, by its subject. Why, they may ask, spend several years and many pages examining honour when the problems of contemporary Africa are so often attributed to *lack* of honour, to corruption and cruelty and greed? The contention here is that such thinking is mistaken. Human beings seldom do things they believe to be wrong. They do wrong things because they believe them to be right. That is why honour is so important. It is an immensely powerful motivator. It expresses a group's highest values. But what was honourable to a Homeric hero is not necessarily honourable to modern people. To understand an alien code of honour is a challenge to the imagination. The first step is to suspend one's own value system.

Part One

Hero and Householder

2   Men on Horseback

One version of heroic honour took shape in the broad belt of open grass-land south of the Sahara Desert stretching from the Atlantic coast to the foothills of Ethiopia. Here horses could flourish, safe from equatorial dis-eases. Traders could range the savanna and cross the desert from the Mediter-ranean coast, bringing Islam, literacy, and knowledge of the outside world. Towns could be built with sun-baked mud. Equestrian aristocracies could dominate peasants. Rulers could weld these components into kingdoms and empires.

These open grasslands fostered sub-Saharan Africa's best-documented no-tions of honour, both vertical and horizontal. Probably originating in hunting and warfare, they appear first in praises sung at royal courts, then in the un-written codes of warrior elites. By the eighteenth century, professional bards had composed these traditions into an epic literature. Many savanna polities were by then officially Islamic, but the heroic code remained essentially pagan. Its formation, before it was profoundly challenged by Islam during the early nineteenth century, is the subject of this chapter.

During 1352–3 the Moroccan traveller Ibn Battuta visited the court of the Mali Empire on the upper Niger. He witnessed four public displays which are the earliest firm evidence of the cultivation of honour in this region. One was a boast of prowess widespread in Africa:

Sometimes one of them will stand before the sultan and mention the deeds which he has performed in his service, saying: 'I did so-and-so on such-and-such a day and I killed so-and-so on such-and-such a day.' Those who know the truth about this ex-press their affirmation by seizing the string of the bow and releasing it as one does when he is shooting. When the sultan says to him: 'You have spoken the truth' or thanks him, he removes his clothes and sprinkles himself with dust. This is good manners among them.[1]

On a second occasion, at a Muslim festival, the preacher proclaimed 'an exhortation and a reminder and praise for the sultan'.[2] Later in the same festival, 'Dugha the interpreter', who was also the sultan's spokesman, 'plays the instrument which is made of reed with little gourds under it, and sings poetry in which he praises the sultan and commemorates his expeditions and exploits.'[3] This performance was followed by an older form of panegyric, whose performers Ibn Battuta described as *jula*, clearly the term *jeli* later used throughout Mali's former dominions for a professional bard or griot:

Each of them has enclosed himself within an effigy made of feathers, resembling a [bird called] *shaqshaq*, on which is fixed a head made of wood with a red beak... I was told that their poetry was a kind of exhortation in which they say to the sultan: 'This *banbi* [dais] on which you are sitting was sat upon by such-and-such a king and of his good deeds were so-and-so... so you do good deeds which will be remembered after you.'... I was informed that this act was already old before Islam.[4]

Ibn Battuta's account of Mali's court suggests that praise-singing was a long-established means of celebrating honour, primarily arising from ancestry and martial prowess, although generosity was also mentioned. Mali, perhaps created early in the thirteenth century, was only the latest large-scale society in the region, but neither archaeological nor literary records of its predecessors contain evidence concerning honour. The only savanna kingdom prior to Mali where such evidence may exist was Kanem, originally a loose confederation north-east of Lake Chad, perhaps created during the sixth century.[5] Early in the twentieth century a British official in the successor state of Borno recorded a praise-song allegedly addressed to Sultan Hummay, who ruled the recently Islamised kingdom from c.1075 to 1087.[6] The official doubted if the song could be in its original form, but its description of Hummay as 'Islam's disposer' and 'Angel of God' suggests an early stage of Islamisation, while its celebration of his

---

[1] N. Levtzion and J. F. P. Hopkins (eds.), *Corpus of early Arabic sources for West African history* (Cambridge, 1981), p. 292.

[2] Ibid.

[3] Ibid., p. 293.

[4] Ibid.

[5] Dierk Lange, *Le Diwan des Sultans du [Kanem-]Bornu: chronologie et histoire d'un royaume africain* (Wiesbaden, 1977), p. 141.

[6] Ibid., p. 111.

ancestry, triumphs, and cruelty all display a vigorous heroic ethos:

> You put to flight a warrior, Dalla, son of Mukka, chief of the land of Mobber,
>   during the freshness of the rainy season . . .
> And captured (from his following) a thousand slaves:
> And took them and scattered them in the open places of Bagirmi:
> The best you took (and sent home) as the first fruits of battle:
> The children crying on their mothers you snatched away from their mothers:
> You took the slave wife from a slave,
> And set them in lands far removed from one another.[7]

One other savanna region with a recorded tradition of early praise-singing was Hausaland, located west of Borno and divided in the early second millennium into numerous rival kingdoms. One of these, Kano, preserved traditions and a king-list that were incorporated in the late nineteenth century into a written chronicle that is chronologically accurate for at least the previous four hundred years during which it can be compared with other sources. It represents Kano's twelfth- and thirteenth-century rulers as warriors, lists the heroes who fought for them, and by the reign of Sarki Yaji (?1349–85), 'Conqueror of the rocky heights, scatterer of hosts, lord of the town', suggests the existence of a praise-singing tradition.[8] A similar poem, perhaps from the fifteenth century, survives from the neighbouring Katsina kingdom.[9]

Royal courts were probably not the only venues for the display of honour. Individuals in more recent savanna societies have had personal praise-names, referring to their ancestry, qualities, and deeds, which were proclaimed as formal greetings, challenges, and encouragements, as well as at the moment of death. Wrestling competitions, the region's favourite sport, were occasions for elaborate praise-singing. Ancient hunters' societies had their own bards, their more democratic traditions of panegyric and lament for great hunters, and, at least in the twentieth century, their forms of oral but nonhistorical narrative incorporating such laments.[10]

---

[7] J. R. Patterson, *Kanuri songs* (n.p., n.d.), pp. vi, 2–3. According to Lange, *Diwan*, p. 74 n21(2), Bagirmi may have existed by at least the thirteenth century.

[8] H. R. Palmer, *Sudanese memoirs* (reprinted, 3 vols. in 1, London, 1967), vol. 3, pp. 101–6. For the reliability of the chronicle, see John O. Hunwick, 'Not yet *the* Kano Chronicle,' *Sudanic Africa*, 4 (1993), 95–6; M. G. Smith, *Government in Kano 1350–1950* (Boulder, 1997), p. 138.

[9] Yusufu Bala Usman, *The transformation of Katsina (1400–1883)* (Zaria, 1981), p. 13.

[10] Solange de Ganay, *Les devises des Dogons* (Paris, 1941), pp. vii, 1–3, 47; Sigrid Paul, 'The wrestling tradition and its social functions,' in William J. Baker and James A. Mangan (eds.), *Sport in Africa: essays in social history* (New York, 1987), pp. 25–6; Gordon Innes, with Bakari Sidibe (eds.), *Hunters and crocodiles: narratives of a hunter's bard* (Sandgate, 1990), introduction.

These popular traditions probably underlay the savanna's code of honour, but its crystallisation appears to have accompanied the formation of aristocracies within Mali, Kanem-Borno, Hausaland, and other major states during the early and middle centuries of the second millennium. Three cultural innovations fostered this stratification. One was the establishment of Islam as a court religion. Traders probably brought the new faith across the desert during the eighth century, initially converting their African counterparts and then, in the eleventh century, several rulers, including the king of Kanem and the ancestors of Mali's sovereigns. The Kano Chronicle dates the arrival of Islam there to 'Yaji's time' (?1349–85), although some scholars suspect an earlier date.[11] Although rulers and courtiers remained eclectic, as Ibn Battuta witnessed in Mali, Islam nevertheless helped to distinguish them culturally from their rural subjects. Even more important to the emergence of aristocracies was their adoption of war-horses. Small ponies, ridden without saddles, stirrups, or bridles, existed in the savanna during the late first millennium A.D., but larger war-horses probably arrived by the thirteenth century, perhaps first in Borno. The Kano Chronicle claims that Yaji's son Kanajeji (?1390–1410) 'was the first Hausa Sarki [King] to introduce "Lifidi" [quilted cotton armour] and iron helmets and coats of mail for battle.' While ponies remained quite common, the great expense of war-horses and their accoutrements confined them to an elite.[12] Free bowmen long remained the core of Mali's army, but horses and the military officers who rode them were conspicuous in the court ceremonial that Ibn Battuta witnessed, while travellers' accounts of the kingdom recorded in 1337–8 described a burgeoning equestrian culture:

Their brave cavaliers wear golden bracelets. Those whose knightly valour is greater wear gold necklets also. If it is greater still they add gold anklets. Whenever a hero (*batal*) adds to the list of his exploits the king gives him a pair of wide trousers, and the greater the number of a knight's exploits the bigger the size of his trousers.[13]

The magnificent equestrian terracotta statuettes of this period excavated from the Niger Valley identify horsemanship with social distinction and display an admiration of the animal expressed also in savanna poetry:

> Mouth full of chain and back full of saddle,
> Your forefeet dig a grave and your hind feet close it.
> Your tail fans misfortune away from your neck.

---

[11] John Iliffe, *Africans: the history of a continent* (Cambridge, 1995), pp. 51–3; Palmer, *Memoirs*, vol. 3, p. 104; M. Adamu, 'The Hausa and their neighbours in the central Sudan,' in D. T. Niane (ed.), *UNESCO general history of Africa* (London, 1984), vol. 4, p. 289.

[12] Robin Law, *The horse in West African history* (Oxford, 1980), esp. ch. 1; Palmer, *Memoirs*, vol. 3, p. 107.

[13] Levtzion and Hopkins, *Corpus*, p. 265.

> Your spine tramples misfortune,
> The pupil of your eye blinks at misfortune,
> Your nose snorts at misfortune,
> Your ears twitch at misfortune,
> Your head tosses at misfortune.[14]

Savanna horsemen, unlike their pony-riding predecessors, were not mounted archers; they increasingly (although never completely) abandoned missile weapons in favour of close combat with lance and sword, despising those who practised less-demanding tactics. 'Only when it is breast to breast does one know a great man,' said a Hausa proverb.[15] This was probably the route by which the hunter's more democratic ethos became the jealous and exclusive honour of an equestrian aristocracy.

This growing stratification was the third innovation of the period. Throughout the savanna lands from the Atlantic to the Niger that fell under Mali's hegemony, society came to be divided into freemen (*horon*), slaves (*jon*), and specialised craftsmen (*nyamakala*). Slaves had been exported northwards since at least the eighth century A.D., but war-horses made it more necessary and possible for military aristocracies to capture slaves from surrounding agricultural peoples, with whom Mali was said to be permanently at war. This, in turn, fostered local employment of slaves at all levels; Ibn Battuta described some three hundred participating in court ceremonies, but many more were farmworkers and concubines.[16] Craft specialists – workers in iron, leather, or wood; griots; and their womenfolk who were often potters or midwives – came over time to be excluded from marriage or eating with freemen and to suffer varying degrees of stigmatisation, an obscure process perhaps fully systematised only in the twentieth century.[17] Such specialisation presumably fostered class-based notions of honour. So, in particular, did the griots who became the custodians of their patrons' ethos and probably elaborated it into epic literature.

Mali left no written records, so that it is impossible to reconstruct the practice of aristocratic honour there. For that we must turn to later savanna societies

---

[14] David C. Conrad (ed.), *A state of intrigue: the epic of Bamana Segu according to Tayiru Banbera* (Oxford, 1990), p. 89. For the statuettes, see Boubé Gado, 'Un "village des morts" à Bura en République du Niger,' in Jean Devisse (ed.), *Vallées du Niger* (Paris, 1993), pp. 365–74; *African Arts*, 28, 4 (Autumn 1995), 38, 48, 50, 72.

[15] Quoted in Joseph P. Smaldone, *Warfare in the Sokoto Caliphate* (Cambridge, 1977), p. 200 n45.

[16] E. Savage, 'Berbers and Blacks: Ibadi slave traffic in eighth-century North Africa,' *JAH*, 33 (1992), 351–68; Levtzion and Hopkins, *Corpus*, pp. 272, 290–1; Paul E. Lovejoy, *Transformations in slavery* (Cambridge, 1983), pp. 28–35.

[17] Tal Tamari, *Les castes de l'Afrique occidentale* (Nanterre, 1997), ch. 2; David C. Conrad and Barbara E. Frank, 'Introduction,' in their *Status and identity in West Africa: nyamakalaw of Mande* (Bloomington, 1995), pp. 1–23.

1. *Terracotta equestrian figure from the Inland Delta of the Niger, Mali.*
Thirteenth to fifteenth century, Ceramic. H × W × D: 70.5 × 14.9 × 19.7 cm.
Museum purchase, 2 December 1986. Photograph by Franko Khoury. National
Museum of African Art. Smithsonian Institution.

with near-contemporary written sources. One was Mali's major successor, the Songhai Empire, which dominated the middle Niger Valley from the mid fifteenth century until it was conquered by a Moroccan expedition in 1591, leaving its dynastic traditions in the seventeenth-century chronicles of Timbuktu. Although Songhai's wealth rested on trade and agriculture, its rulers seem to have eschewed both. They were a massively polygynous and factionalised military elite whose power rested on war-horses purchased from the north with slaves. The true founder of the state, Sonni Ali Ber (1464–92), was at best a syncretic Muslim. His eventual successor, Askiya Muhammad (1493–1528), expiated his violent seizure of the throne by a spectacular pilgrimage to Mecca and a holy war against surrounding pagans, but he preserved a reputation as a great magician and never let his piety threaten his prowess.[18]

For Songhai's equestrian nobility, mounted warfare with counterparts in other kingdoms was a dangerous sport governed by a code of honour. When fifteen of a party of twenty-four Songhai horsemen were killed by a much larger enemy force, so the chronicle records, the victors treated the wounded 'and looked after them most solicitously, then set them free and sent them back to Askiya Dawud, saying that such valorous folk did not deserve to die.'[19] Appearances were vital to Songhai's noblemen. They affected insouciance. One general refused to interrupt his *mankala* board-game to counter the advancing enemy, was denounced for cowardice, and then routed the foe. Noblemen also cultivated personal display. Two princes were so handsome that 'when they went to Timbuktu people followed them about just to gaze at their good looks.'[20] Court etiquette was elaborate:

Among the whole army, only the *Jenne-koi* [Chief of Jenne] had the right to seat himself on a carpet at audiences with the sovereign; further, the *Jenne-koi* alone had the privilege of not covering his head with dust in his presence and could be content to cover himself with flour. Everyone must remove his head-dress at the moment of covering himself with dust except the *Kurmina-fari* [Governor of Kurmina]. Only the *Dendi-fari* might permit himself to address his views to the sovereign with complete freedom. Only the *Bara-koi* had a right of veto, of which the prince must take account whether he liked it or not. Only the *Dirma-koi* was authorised to enter the royal palace without dismounting from his horse.[21]

The ruling family sometimes settled their interminable rivalries on the battlefield or in single combat, but more often they vied in the language of precedence,

---

[18] John O. Hunwick, *Timbuktu and the Songhay Empire: Al-Sadi's Tarikh al-sudan down to 1613 and other contemporary documents* (Leiden, 1999), pp. xxii–lxv.

[19] Ibid., p. 147

[20] Ibid., pp. 128, 178.

[21] Mahmoud Kati, *Tarikh el-fettach* (trans. O. Houdas and M. Delafosse, Paris, 1913), pp. 13–14. See also Hunwick, *Timbuktu*, p. 341.

privilege, and honour, in which holding true to one's word was crucial. In the mid 1520s, Askiya Muhammad appointed a young but valiant son, Balla, to an administrative post with the privilege of beating a drum, which his jealous brothers vowed to split:

When he reached them those who would customarily dismount to greet such a person did so, except for Fari-mondyo Musa [the eldest brother]. He greeted him from on horseback with a slight nod of his head, saying, 'I have said nothing, but you know that if I speak, I keep my word.' None of them dared harm him, and thus enmity rose between them, because of his haughtiness and the way in which he outshone them by his bravery in many engagements and combats.[22]

Shortly afterwards Musa deposed his father and won a succession war in which his son captured Balla, who declared, 'There are three things that I will never do: I will not address [your father as] askiya, I will not put dust on my head for him, and I will not ride behind him.'[23] He was buried alive. Songhai's horsemen were notoriously proud. Their language, it is said, had no word for honourable behaviour, since to act honourably was simply to act normally. But it had a word for shame, *haawi*, which 'crystallises the strongest social values; cowardice, theft, adultery, neglect of the rules of hospitality or familial deference are so many situations generating shame.'[24] A disgraced official seized into slavery killed himself when recognised. Others were humiliated by being paraded around the town on donkeys.[25] The language also had a word for sexual prudery, which coexisted in savanna cultures with intense pride in virility. When Askiya Muhammad was deposed by his son Musa,

he wept and cursed his son, begging God not to let him die before he had exposed Musa's shameful parts. And God granted this prayer, for, as Askiya Musa passed one day on horseback through the market at Gao, spurring his horse, it threw him to the ground, one foot remained suspended from the stirrup-strap, his clothes were thrown back over his head, the string of his breeches broke, his shameful parts were exposed, and everyone in the market could see them as the frightened horse dragged him along in flight.[26]

Songhai suffered collective humiliation in 1591 when some four thousand Moroccan troops, mostly armed with muskets, destroyed a Songhai force ten times more numerous at the Battle of Tondibi. Askiya Ishaq II, persuaded to flee the field, was promptly deposed. A body of ninety-nine warriors fought to the death. A successor kingdom was created, but the Songhai-speaking peoples

[22] Hunwick, *Timbuktu*, p. 116.
[23] Ibid., p. 121.
[24] Jean-Pierre Olivier de Sardan, *Les sociétés Songhay-Zarma* (Paris, 1984), pp. 35–6.
[25] Hunwick, *Timbuktu*, pp. 139, 130, 177.
[26] Mahmoud Kati, *Tarikh*, p. 340.

were now fragmented.[27] The chief heirs to their military tradition were Songhai-speaking Zarma groups, whose horsemen, when not fighting one another or their neighbours, were notorious during the nineteenth century for their slave raids. Zarma society was highly stratified, initially between freemen and slaves, then between noble freemen and commoners, and finally among the nobility between fathers of families, women, and young men. Honour was the behaviour appropriate to a nobleman:

A fine action, a decorous deportment, a sign of generosity, the thousand customary expressions of reserve, of modesty, of elegance, of good taste or good manners, of grandeur of spirit or sense of propriety, will be characterised as 'noble'. . . . Conversely, 'captive' connotes the vulgar, the rootless; it is associated with frailty of character or absence of shame, with coarseness or lack of breeding.[28]

A Zarma nobleman might be expected to quote seven generations of ancestors. Noble behaviour was not confined to noblemen. A peasant might display courage and pride. A nobleman, however, was trained and expected to do so; he was a professional among amateurs:

> Mayatachi Teko . . . said . . .
> 'A man, if he does not flee one day, does not return another day!'
> Issa said that he would not know how to flee.[29]

For peasants, warfare was a calamity; for noblemen, it was a means of accumulation and heroic action, to be fought with horse and lance, sword and shield, leaving bow and poisoned arrow to peasants. A captured peasant would be enslaved; a captured nobleman would often be ransomed.

There is no suggestion in Songhai's aristocratic code that honour required noblemen to display respect for inferiors. Rather, their arrogant brutality was essentially pagan. The same was true of another sixteenth-century savanna kingdom, Borno, the successor state to Kanem, for which contemporary evidence survives in a chronicle of campaigns waged by Mai Idris Alauma (1564–96) against surrounding pagans:

As for their women and young children, some of them rushed outside the stronghold, in fear and cowardice, in the same manner as the cattle, while the men of the enemy became divided into two kinds, one of which stayed at the entrance of the stronghold, or near it, or opposite to it, for the purpose of war and battle, until they were killed by the muskets, in an instant, as though made to drink poison. . . .

---

[27] Ibid., pp. 264–77; Lansine Kaba, 'Archers, musketeers, and mosquitoes: the Moroccan invasion of the Sudan and the Songhay resistance (1591–1612),' *JAH*, 22 (1981), 457–75.

[28] Olivier de Sardan, *Les sociétés*, p. 29. My account is based chiefly on this book.

[29] 'The epic of Issa Korombé,' in John William Johnson, Thomas A. Hale, and Stephen Belcher (eds.), *Oral epics from Africa* (Bloomington, 1997), p. 145.

However, the cowards and the weak fell behind, or even hid themselves, lest they should be seen by the musketeers and lest these should annihilate them as they had annihilated the courageous ones. They waited for the fall of the darkness of night, with their remaining women and children ... when they took flight. ...

And when the troops of the Muslims saw them in these circumstances, they attacked them most furiously and struck them in one blow. Upon that the men fled ahead, abandoning the women and children completely, as pawns to be captured and seized. The people did not cease from catching them and capturing them as long as any remained, and that day only a few of the women and children escaped.[30]

The muskets – the first seen in the savanna – were handled by Ottoman musketeers and royal slaves. Borno's nobility remained cavalrymen, finely mounted on the kingdom's famous horses, reinforced by clients and professional military slaves, armoured in the chain-mail of the Crusades, and sometimes so encumbered with rich clothing that they had to be lifted into the saddle. One Mai of Borno died because his horse was too exhausted to carry his rider's weight to safety, but generally horsemen were as quick out of battle as into it.[31] Like one group defeated by Idris Alauma, they 'spurred their horses, and left the infantry behind like a worn-out sandal abandoned and thrown away.'[32] A nobleman's song caught the ethos:

> The peasant is grass, fodder for the horses.
> To your hoeing, peasant, so that we can eat.[33]

Although the Kano Chronicle is not a contemporary document like those of Timbuktu and Borno, it too describes the emergence in fifteenth-century Hausaland of a dominant equestrian nobility. It credits Mohammed Rumfa (?1463–99) with introducing, probably from Borno, a hierarchy of official titles (*sarauta*) supported by tributary fiefs, distinguishing title-holders (*masu sarauta*) from commoners (*talakawa*). The same period saw a great expansion of slavery and interminable warfare among the rival Hausa kingdoms.[34] In 1659 the earliest known Hausa poet, Dan Marina, writing in Arabic, captured the heroic ethos by praising his master, the King of Katsina, as both Commander of the Faithful and

[30] Dierk Lange (ed.), *A Sudanic chronicle: the Borno expeditions of Idris Alauma (1564–1576)* (Stuttgart, 1987), pp. 85–6.

[31] Ibid., pp. 25, 38; Louis Brenner, *The Shehus of Kukawa: a history of the al-Kanemi dynasty of Bornu* (Oxford, 1973), ch. 5; Dixon Denham and Hugh Clapperton, *Narrative of travels and discoveries in Northern and Central Africa, in the years 1822, 1823, and 1824* (2 parts, London, 1826), part 1, pp. 63–4, 327–8.

[32] Quoted in Smaldone, *Warfare*, p. 48.

[33] Quoted in Elizabeth Isichei, *A history of Nigeria* (London, 1983), p. 223.

[34] Palmer, *Memoirs*, vol. 3, pp. 111–19; Smith, *Government in Kano*, ch. 2.

Elephant-Slayer.[35] Ostentations displays of honour and dishonour were common. Katsina's elite wealth led it to be described in the late eighteenth century as 'a city of vainglory'. A sixteenth-century king of Kano celebrated his defeat of Bornoese invaders by ordering his griot to declaim his praises from the city wall for forty days. A century later, a successor 'assembled many maidens, put the Madawaki [a senior official] on a donkey, and handed it over to the maidens, to drive round the town. . . . The Madawaki died of chagrin.'[36]

Although infantry commonly bore the brunt of savanna warfare, it was nevertheless a horseman's world. Perhaps the best evidence of their dominance is that the firearms introduced into Borno in the sixteenth century disappeared from subsequent reports until the early nineteenth century, when the state possessed only a small and motley collection. Antipathy to firearms was widespread in the savanna. Songhai warriors who captured Moroccan muskets at Tondibi threw them into a river.[37] Even further west in Senegambia, with easier access to supplies, firearms became common only during the 1690s. Galam, on the upper Senegal, was the first inland state to rely extensively on muskets, followed later in the eighteenth century by the Bamana kingdoms of the middle Niger. Generally, however, horsemen dominated savanna battlefields well into the nineteenth century, and sometimes into the twentieth.[38]

It was during these centuries of equestrian power that the horsemen's fierce honour code was elaborated into heroic epic. How this happened is still disputed among historians.[39] In their modern form, the savanna's oral epics are historical narratives declaimed in public by professional griots, usually to musical accompaniment. In the past, these performances probably took place chiefly at royal courts and noble homesteads, where their purpose was both to entertain

---

[35] Hamidu Bobbayi and John O. Hunwick, 'Falkeiana I: a poem by Ibn al-Salbagh (Dan Marina) in praise of the Amir al-Muminin Kariyagiwa,' *Sudanic Africa*, 2 (1991), 126–9.

[36] Usman, *Transformation*, p. 59; Palmer, *Memoirs*, vol. 3, pp. 113, 120.

[37] Denham and Clapperton, *Narrative*, part 1, p. 209; D. Laya, 'The Hausa states,' in B. A. Ogot (ed.), *UNESCO general history of Africa* (London, 1992), vol. 5, p. 471.

[38] Philip D. Curtin, *Economic change in precolonial Africa: Senegambia in the era of the slave trade* (2 vols., Madison, 1975), vol. I, pp. 323–5; Richard L. Roberts, *Warriors, merchants, and slaves: the state and the economy in the middle Niger valley, 1700–1914* (Stanford, 1987), pp. 35, 60; John K. Thornton, *Warfare in Atlantic Africa, 1500–1800* (London, 1999), p. 39.

[39] This paragraph relies chiefly on Ivor Wilks, 'The history of the Sunjata epic: a review of the evidence,' and Ralph A. Austen, 'The historical transformation of genres: Sunjata as panegyric, folktale, epic, and novel,' in Ralph A. Austen (ed.), *In search of Sunjata: the Mande oral epic as history, literature and performance* (Bloomington, 1999), chs. 2 and 4; Stephen Belcher, *Epic traditions of Africa* (Bloomington, 1999). For an alternative analysis, see Stephen Paul Dušan Bulman, 'Interpreting Sunjata: a comparative analysis and exegesis of the Malinke epic,' PhD thesis, University of Birmingham, 1990.

and to excite the hearer to heroic behaviour, 'so that, in the morning, he would show himself worthy of his ancestors'.[40] Griots thus propagated family honour. Unlike European bards, they did not rely on formulae but dramatised series of incidents, interspersing songs and perhaps passages of praise-singing. Their long historical narratives differ from the shorter, personalised, and usually allusive praise-songs performed in many parts of Africa, apparently described by Ibn Battuta in Mali, and recorded from Kanem-Borno. Epics differ also from hunters' narratives, which lack the historical character (and often the refinement) of epic. No epic performance is mentioned in any contemporary source discussed in this chapter prior to the seventeenth century, nor did either Songhai or Borno create epic traditions until, in the case of Songhai, relatively recently. But if, as therefore seems possible, epic took shape only at a relatively late stage in savanna history, it certainly incorporated elements of earlier oral literature: passages of praise-singing, songs and incidents from hunters' narratives, stock characters of folklore, and probably much oral history, all presumably brought together by the griots' skill and given an emphasis on noble behaviour pleasing to aristocratic patrons. In other cultures, such literary creativity – especially the imagination of a past heroic age – often either followed 'some change in political conditions, when public attention is turned from a depressing or unsatisfactory present to what has gone before and thinks of it with admiration and longing,' or took place when heroic values were threatened by an alternative value system such as a world religion.[41] In the West African savanna, it is tempting to think that heroic epic was formed in response either to Mali's collapse in the fifteenth century or Songhai's in the late sixteenth, to the growing influence of Islam, or to some combination of these. At present, however, this is speculation.

Such a process might explain the character of the savanna's most famous epic, the story of Sunjata, reputed founder of the Mali Empire in the early thirteenth century, an epic recorded in at least thirty-five versions and known throughout the savanna west of the Niger. Ibn Battuta probably heard reference to Sunjata in 1352–3, and he was mentioned in 1393–4 (under another Malinke name) by the Tunisian historian Ibn Khaldun. He is not heard of again until French officers first recorded his story in the late nineteenth century. Yet the epic itself incorporates apparently ancient songs and praises that may have been sung before or after his death, as modern griots claim. The story also includes incidents characteristic of hunters' narratives and folklore that were, or became, stock elements in other savanna epics, and it has the strong magical component

---

[40] D. T. Niane, *Sundiata: an epic of old Mali* (trans. G. D. Pickett, London, 1965), p. 63.

[41] Sir Maurice Bowra, *The meaning of a heroic age* (Newcastle upon Tyne, 1957), pp. 15, 21–3. See also Victor W. Turner, 'An anthropological approach to the Icelandic saga,' in T. O. Beidelman (ed.), *The translation of culture: essays to E. E. Evans-Pritchard* (London, 1971), pp. 349–74.

characteristic of African expressions of heroic honour. Malinke, however, see the story as specifically historical.[42] In outline, it tells that Sunjata's father ruled a small Malinke chiefdom, while his mother came from a background of pagan magic.[43] Herself deformed, she bore a monstrous child unable to walk until the age of ten, when he overcame his disability by sheer willpower. Now a threat to his father's successor on the throne, he was driven into exile with his mother (or, in other versions, his griot) and travelled through the small chiefdoms of the upper Niger, displaying his arrogant egotism, his prowess as hunter and warrior, and his intelligence in the *mankala* board-game. In his absence, a fearsome Soninke sorcerer-king, Sumanguru, conquered Malinke country. Its people begged Sunjata to return and liberate them. Assembling a cavalry army, he attacked Sumanguru but was unable to prevail against his magic until its point of weakness was discovered by Sunjata's sister, who had been forced to share the tyrant's bed. When the armies met again, Sunjata wounded Sumanguru with a wooden arrow tipped with a white cock's spur and drove him from the field. The hero then united the Malinke under his rule and launched their expansion to create the savanna's greatest territorial empire. As a modern griot put it, Sunjata ennobled Mande country.[44]

Sunjata's story stands alone. It is not part of any larger history of Mali. With its sole focus on the hero, its numerous borrowings from folklore and hunters' tales, and its strong magical elements, it is anything but a straightforward epic. More accurately, perhaps, it is transitional towards epic and possibly central to the formation of the epic tradition. Built around Sunjata as culture-hero, the story gathers elements legitimising Malinke culture and the dominance of its equestrian rulers. Sunjata had created their empire, introduced their horses, and stratified their society by incorporating Sumanguru's followers as craftsmen and griots. All major Malinke patronymic groups had roles in the epic, thus fixing their social identities.[45] Yet the story did not legitimise Islam, for, until later accretions traced Sunjata's descent from the Prophet's black *muezzin*, Bilali, the hero rather embodied the values of the heroic order, especially in youth when his reckless prowess in battle led old warriors to declare, 'There's one that'll make a good king'.[46] Along with superhuman prowess went the superhuman egotism that made the young hero so dangerous: 'Modesty is the portion of the average

[42] Wilks in Austen, *In search*, pp. 26, 33–49; Austen in ibid., pp. 69–73.

[43] The most convenient version is Niane, *Sundiata*. For its relationship to other versions, see Stephen P. D. Bulman, 'Sunjata as written literature,' in Austen, *In search*, pp. 242–3.

[44] Wa Kamissoko, 'Les funérailles de Soundjata,' in Youssouf Tata Cisse and Wa Kamissoko, *La grande geste du Mali* (2 vols., Paris, 1988–91), vol. 2, p. 138.

[45] Bulman, 'Interpreting Sunjata,' pp. 452–66; Austen in Austen, *In search*, p. 79; Jan Jansen, *Epopée, histoire, société: le cas de Soundjata* (Paris, 2001), pp. 107–24.

[46] Niane, *Sundiata*, p. 37.

man, but superior men are ignorant of humility.'[47] On the decisive battlefield, however, the hero's egotism was restrained by the iron laws of honour. Before they joined battle, Sunjata and Sumanguru exchanged conventional boasts and challenges, for, as the griot observed, 'One does not wage war without saying why it is being waged.'[48] And once triumphant, Sunjata displayed not the destructive danger of a hero but the ordered restraint of a king.

Women played a large role in Sunjata's story, as is common in the epic literature of the savanna.[49] They were royal women, Sunjata's forceful mother and self-sacrificing sister, who supported his rise to power in this masculine view of women's place in an honour culture. There was no anguished sexual modesty here. Sunjata's sister exploited her sexuality to discover Sumanguru's weakness, while a later epic pictured a pagan leader telling his wife:

> A noble man must not be jealous
> About women
> Those days people thought
> Jealousy is little men's conduct
> They did not consider women of any worth
> Let alone be jealous about them.[50]

A wife's weakness or treachery might threaten male honour, as a later hero, Samba Gelajo, was dishonoured when his wife forced him to die in his bed by poisoning his food.[51] But the main gender relationship in epics, as in Malinke society, was between a man and his mother who found her fulfilment in his heroism:

> Ah! said the mother, my Samba,
> if it is true that I obeyed your father,
> and that your father married me in order to have you,
> and not for my beauty,
> nor for my wealth . . .
> then, my Samba, may God give you what you are going to seek.[52]

Nothing allows us to penetrate either to a feminine view or to the ordinary women who, as a sixteenth-century visitor to the western Malinke put it, 'cultivate and labour and sow and feed their husbands.'[53]

---

[47] Ibid., p. 34.

[48] Ibid., pp. 59–60.

[49] David C. Conrad, 'Mooning armies and mothering heroes: female power in Mande epic performance,' in Austen, *In search*, ch. 9.

[50] Oumarou Watta, *Rosary, mat and molo: a study in the spiritual epic of Omar Seku Tal* (New York, 1993), p. 58.

[51] Oumar Kane, 'Samba Gelajo-Jegi,' *BIFAN*, 32B (1970), 924.

[52] Amadou Ly (ed.), *L'épopée de Samba Gueladiegui* (n.p., 1991), p. 94.

[53] Quoted in Paul Pélissier, *Les paysans du Sénégal* (Saint-Yrieix, 1966), p. 555.

We do not know whether Sunjata's epic was a transitional master-narrative that mobile griots carried through the savanna, stimulating local heroic literatures, or whether Sunjata's memory gained epic form simultaneously with many other narratives. The earliest certain date for a local epic tradition is 1850, when a French traveller in the Senegal Valley recorded the story of Samba Gelajo, who had lived a century earlier.[54] He was a Fula from an ethnic group (also known as Fulani or Fulbe) who during the second millennium had spread eastwards from the Senegal Valley as far as Borno, mainly as pastoral clans symbiotic with local cultivators. Physically somewhat distinct, Fula regarded themselves as freeborn noblemen superior to agriculturalists, whom they reduced where possible to slavery or serfdom. Pastoral life was solitary and austere. Freemen cultivated a code of honour, often called *pulaaku*, which varied in detail but commonly stressed personal freedom, self-control, reserve, truthfulness, stoicism, courage, an acute sense of shame, and elegance of physique and manners, a code consciously distinct from the assertive and grandiose style of equestrian noblemen.[55] Young men were trained in *pulaaku* through the responsibilities of herding and through a reciprocal flagellation ritual (*sharo*), which required the same self-mastery as the often agonising initiation rites of other African peoples.[56] When elaborated by a mounted aristocracy, *pulaaku* gave birth to an epic literature.

The elaboration probably took place in Masina, the internal flood-plain of the Niger and superb pastoral country that Fula entered by the fifteenth century. Initially subordinate to Songhai and later to the Bamana rulers of Segu, these relatively settled Fula adopted horses, obeyed powerful clan-heads known as *ardoen*, and probably acquired non-Fula griots and models of oral literature. Among Masina's epic heroes, some may have lived in the seventeenth century; others certainly lived during the reign of Da Monzon of Segu (c.1808–28), in which the epics specifically situate themselves. Only after 1818 were Islam and state power imposed upon the Fula of Masina, so that it is tempting to see their epic literature as a nineteenth-century celebration of a last generation of freedom and pagan heroic values.[57] The epics, unlike the story of Sunjata, are

---

[54] Stephen Belcher, 'Constructing a hero: Samba Gueladio Djegui,' *RAL*, 25, 1 (Spring 1994), 76–7.

[55] See Paul Riesman, *Freedom in Fulani social life: an introspective ethnography* (trans. M. Fuller, Chicago, 1977), ch. 7; Ver Eecke, 'Pulaaku,' ch. 3; Anneke Breedveld and Mirjam de Bruijn, 'L'image des Fulbe: analyse critique de la construction du concept de *pulaaku*,' *CEA*, 36 (1996), 791–821.

[56] Described in H. S. W. Edwardes, diary, 11 June 1921, Edwardes Papers, RH.

[57] For these complicated issues, see Stephen Belcher, 'Heroes at the borderline: Bamana and Fulbe traditions in West Africa,' *RAL*, 29, 1 (Spring 1998), 43–65.

not biographies of heroes, nor, unlike Segu's epics, do they form a historical sequence. Rather, they are magnificent poetic accounts of incidents in which the heroes display *pulaaku*, pursuing not duty to God or lady but personal reputation:

As intransigent towards himself as to others, he permits no weakness, no complaisance; infallibly vigilant with regard to himself, he holds aloof from all indulgence as from all sentimentalism in order to remain faithful, with a pure and harsh objectivity, to the image he has formed of the 'free' man – that is to say, of the Fula worthy of this name – which it is his ideal to incarnate on all occasions.[58]

Three such heroes dominated Masina's epics. One was Hambodedio – Hama the Red, an allusion to lighter skin and racial superiority – the ruler of Kounari and the most powerful of early nineteenth-century *ardoen*. In one narrative, with strong echoes of Sunjata's epic, Hambodedio's wife, jealous for his honour, provoked him into challenging other heroes in the marketplace. When one accepted the challenge, Hambodedio first defeated him at the *mankala* board-game, next fought an inconclusive ritual duel that merely demonstrated equal magical power, then drove his adversary from the field with a horse tether (a traditionally humiliating instrument for punishing a slave), and finally subjected him to the ultimate disgrace of torture.[59]

Silamaka – his name meant *The Sword* – was a younger, romantic, and tragic figure whose failure and death in the cause of honour likened him more to Japanese heroes than to Sunjata.[60] One story described him raiding Hambode-dio's cattle, to avenge an insult, and then, to demonstrate that he was no mere brigand, remaining at the point of theft and returning the cattle when the chief preferred to request them rather than risk shameful failure in an attack.[61] The climax of Silamaka's career was his rebellion against the indignity of taxation by Segu, a rebellion that provoked full-scale invasion of Masina and heroic resistance – including ritual combat with the Segu champion – until Silamaka was killed by the only means to which he was vulnerable: a poisoned arrow dropped from a tree by an albino slave boy:

Objectively, it is merely suicidal to fight against 'the power of Segu', which possesses a regular army of 50,000 horsemen, while Silamaka disposes of only his 500 age-mates. But Silamaka 'fears shame, not the blows of the lance'! And despite the inequality of the combat, he provokes it and enters it without hesitation, with complete calm and even a touch of humour.

---

[58] Christiane Seydou (ed.), *La geste de Ham-Bodêdio ou Hama le Rouge* (Paris, 1976), p. 30.

[59] Ibid., pp. 133–225; Johnson and others, *Oral epics*, pp. 149–61.

[60] Ivan Morris, *The nobility of failure: tragic heroes in the history of Japan* (London, 1975).

[61] Amadou Hampate Ba and Lilyan Kesteloot (eds.), 'Une épopée peule: "Silamaka",' *L'homme*, 8 (1968), 18–22; Johnson and others, *Oral epics*, pp. 172–84.

He exposes his people to Segu's destructive vengeance, for this war is lost in advance. Yet not for an instant does one feel the least reserve penetrate the admiration of the griot who recounts the adventure. The hero's temerity is not resented as a crime. On the contrary it reflects glory on the whole of Masina.[62]

The most remarkable of Masina's epic heroes was Poullori, for he was not a nobleman but a slave born in his master's household on the same day as the son Silamaka, brought up with him, taken to war with him, his master's companion in life and his avenger in death:

> One would not know which is the master,
> One would not know which of them is the slave.
> Silamaka and Poullori
> Were never separated.[63]

As warrior-companion in a relationship of reciprocity much admired in the savanna,[64] Poullori shared vicariously in his master's honour and was doubly jealous of it. In return, Silamaka avenged Poullori when Hambodedio described him as 'a rope's end'. Yet the distinction between master and slave was never forgotten. At the end of the story, in a statement mingling pride and resentment, Poullori recalled that only three times had Silamaka reminded him that he was a slave: once when he tried on Silamaka's sandals and found 'that mine was not the small foot of a noble'; once while bathing, when 'I had to expose myself while he remained in the water'; and on the day of Silamaka's death, when he sent Poullori with a message and 'stopped me from sharing his fate'. When he learned this, Poullori turned his horse against his master's enemies:

> No one ever learned
> Where this procession disappeared.
> Those thousand horses, in legend,
> Rose to the sky with Poullori.
> And today, as clouds march by
> As thunder strikes and the rains pelt down,
> When lightning flashes and the echo answers,
> The Bambara say, 'There is Poullori,
> Still chasing the horsemen of Segu.'[65]

---

[62] Hampate Ba and Kesteloot, 'Une épopée,' p. 8 (and text in pp. 22–35); Johnson and others, *Oral epics*, pp. 166–71.

[63] Christiane Seydou (ed.), *Silâmaka et Poullôri: récit épique peul raconté par Tinguidji* (Paris, 1972), p. 79.

[64] J. P. Olivier de Sardan (ed.), *Quand nos pères étaient captifs . . . :récits paysans du Niger* (Paris, 1976).

[65] Johnson and others, *Oral epics*, p. 171; Seydou, *Silâmaka*, pp. 77–173.

Heroic honour, to the Fula of Masina, was the honour of *pulaaku*, of the pastoralist, the wholly autonomous individual. In Segu, by contrast, honour existed within the state. The Bamana people of the middle Niger, Mande-speaking agriculturalists, created the kingdom by the early seventeenth century amidst the collapse of Songhai. A century later it fell under the control of a powerful monarchy reliant on military slaves and freemen who fought not as cavalry but as archers and, increasingly during the eighteenth century, as infantry musketeers.[66] Segu's oral epics, which provide much of the evidence for notions of honour there, form a cycle ending with the last years of Da Monzon (c.1808–28). This suggests that the epics may have been formed at much the same time as Masina's. There was complex interaction between them. If Masina took its griots from Segu or some other kingdom, Segu took incidents and characters (including Hambodedio and Silamaka) from Masina. Indeed, the distinctiveness of Segu's epics – along with their very prominent magical element – was that the heroes attracting most sympathy were either opponents of Bamana power, slaves, or foreign mercenaries. Segu's kings, by contrast, were sinister figures, treacherous and cruel. Heroic values, it appears, were incompatible with reason of state. In the epic account of Segu's capture of Dionkoloni, for example, the victor was Da Monzon, but the romantic hero was a warrior-lover named Silamakan Koumba, whom the griots confused with Silamaka, while the tragic hero was the enemy chief of Dionkoloni, who blew himself up rather than suffer capture and sacrifice at Segu:

> When death arrives, take to your deathbed,
> Stretch yourself on it!
> If dishonour threatens you,
> You will know then
> How to shun it.
> That is what is agreeable in old age.
> It is why we, the griots, say:
> 'A broken leg can mend,
> A broken arm can mend,
> But a man's courage
> Is all he has.'[67]

In the equally fine story of Da Monzon's defeat of Samanyana, the heroine was a slave woman sent (like Sunjata's sister) to seduce the enemy king and secure the articles needed to ensorcel him. When she returned successfully, Da Monzon killed her lest she might similarly betray Segu.[68]

---

[66] Roberts, *Warriors*, pp. 28–35.
[67] Gérard Dumestre (ed.), *La geste de Ségou* (Paris, 1979), p. 325.
[68] Conrad, *State of intrigue*, p. 263.

The Fula epic tradition may have originated in Masina but it spread westwards (although not eastwards) as far as the Senegal Valley. The story of Samba Gelajo, first recorded there in 1850, concerned a real historical figure, a member of the Fula ruling family of Futa Toro, who tried repeatedly but ultimately unsuccessfully between 1731 and 1751 to usurp the throne from his senior cousin, Konko Boubou Moussa, before dying in exile.[69] Like Masina's heroes, Samba Gelajo belonged to the last pagan generation before Islam dominated the region. The epic transformed him into an archetypal heroic egotist who, like Sunjata, narrowly avoided early death (by being brought up as a girl), escaped to prove his manhood by killing a monster and engaging in chivalrous combat with rival heroes, and returned to claim his rightful throne by overthrowing his uncle and humiliating him as a beggar, before deliberately accepting his predicted death at the hands of a treacherous wife by eating food he knew to be poisoned.[70] His turbulent and brutal career exemplified a particular notion of honour, that of the military adventurers who, as will be seen, proliferated in the nineteenth century.

Further east in the savanna, in the modern Republic of Sudan, similar processes were taking place. In 1504 the rainlands south of the desert where White and Blue Niles meet came under the control of an African group known as the Funj who established a state based on Sinnar. Although they officially adopted Islam, few Funj were literate or observed Islamic rites. At their peak between about 1650 and 1750, they were a hereditary nobility of armoured, sword-wielding horsemen divided into extensively intermarried, territorially based kinship groups that collectively chose a sultan from the royal matrilineage.[71]

During the eighteenth century, this aristocratic order was undermined from two directions. On the one hand, the growing power of the central government's slave forces provoked a noble reaction that overthrew the sultan in 1718 and initiated a century of dynastic strife and treachery reminiscent of contemporary Segu. On the other hand, contact with the outside world encouraged commerce, urbanisation, expansion of Islam, increasing domestication of women, and an alternative leadership of Muslim clerics, many of whom rejected the ostentation of noble lifestyles. As the central administration became more reliant on literate Muslims, provincial noblemen converted themselves into local warlords.[72] And,

---

[69] Ly, *Samba Gueladiegui*, pp. 179–94.

[70] Ibid., passim; Johnson and others, *Oral epics*, pp. 185–99.

[71] Jay Spaulding, *The heroic age in Sinnar* (East Lansing, 1985), part 1.

[72] Ibid., pp. 139–42, 151–61, 199–214; Neil McHugh, *Holymen of the Blue Nile: the making of an Arab-Islamic community in the Nilotic Sudan, 1500–1850* (Evanston, 1994), pp. 51–2, 62–3, 97–9, 104–5.

as in Masina and Futa Toto, it was precisely this moment in the late eighteenth century when the pagan order was disintegrating into violence that traditions were to identify as their heroic age:

The archtypical [sic] hero of Hamaj Sinnar [1762–1821] as he appears in the literature of the day was the 'knight' (*faris*), always a warrior on horseback, ideally of noble birth, preferably not a slave, and certainly not a man of common origin. The knight was contemptuous of death, loyal to his family, his friends, his troops, and his honor; he sought fame, fulfilled his oaths, and never abandoned a just cause even if he defended it against the world. He was temperate in his bodily appetites, avoided vice, and governed his subordinates with justice and moderation. Whenever circumstances permitted, he gave generously. Desirable but less essential positive attributes were wealth, literacy, and Islamic piety. The failings of knights, as they appear in the judgment of contemporary sources, were often an excessive or immoderate display of otherwise admirable qualities.[73]

Later and more popular traditions, by contrast, populated this world with egotistical adventurers like Samba Gelajo: men such as Regeb, 'so mighty a man that he used red pepper for snuff,' who after a life of outlawry was impaled at Khartoum,[74] or the nomad sheikh and warrior Ali Abu Huneik:

Last of all came Ali on his mare, smitten in the jaw with a spear so that it projected from the other jawbone; with his right hand he held the spear steady and with his left the reins. . . .

Then said Ali to the king, 'Saddle me a stout charger and bring me a rope'; and when they did so he mounted the charger, and tying one end of the rope to the spear shaft, he bade the slaves tie the other to a tree. Then he called out and boasted and spurred the charger: the spear came out and in its teeth part of his jawbone, and so he got the name of Abu Huneik, the little jawbone.[75]

Jay Spaulding, who has recreated this distant world, has compared it to the Jahiliyya, the period of Arab antiquity preceding the Prophet's mission, a time of heroism and futility when the tribal world of Arabia had been dislocated but not yet reintegrated by economic and intellectual change, an age ruled by notions of honour that were to infuse Islam.[76] It is an accurate comparison, not only for the Funj Sultanate but for the entire savanna region on the eve of the nineteenth century as zealous Muslims prepared to contest power and confront the heroic tradition with their distinctive notions of virtue and honour.

---

[73] Spaulding, *Heroic age*, p. 300.
[74] L. F. Nalder, 'Tales from the Fung Province,' *Sudan Notes and Records*, 14 (1931), 67.
[75] Ibid., p. 74.
[76] Spaulding, *Heroic age*, pp. xi–xii; Farès, *L'honneur*, pp. 191–2.

3   Honour and Islam

From the eleventh century, several West African savanna states were officially Islamic, some quite profoundly so, but their Islam was generally syncretic until the eighteenth century and had little impact on their equestrian ethos. During the eighteenth century, however, the distinction between warriors who fought and Muslims who prayed disintegrated, and armed zealots began to seize power in holy wars.

The zealots' impact on codes of honour was ambiguous. On the one hand, Islam rejected many aspects of pagan honour, especially its glorification of the hero, for whom Muslims substituted the Prophet, and its egotistical pursuit of rank and personal reputation, against which Muslims posed ideals of virtue and respectability. On the other hand, not all holy wars succeeded, all stimulated resistance, Muslims often triumphed by adopting their adversaries' military values, and their new theocracies not only denounced but incorporated heroic traditions, a process documented in the reformers' writings and their opponents' oral literature. The outcome exemplified the fate of African notions of honour in the modern world: absorption and transmutation into other ideologies. And it was those new ideologies like Islam that could absorb the old notions of honour that were to be most successful.

These changes were most extensive in the West African savanna, but they can be seen in the other nucleus of sub-Saharan Islam: the East African coast. Seaborne traders brought Islam to this region by the ninth century A.D., probably first to the Kenya coast, where Swahili (a Bantu language) evolved and was carried southwards to become the common coastal language.[1] Unlike the contemporary

---

[1] Thomas Spear, 'Early Swahili history reconsidered,' *IJAHS*, 33 (2000), 257–90.

cultures of the Niger Valley, East Africa's coastal peoples had a less populous hinterland and no horses, which could not survive in the environment. Each major port became self-governing under Muslim notables claiming affiliations with the Middle East.

Written Swahili poetry, which can perhaps be traced back as far as the sixteenth century,[2] could be one of the most valuable sources for expert study of the history of honour in Africa. To an inexpert eye, some of the earliest poetry embodies a heroic tradition focused especially on Liyongo Fumo, a man from the Kenya coast whose life has been dated anywhere between the twelfth and seventeenth centuries. A man of gigantic strength, associated with dance and drinking, with love-songs and largess, he had also the hero's dangerous egotism, while his popularity was feared by his brother, the ruler of a coastal town, who eventually had him murdered with a copper dagger, which alone could kill him.[3] The earliest written evidence of this tradition is a poem, *Takhimisa ya Liyongo*, by Sayyid Abdallah bin Nassir (c.1730–1820), which put into Liyongo's mouth a song of defiance possibly incorporating oral sources but most interesting as a later poet's representation of a heroic code of honour.[4] Although the text and its translation present difficulties, it mainly used two words with the broad meaning of honour. One was *cheo*, as in Liyongo's declaration, 'He who strives for honour [*cheo*] is honoured as he strives.'[5] *Cheo* was a Bantu word with the wider meaning of a measure and hence of 'position, station in the world, sense of honour,' as the earliest Swahili dictionary of 1882 defined it.[6] The other word was *jaha*: Liyongo declared that a hero 'strives for his honour [*jaha*] till his eyes are closed.' *Jaha*, a loan-word from Arabic, connoted power and authority.[7] The poem also made one use of a third word for honour, *murua*, also of Arabic derivation and connoting 'pleasing manners, honour, respect, reverence' in modern Swahili.[8] It appears possible, then, that

---

[2] Kyallo Wadi Wamitila, *Archetypal criticism of Kiswahili poetry, with special reference to Fumo Liyongo* (Bayreuth, 2001), pp. 45–7.

[3] Ibid., pp. 93–8.

[4] The full text is in C. Meinhof, 'Das Lied des Liongo,' *Zeitschrift für Eingeborenen-Sprachen*, 15 (1924–5), 241–65. I have also used the partial translations in Lyndon Harries, *Swahili poetry* (Oxford, 1962), pp. 188–93, and Wamitila, *Archetypal criticism*, pp. 127, 199, 200, 204.

[5] Harries, *Poetry*, pp. 190–1; Meinhof, 'Das Lied,' pp. 251–2.

[6] [J.] L. Krapf, *A dictionary of the Suahili language* (London, 1882: reprinted, Ridgewood, N.J., n.d.), p. 37.

[7] Wamitila, *Archetypal criticism*, p. 200; Krapf, *Dictionary*, p. 110. Meinhof, 'Das Lied,' p. 263, translated *jaha* here as power, although in verse 18 (p. 259) he translated *jana* (perhaps a misprint for *jaha*) as honour.

[8] Frederick Johnson, *A standard Swahili-English dictionary* (Oxford, 1939), p. 300 (s.v. *mrua*). Meinhof ('Das Lied,' p. 260) translated *murua* as bravery. He also (p. 252) hesitantly translated *sono* (in verse 5) as honour, although Harries, *Poetry*, p. 191, translated it as friendship. Dictionaries do not support either of Meinhof's translations.

by the early nineteenth century an indigenous notion of honour as rank and prowess (*cheo*) coexisted with imported ideas of honour as power (*jaha*) and, perhaps less strongly, as civility (*murua*). This, of course, needs to be tested against other sources of the period.

Neither celebrations of valour nor love-poetry died with Liyongo. In the early nineteenth century, Muyaka bin Haji wrote passionately on both subjects, exhorting his fellow-townsmen in Mombasa to resist subjugation by the ruler of Oman.[9] Yet the Swahili epic tradition – in striking contrast to West African epic poetry – borrowed most of its materials directly from Arabic accounts of Muhammad and his companions. The earliest known Swahili manuscript of an epic poem, tentatively dated to 1728, versified an Arabic account of the Prophet's supposed triumph over a Byzantine Emperor.[10] Many later Swahili epics used similar materials or imitated them. Even their romantic knight-errant, Mikidadi, was a companion of the Prophet. Such borrowed heroes epitomised the growing dominance of Islamic values within coastal society, especially during the nineteenth century when the Arab rulers of Oman and Zanzibar asserted control over the coast and when the incorporation of Arabic loan-words into Swahili accelerated.[11] Islam and Arabness (*ustaarabu*) became essential components of a somewhat different notion of honour, *heshima*, an Arabic loan-word apparently associated especially with the Swahili dialect of Zanzibar and the adjacent Mrima coast.[12] *Heshima* included honour in the objective sense of rank, the behaviour appropriate to it, and the respect due to such behaviour. Conservative patricians saw this as its only meaning: 'The higher person keeps his hishima only when he acts like a higher person; the lower person keeps his when he acts like a lower person.'[13] For others, however, *heshima* also acquired a subjective meaning of character, respectability, and Islamic virtue, as a twentieth-century analysis explained:

Heshima has a second and more complex meaning, that of 'honor'. Honor is an inner quality: its possession and expression may indeed suggest to others that a person should be given outer reputation, but the two qualities are different, perhaps two sides of one coin but not identical. Heshima is the essential quality of a 'true patrician' (*mngwana*

---

[9] Mohamed H. Abdulaziz, *Muyaka: 19th century Swahili popular poetry* (Nairobi, 1979).

[10] Jan Knappert, *Four centuries of Swahili verse* (London, 1979), pp. 109–14; Wamitila, *Archetypal criticism*, p. 47.

[11] Spear, 'Early Swahili history,' p. 272.

[12] Even in the late twentieth century, the primary word for honour in Mombasa was not *heshima* but *fakhri*. See Swartz, *The way*, pp. 16, 158–60, 168; Bacuez, 'Honneur,' p. 26 n3. *Cheo*, meanwhile, apparently lost its meaning of honour, while retaining that of rank. See, for example, Ch. Sacleux, *Dictionnaire Swahili-Français* (Paris, 1939), pp. 140, 278.

[13] Abdul Hamid M. el Zein, *The sacred meadows: a structural analysis of religious symbolism in an East African town* ([Evanston] 1974), p. 63.

wa haki), not merely of a member of a patrician lineage as such. (. . . a slave formerly could acquire heshima in certain situations.) It is not a quality of an isolated individual, but an aspect of relations of communication and exchange. By behaving with courtesy, sensitivity, and goodness toward someone else, a person both acquires heshima and bestows it on the person addressed, who, by responding seemingly and graciously, in turn affirms his own heshima and emphasizes its possession by the original giver.[14]

During the nineteenth century, this transition from nobility of rank to nobility of character was only at an early stage, for the commercially expansive, slave-owning, mobile, turbulent Mrima respected not only a man's character and piety but also the deeds of his ancestors, the size of his following, the length of his purse, and the strength of his arm. Yet *ustaarabu*, with Islam at its core, provided a model to which even slaves might seek to acculturate themselves and thereby claim a degree of honour, however much their masters might contest it and deprecate the Africanised Islamic rituals and competitive displays of wealth by which the underclasses asserted their dignity.[15]

The transition from *cheo* to *heshima* had especially important consequences for women. Because virtually all coastal women were born in Africa, their culture had long been more purely African than that of men, and they had enjoyed greater freedom than was normal in the Islamic world. Muyaka bin Haji's poetry, for example, described a disreputable female world coexisting with concern for rank and reputation.[16] During the nineteenth century, however, the male belief that a woman's chastity was essential not only to her own honour but to that of her lineage became insistent among those claiming *heshima*. By the end of the century, respectable coastal women were veiled in public and those in the most conservative households were secluded.[17] The advice Mwana Kupona supposedly wrote to her daughter in c.1858 emphasised not only modesty, obedience, and household management but also a woman's obligation to perform the religious duties of Islam; however, the poem's silence on the care of children must make the author's gender uncertain.[18]

In West Africa the dominant Muslim political tradition before the eighteenth century was quietist, as the faith recommended where Muslims were too few to

---

[14] John Middleton, *The world of the Swahili* (New Haven, 1992), p. 194.

[15] Jonathon Glassman, *Feasts and riot: revelry, rebellion, and popular consciousness on the Swahili coast, 1856–1888* (Portsmouth, N.H., 1995), pp. 22–4, 79–80, 133–45, 158–74.

[16] Carol M. Eastman, 'Women, slaves, and foreigners: African cultural influences and group processes in the formation of northern Swahili coastal society,' *IJAHS*, 21 (1988), 1–20; Abdulaziz, *Muyaka*, pp. 173, 241.

[17] Margaret Strobel, *Muslim women in Mombasa, 1890–1975* (New Haven, 1979), pp. 74–6; Middleton, *World*, pp. 114–15, 150, 192–3.

[18] Harries, *Poetry*, pp. 72–87.

challenge non-Muslim rulers with hope of success. This tradition was first broken when Askiya Muhammad usurped Songhai's throne in 1493 with Muslim support. Two centuries later, a Berber cleric from Mauritania invaded the Senegal Valley and provoked the region's first holy war. By then Islam had sufficient followers to make apolitical quietism unacceptable to zealous critics of their rulers' 'mixed Islam', especially where Fula clerics combined their religious beliefs with the austere principles of *pulaaku*. The first West African state created by such a cleric, in c.1698, was Bundu, located between the upper Senegal and the Faleme. The next, Futa Jalon, further to the south, emerged from a holy war launched by Torodbe (largely Fula) clerics in 1726. A sequence of similar jihads followed, notably in Futa Toro in 1776, Hausaland in 1804, Masina in 1818, and a complicated series of 'maraboutic wars' among Wolof and Mandinka in Senegambia.[19]

In Masina, the flood-plain of the middle Niger, pagan Fula pastoralists, led by heroes like Silamaka, had contested domination by the Bamana kingdom of Segu during the eighteenth century. In 1818 a Muslim Fula cleric, Shehu Amadu, made his small following the spearhead of a widespread Fula insurrection, blending Islamic principles and Fula notions of honour into an amalgam that largely explained Islam's success in an otherwise inhospitable region. To reconstruct this process is both possible and difficult because the evidence consists of oral traditions collected in the mid twentieth century by a Malian scholar, Amadou Hampate Ba, who presented them somewhat uncritically, 'quoting' speeches and writings of which no contemporary record existed and ignoring the possible influence of Masina's epic literature.[20]

According to these traditions, Masina's jihad began over a point of honour. Convinced that he was called to destroy idolatry, Shehu Amadu demanded the allegiance of Fula clan-heads (*ardoen*). One replied by seizing a cloth from a disciple of the Shehu to demonstrate 'that so long as an *ardo* remains alive in the land of Masina and its environs, no "blackener of writing-boards" will command the territory.' Amadu had the *ardo* killed. His father complained to the King of Segu, who attacked Amadu's community at Noukouma and was defeated.[21] The victorious Muslims established a Caliphate, the *dina*, ruled by a council of forty *marabouts*, with the Shehu as spiritual guide, and divided into five provinces under military *amirs*. Such centralised control over a hitherto

---

[19] Nehemia Levtzion and Randall L. Pouwels (eds.), *The history of Islam in Africa* (Athens, Ohio, 2000), pp. 96–8, 70, 133–44.

[20] Amadou Hampate Ba and Jacques Daget, *L'empire peul du Macina (1818–1853)* (reprinted, Abidjan, 1984). See also Bintou Sanankoua, *Un empire peul au XIXe siècle: le Diina du Maasina* (Paris, 1990).

[21] Hampate Ba and Daget, *L'empire*, pp. 29–40.

fragmented region provoked much resistance from Fula noblemen dedicated to the pagan code of honour, which became known as *jahiliyyaku*.[22] The most recalcitrant was Gelajo of Kounari, son of the legendary Hambodedio, who rallied to the *dina* after its victory at Noukouma but resented its interference in his control of Kounari, which, he complained, offended his family honour. Tradition says the Council replied coldly that it 'contests neither your illustrious birth nor your military merits, but it does not see this as a question of giving you precedence in a matter where military valour and birth constitute essential qualifications. What is demanded of chiefs is faith and learning. Yet, without insulting you, your faith is tepid and your learning nil.'[23] Gelajo was indeed insulted. 'I shall not let myself be intimidated,' he apparently declared. 'Without honour, what can I make of life? To die is an inevitable law, but to let oneself be dishonoured without reaction is to lack courage and virtue. I have faith in my lance. . . . I shall make war without mercy on the *marabouts*.'[24] Such defiance of unwarlike clerics was widespread among the military nobility. *Ardo* Ngourori long refused even ostensible submission to Shehu Amadu: 'He is a beggar and I am a bird of prey.' According to tradition it was only when Amadu displayed personal courage that Ngourori accepted Islam and took a humiliating place among the pupils at a Koran school.[25]

Yet the nobility found a place in the *dina* as military commanders below the rank of *amir*. The core of Masina's army was still a cavalry force of lancers, although by the 1850s the infantry had acquired some poor-quality firearms. In battle everything still depended on the first cavalry charge, after which discipline disintegrated and 'each fought ultimately for his own account and sought to distinguish himself by some brilliant action, regardless of the final result of the battle taking place.'[26] These tactics defeated Masina's immediate neighbours but were wholly inadequate when a disciplined Tukulor army from Futa Toro invaded the region in 1862.

The *dina* struggled throughout its history to impose Islamic restraints on the military nobility. The Council claimed sole right to launch expeditions. Before appointing an *amir* to command a province, it humbled him by requiring him to declare and settle his debts, a procedure likened to making him expose his private parts.[27] In practice, however, the heroic ethos continued to dominate the battlefield, as tradition describes it. Before Gelajo rebelled, 'He declared war on

---

[22] Sanankoua, *Un empire*, p. 47.

[23] Hampate Ba and Daget, *L'empire*, pp. 117–18.

[24] Ibid., p. 119.

[25] Ibid., pp. 107–14.

[26] Ibid., p. 73. See also Irene Aschwanden, *Organisation und Strategie der Fulbe Armee von Macina im 19. Jahrhundert* (Berne, 1972).

[27] Hampate Ba and Daget, *L'empire*, pp. 74–5.

Shehu Amadu in the forms which tradition demanded of men of noble stock.'[28] His rebel brother refused to flee when cornered by the *dina*'s forces, for 'I shall never owe my survival to the swiftness of my steed, but to the point of my lance and the edge of my sword'. When he turned instead to attack, the *dina*'s commander replied: 'Do not charge thus like a fool, so that it can be said that it took thirty of us to kill you. I am your man. Let us face one another in single combat.' Childhood friends, they fought on horseback all day without result, then met again and died by simultaneous blows.[29] The legacy of epic tradition is doubtless especially strong in this story, but military honour was compelling. In the final resistance to Tukulor invasion, Shehu Amadu's grandson, famed for his reckless courage and sense of honour, led a desperate charge in which, according to contemporary evidence, he planted his family's three lances in the breasts of three Tukulor chiefs, 'For my grandfather, for my father, and for me!' Wounded and captured, he begged for death and received it.[30]

The *dina* was a remarkably fervent theocracy that challenged the heroic order at many points. Attendance at public prayer five times a day was compulsory, at least in the capital. Shehu Amadu himself, as a later panegyric declared, was a new kind of hero, blending *pulaaku* with piety:

> There are heroes desirous of anonymity,
> They do not envy glory or publicity,
> Their concern is the Day of Judgment.[31]

Griots largely disappeared, their lavish praises judged to verge on blasphemy. The *dina* initially freed slaves who fought with distinction for Islam. Yet Shehu Amadu refused to interfere with Fula customs not specifically condemned by Islamic law. When the Council proposed to abolish the stigmatisation of craftsmen, he is said to have offered its members a stew containing lizards and other disgusting ingredients that the Koran did not forbid. Apart from empowering clerics, the *dina* did not fundamentally change Masina's social order.[32] Instead, Islam achieved a rewarding rapprochement with the distinctive Fula blend of *pulaaku* and heroic honour.

By contrast with Masina, the history of nineteenth-century Hausaland is not complicated by a legacy of epic literature, for little existed except versifications of incidents from the Prophetic age, perhaps because Hausa culture suffered no

---

[28] Ibid., p. 123.

[29] Ibid., p. 126.

[30] Eugène Mage, *Voyage au Soudan occidental (1863–1866)* (reprinted, Paris, 1980), p. 112.

[31] Amadou Wangara, 'Chant de Cheikou Amadou,' in Hampate Ba and Daget, *L'empire*, p. 291.

[32] William Allen Brown, 'The Caliphate of Hamdullahi ca. 1818–1864,' PhD thesis, University of Wisconsin, 1969, pp. 9, 79, 124–6, 137; Hampate Ba and Daget, *L'empire*, pp. 67–8.

radical discontinuity, such as the collapse of Mali and Songhai, until its ruling class was so comprehensively supplanted by the jihad of 1804 that the holy war itself became the heroic age, abundantly documented by the writings of its leaders. Nevertheless, beneath this surface, Islam triumphed in nineteenth-century Hausaland, as in Masina, not only by contesting heroic values but also by absorbing them into a new synthesis of honour and virtue.

The jihad of 1804 that created the Sokoto Caliphate was launched initially against the Hausa kingdom of Gobir but was extended throughout Hausaland. Its originators, led by Usuman dan Fodio, were Muslim teachers of Fula origin whose ancestors had probably settled in Hausaland before the sixteenth century.[33] By the late eighteenth century, they were attracting so many adherents that the ruler of Gobir tried to ban further conversions, leading Usuman to withdraw his community to the border of the kingdom and prepare for Gobir's attack. The prospect aroused largely traditional responses in men of warrior age like his twenty-three-year-old son and cavalry commander, Muhammad Bello:

Little by little, war is going to break out in this place, a dust raising war. Tell them my desire, I will not accept humiliation, for disgrace is a heavy burden to bear. . . . In truth I wish to fulfil my promise to . . . fall upon the Gobirawa with strenuous war, and destroy them in all haste if indeed death do not first come upon me.[34]

At the major initial battle at Lake Kwatto, which Usuman likened to the Prophet's decisive victory at Badr, Bello and his companions defeated the panoply of a Hausa cavalry army:

As we approached the enemy we marched in lines. The enemy, too, prepared and took up their positions. In truth they had put on chain and quilted armour about one hundred in number. They drew up in line with round shields, and square shields, and made their preparations. We formed our line of battle against them. We gazed at each other, and each man's eye looked into his enemy's. Then we shouted three times 'Allah akbar' and charged them. They beat their drums and charged to meet us. The lines met. . . .

Our weapon at that time was the bow and arrow. Our horsemen did not exceed twenty but the Gobirawa had war horses not to be numbered except by God. . . . The fight continued and the opposing lines were intermingled. God broke the army of the heathen. They fell back. They retreated, they ran and scattered.[35]

---

[33] The best outline account of the jihad is Murray Last, 'Reform in West Africa: the *jihad* movements of the nineteenth century,' in J. F. A. Ajayi and Michael Crowder (eds.), *History of West Africa* (2 vols., 2nd edn, Harlow, 1987), vol. 2, pp. 15–28.

[34] Muhammad Bello to the Mallams of Gobir, in E. J. Arnett, *The rise of the Sokoto Fulani, being a paraphrase and in some parts a translation of the 'Infaku'l Maisuri' of Sultan Mohammed Bello* (Kano, 1922), p. 49.

[35] Ibid., pp. 56–7.

Bello's father, by contrast, was no fighting man and even at this crisis was preoccupied with the morality of violence, purity of motive, and what was perhaps sub-Saharan Africa's first attempt to discipline warfare. On the eve of the Battle of Lake Kwatto, Usuman is said to have told his followers, 'If I fight this battle that I may become greater than my fellow, or that my son may become greater than his, or that my slave may lord it over his, may the Kafiri wipe us off the land.'[36] A year later he is said to have required his commanders to swear 'that they would not be corrupted or changed by power, as were the Israelites in the desert, but they would avoid worldly aspirations, envy, mercilessness, feuds, the pursuit of wealth.'[37] To guide his followers he wrote a treatise on jihad urging them not to fight as 'martyrs of only this world,' as 'one who has fought only for the spoils or to vaunt his bravery or out of chauvinism, or to protect his wealth or his people, or to preserve his honour or the like'. 'Do not be cowardly in battle,' he quoted, 'and do not mutilate when you have the upper hand. Do not go too far when you are victorious and do not defraud when collecting booty. And make jihad free from worldly motives'. Like the founders of Islam, Usuman valued honour and incorporated it into his teachings, but he ranked it last among his 'universal rules', below religion and the preservation of the soul, the intellect, and lineage, and on a par with wealth.[38] Like the founders, too, he sought to purge honour of bravado, condemning the Fula *sharo* ordeal and criticising Hausa for their brutality in beating youths who cried or showed fear during circumcision.[39] 'Self-conceit, vanity, jealousy, envy, covetousness, ostentation, vain glory, seeking wealth, if it is for display' headed the ten 'qualities of destruction' which he condemned.[40] In a chapter 'On the law concerning boasting at the time of shooting arrows, reciting *rajaz* poetry, declaiming one's genealogy (*tasmiya*) and shouting in a jihad', he pronounced all these to be lawful on the battlefield because the Prophet himself was recorded to have declared his ancestry when shooting and to have quoted poetry during a raid. 'But', Usuman warned, 'mention of God's name rather than anything else the archer may shout, is more desirable.'[41]

Much of this virtuous restraint was preserved by the young men who exercised power after gaining victory and establishing a Caliphate. Their leader and

[36] C. L. Temple, in J. A. Burdon, *Northern Nigeria* (2nd edn, London, 1972), p. 67.

[37] Murray Last, *The Sokoto Caliphate* (London, 1967), p. 36.

[38] Uthman ibn Fudi, *Bayan wujub al-hijra ala 'l-ibad* (trans. F. H. el Masri, Khartoum, 1978), pp. 80 (quoting al-Shabrakhiti), 100, 49.

[39] Beverly B. Mack and Jean Boyd, *One woman's jihad: Nana Asma'u, scholar and scribe* (Bloomington, 2000), p. 45; Yusuf Wali, 'The translation of the Nur-al-Albab (of Usuman ibn Fudi),' *Kano Studies*, NS, 2, 1 (1980), 16–17.

[40] Arnett, *Rise*, p. 37.

[41] Uthman, *Bayan*, p. 101.

exemplar, Muhammad Bello, fought forty-seven major campaigns during his twenty years on the throne (1817–37), lived and died in a frontier *ribat*, and was a distinguished administrator and polymath, but the elegy written by his sister Nana Asma'u stressed rather his virtue:

> He was upright, exceedingly generous, patient:
> He spread learning and explained matters.
> He was wise. He could turn back prodigals
> And used his wits to remedy any situation . . .
> He had a fine character, he was merciful to the poor,
> He honoured and befriended people.
> He was gracious to strangers and generous to them.[42]

Until 1881, at least, Bello's successors in Sokoto generally preserved his austere lifestyle and easy access to petitioners. Yet the claims of heroic honour were not easily set aside. The new rulers initially obeyed Usuman's injunction not to imitate elaborate Hausa titles but soon became 'captives of the historical situation' and took over their predecessors' offices, property, and titles, which even Usuman eventually recognised as unavoidable.[43] In outlying emirates, the Fula often preserved among themselves something of their egalitarian traditions, but in the wealthy former Hausa kingdoms the emirs' kinsmen and slaves might virtually monopolise office. In Kano, for example, the ruling family had by the later nineteenth century 'stamped out all vestiges of the egalitarianism that had been a part of the Jihad movement . . . and had re-established the hierarchy and the court protocol that had been part of the pre-Jihad government.'[44]

The most profound adaptation to Hausa culture was the adoption of cavalry warfare. At Lake Kwatto only twenty horses had supplemented the jihad's bowmen. Their riders made it a point of honour to fight without elaborate Hausa armour. Yet their early losses, the recruitment of horsemen, and the capture of enemy mounts changed these tactics until the jihad armies were dominated by cavalrymen and their distinctive ethos.[45] Their expensive horses became 'the visible and outward manifestation of rank and wealth, power and swagger.' Horses could sometimes be bought only with slaves. A horse – especially a black horse – was a gift of special honour. Kano sent one each week as tribute to the Caliph, while an emir's death was reported to Sokoto by the arrival of

---

[42] Jean Boyd and Beverly B. Mack (eds.), *Collected works of Nana Asma'u, daughter of Usman dan Fodiyo (1793–1864)* (East Lansing, 1997), p. 87.

[43] Last in Ajayi and Crowder, *History*, vol. 2, pp. 25–6; Smith, *Government in Kano*, pp. 206–7, 226.

[44] Tanimu Abubakar (ed.), *The essential Mahmud: selected writings of Mahmud Modibbo Tukur* (Zaria, 1990), p. 171.

[45] Smaldone, *Warfare*, pp. 30–2.

his riderless horse.[46] As in the western savanna, the style of horsemanship admired was dashing and brutal, with much sudden reining-in from a wild gallop. Ceremonial boasting before combat survived Usuman's displeasure, at least in outlying emirates, along with discreet self-exposure to danger. 'Now and then', a European observer wrote of Bello's forces in 1826, 'a single horse would gallop up to the ditch, and brandish his spear, the rider taking care to cover himself with his large leathern shield, and return as fast as he went.'[47] A distinct category of young noblemen emerged seeking advancement by military adventure. During the 1880s, for example, one such refugee Fula warrior gained the Emir of Kano's permission to challenge an enemy champion, killed him, won a leading place in Kano's forces, had three horses killed beneath him in battle, insulted the officer who refused him a fourth, and was banished, only to settle in Katsina.[48] This ethos found expression in the vainglorious poetry, celebrating the slaughter of Gobir's forces, written by Muhammad al-Bukhari, a son of Usuman dan Fodio who had taken a leading role in the jihad campaign at age nineteen but was later passed over for the Caliphate.[49] Much violence found an outlet in brutal annual slaving expeditions against surrounding agricultural peoples, but even the virtuous Nana Asma'u celebrated its use in defence of the jihad:

> God the Beneficent destroy Mayaki and Nabame
> Destroy them completely . . .
> Destroy the unbelievers of Hausaland who are in revolt,
> Fomenting rebellion with obduracy.
> Destroy those who have set out to destroy religion
> Everywhere, let them perish.[50]

Although the initial jihad forces were multiethnic, victory gave Fula leaders a near-monopoly of power. Only one emir, Yakubu of Bauchi, was not Fula, and

---

[46] C. L. Temple, *Native races and their rulers: sketches and studies of official life and administrative problems in Nigeria* (2nd edn, London, 1968), p. 131; Bryan, 'Report on the recruiting expedition to Bauchi,' 1898, CO 446/4/27; E. J. Lugard, 'Journal jottings,' 6 February 1904, RH Mss.Brit.Emp.s.61; Denham and Clapperton, *Narrative*, part 2, p. 67; Smith, *Government in Kano*, p. 301.

[47] Paul Staudinger, *In the heart of the Hausa states* (trans. J. Moody, 2 vols., Athens, Ohio, 1990), vol. 2, p. 161; Rupert M. East, *Stories of old Adamawa* (reprinted, Farnborough, 1967), pp. 71–3; Hugh Clapperton, *Journal of a second expedition into the interior of Africa* (reprinted, London, 1966), p. 186.

[48] Smith, *Government in Kano*, p. 325.

[49] Ahmad Muhammad Kani, 'The intellectual and political contributions of Muhammad al-Bukhari (d.1258 A.H.) to the Sokoto Caliphate,' in Ahmad Muhammad Kani and Kabir Ahmed Gandi (eds.), *State and society in the Sokoto Caliphate* (Sokoto, 1990), pp. 227, 233–4.

[50] Boyd and Mack, *Collected works*, pp. 208–9. Mayaki was the son of the ruler of Gobir, Nabame the son of the ruler of Kebbi.

he had been among Usuman's most loyal disciples. Several ousted Hausa rulers created defiant successor states beyond the Caliphate's borders.[51] Usuman's death in 1817 precipitated a widespread Hausa revolt, including many who had supported the jihad and resented exclusion from its fruits. Several areas of dissidence survived within the Caliphate throughout the nineteenth century.[52] Generally, however, Fula were able to insist upon their ethnic dominance over 'Habe', their pejorative term for conquered blacks. The new rulers were much concerned with genealogy and dynastic marriage.[53] Even Usuman allowed them privileged status before the law, quoting an authority: 'The Caliphs used to chastise men according to their status; so if any of those known to be men of honour should stumble, they would help him up again and let him off.'[54] Fula power was most brutal in frontier regions like Adamawa, but even in wealthy and sophisticated Kano City the Fula generally went armed, while Habe were forbidden the use of arms and horses and were required to remove their shoes on entering the Fula quarter.[55] 'The Fulbe marry the handsome daughters of the subjugated tribe,' a traveller noted, 'but would not condescend to give their own daughters to the men of that tribe as wives.'[56] Hausa resentment occasionally flared into violence, as when a peasant brutalised by a Fula horseman dragged his tormenter into a fire in which both died, thereby precipitating a local revolt.[57] More commonly these tensions were restrained by the vertical relations of clientage that pervaded the society. 'They may be said to march through life in single file,' observed an early British official, 'receiving personal homage from those below, and rendering personal homage to those above.' Honour accrued from supporting a host of clients, as it also accrued from open-handed largess to the numerous poor.[58]

[51] A. Y. Abubakar, 'The establishment and development of emirate government in Bauchi 1805–1903,' PhD thesis, Ahmadu Bello University, Zaria, 1974, pp. 357–60; M. G. Smith, 'A Hausa kingdom: Maradi under Dan Baskore, 1854–75,' in Daryll Forde and P. M. Kaberry (eds.), *West African kingdoms in the nineteenth century* (London, 1967), pp. 93–122.

[52] Clapperton, *Journal*, pp. 154–5, 207–8; Adell Patton, Jr., 'Ningi raids and slavery in nineteenth century Sokoto Caliphate,' *Slavery and Abolition*, 2 (1981), 114–45.

[53] Philip Burnham and Murray Last, 'From pastoralist to politician: the problem of a Fulbe "aristocracy",' *CEA*, 34 (1994), 313–14; Smith, *Government in Kano*, p. 29; Last, *Sokoto Caliphate*, p. 223.

[54] Uthman, *Bayan*, p. 139.

[55] Smith, *Government in Kano*, p. 242; C. S. Whitaker, Jr., *The politics of tradition: continuity and change in Northern Nigeria, 1946–1966* (Princeton, 1970), p. 382.

[56] Heinrich Barth, *Travels and discoveries in North and Central Africa . . . in the years 1849–1855* (reprinted, 3 vols., London, 1965), vol. 1, p. 525.

[57] Guy Nicolas, 'La question de la vengeance au sein d'une société soudanaise,' in Raymond Verdier (ed.), *La vengeance: études d'ethnologie, d'histoire et de philosophie* (4 vols., Paris, 1980), vol. 2, p. 32.

[58] Temple, *Native races*, p. 35; John Iliffe, *The African poor: a history* (Cambridge, 1987), ch. 3.

The line between largess, clientage, and corruption was a special concern to the reformers and was, as always, a sensitive indicator of honour and virtue. The exchange of gifts was probably very widespread in Hausaland before the jihad, as elsewhere in sub-Saharan Africa and other premodern societies, creating a diffuse web of relationships and obligations. To refuse to give or receive such presents might imply not merely discourtesy but enmity. Especially important was the gift exchange between superiors and inferiors, which established ties of patronage and clientage. Among these were the gifts known as *gaisuwa*, made by those seeking office, and *kurdin sarauta*, presented on taking it up. In his critique of the Hausa kingdoms Usuman dan Fodio denounced both these and the practice of bribery (*toshi*). Muhammad Bello 'flung back at the givers money offered for titles,' according to Nana Asma'u, who also praised her husband, Bello's vizier, for checking corruption in Sokoto. The reformers' attack failed, however, for all these practices remained common throughout the nineteenth century; senior officials, including the viziers themselves, continued to collect large sums from those seeking their favour.[59] Equally unsuccessful was the attempt to eradicate praise-singing, on the grounds that only the Prophet should receive such honour. Even Usuman dan Fodio, who denounced the practice, attracted many praise-names, and the custom continued at emirate courts and social occasions.[60] Another enduring aspect of heroic honour was the extreme sensitivity to insult, which foreign visitors noted. Swords were more likely to be drawn in such disputes than in war, despite emirs' attempts to replace private vengeance – which Bello condemned as characteristic of *jahiliyya* – by Islamic justice.[61]

Expert study of the vocabulary of honour in the Hausa and Fulfulde languages might reveal the same shift of emphasis from objective rank and prestige towards subjective virtue and respectability contained in the Swahili transition from *cheo* to *heshima*. The first Hausa–English dictionary, published in 1876, gave two main words for honour: *yabo*, whose connotations were fame, praise, and (more distantly) companionship, and *girima*, which connoted greatness. A supplement in 1888 added the Arabic loan-word *daraja*, meaning honour or glory, which was also adopted during the nineteenth century into the Fulfulde language to

---

[59] M. Hiskett, '*Kitab al-farq*: a work on the Habe kingdoms attributed to Uthman dan Fodio,' *Bulletin of the School of Oriental and African Studies*, 23 (1960), 567–9, 576–7; M. G. Smith, 'Historical and cultural conditions of political corruption among the Hausa,' *CSSH*, 6 (1963–4), 170–1, 176–7, 183–5; Boyd and Mack, *Collected works*, pp. 92, 201.

[60] Mervyn Hiskett, *A history of Hausa Islamic verse* (London, 1975), pp. 1–12, 17; Alhaji Shehu Shagari and Jean Boyd, *Uthman dan Fodio: the theory and practice of his leadership* (Lagos, 1978), p. x.

[61] Staudinger, *In the heart*, vol. 2, pp. 57, 194–5; Arnett, *Rise*, p. 11.

describe the prestige enjoyed by the rulers, scholars, and wealthy commoners forming the newly differentiated Fula ruling class.[62] Among the Hausa subjects, by contrast, the common word for honour, *martaba*, appeared only in twentieth-century dictionaries, while the major trend – which cannot at present be dated – seems to have been towards an Islamic notion of uprightness and respectability encapsulated in the word *kirki*, also contained for the first time in twentieth-century dictionaries.[63] *Kirki* combined horror of shame and positive evaluation of courtesy with emphasis on patience, sobriety, wisdom, scrupulous behaviour, truthfulness, and respect for others.[64] It epitomised the good man, the virtuous householder, a bourgeois ethic contrasting with the heroic honour of the defeated Hausa nobility, and it became associated especially with urban scholars and merchants, as in Nana Asma'u's elegy for Malam Dandi of Sokoto:

> O God the Infinitely Pure, forgive Malam Dandi.
>> He was God-fearing, a Muslim gentleman.
> He was patient and benefitted Muslims, his neighbours,
>> And did well in all he set out to do.
> He was a good man, a man of great piety and kindness,
>> All who knew him agree on this.
> He helped peasants, his relatives, those unrelated to him,
>> Never discriminating in favour of any section.
> He was a follower of the Shehu and Bello and he obeyed the *Sharia*
>> He gave freely of his possessions.
> He spoke truthfully and was righteous:
>> Shehu's disciple.[65]

During the nineteenth century Hausaland's important merchant class remained distinctly subordinate to the ruling Fula elite. Merchants did not fight, any more than noblemen traded; those who captured slaves did not market them.[66] Merchants deferred to the nobility, often as clients, and suffered heavy exactions through forced loans and inheritance taxes. Mohamman Mai Gashin

---

[62] James Frederick Schön, *Dictionary of the Hausa language* (London, 1876), part 1, pp. 76, 263, and part 2, p. 67; idem, *Appendix to the dictionary of the Hausa language* (London, 1888), p. 32; Ver Eecke, 'Pulaaku,' pp. 188–92, 202, 225–6.

[63] Charles Henry Robinson, *Dictionary of the Hausa language* (2 vols., 4th edn, Cambridge, 1925), vol. 1, pp. 221, 293; G. P. Bargery, *A Hausa–English dictionary and English–Hausa vocabulary* (London, 1934), pp. 611, 775.

[64] Anthony H. M. Kirk-Greene, *Mutumin Kirkii: the concept of the good man in Hausa* (Bloomington, 1974).

[65] Boyd and Mack, *Collected works*, p. 281.

[66] Mahdi Adamu, 'The delivery of slaves from the Central Sudan to the Bight of Benin in the eighteenth and nineteenth centuries,' in Henry A. Gemery and Jan S. Hogendorn (eds.), *The uncommon market: essays in the economic history of the Atlantic slave trade* (New York, 1979), p. 171.

Baki, who made a fortune from slaves and ivory in Adamawa in the 1840s and 1850s, gave credit to Kano's penurious princes, 'receiving in return little more than empty promises,' while Muminu, a rich merchant and banker in late nineteenth-century Bauchi, listed the heir-apparent and several senior officials among his twenty-one debtors.[67] Merchants needed both to display modesty and to legitimise their wealth by generosity – they were favourite targets for praise-singers – and by maintaining a large clientele of kinsmen, agents, and trusted slaves who were bound to them by *amana* (professional integrity) and were essential both to their commercial operations and to their credit worthiness.[68] A merchant's reputation was vital to his success; stories were told of men who died mad because 'I broke trust'.[69] To gain such trust in alien towns, merchants operated through resident brokers from their own community familiar to the local population in a network of diasporas that underlay commerce throughout the savanna.[70] Trade had its heroic qualities, for like warfare it involved risk, attracted the adventurous, and needed luck: the Hausa word *arziki* meant fortune in both senses.[71] But merchant honour probably approximated increasingly to the ideal of *kirki*. That may have been true also of Hausa craftsmen, who were not stigmatised. A town's occupations each had an appointed head and the right to regulate its trade. Wage labour carried less stigma than was normal in precolonial Africa; it was common in transport work and quite widely used in agriculture.[72] Urban popular culture had its own heroes, as in the boxing and wrestling contests denounced by reformers and patronised especially by the much-despised butchers.[73] But further research might reveal a broad trend towards Muslim respectability.

More is known about female honour. Nineteenth-century Hausa women generally married young, at about thirteen or fourteen, to men chosen by their parents, which in this bilateral society led to a noncompanionate marriage pattern broken on either side by frequent divorce.[74] This had probably been true before the jihad. On the other hand, women had then enjoyed a greater economic

[67] E. R. Flegel, *The biography of Madugu Mohamman Mai Gashin Baki* (trans. M. B. Duffill, Los Angeles, 1985), p. 18; Abubakar, 'Establishment,' pp. 658–9.

[68] Ibrahim A. Tahir, 'Scholars, sufis, saints and capitalists in Kano, 1904–1974: the pattern of bourgeois revolution in an Islamic society,' PhD thesis, University of Cambridge, 1975, pp. 223–4, 283; Ahmed Beita Yusuf, 'Capital formation and management among the Muslim Hausa traders of Kano, Nigeria,' *Africa*, 45 (1975), 178–80.

[69] M. F. Smith, *Baba of Karo: a woman of the Muslim Hausa* (London, 1954), pp. 181–2.

[70] Philip D. Curtin, *Cross-cultural trade in world history* (Cambridge, 1984), pp. 53–7.

[71] Claude Raynaut, *Structures normatives et relations électives: étude d'une communauté villageoise haoussa* (Paris, 1972), p. 52.

[72] John Iliffe, *The emergence of African capitalism* (London, 1983), pp. 7–13.

[73] Paul in Baker and Mangan, *Sport,* p. 27.

[74] See esp. Smith, *Baba,* passim.

role than was normal in the savanna, for their engagement in urban trade had been equalled only in Malinke trading communities and coastal towns. In addition, elite women and senior wives had exercised leadership within the female sphere, sometimes holding titled offices, and Hausa cities had contained a *demi-monde* of gambling, dancing, drinking, and sexual licence surrounding the *karuwai*, the 'free' (temporarily unmarried) women, distinct from prostitutes, whose lifestyle challenged conventions.[75] Much of this was anathema to reformers, but they had to reckon with the traditionally high status and economic independence of their own Fula women. Influenced perhaps by this and the teaching of his Qadiriyya brotherhood, Usuman dan Fodio insisted that women had the same right and duty as men to education in the Islamic religion. Their husbands, he told them,

require of you what neither God nor his messenger make obligatory for you by birth, such as cooking, washing clothes, and other things which are mostly what they desire; while not requiring of you what God and his Apostle (may God bless him and grant him salvation) oblige for you in the way of obedience to God and obedience to his Apostle. Yes, it is obligatory for the wife to obey her husband both in private and in public, even if her husband is very wretched or a slave. And it is forbidden for her to go against her husband except when he commands her to disobey God Most High. Then it becomes necessary for her to refuse to obey, because there is no obedience to the created in disobedience to the Creator.[76]

These teachings were implemented especially by Usuman's highly educated daughter, the poet Nana Asma'u, who organised the training of women teachers to work among the wives of the elite, although women had only an ancillary place in public worship, their former titled offices were either abolished or reallocated to men, and education did not reach the bulk of Hausa women.[77] Nana Asma'u's writings provide a rare opportunity to penetrate beyond male views of female honour and glimpse what women honoured in one another:

I have composed this elegy for Halimatu
Who was a very kind good neighbor.
She was a fine woman with lots of common sense;

---

[75] Beverly B. Mack, 'Harem domesticity in Kano, Nigeria,' in Karen Tranberg Hansen (ed.), *African encounters with domesticity* (New Brunswick, N.J., 1992), p. 77; M. G. Smith, *The affairs of Daura* (Berkeley, 1978), pp. 42, 134.

[76] Wali, 'The translation of the Nur-al-Albab,' p. 14.

[77] Jean Boyd, 'Distance learning from purdah in nineteenth-century northern Nigeria: the work of Asma'u Fodiyo,' *JACS*, 14 (2001), 7–22; Smith, *Affairs*, p. 42; Douglas Edwin Ferguson, 'Nineteenth-century Hausaland, being a description by Imam Imoru of the land, economy, and society of his people,' PhD thesis, University of California at Los Angeles, 1973, p. 261.

> She loved children and adults, treating them fittingly with respect.
> She was religious and kept close relationships in good repair,
> Acting always with never ending patience.[78]

Yet Nana Asma'u endorsed her father's belief that both Islam and female honour required that wives should wherever possible be secluded. Although the Kano Chronicle attributed this practice to Muhammad Rumfa in the fifteenth century, it appears to have been rare until Usuman advocated it:

> A woman should protect her honour and stay at home . . . and show a pleasant and gracious manner to her husband . . . giving him due respect . . . it is compulsory to feed and clothe such a woman and give her her dowry (*sadaki*). A wife who goes out [without good reason] loses her right to her dowry and cannot claim food and clothing from her husband. . . . Womenfolk take heed! Do not do communal farm work and do not assist in herding . . . cover yourself up and spin the thread you need to cover yourself with. . . . The best thing is to let the men-folk go to the market, but if circumstances compel you to go you must dress in a restrained manner, covering yourself up from head to toe.[79]

Usuman had difficulty in making this acceptable to his own senior wife, who had grown up in the freer Fula environment, but, as in India at the same period, seclusion became a matter of social prestige, being practicable only for those who could afford the slaves needed to free women from outdoor labour.[80] By the late nineteenth century, free women had withdrawn from agricultural work in some parts of the Caliphate, although European visitors were surprised by the freedom of movement and behaviour enjoyed by ordinary townswomen, especially in Kano, which was famous for its women's beauty and gaiety.[81] 'With the exception of the wives of the king,' it was reported, 'and one or two of his chief ministers [and, doubtless, important clerics], they are not kept in seclusion, but are allowed to go about as they please.'[82] There are indications of sensitive notions of sexual honour among the elite. One account describes an adulterous woman demanding execution so insistently that Muhammad Bello was obliged to comply. A tale of the period describes a noble courtship in which the couple agreed that one might kill the other if seen with a member of the opposite sex. Islam gave wives legal protection of their property, but less protection against domestic violence, which court records show to have been

---

[78] Boyd and Mack, *Collected works*, p. 196.

[79] Quoted in Jean Boyd, *The Caliph's sister: Nana Asma'u (1793–1865), teacher, poet and Islamic leader* (London, 1989), pp. 5–6.

[80] Ibid., p. 4; Hiskett, *History*, p. 104; Rosalind O'Hanlon, *A comparison between women and men: Tarabai Shinde and the critique of gender relations in colonial India* (Madras, 1994), pp. 22–8.

[81] Ferguson, 'Hausaland,' pp. 63–4; Barbara J. Callaway, *Muslim Hausa women in Nigeria: tradition and change* (Syracuse, 1987), pp. 59–60; Staudinger, *In the heart*, vol. 2, pp. 62–3.

[82] Charles Henry Robinson, *Hausaland* (London, 1896), p. 205.

common.[83] In the sphere of female honour, as of male, Hausaland's Islamic reformation absorbed as much of the old order as it destroyed. Its capacity to do so helps to explain its success.

Where the western savanna meets the sea between the Senegal and Casamance estuaries, elaborate notions of honour have been studied with greater care than anywhere else in sub-Saharan Africa, notably by the Senegalese sociologists Boubakar Ly and Assane Sylla.[84] The unified Wolof state, which the Portuguese found here in the fifteenth century, fragmented in the 1530s into six major kingdoms with outwardly Islamic courts but largely pagan people, a fragmentation characteristically attributed to a dispute over honour.[85] The neighbouring state of Futa Toro in the Senegal Valley had a long Islamic history, but its Denianke (Fula) rulers, who seized power at the beginning of the sixteenth century, practised at best a mixed Islam.[86] Wolof and Tukulor societies shared the Malinke specialisation into freemen, craftsmen, and slaves. Freemen, in turn, were divided between the ruling nobility and peasant commoners. Ancestry was fundamental, determining not only rank and endogamy but expected behaviour and personality traits. 'Character reveals birth', it was said, and poetry focused not on the individual but his ancestors.[87]

The most distinctive social group were the *sebbe* (sing. *ceddo*), professional warriors, horsemen who – unusually in the savanna – adopted the firearms that became widely available from the 1690s. Whether freemen or royal slaves, they were deeply engaged in slave-raiding and were notorious for their violence and pride, their addiction to alcohol, and their reckless courage. The Senegalese *abbé* Boilat described them with loathing in 1853:

The word *thiédo* is the opposite of *marabout* [Muslim cleric]; it signifies an unbeliever, an impious person, a man without faith or probity.... Living only by theft and pillage on the main roads, they are especially fitted for warfare.... None receives pay, but they

---

[83] Alhaji Shehu Malami, *Sir Siddiq Abubakar III, 17th Sultan of Sokoto* (Ibadan, 1989), pp. 21–4; Richard P. Brady, 'Hierarchy and authority among the Hausa,' DPhil thesis, University of Oxford, 1978, p. 274; Allen Christelow (ed.), *Thus ruled Emir Abbas: selected cases from the records of the Emir of Kano's Judicial Council* (East Lansing, 1994), pp. 14–15, 166–7, 177 n28, 178.

[84] Ly, 'L'honneur dans les sociétés' and 'L'honneur et les valeurs'; Assane Sylla, *La philosophie morale des Wolof* (Lille, 1980).

[85] Mamadou Diouf, *Le Kajoor au XIXe siècle: pouvoir ceddo et conquête coloniale* (Paris, 1990), p. 37.

[86] Nehemia Levtzion, 'Islam in the Bilad al-Sudan to 1800,' in Levtzion and Pouwels, *History*, pp. 77–8.

[87] Ly, 'L'honneur dans les sociétés,' p. 46; George Joseph, 'The Wolof oral praise song for Semu Coro Wende,' *RAL*, 10 (1979), 152–3.

have part of the booty they take in war. Today all have muskets and swords. Lacking any belief, they are addicted to all the vices, and especially to drinking brandy. I have seen *thiédos* pass whole days drinking this horrible liquor and collapse dead drunk. . . .

The religion of a *thiédo* consists only in *grisgris* [amulets] which render him invulnerable in wars and raids.[88]

Along with this lifestyle went dedication to a particularly ostentatious heroic code:

The *alamari* is a very ancient war dance, which is danced on the eve of an expedition's departure for war. The warrior who enters the circle of the dance first goes to seize a lance stuck into the ground before the commander who presides over the assembly. The woman who loves him enters the circle in her turn and goes towards him. Then both dance, he enumerating the exploits which he will accomplish, she holding his wrist as if to help him to support the lance which he brandishes above their heads. Once the dance is ended and the lance stuck again into the ground where it was found, the warrior and his lover, face to face, take one another by the hand, taking the haft of the lance between their palms, and the warrior tells the woman that he makes her his witness to the undertakings he has made.[89]

During the *alamari* was sung the *gumbala*:

> The gourds of *pata* have sounded
> The drums of Alamari have sounded
> He who is afraid is not invited.
> God, for the sake of my mother's prayers
> God, for the sake of my father's fasts
> Do not slay me with a small and shameful death
> That of dying in a bed
> Amidst the tears of children
> And the moans of the elders
> And the marabout's appeals to God.
> Kill me when
> Swallowed bullets are spat.[90]

The epic hero Samba Gelajo had danced the *alamari* even in his enemy's camp on the night before battle, protected by the laws of hospitality.[91] A *ceddo* never violated those, never retreated, was never taken prisoner, never returned defeated from a battlefield, never displayed weakness, never admitted pain:

The true incarnation of *ceddaagu* would be quasi-insensibility to physical pain, for the *ceddo* of quality would be by definition invulnerable (*tunndoowo*) to iron, whether it be

---

[88] David Boilat, *Esquisses sénégalaises* (reprinted, Paris, 1984), pp. 308–9.

[89] Henri Gaden, *Proverbes et maximes peuls et toucouleurs* (Paris, 1931), pp. 225–6.

[90] Abdoul Aziz Sow, 'Fulani poetic genres,' *RAL*, 24 (1993), 63.

[91] Ly, 'L'honneur et les valeurs', vol. 2, p. 402 n1.

the dagger or the ball, having in this respect and from tender years received appropriate treatment, which is jealously transmitted from father to son . . . on hearing the *gumbala* evoking his noble and warrior past, the *ceddo* will unsheathe his dagger and, in default of an enemy to slay, will cut off his ear to offer to the artists.[92]

In the mid nineteenth century, the French Governor Faidherbe told of a *ceddo* who refused to eat or drink for ten days because his hands were manacled and he declined 'to lap like a dog'.[93]

The Wolof nobility shared much of this ethos well into the nineteenth century, although in a more courtly form. Equestrian noblemen noted for spectacular and ruthless horsemanship, they cultivated the style of the *samba linguère*, the gentleman of courage, loyalty, virility, taste, diplomacy, grace of manner, reckless generosity, and sensitivity to insult. Among the Tukulor, by contrast, the similar nobility of the Denianke regime were overthrown in 1776 in a jihad led by Muslim zealots known as Torodbe who evolved into a ruling class, much interpenetrated with the old nobility, practising an unusually harmonious blend of aristocratic honour and Islamic virtue. As analysed by Boubakar Ly, the basis of Torodbe honour (*jom*) was ancestry, family loyalty, and behaviour governed by rank. As a proverb said, 'Clothes hide the body but not the genealogy.' Such behaviour required courage, daring, and quickness to retaliate. 'If someone has bitten you,' ran another proverb, 'he has reminded you that you have teeth.'[94] Honourable behaviour also demanded hospitality and generosity, virility in men and chastity in women. But in addition *jom* had a new earnestness. As in Hausaland, this drew heavily on a notion of shame, *gacce*, which also meant self-respect. Fear of shame discountenanced boasting and conspicuous ambition. To shame another was to shame oneself.[95] Above all the new ethos counselled dignity, gravity, and moderation. Boubakar Ly's analysis of this blend of honour and virtue among Tukulor (and later among Wolof) catches the process of change exactly:

All religions of which humility is one of the fundamental elements of dogma have combatted honour in its more 'prideful' aspects. It is the case with Christianity; it is the case with Islam. Islam in pre-Islamic Arab society combatted honour in its aspects most contrary to humility at the same time as it assimilated those values most compatible with dogma.

It had to be the same in Wolof and Tukulor societies. There Islam had to combat the practices of agonistic glorification and self-glorification, to end by accommodating

[92] Yaya Wane, *Les Toucouleurs du Fouta Tooro (Sénégal): stratification sociale et structure familiale* (Dakar, 1969), pp. 40–2.

[93] Vincent Monteil, *Esquisses sénégalaises* (Dakar, 1966), p. 88.

[94] Ly, 'L'honneur et les valeurs,' vol. 1, pp. 79–87; Gaden, *Proverbes*, pp. 103, 8.

[95] Ly, 'L'honneur et les valeurs,' vol. 1, pp. 40–1, 114, 166, 169.

itself to them, or it had to accept them because Arabian Islam itself had accommodated to them.

However that may be, one can see at the level of Wolof and Tukulor societies – warrior societies despite their Islamisation – two fundamental models of values, those which tend towards the glorification and affirmation of the person (with all his social content) and those which tend towards humility.... It seems that the Wolof and Tukulor *marabouts* introduced into the animist *ceddo* milieu of the Wolof and Tukulor a new type of personality based on the old type. Islamic honour and dignity seem to be superimposed and amalgamated with traditional noble honour and dignity.[96]

As a proverb said, 'It is the old garments that preserve the new.'[97]

Futa Toro's rulers and warriors did not acknowledge that their inferiors could possess honour, although, as Ly pointed out, 'People of caste [and] captives have adopted the dominant values of the nobility and freemen.'[98] Exceptionally, a man who was not fully free (*gor*) but behaved in the manner of a freeman might be called *gore*. But honourable behaviour for subordinate groups consisted chiefly in performing their appropriate specialities.[99] Self-awareness of honour in this sense has been demonstrated not only for griots who specialised in the power of speech but also for other craft groups who emphasised the indispensable nature of their skills, competed with one another for relative status, and celebrated their past heroes in poetry.[100]

During the nineteenth century, the Islamic pressures that had changed notions of honour in Futa Toro affected also the Wolof, where Islam, although long established, had hitherto been shallow and eclectic. Here there was no triumphant jihad but several confused and violent decades of 'maraboutic revolutions', which gradually created a new synthesis of honour and virtue, more egalitarian than that of the Torodbe nobility.[101] Similar changes also took place further south among the Mandinka chiefdoms of the Gambia.[102] In some frontier areas there, as in the Kaabu kingdom south of the River Gambia, the *nyancho* military nobility had hitherto observed a particularly disciplined and exclusive code of heroic honour, and everywhere before the nineteenth century the Mandinka

---

[96] Ibid., vol. 2, pp. 513–15.

[97] Gaden, *Proverbes*, p. 281.

[98] Ly, 'L'honneur dans les sociétés,' p. 44; Ly, 'L'honneur et les valeurs,' vol. 2, p. 500.

[99] Ly, 'L'honneur et les valeurs,' vol. 1, p. 82, and vol. 2, p. 500.

[100] Emil A. Magel, 'Hare and hyena: symbols of honor and shame in the oral narratives of the Wolof of the Senegambia,' PhD thesis, University of Wisconsin–Madison, 1977, pp. 92–4, 107; Sow, 'Fulani poetic genres,' pp. 65–71.

[101] Martin A. Klein, 'Social and economic factors in the Muslim revolution in Senegambia,' *JAH*, 13 (1972), 419–41.

[102] The following account is based on Djibril Tamsir Niane, *Histoire des Mandingues de l'ouest: le royaume du Gabou* (Paris, 1989); Charlotte A. Quinn, *Mandingo kingdoms of the Senegambia* (London, 1972).

aristocrats were either pagans or practised 'mixed Islam'. For some centuries, however, quietist Muslim communities had lived under their rule. During the first half of the nineteenth century, this relationship broke down, chiefly perhaps through the gradual expansion of Islam and the example of successful jihads elsewhere, but also as a result of the decline of the Atlantic slave trade and the growth of groundnut exports, which shifted wealth and the ability to buy firearms from nobility to peasantry. Major conflict between Muslims and traditionalists – or Marabouts and Soninke, as the parties became known – began in the 1840s and drew in all the region's fighting men. Most prominent among them, in legend, was Kelefa Saane, a turbulent *nyancho* prince of Kaabu, who felt compelled by honour to aid a fellow *nyancho* ruler, knowing that it would mean his death. 'The *nyancho*', he declared, 'holds three things in horror: wealth, feebleness, and to die old':[103]

> As the prince lay dying,
> Koriyang Musa played the *kora*
> Till dawn broke.
> After a little while Kelefa would raise his head
> And ask, 'Griot Musa, I didn't disgrace myself, did I?'
> And the griot would answer, 'You did not disgrace yourself.'[104]

Shortly afterwards the Fula state of Futa Jalon attacked Kaabu's capital to aid its Fula subjects against their *nyancho* rulers. *Nyancho* warriors buried themselves to the waist so that they could not run, princesses threw themselves into wells to escape dishonour, their servants threw their jewels after them, and the king blew up his arsenal, his capital, its invaders, and himself. Confused and brutal fighting engulfed the region. On the Marabout side, the lawless violence was epitomised by Fode Kaba, border chieftain, slave-raider, and converter by the sword. 'Ever since I knew myself to be a man,' he wrote in 1886, 'my occupation is a warrior and I make it my duty to fight against Sonninkeys who profess no religion whatever.'[105] War chiefs took power in many Muslim villages. No man went unarmed. Yet gradually Islam won the young and inserted its disciplined sobriety into traditional notions of military honour. 'They are all very strict Mahomedhans', the first British commissioner on the northern bank of the Gambia reported in 1893:

... The men are ... for the most part reticent, and morose, although they brighten up when spoken to. They have a quiet rather dignified manner.... At a palaver once the

---

[103] Niane, *Histoire*, p. 161.

[104] Bamba Suso, 'Kelefa Sane,' in Gordon Innes (ed.), *Kelefa Saane: his career recounted by two Mandinka bards* (London, 1978), p. 65.

[105] Great Britain, *Correspondence respecting the affairs of the Gambia*, PP, 1887, LIX, 393.

ice is broken, they express their opinion slowly and deliberately. Being Mahomedhans they drink no spirits, and I must say that I have never travelled anywhere, and seen so little fighting and wrangling. . . . They will not hire themselves or their slaves to anyone. . . . Both men and women go about well dressed in the Arabic style. . . . The mosque is always a conspicuous building, and every four hours the men go there to pray. . . . Here the people manage their own affairs, live quietly and soberly together.[106]

Fifty years of warfare in Senegambia had transmuted heroic honour into Muslim respectability.

[106] Ozanne to Administrator, 16 May 1893, CO 87/143/12599.

4   Christian Ethiopia

In contrast to the West African savanna, Ethiopian records from as early as the fourteenth century display that tension between religious humility and the 'prideful' aspects of honour that Boubakar Ly described. Yet the Christian challenge was less effective than the Muslim. Rather than restraining the heroic ethos, Ethiopian Christianity tended to be absorbed by it. Saints acted like heroes rather than heroes acting like saints. Until the end of the nineteenth century, an unwritten code of honour derived from rank and military prowess showed little of the evolution towards virtue and respectability seen in Muslim societies. The reasons need expert study but perhaps included Christianity's lack of the specific rules of public behaviour contained in the Koran; the schizophrenia between Old and New Testament models resulting from the isolated Ethiopian Church's dependence on the Bible; the difficulty of containing violence in Ethiopia's physical environment; the unimportance of trade and towns; the fact that noblemen were not only horsemen but landowners more sharply differentiated from the peasantry than elsewhere in Africa; and the individualism fostered by the bilateral kinship system.

The two earliest surviving Ethiopian texts relating to honour concern the warrior-emperor Amda Siyon (1314–44). One was a soldiers' praise-song:

> Emperor, gainer of victory,
> His ancestor was the striker of Adal.
> When he appeared in Adal,
> The entrails [of the enemy] fell out
> Like a hyena that has eaten poison.
> Vulture, David's vulture,
> Follow behind me here!

> I shall give you shredded flesh to eat,
> I shall give you red blood to drink . . .
> We are called the Emperor's Jackals.[1]

The other text was the chronicle of Amda Siyon's campaign against the Muslim ruler of Ifat, an ostensibly eyewitness account, which was at least written close to the event. It, too, celebrated heroic valour:

[T]he king stood alone like a firm foundation, like a wall of hard stone, and called out to his soldiers, 'Stand in patience for a time, and see how I fight and how I die, and (see also) what God will do to-day by my hand.' . . . They surrounded him with their swords and he, his face set hard like stone and his spirit undaunted by (the prospect of) death, clove the ranks of the rebels and struck so hard that he transfixed two men as one with a blow of his spear, through the strength of God. . . . Men's blood flowed like water, and bodies lay like grass on the earth.[2]

Yet the (presumably ecclesiastical) chronicler also insisted that Amda Siyon was motivated not by the self-regarding honour of a hero but by the Christian duty of a crusader. 'Our story is (written) not (from) vainglory nor to display (our power) to the sight of men,' the chronicler wrote, 'but that we may tell of the goodness of God.'[3] The motive, not the action, was what justified the emperor's behaviour. '"If you have killed ten Christians",' Amda Siyon warned his adversary, '"then I will kill from among your side a thousand Moslems".'[4] And the Christian standard was that of the Old Testament, to which Ethiopians attached the same veneration as to the New. The chronicler specifically compared his hero to Saul and David. Two centuries later, in the chronicle of another warrior-emperor, Galawdewos (1540–59), the crusader had become the settled image of the ideal emperor:

He did not pride himself on his victories and he had no shame in his defeats. He remembered this saying of the Wise to His children: 'The victor is no more worthy of glory or praise than the vanquished merits shame, ridicule or contempt, for God alone, Whose Name is glorified, is always victor and never vanquished.'[5]

Concern with quality of motive rather than action meant that Ethiopian Christianity in practice set few constraints on heroic honour. Unlike the medieval European Church, that of Ethiopia created little ritual to discipline the military

[1] Enno Littmann, *Die altamharischen Kaiserlieder* (Strassburg, 1914), pp. 24–5; Bahru Zewde, 'The military and militarism in Africa: the case of Ethiopia,' in Eboe Hutchful and Abdoulaye Bathily (eds.), *The military and militarism in Africa* (Dakar, 1998), p. 261.

[2] G. W. B. Huntingford (ed.), *The glorious victories of Amda Seyon* (Oxford, 1965), pp. 89–92.

[3] Ibid., p. 96.

[4] Ibid., p. 57.

[5] William El. Conzelman, *Chronique de Galawdewos (Claudius), Roi d'Ethiopie* (Paris, 1895), p. 127.

life, other than blessing and absolving armies before battle. A pious soldier might enter a church to beg protection before a campaign or forgiveness after it, but there was nothing comparable to Europe's code of chivalry to restrain his actions.[6] Instead, Ethiopian Christianity gained strength by absorbing the heroic ethos. Painting, for example, often depicted kings, saints, and archangels in virtually indistinguishable warrior poses.[7] Heroic Christianity took its most spectatular form in the ascetic contendings of monastic holy men, generally drawn from the same nobility as warrior-heroes. St. Takla Haymanot (traditional dates 1215–1313), the most venerated, spent long periods in the desert, where, according to his sixteenth-century hagiography,

he tasted no food of any kind whatsoever except on the Sabbath; and on the Sabbath he ate the wild herbs of the desert, without making any choice of them, and he did not eat those which were the best, but he ate the poorest and bitterest of the herbs. And he said unto his belly, 'If thou art willing, I will give up water, and I will not drink anything at all until the days of the fast be at an end.'[8]

Abbot Isaiah of Gunda-Gunde, in the sixteenth century, is said to have had himself flogged 1,300 strokes a day until his death at the age of eighty-seven.[9] Takla Maryam, a fifteenth-century monk,

strengthened greatly his mind in the love of our Lord, and he meditated how he could suffer because He suffered, and how he could be pierced with nails because He was pierced with nails. And he said unto himself, 'If I make [holes] in the palms of my hands, and in the soles of my feet, men will see them and know that I am suffering; therefore it will be better for me to make them in my knees.' Then he brought instruments of iron which were made sharp like unto a bradawl, and he drove them into his knees with a stone; and he wept tears because of the intensity of his suffering. And he praised the Lord Christ, who straightway came unto him and smiling [said unto him] ... 'Whosoever kisseth and toucheth these thy knees shall receive redemption, and salvation, and remission of sins, and thy knees shall redeem many souls; when they stand still they shall protect [with] loving kindness and mercy, and when they move about cities and lands shall be sanctified.'[10]

Such ascetic heroes protected ordinary people from evil as martial heroes protected them from enemies. But the two behaviour patterns could therefore

---

[6] Donald N. Levine, *Wax and gold: tradition and innovation in Ethiopian culture* (reprinted, Chicago, 1972), p. 174; Reidulf Knut Molvaer, *Tradition and change in Ethiopia: social and cultural life as reflected in Amharic fictional literature ca.1930–1974* (Leiden, 1980), p. 94.

[7] I owe this point to Dr C. R. Barnes.

[8] E. A. Wallis Budge (ed.), *The life of Takla Haymanot* (2 vols., London, 1906), vol. 1, pp. 92–3.

[9] Aleksander Ferenc, 'Les actes d'Isaie de Gunda-Gunde,' *Annales d'Ethiopie*, 10 (1976), 278.

[10] E. A. Wallis Budge (ed.), *The lives of Maba' Seyon and Gabra Krestos* (London, 1898), pp. 81–2. For a general account of monastic asceticism, see Steven Kaplan, *The monastic holy man and the Christianization of early Solomonic Ethiopia* (Wiesbaden, 1984), pp. 77–81.

remain distinct, as they had in the West African savanna in the days of Islamic quietism.

In modern dictionaries, the most common Amharic word for honour, *keber*, appears to have connotations even broader than its English equivalent; it not only embraces respect and glory but is also cognate with a rich person (*käbbärte*), a respectable person (*yätäkäbbärä*), enforcing the law (*askäbbärä*), a large drum (*käbäro*), and celibacy or virginity (*keberenna*).[11] Surprisingly, these cognates do not include courage or masculinity, for which there were separate terms.[12] Masculinity and courage, it appears, were qualities cultivated by men of all social ranks.[13] *Keber* was associated with an elite.

This notion of honour was rooted in Ethiopia's socio-economic structure and military system. The economy's core was production of grain with a light plough drawn by one or two animals. This was sufficiently productive to support a leisured class but did not require the large plough-teams and labour forces that bred Europe's manorial feudalism. Instead, Ethiopian land was controlled mainly by peasant families paying tribute to political overlords. Peasants lived in elementary households with a bilateral kinship structure in which people could claim descent and inheritance from both their father's and mother's families. This dispersed property at death, prevented the emergence of strong corporate descent groups, and fostered the individual freedom and mobility that underlay the widespread cultivation of masculinity and courage.[14]

The nobility (*makuannent*) were an office-holding and tribute-collecting class. They owed appointment to a combination of royal favour and family distinction, for although office was not in principle hereditary, in practice tribute-collecting rights and consequent local power often became so, while noblemen also owned virtually freehold land (*rim*). Rather than dispersing their property at death, they often appointed a major heir to inherit the family's leadership, the bulk of its property, its attached duties of military service, and powerful claims to office. By these means, major families built up hereditary estates, corporate identities, and regional powers that survived across the generations, in turn fostering dynastic marriages, a degree of class solidarity, distinctive notions of

[11] Thomas Leiper Kane, *Amharic-English dictionary* (2 vols., Wiesbaden, 1990), vol. 2, pp. 1416–18. I am grateful to Dr. Barnes for providing me with this source and advising me on it.

[12] *Guabaznat* and *wandnat*: Levine, *Wax and gold*, p. 106.

[13] See Donald N. Levine, 'The concept of masculinity in Ethiopian culture,' *International Journal of Social Psychiatry*, 12 (1966), 18–19.

[14] See Allan Hoben, *Land tenure among the Amhara of Ethiopia* (Chicago, 1973); Donald Crummey, *Land and society in the Christian kingdom of Ethiopia from the thirteenth to the twentieth century* (Oxford, 2000), pp. 2, 9–12.

honour, and pride of blood.[15] Men were taught to memorise seven generations of ancestors. Genealogists had an important role in the courts.[16] 'Though ability and fortune might carry any man high in the political hierarchy,' a sensitive analyst has written,

> he would not thereby automatically be accepted as one of the *makuannent*. A self-respecting man of noble family would resist marrying his daughter to a commoner or person of dubious parentage, no matter how high a rank the latter obtained. For the Abyssinian nobility did form a self-conscious status group with a certain hereditary base. Its members shared a sense of superiority, a consciousness of kind, an attitude towards commoners such as that expressed by the governor Takla Giyorgis to the Jesuit Barradas: 'Father, these villeins are like camels, they cry and groan when they are loaded, but in the end they carry the load that is put on them.' They set themselves off from the commoners, not only because of their style of life and subculture, but also because they came from well-known families.[17]

The wide but permeable divide between nobility and commoners was paralleled in the military system. Officers of state bore military titles and were expected to be active warriors. Soldiers, it was said, could not fight unless they saw their king among them. Early in the seventeenth century the Emperor Za-Dengel, whose purely ecclesiastical education had not taught him even how to mount a horse, so offended his soldiers that they killed him and outraged his corpse.[18] Three centuries later Emperor Yohannes IV was killed while personally leading an attack on a Mahdist stronghold, after which his army disintegrated, turning victory into rout. His staff had attracted fire by their silver shields and bright silks, for honourable warriors sought visibility rather than concealment.[19]

Preparation for the pursuit of honour began for noblemen in early childhood, when boys were expected to defend themselves and their social rank. Noble youths might learn to read, although seldom to write, and might have instruction in music and the scriptures, but – unless, like Za-Dengel, they were destined for the church – from an early age they would learn the arts of war and

---

[15] Donald Crummey, 'Family and property amongst the Amhara nobility,' *JAH*, 24 (1983), 207–20; idem, *Land and society*, pp. 2, 10–12, 115–23; idem, 'Three Amharic documents of marriage and inheritance from the eighteenth and nineteenth centuries,' in Taddese Beyene (ed.), *Proceedings of the Eighth International Congress of Ethiopian Studies* (2 vols., Addis Ababa, 1988–9), vol. 1, pp. 318–22.

[16] Sven Rubenson, *King of Kings Tewodros of Ethiopia* (Addis Ababa, 1966), p. 16; Patrick Gilkes, *The dying lion: feudalism and modernization in Ethiopia* (London, 1975), p. 35.

[17] Levine, *Wax and gold*, pp. 163–4.

[18] J. Perruchon, 'Règnes de Yaqob et Za-Dengel (1597–1607),' *Revue Sémitique*, 4 (1896), 355, 362.

[19] Augustus B. Wylde, *Modern Abyssinia* (London, 1901), p. 41.

horsemanship. In their early teens they would marry, receive nominal administrative offices, and kill, for, in the absence of a traumatic adolescent initiation,
a first kill of man or beast was the most important step into manhood.[20]

This was the training of a professional military class. Unlike many African
armies, Ethiopia's army was not simply every man of fighting age, although
in later centuries every such man was liable to military service if summoned.
Rather, the army's core were professional soldiers. Amda Siyon's power, in the
early fourteenth century, already rested on a central mercenary army, although
his campaigns also attracted many untrained auxiliaries. 'In all the Prester's
[Emperor's] country there are *chavas*, who are men-at-arms, because in these
kingdoms the peasants do not go to the wars,' a missionary observed in the
1520s.[21] Shortly thereafter warfare with Muslims and neighbouring Oromo
peoples led to the army's expansion, decentralisation, and rearmament with
firearms and horses. By 1634 it had some fifteen hundred matchlock muskets.
Firearms multiplied in subsequent decades, but not until the late nineteenth
century did they dominate warfare. For the previous four centuries, military
predominance lay with horsemen, whose ethos underlay the aristocratic code of
honour as it did in the West African savanna. In the mid seventeenth century,
the Emperor was thought to command some five thousand horsemen; the first
charge, it was said, decided the battle, for musketeers took so long to reload
that they could not stand against cavalry. 'A superiority is generally felt and
conceded to the horseman over the gunner,' it was noted in the 1840s, 'and the
killing horse to horse is more boastfully announced.'[22]

An Ethiopian nobleman identified himself with his horse and might adopt its
name, to be used especially in praise-songs. Professional *asmaris* performed the
same roles as West African griots, although their art never developed into epic
poetry, perhaps because written chronicles took its place and because Ethiopia's
heroic culture never receded into the past. Warriors – although not great
noblemen – also praised themselves when parading before battle, launching
attacks, and reporting victories, when they also threw down trophies taken from

---

[20] Reidulf K. Molvaer, *Socialization and social control in Ethiopia* (Wiesbaden, 1995), pp. 56,
103; Tsehai Berhane-Selassie, 'The political and military traditions of the Ethiopian peasantry
(1800–1941),' DPhil thesis, University of Oxford, 1980, ch. 3.

[21] C. F. Beckingham and G. W. B. Huntingford (eds.), *The Prester John of the Indies* (2 vols.,
Cambridge, 1961), vol. 2, pp. 411–12. Generally, see Merid W. Aregay, 'Military elites in medieval Ethiopia,' *JES*, 30 (1997), 41–5; Zewde in Hutchful and Bathily, *Military and militarism*,
pp. 260–5.

[22] Walter Chichele Plowden, *Travels in Abyssinia and the Galla country* (London, 1868), p. 64.
Generally, see Merid W. Aregay, 'A reappraisal of the impact of firearms in the history of warfare
in Ethiopia (c.1500–1800),' *JES*, 14 (1976–9), 98–121; Richard Pankhurst, *Economic history
of Ethiopia 1800–1935* (Addis Ababa, 1968), pp. 560–1.

the emasculated enemy dead and wounded.[23] This equestrian-dominated war-fare was highly individualistic, in the heroic manner. Only certain specialised formations had collective training. Single combat was a favoured route to hon-our. Late in the eighteenth century, when Ras Welled, a future ruler of Tigray, was an outlaw fighting for his life,

> he challenged any two chiefs in the army opposed to him to fight on horseback; and, two men of distinguished bravery having been made choice of for the purpose, he went down into the plain to meet them, and killed both with his own hand; possessing, notwithstanding his small and delicate form, such peculiar skill in the management of two spears on horseback, that it was said in the country to be unequalled. This unexampled exploit raised his character as a warrior to the highest pitch; and the particulars of the combat still continue to form a favorite topic of conversation among his followers.[24]

Such conspicuous skill and courage could win breathtaking advancement even for men of the lowest rank. The later Ras Gobana, who conquered much of Oromo country for the Emperor Menelik in the late nineteenth century, was himself an exiled Oromo royal working as a reaper on the Emperor's estate until he caught his master's eye by unhorsing all competitors in a joust. Habtä Giyorgis, the most powerful Ethiopian of the early twentieth century, was an Oromo captive who won Menelik's favour by protecting him from a lion. This extreme mobility bred conflict between hereditary noblemen and the *zemanay*, the parvenu. Ras Alula, Ethiopia's most gifted commander against the Italians during the 1890s, was never accepted by the Tigrayan aristocracy because of his low and alien birth.[25]

Despite its individualism, warfare had its rules. Honour demanded that Ethiopian armies customarily fought hand-to-hand in the open field, despite their country's suitability for defensive fortifications and guerilla tactics. Oromo were thought treacherous because they fired from ambush and even attacked at night. While opposing forces traded insults, commanders addressed one another in due form before joining battle. Prior to the Battle of Embabo in 1882, King Takla Haymanot of Gojjam sent King Menelik of Shoa a verbal message rather than a letter, 'because you would be able to read it alone, tear it up, and flee, as if you had learned nothing. I have wished to say all this to you by word of

---

[23] Littmann, *Die Kaiserlieder*, pp. 6–8; Plowden, *Travels*, pp. 51–3; Mansfield Parkyns, *Life in Abyssinia* (2nd edn, London, 1868), p. 443 n.

[24] Henry Salt, *A voyage to Abyssinia* (reprinted, London, 1967), pp. 326–7.

[25] Enrico Cerulli, 'Folk-literature of the Galla of southern Abyssinia,' in E. A. Hooton and Natica I. Bates (eds.), *Varia Africana III*, Harvard African Studies, vol. 3 (Cambridge, Mass., 1922), p. 71; Tamene Bitima, 'On some Oromo historical poems,' *Paideuma*, 29 (1983), 319; Haggai Erlich, *Ras Alula and the scramble for Africa* (Lawrenceville, N.J., 1996), p. 155.

mouth, so that, if you come to flee, all your chiefs and soldiers will despise you.' Menelik replied by refusing to trust messengers who came without the king's seal: 'Since he calls himself a king, propriety forbids him to send me a message which is not written and sealed with his seal.'[26] Concern with etiquette also shaped behaviour between individual members of the military class. Defence of honour and status was obligatory. 'Since the day of my birth, no man dared to lay hands upon me,' Emperor Tewodros declared.

Earlier in his life Tewodros had rebelled against his master and father-in-law when sent only a piece of meat instead of an animal: 'Why am I given a *shent* (thigh) like a servant?' Men were known to kill one another over the distribution of meat at a feast.[27] Insult was an art, whether crude vituperation, the mutual taunting that accompanied *mankala* board-games, or the refinement of 'wax and gold', the covert insult beneath the commonplace. To recognise the insult was itself an art in which an apt verbal riposte was even more honourable than physical retaliation.[28] Single combat was a remedy recognised by law, but it threatened the victor with vendetta. Feud was common, although the state discouraged it, sometimes punishing both parties in a dispute threatening public tranquility. Emperor Tewodros (1855–68) decreed that state executions should replace private vengeance on murderers, although this no doubt took effect slowly. By the late nineteenth century, some provincial governors were seeking to prohibit homicide as a step towards manhood.[29]

As insult suggests, there was more to aristocratic honour than mere valour. The nobleman was *telek saw*, a Big Man,[30] whose enclosure swarmed with servants and retainers, each with a specialised function and a personal relationship, however unequal, with the master. No Big Man would have demeaned himself by appearing in public alone:

Dejazmach Mikael left Adwa, his capital town, with thousands of musketeers and thousands of horsemen; with numerous tambours, drums, trumpets, violins and small lyres. We cannot count the people of Tigray and Amhara who followed him on foot. He left Adwa, his face resplendent as the sun, his person ornamented with vestments of pure

[26] Guèbrè Sellassié, *Chronique du règne de Ménélik II, Roi des Rois d'Ethiopie* (trans. Tèsfa Sellassié, 2 vols., Paris, 1930–1), vol. 1, p. 178.
[27] Wilfred Thesiger, *The life of my choice* (London, 1987), p. 39: Berhane-Selassie, 'Traditions,' p. 268; Parkyns, *Life*, p. 206.
[28] Molvaer, *Socialization*, pp. 61, 219, 244–86, 315; Thomas Q. Reefe, 'The biggest game of all: gambling in traditional Africa,' in Baker and Mangan, *Sport*, p. 57; Levine, *Wax and gold*, p. 9.
[29] Plowden, *Travels*, pp. 55, 98–101; C. F. Beckingham and G. W. B. Huntingford (eds.), *Some records of Ethiopia 1593–1646* (London, 1954), p. 58; Svein Ege, *Class, state, and power in Africa: a case study of the Kingdom of Shäwa (Ethiopia) about 1840* (Wiesbaden, 1996), pp. 170, 185; Parkyns, *Life*, p. xxiii; Wylde, *Modern Abyssinia*, pp. 364, 388–9.
[30] Berhane-Selassie, 'Traditions,' p. ii.

and dazzling gold. No dignitary had arisen under the heavens to compare with him for strength and grandeur, for generosity in distributing wealth, or for [skill in] rendering good judgments.[31]

To his dependants, a man of honour was expected to be open-handed to the point of recklessness. With his peers, the exchange of gifts was as finely calibrated as the exchange of insults. 'It is tantamount to an affront should one refuse a present from a superior,' a diplomat explained; 'if the refusal is on the part of the superior, it is an expression of grave displeasure.'[32] Rank, deference, and largess were most spectacularly displayed in feasting. At one continuous, three-day banquet hosted by King Menelik of Shoa in 1887, over 20,000 people were said to have eaten, which was not exceptional. To be denied a master's hospitality 'is spoken of with great emotion and resentment.'[33]

In the elaborate etiquette of feasting, princes distinguished themselves from office-holders, senior officers from juniors, noblemen from gentlemen (*balabbat*: 'he who has a name'). Men were frankly unequal before the law: a captured royal was generally ransomed or honourably confined, while an office-holder might be ceremonially but lightly flogged, fettered with 'a very slender chain', or publicly stripped of his clothes.[34] Mutilation, inflicted on noblemen chiefly for reasons of state, was a routine punishment for commoners. This class consciousness among the nobility, although less pronounced than in medieval Europe, nevertheless found many cultural expressions. Noblemen refused to touch a plough. Like the Torodbe aristocracy of Futa Toro, they left the more extravagant displays of heroic behaviour to their subordinates, cultivating instead a quiet and sober reserve. They distinguished themselves by dress, ornament, and a more sophisticated cuisine; a late nineteenth-century royal court convicted a merely rich man of treason for serving mead rather than beer.[35] Dejazmach Farris, 'the soldiers' idol' of the mid nineteenth century, was as skilled with the harp as the spear. At an annual court festival, the Master of Ceremonies honoured senior officers with gifts of cloth and flowers. The word *chawa*, originally meaning a bearer of arms, came to signify a man of culture and good behaviour.[36]

[31] I. Guidi (ed.), *Annales Regum Iyasu II et Iyo'as* (Rome, 1912), p. 214.

[32] Armbruster to Phipps, enclosed in Graham to Grey, 26 September 1908, FOCP 9505/170.

[33] Jules Borelli, *Ethiopie méridionale* (Paris, 1890), pp. 255–6; Berhane-Selassie, 'Traditions,' p. 266.

[34] Bairu Tafla (ed.), *A chronicle of Emperor Yohannes IV (1872–89)* (Wiesbaden, 1977), p. 115; Beckingham and Huntingford, *Prester John*, vol. 2, pp. 424, 431.

[35] Crummey, *Land and society*, p. 128; Levine, *Wax and gold*, p. 156; Parkyns, *Life*, chs. 22–23; Berhane-Selassie, 'Traditions,' p. 260.

[36] Plowden, *Travels*, p. 82; Joseph Varenbergh, 'Studien zur abessinischen Reichsordnung (*Serata Mangest*),' *Zeitschrift für Assyriologie*, 30 (1915–16), 35–6; Zewde in Hutchful and Bathily, *Military and militarism*, p. 273.

These differences of rank coexisted with much social mobility and the vertical ties of clientage linking the Big Man to the followers on whose support his status depended. Those ties were easily broken, for they rested on every free man's right to choose and change his lord, a right derived ultimately from the peasantry's ownership of land. Loyalty, of course, was admired. A mutinous regiment might be publicly disgraced and there were many displays of personal devotion, such as that surrounding the death of Yohannes IV, when 'Ras Areya was last seen standing alongside the box containing the king's body, after having expended all his ammunition, with his shield and sword in his hands, defending himself, till at last he was speared by a Dervish from behind, and died fighting gamely like the fine old warrior that he was.'[37] Yet such devotion was not always expected, nor was it necessarily a matter of honour. No oath of fealty bound the client. 'They are ordinarily changeable and inconstant,' a seventeenth-century European observer complained, 'and so today they are with one lord and tomorrow will leave him and take another. They readily swear to any agreement and then break it as if they had not sworn. Hence arise incessant rebellions and most often, if things go badly for the rebel and his followers, they ask the Emperor's pardon and obtain it.'[38] There was no punishment for a common soldier who deserted, provided he left his gun behind, nor was it dishonourable to preserve one's life by flight before a stronger enemy, and although an officer who successfully charged a senior with cowardice could claim his rank, yet a chief with no stomach for battle might retain royal favour.[39] Moreover, allegiance was contingent on the patron retaining the power to protect and advance his client. Rulers did not expect the degree of loyalty to which their European counterparts aspired.[40] Forgiveness could often be gained by skilful betrayal:

Hailoo . . . purchased restoration to royal favour at the expense of a deed of the blackest treachery. This he recounted not only without a blush, but with extraordinary satisfaction at his fancied heroism. Apprehending a similar fate with him whose cause he had espoused, he fled across the border, and found a safe asylum with Wodoge Girmee, a powerful Galla [Oromo] chieftain, long in open revolt, and one of the bitterest enemies of the monarch. Basely assassinating his benefactor, whilst seated unsuspectingly in the open field, he sprang upon his horse, and casting the head of his victim at the royal footstool in token of his villany, was rewarded by advancement.[41]

[37] Wylde, *Modern Abyssinia*, p. 43.
[38] Beckingham and Huntingford, *Some records*, p. 58.
[39] Samuel Gobat, *Journal of a three years' residence in Abyssinia* (2nd edn, London, 1847), p. 260; Beckingham and Huntingford, *Some records*, p. 78; H. Weld Blundell, *The royal chronicle of Abyssinia 1769–1840* (Cambridge, 1922), p. 294; Nathaniel Pearce, *The life and adventures of Nathaniel Pearce, written by himself* (2 vols., London, 1831), vol. 1, pp. 158–9.
[40] I owe this point to Dr Barnes.
[41] W. Cornwallis Harris, *The highlands of Aethiopia* (2nd edn, 3 vols., London, 1844), vol. 2, pp. 101–2.

Kädda – rebellion, treason, even apostasy – could be pardoned if the terms of power and mutual advantage shifted. As always in Ethiopia, the new relationship was dramatised in ceremony:

The Gusmati Ischias and two of Nebrid Aram's sons, who had been among the Tigre rebels, came from the Amhara, with stones about their necks, to ask forgiveness, at Mucculla, where the Ras was keeping the yearly holyday. The Ras, upon seeing the Gusmati, rose from his sofa, and kissed him, saying, 'Although it is far from the first time you have rebelled against me, yet I forgive you from my heart,' and immediately gave orders that the Gusmati Ischias's districts should be returned to him.[42]

Neither the pardon nor the reinstatement was always so complete, and occasionally they were denied, but often a relationship sufficiently honourable to both sides could be restored. 'If a pool of water is clear at the top,' said a proverb, 'it does not matter what is underneath.'[43]

The aristocratic code was not the only notion of honour followed in highland Ethiopia, although it certainly was the best documented. There was no rival bourgeois ideal of virtue, for trade was left to Muslims and craftsmanship to stigmatised communities who did not consider themselves inferior but were despised by Christian highlanders. There was, however, the alternative code of the adult peasant householder, which shared some aristocratic notions while emphasising others more germane to common people. Courage, emphasised in folklore, remained central, for peasants were quick to defend homestead or locality, whether against military exactions or novel demands for tribute.[44] Should exploitation threaten peasant subsistence, it might provoke revolt, generally under the leadership of some dissident nobleman or millenarian visionary.[45] The most sustained resistance to state power, however, came not from Christians but from the Falasha or Beta Israel, who defended their independence and Jewish faith throughout the fifteenth and sixteenth centuries in the Lake Tana region and the high mountains of Semien, some killing themselves or one another to escape capture, declaring, 'It is more meritorious to die honourably than to

[42] Pearce, *Life*, vol. 1, pp. 89–90.

[43] Quoted in 'Report on Abyssinia by Lord Noel-Buxton and Lord Polworth,' enclosed in Peterson to League of Nations, 26 April 1932, FO 401/28/XVII/82.

[44] Levine, 'Concept,' p. 18; Molvaer, *Socialization*, p. 73; R. A. Caulk, 'Armies as predators: soldiers and peasants in Ethiopia, c.1850–1935,' *IJAHS*, 11 (1978), 473; Crummey, *Land and society*, p. 86.

[45] Andrzej Bartnicki and Joanna Mantel-Niecko, 'The role and significance of the religious conflicts and people's movements in the political life of Ethiopia in the seventeenth and eighteenth centuries,' *Rassegna di Studi Etiopici*, 24 (1969–70), 5–39.

live in shame.'[46] Christian peasants ruined by disaster or threatened by the law might also take to the hills and join the brigand groups that both preyed on the poor and won their admiration by their violent assertion. Most often, however, peasant courage was expressed in endurance, whether of toil, of natural disaster like famine, or especially of pain, whether from disease, the terrible physical punishments of the law, or the competitive mutual flogging by which men and youths in some areas displayed courage.[47] Alongside endurance, male peasant honour embraced manliness, self-control, independence, industry, and ability to support and manage a household: 'Having worked, to eat,' as it was expressed. Cunning, too, was a quality much admired in folklore and no more considered dishonourable than it was among the nobility.[48] To work for wages was discreditable, but service to a patron was not, provided it was freely chosen.

Women, too, doubtless had their own notions of honour, but these can scarcely be glimpsed in the exclusively male records. In principle, women had stronger rights than in many peasant societies. They could inherit land, retain possession of it within marriage, claim half of the property accumulated during a marriage, take custody of very young children in the event of divorce, and litigate on their own behalf. In practice, however, even aristocratic women did not enjoy equal rights over property and often lost control of it to men.[49] A double standard of sexual behaviour by husband and wife was normal, divorce and remarriage were easy and frequent, and twentieth-century evidence suggests that peasant women commonly married very young, often most unhappily, and were frequently left widowed or unsupported. The sorrows of women are a stock theme of Amharic literature. Male control of plough-oxen left much agricultural drudgery and all food-processing to women, whose work men despised.[50] At the courtly level, literature celebrated female beauty, notably that of the eighteenth-century Queen Mentewwab whose career demonstrated the powerful role noblewomen

[46] C. Conti Rossini (ed.), *Historia Regis Sarsa Dengel (Malak Sagad)* (Paris, 1907), p. 118. Generally, see Steven Kaplan, *The Beta Israel (Falasha) in Ethiopia from earliest times to the twentieth century* (New York, 1992), ch. 4; James Quirin, *The evolution of the Ethiopian Jews* (Philadelphia, 1992), pp. 52–85.

[47] Donald Crummey, 'Banditry and resistance: noble and peasant in nineteenth-century Ethiopia,' in his *Banditry, rebellion and social protest in Africa* (London, 1986), ch. 6; Théophile Lefebvre and others, *Voyage en Abyssinie* (6 vols., Paris [1851]), vol. 1, pp. 369–77, and vol. 2, pp. 42–3, 87; Levine, *Wax and gold*, p. 64.

[48] Levine, *Wax and gold*, pp. 75–83; Molvaer, *Socialization*, pp. 168–9, 207.

[49] Levine, 'Concept,' p. 19; Donald Crummey, 'Women, property, and litigation among the Bagemder Amhara, 1750s to 1850s,' in Margaret Jean Hay and Marcia Wright (eds.), *African women and the law: historical perspectives* (Boston, 1982), pp. 19–32.

[50] Molvaer, *Socialization*, pp. 23–4; Gobat, *Journal*, p. 170; Iliffe, *Poor*, pp. 15–16; Molvaer, *Tradition*, p. 96; [B.] Graham, 'Report on the agricultural and land produce of Shoa,' *Journal of the Asiatic Society of Bengal*, 13, 1 (1844), 290; Levine, 'Concept,' p. 19.

could play in politics.[51] But Ethiopian art associated women overwhelmingly with the domestic sphere, which males saw as their proper place of honour:

Now Sara [the mother of St. Takla Haymanot] was beautiful in form and feature, and she was exceedingly well instructed, and all those who looked upon her form and heard her speech marvelled thereat. Whilst she was [living] in the house of her father-in-law she kept her face veiled, according to the custom [of the country], and she laid down a law for her tongue, and she worked hard at weaving with her hands and arms.[52]

That Sara was 'exceedingly well instructed' was probably unusual. Her modesty was no doubt more common, for there was much emphasis on premarital virginity, the term being cognate with honour. Ecclesiastical teaching generally stressed the shamefulness of the body and the frailty and impurity of women, who were not allowed to enter beyond the outer circle of a church.[53] There were no Ethiopian women saints, although there were many elderly nuns. Sara's industry, too, was part of her honour, as was endurance, especially the uncomplaining endurance of childbirth, for fertility was essential to a woman's respect. That Sara was remembered only for bearing her son illustrated the secondary place that women held in Ethiopian life. As Amda Siyon's chronicle made clear, their role in male eyes was to accompany the hero to battle, to pray for his success, and to support his courage:

And the younger queen [Amda Siyon's wife] said to the elder [his mother], 'Restrain him, for the sake of Christ, and prevent him from going.' But the elder queen said to the younger, 'If he wishes to go, I will not restrain him. And how should I restrain him when the rebels are approaching to kill him in his tent? Away (with such a thought): I will not restrain him. Let him go forth and die the death of a man.'[54]

---

[51] Guidi, *Annales*, pp. 20–1; Crummey, *Land and society*, p. 95.
[52] Budge, *Takla Haymanot*, vol. 1, p. 16.
[53] Ed. Combes and M. Tamisier, *Voyage en Abyssinie, 1835–1837* (4 vols., Paris, 1838), vol. 3, p. 202; Levine, *Wax and gold*, p. 100; Stanislas Kur (ed.), *Actes de Samuel de Dabra Wagag* (Louvain, 1968), p. 49; Alice Louise Morton, 'Some aspects of spirit possession in Ethiopia,' PhD thesis, University of London, 1973, p. 71.
[54] Huntingford, *Glorious victories*, p. 84.

5 Honour, Rank, and Warfare Among the Yoruba

On the West African savanna's southern border with the forest, the Yoruba people of modern Nigeria began to acquire literacy only in the nineteenth century. Evidence of their earlier notions of honour comes only from oral praise-poems (*oriki*) and the traditions gathered chiefly by the first literate Yoruba, especially the pioneer historian Samuel Johnson.[1] For the nineteenth century, the journals of Yoruba clergymen and evangelists and the writings of European missionaries and travellers add contemporary evidence. These sources suggest that Yoruba society before the nineteenth century was dominated by rank, by vertical honour derived from it, and by horizontal honour gained chiefly through civil distinction, the management of a household, and virtuous character. These forms of honour contrasted with the military notions prevalent in the savanna, although cavalry officers had introduced those notions also into Yorubaland. During the nineteenth century, however, the Yoruba suffered almost continuous warfare so that honour gained by military achievement became dominant, although it was still expressed in the pursuit of rank and coexisted with the separate codes of household heads and women. The dominance of military values helped to explain the failure of Christian missionaries who refused to compromise with them, in contrast to the greater accommodation and success of Islam.

Until the nineteenth century, honour in the several Yoruba kingdoms seems to have adhered closely to rank and civic virtue. Of the two main words for honour listed in the vocabulary published in 1852 by the Yoruba clergyman Samuel Crowther, the more common, *ola*, connoted respect, dignity, and authority. 'What underlies *ola*,' a modern authority has written, 'is the notion

---

[1] Samuel Johnson, *The history of the Yorubas* (reprinted, London, 1973).

of recognition, of being acknowledged superior . . . *Ola* . . . is ultimately the capacity to attract and retain the gaze of other people.' It was distinct from fame (*okiki*) and glory (*ogo*).[2]

The man who most attracted the gaze of others in a Yoruba kingdom was certainly the king (*oba*), 'the unquestioned magnetic center of the social universe' whose installation made him 'a being of a different kind'.[3] The Alafin of Oyo, the ruler of the most powerful kingdom embracing about half the Yoruba territory and people, headed a royal lineage whose princes claimed the highest rank beneath the throne, commanded a household bureaucracy of titled slaves, and was surrounded by great ceremony.[4] In 1826 the Alafin assured European visitors that his subjects 'preferred a ruler with a smart and gorgeous exterior, even if he happened to be the most odious tyrant.'[5] At the three annual festivals at which he appeared in public, even the greatest chiefs lowered their cloths to the waist in homage: 'three times they have to run to the main entrance gate, sprinkle earth on their heads and on their naked bodies, and run back half way towards the throne, prostrating themselves on the bare ground, on the stomach and on the back!'[6] At the Alafin's death not only were slaves and attendants killed to serve him in the next world, but his official mother, his eldest son and the son's mother, three other princes, the hereditary master of the horse, the chief eunuch of the royal quarters, and several other notables were required to commit suicide after processing through the streets distributing largess and taking leave of their households at ceremonial feasts. Any who evaded this duty would be killed by relatives to avoid collective disgrace.[7]

Kings and their households shared power with the hereditary chiefs of the capital's main lineages or quarters, men whose rank and power were measured by the size of their followings. 'According to the universal custom of the country,' wrote Johnson, 'whenever a chief is out, all his subordinates must go out with him.'[8] Chiefs distinguished themselves by elaborate robes borrowed from the Muslim styles to the north, whereas the poor of early nineteenth-century Oyo

---

[2] Samuel Crowther, *A vocabulary of the Yoruba language* (London, 1852), pp. 209, 213, 234, 240; Barber, *I could speak*, p. 203.

[3] Karin Barber, *The generation of plays: Yoruba popular life in theater* (Bloomington, 2000), p. 21; idem, 'Documenting social and ideological change through Yoruba oriki: a stylistic analysis,' *JHSN*, 10, 4 (June 1981), 41.

[4] Johnson, *History*, pp. 40–78; Robin Law, *The Oyo Empire, c.1600–c.1836: a West African imperialism in the era of the Atlantic slave trade* (Oxford, 1977), part 2.

[5] Richard Lander, *Records of Captain Clapperton's last expedition to Africa* (reprinted, 2 vols., London, 1967), vol. 1, p. 112.

[6] Johnson, *History*, pp. 52–3.

[7] Ibid., pp. 55–7, 398.

[8] Ibid., p. 46.

wore skins. Great men, whether kings or chiefs, were made the subjects of *oriki*, allusive praise-poems composed by professional bards or women married into the lineage, celebrating the subject's rank and appearance, his achievements, his personality, and above all his individuality. *Oriki* of the late eighteenth and early nineteenth centuries suggest that honour was then a multifaceted quality embracing authority, esteem, courage, wealth, decency, and moderation – attributes that made up *iwapele*, good or gentle character – all expressed within a richly sensuous ambience, a vast range of personal relationships, a complex private as well as public life, and a deep embeddedness in a local culture and community that shared in the great man's distinction:

> The beauty of cloth dyed in indigo does not fade
> Adewale, indigo is what gives the cloth its worth
> My father, *egbe* are the best kind of beads
> If I were an *egbe* bead
> Akanni, I would be right in the middle
> Adewale, you stand out among your peers most distinctly.[9]

This notion of civil honour was not unique in precolonial Africa – it had parallels in the Kuba kingdom, for example[10] – but it contrasted with the military ethos of the West African savanna.

Ranking beneath major chiefs were senior men heading compounds occupied by the complex households in which most Yoruba townspeople lived. 'They are chiefs in their respective domains, where they transact all business affecting the welfare or interest of the people in their respective households,' Johnson wrote. 'All important cases are judged and decided in the master's piazza, and he is responsible to the town authorities for the conduct of the inmates of his compound.... His word is law.'[11] In principle, younger men owed deference not only to their compound head but to elder brothers and all those senior to them. According to Johnson, men seldom married and gained full adulthood before the age of thirty. The women of the compound, similarly, owed deference not only to its head but to all its male members and all women who had entered the lineage by marriage before them. Only with age and the birth of children did women gain authority and sometimes a high degree of economic independence.[12] At the

---

[9] Barber, *I could speak*, p. 201. See also Barber, 'Documenting,' pp. 46–8; Bolanle Awe, 'Praise poems as historical data: the example of the Yoruba *oriki*,' *Africa*, 44 (1974), 331–49; Wande Abimbola, 'Iwapele: the concept of good character in Ifa literary corpus,' in his *Yoruba oral tradition* (Ibadan, 1975), p. 395.

[10] See this volume, p. 94.

[11] Johnson, *History*, p. 100.

[12] Ibid., p. 103; Barber, *I could speak*, pp. 105–16; N. A. Fadipe, *The sociology of the Yoruba* (Ibadan, 1970), ch. 4.

bottom of this society were the poor, whose condition was considered shameful, and the slaves who became increasingly numerous once Yoruba engaged deeply in the Atlantic slave trade during the seventeenth and eighteenth centuries.

The most alien element in the eighteenth-century social order were the Eso, Oyo's seventy professional military officers. Commanding trained bands of cavalry and archers, they probably emerged in the wake of mounted invasion from the north during the sixteenth century. They may have been responsible for a new style of praise-singing and, although proverbial for their endurance, courage, and loyalty to the Alafin, they may also have helped to destabilise Oyo's power balance during the eighteenth century. Certainly they embodied the arrogant equestrian honour of the savanna, mocked in the Yoruba proverb, 'One who mounts a horse has to come down.'[13] 'We had a visit from one of the Eyeo [Oyo] war chiefs, who came in state . . . curvetting and leaping his horse,' the first European to traverse Yorubaland recorded in 1826. Some two hundred horsemen and four hundred infantry then accompanied him to the capital.[14] Yoruba culture admired moderation in all things, including valour. 'Strike when necessary, run when necessary' was a drum message.[15] Eso professed a different ethos:

> One of two things befits an Eso
> The Eso must fight and conquer [or]
> The Eso must fight and perish.[16]

'So much is this title thought of by military men and others,' Johnson recorded in the 1890s, 'and so great is the enthusiasm it inspires, that even the children and grandchildren of an Eso hold themselves bound to maintain the spirit and honour of their sires. The Eso is above everything else noble in act and deed.'[17]

The nineteenth century brought profound change. Yoruba called it the Age of Confusion, when Oyo disintegrated in civil war, its people resettled in military towns like Ibadan and Ijaye that struggled for predominance, trade, slavery, and the use of firearms expanded, and self-made military men challenged rank and civic honour.[18] They did not destroy the old order entirely. Kingship

---

[13] Robin Law, 'A West African cavalry state: the kingdom of Oyo,' *JAH*, 16 (1975), 1–15 (quotation on p. 1 n3); P. F. de Moraes Farias, 'History and consolation: royal Yoruba bards comment on their craft,' *History in Africa*, 19 (1992), 279.

[14] Clapperton, *Journal*, p. 2; Lander, *Records*, vol. 1, p. 103.

[15] Tunde Olowookere and Gbenga Fagborun, 'Systems of communication in Yoruba wars,' in Adeagbo Akinjogbin (ed.), *War and peace in Yorubaland, 1793–1893* (Ibadan, 1998), p. 240.

[16] Quoted in Johnson, *History*, p. 73.

[17] Ibid., p. 74.

[18] J. D. Y. Peel, *Religious encounter and the making of the Yoruba* (Bloomington, 2000), p. 49.

retained prestige, the new military honour owed something to the Eso ethos, and rank remained vital, although now it was rank achieved by prowess rather than ancestry or virtue. It is not surprising that Christian missionaries found nineteenth-century Yorubaland a disappointingly barren field.

It was a harsh time for kings. Oyo's disintegration in the early nineteenth century left the Alafin dependent on army commanders in Ijaye and Ibadan. In 1859 the military ruler of Ijaye, Kurunmi, refused to recognise a new Alafin, precipitating warfare that destroyed Ijaye and left Ibadan as the dominant power. In 1866 Ibadan's senior chief, the Bashorun Ogunmola, desired the Alafin to supply him with posts and grass to extend his house, an unsubtle demand for tribute; the Alafin sent the posts enclosed in mats commonly used to wrap corpses. Eleven years later Ibadan's ambitions provoked a coalition against it and a war, the Kiriji War, which smouldered until the British imposed their overrule in 1893, after the Alafin's attempts at mediation had been spurned by all sides.[19] Another king claiming even older authority, the Oni of Ife, watched his capital twice destroyed. Ibadan's opponents in the Kiriji War claimed to fight 'for all the crowned kings in the world' against 'a people without a king or even a constitution.'[20] Yet monarchy retained prestige. Even Ibadan paid tribute to Oyo throughout the century and deferred to its spokesmen in formal negotiations.[21]

Power, nevertheless, passed decisively to military men. During the fighting accompanying Oyo's disintegration, its army fragmented into the personal followings of individual commanders. Several clustered at Ibadan, a military republic with a hierarchy of chiefly ranks through which successful commanders won promotion. Military success gained not only rank and honour but also slaves and other booty with which to reward subordinates, attract followers, produce food and export crops, purchase firearms, and staff the warlord's army. A missionary wrote that nobody could claim to be a great warlord unless he had at least one thousand slaves.[22] Such leadership required great strength and courage to survive the rigours of campaigning, to face a possibly agonising death if captured, and to risk obligatory suicide if defeated by an enemy or

---

[19] Johnson, *History*, pp. 331, 372, 462–73, 584–603; S. Johnson, journal, 13 October 1881–29 November 1883, CMS G3/A2/O/1884/101.

[20] Bolanle Alake Awe, 'The rise of Ibadan as a Yoruba power in the nineteenth century,' DPhil thesis, University of Oxford, 1964, p. 261; S. A. Akintoye, *Revolution and power politics in Yorubaland, 1840–1893: Ibadan expansion and the rise of the Ekitiparapo* (London, 1971), p. 156 n20.

[21] Bolanle Awe, 'Ibadan, its early beginnings,' in P. C. Lloyd, A. L. Mabogunje, and B. Awe (eds.), *The city of Ibadan* (Cambridge, 1967), p. 16; Johnson, *History*, p. 470.

[22] Toyin Falola and Dare Oguntomisin, *The military in nineteenth-century Yoruba politics* (Ife, 1984), p. 57.

rival. It required the open-handed generosity and ostentation that led a young spectator at Seriki Iyapo's triumphal entry into Ibadan in 1875 to declare, 'If I enjoy such a glory for only one day and I die the next, I shall be content.'[23] It required 'that air of toughness and imminent anger that characterizes "big" men in Yoruba society.'[24] Karin Barber has shown that in the *oriki* of nineteenth-century warlords, in contrast to the multifaceted verses of the late eighteenth century,

we find tremendous, overwhelming emphasis on one attribute – military might. Nothing reveals the brutalising, and energising, effect of the military machine on popular consciousness so well as this new poetic style. The delicate, weaving movement of thought in the 'standard' *oriki* is replaced by a headlong, cumulative, exclamatory exuberance incessantly hammering in the same point. The leaders are seen as towering, monolithic, almost asocial beings, and the self-renewing need of the military state for ever more conquests to fuel it is pictured in terms of the leaders' driving personal blood-lust. Intensely highly charged language, packed with hyperbole, glorifies the qualities that lead to military success: toughness, ferocity, indestructability, ruthlessness, cruelty, possession of all types of hitherto unknown firearms, huge retinues of warboys. The deeds that are commemorated are all public ones – lists of conquered towns and humiliated enemies – as if there were no longer any room for the private and personal. Everything the Ibadan leader does is on a colossal scale.[25]

Balogun Ibikunle's *oriki* exemplified the new style:

> When in fighting mood, both eyes and nose are usually blood red,
> Always in bloody mood at the theatres of war.
> A really hefty personality.
> With strong plump hand and feet of a gorilla . . .
> He was dared to camp in the forest,
> Balogun camped in the forest and despoiled it.
> He was dared to pitch his tent in the field
> Balogun pitched his tent in the field,
> He ravaged and rent the whole field as would a cloth.[26]

Ibadan attracted 'wild, wicked and warlike men' from every part of Yorubaland, besides incorporating many captured slaves into its warbands.[27] Young boys, known as 'Father-said-I-should-not-run-away', served as attendants 'in order to familiarize them with the horrors of war.' Eventually they

[23] Johnson, *History*, p. 395.
[24] David Laitin, *Hegemony and culture: politics and religious change among the Yoruba* (Chicago, 1986), p. 59.
[25] Barber, 'Documenting,' p. 48.
[26] Quoted in Awe, 'Praise poems,' p. 344.
[27] J. Johnson to Secretary, Aborigines Protection Society, 26 May 1892, CO 879/36/428/122.

entered service with their compound's military chief, who allocated them ranks, fed them, but did not pay them, leaving them to support themselves by predation. The future Bashorun Latosisa, the most belligerent of Ibadan's military rulers, launched his career by capturing a woman, whom he married, and her children, whom he sold.[28] Ibadan was immensely violent. Until Ogunmola imposed a degree of order during the 1860s,

> a young man did not consider himself fully dressed without a short sword or knife girded to his side, a jack knife buckled to his left wrist, and wielding in his right hand a large-headed club or cudgel ringed or pegged with iron; consequently street fighting was a common affair. To spend a good day out without wounds and bruises to show for it was not considered manly.[29]

Yet Ibadan's warbands were not merely thugs. They inherited the professionalism of Oyo's cavalrymen and were markedly more skilful in warfare than their enemies.[30] The system rewarded skill and, above all, success, for there was a prejudice against men of distinguished ancestry, who were resented as arrogant, and most senior officers rose from the ranks, at least until late in the century.[31]

Nineteenth-century Yoruba notions of honour were shaped by prevailing technology. When Oyo disintegrated, most Yoruba moved southwards into the forest where cavalry no longer dominated. To own a horse still carried prestige, but the vital weapons now were flintlock muskets, introduced during the early 1820s.[32] There is no indication that they were considered unmanly. Slow to load, fired from the hip or at arm's length, and with an effective range of perhaps 100 metres, they severely limited military tactics. Ibadan's trained forces preferred the open field and fired in an advancing succession of ranks, perhaps eventually charging with their swords. Less professional warriors generally defended walled towns, the larger of which were virtually impregnable to musketeers, who instead mounted sieges that might last several years.[33] Single combat with flintlocks was barely conceivable – the only single combat noted from nineteenth-century Yorubaland was between two cavalrymen and 'recalled similar warfare of ancient times'[34] – but muskets had to be fired from

---

[28] Toyin Falola, *The political economy of a pre-colonial African state: Ibadan, 1830–1900* (Ile-Ife, 1984), pp. 138–9; Johnson, *History*, pp. 131, 324–6, 502.

[29] Johnson, *History*, pp. 374–5.

[30] J. F. A. Ajayi, 'The aftermath of the fall of Old Oyo,' in Ajayi and Crowder, *History*, vol. 2, p. 174; Johnson, *History*, p. 340.

[31] Johnson, *History*, pp. 305, 367, 500.

[32] Ibid., pp. 206–10.

[33] J. F. Ade Ajayi and Robert Smith, *Yoruba warfare in the nineteenth century* (Cambridge, 1964), pp. 17–19, 87–90; Akintoye, *Revolution*, p. 116.

[34] Johnson, *History*, p. 604.

a standing position, and there was much opportunity to dash towards the enemy, discharge a musket, and race back: 'This feat elicited great applause.'[35] Major casualties occurred when a walled town was stormed; Dahomey lost nearly three thousand dead in ten successive assaults on Abeokuta in 1851.[36] These tactics changed after 1881 when Ibadan's opponents in the Kiriji War imported breech-loading rifles, of much greater range and accuracy, which 'struck terror into the Ibadans', who were reduced to 'crawling along valleys, picking out shelters till they could approach near enough within the range of their Dane guns [i.e., flintlocks], to return the fire.'[37] Three years later, when Ibadan too had obtained breech-loaders,

the new weapons . . . led to the discouragement of battles in which opposing sides had to bare their chests open to each other. Thus pitched battles were avoided and hand-to-hand fighting method to which warriors fought at close quarters was cautiously employed only when combatants had expended their ammunitions. Also new methods of fighting such as shelling with barrages of gunfire, concealment of troops in trenches etc, accompanied with training and drilling of soldiers were employed in response to the introduction of the new weapons.[38]

Within two years, the resulting stalemate had forced the two sides to end their eight years of war.

Notions of military honour varied with circumstances. When Owu was destroyed at the beginning of the nineteenth-century wars, its men fought to the death or committed suicide to escape captivity. That model was followed in two Ekiti towns captured by Ibadan in 1855, where the defenders first killed their wives and children, and on other occasions.[39] The leader of the Kiriji War against Ibadan, Ogedemgbe, 'had to expose himself in every battle as any of the meanest soldiers in order to get his countrymen to follow him. His body was covered with scars from wounds.'[40] Johnson recorded one clear example of cowardice and betrayal, when an Oyo official fled a town under attack, took refuge in Dahomey, and encouraged its king to destroy Yoruba towns; he was eventually handed back and executed in the marketplace at Oyo.[41] Charges of

[35] Townsend, journal, 1 February 1845, CMS C.A2/O.85/227.
[36] Edouard Dunglas, 'La première attaque des Dahoméens contre Abéokuta (3 mars 1851),' *Etudes Dahoméennes*, 1 (1948), 19; Ajayi and Smith, *Yoruba warfare*, pp. 39, 50–1.
[37] Johnson, *History*, pp. 459–60.
[38] Oguntomisin in Akinjogbin, *War and peace*, p. 105.
[39] Kemi Morgan, *Akinyele's outline history of Ibadan: part one* (Ibadan, n.d.), p. 47; Akintoye, *Revolution*, p. 47; White, journal, 3 December 1855, CMS C.A2/O.87/49; King to ?, 1 December 1857, CMS C.A2/O.61/15.
[40] Johnson, *History*, p. 636.
[41] Ibid., p. 228.

cowardice were often levelled against leaders who counselled restraint; even Balogun Ibikunle, despite his 'bloody mood' and renowned courage, was taunted in songs, fined by the other chiefs for 'betraying cowardice', had a crow affixed to his house at night by soldiers as a sign of contempt, and was finally obliged to abandon his opposition to attacking Ibadan's kinsmen in Ijaye.[42] Generally, however, courage had a different quality from the cavalry ideal. The citizen-soldiers of most Yoruba towns were amateurs who saw nothing wrong 'if a man having served some time at the war finds his supplies getting low, he quietly shoulders his firelock and returns to his home, until by work or otherwise, he acquires money enough to purchase a fresh supply or provisions, or a new harvest has replenished his barns.'[43] The authorities in Abeokuta sometimes had to prohibit trade in order to force its men to war. Even in Ibadan, with its more professional soldiers and *condottiere* spirit, violence was needed at the end of the Ijaye War and during the breech-loader crisis in the Kiriji War in order to compel men to fight. Ogedemgbe's followers, an Ibadan man explained in 1884, 'are fighting for their freedom and their country, and they do not care whether they live or die; but we are fighting to catch slaves and we do not want to die.'[44]

If courage was flexible, so also was loyalty. Personal duty to one's patron and loyalty to one's town were obligations not lightly renounced. Ogedemgbe was thought to have resisted appeals to fight Ibadan early in the Kiriji War because he had been trained there, had sworn not to oppose the town, and had received his war-standard from its commander.[45] Yet during the divided loyalties and ruthless competition of the nineteenth century, fighting men changed towns, whether as refugees, captives, or ambitious soldiers, almost as often as they changed patrons. Elepo, widely considered Ibadan's finest general, helped his patron Oluyole to power there but was deserted by him when attacked by jealous rivals, whereat Elepo moved to Ijaye and died fighting Ibadan's allies.[46] A British visitor to Abeokuta noted that 'Both parties are perfectly well acquainted with each other's movements, many men having in both camps friends to whom they are bound by oath. It will sometimes happen that a chief refuses to go forth to war, pleading brotherhood with the enemy; and the reason is rarely

[42] Ibid., p. 333.
[43] Jones to Officer Commanding, Second West Indian Regiment, 6 June 1861, in Ajayi and Smith, *Yoruba warfare*, p. 135.
[44] Wright and others to Committee, 7 November 1861, MMS 263/B/25; Townsend to Venn, 25 February 1864, CMS C.A2/O.85/111; Akiele, journal, 30 January 1886, CMS G3/A2/O/1887/114; Wood to Lang, 10 December 1884, CMS G3/A2/O/1885/13.
[45] Johnson, *History*, pp. 440–6. But contrast Akintoye, *Revolution*, p. 78.
[46] Johnson, *History*, pp. 289–91, 302–3.

disregarded.'[47] This was indeed the case in Abeokuta during the Kiriji War, when Chief Ogundipe smuggled powder to his friend Latosisa, commanding the enemy forces. At the same period many young men from Ekiti fought enthusiastically for Ibadan against their own people.[48] Moreover, the violent competition among leaders meant that few towns launched campaigns with unanimous agreement. Ibikunle, Ibadan's senior chief, opposed the attack on Ijaye in 1860 and was believed to betray his forces' movements to the enemy, while Ijaye's warchiefs so opposed the dictator Kurunmi's intransigence that they threatened to surrender the town's gates to Ibadan and are said to have agreed with its cavalrymen to use only blank ammunition.[49]

The one indispensable qualification for honour was success: 'ever winning in every case,' as Ibikunle's *oriki* put it.[50] Eso principles required that an honourable commander must not survive defeat. Abeokuta's people obliged their general, Anoba, to kill himself after defeat at the beginning of the Ijaye War, and Kurunmi committed suicide to avoid capture at its end.[51] Yet many commanders did survive defeat. In the Batedo War of 1844 Kurunmi defeated Ibikunle and captured Ogunmola, both of whom survived as valiant fighting men.[52] Moreover, victory could be almost as dangerous as failure because of the jealousy provoked by success. Ibadan leaders forced to commit suicide under threat of murder or despoliation were as often victimised by jealous competitors as they were ruined by defeat. Aijenku, a hero of Ibadan's victory over Ijaye, and the young warchief Iyapo, son of Ibikunle, were both forced by a jealous superior to blow out their brains, the alternative being not only their own deaths but the destruction of their households. 'My father was an Eso and I was born an Eso,' Iyapo declared, 'and like an Eso I will die.'[53]

Honour, in various forms, was often cited during negotiations to end Yoruba wars, although perhaps mainly to justify decisions made for security reasons. At the end of the Ijaye War in 1865, for example, the Alafin of Oyo arranged for Ibadan and Abeokuta forces to withdraw simultaneously from their war camps, but – according to Johnson's possibly tendentious account – Abeokuta's men

[47] Richard F. Burton, *Abeokuta and the Cameroons Mountains* (2 vols., London, 1863), vol. 1, p. 293.

[48] Akintoye, *Revolution*, pp. 123, 52.

[49] Hinderer to Venn, 27 December 1861, CMS C.A2/O.49/56; Dare Oguntomisin, *Kurunmi of Ijaye 1831–1862* (Ikeja, 1986), p. 64.

[50] Awe, 'Praise poems,' p. 343.

[51] Johnson, *History*, p. 341; Toyin Falola and G. O. Oguntomisin, *Yoruba warlords of the nineteenth century* (Trenton, N.J., 2001), p. 64.

[52] Morgan, *Akinyele's history*, p. 93.

[53] Johnson, *History*, pp. 410–12, 417–19; Falola and Oguntomisin, *Military*, pp. 59–60.

attacked the retreating Ibadan forces and Ibadan had to take one of Abeokuta's villages before 'honour had been satisfied on both sides.'[54] This precedent weighed on those trying to end the Kiriji War in 1881. Initially neither party would seek mediation, 'for fear of losing prestige'. Negotiations in 1882–4 and again in 1886 broke down over which side should first vacate its war camp. 'Each party is . . . mistrustful of the other, and also ashamed to be the first to make peaceful overtures,' a British representative explained in 1889. Only British intervention enabled all to withdraw without losing honour.[55]

The main victims of nineteenth-century violence were ordinary people, especially the weak, towards whom military honour appears to have shown no chivalry. The military 'look down upon the working class, especially the farmers, with great contempt,' a missionary reported from Ibadan, where offences by soldiers were punished more leniently than those by civilians. 'The poor or working class and the aged ones,' he added, 'are crying and sighing for peace.'[56] Victims occasionally took violent revenge against oppressors or the public:

[There] was a conflagration this morn[in]g a man called Aina actually set the town on fire. [T]he girl who saw him and exclaim of it and made known of it was wounded by him, he also hurts many who mad[e] the attempt to extinguish it. There was a great stir in the town that day the man too was killed in the sine [scil: scene] the cause of the action was one of the chiefs deprives him of his kola trees which are valuable among the people here. [H]e wounded the chief too meaning to kill him only the wound was not fatal.[57]

Other victims killed or wounded themselves in order to salvage pride, assert innocence, or throw guilt on to the persecutor. 'It is a custom here,' it was reported from Ode Ondo in south-eastern Yorubaland, 'in cases of irritation, misfortune, shame and the like, to show one's courage by putting an end to one's life, or by attempting to do so.'[58] In other ways, too, the poor had their own notions of honour. Wage-labour, especially in agriculture, was widely considered demeaning for a freeman in this slave-owning society – 'the citizens of this place look at any one who wants to employ them as a real insult to them' – although such labour could be obtained for a price, especially in more commercialised

---

[54] Johnson, *History*, pp. 358, 363.
[55] Ibid., pp. 466, 547–67; I. A. Akinjogbin, 'Wars in Yorubaland, 1793–1893: an analytical categorisation,' in his *War and peace*, p. 48; Macdonald to Salisbury, 18 October 1889, CO 879/33/399/14.
[56] Hinderer, journal, 4 October 1851, CMS C.A2/O.49/104.
[57] Cross, journal, 26 July 1884, CMS G3/A2/O/1885/9.
[58] Lijadu, journal, 16 January 1891, CMS G3/A2/O/1892/15.

areas and nonagricultural occupations like porterage.[59] Small-scale trade relied considerably on public honesty, especially in the practice of leaving food by the roadside for passers-by to take in return for depositing currency. Much larger-scale trade relied on credit ('trust') from European merchants. The expanded commerce of the nineteenth century created a new category of Big Men whose standing rested on wealth, especially in Lagos where they sought to convert their wealth into honour by largess and patronage. In militarised Ibadan, by contrast, the warchiefs were themselves active traders but despised civilian merchants, excluding them from office and mulcting them in time of war.[60] Predictably, in such an acquisitive society at a time of disorder, nineteenth-century Yorubaland was highly corrupt, the constant exchange of gifts shading into direct bribery, which was especially evident in the courts, where gifts to a judge were seen as part of the costs of litigation and a recognised set of gestures was said to signal the offers. Yet, as in later times, powerful men also sought honour by denouncing corruption. 'Here is his money. I do not need it,' Ogunmola of Ibadan declared when punishing a litigant who tried to bribe him. 'Bribery is not good, it is worse than poison.'[61]

The Age of Confusion created conflict within the large compounds in which most urban Yoruba lived. The conflict centred on questions of generation, gender, and adulthood, for the authority of compound heads over women and the young conflicted with new opportunities for junior members to secure independence, young men by seeking their fortunes as warboys or palm-oil traders, young women by escaping unwelcome marriages by fleeing to the British colony at Lagos, and both by adopting Islam or Christianity. Evidence of family conflict and householder honour comes especially from the persecution of Christian converts, which in otherwise tolerant Yorubaland chiefly meant family pressure – sometimes very brutal pressure – on deviant members.[62] In Ode Ondo during 1890, for example,

An old man rudely entered the church while I was preaching, to force out his son (a lad about 18 years old) from the church . . . when the young man returned home, he bound him and flogged him severely. . . . He said he had permitted a nephew of his to attend

---

[59] W. Allen, 19 November 1879, quoted in Peel, *Religious encounter*, p. 67; Edward Graham Norris, *Wirtschaft und Wirtschaftspolitik in Abeokuta 1830–1867: Aspekte der Ethnographie und Geschichte eines Yoruba-Staates im neunzehnten Jahrhundert* (Wiesbaden, 1978), pp. 46–7.

[60] Barber, *I could speak*, pp. 195–203; Kristin Mann, 'The rise of Taiwo Olowo: law, accumulation and mobility in early colonial Lagos,' in Kristin Mann and Richard Roberts (eds.), *Law in colonial Africa* (Portsmouth, N.H., 1991), ch. 3; Falola, *Political economy*, ch. 5; Falola and Oguntomisin, *Military*, p. 57.

[61] Fadipe, *Sociology*, pp. 226, 235–6; Falola and Oguntomisin, *Warlords*, p. 44.

[62] This account is based on John Iliffe, 'Persecution and toleration in pre-colonial Africa: nineteenth-century Yorubaland,' *Studies in Church History*, 21 (1984), 357–78.

Christian instruction, but he could not permit the young man who is his own son, for if they both became Christians, he would have no one after his death, who will keep up the worship of the Osonyin [god of medicine] which he had inherited from his ancestors, and regard as indispensable to the well being of his family.[63]

Young women were even more vulnerable. All the recorded victims of persecution in Ibadan in the mid 1850s appear to have been young women. When a missionary in Ijaye protested at a husband beating his Christian wife for refusing to eat sacrificial meat, Kurunmi replied briefly, 'Is she not the man's wife?'[64] Yet victims were not invariably young or female, for wives might persecute their husbands, daughters their mothers, or children their fathers into abandoning Christianity.[65] The difference was that the authorities recognised an adult man's right to control his own actions as well as those of his wives, children, and slaves. When a man tried to force his adult younger brother to abandon Christianity, his chief 'sent to the brother to trouble him no more, stating that it was folly to take steps with a man of age and sound judgment.'[66]

Adulthood and masculinity were especially at issue in sexual matters. It has been estimated that if Yoruba men did not generally marry until their early thirties, women generally married at seventeen or more, 30 per cent of married men were polygynous, and women abstained from sexual intercourse for three years after giving birth – all broadly reasonable assumptions in this society – then at any moment 42 per cent of males over seventeen were single, 58 per cent of married men had no sexually available wife, and as much as 60 per cent of all male sexual activity took place outside marriage, especially perhaps within the extended family and with slave women.[67] A Yoruba clergyman in Ode Ondo perhaps exaggerated only slightly when writing in 1884 that 'in the present state of things, it is nearly impossible for our young men to have wives among their countrymen, except they take one of the widows of their deceased relatives.'[68] Amidst the intense competition for women, the normal punishment for adultery among commoners was said to be a fine, but cases of extreme sexual jealousy are recorded. In Abeokuta in 1855, for

[63] Phillips, journal, 16 February 1890, CMS G3/A2/O/1890/166.

[64] Anna Hinderer, *Seventeen years in the Yoruba country* (London, 1872), pp. 131–7; R. H. Stone, *In Afric's forest and jungle or six years among the Yorubans* (Edinburgh, 1900), p. 59.

[65] Maser, journal, 9 July 1858, CMS C.A2/O.68/125; S. Crowther, journal, 25 December 1856, CMS C.A2/O.32/65; J. Johnson, 'From Ibadan to Oyo and Ogbomoso' [1877] CMS C.A2/O.56/51.

[66] King to Snaith, 25 April 1853, CMS C.A2/O.61/3.

[67] John C. Caldwell, Pat Caldwell, and I. O. Orubuloye, 'The family and sexual networking in sub-Saharan Africa: historical regional differences and present-day implications,' *Population Studies*, 46 (1992), 389–90.

[68] Phillips to Lagos Finance Committee, 10 November 1884, CMS G3/A2/O/1885/3.

example, a cuckolded husband killed himself, thereby procuring the execution of the offending man.[69] The most severe penalties resulted from adultery with the hundreds of royal wives. In Oyo offending men were customarily sent to the Alafin's court for emasculation; during the 1890s his servants included twenty-one eunuchs. Kurunmi of Ijaye was pathologically cruel towards offending wives and their lovers. Several nineteenth-century wars, including the Kiriji War, were supposedly precipitated by offences against women.[70]

Yet women had their own notions of honour, more clearly than in either the savanna or Ethiopia. These notions probably included premarital virginity, which was thought to guarantee a fertile marriage. 'The virgin woman who immediately gets pregnant does not know suffering in her husband's house,' said a proverb.[71] Mature Yoruba women were highly independent, even by the standards of the West African forest. They were especially prominent in religious cults. Their share in agricultural labour was less than was normal in Africa and was concentrated mainly at harvest, but they were active in craft industries and almost monopolised small-scale trade, from which they sought especially to support their children. As a later Yoruba wrote, 'There is nothing that a Yoruba woman would not do for her children.' Royal palaces had numerous female officers and each town had women chiefs to control markets and adjudicate in female affairs.[72] A few exceptional women such as Tinubu in Abeokuta and Efunsetan in Ibadan achieved great success in the import-export trade, which was open to both sexes. Both became Iyolade (chief of the women) in their respective towns through their services during wartime, for women financed warboys, supplied food and munitions, maintained morale, and occasionally assisted in military actions. Yet both experienced difficulty in converting wealth into public status and male respect. Tinubu was expelled from Lagos for her political activities, while Efunsetan was murdered for refusing to give Ibadan's senior chief further credit in time of war.[73]

---

[69] S. A. Crowther to Hutchinson, 10 September 1856, CMS C.A2/O.31/78; Macaulay, journal, 17 July 1855, CMS C.A2/O.65/92.

[70] Bower to CS, 3 December 1895, CO 879/45/509/6; MacGregor to Chamberlain, 19 June 1900, CO 879/62/627/1; Phillips, journal, 3 September 1853, CMS C.A2/O.77/7; Bolanle Awe and Omotayo Olutoye, 'Women and warfare in 19th century Yorubaland: an introduction,' in Akinjogbin, *War and peace*, p. 124.

[71] Elisha P. Renne, 'Changes in adolescent sexuality and the perception of virginity in a southwestern Nigerian village,' *Health Transition Review*, 3 (1993), 121–33.

[72] Peel, *Religious encounter*, p. 103; LaRay Denzer, 'Yoruba women: a historiographical study,' *IJAHS*, 27 (1994), 1–12; Lawrence A. Adeokun, 'Marital sexuality and birth-spacing among the Yoruba,' in Christine Oppong (ed.), *Female and male in West Africa* (London, 1983), p. 129.

[73] Robin Law, '"Legitimate" trade and gender relations in Yorubaland and Dahomey,' in his *From slave trade to 'legitimate' commerce* (Cambridge, 1995), pp. 202–8; Awe and Olutoye in

That the success of innovations in nineteenth-century Yorubaland depended heavily on their accommodation to the dominant military ethic is illustrated by the different fortunes of Islam and Christianity. Islam had probably reached Yorubaland by the fifteenth century, but it suffered acutely early in the nineteenth century when Muslims supported Sokoto's intervention in the conflict that destroyed Oyo. Several Yoruba towns proscribed or persecuted Muslims at that time. Ibadan's leaders destroyed the town's first mosque.[74] After Sokoto's aggression was halted in 1840, however, Islam expanded rapidly. Ibadan was said to have at least twenty-four mosques in 1877 and seventy in 1908.[75] Islam's chief initial attractions were probably its prayers and protective amulets for fighting men. Warchiefs in Ibadan were especially responsive; by 1875 Ibadan's Muslims were said to include 'more than half of the ruling chiefs'. Muslims showed an eager readiness to defend their towns. When the British defeated Ijebu in 1892, its warriors immediately adopted Islam en masse.[76]

By contrast, Christianity in Yorubaland generally conflicted with notions of military honour, rejecting the accommodation achieved in Ethiopia and later in Buganda. Despite many advantages, including recaptured Yoruba slaves trained as clergymen and evangelists, the missionaries who settled in Yorubaland in 1846 had by 1890 gained the adherence of only about 1 per cent of the population.[77] Not a single Christian held an important indigenous office outside Lagos. A major reason for this failure was the missionaries' frontal assault on notions of honour. Not only did Christianity reject polygyny, but it also challenged the compound head's authority, attacked the culture of display, and denounced the militarism that attracted many young men who elsewhere in Africa often became the first Christians. The European missionaries, often German pietists, encouraged converts to defend their towns against attack, for which they gained credit in Abeokuta during Dahomeyan invasions, but proscribed other forms of military action, not always successfully. In Abeokuta Christianity was sometimes known as *abukon*, meaning disgrace.[78] In Ibadan the mission school

Akinjogbin, *War and peace*, ch. 10; Earl Harold Phillips, 'The Church Missionary Society, the imperial factor, and Yoruba politics, 1842–1873,' PhD thesis, University of Southern California, 1966, p. 321; Johnson, *History*, pp. 391–2.

[74] T. G. O. Gbadamosi, *The growth of Islam among the Yoruba, 1841–1908* (London, 1978), pp. 4–13; Morgan, *Akinyele's history*, p. 107.

[75] 'Report from Revd J. Johnson,' August 1877, CMS C.A2/O.56/50; *CMS Gazette*, 1908, p. 301.

[76] Hinderer, journal, 4 October 1851, CMS C.A2/O.49/104; F. H. el-Masri, 'Islam,' in Lloyd, Mabogunje, and Awe, *Ibadan*, p. 253; Norris, *Wirtschaft*, p. 165; Olubi to Fenn, 28 December 1875, CMS C.A2/O.75/43; Cole, journal, 3 December 1872, CMS C.A2/O.29/12; J. F. Ade Ajayi, *A patriot to the core: Bishop Ajayi Crowther* (Ibadan, 2001), p. 96.

[77] Peel, *Religious encounter*, p. 242.

[78] *Wesleyan Missionary Notices*, 1864, pp. 117–20 (reprinting *Iwe Irohin*, 22 March 1864); Peel, *Religious encounter*, pp. 138–9; King, journal, 2 January 1854, CMS C.A2/O.61/52.

stagnated – 'they think "book" will make them cowards' – and a Yoruba clergyman reported in 1877 that 'Christians hold a low social position and are
accounted and spoken of as a lazy, idle and coward people because of their
refusal to go out with war and slave making expeditions.'[79] 'Christianity is not
for one of his capacity, but for beggars or slaves,' a convert's family told him,
'and hence he should not let his father's house go to ruins, but he must inherit
the wives left by his father and brother; and in times of war to be their leader,
and they will show him all honour and respect.'[80] Only after colonial rule made
militarism redundant did Yoruba pastors convincingly appropriate the warrior
ideal and compare themselves to Eso.[81]

Christianity contested both Yorubaland's notions of honour: its eighteenth-
century order of rank and civic reputation and its nineteenth-century order of
military heroism. And Christianity lost, as other social and ideological innovations were to lose unless they could accommodate to, absorb, and transmute
Africa's honour cultures.

[79] Hinderer, *Seventeen years*, p. 86; 'Report from Revd J. Johnson,' August 1877, CMS
C.A2/O.56/50.
[80] S. Johnson, journal, 24 December 1877, CMS C.A2/O.58/9.
[81] Peel, *Religious encounter*, p. 246.

6   Honour and the State in West and Central Africa

In contrast to Yoruba states, the kingdoms of the forest and its fringes in West and Equatorial Africa relied wholly on spearmen or musketeers. Here the state itself was the fount of honour. The individual was gradually subordinated to the political community and, as in the Ancient World, heroic egotism, expressed elsewhere in single combat, gave way increasingly to soldierly duty or civil litigation.[1] During the nineteenth century, this process went further as men possessing administrative skills or wealth also pursued honour through service to the state. For women, too, the state provided opportunities for an elite to play a public role matched elsewhere in precolonial Africa only in the Great Lakes region. These distinctive notions of honour will be analysed first in the Asante kingdom, where the evidence from European descriptions and later oral testimonies is particularly rich. Other kingdoms will then be compared with Asante.

Asante (in modern Ghana) straddled the forest-savanna border at the only point in Africa where gold deposits coincided with well-watered agricultural land. The local Akan-speaking people probably worked gold from early in the second millennium A.D. In the late fifteenth century, they sold it to Portuguese traders on the Gold Coast, first in return for slaves and then, from the 1660s, for firearms with which military clans created the Asante state. During the eighteenth century, this state expanded northwards into the savanna and southwards towards

---

[1] For the comparison, see Hugh Lloyd-Jones, 'Honour and shame in ancient Greek culture,' in his *Greek comedy, Hellenistic literature, Greek religion, and miscellanea* (Oxford, 1990), p. 269; Douglas L. Cairns, *Aidos: the psychology and ethics of honour and shame in ancient Greek literature* (Oxford, 1993), pp. 164–5.

the coast to rule some 250,000 square kilometres.[2] The capital at Kumase was surrounded by the six confederate chiefdoms forming the original kingdom, then by a circle of incorporated Akan-speakers, and finally by conquered tributary peoples. Nineteenth-century conflict with the British on the Gold Coast was to end in British occupation of Kumase in 1896.[3]

As in Oyo, honour in Asante was enjoyed primarily in its vertical dimension as an attribute of rank. At the apex of the hierarchy, the Asantehene, although far from absolute, was a highly visible ruler, active in politics and justice. He was the focus of the praise-poetry sung during the annual Odwira festival:

> Behold the Great One!
> Who dares go to provoke him?
> Whoever provokes Osee Tutu
> invites war.
> He is the creator of a new nation
> as solid as fresh nut.
> A mighty man
> feared by mighty men.[4]

The ceremony surrounding an Asantehene was perhaps the continent's most spectacular:

As soon as the King descended from his basket, he commenced dancing.... He was dressed in a beautiful, elaborately-wrought country cloth, and was literally laden with gold; his head, neck, arms, wrists, fingers, legs, ankles, and feet, all profusely ornamented with studs, chains, bracelets, rings, &c., in great variety. Crowding near him were scores of men bearing massive gold-handled swords, to which were attached, hanging by a piece of native string, large gold ornaments in the shape of birds, beasts, fishes, fruits, barrels, human heads, vases, &c., some of them weighing at least three or four pounds.... Mixed up with them were bearers of elephants' tails, and a number of men with large oblong shields, and others holding immense umbrellas of variegated satin; and as the King danced, the whole mass kept in motion, while his executioners vociferated his strong names, and the horns gave out their loudest tones, and the drums were beaten with re-doubled energy, and the thousands of spectators shouted applause.[5]

Next to the Asantehene at state occasions was the queen mother – not normally his physical mother, but a close matrilineal relative – who was the second

---

[2] James Anquandah, 'Urbanization and state formation in Ghana during the Iron Age,' in T. Shaw, P. Sinclair, B. Andah, and A. Okpoko (eds.), *The archaeology of Africa* (London, 1993), pp. 644–51; Ivor Wilks, *Asante in the nineteenth century: the structure and evolution of a political order* (Cambridge, 1975), pp. 18–25, 80, 110–11.

[3] Wilks, *Asante*, pp. 46–79, 654–6.

[4] Kwame Arhin, 'The Asante praise poems: the ideology of patrimonialism,' *Paideuma*, 32 (1986), 192. Osei Tutu was the first Asantehene.

[5] The Revd William West, 9 June 1862, in *Wesleyan Missionary Notices*, 1862, p. 154.

person in the kingdom and acted when necessary as regent. Every territorial chief had a similar female relative to serve in his absence, act as a repository of custom, and exercise authority over women.[6] In this matrilineal society, an Asantehene's sons could not succeed to the throne but often held high office as military commanders or chiefs. The highest rank after the queen mother, however, was occupied by the hereditary rulers of the confederate chiefdoms, who jealously defended their right to mobilise and command their subjects in war against the centralising ambitions of Asantehenes who sought to subordinate these forces to the capital's professional military officers.[7] Divisional and village chiefs in the confederate chiefdoms exercised both administrative and military leadership, while at the lowest level the household head controlled the women, younger men, and slaves of his family. Among both Asante and other Akan-speaking peoples, matriliny allowed women considerable autonomy. A girl impregnated before her nubility rites might be excoriated, along with her lover and her family, but the making and breaking of marriages was relatively easy, postmenstrual women could exercise public functions, and women always remained primarily members of their own matrilineages.[8] Adultery, however, was a dispute between men over property in a woman; nothing dramatised rank more vividly than the scale of penalties for the offence, ranging from the terrible lingering death of the man who interfered with an Asantehene's wife to the graduated financial compensation due to commoners, while powerful men 'flaunted their ability to pay for misdemeanours.'[9]

Underlying this society was its military technology. Asante never used cavalry, even in the savanna, but relied on the flintlock muskets that every man was expected to own. They were unreliable, inaccurate, short in range, and slow to reload, but some Asante forces, at least, sighted their weapons and fired from the shoulder.[10] The army was the male nation in arms, mobilising at its peak perhaps forty thousand to eighty thousand men. In open country, musketeers

---

[6] Kwame Arhin, 'The political and military roles of Akan women,' in Oppong, *Female and male*, pp. 93–5.

[7] Agnes Akosua Aidoo, 'Political crisis and social change in the Asante kingdom, 1867–1901,' PhD thesis, University of California at Los Angeles, 1975, pp. 54–60, 71–4.

[8] T. C. McCaskie, *Asante identities: history and modernity in an African village, 1850–1950* (Edinburgh, 2000), pp. 181–2; Jean Allman and Victoria Tashjian, *'I will not eat stone': a women's history of colonial Asante* (Portsmouth, N.H., 2000), pp. xxviii, 46–60.

[9] *Asantesem*, 2 (April 1975), 19; R. S. Rattray, *Religion and art in Ashanti* (Oxford, 1927), ch. 9; T. C. McCaskie, 'The consuming passions of Kwame Boakye: an essay on agency and identity in Asante history,' *JACS*, 13 (2000), 55.

[10] The evidence on this last point is contradictory: see Robert S. Smith, *Warfare and diplomacy in pre-colonial West Africa* (London, 1976), p. 115; C. H. Armitage and A. F. Montanaro, *The Ashanti campaign of 1900* (London, 1901), p. 131. Generally, see Emmanuel Terray, 'Contribution à une étude de l'armée asante,' *CEA*, 16 (1976), 297–356; Wilks, *Asante*, pp. 80–3.

generally fought in loose skirmishing order divided into three ranks, each firing in turn while the others reloaded and then moved to the front, so that the whole body was continuously advancing. 'To advance every time he fires he feels to be imperative,' the first British observer, Bowdich, reported in 1817.[11] Withdrawal even to reload was in principle cowardice. In practice, however, much fighting was on narrow forest paths where ambush was the most formidable tactic. Casualty rates were relatively high, for Asante, unlike Yoruba, did not construct fortifications. Their tactics put a premium on courage, discipline, and morale, the areas in which, as foreign observers agreed, Asante excelled.[12] The hero (*obarima*, connoting also the penis) personified military honour.[13] Bowdich recorded two relatively poor men 'very suddenly elevated for extraordinary courage' to positions of command. Many families defended privileges gained through past heroism, passing down charm-encrusted war-coats as heirlooms.[14] Cowardice, by contrast, might earn death, although the sentence might be commuted to a money payment and public humiliation in which the offender was dressed as a woman and any man might seduce his wife without paying damages.[15] Yet courage was more disciplined than the individual heroics fostered by cavalry warfare. Tradition told of past disputes settled by single combat, but no example in war has been noted, nor would it have been feasible with muzzle-loading muskets. Conflict between individual egotism and collective constraint pervaded Asante society.[16] Military discipline was severe. Not only did cowardice and malingering earn death, but so did disobedience, disclosing casualty levels, and misappropriating booty. Battle police armed with swords and whips drove forward anyone seen to retreat. 'If I fight I die, if I run away I die, better I go on and die,' ran a song popular in early nineteenth-century Kumase.[17] Morale was buttressed by divination, ritual, magic – especially protective amulets – and care for serving troops. 'The Ashantees make very great effort to bury their dead and to carry their wounded back,' a British observer

---

[11] T. Edward Bowdich, *Mission from Cape Coast Castle to Ashantee* (3rd edn, London, 1966), p. 299.

[12] Terray, 'Contribution,' p. 339; Thornton, *Warfare*, pp. 71–3; Wilks, *Asante*, pp. 82–3; Bowdich, *Mission*, p. 298.

[13] McCaskie, 'Consuming passions,' p. 44.

[14] Bowdich, *Mission*, p. 295; Kwame Arhin, 'Asante military institutions,' *Journal of African Studies*, 7 (1980), 25; McCaskie, 'Consuming passions,' p. 46.

[15] Bowdich, *Mission*, pp. 73, 257; R. S. Rattray, *Ashanti law and constitution* (Oxford, 1929), p. 126.

[16] Rattray, *Ashanti law*, p. 75; T. C. McCaskie, 'People and animals: constru(ct)ing the Asante experience,' *Africa*, 62 (1992), 236.

[17] Sir Francis Fuller, *A vanished dynasty: Ashanti* (2nd edn, London, 1968), p. 13; Bowdich, *Mission*, p. 299.

noted, and a medical corps did what little it could for the wounded.[18] Asante endurance of pain was legendary, although its counterpart was such cruelty to prisoners that Muslims deserted an Asante army in 1818 rather than 'witness the horrid butcheries in the camp'.[19] To endure such cruelty without flinching won lasting admiration.

Military honour was equally unforgiving for commanders. Asante's strategy was generally cautious, conscious of surrounding enemies and the difficulties of manoeuvre in a forest environment, but an Asantehene opposing a majority demand for war or withdrawing an army without decisive battle risked accusations of cowardice and deposition, as Kofi Kakari found in 1872–3 when he did both after swearing at his accession that 'My trade shall be war'.[20] Such oaths replaced the vaunts of personal prowess common in Ethiopia. A man could protest a grievance by an oath alluding to an incident humiliating to a chief's office, thereby obliging the chief to hear the case at the risk of the complainant's life. Similarly, a commander might swear before a campaign:

I speak the great forbidden name that, if I do not go to this war on which you have sent me forth, or if I go and show my back to the enemy, if I send a bullet and it falls short, and I do not follow it, and if I run away, then have I violated the great forbidden word.[21]

This practice emphasised the importance of their given word to men of honour. When, in 1872, Kofi Kakari's commanders 'took oaths to march to the Coast' but returned unsuccessful, the Asantehene dismissed the commander-in-chief with the reminder that 'You swore you would not return till you could bring me the walls of Cape Coast.' That was not a moment to exact more severe penalties, but a general had been executed in similar circumstances a decade before.[22] Etiquette was said to require a commander to play the *aware* board-game during battle but to surround himself with the barrels of gunpowder which he would ignite if faced by capture or defeat.[23] Many commanders were doubtless less ostentatious, but several committed ritual suicide, an action particularly admired by a society that regarded suicide as disgraceful unless performed for the sake of honour. In 1875 Asante's most distinguished general, Asamoa Nkwanta, and two of his subordinates blew themselves up after suffering initial reverses, whereupon his deputy sat on his stool in the middle of the enemy town and

---

[18] Terray, 'Contribution,' pp. 331–2.
[19] Joseph Dupuis, *Journal of a residence in Ashantee* (2nd edn, London, 1966), pp. 98–9.
[20] Henry Brackenbury, *The Ashanti War: a narrative* (reprinted, 2 vols., London, 1968), vol. 1, pp. 43–52; Wilks, *Asante*, p. 478.
[21] Rattray, *Ashanti law*, p. 123.
[22] Wilks, *Asante*, pp. 503, 506, 222.
[23] Terray, 'Contribution,' p. 339.

challenged his men to defend him, as they did successfully.[24] By contrast, there is no mention of feud or duelling in Asante. Manifold opportunities to demonstrate courage in war made artificial means unnecessary, while state power made them impracticable.[25]

Similar principles extended into civilian life. Asante was a rare African society that expected a man to defend his honour in court rather than by violence. That honour was sensitive, especially among the nobility, the *bakoma*, from which derived a word meaning 'to be imperious, violent, stubborn, wilful, arbitrary'. 'The manners of the higher orders of captains, always dignified, are courteous and hospitable in private, though haughty and abrupt in public,' Bowdich reported.[26] One means of asserting status was *mpoatwa* – 'challenge, setting at defiance, defamation' – a form of insult, generally verbal but possibly by gesture, used to claim or deny rank.[27] Bowdich described a prince, whose status in a matrilineal society was ambiguous, telling a warchief's son, with some truth, 'that in comparison with himself, he was the son of a slave.' At which point the commander seized the prince and destroyed his house so that the Asantehene had to redeem him. Later in the century, Asantehene Mensa Bonsu insulted the corpse of a confederate chief, whose successor swore never to serve Kumase again and kept his vow.[28] Yet, as in many oral societies, ordinary people, too, were intensely sensitive to insult. Under Akan law, any false and discreditable imputation was slanderous, without need to prove material damage as in Britain, which led a later nationalist lawyer to claim that '[t]he delicate feelings of the average African are not half as blunted and atrophied as those of the average European.'[29] The anthropologist Rattray, in the 1920s, believed that personal abuse was Asante's most important cause of quarrels and lawsuits:

The Ashanti was (and is), to our way of thinking, extremely sensitive to personal invective of every kind. To have 'a good name' was wellnigh essential to his existence; to have 'a bad name' rendered life, in the narrow community in which he passed his days, unbearable. He was incapable of withstanding an atmosphere of adverse public opinion; public ridicule readily drove him to commit suicide. This last sanction was, perhaps, the strongest deterrent known to Ashanti law. These were probably the reasons why

[24] *Asantesem*, 3 (June 1975), 9; Wilks, *Asante*, pp. 226, 515.

[25] Rattray (*Ashanti law*, p. 286) wrote, 'There is not a trace of the vendetta.'

[26] Emmanuel Terray, *Une histoire du royaume abron du Gyaman des origines à la conquête coloniale* (Paris, 1995), p. 821; Bowdich, *Mission*, p. 249.

[27] J. G. Christaller, *A dictionary of the Asante and Fante language* (Basel, 1881), p. 382; McCaskie, *Identities*, p. 29.

[28] Bowdich, *Mission*, p. 253; Aidoo, 'Political crisis,' p. 427.

[29] J. B. Danquah (ed.), *Cases in Akan law* (London, 1928), p. xxiii. See also John Mensah Sarbah, *Fanti customary laws* (3rd edn, London, 1968), p. 113.

personal abuse or personal slander were invariably and immediately followed by 'legal proceedings'.

If ridicule was an especially painful offence, it was also an especially effective punishment. Just as a coward might be treated as a woman, a malicious gossip might be smeared with charcoal, given a live fowl to hold beneath the teeth, and paraded through the town beating a gong.[30]

The military system formed the basis of Asante's political order and notions of honour, but by the nineteenth century there were two other major sources of distinction. One was a cadre of centrally appointed administrators rivalling the hereditary nobility. Bowdich noted their emergence in 1817. 'The Aristocracy,' he wrote, 'was originally formed of the peers and associates of Sai Tootoo [Osei Tutu] the founder of the monarchy. . . . The Aristocracy has been gradually re-trenched since Sai Cudjo [Osei Kwadwo, 1764–77] pointed out the way.'[31] Each administrative department evolved as a complex of offices, staff, and supporting estates, normally transmitted patrilineally to facilitate specialised training. The most powerful department was the Gyaase, originally a military unit (probably a royal bodyguard) whose commander, the Gyaasewahene, became the chief household officer overseeing the treasury.[32] Studies of official careers have shown a distinct ethos of administrative honour and public service among some office-holders. Asante Agyei (born c.1788), for example, risked his diplomatic career and perhaps his life by defending the impartial administration of justice. Kwame Butuakwa (c.1770–c.1835) and Boakye Tenten (c.1818–84) loyally implemented the changing policies of successive Asantehenes.[33] Not receiving regular salaries, these officials were frequently accused of corruption, doubt-less often with justice, but several were not remembered as especially venal or wealthy men.[34] This sense of public duty was probably built upon an older ethos of personal loyalty to a chief. In 1867, for example, the dying Asantehene Kwaku Dua I charged his kinsman and general, Owusu Koko, to secure the throne for the child prince Agyeman Kofi, an obligation which Owusu Koko pursued for sixteen years at the ultimate cost of his life.[35]

Among the most important administrative departments was the corporation of state traders. It enjoyed a privileged position in external trade in kola, gold,

---

[30] Rattray, *Ashanti law*, p. 326.

[31] Bowdich, *Mission*, p. 252 n. See also Wilks, *Asante*, pp. 127–30, 445–7.

[32] Aidoo, 'Political crisis,' pp. 77–81; Wilks, *Asante*, pp. 415–16.

[33] *Asantesem*, 3 (June 1975), 5–6; ibid., 2 (April 1975), 5–6; ibid., 6 (December 1976), 5–13.

[34] Ibid., 2 (April 1975), 6; ibid., 4 (February 1976), 19; ibid., 5 (November 1976), 7–9.

[35] Ibid., 4 (February 1976), 7–10.

slaves, and firearms, but not a monopoly, for chiefs and commoners also participated, while retail trade within Asante was in private hands. Rather than discour-
aging private enterprise and accumulation, the state exploited it through taxation
and extortion, especially death duties.[36] Private wealth was therefore a second
source of civil distinction, harder to control than administrative power but skilfully channelled into the scheme of public honour. Yamoa Ponko (c.1730–85)
was among the first to display his wealth before the Asantehene and earn the
obirempon (great man) title and the right to be preceded by a servant carrying an
elephant's tail. The Asantehene honoured him further by attending his funeral,
then seized his self-acquired fortune.[37] Not only the rich but noblemen, tributary
rulers, and friendly princes received the regalia by which Asante sought to assert
prestige and authority throughout the region. In 1807, for example, the King of
Banda received a palanquin, six ceremonial swords, and a drum. Ten years later,
by contrast, a leader in Juaben, anxious to defend his autonomy from Kumase,
refused 'a gold headed sword, with other marks of dignity . . . alleging, that the
honors he already possessed at home became him better.'[38] Appearances were
crucially important in this honour culture. Many patterns of the magnificent,
locally woven *kente* cloths were unique to individuals, groups, or clans. Musical instruments were allocated by rank. Commoners might not wear gold or
silver rings, sit on carved stools, wear sandals, or sport anything implying self-
elevation. Many possessed only a coarse cloth for daily wear and a dyed one
for mourning. Even a rich man was wise to conceal his wealth unless he could
demonstratively put it to the service of the state. Above all, he must pass it on
to the community and the state at his death. To have consumed or wasted it –
to have 'boiled and eaten the elephant tail' – was ultimately shaming.[39]

Although the new administrative class reduced the autonomy of the military
nobility, it did not threaten the priority of rank or the military basis of honour.
Within the confederate chiefdoms, political and military authority remained
with the hereditary nobility. Within the central Kumase chiefdom, below the
Asantehene himself, it passed to appointed officials and military commanders.
The two were in practice closely identified. The Gyaase was not only the core of

---

[36] Gareth Austin, '"No elders were present": commoners and private ownership in Asante, 1807–
96,' *JAH*, 37 (1996), 10–22; Ivor Wilks, 'The golden stool and the elephant tail: an essay on
wealth in Asante,' *Research in Economic Anthropology*, 2 (1979), 1–36.

[37] *Asantesem*, 9 (June 1978), 28–30.

[38] Wilks, *Asante*, p. 77; Bowdich, *Mission*, pp. 245–6.

[39] Rattray, *Religion*, ch. 24; J. H. Kwabena Nketia, 'History and the organization of music in
West Africa,' in Klaus P. Wachsmann (ed.), *Essays on music and history in Africa* (Evanston,
1971), p. 17; Kwame Arhin, 'The political economy of the expansionist state,' *Revue Française
d'Histoire d'Outre-Mer*, 68 (1981), 27–8; T. C. McCaskie, *State and society in pre-colonial
Asante* (Cambridge, 1995), p. 47.

the Asantehene's household administration in peace but also his bodyguard in war. Its most famous chief, Opoku Frefre (c.1755–1826), was not only the head of the civil service and a man wealthy enough to earn the elephant's tail but a general who committed suicide after defeat in battle.[40] As the anthropologist Kwame Arhin insisted, nineteenth-century Asante was a society dominated by militarism and rank into which new offices were absorbed.[41]

Wealth, however, was not so easily controlled. As warfare slackened and trade with the coast increased during the mid-nineteenth century, it became easier to acquire wealth outside the framework of the state. Kwasi Brantuo (c.1791–1865) gained the elephant's tail without probably ever firing a shot in anger. By the 1860s rich men were escaping the state's exactions by taking refuge in British territory.[42] Opposition increased after 1874, when British invasion severely weakened the kingdom. Nine years later, popular insurrection in Kumase overthrew the Asantehene with the support, if not the inspiration or leadership, of wealthy men who looked to the relatively liberal Gold Coast regime as their model.[43] The Asantehene who was enstooled in 1888 was required (by some accounts) to renounce the right to levy death duties.[44] And when his regime once more displayed authoritarian tendencies, wealthy Asante in the Gold Coast urged the British to replace it by a liberal, Christian, modernising protectorate. 'We do not want to hear the names of these down trodden degraded native African Kings and Chiefs,' they complained. '...Down with native drums, native umbrellas, native swords and elephant tails: useless and good for nothing.'[45] The culture of rank and honour was in question.

Kingdoms in two regions of West and Central Africa warrant comparison with Asante. One, slightly to its east, was Dahomey. The other was the Bantu-speaking group of states that Jan Vansina named the Kingdoms of the Savanna, ringing the equatorial forest from Kongo and Tio in the west, through Kuba, Lunda, and Lozi in the south, to Luba, Kanyok, Bemba, and Kazembe in the east.[46] In all these kingdoms, as in Asante, honour was primarily vertical, emanating from rank in the state hierarchy. All were strongly differentiated between

[40] Aidoo, 'Political crisis,' pp. 55–6; *Asantesem*, 11 (July 1979), 38–53.

[41] Kwame Arhin, 'Rank and class among the Asante and Fante in the nineteenth century,' *Africa*, 53 (1983), 2–22. See also Wilks, *Asante*, p. 677.

[42] T. C. McCaskie, 'Accumulation, wealth and belief in Asante history, I: to the close of the nineteenth century,' *Africa*, 53 (1983), 33, 36.

[43] Wilks, *Asante*, pp. 530–43; Aidoo, 'Political crisis,' chs. 7–9.

[44] Wilks, 'Golden stool,' p. 31.

[45] Ivor Wilks, 'Dissidence in Asante politics: two tracts from the late nineteenth century,' in his *Forests of gold: essays on the Akan and the kingdom of Asante* (Athens, Ohio, 1993), p. 180.

[46] Jan Vansina, *Kingdoms of the savanna* (Madison, 1966).

rulers and subjects. All witnessed intense competition for honour among the elite. Yet with these similarities went four main variations. States varied in the extent to which the kingship monopolised access to honour. They differed in the degree to which military activity was the dominant source of prestige. Distinct patterns of social stratification affected the means by which honour could be acquired and displayed. And the challenges to traditional social distinctions varied to some degree from one kingdom to another.

The monarchy most successful in monopolising power and access to honour was Dahomey, which emerged from obscurity in the 1720s. Relatively small, its success depended on mobilising all its resources, especially of personnel, with an efficiency exceptional in precolonial Africa. Its throne was unusually stable, each reign averaging some twenty-four years. There were no federated chiefdoms or powerful councils to check royal power. The king appointed all officials, although he often chose the previous holder's eldest son. He had sole power of life and death, displaying it in bloody annual ceremonies. He gradually gained much control over religious institutions and intervened directly in village life through his officials. 'The king and the king's service: nothing else exists,' a French official reported in 1895. It was virtually the only route to honour.[47]

In the Luba kingdom south-east of the equatorial forest, similarly, 'power is eaten whole,' as a proverb put it. The state's core had existed since at least 1600 and its ruler became notorious for displays of naked power.[48] Luba princes created the Lunda empire to the west and the authoritarian Bemba kingdom to the east, although further south among the Lozi they shared power with aristocratic councillors and judicial tribunals.[49] Diffusion of power among an immigrant elite also characterised the Kongo and Kuba kingdoms,[50] while the extreme end of the spectrum of royal power was occupied by the sparsely populated Tio kingdom of the lower Congo, whose rulers' authority was largely ritual. There honour was pursued less by state service than by personal retaliation:

Tio easily came to blows.... It seems to have been usual for people who were not related or neighbours to go from arguments to blows, from blows to woundings and

[47] Robin Law, *The Slave Coast of West Africa 1550–1750: the impact of the Atlantic slave trade on an African society* (Oxford, 1991), chs. 7–8; Melville J. Herskovits, *Dahomey: an ancient West African kingdom* (2 vols., New York, 1938), vol. 2, pp. 21, 294; Edouard Foà, *Le Dahomey* (Paris, 1895), p. 184.

[48] Thomas Q. Reefe, 'The societies of the eastern savanna,' in David Birmingham and Phyllis M. Martin (eds.), *History of Central Africa* (3 vols., London, 1983–98), vol. 1, p. 185. The proverb is quoted in David B. Coplan, *In the time of cannibals: the word music of South Africa's Basotho migrants* (Johannesburg, 1994), p. 37.

[49] Iliffe, *Africans*, pp. 103–5; Max Gluckman, *The judicial process among the Barotse of Northern Rhodesia* (2nd edn, Manchester, 1967), ch. 1.

[50] Anne Hilton, *The kingdom of Kongo* (Oxford, 1985), pp. 35–9; Jan Vansina, *The children of Woot: a history of the Kuba peoples* (Madison, 1978), chs. 8–9.

finally, sometimes, to murder. This immediately started a feud which might escalate into war. The very existence of feuds and their frequency were a sign of the weakness of the political structures and of the key position the social structure retained in the overall organization. . . . For whenever a person had been killed, kinship solidarity was stronger than political control. There had to be a feud.[51]

A state's control of feud indicated its command over access to honour. The late nineteenth-century Lozi monarchy, for example, enjoyed partial control, leaving offended groups to take vengeance in some homicide cases but intervening in others and then demanding obedience. The more powerful Kuba kingship required a group committing homicide to hand over a person in compensation to the state rather than to the victim's family. In Dahomey, as in Asante, personal vengeance was suppressed, supposedly by one of the earliest kings.[52]

Notions of honour also varied in their relationship to military systems. The forest-edge environment prevented these kingdoms from using cavalry. Dahomey, like Asante, owed its power to the early adoption of flintlock muskets. The Kongo kingdom, on the coast, secured firearms gradually from the sixteenth century, while the Tio probably secured them soon afterwards. Inland states acquired them only during the second half of the nineteenth century, relying previously on spears, although the Kuba, with no serious African enemies, had no guns until the twentieth century.[53] This sequence affected degrees of militarisation. Dahomey had a professional mercenary force by 1724, reinforced by a female palace guard expanded early in the nineteenth century into the famous corps of Amazons, plus universal adult mobilisation in emergency. Regular soldiers of both sexes there were mainly slaves, marched in ranks, fired in volleys – the Amazons from the shoulder – and had the discipline to storm walled towns like Abeokuta. These tactics were sufficiently disciplined to rule out single combat, but warfare still contained much display. Kings harangued departing troops from a 'Mound of Oaths' at which soldiers danced, imitated combat, swore to destroy the enemy, and were honoured if they did so. A defeated Dahomeyan commander was not expected to return alive, while

[51] Jan Vansina, *The Tio kingdom of the middle Congo, 1880–1892* (London, 1973), p. 355.

[52] Max Gluckman, *The ideas in Barotse jurisprudence* (reprinted, Manchester, 1972), pp. 211–12; Jan Vansina, 'A traditional legal system: the Kuba,' in Hilda Kuper and Leo Kuper (eds.), *African law: adaptation and development* (Berkeley, 1965), pp. 112–13; A. le Herissé, *L'ancien royaume du Dahomey* (Paris, 1911), p. 73.

[53] Law, *Slave Coast*, p. 271; Thornton, *Warfare*, pp. 108–9; Jan Vansina, *Paths in the rainforests: toward a history of political tradition in equatorial Africa* (London, 1990), pp. 202–3; Thomas Q. Reefe, *The rainbow and the kings: a history of the Luba empire to 1891* (Berkeley, 1981), p. 161; John C. Yoder, *The Kanyok of Zaire: an institutional and ideological history to 1895* (Cambridge, 1992), p. 86; Andrew D. Roberts, *A history of the Bemba* (London, 1973), p. 201; J. Vansina, 'Du royaume kuba au "territoire des Bakuba",' *Etudes Congolaises*, 12, 2 (April 1969), 10.

ransomed soldiers might be executed for cowardice in letting themselves be captured. All Dahomey's important state officials had military functions.[54] In this the kingdom differed in degree rather than kind from the Bemba, Kanyok, or Luba states, who employed disciplined and partly regular armies of spearmen.[55] Other states, however, were distinctively civilian. The Kuba kingdom, although created by conquest, probably mobilised its grand army only twice in the three hundred years before colonial invasion, set a high value on justice and conciliation, and cultivated a civil honour comparable to that of eighteenth-century Yorubaland.[56] The Tio, although using muskets, fought in the ceremonial manner more common among stateless peoples. Having agreed on a battlefield, prepared it, and supplied themselves with food and drink, 'Both sides formed a line of attack. . . . One man would leave the line and in front of it wave his spear in the air, or throw his knife up, singing and dancing, challenging the enemy. The others behind repeated the song. Then there was a general advance.' As soon as someone was killed or wounded, or one side ran out of gunpowder, a horn was blown and everyone went home. Such fighting was called 'war of the borders'. 'Great' war was different in that captives were taken and sold and settlements (but not crops) were destroyed. 'Still, no Tio remembered a war in which more than five or six prisoners were taken.'[57]

Patterns of stratification formed a third area of variation from Asante's profile of honour. Dahomey gradually acquired an enormous royal family embracing the children of all royals, male or female; in 1908 at least twelve thousand people were classified as princes. Partly in consequence, the commoners who had shared power with early rulers were largely replaced during the nineteenth century by officers of royal birth, creating an ever more rigid stratification in which the dubiously advantageous gift of a royal bride was supposedly the greatest of honours.[58] The Mwissikongo matrilineages who created the Kongo kingdom also enjoyed a virtual monopoly of high political offices, while the Lunda conquerors who established the Yaka kingdom over Kongo speakers

[54] Robin Law, 'Warfare on the West African Slave Coast, 1650–1850,' in R. Brian Ferguson and Neil L. Whitehead (eds.), *War in the tribal zone: expanding states and indigenous warfare* (Santa Fe, 1992), pp. 114–21; Edna G. Bay, *Wives of the leopard: gender, politics, and culture in the kingdom of Dahomey* (Charlottesville, 1998), pp. 134, 137, 201–7, 317; Dunglas, 'La première attaque,' pp. 7–19; Townsend to Dawes, 29 November 1866, CMS C.A2/ O.85/144.

[55] A. L. Epstein, 'Military organisation and the pre-colonial polity of the Bemba,' *Man*, NS, 10 (1975), 204–8; Yoder, *Kanyok*, pp. 82–4; Reefe, *Rainbow*, pp. 108–10.

[56] Vansina, *Children*, pp. 143–5; J. Vansina, 'Les valeurs culturelles des Bushong,' *Zaire*, 8 (1954), 899–910.

[57] Vansina, *Tio kingdom*, pp. 362–4.

[58] Le Herissé, *L'ancien royaume*, p. 35; Bay, *Wives*, pp. 26, 52, 63, 126, 248.

abandoned their matrilineal traditions in order to consolidate power among their descendants.[59] The Lozi elite described their subjects as 'that black thing':

Lozi are always disputing their own and others' relative ranking. Lozi society and thought are permeated with the ideas of *bulena* (kingship, chieftainship, rank, overlordship) and of the proper and appropriate behaviour between persons of different rank (*likute*, politeness, respect, appropriateness, good taste). . . . High praise of a man is to say *unani likute* (he has *likute*); a boor is damned, *utokwa likute*, he lacks *likute*. This is said of an impertinent underling and of an important person who reviles, or is impolite to, or is familiar with, his subordinates. . . . Rank – the relationship of lord (*mubua*) and underling (*mutanga*); of parent (*mushemi*) and child (*mwana*); of warden or owner (*muug'a*) and a person (*mutu*) or thing (*nto*) – is implicit in every Lozi relationship.[60]

Power-holders displayed special contempt for the weak. Many Kuba villages had a 'street of small children' reserved for unmarried men, who in that largely monogamous and early-marrying society were the poor and servile. Bemba and related matrilineal peoples extorted extreme deference and service from aspiring bridegrooms, while in Dahomey, characteristically, the village youth formed a compulsory association whose state-confirmed head vowed:

I shall work to serve the King and all the young people of my village will work with me. We shall cultivate the fields which will feed him; we shall construct the roofs which will shelter his people; we shall build the walls which will render his kingdom invincible. Glory to the King.[61]

For women, as in Asante, the state and its associated stratification gave unusual autonomy and influence to an elite. From the later nineteenth century, a sister of the Lozi king ruled an almost independent southern province, while other royal women there exercised substantial power. 'When I go into council,' a princess told a later anthropologist, 'I change – I am a man.'[62] Most Kingdoms of the Savanna were matrilineal societies where, as among the Bemba, women

[59] Hilton, *Kingdom*, pp. 35–45; Joseph N'soko Swa-Kabamba, *Le panégyrique mbiimbi: étude d'un genre littéraire poétique oral yaka* (Leiden, 1997), pp. 30–1.

[60] Max Gluckman, 'The Lozi of Barotseland,' in Elizabeth Colson and Max Gluckman (eds.), *Seven tribes of British Central Africa* (London, 1951), pp. 42–3. See also François Coillard, *On the threshold of Central Africa* (3rd edn, London, 1971), p. 279 n1.

[61] E. Torday and T. A. Joyce, *Notes ethnographiques sur les peuples communément appelés Bakuba, ainsi que sur les peuplades apparentées* (Brussels, 1910), pp. 162–3; Audrey I. Richards, *Land, labour and diet in Northern Rhodesia: an economic study of the Bemba tribe* (2nd edn, London, 1961), pp. 124–7; Bellarmin Coffi Codo, 'Les associations de classe d'âge (les Donkpè) dans l'ancien royaume du Danxomé et leurs mutations sous la colonisation,' in Hélène d'Almeida-Topor, Catherine Coquery-Vidrovitch, Odile Goerg, and Françoise Guitart (eds.), *Les jeunes en Afrique* (2 vols., Paris, 1992), vol. 1, p. 179.

[62] Gerald L. Caplan, *The elites of Barotseland 1878–1969: a political history of Zambia's Western Province* (London, 1970), pp. 6, 20; Gluckman in Colson and Gluckman, *Seven tribes*, p. 24.

had considerable freedom to contract marriages, control property, and defend their rights. Yet Bemba women were still taught at initiation that their honour lay in subservience to husbands and seniors. Kuba royal women enjoyed a leisured lifestyle, but Kuba men were extremely jealous of their wives, both sexually and as property, and Kuba masks representing women often display tears.[63] The position of women in Dahomey was especially revealing because the kingdom's lack of manpower encouraged their employment in many roles normally reserved to men. The Amazons were the most conspicuous example, but they were only one element among the thousands of women staffing royal palaces. These included royal women headed by the queen mother who enjoyed much freedom and influence, women who supervised and represented male officials posted to the provinces, but also – and increasingly – women (often slaves) employed in agricultural labour, plus in the lowest ranks the female sex slaves whom the state provided for junior men denied opportunity to marry. Yet Dahomey also had special rules of kindness to childless women.[64]

Ruling classes sought to reinforce their claims to honour by display. Kuba nobles coveted not only elegance of body and movement but also splendour of dress, their king affecting a vast ceremonial costume weighing nearly seventy kilogrammes. The insignia of a Luba chief might be a crest of red parrot feathers, a leopard's skin and teeth, a bead collar, a ceremonial axe, ivory amulets, and a staff. Kongo notables, hitherto distinguished by garments of fine skins and palm-cloth, eagerly adopted Portuguese fashions, displaying an obsession with dress that was to survive beyond colonial rule.[65] Sumptuary laws were strict:

Among the Barotse [Lozi] to use the eland tail or leopard skin, to wear ivory bangles, to decorate one's fence with royal lashing or one's implements with royal markings, to use a royal name for one's dog or dugout, to commit adultery with a queen, or to speak ill of the king were all more heinous and less forgivable offences than to rise in armed revolt against him.[66]

Yet display not only distinguished elite from mass; it was a language in which elite members competed for honour. Kuba noblemen rivalled one another in patronising the craftsmen who carved their superb household possessions, a pattern that was repeated elsewhere in a region famed for producing much of

[63] J. S. la Fontaine, *Initiation* (Manchester, 1986), pp. 173–7; Vansina, *Children*, pp. 170–1; Vansina, 'Les valeurs,' p. 908; Elizabeth Isichei, *A history of African societies to 1870* (Cambridge, 1997), p. 82.

[64] Bay, *Wives*, pp. xii, 8, 71–6, 148–9, 198–9, 239–40; Herskovits, *Dahomey*, vol. 1, pp. 341–2.

[65] Vansina, 'Les valeurs,' pp. 899–900; Vansina, *Children*, p. 130; Patrice Mufuta (ed.), *Le chant kasala des Luba* (Paris, 1968), pp. 27–8; Filippo Pigafetta and Duarte Lopes, *Le royaume de Congo et les contrées environnantes (1591)* (trans. W. Bal, 3rd edn, Paris, 2002), pp. 189–92.

[66] Gluckman, *Ideas*, p. 60.

Africa's finest sculpture. To excite jealousy was considered the supreme proof of prestige. Yet Kuba valued intelligence above wealth and competed above all in verbal skills, for these were oral cultures in which courtesy and insult were exchanged with a refinement that made European visitors feel boorish.[67] Oral literature, as in Asante, was chiefly praise-poetry, although shading at times towards epic. Dahomey, characteristically, attempted to create a single, authorised version of the past embodied in the praises of successive kings. Kuba and Luba rulers preserved authorised legends, but Luba also praised individuals and their ancestors in an allusive form similar to Yoruba *oriki*. It was known as *kasala*, 'free verse made from names', and was sung to stimulate courage in battle, to foster energy in cultivation, or to mourn the dead.[68] This tradition extended to the Lunda kingdoms, notably Kazembe's and the Yaka court, where *mbiimbi*, the royal praises deliberately emphasising the brutality of the Lunda conquest, were fashioned by professional bards into a historical panegyric that as yet lacked the distancing from contemporary culture characterising true epic.[69] Luba and Lunda titles and insignia conferred prestige across a vast area to the south and east of the equatorial forest, much as Asante regalia ennobled its recipients throughout Akan-speaking territory.

The most revealing example of the use of symbols to embody honour and differentiation was the adoption of Christianity in the Kongo kingdom. The other states considered in this chapter rejected early missionary work. Asante's rulers feared that it would destroy their sons' valour and their slaves' obedience. King Glele of Dahomey declared 'that when negroes learned to read and write like white men they could not be taken to war.'[70] The King of Kongo, by contrast, accepted baptism from Portuguese missionaries in 1491 and his successor, Mbemba Nzinga (Afonso I, 1509–43), sought to make Kongo a Christian kingdom. The chief reason was probably that the immigrant Mwissikongo rulers had little control over their subjects' religious institutions, so that Mbemba Nzinga saw Christianity as a potential state cult, building the first church in the royal graveyard.[71] The king and nobility adopted much Portuguese material culture. Many observed Christian rites, competing for prominent ritual roles, blending them with state ceremonies, and disputing issues of precedence

---

[67] Vansina, *Children*, p. 170; Vansina, 'Les valeurs,' p. 904; Richards, *Land*, p. 30.

[68] Melville J. Herskovits and Frances S. Herskovits, *Dahomean narrative: a cross-cultural analysis* (Evanston, 1958), pp. 20–1; Vansina, *Children*, pp. 34–40; Reefe, *Rainbow*, ch. 3; Mufuta, *Le chant* kasala.

[69] Jacques Chileya Chiwale, *Royal praises and praise names of the Lunda Kazembe of Northern Rhodesia*, Rhodes-Livingstone Communication No. 25 (Lusaka, 1962); Swa-Kabamba, *Le panégyrique* mbiimbi, ch. 3.

[70] McCaskie, *State and society*, pp. 139–40; Burton to Russell, 23 March 1864, FOCP 1392*/1.

[71] Hilton, *Kingdom*, pp. 90–103.

and honour with as much anxiety as Louis XIV's courtiers.[72] Some noblemen maintained this zeal in the nineteenth century, long after missionary work had virtually ceased. During the seventeenth century, Christianity also penetrated quite deeply among commoners in the coastal province of Soyo, but elsewhere the new faith won little rural response except a desire for baptism as a protection against witchcraft.[73] Christianity thus succeeded in Kongo insofar as it accommodated to the honour culture, an accommodation more acceptable to early modern Catholic missionaries than to their nineteenth-century Protestant successors in Yorubaland.

Yet this should not suggest that only elites claimed honour, for the fourth area of comparison with Asante concerned alternative routes to social distinction. Kongo terms for honour ranged from the deferential respect paid to a Big Man (*vumina*) to a more widely enjoyed good reputation (*jitu*), the latter perhaps equating with the Lozi term for an upright man, *mutu yalukile*.[74] Perhaps the best illustration of widespread concern for honourable reputation was the use of ordeals to demonstrate innocence, especially the *mwavi* poison ordeal associated with kingdoms of Luba and Lunda origin.[75] David Livingstone observed in the mid nineteenth century that 'persons accused of witchcraft, in order to assert their innocency, will often travel from distant districts to ... drink the infusion of a poisonous tree.' Kuba 'cheerfully ask to drink the poison so as to clear their names,' as also did Tio.[76] It was a counterpart to the defence against defamation that Asante mounted in court.

Opposition to inegalitarian structures also existed. In Dahomey, it is true, revolts were said to have been led only by princes, while folk wisdom counselled reticence, discretion, and silent endurance. Lozi, too, rebelled only under royal leadership.[77] Yet exploitation provoked a major revolt in the Kongo kingdom in c.1652, while fifty years later popular dissatisfaction with decades of civil war

---

[72] Luca da Caltanisetta, *Diaire congolais (1690–1701)* (trans. F. Bontinck, Louvain, 1970), pp. 5–6, 13–14, 197–9.

[73] L. Jadin (ed.), 'Andrea de Pavia au Congo, à Lisbonne, à Madère,' *Bulletin de l'Institut Historique Belge de Rome*, 41 (1970), 440–4; Richard Gray, *Black Christians and white missionaries* (New Haven, 1990), pp. 35–56; da Caltanisetta, *Diaire*, pp. 51, 63, 110–12.

[74] W. Holman Bentley, *Dictionary and grammar of the Kongo language* (London, 1887), pp. 108, 285, 455; Gluckman, *Judicial process*, p. 125.

[75] Gloria M. Waite, *A history of traditional medicine and health care in pre-colonial East-Central Africa* (Lewiston, N.Y., 1992), p. 51.

[76] David Livingstone, *Missionary travels and researches in South Africa* (new edn, London, 1899), p. 291; Vansina in Kuper and Kuper, *African law*, p. 114; Vansina, *Tio kingdom*, pp. 350–1.

[77] Paul Hazoume, *Doguicimi* (trans. R. Bjornson, Washington, D.C., 1990), p. 130; Herskovits and Herskovits, *Narrative*, pp. 44–5, 74–5; Gluckman in Colson and Gluckman, *Seven tribes*, p. 23.

there produced sub-Saharan Africa's first Christian millenarian movement.[78] More subtle challenges to rank came, as in Asante, from the impact of trade. The challenges were largely contained. Dahomey tolerated private merchants but prevented them from gaining sufficient strength to threaten the established order. In the more fluid Luba society, wealthy men bought their way into chieftainship. Overseas commerce helped to destabilise the Kongo kingdom, but the state most clearly subverted by trade was, significantly, the weakest, the Tio kingdom, whose largely ritual monarch was barred from trade so that profit and power passed to successful merchants and provincial chiefs.[79] With these exceptions, however, rank and military power enforced their right to respect within these kingdoms until they were more profoundly challenged by colonial conquest.

---

[78] John K. Thornton, *The kingdom of Kongo: civil war and transition 1641–1718* (Madison, 1983), p. 41; idem, *The Kongolese Saint Anthony: Dona Beatriz Kimpa Vita and the Antonian movement, 1684–1706* (Cambridge, 1998). The so-called Jaga Invasion of 1568 was probably in part a peasant revolt: J. Vansina, 'The Kongo kingdom and its neighbours,' in Ogot, *UNESCO history*, p. 558.

[79] Robin Law, 'Royal monopoly and private enterprise in the Atlantic trade: the case of Dahomey,' *JAH*, 18 (1977), 565; Mufuta, *Le chant* kasala, p. 118; Hilton, *Kingdom*, ch. 5; Vansina, *Tio kingdom*, pp. 309–12.

7   Honour Without the State

Precolonial Africans were fairly evenly divided between states and stateless societies, with a continuum and much interaction between the two. Lacking a state as fount of vertical honour, stateless peoples competed for honour in its horizontal dimension, as the respect of their peers. For them honour was not the code of a class, but male honour related strongly to age and notions of masculinity, distinguishing the heroic behaviour expected of the young warrior from the civic honour appropriate to the adult householder, although these were commonly two stages in the life of one man. Ideals of female honour were not dichotomised in this way but changed more gradually with growing maturity. Where age was so important, initiation into adulthood, marriage, and parenthood created claims to respect. Lack of a state to impose law made vengeance a more common means of defending honour. Intense competition made stateless societies far from egalitarian and shaped their responses to innovation. And the dichotomy between hero and householder found expression in an oral literature warranting comparison with that of the West African savanna.

Our understanding of African stateless societies comes chiefly from twentieth-century anthropologists, supplemented by oral material and by documents seldom earlier than the nineteenth century. This often prevents chronological precision and the analysis of change possible in centralised states. The anthropologists demonstrated that statelessness was not anarchy but that acephalous peoples used various means to maintain order.[1] One was for descent groups

---

[1] For surveys, see John Middleton and David Tait, 'Introduction,' in their *Tribes without rulers: studies of African segmentary systems* (London, 1958); Robin Horton, 'Stateless societies in the history of West Africa,' in Ajayi and Crowder, *History*, vol. 1, ch. 3.

and territorial divisions to balance one another, restraining violence by fear of retaliation; this happened among the Somali of north-eastern Africa, the Nuer and Dinka of the southern Sudan, and the Tiv of central Nigeria. Another pattern prevailed where balanced corporate groups were assisted in maintaining order by overlapping clans, exogamous marriage ties, and religious cults; this was the case with the Tonga peoples surrounding the Zambezi Valley and the Voltaic-speaking peoples north of Asante. Ritualists provided a third source of mediation, as among the Oromo fringing the Ethiopian plateau, the Jola of the Casamance estuary in Senegal, and some Igbo people of southern Nigeria. Other Igbo used a fourth device, a hierarchy of titles conferring social prestige and authority; Igbo bought their way up the ladder, but other peoples often ascended it through initiation, as in the Poro association of men and the Sande and Bundu associations of women which had been powerful among stateless peoples from modern Sierra Leone to Côte d'Ivoire since at least the sixteenth century and perhaps since the Mali Empire. More mobile, colonising peoples, especially in forest areas, might follow a fifth pattern where such order as existed was provided by Big Men, community leaders with large households and warrior reputations who competed for local predominance; the Baoule of Côte d'Ivoire and the Beti and Fang groups in the western equatorial forest, organised in this way, were among the continent's most strenuously competitive peoples.

Along with kinship and personal achievement, age was especially important to the social organisation and values of stateless peoples. In many East African pastoral societies, young men were initiated together into an age-set that passed through successive grades of seniority from junior warrior to senior elder, each grade having its appropriate behaviour. This structure regulated the generational conflict common in stateless, polygynous societies where fathers and sons – or, more often, unrelated men of these two generations – competed for wives and where wide age differentials bred tensions between husbands and wives and between co-wives of the same husband. Control of their sons' labour was a vital but elusive resource for household heads. They sought it partly by ideological domination but chiefly by controlling access to adulthood through command of marriageable women. Africa's stateless societies often bore out Freud's dictum: 'A hero is a man who stands up manfully against his own father and in the end victoriously overcomes him.'[2]

The first stage in this pursuit of heroism was commonly the physical and emotional test of initiation, generally at the transition from youth to adulthood. Although not entirely confined to stateless societies organised mainly by

---

[2] Quoted in Sùżette Heald, *Manhood and morality: sex, violence and ritual in Gisu society* (London, 1999), p. 70.

descent, it was especially common among them. It reaffirmed a society's categories and boundaries, dramatised the initiate's transition from one category to
another, fostered the community's solidarity, transmitted its values – as much to
spectators as initiates – and gave elders power over the young.[3] For initiates, the
rites were public tests of courage, self-control, and endurance of pain that could
win or lose them honour, possibly for life, while preparing them to withstand
future pain.

The test could be cruelly demanding. The most common was circumcision,
as described for the Gishu of Uganda:

> The boy stands in the compound of his father or senior relative and must remain abso-
> lutely still while his foreskin is cut and then stripped from around the *glans penis*. He
> is required to display total fortitude under the knife, betraying no signs of fear; even
> what might be regarded as involuntary twitches and tremblings, such as the blinking
> of the eyes, are evaluated negatively. Success, however, is triumphantly celebrated; the
> watching men roar in unison while the women rush forward ululating as they dance.
> The boy is then allowed to sit and the onlookers come forward one by one to call
> him a man.[4]

This twentieth-century observer reckoned that between 70 and 80 per cent of
men aged eighteen to twenty-five passed the test successfully, although the
nervous shock alone could occasionally be fatal.[5] Among Kenya's Samburu
pastoralists, an initiate who flinched during the four minutes or more of his
ordeal might damage his own and his family's honour for a generation.[6] Many
further refinements of pain were added to male circumcision, while other operations, such as the parallel cuts made in the foreheads of Nuer and Dinka
youths, could be equally agonising. 'The initiates themselves, still and serene,
first attempt to chant their boastful words of courage, but soon pass out from
excessive bleeding,' a Dinka later recalled. '... But so flattering is the whole
situation that even a coward acquires enough courage to endure the pain. ... I
have never heard of a man who showed fear of initiation.'[7] Even more severe
and equally crucial to personal and family honour were some forms of geni-
tal mutilation inflicted on young women, although this was less common and

[3] See la Fontaine, *Initiation*, esp. ch. 5.

[4] Heald, *Manhood*, p. 33.

[5] Ibid., p. 31; I. M. Pande, 'Medical aspects of ritual circumcision,' *East African Medical Journal*,
   32 (1955), 28.

[6] Spencer, *Samburu*, pp. 103–6; David D. Gilmore, *Manhood in the making: cultural concepts of
   masculinity* (New Haven, 1990), p. 135.

[7] Francis Mading Deng, *The Dinka of the Sudan* (New York, 1972), p. 70. See also E. E. Evans-
   Pritchard, *The Nuer: a description of the modes of livelihood and political institutions of a Nilotic
   people* (Oxford, 1940), pp. 249–54.

seldom public.[8] Perhaps less painful, but almost as traumatic, were the many ordeals inflicted on young people, such as the Poro and Sande forest schools that inculcated obedience to elders.[9]

'To see a Dinka before and after initiation,' one wrote, 'is to witness the remarkable power of symbolism and ritual, as the dignity of bearing, the responsible conduct, and the overall poise of a gentleman take over the carefree, servile status of boyhood.'[10] Yet initiation did not necessarily confer adulthood. Among such pastoralists as the Samburu and the related Maasai, initiation was rather a means of deferring adulthood, for as junior warriors the initiates were mobilised in military camps and forbidden to marry for a decade or more, enabling their elders to monopolise wives and property.[11] Oral accounts of the military training of young Meru warriors on Mount Kenya have shown its extreme severity, with deliberate humiliation, repeated beating, and forced competition with their seniors, all designed to stimulate aggressive striving for higher status. Such discipline and enforced adolescence were made acceptable by idealising the warriors' lifestyle. They cultivated group solidarity, affected elegance of dress, displayed extreme sensitivity to insult, and eventually enjoyed legitimate access to unmarried girls and illicit relations with elders' wives.[12] Other stateless peoples with warrior traditions allowed young men a similar status, partly in order to control them. Until they married in their twenties, Beti men competed in the splendour of their bodies and the elaboration of their hairstyles as well as in their fighting skills, their dancing vigour, and their sexual adventures. The leader of Beti fashion at the time of European conquest, Mboo Manga, was 'celebrated for his beauty and his insolence,' although later eclipsed by Charles Atangana, 'so handsome a young man that if you saw him, you could only clap your hands.'[13] Their culture set a high value on singularity, but distinction required more of a young man than elegance. It required strength and courage. Kabre youths in the hills of modern Togo competed in public wrestling competitions, as did Beti, Igbo, and Jola villagers, both male and female.

[8] La Fontaine, *Initiation*, p. 109 and ch. 8. For first-hand experiences, see Jean Davison, *Voices from Mutira: lives of rural Gikuyu women* (Boulder, 1989), pp. 66–7, 120, 149.

[9] La Fontaine, *Initiation*, pp. 95–9; William P. Murphy, 'Secret knowledge as property and power in Kpelle society: elders versus youth,' *Africa*, 50 (1980), 193–207.

[10] Francis Mading Deng, *The man called Deng Majok: a biography of power, polygyny, and change* (New Haven, 1986), p. 25.

[11] Spencer, *Samburu*, pp. 96, 133–5; P. T. W. Baxter and Uri Almagor, 'Introduction,' to their *Age, generation and time: some features of East African age organisations* (London, 1978), pp. 16–20.

[12] Jeffrey A. Fadiman, *An oral history of tribal warfare: the Meru of Mt. Kenya* (Athens, Ohio, 1982), chs. 3 and 4; Paul Spencer, *The Maasai of Matapato* (Manchester, 1988), chs. 6–8.

[13] Philippe Laburthe-Tolra, *Les seigneurs de la forêt* (Paris, 1981), pp. 297–308, 323.

2. *A young Kuba man* (painted by Norman Hardy from photographs, c. 1907). From John Mack, *Emil Torday and the art of the Congo, 1900–1909* (London, n.d.), plate 2. Reproduced by permission of the Syndics of Cambridge University Library.

Young Beti men, like Fula and Samburu, held mutual flagellation contests. The favourite male pastime almost everywhere, except among pastoralists, was hunting, a collective enterprise providing opportunities to win prestige out of all proportion to the food it yielded.[14]

This emphasis on competition, achievement, and physical prowess was preparation for warfare in societies where virtually every man was a warrior. Stateless societies were not necessarily violent. Among the Kikuyu of highland Kenya, tradition 'had little to say about war, none of it admiring.' Iraqw agriculturalists of north-central Tanzania, although long harried by pastoral neighbours, were not militarised and, although capable on occasion of defending their homes, commonly preferred to hide. Yet a sixteenth-century Ethiopian monk attributed his kingdom's recent defeats by their stateless Oromo neighbours to the fact that among the latter 'all, from small to great, are trained in warfare,' in contrast to Ethiopia's reliance on professional troops.[15] Nineteenth-century Beti, Jola, and Igbo men always went armed. As among the Tio, some warfare had almost a sporting quality. A place and time might be agreed in advance. Insults might precede blows. 'Much of the fighting' among Kofyar hillsmen of central Nigeria 'took place in a no man's land and consisted of blowing war horns, waving shields, and rapid spear-throwing forays toward enemy lines. Death or serious injury to either side ended battle for that day.'[16] Casualties might be limited by using only sticks or clubs when fighting neighbouring groups. The Konso of south-western Ethiopia thought it disgraceful to kill women, children, or the old or to burn towns, use bows or barbed spears, attack at night, or fight anywhere but in open country. Killing by stealth or ambush rather than fair fight was similarly 'an offence against Nuer standards of chivalry.' Even Maasai, when fighting one another, gave warning of attacks, initiated hostilities by leaders harranguing and fighting one another, and spared elders, women, and children.[17]

---

[14] Charles Piot, *Remotely global: village modernity in West Africa* (Chicago, 1999), pp. 91–2; Paul in Baker and Mangan, *Sport*, pp. 24–5, 29–32, 38; Laburthe-Tolra, *Les seigneurs*, pp. 274, 294; Spencer, *Samburu*, p. 111; this volume, p. 42; Mary Douglas, *The Lele of the Kasai* (London, 1963), pp. 36–9.

[15] Bruce Berman and John Lonsdale, *Unhappy valley: conflict in Kenya and Africa* (2 vols., London, 1992), vol. 2, p. 342; Robert J. Thornton, *Space, time, and culture among the Iraqw of Tanzania* (New York, 1980), p. 32; Bahrey's 'Histoire des Galla,' in C. Conti Rossini (ed.), *Historia Regis Sarsa Dengel (Malak Sagad)* (Paris, 1907), p. 206.

[16] Robert McC. Netting, *Hill farmers of Nigeria: cultural ecology of the Kofyar of the Jos Plateau* (Seattle, 1968), p. 48.

[17] C. R. Hallpike, *The Konso of Ethiopia: a study of the values of a Cushitic people* (Oxford, 1972), pp. 28, 55–6; P. P. Howell, *A manual of Nuer law* (London, 1954), p. 55; Alan H. Jacobs, 'The traditional political organization of the pastoral Masai,' DPhil thesis, University of Oxford, 1965, pp. 366–7.

Such small-scale fighting merged into raiding for profit. Nuer fought one another with clubs on the slightest provocation but used spears in cattle raids on neighbouring Dinka. 'When ownership of cattle is in dispute Nuer throw over caution and propriety, showing themselves careless of odds, contemptuous of danger, and full of guile. . . . Skill and courage in fighting are reckoned the highest virtues, raiding the most noble, as well as the most profitable, occupation.'[18] Forest peoples, with no cattle to covet, raided instead for women, often the only way a young man could gain a wife. This was the main form of warfare among the Beti, whose warriors hoped also to return with enemy heads and genitals.[19] The most elaborate cult of heroism was that of the Oromo, for whom only killing conferred full manhood:

Any man who had not killed a man and never took the trophy of the dead would not butter the hair of his head, and his wife would not be able to draw water (from a well) except after all the women, whose husbands had killed, had done so. The girls of the country also would mock at him, saying: 'You and we are the same; our youth is better than your bravery.'[20]

Oromo men enjoyed three moments of signal honour. The first was when they returned singing from a kill:

> I have descended to the narrow valley
> and I have pulled down the horsemen!
> My god-father will dress my hair;
> the beautiful girls will adorn my comb;
> my friends will kiss my mouth.
> The children will say to me, 'You have killed well!'
> . . . As to my life, what have I thought about it?[21]

The second moment came when Oromo died and their relatives marked their graves with standing stones to 'witness' each kill. The third was when their deeds were celebrated in poems also recalling heroic ancestors.[22]

New initiates might fight for sport or trophies, but serious warfare was for adult men, who commonly formed the front line of battle. Alongside raid and counterraid – 'wars of honour', as they have been called in the Cameroun Grassfields – Western Bantu languages have for over a thousand years distinguished more destructive warfare, often launched against stateless peoples

[18] Evans-Pritchard, *Nuer*, pp. 49–50.
[19] Laburthe-Tolra, *Les seigneurs*, pp. 318–27.
[20] Bairu Tafla, *Chronicle of Yohannes IV*, p. 117.
[21] Cerulli in Hooton and Bates, *Varia Africana III*, p. 102.
[22] Eike Haberland, *Galla Süd-Aethiopiens* (Stuttgart, 1963), pp. 209, 495; Cerulli in Hooton and Bates, *Varia Africana III*, p. 58.

by neighbouring kingdoms or predatory bands seeking slaves.[23] It is hard to know how much violence in stateless societies was a response to this aggression rather than to lack of political authorities. Oromo heroic culture took shape on Ethiopia's frontiers. Dahomey's disparate northern neighbours appear to have consolidated into the Mahi people while resisting the kingdom's slaving expeditions. Peoples of central Nigeria militarised in defence against the Sokoto Caliphate's horsemen. Nineteenth-century Igbo went armed because they feared slave-raiders.[24] Yet Beti went armed because they feared other Beti, just as Maasai feared other Maasai and the wild animals threatening their herds. Probably both external aggression and social organisation were responsible for the violence of stateless societies and the heroic codes it fostered.

These codes demanded more than military valour. They demanded unhesitating response to insult. Slander might be ritualised, as in the esoterically libellous songs exchanged between rival groupings at Gouro funerals in Côte d'Ivoire or the Somali poetic insults which, if not countered by apt rejoinder, might breed vengeance or feud.[25] More commonly, however, insult was vulgar, and response was violent. 'A Nuer will at once fight if he considers that he has been insulted,' an anthropologist reported, 'and they are very sensitive and easily take offence. When a man feels that he has suffered an injury there is no authority to whom he can make a complaint and from whom he can obtain redress, so he at once challenges the man who has wronged him to a duel and the challenge must be accepted.' Nuer usually fought with clubs until one was incapacitated, no third party being allowed to interfere.[26] 'Redress for insults was settled out of court,' Jomo Kenyatta wrote of his fellow Kikuyu, 'no man with any dignity would take another to court for an insult.... The proper procedure was duelling or fencing.' Dinka and Beti reacted with similar violence.[27]

Duty to respond shaded into duty to avenge. Whereas states like Asante generally sought to subordinate private vengeance to judicial process, stateless peoples had no recourse to political authority. This did not mean that

[23] Jean Pierre Warnier, 'Traite sans raids au Cameroun,' *CEA*, 29 (1983), 12–13; Vansina, *Paths*, p. 80.

[24] Law in Ferguson and Whitehead, *War*, p. 125; Isichei, *History of Nigeria*, pp. 210–11; Winston McGowan, 'African resistance to the Atlantic slave trade in West Africa,' *Slavery and Abolition*, 11 (1990), 15–16.

[25] Ariane Deluz, 'Histoire inattendue: insultes et récit épique,' *Journal de la Société des Africanistes*, 55 (1985), 187–202; Said S. Samatar, *Oral poetry and Somali nationalism: the case of Sayyid Mohammad Abdille Hasan* (Cambridge, 1982), p. 4.

[26] Evans-Pritchard, *Nuer*, p. 151.

[27] Jomo Kenyatta, *Facing Mount Kenya: a tribal life of the Gikuyu* (reprinted, London, 1961), p. 226; Francis Mading Deng, *Tradition and modernization: a challenge for law among the Dinka of the Sudan* (New Haven, 1971), pp. 209, 217; Laburthe-Tolra, *Les seigneurs*, p. 328.

every homicide had to be avenged in blood. Within the kin-group or neigh-bourhood there was generally machinery for reconciliation and compensation; otherwise, the group could not have endured. Among Nuer, bloodwealth com-pensation – the customary sum was forty cattle – could be paid for homicide within a tribe, but no mechanism existed for paying it for a victim from an-other tribe. In Kabre hill towns a murderer's family could forestall revenge for killing a fellow-townsman by themselves confessing it to the town's priests and elders.[28] Where autonomous kin-groups or villages interacted extensively or were strongly linked by ritual or marital alliances, systems of compensation might exist, as among Somali pastoralists, the Tonga, and some Voltaic peo-ples.[29] Often, however, the instinctive response to homicide from outside the small community was the revenge killing of the murderer or a close kinsman:

The first step in a murder case was that the family group of the murdered man took up arms and invaded the murderer's homestead with the object of killing the murderer or one of his close relatives, and letting them realise that the murdered man had a family group capable of inflicting retribution on behalf of one of its members. If the invaders succeeded in killing the murderer or one of his kinsfolk, the case was settled there and then, for the two lives were considered equal.[30]

Kenyatta's account for the Kikuyu was paralleled among the Gishu of Uganda, where a single revenge killing normally ended the matter.[31] If not, the result might be endemic small-scale warfare between communities lacking desire or machinery for reconciliation. Tiv villages were in this relationship to their neighbours.[32] Such vengeance or warfare signified lack of order and was distinct from feud, which implied long-lasting animosity and sporadic violence between corporate groups that recognised some means and obligation to compose dis-putes.[33] Feud was less common in sub-Saharan Africa than in the Mediterranean region and did not foster elaborate codes of behaviour. It was reported between Somali clans, among Mandari, Nuer, and Dinka tribes in southern Sudan, and most vividly among the Massa and Moussey of the Logone plains south of Lake

---

[28] Howell, *Manual*, pp. 40, 48; Raymond Verdier, 'Pouvoir, justice et vengeance chez les Kabiye,' in his *La vengeance*, vol. 1, pp. 209–10.

[29] I. M. Lewis, *The modern history of Somaliland* (London, 1965), p. 11; E. Colson, 'Social control and vengeance in Plateau Tonga society,' *Africa*, 23 (1953), 199–212; M. Fortes, 'The political system of the Tallensi,' in M. Fortes and E. E. Evans-Pritchard (eds.), *African political systems* (London, 1940), pp. 241–8, 269–71.

[30] Kenyatta, *Facing*, p. 227.

[31] Jean la Fontaine, 'Homicide and suicide among the Gisu,' in Paul Bohannan (ed.), *African homicide and suicide* (Princeton, 1960), p. 97.

[32] Paul Bohannan, *Justice and judgment among the Tiv* (London, 1957), p. 146.

[33] Middleton and Tait, *Tribes*, pp. 20–1; Jacob Black-Michaud, *Cohesive force: feud in the Mediter-ranean and the Middle East* (Oxford, 1975), pp. x, 27–30.

Chad, whose feuds might extend to chains of fifty or more killings:

> One cannot accept the murder of a relative, any more than one can remain inactive under an insult. . . . To accept is to admit one's inferiority and culpability, to leave the field free for physical violence or magical aggression. One must 'exchange' the death of one of one's own for that of a member of the murderer's clan according to a classificatory principle which is strict and almost without hatred. . . . Vengeance is a duty; it incubates and follows its course 'like fire in a bale of corn'. Only the contemptible seek to escape it, but the village women will take care that they do their duty. Massa and especially Moussey societies traditionally value warlike qualities; a coward is buried like a woman. . . . What is striking in traditional accounts . . . is the gratuity, one may almost write the placidity with which vengeance between individuals of different clans is executed, without hatred.[34]

Stateless peoples found violent defence of honour difficult to restrain. A Nuer who had killed hastened to a ritualist, both to purify himself against mystical consequences and to seek sanctuary until the victim's kinsmen could properly permit the ritualist to initiate negotiations for compensation, which would not necessarily settle the matter permanently because it was less honourable than retaliation. Beti turned to noted local arbiters or those allied to both disputing villages by kinship or marriage. Earth-priests with ritual authority cutting across political divisions mediated in Voltaic areas. Yet the stateless Gamo people south of the Ethiopian plateau had no word for vengeance, regarding such violence as an offence against both supernatural forces and society. Instead they required the close kinsmen of offender and victim to distance themselves and allow the assembly of adult men to arrange compensation and reconciliation.[35] Against the honour of the hero, they set the honour of the householder.

Not all stateless peoples admired heroes. In the mid twentieth century Elizabeth Colson described an entirely different ethic among the Tonga people whose plateau villages overlooked the Zambezi. Tonga did not claim to have been great warriors. They admired neither heroic valour – for which they had no word – nor last-ditch defence, valuing rather the cunning of the folktale hare, which others might have thought cowardice. They admired a different courage:

> Tonga respect men and women who meet daily life with fortitude avoiding violence and contention, earning their own living, giving assistance when need be to their

---

[34] Igor de Garine, 'Les étrangers, la vengeance et les parents chez les Massa et les Moussey,' in Verdier, *La vengeance*, vol. 1, pp. 98–9. See also Samatar, *Oral poetry*, p. 36; Middleton and Tait, *Tribes*, p. 28; Evans-Pritchard, *Nuer*, pp. 150–62.

[35] Evans-Pritchard, *Nuer*, pp. 152–8; Laburthe-Tolra, *Les seigneurs*, pp. 344–7; Rüdiger Schott, 'Vengeance and violence among the Bulsa of northern Ghana,' in Verdier, *La vengeance*, vol. 1, pp. 187–91; Jacques Bureau, 'Une société sans vengeance: le cas des Gamo d'Ethiopie,' in ibid., pp. 213–24.

kin and neighbours. Of them they say . . . 'they have strong hearts'. These are the people they describe as . . . 'upright people' or 'those to be respected'. Their virtues are the standard virtues which give no special renown outside one's own small community. . . . Parents . . . insist upon the need to acquire fortitude as they insist upon the need to learn to work and to be able to take one's place in society.[36]

Central to 'the quiet virtue of fortitude' was endurance of pain:

It is . . . expected that people will bear pain without complaint. Women proudly boast that they have not cried out in childbirth though they say the pain is like a flame. Men and women brutally injured by some accident and those wretchedly ill bear their pain with stoicism. Babies wail and scream in minor discomforts, small children rend the air with their protests, older children have already learned to suppress signs of acute distress, even though they have a searing burn or a limb swollen with infection. Adults half-mad with pain still refuse to cry out. They also seek to cause as little trouble as possible to those who must care for them, dragging themselves to work while they can, lying quietly to one side when they cannot. When they have no hope of recovery, and the illness is such that they find their dependence unendurable, they have a further resource. For a few days they refuse to accept food or drink; then, having arranged their affairs, they pass into a coma which presages death.[37]

This pacific ethic was not unique – it was shared, for example, by the Senoufo of northern Côte d'Ivoire[38] – but, more commonly among stateless peoples, it coexisted with the heroic ethos of the young, forming an indigenous code of respectability appropriate to the adult householder, a counterpoint of serenity and violence found also in African sculpture.[39] When a Kikuyu man's first child was circumcised and ready to marry, the father became a junior elder through a ceremony that 'signifies that he is now a peaceful man, that he is no longer a carrier of spear and shield, or a pursuer of the vanity of war and plunder. That he has now attained a stage where he has to take the responsibility of carrying the symbols of peace and to assume the duty of peace-maker in the community.'[40] Such an honourable householder was, first, an independent landholder. 'There is a great desire in the heart of every Gikuyu man,' Kenyatta explained, 'to own a piece of land on which he can build his home, and from which he and his family can get the means of livelihood.'[41] To clear land and create a homestead required the arduous labour prized by the householder ethic throughout the

---

[36] Elizabeth Colson, 'Heroism, martyrdom, and courage: an essay on Tonga ethics,' in Beidelman, *Translation*, p. 32.

[37] Ibid., p. 31.

[38] Sinali Coulibaly, *Le paysan senoufo* (Abidjan, 1978), pp. 52–4.

[39] For example, Anita J. Glaze, *Art and death in a Senufo village* (Bloomington, 1981), p. 197.

[40] Kenyatta, *Facing*, p. 203. I am grateful to Dr J. M. Lonsdale for showing me the importance of Kenyatta's work on this subject.

[41] Ibid., p. 55.

continent. Among the Voltaic Tallensi, for example, 'it was the good farmer and not the bold fighter who was held up as the ideal of a worthwhile life.'[42] The decisive point in becoming an adult Beti man was not initiation but the erection of the first wife's house, while the young Gishu who had braved the agony of circumcision was handed not a spear but tools to build a homestead.[43] Marriage, preferably polygynous, was essential to the honourable householder, who demonstrated by managing his homestead that he was fit to share in the management of society:

There is a fundamental idea among the Gikuyu that the larger the family is the happier it will be. In Gikuyu the qualification for a status to hold a high office in the tribal organisation is based on family and not on property as is the case in European society. It is held that if a man can control and manage effectively the affairs of a large family, this is an excellent testimonial of his capacity to look after the interests of the tribe.[44]

Such benevolent elderhood demanded restraint, etiquette, and the 'coolness' essential to harmony in close-knit communities.

The most successful exponents of householder honour in stateless societies might in middle age become Big Men, a Melanesian term especially applicable to mobile and competitive forest peoples like the Beti.[45] A Big Man's status rested chiefly on wealth in people. A nineteenth-century Beti notable might have twenty wives and father fifty children.[46] Wives bore sons to work and fight, daughters to labour and attract further dependents. As neighbouring Fang people said, 'Another kinsman means another gun.'[47] The Big Man's household also commonly contained slaves (generally absorbed as poor relations), pawns taken as security for loans, and the clients whom no Big Man could neglect. To acquire and hold dependents, the Big Man had to distribute wealth: 'treasure' or cattle to pay bridewealth, food to support the poor or feast the community, and increasingly the European trade goods that nineteenth-century Beti and their neighbours pursued as avidly as they pursued women.[48] Such wealth aroused envious suspicion of magic practised at others' expense, perhaps by sacrificing a relative's life. At times of great tension Big Men might become targets of

[42] Meyer Fortes, *The dynamics of clanship among the Tallensi* (London, 1945), p. 235.

[43] Laburthe-Tolra, *Les seigneurs*, p. 207; Heald, *Manhood*, p. 44.

[44] Kenyatta, *Facing*, p. 175.

[45] M. D. Sahlins, 'Poor man, rich man, big-man, chief: political types in Melanesia and Polynesia,' *CSSH*, 5 (1963), 285–303.

[46] M. Heepe (ed.), *Jaunde-Texte von Karl Atangana und Paul Messi* (Hamburg, 1919), p. 142; Laburthe-Tolra, *Les seigneurs*, p. 152.

[47] Georges Balandier, *The sociology of Black Africa* (trans. D. Garman, London, 1970), p. 152 n.

[48] Albert Wirz, *Vom Sklavenhandel zum kolonialen Handel: Wirtschaftsräume und Wirtschaftsformen in Kamerun vor 1914* (Zurich, 1972), pp. 103–5.

community attack, usually by the disaffected young, but more often envy co-existed ambivalently with admiration for those who displayed and distributed their wealth.[49] Displays were most extravagant among the seaboard communities of the Gold and Ivory Coasts, where they dated from at least the seventeenth century. Candidates for the Agbadzi association feasted its members and then laid out their riches:

chests full of money, carved stools, coronets, jewels, etc. In gesture and dance they mime the exertions thanks to which they have acquired this wealth which they can display today. A hand stretched out flat is the symbol of domination, clawing fingers express the strength of the leopard. The mechanic displays his tools, the cocoa-grower mimes the actions of harvesting.[50]

Beti, similarly, 'danced the *bilabi*':

They came, perhaps a hundred strong with fanfare and with elaborate gestures of courtesy. Then the visiting headman started to dance and began insulting his host: 'Oh Nko'o . . . I have pity on you, poor and unhappy that you are. . . . Your family has never had salt to eat. I will take you today into my family so that you can work on my plantations.' At this point he produced several bars of salt and presented them casually to his host, while his own followers vigorously applauded.

As the dancing continued the host would rise and begin a dance of his own. 'Oh, Tchungi (the challenger), here are ten baskets of fish for you and your kinsmen. I doubt if you have ever eaten them before because your men are such poor fishermen.' The gifts became increasingly more elaborate, and the insults and feasting continued for three to five days. Almost any object, including wives, could be given at a *bilabi*. Representatives of both sides kept an exact tally of what had been given. . . . The contest ended when one headman could not assemble resources enough to hold a more extensive *bilabi* than his rival last offered.[51]

Gambling offered further opportunities for competitive display: wealth, wives, freedom, and lives were staked on the *mankala* board-game, in which a reputation for undiscovered cheating was coveted.[52] Yet the supreme occasion to assert honour was death. Some stateless peoples, it is true, disposed of their dead with brutal simplicity, but more regarded a fitting death and funeral as a necessary end for a person of honour. At a nineteenth-century Jola funeral,

---

[49] Robert W. Harms, *River of wealth, river of sorrow: the central Zaire basin in the era of the slave and ivory trade, 1500–1891* (New Haven, 1981), ch. 11; Douglas, *Lele*, chs. 12–13.

[50] Marguerite Dupire and Jean-Louis Boutillier, *Le pays Adioukrou et sa palmeraie* (Paris, 1958), p. 30. See also Harris Memel-Fotê, 'La fête de l'homme riche dans le Golfe de Guinée au temps de l'esclavage,' *CEA*, 33 (1993), 368.

[51] Frederick Quinn, 'Beti society in the nineteenth century,' *Africa*, 50 (1980), 299–300. For a similar potlatch on the East African coast, see Lyndon Harries (ed.), *Utenzi wa Mkunumbi* (Dar es Salaam, 1967).

[52] Reefe in Baker and Mangan, *Sport*, ch. 3.

3. *Wagas*. From C. R. Hallpike, *The Konso of Ethiopia* (Oxford, 1972), plate X. Reproduced by permission of the Syndics of Cambridge University Library.

the deceased, richly dressed, seated before his house, and surrounded by his possessions, was asked repeatedly by his kinsmen why he was leaving them and how they had harmed him; then, the drums beat, the mourners danced, the corpse was buried, and for eight days the triumphal entry to the land of the dead was celebrated.[53] For many stateless peoples – as for great kingdoms – the supreme compliment to a Big Man was to bury wives or slaves to form his household. Yet the most complete and lasting memorials were the magnificent wooden *waga* statues erected by the Konso of southern Ethiopia to represent the several attributes of a man of honour:

> In the statues are displayed the man, his wives, and his slaughtered enemies. If he has killed a game animal there will also be a carved representation of that. . . . In front of the group there may be a cluster of small stones. These indicate the number of fields the man has bought, showing that he was hard-working and thrifty. I once counted about 150 in front of one man's *wagas*, but this was exceptional. . . . The *waga* statues are the symbols of individual achievement.[54]

For Beti women, by contrast, funerals were times of terror, lest a dead husband's brothers might bury them with him.[55] A stateless society was generally a man's world. Unmarried Beti and Igbo women were required to go naked. Kikuyu paid one hundred goats in bloodwealth for a man and thirty for a woman. With some exceptions among intensive agriculturalists like Jola and Kabre, the sexual division of labour imposed a heavy burden of agricultural drudgery upon women; to make a man do women's work was a particularly feared punishment and often a distinguishing mark of slavery.[56] Along with cattle and slaves, women were the only investments available to most African men, and competition was intense. Late nineteenth-century Beti women might be affianced at birth, paid in compensation for homicide, or wagered in gambling contests.[57] Several forms of marriage generally existed. The most prestigious was often an exchange of brides between lineages, as practised by Tiv and by Beti notables. A respectable marriage commonly required payment of bridewealth, which inhibited subsequent divorce, especially in cattle-owning societies of southern and

---

[53] Boilat, *Esquisses*, pp. 431–3.

[54] Hallpike, *Konso*, pp. 137–8.

[55] Jeanne-Françoise Vincent, *Traditions et transition: entretiens avec des femmes beti du Sud-Cameroun* (Paris, 1976), p. 12.

[56] Laburthe-Tolra, *Les seigneurs*, p. 297; T. J. Dennis, journal, 24 April 1895, CMS UP/89/F1; Kenyatta, *Facing*, p. 228; Bohannan, *Justice*, p. 68; Ralph A. Austen and Jonathan Derrick, *Middlemen of the Cameroons Rivers: the Duala and their hinterland, c.1600–c.1960* (Cambridge, 1999), p. 116.

[57] Laburthe-Tolra, *Les seigneurs*, pp. 243, 247.

eastern Africa where women were consequently more strictly controlled than in the west.[58] Yet bridewealth was often beyond a young man's means; consequently, numerous peoples reluctantly recognised a less respectable marriage by bride-service or even elopement, subsequently regularised by negotiation. As a last resort, women might be captured by raiding. 'Marriage is war', said a Beti proverb.[59]

Male notions of honour emphasised virility. Among the Beti, a woman of the bride's family might test a suitor's manhood before the marriage.[60] Denied marriage by their elders' polygyny, young men might find a surrogate in a communal wife – an honoured position among the Lele of the Congo[61] – or, more commonly, pursue risky sexual adventures. 'The characteristic sin of Nyakyusa society' on the northern shore of Lake Nyasa '. . . was for a son to seduce one of his father's young wives.' Nuer thought it no shame for an adulterer to flee if caught *in flagrante*.[62] If the woman was a Big Man's wife or belonged to an enemy community, the penalties could be terrible for both parties. 'When I was small,' an elderly Beti woman recalled in 1967, 'I heard tell of a woman buried alive for adultery with her polygamous husband's son. She cried for nine days; on the tenth she was dead.'[63] More often an offended husband demanded compensation, but there was little sense that the woman's behaviour shamed her own family, as in Mediterranean societies. Men, especially in West Africa, did not necessarily expect their brides to be virgins, although East African attitudes could be more severe and premarital pregnancy was widely deprecated.[64]

As always, it is more difficult to discover what women honoured in themselves and one another. The lack of institutionalised hierarchy in stateless societies meant that women lacked the elite positions available in Asante. Within the female sphere their status rose with age. They could control associations

[58] Bohannan, *Justice*, p. 72; Laburthe-Tolra, *Les seigneurs*, p. 241; Adam Kuper, *Wives for cattle: bridewealth and marriage in southern Africa* (London, 1982); John C. Caldwell, Pat Caldwell, and Pat Quiggin, 'The social context of AIDS in sub-Saharan Africa,' *Population and Development Review*, 15 (1989), 198–212.

[59] Monica Wilson, *For men and elders: changes in the relations of generations and of men and women among the Nyakyusa-Ngonde people 1875–1971* (London, 1977), pp. 59–62, 152–3; Caroline H. Bledsoe, *Women and marriage in Kpelle society* (Stanford, 1980), p. 83; Laburthe-Tolra, *Les seigneurs*, p. 351.

[60] Laburthe-Tolra, *Les seigneurs*, p. 249.

[61] Douglas, *Lele*, pp. 76, 128–9.

[62] Wilson, *For men*, p. 94; Evans-Pritchard, *Nuer*, p. 166.

[63] Vincent, *Traditions*, p. 78.

[64] Meyer Fortes, *The web of kinship among the Tallensi* (London, 1949), p. 100; Bledsoe, *Women*, p. 90 n6; E. E. Evans-Pritchard, *Kinship and marriage among the Nuer* (Oxford, 1951), pp. 53, 56; Deng, *Dinka*, p. 28; Kenyatta, *Facing*, p. 160.

like Sande and Bundu, occupy ritual roles, perhaps mobilise collective action against offensive males, and take an important part in trade in West Africa, where unusually equal relationships between women and men existed among loosely structured and individualistic peoples like Baoule and Jola.[65] Women sometimes had an ancillary role in warfare. Among Dinka, for example, 'Women keep close behind their fighting men, gathering the fallen spears and handing them back. When men are speared and forced to the ground, women fall on them to protect them from the enemy.'[66] More commonly, however, women probably prided themselves most on fertility – the body of a childless Igbo woman might be mutilated before burial[67] – the endurance of pain and danger in childbirth for which initiation might prepare them, and the industry in home and field that enabled them to take the main responsibility for raising children. 'Women that I had occasion to assist,' a pioneer West African midwife recalled, '... all had the same behaviour when faced with the pain of childbirth, with rare exceptions.... Because of the value given to personal honor, [they] ... make it a point of honor to give birth without expressing their suffering.'[68]

Both a woman's reputation and her life might be endangered by accusations of witchcraft in stateless village societies where interpersonal relationships were close and political authorities lacking. The common recourse was to demonstrate innocence by submitting to a poison ordeal or similar test. In parts of eastern Africa, *mwavi* was also taken by those accused of theft.[69] Both were particularly shameful crimes in village eyes, and shame was a common and powerful punishment among those whose lives were so open to their neighbours' judgment. Igbo tied petty thieves in a public place as targets of ridicule. Meru warriors who deserted their posts were marched through the countryside carrying bananas like women.[70]

Two further points illustrate the particular nature of honour among stateless peoples. One was its role in shaping their responses to world religions.

---

[65] Mona Etienne, 'Gender relations and conjugality among the Baule,' in Oppong, *Female and male*, ch. 22; Louis-Vincent Thomas, *Les Diola* (2 vols., Dakar, 1959), vol. 1, pp. 251–68.

[66] Deng, *Dinka*, p. 76.

[67] G. T. Basden, *Niger Ibos* (reprinted, London, 1966), p. 213.

[68] Aoua Keita, quoted by Jane Turrittin, 'Colonial midwives and modernizing childbirth in French West Africa,' in Jean Allman, Susan Geiger, and Nakanyike Musisi (eds.), *Women in African colonial histories* (Bloomington, 2002), pp. 77–8.

[69] Ian Linden (ed.), 'Mponda mission diary, 1889–1891: daily life in a Machinga village,' *IJAHS*, 7 (1974–5), 505 (entry for 20 March 1890) and 720 (entry for 25 November 1890).

[70] Daryll Forde, 'Justice and judgment among the southern Ibo under colonial rule,' in Kuper and Kuper, *African law*, p. 91; Fadiman, *Oral history*, p. 107.

Although stateless pastoralists like Fula, Somali, and Oromo widely accepted Islam, cultivators generally resisted it, partly because Islam disdained agricultural rituals and divinities and partly because it was often associated with predatory neighbouring states. If an itinerant *marabout* prayed in the Serer region of Senegambia, he was forced to scrape up the sand on which he had knelt.[71] The same resistance often faced nineteenth-century Christian missionaries, but they were less of a political threat and might even offer protection to stateless peoples oppressed by powerful neighbours. That was the situation west of Lake Nyasa in the late 1870s when Tonga people welcomed Scottish missionaries, who found that the competitive pursuit of distinction and the generational tensions of stateless Tonga society encouraged response to Christianity. Every freeborn Tonga man was a potential headman of his own village; almost every village demanded a school to match its rivals; through the schools the young sought advantage over their elders and one another. By 1890 the mission had only 53 communicants but 2,279 schoolchildren.[72] It was a pattern later repeated especially among Igbo and Beti, for in Africa – with the sole exception of Buganda – all early mass conversions to Christianity took place through schooling among stateless peoples.[73]

Distinctive notions of honour found expression also in a distinctive epic literature paralleling that of West Africa's equestrian aristocracies. Among equatorial forest peoples, bards told of heroes – Mwindo of the Nyanga and Mubila of the Lega in eastern Congo, Lianja of the Mongo in northern Congo, Jeki la Njambe of coastal Cameroun, and the mortals and immortals of Fang *mvet* poetry in Gabon – who had a counterpart in Ozidi of eastern Nigeria. Unlike savanna heroes, these were more mythological than historical figures, close to the protagonists of folktales and hunters' stories, although their reliance on supernatural forces was only a more extreme form of Sunjata's and their personification of heroic ideals was essentially similar to his.[74] As products of stateless societies, these epics centred on relationships between fathers and sons. Lianja and Ozidi personified filial piety, avenging murdered fathers through dramatic

---

[71] Boilat, *Esquisses*, p. 64.

[72] J. Van Velsen, *The politics of kinship: a study in social manipulation among the lakeside Tonga of Nyasaland* (Manchester, 1964), pp. 18–19, 201, 297; John McCracken, *Politics and Christianity in Malawi, 1875–1940: the impact of the Livingstonia Mission in the Northern Province* (Cambridge, 1977), pp. 73–85.

[73] Elizabeth Isichei, *A history of the Igbo people* (London, 1976), ch. 11; Philippe Laburthe-Tolra, *Vers la lumière? ou le désir d'Ariel: à propos des Beti du Cameroun: sociologie de la conversion* (Paris, 1999).

[74] Belcher, *Epic traditions*, ch. 2. C. M. Bowra, *Heroic poetry* (London, 1952), p. 25, described such literature as shamanistic rather than epic.

contests with men and monsters.[75] *Mvet*, by contrast, often turned on generational conflict:

> As soon as Mekui-Mengômo-Ondo was old enough to marry,
> He asked his father, 'When shall I marry?'
> His father answered him, 'A son of Ekañ never asks his father
>   when he will marry.'[76]

When Mekui persisted, his father called on the lord of the immortals to exile the
youth as a slave, in which capacity he performed wonderful deeds and married a
headman's daughter. Similarly Mwindo, the most characteristic of these heroes,
was born miraculously, faced death at his father's hands, escaped with the aid of
maternal relatives, allied with forest animals, fought and overcame ogres, and
returned to divide the kingdom with his father.[77] Yet the violence and egotism
that made Mwindo a hero were disastrous in a ruler. The spirits had to teach
him restraint: 'You, Mwindo, never accept being criticized; the news about your
toughness, your heroism, we surely have heard the news, but over here, there
is no room for your heroism.'[78] Chastened, he returned with the adult virtues
of householder and chief. His epics, their interpreter has explained, 'are not
simply narratives of battle, tension, and heroic deed, but of appeasement, of
resolution of conflict, and of harmony.'[79] They dramatise the twin notions of
heroic and householder honour coexisting among stateless peoples.

[75] Belcher, *Epic traditions*, pp. 34–8, 45–7.

[76] Johnson, Hale, and Belcher, *Oral epics*, p. 257.

[77] Daniel Biebuyck and Kahombo C. Mateene (eds.), *The Mwindo epic from the Banyanga* (Berkeley, 1969).

[78] Ibid., p. 138. Ozidi was similarly chastened: J. P. Clark (ed.), *The Ozidi saga* (Ibadan, 1977), p. xx.

[79] Daniel P. Biebuyck, *Hero and chief: epic literature from the Banyanga* (Berkeley, 1978), p. 4.

8   The Honour of the Slave

The existence of honour among precolonial Africa's numerous slaves was the best demonstration of its presence at all social levels. Slaves have often been regarded as personifying dishonour. In pre-Islamic Arabia, for example, they allegedly had no honour because they had no ancestry: they were by definition kinless strangers. Proslavery apologists in the United States insisted that slaves had renounced honour when they or their ancestors had preferred slavery to death.[1] Following these lines of thought, the sociologist Orlando Patterson defined slavery as 'the permanent, violent domination of natally alienated [i.e., kinless] and generally dishonored persons.' As a Jamaican, Patterson was exceptionally alert to honour in African cultures and recognised that slaves did not accept their dishonoured status. But students of the Mediterranean had argued that a claim to honour not accepted by others was vanity. That was the slave's situation. 'What was universal in the master-slave relationship,' Patterson concluded, 'was the strong sense of honor the experience of mastership generated, and conversely, the dishonoring of the slave condition.'[2]

There is truth in this argument with respect to sub-Saharan Africa. Masters there did commonly deny honour to their slaves. Freedom was necessary to honour in its fullest sense. But Patterson linked honour inseparably to power and considered only its vertical dimension, as a relationship between unequals.[3] Honour, however, had also a horizontal dimension: even when slaves could not assert a right to respect by their masters, they might assert it among

---

[1] Farès, *L'honneur*, p. 156; Greenberg, *Honor*, pp. 108–10.

[2] Patterson, *Slavery and social death*, pp. 13, 82–3, 11; Julian Pitt-Rivers, 'Honour and social status,' in Peristiany, *Honour and shame*, p. 22.

[3] Patterson, *Slavery and social death*, p. 10.

themselves – as has been shown in the southern United States[4] – and in the wider society, for African peoples possessed multiple notions of honour, especially when most African slaves were women whose views of honour differed from those of male masters. Moreover, slaves were more diverse in Africa than in the Americas. There were many ways of becoming a slave. The condition was not necessarily permanent. Slaves contested it. And even masters were sometimes obliged to recognise that slaves possessed honour. In sum, many African slaves could assert a limited right to respect, often at great cost. This must be substantiated from scattered evidence of their words and actions.

Like the Ancient Mediterranean World, but unlike American slave societies, sub-Saharan Africa was not divided sharply between slave and free. Slavery and freedom were extreme points of a spectrum of rights in people: chiefs in subjects, patrons in clients, husbands in wives, parents in children.[5] Languages were rich in terms describing degrees of dependence.[6] Slaves, moreover, might be captured in war, kidnapped, bought, born into slavery, inherited, sentenced for crime or witchcraft, received in settlement for debt, self-enslaved in need, or acquired in many other ways. Details varied, but slaves had a place in four main social formations: stateless societies, non-Islamic states, Islamic societies, and early European colonies.

In stateless societies a slave was normally a person alienated from his or her kinship group and subordinated to another. Women became junior wives or concubines, their descendants joining the father's lineage, perhaps with residual stigma. Male slaves, normally acquired when young, performed menial duties and might have little chance of marriage; their descendants, if any, belonged to the master's lineage and might over time rise in status, although again with residual stigma. Those born within the new kinship group could not generally be sold. Kinship idiom might conceal real exploitation:

A slave is a man who will do as he is told. If you send him to draw palm wine in the rain, he goes. You call him brother, age-mate, put your arm round his neck, give him palm wine and meat, so that he is happy. He thinks you love him. Then, when your mother's brother dies, you kill him.[7]

---

[4] Wyatt-Brown, *Shaping*, pp. 3, 303. The most famous conflict was described in B. Quarles (ed.), *Narrative of the life of Frederick Douglass, an American slave* (Cambridge, Mass., 1960), pp. 104–5.

[5] Igor Kopytoff and Suzanne Miers, 'African "slavery" as an institution of marginality,' in Suzanne Miers and Igor Kopytoff (eds.), *Slavery in Africa: historical and anthropological perspectives* (Madison, 1977), pp. 7–11; Moses Finley, *The ancient economy* (London, 1973), pp. 67–9.

[6] E. M'Bokolo, 'From the Cameroon grasslands to the Upper Nile,' in Ogot, *UNESCO history*, vol. 5, p. 532; Vansina, *Tio kingdom*, pp. 365–71; Jean-Loup Amselle, *Les négociants de la savane: histoire et organisation sociale des Kooroko* (Paris, 1977), p. 32.

[7] Douglas, *Lele*, p. 36. Generally, see Miers and Kopytoff, *Slavery*, pp. 12–39.

Non-Islamic states also incorporated many slaves into kinship groups; however, they also employed them widely as soldiers, agricultural labourers, and administrators. Captives proved to be many of Ethiopia's ablest nineteenth-century generals, while Oyo was only the most prominent kingdom to rely on slave officials, even in the highest posts. Assimilation over the generations was normal, although seldom complete; Dahomey, for example, regarded everyone born on its soil as legally free but still dependent upon former masters. Assimilation was a means of control, as was the paternalism cultivated by slave-owners. Behind these, moreover, lay the violence that states sought to monopolise. In Dahomey only the state could kill or imprison a slave.[8]

In Islamic societies, similarly, slaves were marginal at all levels, rather than purely an underclass. They governed some provinces of medieval Mali and held high civil and military offices in most Muslim states. Slaves also provided many professional soldiers like the *sebbe* of Senegal, numerous concubines, domestic servants, craftsmen, and urban labourers, together with the thousands of tributary cultivators settled in slave villages in the West African savanna since at least the time of Songhai. Some authorities have estimated that the Sokoto Caliphate, the world's last great slaveholding society, may have included two and a half million slaves among its ten million people.[9] Its closest East African counterparts were the plantation islands of Zanzibar and Pemba, with possibly more than one hundred thousand slaves at their nineteenth-century peak.[10] These societies acquired slaves cheaply from neighbouring non-Islamic peoples; employed them under relatively loose work-discipline; controlled them by Islamic law, which recognised slaves' rights as well as disabilities; and assimilated them through shared culture, Islamisation, and the non-Islamic distinction between newly acquired and home-born slaves. This did not preclude violence. In Zanzibar '[n]one but women and slaves leave the house unarmed', while the Sokoto Caliphate was notorious for the cruelty of its punishments and the horror of its prisons.[11]

Nevertheless, Muslim slavery differed significantly from the European-imposed system of the Cape Colony, which the Dutch founded in 1652.

[8] Bitima, 'Oromo poems,' p. 319; Law, *Oyo Empire*, pp. 67–71; Emmanuel Terray, 'La captivité dans le royaume abron du Gyaman,' in Claude Meillassoux (ed.), *L'esclavage en Afrique précoloniale* (Paris, 1975), pp. 437–43.

[9] Nehemia Levtzion, 'The early states of the Western Sudan to 1500,' in Ajayi and Crowder, *History*, vol. 1, p. 154; Humphrey J. Fisher, *Slavery in the history of Muslim black Africa* (London, 2001), p. 263; Michal Tymowski, 'Les domaines des princes du Songhay,' *Annales E.S.C.*, 25 (1970), 1640–4; Paul E. Lovejoy and Jan S. Hogendorn, *Slow death for slavery: the course of abolition in Northern Nigeria, 1897–1936* (Cambridge, 1993), p. 1.

[10] Frederick Cooper, *Plantation slavery on the east coast of Africa* (New Haven, 1977), p. 56.

[11] Richard F. Burton, *Zanzibar; city, island, and coast* (2 vols., London, 1872), vol. 1, p. 384; Denham and Clapperton, *Narrative*, part 2, pp. 101, 107.

The Cape imported some sixty-three thousand slaves from India, Indonesia, Madagascar, and East Africa, employing most as estate labourers under relatively rigorous work-discipline and an exceptionally brutal law designed to control an adult male slave force, which in the eighteenth century outnumbered European men by three or four to one.[12] Although slave-owners used the language of patriarchy, the Cape's colonial administration and agrarian economy offered few opportunities for slave advancement, its lack of women slaves obstructed family life, the diversity of slave origins inhibited the formation of a slave culture, and the cultural distance between slaves and masters restricted assimilation. The result was a particularly harsh and dehumanising regime in which issues of honour were fiercely contested.

Slave-owners in Africa, as elsewhere, tried to deny slaves a right to respect. Their methods varied with the prevailing culture. Whereas Beti cut one ear from an adult male slave, scored his body, and made him go naked, Dutch colonists required him to cover his body but not his feet. Slaves were commonly equated with animals, Funj masters branding them with the same marks.[13] Slave women everywhere suffered sexual exploitation:

Cheikna Keita's old slave retainer [in modern Mali] was first taken as a teenage girl. During her first weeks of captivity, she and her friends were raped every night by *sofa* [slave soldiers]. The first time she was sold, she found herself in a situation where she would be taken into a hut at night by a group of men in the family and used sexually until the men were tired. Once in a family, however, she was treated with respect.[14]

In that she was fortunate: no man in the Cape Colony, free or slave, is known to have been convicted of raping a slave woman. African masters humiliated male slaves by requiring them to do women's work.[15] In lineage systems, slaves were commonly separated from their past and given a new identity. In larger societies, contemptuous nicknames for slaves were common from Songhai to the Cape. So were ignominious forms of burial, if indeed a slave's corpse was not merely thrown into the bush.[16]

[12] Robert C.-H. Shell, *Children of bondage: a social history of the slave society at the Cape of Good Hope, 1652–1838* (Johannesburg, 1994), pp. 40–1. See also Nigel Worden, *Slavery in Dutch South Africa* (Cambridge, 1985).

[13] Laburthe-Tolra, *Les seigneurs*, pp. 301, 343; Shell, *Children*, p. 225; El Zein, *Sacred meadows*, p. 219; Spaulding, *Heroic age*, cover design.

[14] Martin A. Klein, *Slavery and colonial rule in French West Africa* (Cambridge, 1998), p. 247.

[15] Robert Ross, *Beyond the Pale: essays on the history of colonial South Africa* (Hanover, N.H., 1993), p. 114; Vansina, *Children*, p. 167.

[16] Miers and Kopytoff, *Slavery*, pp. 24–5; Olivier de Sardan, *Les sociétés*, p. 33; Shell, *Children*, pp. 240–6; El Zein, *Sacred meadows*, p. 78; Basden, *Niger Ibos*, pp. 275–6.

Masters might humiliate even privileged slaves to remind them of their status. In 1823 Borno's ruler required the slave commanding his army to return a horse – a most prestigious gift – presented by mistake:

he took such great offence, that he sent back all the horses which the sheikh had previously given him, saying that he would in future walk or ride his own. On this the sheikh immediately sent for him, had him stripped in his presence, and the leather girdle put round his loins; and, after reproaching him with his ingratitude, ordered that he should be forthwith sold to the Tibboo merchants, for he was still a slave.

After acknowledging his fault, begging forgiveness with his soldiers' support, and receiving pardon, 'Barca Gana, in new tobes and a rich bornouse, rode round the camp, followed by all the chiefs of the army.'[17] The incident captured both the ambiguity of privileged slave status and the difficulty of denying it honour. Masters acknowledged this whenever they used humiliation as a disciplinary weapon. In 1879 the Wolof ruler of Kajoor bewailed his military slaves' insubordination. 'I shall reduce them to nothing,' he declared, 'after having dishonoured them.' Fifty years earlier a Cape master had chained one Spatie by the neck 'to shame the slave into compliance'.[18] The dilemma was especially clear when slaves formed a hierarchy useful to the master, for not only could privileged slaves claim honour from equals and inferiors but their master could not deny it without harming his interests. The chief slave of mid-seventeenth-century Borno, praised as 'the rallying point of the spearmen: the hub of war,' was no servile Sambo, nor was his nineteenth-century successor who had five men with musical instruments riding behind him and a dozen running before singing his praises.[19]

Sambo remained, nevertheless, a slave-owners' ideal, embodied in a Cape Colony advertisement for a slave 'possessing a moderate share of active docility'.[20] To be born into slavery could foster acquiescence. 'I know that as often as I have been in the world I have been a slave, and as often as I shall come I must be a slave,' a mason on the Gold Coast confessed in c.1739; all he could pray for was to be slave to a king.[21] Servitude itself could breed servility, especially in the lowest strata of slaves. When the Cape emancipated slaves in 1834, one

[17] Denham and Clapperton, *Narrative*, vol. 1, pp. 172–3.
[18] Diouf, *Kajoor*, p. 257; 'Report of the Assistant Guardian of Slaves for the District of Graff-Reinet for six months, ending the 24 June 1830,' CO 53/50/10.
[19] Patterson, *Kanuri songs*, p. 14; Denham and Clapperton, *Narrative*, vol. 1, pp. 105–6.
[20] Andrew Bank, 'Slavery in Cape Town, 1806 to 1834,' MA thesis, University of Cape Town, 1991, p. 92.
[21] Ray Kea, '"But I know what I shall do": agency, belief and the social imaginary in eighteenth-century Gold Coast towns,' in David M. Anderson and Richard Rathbone (eds.), *Africa's urban past* (Oxford, 2000), p. 170.

recalled his previous self-hatred: 'I even rubbed myself over with white clay to try to gain acceptance with my master.'[22] 'The "model" of the slave,' in the West African savanna,

is, at all events for the freeman (but many slaves conform to this model), the 'importunate' (*nyaarekwo*), one who seeks, by his devices, the services he renders, by flattery or begging, to extract some money from the noble. He is also someone of easy vulgarity, with insult on his lips. In a word, he is someone who knows no shame. Shame (*haawi*) is perhaps the cardinal value of 'nobility' which by negative symmetry defines 'slavery'.[23]

Here, as on the East African coast, slaves were stereotyped as 'black, fat, coarse, naive, irresponsible, uncultivated, shameless, dominated by their needs and their emotions.' West African folktales represented slaves as hyenas: greedy, untrustworthy, and shameful. Above all, slaves *danced*, publicly and obscenely. 'If you dance too skilfully,' said a proverb from the Gold Coast, 'you betray your slave parentage.'[24]

Yet the few surviving statements by low-status slaves often demonstrate consciousness and resentment. Such testimony was given in 1893 to a Gambian court investigating whether women in a British subject's household were truly slaves. One pointed to punishment. 'I know I am a slave because they never tie free people or put them in irons,' she explained. '. . . Another reason I know that I am a slave is that when prisoner was abusing me he would say if I did not know that I was his slave.'[25] A second woman stressed powerlessness:

I used to work for prisoner. He never paid me. Prisoner never made a bargain with me. It was not my will or pleasure to go to prisoner. I could not help myself. I am a slave. Prisoner hold me and my child good.
. . . I have a child. . . . Fafu James took the child to Bathurst saying she was a slave. It was not with my consent. I cried.[26]

A third woman echoed these testimonies:

It was against my wish that prisoner came to me at night being a slave I was afraid. . . . Prisoner himself used to tell us that we are slaves. That is all the reason I

---

[22] *South African Commercial Advertiser*, 6 September 1834, quoted in Elizabeth Elbourne, 'Freedom at issue: vagrancy legislation and the meaning of freedom in Britain and the Cape Colony, 1799 to 1842,' *Slavery and Abolition*, 15, 2 (August 1994), p. 124.

[23] Olivier de Sardan, *Les sociétés*, p. 35.

[24] Riesman, *Freedom*, p. 117; Magel, 'Hare and hyena,' introduction; Olivier de Sardan, *Quand nos pères*, pp. 19 n3, 166; Kwesi Yankah, *Speaking for the chief: Okyeame and the politics of Akan royal oratory* (Bloomington, 1995), p. 66.

[25] Dado Bass, in *Regina v. James Edwin*, Supreme Court, Bathurst, July 1893, CO 87/144/14153.

[26] Maladdo Mangah, in ibid.

have for saying that I am a slave. It is not because I beat that I say I am a slave. All the world beats. Not because I make rice farm. If you are in the hands of a person if you are a free born you will know. . . . Prisoner did not flog us when his house was burnt, but he refused to give us corn and that is worse than flogging. . . . The flogging I had from prisoner was painful. The marks on my right shoulder are scars from the flogging.[27]

When the Cape Colony appointed a Protector of Slaves in 1823, several slaves asserted honour by complaining that fellow-slaves had attacked their character.[28]

Not all African slaves felt the stigma that servitude is said to have borne elsewhere. They might see their enslavement as merely the luck of war, or even hold their captors to bear the dishonour if '[t]hey did not fight as people who take a town openly, but caught us like chickens, secretly.'[29] Some, moreover, chose servitude as a means of advancement, whether by voluntarily serving an Alafin of Oyo or like the youth in Mozambique who, finding 'he was all alone in the world, had neither father nor mother, nor any one else to give him water when sick, or food when hungry,' sold himself to a Portuguese master for three pieces of cloth with which he purchased other slaves.[30] Others chose slavery in preference to worse alternatives. The Luba boy who recalled, 'I did not want to be free, for I would only be caught and sold again,' was one of many who found refuge in slavery from the insecurity of nineteenth-century eastern Africa.[31] Female relatives of hereditary royal slaves in Jaara (in modern Mali) positively boasted their status:

> Allah has not created anything so noble as the servile condition . . .
> Serving people are people of their word.
> If they accept something,
> It is for ever,
> And if by contrast they reject it,
> That is definitive.[32]

That most slaves nevertheless resented servitude was clear from their resistance to enslavement. On the West African coast, the Balanta, Baga, and

---

[27] Nyahling Dahbo, in ibid.

[28] McKenzie, 'Gender,' p. 150.

[29] S. F. Nadel, *A black Byzantium: the kingdom of Nupe in Nigeria* (reprinted, London, 1969), p. 312; 'The life and travels of Dorugu, dictated by himself,' in J. F. Schön, *African proverbs, tales and historical fragments* (London, 1886), p. 14.

[30] Law, *Oyo Empire*, p. 69; David Livingstone and Charles Livingstone, *Narrative of an expedition to the Zambesi and its tributaries, 1858–1864* (London, 1865), p. 49.

[31] Marcia Wright (ed.), *Strategies of slaves and women: life-stories from East/Central Africa* (New York, 1993), p. 2.

[32] Mamadou Diawara, *La graine de la parole* (Stuttgart, 1990), p. 139.

Kru peoples successfully defended their freedom throughout the Atlantic trade, sometimes killing themselves to avoid capture. In 1855 nine prisoners captured by Ibadan hanged themselves rather than serve as slaves.[33] Raided communities in the interior might rally to release captives, although this was rare on the Atlantic coast where most slaves were aliens and local people participated in the trade. Slave mutinies on ships bound for the Americas were common, especially before they left port when slaves made a last grasp at freedom. Mutinies at sea were more difficult to effect and less successful. The 3,341 French slaving expeditions of the eighteenth century experienced 155 *reported* slave revolts; in 75 cases the rebels escaped.[34]

Until the late eighteenth century, most slave rebellions in the Americas were led by newly arrived African slaves with military experience and aristocratic traditions of honour. Spanish colonies tried to exclude Wolof slaves as 'haughty and rebellious', 'with vain presumptions to be knights.' Akan slaves from the Gold Coast made Jamaica notoriously turbulent, Kongo Christians launched the Stono revolt of 1739 in South Carolina, and Yoruba and Hausa Muslims enslaved during the Sokoto jihad and its aftermath launched several revolts in Brazil between 1807 and 1835. By then, however, a new type of skilled and literate leadership had emerged seeking to attack slavery itself, as in the Saint-Domingue rebellion of 1791.[35] Slave rebellions in Africa showed some parallels with this sequence, although they were generally smaller in scale, perhaps because slaveholdings were smaller or surrounded by large free populations, because Africa's slaves came mainly from stateless societies without strong military organisation, because opportunities for assimilation and advancement often existed, and because escape was usually an easier alternative to rebellion. In addition to coups d'état by slave soldiers, as in eighteenth-century Segu, there were several localised insurrections during the peak of the Atlantic

---

[33] McGowan, 'African resistance,' pp. 7–8, 24; Stone, *In Afric's forest*, pp. 12–13; Barber, journal, 10 September 1855, CMS C.A2/O.21/11.

[34] Fisher, *Slavery*, p. 132; Elise Kootz-Kretschmer, *Die Safwa* (reprinted, 3 vols., Nendeln, 1969–73), vol. 2, pp. 169–70; McGowan, 'African resistance,' pp. 18–24; Serge Daget, *La traite des Noirs* (Evreux, 1990), p. 106.

[35] Michael Mullin, *Africa in America: slave acculturation and resistance in the American South and the British Caribbean, 1736–1831* (Urbana, 1992), pp. 2, 40–3, 268; Elizabeth Donnan (ed.), *Documents illustrative of the history of the slave trade to America* (4 vols., Washington, D.C., 1930–5), vol. 1, p. 342; John Thornton, *Africa and Africans in the making of the Atlantic world, 1400–1680* (Cambridge, 1992), p. 293; idem, 'African dimensions of the Stono Rebellion,' *American Historical Review*, 96 (1991), 1101; João José Reis, *Slave rebellion in Brazil: the Muslim uprising of 1835 in Bahia* (trans. A. Brakel, Baltimore, 1993); Robin Blackburn, *The overthrow of colonial slavery, 1776–1848* (London, 1988), chs. 5 and 6.

trade, whether against European traders, as in the Gambia in 1681–2 and Senegal in 1698, or against African slaveholders, as in the Galinhas country in 1825.[36] Larger movements took place when the decline of the Atlantic trade created large slave concentrations in West Africa, leading to rebellion in Asante in 1818, an abortive revolt in Dahomey in 1855, and numerous disturbances on the coast for two decades after 1848.[37] East Africa had similar experience during the nineteenth century, culminating in a substantial revolt near Pangani on the mainland coast in 1873.[38] These movements seem to have aimed only to free the slaves concerned, but larger ambitions may have entered slave revolts from West Africa's Islamic reform movements, which both taught the illegality of enslaving Muslims and established theocracies with large slave concentrations. Thus the Sokoto jihad both inspired slave revolts, as in Oyo in 1817, and created emirates that became targets of revolt.[39] The largest rebellions took place in Futa Jalon, a relatively small theocracy with a high concentration of slaves ethnically distinct from the Fula rulers. One revolt there in 1756 established an independent slave settlement at Kondeah. A second in 1785 decapitated numerous masters, burned rice fields, and created an independent slave community that survived for eleven years. Then during the 1840s an Islamic teacher, Mamadu Juhe, gained a following of slaves and marginal Fula known as Hubbu (God-lovers) who resisted repression, took refuge in the mountains, and pillaged the capital before they were destroyed in 1884. The fact that the Hubbu themselves possessed slaves, however, suggests the limits to their aspirations.[40]

A wider vision, more akin to that in the Americas, emerged in the Cape Colony early in the nineteenth century. Previous slave resistance there had achieved little more than unsuccessful conspiracy, but after the British abolished the slave trade in 1807, slaves began to attack slavery itself.[41] In 1808 a mulatto

---

[36] This volume, p. 28; J. M. Gray, *A history of the Gambia* (Cambridge, 1940), p. 98; Anne Raffenel, *Nouveau voyage dans le pays des nègres* (2 vols., Paris, 1856), vol. I, p. 150; McGowan, 'African resistance,' p. 24.

[37] Bowdich, *Mission*, pp. 381–2; Patrick Manning, *Slavery and African life* (Cambridge, 1990), pp. 144–5.

[38] Glassman, *Feasts*, pp. 109–13.

[39] Law, *Oyo Empire*, pp. 255–60; Paul E. Lovejoy, 'Fugitive slaves: resistance to slavery in the Sokoto Caliphate,' in Gary Y. Okihiro (ed.), *In resistance: studies in African, Caribbean, and Afro-American history* (Amherst, 1986), ch. 6.

[40] Boubacar Barry, *La Sénégambie du XVe au XIXe siècle* (Paris, 1988), pp. 180–2, 216–20; Roger Botte, 'Révolte, pouvoir, religion: les Hubbu du Futa-Jalon,' *JAH*, 29 (1988), 391–413.

[41] Shell, *Children*, p. 264; Robert Ross, *Cape of torments: slavery and resistance in South Africa* (London, 1983), chs. 5 and 8.

slave craftsman, Louis of Mauritius, learning from an Irish seaman 'that there were no slaves in his country,' resolved, in the court's words,

to incite as much as possible the slaves in the interior to insurrection and rebellion, and having assembled and armed them with such arms as were to be procured in the country, to march to Cape Town, take the first Battery, and having thus posted themselves to dispatch a letter from thence to His Excellency the Governor demanding the liberty of the slaves of this Colony.[42]

Louis rallied some three hundred farm slaves, but British forces dispersed and captured them without bloodshed. Greater violence attended a second revolt in 1825 when Galant, an assertive home-born farm slave, persuaded his fellows that their masters were withholding freedom that the government had granted:

Galant said . . . no one would read the newspaper to him, and there came so many newspapers in which it was said that the slaves were free and that the farmers would not let them go, and that he would now press on with the people whom he had stirred up to the Salt River at Cape Town, and that if the Commando should prove too strong for him, he would then proceed to the Great [i.e., Orange] River and fetch a Commando thence.[43]

In the event, the rebels killed Galant's master and two other Europeans before a commando captured them.

Louis and Galant aspired to destroy slavery. More slaves sought to escape it. Of the first 174 who landed in 1658 at the Cape Colony, 7 escaped within a month and another 21 soon followed them. In 1834, when slavery was formally abolished there, 427 of the 35,745 slaves were listed as runaways. Most fugitives were young men, especially recently enslaved field-hands.[44] In the Cape the most common reason for flight was punishment and fear of punishment, especially flogging. Refusal of food, clothing, or a mate, or threatened sale away from family or comrades, were further reasons, as in tropical Africa. Some slaves took advantage of a master's death or political disruption.[45] The most vivid account of slavery and escape was given in old age by Alfred Diban,

---

[42] George McCall Theal (ed.), *Records of the Cape Colony* (36 vols., London, 1897–1905), vol. 6, pp. 410, 412.

[43] Evidence of Abel in Galant's trial, March 1825, in ibid., vol. 20, p. 308.

[44] H. B. Thom (ed.), *Journal of Jan van Riebeeck* (3 vols., Cape Town, 1952–8), vol. 2, pp. 266–329; John Edwin Mason, Jr., '"Fit for freedom": the slaves, slavery, and emancipation in the Cape Colony, South Africa, 1806 to 1842,' PhD thesis, Yale University, 1992, pp. 404–8.

[45] Worden, *Slavery*, pp. 123–8; Ross, *Cape of torments*, pp. 33–4; Wood to Lang, 18 June 1887, CMS G3/A2/O/1887/152; Young, journal, 18 September–22 October 1880, CMS G3/A2/O/1881/12; Lovejoy in Okihiro, *In resistance*, p. 77.

who was kidnapped as a youth in about 1896 and sold to a Fula cattle-owner. 'For four months,' he recalled,

I was chained, my left wrist tied to my right foot, in order to prevent me climbing trees and detaching the end of the chain tied to the highest branch of a thorn tree. Then I was 'freed' and set to menial tasks like washing linen, cutting wood – this for three months. Finally I was allowed to graze the herds in the bush in company with my 'master'.... Every day the idea of getting away haunted me and turned into an obsession.[46]

When he tried to escape while herding, his master recaptured him and knocked him unconscious but did not otherwise punish him. At his third unsuccessful attempt, however,

Bardamou [his master] bound me to death with my arms and legs behind me. He soaked the cords in water and left me in the courtyard. As the sun rose, the cords were tightened considerably. They penetrated deeply into my flesh. In the heat of the sun my limbs began to bleed. The cords were moistened for a second time. I had never suffered so much. Then towards mid-day my 'master' went to get a large stick and began to beat me from all directions, so savagely that my skin was broken.[47]

Soon afterwards he fled again towards his home and was sheltered by Niger fishermen who handed him over to a missionary.

Not all fugitive slaves headed for home. Many had been transported long distances to make that impossible. Instead, 'maroon' communities of escaped slaves proliferated almost everywhere that slavery flourished. Most bordered settled regions or occupied inaccessible points within them, for maroons were often partly parasitic on the societies they had fled. Maroon communities were especially numerous in eastern Africa, initially on offshore islands – one existed in the Comoros by the twelfth century – and later in the sparsely populated coastal hinterland which offered refuge, ample land, and opportunity to prey on trade routes. In the late nineteenth century, the lower Juba and Shebelle valleys of northern Kenya and Somalia housed some sixty maroon villages with perhaps twenty thousand to thirty thousand inhabitants, mostly led by a freed slave named Nassib Bunda who called himself Sultan. The West African coast and hinterland were similarly lined with maroon communities, the largest being probably Kisama, south of Luanda, which flourished in the eighteenth century.[48] In the West African interior, in addition to the Hubbu community,

---

[46] Joseph Ki-Zerbo, *Alfred Diban: premier chrétien de Haut-Volta* (Paris, 1983), pp. 29–30.
[47] Ibid., pp. 33–4.
[48] G. S. P. Freeman-Grenville (ed.), *The East African coast* (Oxford, 1962), p. 19; Lee V. Cassanelli, 'The ending of slavery in Italian Somalia,' in Suzanne Miers and Richard Roberts (eds.), *The end of slavery in Africa* (Madison, 1988), pp. 321–2; Joseph C. Miller, *Way of death: merchant capitalism and the Angolan slave trade 1730–1830* (London, 1988), p. 386.

there were several maroon settlements in inaccessible pockets within the Sokoto Caliphate. The only significant group within the Cape Colony led a free and brutal existence in the cliffs east of Cape Town for over a century.[49] Maroon communities were not romantic. Many were part-time bandits, owned slaves, and returned deserters to neighbouring owners. It would be interesting to know whether, as in the Americas,[50] maroons came disproportionately from stateless peoples and whether heroic honour inspired rebellion while householder honour fostered maroonage. But there is no serious evidence and several groups started as rebels and ended as maroons.

Although collective rebellion and maroonage were spectacular, most slaves had to defend their honour and humanity by mundane individual struggle. Some cultivated surly indifference:

How were you always treated by your Master?
Answer. Not well and not badly.
How were the other people treated?
Answer. If they deserved it, they were flogged.
How was it with respect to victuals?
Answer. It was not so bad.[51]

Many employed the 'weapons of the weak': deliberate incomprehension, malingering, noncompliance, petty crime, sabotage, ridicule. 'All they do is what they want to do,' a Swahili account complained.[52] The classic slave crime was arson, always difficult to trace. Cape slaves incinerated much of Stellenbosch, so that it was a neat riposte for the Dutch authorities to make black freedmen responsible for Cape Town's fire brigade. Masters often lived in fear of violence. The first slaves imported into Cape Town created panic within four months of arrival: 'Everyone should . . . be on his guard to prevent being murdered by them.'[53] The most terrible punishments faced slaves who raised their hands against masters.[54] Yet actual violence against slave-owners was rare in Zanzibar and did not stop them arming trusted slaves, while detailed evidence from the Cape Colony reveals few planned attacks before Galant's rebellion.[55]

---

[49] Lovejoy in Okihiro, *In resistance*, pp. 81–2; Ross, *Cape of torments*, ch. 5.

[50] Blackburn, *Overthrow*, p. 20.

[51] Evidence of Lea in Galant's trial, March 1825, in Theal, *Records*, vol. 20, p. 291.

[52] Lyndon Harries (ed.), *Swahili prose texts* (London, 1965), p. 209.

[53] Worden, *Slavery*, p. 132; Robert Ross, *Status and respectability in the Cape Colony, 1750–1870: a tragedy of manners* (Cambridge, 1999), p. 34; Thom, *Journal of Jan van Riebeeck*, vol. 2, p. 361.

[54] Hope Masterton Waddell, *Twenty-nine years in the West Indies and Central Africa, 1829–1858* (2nd edn, London, 1970), p. 572; Worden, *Slavery*, pp. 117, 132–3.

[55] Cooper, *Plantation slavery*, p. 190; Worden, *Slavery*, p. 133.

Newly acquired slaves, especially in large numbers, were the most dangerous. Following Dahomey's unsuccessful assault on Abeokuta in 1864, Dahomeyan captives were described as 'like the wild beasts setting fire to the houses, and killing their masters and even young children.'[56] Frenzied violence was a recognised response to desperation among Yoruba. When the Bale of Ibadan ordered a fugitive slave back to his master in 1855, 'he not willing to return to his master took his knife and stuck 5 of balle's people with the knife and intended to kill balle himself: not being able to get the balle, he run the knife through his own bowel and was finished by balle.' Indonesian slaves at the Cape occasionally 'ran amok' in this way. Yet most victims of slave violence were other slaves or the perpetrators themselves.[57]

Suicide was a common response to enslavement, cruelty, and offended honour. In the Atlantic trade, many slaves killed themselves before embarkation, drowned themselves by jumping overboard, refused food and starved to death, or died of 'fixed melancholy'.[58] The Cape Colony averaged between fifteen and twenty reported slave suicides a year during the eighteenth century, overwhelmingly by foreign-born males who hanged themselves. Some were escaping cruel punishments for crimes or desertion. In 1761 a sixteen-year-old boy killed himself for fear of being flogged. Twelve years earlier, a negligent Gold Coast slave had hanged himself 'to avoid the shame and humiliation of public punishment,' leaving his son to plot a revenge killing. Fear of being sold to brutal masters was another motive, while women might commit suicide when children or husbands were taken from them.[59] Some were moved by humiliation and loss of liberty, as in Ibadan in 1883:

> It was one of the Are's slaves, who had been in shackles: he stabbed himself with a knife in his belly, and the bowels came out, intending to kill himself . . . the man at first refused that I should dress the wound for him . . . but the man on whose charge they were put, begged him, and promised after this, never to put shackles on his feet, so he agreed that I should dress the wound.[60]

In 1739 a Cape slave threatened to kill his master's family and himself 'since slavery deprived him of all desire to live. He particularly resented not only the

---

[56] Maser to Venn, 2 May 1864, CMS C.A2/O.68/53.

[57] Barber, journal, 23 November 1855, CMS C.A2/O.21/12; Edna Bradlow, 'Running amok and its historical significance: a Cape case study,' *Cabo*, 5, 1 (1990), 8–11; Ross, *Cape of torments*, p. 9.

[58] Donnan, *Documents*, vol. 1, pp. 402–3, and vol. 2, pp. 280, 460; Miller, *Way of death*, pp. 424–7.

[59] Worden, *Slavery*, pp. 135–6; Kea in Anderson and Rathbone, *Africa's urban past*, pp. 171–2; Gustav Nachtigal, *Sahara and Sudan* (trans. A. G. B. Fisher and H. J. Fisher, 4 vols., London, 1971–87), vol. 1, p. 324; Peeler, journal, 24 February 1879, CMS C.A3/O.29/3.

[60] W. S. Allen, journal, 7 February 1883, CMS G3/A2/O/1884/103.

imposition of work, but also the lack of freedom to go where he wanted, to wear his own clothes and to have female company.' Prevented from carrying out his threat, he was instead executed with particular cruelty.[61]

James Froude once said that slavery demonstrated only the Negro's power of endurance.[62] Certainly African slaves, in Africa as in Asia and the Americas, displayed extraordinary endurance of pain, thanks perhaps in part to their training in fortitude through initiation. 'Once, on looking over some of old Cracker's [John Leadstine's] Slaves,' a European trader wrote of Sierra Leone in 1721,

> I could not help taking notice of one Fellow among the rest, of a tall, strong Make, and bold, stern aspect. As he imagined we were viewing them with a design to buy, he seemed to disdain his Fellow-Slaves for their Readiness to be examined, and as it were scorned looking at us, refusing to rise or stretch out his Limbs, as the Master commanded; which got him an unmerciful Whipping from Cracker's own Hand, with a cutting Manatea Strap, and had certainly killed him but for the loss he himself must sustain by it; all which the Negro bore with Magnanimity, shrinking very little, and shedding a Tear or two, which he endeavoured to hide as tho' ashamed of. All the Company grew curious at his Courage, and wanted to know of Cracker, how he came by him; who told us, that this same Fellow, called Captain Tomba, was a leader in some Country Villages that opposed them, and their Trade, at the River Nunes; killing our Friends there, and firing their Cottages. The Sufferers this way, by the Help of my Men, (says Cracker) surprized, and bound him in the Night, about a Month ago, he having killed two in his Defence, before they could secure him.

Tomba, a Baga leader, later initiated a shipboard mutiny within sight of the African coast, himself killing three sailors with a hammer before he was subdued.[63] Flogging was commonplace in every known slave system. Galant's body had fourteen sets of scars, mostly from punishments.[64] His fellow slave Lydia 'got plenty of flogging':

> With what was she flogged?
> Answer. With a sambok and likewise with a bamboo stick, sometimes my master beat her and sometimes my mistress.
> Did you or Lydia ever complain about it?
> Answer. No.
> Why not?
> Merely so.[65]

---

[61] Worden, *Slavery*, p. 136.
[62] Quoted in *The Observer* (Monrovia), 8 July 1880.
[63] John Atkins, *A voyage to Guinea* (2nd edn, London, 1737), pp. 41–2.
[64] Patterson, *Slavery and social death*, p. 4; Theal, *Records*, vol. 20, p. 303.
[65] Evidence of Antony in Galant's trial, March 1825, in Theal, *Records*, vol. 20, p. 245.

In fact many complaints to the Cape Colony's Protector of Slaves after 1823 were about floggings, but mainly excessive or unjustified floggings. Whipping was a common punishment in African societies; Nyahling Dahbo of the Gambia, although scarred by the whip, thought the withholding of food a worse penalty. Many slaves learned by bitter experience to endure flogging and tried by outward indifference to demonstrate that it could not cow them. Yet against this must be set the boy who killed himself from fear of whipping, the many slaves who fled to escape it, and the agony of those whose loved ones suffered it. Fortitude was not insensitivity.[66]

One way for slaves to defend their dignity was to create areas of life partly beyond their masters' control. One, as in the United States, was the family. Yet special problems surrounded family life for slaves in Africa. In the Cape Colony, it was a focus of acute conflict between slaves and masters because slaves sought independent adulthood, while masters regarded them as members of their patriarchal households. Cape law did not recognise slave marriages until 1823 and few took place before emancipation. Moreover, male slaves heavily outnumbered females, provoking male rivalry and sexual crime.[67] Yet slaves struggled to create families. At Galant's trial slaves referred to one another as husbands and wives, while whites spoke only of concubines. One of the largest eighteenth-century slave-owners kept separate living quarters for 'married' slaves.[68] More often, however, slaves who considered themselves married lived on different estates. Such families were necessarily matrifocal. Official documents recorded only the mothers of slave children, intergenerational ties were mainly between women, and when families were broken up, the father was usually the one sold separately. Matrifocal families gave women unusual responsibility and authority, which they were to retain at the Cape even after emancipation.[69] Their fertility was probably low, but infanticide seems to have been rare, and there is much evidence of the women's devotion to their children, whom they struggled to free. Female notions of honour as endurance and responsibility may have enabled women to survive slavery more

---

[66] John Edwin Mason, 'Paternalism under siege,' in Nigel Worden and Clifton Crais (eds.), *Breaking the chains: slavery and its legacy in the nineteenth-century Cape Colony* (Johannesburg, 1994), ch. 2; this volume, pp. 124, 131; Read to ?, 30 August 1808, in *Transactions of the [London] Missionary Society: volume 3* (London, 1813), p. 205.

[67] Pamela Scully, *Liberating the family? Gender and British slave emancipation in the rural Western Cape, South Africa, 1823–1853* (Portsmouth, N.H., 1997), pp. 28, 38; Worden, *Slavery*, pp. 53, 96.

[68] Theal, *Records*, vol. 20, pp. 209, 250, 327; Worden, *Slavery*, p. 58.

[69] Scully, *Liberating*, pp. 30–2; Mason, '"Fit for freedom",' pp. 13, 431–2, 452, 468.

successfully than men, just as women were later to adapt better to South African cities.[70]

In tropical Africa, the problems of family life for slaves were different and somewhat less acute. African masters permitted slave marriages, although they often insisted on arranging them. Agricultural slaves in the West African savanna generally lived in slave villages with huts and fields on which to establish households. This was expected to reconcile them to their condition. '"If you remain quiet",' Alfred Diban was told, '"in a year you will be given a wife and you will also have children." . . . I swore to myself that I would never take a wife in captivity.'[71] Others were less defiant but faced the difficulty that polygynous freemen appropriated many slave women. 'To female slaves, marriage to free men meant liberation,' Toyin Falola has written of nineteenth-century Ibadan, although it also meant a subordinate position within marriage. For male slaves, however, it might mean enforced celibacy. Heinrich Barth, visiting the West African savanna in the mid nineteenth century, believed 'that a slave is very rarely allowed to marry.' That was perhaps an exaggeration, but there is evidence that slaves did not reproduce themselves, partly because the fertility of slave women was often low.[72] Married women slaves were vulnerable to sexual aggression by their owners; in Asante there was a special ceremony by which a master apologised to his slave for committing adultery with his wife. Women were also at risk of sale and separation from their children. One Yoruba woman robbed of her child exploded a keg of gunpowder, killing herself and burning much of the town.[73] Amidst such obstacles, to create and sustain families bred much conflict. In 1881 four Hausa slaves in Yorubaland broke their chains, armed themselves with bottles filled with sand, 'demanded the restoration of their wives,' and regained freedom. Nearly forty years later a slave in Sierra Leone asserted his rights over his family by killing three of his children because 'My master took my wife, my children and my rice.' Women fought the same battles less violently, struggling to redeem their relatives or buy their own freedom in order to return to

[70] Worden, *Slavery*, pp. 52–60; Shell, *Children*, pp. 46–8, 205, 305, 314; Mason, '"Fit for freedom",' p. 508; this volume, p. 296.

[71] El Zein, *Sacred meadows*, p. 76; Lovejoy, *Transformations*, pp. 206–7; Ki-Zerbo, *Alfred Diban*, p. 30.

[72] Toyin Falola, 'Power relations and social interactions among Ibadan slaves, 1850–1900,' *African Economic History*, 16 (1987), 104–5; Barth, *Travels*, vol. 1, pp. 527–8; Robert Harms, 'Sustaining the system: trading towns along the middle Zaire,' and Margaret Strobel, 'Slavery and reproductive labor in Mombasa,' in Claire C. Robertson and Martin A. Klein (eds.), *Women and slavery in Africa* (Madison, 1983), pp. 105–9, 120–1.

[73] Rattray, *Ashanti law*, p. 38; S. Johnson, journal, 24 November 1880, CMS G3/A2/O/1881/98; Peeler, journal, 24 February 1879, CMS C.A3/O.29/3.

their families.[74] Slave families had a strong matrifocal emphasis even in tropical Africa. 'Slaves are like cattle,' an elder in Adamawa declared. 'Whenever
one is born and grows up it stays with its mother; the father is irrelevant.'
Among slaves it was generally women who preserved and transmitted family
traditions.[75]

A second area in which slaves might seek dignity was cultural autonomy,
but here too African experience differed from that in the Americas. In the Cape
Colony, the diverse origins of slaves and the preponderance of imported males
meant that they brought no common culture and barely began to form one until
the later eighteenth century, even in Cape Town. Until then their *lingua franca*
appears to have been Portuguese, the commercial language of the Indian Ocean.
Afrikaans – literally kitchen Dutch – began to replace it late in the eighteenth
century.[76] Such acculturation in dress, lifestyle, and culture as took place in the
seventeenth and eighteenth centuries was mainly to European models, although
it was limited by the masters' opposition to baptising and educating slaves. In
the 1770s only some 5 per cent of privately owned slave children attended
school.[77] Almost nothing is known of slave religion in the Cape Colony until
the late eighteenth century, when Islam, brought from Indonesia, made a major
impact on slaves and especially freedmen in Cape Town. The first Muslim
school opened there in 1793. By 1820 there were three times as many Muslim
as Christian slaves. 'We teach them to believe that their souls are free,' an *imam*
was quoted as saying in 1835, 'and that they must look up to God to make them
free when they die.'[78]

By contrast, a major obstacle to autonomous slave cultures in tropical Africa
was that assimilation was often so easy. On the East African coast, for example, most slaves from the interior sought not to preserve their cultures
but to achieve *ustaarabu* by adopting Islam, the Swahili language, and the

---

[74] *Lagos Times and Gold Coast Advertiser*, 13 July 1881; Ismail Rashid, '"Do Dady nor lef me
make dem carry me": slave resistance and emancipation in Sierra Leone, 1894–1928,' in Suzanne
Miers and Martin Klein (eds.), *Slavery and colonial rule in Africa* (London, 1999), p. 221;
Gollmer, journal, 6 May 1860, CMS C.A2/O.43/134; Marcia Wright, 'Bwanikwa: consciousness
and protest among slave women in Central Africa, 1886–1911,' in Robertson, *Women and
slavery*, p. 264.

[75] El Zein, *Sacred meadows*, p. 76; Catherine Ver Eecke, 'The slave experience in Adamawa:
past and present perspectives from Yola (Nigeria),' *CEA*, 34 (1994), 34; Diawara, *La graine*,
pp. 128–9, 142.

[76] Worden, *Slavery*, pp. 94–5; Shell, *Children*, pp. 61–4.

[77] David Coplan, *In township tonight! South Africa's black city music and theatre* (London, 1985),
pp. 8–11; Shell, *Children*, p. 350.

[78] Yusuf da Costa and Achmat Davids, *Pages from Cape Muslim history* (Pietermaritzburg, 1994),
pp. 50, 63; Timothy Keegan, *Colonial South Africa and the origins of the racial order* (London,
1996), p. 18.

behaviour of a *mwungwana*, a freeman, as coastal slaves described themselves when travelling up-country. This met some resistance from masters, who welcomed acculturation but not the claims to reciprocity and eventual freedom that slaves associated with it. Even the numerous maroon communities were 'outposts of Swahili culture'.[79] Hausa Islamic society in West Africa, similarly, was strongly assimilative. There, it was remembered, 'The bought slaves spoke "Gwari", but their children spoke Hausa.'[80] That assimilation won respect was most clearly displayed by the home-born slaves who served as retainers to West Africa's equestrian nobility in the manner personified by Poullori's relationship to his master Silamaka, with its subtle ambiguity between companionship and inequality. In the real world this relationship existed among the *horso* retainers who participated vicariously in the honour of their noble Zarma masters. In principle it took slaves three generations to become *horso*.[81] Masters prided themselves on attracting such loyalty. The hagiography of St. Takla Haymanot claimed that when his father freed his slaves in hope of being rewarded with a son, they protested, 'What have we done unto thee, O master, and with what deed have we provoked thee to wrath?'[82] It was chiefly in these relationships that East African slaves might acquire *heshima* in their masters' eyes.[83] Yet such ties were not necessarily found even in Islamic societies. Among the Soninke of modern Mali, who were notoriously harsh masters, slaves denied the existence of paternalism – they were 'just bought, that's all' – and retained identity and customs that their masters viewed with deep suspicion. In Futa Jalon, it was remembered, Fula 'feared the slave only when he was suspected of being a sorcerer,' a reputation widely attributed to slaves, especially women slaves, and probably an important restraint on their maltreatment.[84]

The assimilative capacity of tropical African societies created a hierarchy among slaves. When victims were demanded for sacrifice in the Ode Ondo area of Yorubaland in 1880, the longer-established slaves conspired to volunteer the newly acquired, three hundred of whom broke for freedom.[85] It was often such vulnerable slaves who found refuge in nineteenth-century Christian

[79] Jonathon Glassman, 'The bondsman's new clothes: the contradictory consciousness of slave resistance on the Swahili coast,' *JAH*, 32 (1991), 277–312 (quotation on p. 303).

[80] Smith, *Baba*, p. 42.

[81] Olivier de Sardan, *Les sociétés*, p. 42. See this volume, pp. 62–3.

[82] Budge, *Takla Haymanot*, vol. I, p. 20.

[83] This volume, pp. 26–7.

[84] Eric Pollet and Grace Winter, *La société Soninké (Dyahunu, Mali)* (Brussels, 1971), pp. 249, 253 n137; Roger Botte, 'Stigmates sociaux et discriminations religieuses: l'ancienne classe servile au Fuuta Jaloo,' *CEA*, 34 (1994), 116; Nigel Penn, *Rogues, rebels and runaways: eighteenth-century Cape characters* (Cape Town, 1999), p. 44.

[85] Young, journal, 18 September 1880, CMS G3/A2/O/1881/12.

mission communities, which frequently began as settlements of former slaves. Sometimes, as in Yorubaland, slave predominance deterred free people from accepting Christianity or, as among the Igbo, led the first free Christians to segregate themselves. Yet not all ex-slave congregations were dependent. Early missionaries on the coast of modern Kenya ministered rather to assertive maroon communities like that at Fuladoyo, where an African convert headed a town of four hundred escaped slaves described by a missionary as 'the most industrious set I have seen in Africa.' Nigeria's first martyrs were two Christian slaves killed for refusing to participate in their master's religious rites. Just as Islam might enable slaves to reclaim honour in the Cape Colony, so might Christianity do so in tropical Africa.[86]

The paradox of slavery, in Africa as elsewhere, was that masters could assert dominance only by granting concessions to slaves on whose labour and acquiescence that dominance depended. Conversely, most slaves endured their lot so long as customary concessions were respected. Such was the honour of slaves: they had a right to a limited amount of respect accompanied by a measure of dishonour and could enjoy that respect only so long as they had the courage to defend it.

The compromise normally included a customary labour regime. The tradition on the East African coast and in much of the Sokoto Caliphate was that agricultural slaves worked five or sometimes six days a week for their masters. Attempts to impose more rigorous demands, as at Pangani in 1873, might provoke revolt or flight.[87] Urban slaves, by contrast, often worked or traded independently and paid a fixed sum to their owners, making it possible to save for manumission. A claim to purchase freedom was often one concession that masters were obliged to grant to male slaves, women being treated more commonly as concubines. In Hausaland, slaves could conventionally buy their freedom for twice their market value.[88]

Cruelty, too, had its constraints. Almost the only organisation of slaves recorded in sub-Saharan Africa (other than maroon communities) was created in Old Calabar in the Niger Delta in 1850–1, when the very numerous

---

[86] This volume, p. 82; H. S. Macaulay, 'Report for the year 1889. Mission Station – Asaba,' CMS G3/A3/O/1889/29; A. D. Shaw, 'A trip in Giriama,' March 1882, CMS UP/36/F1; Elizabeth Isichei, 'Christians and martyrs in Bonny, Ora and Lokoja (c.1874–c.1902),' in her *Varieties of Christian experience in Nigeria* (London, 1982), pp. 63–5.

[87] Cooper, *Plantation slavery*, p. 157; Lovejoy, *Transformations*, pp. 206–7; this volume, p. 127.

[88] J. Johnson to Wright, 2 August 1879, CMS C.A2/O.56/28; Jan-Georg Deutsch, 'Slavery under German colonial rule in East Africa, c.1860–1914,' Habilitationsschrift, Humboldt University, Berlin, 2000, p. 80; Bank, 'Slavery,' pp. 53–8; Polly Hill, *Population, prosperity and poverty: rural Kano, 1900 and 1970* (Cambridge, 1977), p. 203.

and independent farm slaves took a blood oath 'to resist the encroachments and oppressions of the Duke Town gentry, and to preserve themselves from being killed on all occasions according to old customs,' as a missionary recorded. When some were arrested, others plundered plantations to secure their release. In 1857 these Bloodmen executed a master who had killed several slaves. Having gained this point, however, they did not attack slavery itself but subsequently intervened in Calabar's affairs only to support their respective masters.[89] Many African states allowed slaves to charge masters with excessive cruelty. Lozi slaves, for example, could appeal to the royal court for protection. It was a dangerous course. When two slaves of the Emir of Kano complained of maltreatment to the Caliph of Sokoto during the 1880s, the Emir had one tortured, beheaded, and mutilated, while the other killed himself to escape the same fate.[90] Moreover, custom could weigh equally heavily on the slave. Galant's trial in 1825 revealed that several fellow-slaves had betrayed his plans – as was common in slave conspiracies – and some tried hard to damage his defence. Fear of dreadful punishment was doubtless their main motive. Another may have been the belief that Galant had broken their unwritten rule that personal defiance must not endanger the entire slave community. Some appear to have thought that in attacking their masters they had broken their own moral code.[91] In other situations, however, slaves might think it a point of honour to protect their fellows. 'A slave will much rather suffer death than give up his accomplice,' a Dutch official asserted in 1799, 'he has known them stand what he could not have conceived Human nature to have stood in order to preserve good faith to each other.'[92]

Evidence from the Cape Colony shows that notions of honour frequently coloured relations between slaves and masters. Dutch courts not only punished slaves savagely but entertained their complaints and penalised masters whose behaviour earned the condemnation of fellow slave-owners.[93] After 1823, complaints to the protector of slaves proliferated. In one a respectable, forty-year-old wagon-driver complained that after being beaten for idling, whose justice he acknowledged, he was flogged again for malingering when still in pain, which

[89] Waddell, *Twenty-nine years*, p. 476; Hugh Goldie, *Calabar and its mission* (new edn, Edinburgh, 1901), p. 192; A. J. H. Latham, *Old Calabar 1600–1891* (Oxford, 1973), pp. 95–6.

[90] Gluckman, *Judicial process*, p. 215; Paul E. Lovejoy, Abdullahi Mahadi, and Mansur Ibrahim, 'C. L. Temple's "Notes on the history of Kano",' *Sudanic Africa*, 4 (1993), 25.

[91] Theal, *Records*, vol. 20, pp. 269–82; Shell, *Children*, p. 55; Mason, ' "Fit for freedom",' p. 402.

[92] Margaret Lenta and Basil le Cordeur (eds.), *The Cape diaries of Lady Anne Barnard 1799–1800* (2 vols., Cape Town, 1999), vol. 1, pp. 213–16.

[93] Wayne Dooling, *Law and community in a slave society: Stellenbosch District, South Africa, c.1760–1820* (Cape Town, 1992).

was not only illegal but unjust. His master found it so humiliating that the protector should summon him to answer for the management of his household that he volunteered rather to free the slave and pay a heavy fine and compensation. Slave, master, and protector all observed their disparate notions of honour.[94]

[94] John Edwin Mason, 'Hendrik Albertus and his ex-slave Mey: a drama in three acts,' *JAH*, 31 (1990), 423–45.

The twin notions of heroic and householder honour coexisting in stateless societies appeared with particular clarity in the kingdoms of nineteenth-century
southern Africa. Heroes flourished especially in the Zulu and other states militarised by inter-African competition and resistance to European encroachment.
This military ethos was not confined to an equestrian elite but influenced ideals
of masculinity in entire societies. It is documented in oral recollections and in
praise-poetry, which militarisation reshaped as it did the *oriki* of Yorubaland.
Praise-poetry was predominantly a male genre, for women were more subordinate in these cattle-owning societies than elsewhere in non-Islamic Africa,
which partly explains their positive responses to Christianity. Yet women shared
in householder honour, which can for the first time be analysed in detail from
records of slander cases brought by Africans in courts of the eastern Cape
Colony. These records reveal an indigenous notion of respectability complementing and conflicting with the heroic ethos.

Komfiya kaNogandaya was a hero, *iqawe*, literally 'a proud one you', glossed
in the earliest Zulu dictionary as an ostentatious person, exhibiting grandeur
or pride.[1] He left Qwabe country shortly before 1819 to escape accusations
of sexual misconduct. Like many young men, he sought fortune in the service
of Shaka, king of the newly dominant Zulu people. 'You, boy, whose son are
you?' Shaka demanded. 'I am the son of Nogandaya. . . . We have come to *konza*
[serve]. We have got into trouble.' The king turned to his men: 'Celebrate, Zulu

---

[1] J. L. Döhne, *A Zulu-Kafir dictionary* (Cape Town, 1857: reprinted, Farnborough, 1967), p. 292.
Shaka renamed Komfiya as Zulu, but I use the earlier name to avoid confusion.

people, for I am chosen as a husband.'[2] He tested Komfiya by ordering him to raid his Qwabe people; then the king gave him menial tasks. Komfiya was smearing cow dung on palace floors when Shaka, preparing his troops for a decisive battle with his Ndwandwe rivals, drove a staff into the ground, saying, 'Let there come forward a warrior to pull out this stick. My praises will be given to him as the first to attack in battle.' Komfiya seized the staff. Shaka warned him, 'I shall now watch and see how my dark friend will conduct himself.'[3] Komfiya replied that if three warriors killed Ndwandwe before he did, Shaka might kill him. In fact Komfiya killed first, continuing to fight, although wounded, until his comrades restrained him.[4] Later Shaka set aside ten oxen and declared, 'Let there come forward any man who can match [Komfiya], and he shall have these cattle.' None responded. Komfiya took the cattle.[5] It launched a career earning him five wounds, eighty wives, command of a regiment, and a praise-poem celebrating his prowess:

> Huge chest on which tears were shed,
> Arm, that defended the vitals
> From the warriors of Mzilikazi;
> Huge frame that was like Kranskop,
> Fire that raged like a furnace,
> Raider of fat while it is still boiling.[6]

At the height of his fame, however, Komfiya preempted a wife from Shaka's much-despised brother Mpande, saying, 'A woman will never be married by a coward.' Mpande later took the throne, and Komfiya died in exile just before the Zulu defeat by the British in 1879.[7]

As seen through the nostalgic eyes of the defeated, Komfiya personified the heroic age when Shaka had cultivated military honour – *udumo*, thunder – among his Zulu people.[8] For some two centuries before Shaka usurped the Zulu throne in c.1816, competition for resources had grown among the Nguni-speaking chiefdoms between the Drakensberg and the sea. That the hitherto unimportant Zulu group came to dominate the region was the result of Shaka's ruthlessness in enforcing the military tactics and organisation that competition

---

[2] Evidence of Mkotana kaZulu, 1905, in C. de B. Webb and J. B. Wright (eds.), *The James Stuart Archive of recorded oral evidence relating to the history of the Zulu and neighbouring peoples* (5 vols., Pietermaritzburg, 1976–2001), vol. 3, p. 226.

[3] Evidence of Dinya kaZozowayo, 1905, in ibid., vol. 1, pp. 101–3.

[4] Ibid., vol. 1, p. 102, vol. 2, p. 180, and vol. 3, p. 217.

[5] Evidence of Mandhlakazi kaNgini, 1916, in ibid., vol. 2, p. 181.

[6] Trevor Cope (ed.), *Izibongo: Zulu praise-poems* (Oxford, 1968), p. 178.

[7] Webb and Wright, *James Stuart Archive*, vol. 2, pp. 181–2, and vol. 3, pp. 222–3.

[8] Döhne, *Zulu-Kafir dictionary*, p. 67; C. M. Doke, D. McK. Malcolm, and J. M. A. Sikakana, *English-Zulu dictionary* (Johannesburg, 1971), p. 223.

fostered.[9] Abolishing circumcision, which he held to weaken young men,[10] Shaka required them to serve for two or three years at local military headquarters before he summoned them to the capital, formed them into a regiment under an appointed *induna*, supervised several months of further training, and sent them to build a new headquarters. Thereafter they did an annual period of military service and were always liable to mobilisation. Only when the king authorised it could they marry, perhaps in their late thirties in Shaka's time, although earlier under his successors. Intensive regimental training was necessary because the army's chief weapon was a short stabbing-spear wielded in close combat, an immensely demanding form of warfare that bred among Zulu the same contempt for missile-using enemies displayed by West African cavalrymen, with the difference that every adult male Zulu was a warrior.

Although, as in Asante, regimental duty restrained heroic egotism, the stabbing-spear nevertheless fostered personal prowess and single combat:

Before the Isandhlwana battle [of 1879] the . . . king called the Kandempemvu and Ngobamakosi [regiments] into the cattle enclosure, he being present, and directed them to challenge one another. A man from the Ngobamakosi lot got up and shouted, 'I shall surpass you, son of So-and-so. If you stab a white man before mine has fallen, you may take the kraal of our people . . . you may take my sister'. . . . Having said this, he will then start leaping about (*giyaing*) with his small dancing shield and a stick. . . . Whilst the *giyaing* goes on, he is praised by those of his regiment.[11]

These wagers were not in reality honoured, but they might be remembered when the army returned, decked in the apparel of those they had killed:

When the *impi* [army] got back from a fight [Shaka] used to say, 'Pick out the cowards.' They would be picked and a semi-circle formed. . . . They would then be given assegais and told to stab one another. They would fight two at a time, and even if a man won two or three times, i.e. killing his man, he would himself presently fail and be killed, or he would be put to death by order of the king if he were the only one remaining.[12]

This heroic ethos pervaded male life. It stressed physical strength and beauty, whether displayed in the near-nakedness of daily life or the elaboration of military costume and personal adornment, carefully graded by age and rank. Dance was a further means of display, replacing military drill and demonstrating

---

[9] For accounts of this controversial process, see John Laband, *The rise and fall of the Zulu nation* (London, 1997), ch. 4; Norman Etherington, *The great treks: the transformation of southern Africa, 1815–1854* (Harlow, 2001), chs. 4–6.

[10] Evidence of Ngidi kaMcikaziswa, 1904, in Webb and Wright, *James Stuart Archive*, vol. 5, p. 68.

[11] Evidence of Mpatshana kaSodondo, 1912, in ibid., vol. 3, p. 306.

[12] Evidence of Melapi kaMagaye, 1905, in ibid., vol. 3, p. 87.

athleticism, discipline, and solidarity. Shaka danced regularly with his people, as did Mzilikazi of the Ndebele, a group who avoided Shaka's control in the early 1820s and created a kingdom north of the Limpopo akin to the Zulu state. Together with male display went sexual adventure. Young men in military service risked death by visiting the girls confined within the royal enclosure. Older men displayed virility by accumulating the wives denied to their juniors. Insult demanded violent response. Zulu fought one another with sticks, but Ndebele law acquitted a man who killed in fair fight. Neither kingdom permitted feud or private vengeance; murder, robbery, and witchcraft were all offences against the state for which the penalty might be death – probably a painful death, for torture and cruel execution were common, especially for political offenders.[13] Honour demanded that death be met with dignified ceremony. When Magolwana kaMkatini, the greatest Zulu praise-poet, was executed for mounting a war-party against a private enemy, he donned his formal costume and praised the king before saying, 'Now kill me.'[14] And death could be preferable to dishonour. When Mzilikazi ordered an Ndebele nobleman to quit his presence and live among the poor, he replied, 'Let me be slain like the warrior; I cannot live with the poor . . . and disgrace these badges of honour which I won among the spears and shields of the mighty.' His request was granted.[15]

Ndebele and Zulu societies were sharply stratified. The Zulu royal family was surrounded by an elite (the *amantungwa*) of clans incorporated during the early stages of state formation. They provided twenty-two of Shaka's thirty-six military *indunas* for whom data survive; another twelve were personal favourites like Komfiya, but none came from outlying tributary peoples.[16] Each *induna* was also a civilian chief, but much political authority remained with Zulu or *amantungwa* noblemen whom the king recognised or appointed.[17] To *konza*, to serve by choice a greater man in return for protection and favour, was the core of rank in this dangerous world, creating a duty that took priority even over duty to the king.[18] 'The way of reckoning whether many have been killed

---

[13] Ibid., vol. 1, pp. 7, 37, 101, 339, and vol. 4, p. 294; Charles Bullock, *The Mashona and the Matabele* (Cape Town, 1950), p. 245; evidence of Sir T. Shepstone in Cape of Good Hope, *Report and proceedings, with appendices, of the Government Commission on Native Laws and Customs* (G.4–83: Cape Town, 1883), part 1, p. 5; J. P. R. Wallis (ed.), *The Matabele journals of Robert Moffat, 1829–1860* (2 vols., London, 1945), vol. 1, pp. 23, 29.

[14] Webb and Wright, *James Stuart Archive*, vol. 1, pp. 30–1; Elizabeth Gunner, 'Forgotten men: Zulu bards and praising at the time of the Zulu kings,' *African Languages*, 2 (1976), 75–82.

[15] Robert Moffat, *Missionary labours and scenes in southern Africa* (London, 1842), p. 541.

[16] C. A. Hamilton and J. Wright, 'The making of the Amalala,' *SAHJ*, 22 (1990), 3–23.

[17] Webb and Wright, *James Stuart Archive*, vol. 4, pp. 357–8.

[18] Gluckman, *Ideas*, p. 53.

of any regiment is by the number of men of importance (*izilomo*) who were killed,' it was remembered.[19]

The chief's role was replicated by the heads of the large, dispersed homesteads in which most Zulu lived. Successful management of a homestead was essential to a mature man's honour. Cattle were exclusively the business of men, cultivation primarily that of unmarried men and especially women. In these societies without slaves, women's labour and fertility had a high value expressed in the cattle transferred to their families at marriage as bridewealth compensation. This gave parents a powerful interest in preserving their daughters' virginity, controlling the choice of their husbands, and preserving their marriages. Zulu and their neighbours attached an importance to female virginity that would have astonished many West Africans, although it did not approach the obsession of Mediterranean societies. Young men and women were permitted, and even encouraged, to practise nonpenetrative sex, but a woman made pregnant before marriage might be beaten and ostracised:

In Zululand there were very few *izirobo*. By *isirobo* was meant a girl who had allowed herself to be deflowered.... There were ... very few girls who ... could not take the necessary precautions guarding against the semen of the men passing into her – for she knew she would of course lose value when the amount of *lobola* [bridewealth] was being fixed.

Izirobo were treated with great contempt. People spat at or towards them to show the disgust they felt for them.[20]

The man responsible was normally fined, or possibly killed if the woman was under the king's direct authority. An account survives of a man killing his wife found having sex with a white man who was probably raping her.[21] Unmarried women defended their reputations against slander either by legal action or by mobbing an offender.[22] Small girls were trained to accept inferiority. Young wives were the most exploited members of the homestead. Men looked for fertility, beauty, diligence, modesty, and respectfulness.[23] What women honoured in one another does not appear from the sources. There is evidence that they resented Shaka's requirement that they should marry only substantially older

---

[19] Evidence of Mpatshana kaSodondo, 1912, in Webb and Wright, *James Stuart Archive*, vol. 3, p. 303.

[20] Evidence of Mkando kaDhlova, 1902, in ibid., vol. 3, p. 147. See also Eileen Jensen Krige, *The social system of the Zulus* (2nd edn, reprinted, Pietermaritzburg, 1950), pp. 105–6, 120–3.

[21] Webb and Wright, *James Stuart Archive*, vol. 1, p. 12, and vol. 4, pp. 294, 353.

[22] W. G. Stafford, *Native law as practised in Natal* (Johannesburg [c.1935]), p. 124; Webb and Wright, *James Stuart Archive*, vol. 4, p. 354.

[23] John Wright, 'Control of women's labour in the Zulu kingdom,' in J. B. Peires (ed.), *Before and after Shaka* (reprinted, Grahamstown, 1983), p. 85; Krige, *Social system*, p. 155; Cope, *Izibongo*, p. 21.

warriors; in 1876 Cetshwayo ordered the death of women who refused such husbands. A procedure did exist, however, for legitimising marriage by elopement. Women also disliked the large households of unmarried girls whom Zulu royals maintained for their own service and for distribution to favourites.[24] Royal women might have important roles in palace politics,[25] but for most ordinary women the creation of the Zulu kingdom probably meant greater subordination.

Zulu notions of honour were expressed most powerfully in the praise-poems chanted to exalt the king and his ancestors at public festivals, before or after battles, at royal funerals, and during rites to invoke the spirits of dead kings. Like Yoruba *oriki*, these poems were not narratives but were composed of praise-names and allusions illuminating the subject's character from many angles. While commoners composed their own praises, the kings' were elaborated by expert singers whose predecessors in southern Africa dated back at least to the early seventeenth-century kingdom of Mwene Mutapa.[26] The praises of a warrior like Komfiya might be merely strings of names and attributes, but the royal praises were refined during the nineteenth century into more poetic sequences.[27] This makes them the more treacherous as historical evidence. A king did not have a single praise-poem memorised (or gradually forgotten) by successive singers. Rather, he was associated with a mass of metaphors and allusions which individual singers reordered and reinterpreted for particular occasions. Praise-poems of rulers recorded at different times were strikingly different. In the Ndebele kingdom, for example, mid-nineteenth-century poems contained elements of criticism, whereas later poems were largely royal propaganda. Praise-poetry was acutely sensitive to power, although each reinterpretation drew on the stock of metaphors and allusions surrounding the king concerned.[28]

This helps to understand the impact of Shaka's reign on Zulu notions of honour. As his image crystallised during the nineteenth century, praise-singers surrounded Shaka's name with ferocious metaphors and allusions, as in the *oriki* of nineteenth-century Yoruba warriors.[29] Many versions began with his best-known praise-name, 'Ferocious one', and ended with the words, 'Finisher

---

[24] Webb and Wright, *James Stuart Archive*, vol. 1, p. 343, and vol. 4, pp. 79, 132–4, 266–7.

[25] James Stuart and D.McK. Malcolm (ed.), *The diary of Henry Francis Fynn* (Pietermaritzburg, 1969), p. 300; Cope, *Izibongo*, p. 170.

[26] S. I. G. Mudenge, *A political history of Munhumutapa, c.1400–1902* (London, 1988), pp. 100–1.

[27] This volume p. 141; Cope, *Izibongo*, pp. 53–9. But see also D. K. Rycroft and A. B. Ngcobo (eds.), *The praises of Dingana* (Durban, 1988), pp. 32–3.

[28] Leroy Vail and Landeg White, *Power and the praise poem: southern African voices in history* (Charlottesville, 1991), pp. 55–64, 71, 89–102, 164–92.

[29] Cope, *Izibongo*, pp. 31–2, 50. But see the scepticism of Mbongeni Zikhethele Malaba, 'Shaka as a literary theme,' PhD thesis, University of York, 1986, p. iii.

off! Black Finisher off!'[30] The qualities generally praised were courage and ferocity. The favoured metaphors were aggressive animals:

> You are a wild animal! A leopard! A lion!
> You are a horned viper! An elephant![31]

The prevailing colour was 'dark as the bile of a goat.'[32] The dominant passion was insatiable appetite:

> He who while devouring some devoured other,
> And as he devoured others he devoured some more.[33]

This violent imagery became the convention for all Shaka's nineteenth-century successors. By contrast, the praise-poems of his eighteenth-century predecessors, when collected at the end of the nineteenth century, said little of warfare. One was praised for his hunting, another for his shrewdness, and a third for his beauty.[34] It may be, as in Yorubaland, that an older, more urbane notion of honour was submerged during the nineteenth century by the simpler heroic form,[35] but this is uncertain, for the praises of Shaka's forebears may rather have been reshaped to emphasise the contrasting character of the post-Shakan monarchy; certainly those published in the mid nineteenth century show the contrast less clearly.[36] If such revision occurred, however, it would suggest that heroic notions of leadership and masculinity had at least become more self-conscious.

West of the Drakensberg, among the Sotho-speaking peoples of the highveld and mountains of modern Lesotho, nineteenth-century praise-poetry also emphasised warfare and ferocious metaphor. The praises of the great King Moshoeshoe (c.1786–1870), as recorded in 1919, stressed his career as a warrior, which ended in 1836, and scarcely mentioned the political skills and peaceful methods by which he amalgamated scattered groups into the nucleus of a nation. His kinsmen and successors, regardless of their military qualities, were portrayed in the same heroic idiom.[37]

---

[30] Cope, *Izibongo*, pp. 86–8.
[31] Malaba, 'Shaka,' p. 60.
[32] Cope, *Izibongo*, p. 96.
[33] Ibid., p. 40.
[34] Ibid., p. 69.
[35] Liz Gunner and Mafika Gwala (eds.), *Musho! Zulu popular praises* (East Lansing, 1991), p. 7.
[36] Vail and White, *Power*, p. 68; Lewis Grout, *A grammar of the Zulu language* (Pietermaritzburg, 1859), pp. 419, 425.
[37] M. Damane and P. B. Sanders (eds.), *Lithoko: Sotho praise poems* (Oxford, 1974), esp. pp. 23, 59; Vail and White, *Power*, pp. 59–64.

One reason for this was that the royal praises, although elaborated by expert poets, originated in the self-praises by which warriors and hunters celebrated their manliness. 'The bravest come out from the ranks, one after another,' a missionary wrote in 1868,

and, as they walk, they chant of their own exploits. . . . If the hero is really a brave man they respond to his account with a chant of approval: if the contrary is the case a terrible din commences. . . . 'You're only a braggart devoid of courage, all the praises which you've just uttered are pure lies alone.' And the hero goes back, somewhat embarrassed, into the ranks.[38]

By contrast, the brief surviving praises of Moshoeshoe's two predecessors – perhaps incomplete and certainly impossible to date – lack martial quality,[39] perhaps because during Moshoeshoe's lifetime the Sotho-speaking people experienced a militarisation comparable to the Zulu's. In response to competition for the resources of the highveld and to raids for slaves and cattle by mounted gunmen from the northern Cape Colony, Moshoeshoe, a minor chief, withdrew in 1824 to a mountain fortress where his protection gradually attracted followers. By the 1850s, he had perhaps eighty thousand subjects. By then his state was threatened even more gravely by the Afrikaners of the Orange Free State, who gradually expelled the Sotho from most of their agricultural land into the mountain kingdom. Consequently, their military system differed profoundly from Shaka's, adopting their enemies' guns and horses rather than the Zulu stabbing-spear. By the 1850s, most men of military age owned a horse and a gun, although they also carried battleaxes and long spears.[40] Unlike West Africa's horsemen, Sotho used missile weapons and their oral literature eulogised not horses but cattle and firearms. At circumcision young men were handed a gun with the words, 'Hold to your arms.'[41] Such weapons did not require tight regimental organisation but a decentralised pattern of mobile bands and an equally decentralised political system. Unlike Shaka, Moshoeshoe did not break down his heterogeneous followers' older loyalties but linked them to the throne as groups through ties of marriage, cattle-clientage, consultation, and mutual advantage.

Consequently, Sotho military honour differed significantly from that of the Zulu. It certainly idealised the hero, *mogale*, a word connoting quickness of temper,[42] and it ridiculed the coward:

[38] Théophile Jousse, quoted in Damane and Sanders, *Lithoko*, pp. 25–6.

[39] Ibid., pp. 63–5.

[40] Elizabeth A. Eldredge, *A South African kingdom: the pursuit of security in nineteenth-century Lesotho* (Cambridge, 1993), chs. 3–5 and pp. 62, 154.

[41] Charles Pacalt Brownlee, *Reminiscences of Kafir life and history and other papers* (2nd edn, reprinted, Pietermaritzburg, 1977), p. 191.

[42] T. J. Kriel, *The new English-Sesotho dictionary* (n.p., 1958), p. 109.

> On that day there was a separation of men,
> Yea, the cowards separated themselves, and were seen;
> And they clawed the mountain-sides,
> They splashed the mountain with their liquid excrement.[43]

Certainly, too, boys were surrounded with warlike imagery from their birth and learned self-sufficiency while herding stock, but, unlike many young Africans, they did not incur dishonour if they flinched at circumcision.[44] Sotho male culture lacked some of the brutality often found elsewhere, as did its vocabulary of honour: *hlonepho* and *tlotlo* connoted not thunder but respect and courtesy.[45] Women, too, were less constrained than Zulu women, governing some of their own affairs, marrying men of more equal age, and enjoying greater sexual freedom.[46]

Sotho culture and poetry also lacked the extreme veneration for the king that characterised Zulu military honour. Moshoeshoe neither claimed nor received reverence; missionaries noted that nobody stood to address him or hesitated to interrupt or contradict him. 'I have warriors, but no servants,' he observed. '... These men ... there is not one of them who would not laugh me to scorn if I sought to compel him to draw water for me, to grind corn, to sweep my huts.'[47] Criticism may have disappeared from Sotho praise-poetry later in the nineteenth century, but it was evident in Moshoeshoe's, especially his suspected abandonment of his younger brother, Makhabane, at a critical moment of battle:

> Keep it from entering my herds ...
> It has come with a dirge, a cause of sadness.
> Thesele [i.e. Moshoeshoe], the other one, where have you left him?[48]

Makhabane had been one of the headstrong warrior-chiefs whom no nineteenth-century Sotho ruler could control. Theirs was not the disciplined courage of the regiment but the individual bravery of cattle-raiding and mountain-fighting.

[43] Daniel P. Kunene, *Heroic poetry of the Basotho* (Oxford, 1971), p. 9.

[44] Ibid., p. 5; Coplan, *Cannibals*, p. 97; Hugh Ashton, *The Basuto: a social study of traditional and modern Lesotho* (2nd edn, London, 1967), p. 49.

[45] A. Mabille, *Se-Suto-English and English-Se-Suto vocabulary* (Moria, 1893), pp. 97, 232; Kriel, *English-Sesotho dictionary*, pp. 178–9, 249.

[46] Stimela Jason Jingoes, *A chief is a chief by the people* (London, 1975), p. 218; Damane and Sanders, *Lithoko*, p. 14; Ashton, *Basuto*, p. 40.

[47] Adrian Hastings, *The Church in Africa 1450–1950* (Oxford, 1994), pp. 311–12; Robert C. Germond (ed.), *Chronicles of Basutoland* (Morija, 1967), p. 516.

[48] Damane and Sanders, *Lithoko*, p. 31.

Praise-poetry continued to celebrate such individual heroism well into the twentieth century.

It would be possible to show how the praise-poetry and honour culture of each nineteenth-century southern African kingdom related to its degree and type of militarisation. The Swazi kingdom, for example, was militarised only gradually and incompletely in resistance to Zulu and Afrikaner aggression; it used firearms in open skirmishing order; and its praise-poems, when recorded in 1929, pictured the kings not as aggressive conquerors but as effective defenders of their subjects, both as military leaders and as guarantors of fertility.[49] The most revealing illustration, however, concerned the Tswana people who occupied the highveld to the north of the Sotho and spoke a related language. Substantial chiefdoms, based on accumulations of cattle, had existed here for many centuries, but those that survived into the colonial period took shape during the seventeenth and especially the eighteenth centuries, before the early nineteenth-century militarisation.[50] This was a society of rank and honour in which ruling minorities gained heterogeneous followers either by force or through the environmental insecurity of a region bordering the Kalahari Desert. An early nineteenth-century praise-poem expressed the rulers' pride of rank:

> I oppose the killing of Kgalagadi,
> paupers with nothing of their own;
> a rich man eats those rich like himself,
> a handsome one eats those handsome as he.[51]

Tswana also shared their neighbours' *machismo*. Their brutal initiation rites trained young people of both sexes in the stoical endurance of pain. 'I never saw a Bechuana man throw aside his mantle without exposing on his back the deep, broad marks of the chastisement which he had received while being introduced to Bechuana manhood,' a missionary reported.[52] Male virility and display and the sexual division of labour were strongly emphasised. Yet this was not an autocratic or violent society like the Zulu or Ndebele. The upper strata of adult male householders cherished their freedom of speech at chiefdom

---

[49] P. A. W. Cook, 'History and izibongo of the Swazi chiefs,' *Bantu Studies*, 5 (1931), 181–201; Vail and White, *Power*, pp. 164–8; Philip Bonner, *Kings, commoners and concessionaries: the evolution and dissolution of the nineteenth-century Swazi state* (Cambridge, 1983), pp. 24–5, 105, 120.

[50] Shula Marks and Richard Gray, 'Southern Africa and Madagascar,' in Richard Gray (ed.), *The Cambridge history of Africa: volume 4* (Cambridge, 1975), p. 412.

[51] Praise-poem of the Kwena regent Tshosa (c.1803–7), in I. Schapera (ed.), *Praise-poems of Tswana chiefs* (Oxford, 1965), p. 126.

[52] John Mackenzie, *Ten years north of the Orange River* (2nd edn, London, 1971), p. 376.

assemblies, and history recorded several over-mighty chiefs who had been expelled, assassinated, or deserted by their subjects. That remained true in the nineteenth century, for although aggressive Ndebele and Afrikaner neighbours forced the Tswana to defend themselves, they were never militarised in the manner of Zulu or Sotho.[53] Nor were their praise-poems. The oldest date from the early eighteenth century. Some are ferocious, others are critical, others again honour the diverse traditional qualities of a chief. But they show no trend over time in this respect, presumably varying with their subjects' personalities.[54]

Tswana evidence highlights another aspect of honour in nineteenth-century southern Africa: its interplay with Christianity. As among Yoruba and Asante, missionary work generally found little response in southern African societies whose notions of heroic honour seemed incompatible with nineteenth-century mission teaching. Despite several attempts to establish mission stations in the Zulu kingdom, only a few marginal people were converted, many of whom moved to the British colony in Natal. Missionaries equally detested the Ndebele state, where, despite an ostensible friendliness motivated by material ambitions, the few enquirers met such hostility from their families and the authorities that it was twenty-two years before the pioneer mission baptised a convert. Even in Lesotho, where the open-minded Moshoeshoe invited missionaries in 1833 and some of his sons were early converts, there was a reaction against Christianity when the missionaries opposed retaliation against a military rival.[55] Yet the Tswana response to Christianity was more complex. Several chiefs initially welcomed missionaries, but mainly to secure firearms, trade, diplomatic protection, and contacts with the Cape Colony. 'Even now few of the old and principal people are of the congregation,' a visitor wrote after nineteen years of evangelisation. '... The principal people who have become the best Christians are of other tribes or the poorest of the tribe.'[56] But Christianity did win support in two directions. A young Ngwato prince, Khama, accepted baptism in 1862, seized the throne, and created a tribal church through which he extended his power in alliance with the second Ngwato group to adopt the new

---

[53] Jean Comaroff and John Comaroff, *Of revelation and revolution* (2 vols., Chicago, 1991–7), vol. 1, p. 150; Schapera, *Praise-poems*, pp. 54, 127, 191–2.

[54] Schapera, *Praise-poems*, passim.

[55] Norman Etherington, *Preachers, peasants and politics in southeast Africa, 1835–1880: African Christian communities in Natal, Pondoland, and Zululand* (London, 1978), pp. 24, 35, 45, 86; Ngwabi Bhebe, *Christianity and traditional religion in western Zimbabwe, 1859–1923* (London, 1979), pp. 62–4; Leonard Thompson, *Survival in two worlds: Moshoeshoe of Lesotho 1786– 1870* (Oxford, 1975), pp. 99–104, 148–51.

[56] Anthony Joseph Dachs, 'Missionary imperialism in Bechuanaland, 1813–1896,' PhD thesis, University of Cambridge, 1968, pp. 53–68; Percival R. Kirby (ed.), *The diary of Dr Andrew Smith, 1834–1836* (2 vols., Cape Town, 1939–40), vol. 1, p. 269 (entry for 18 February 1835).

religion: the women, who shared his desire to break the domination of male patriarchs. Whereas men of all ages were deterred from Christianity by its hostility to heroic values and polygyny, the subordination of Tswana women, who did most agricultural labour but had access to land only through men, attracted many to the mission.[57] By 1855, despite male persecution, 'the female portion greatly preponderates in numbers at school, and invariably in progress leave the boys in the rear. The same thing may also be said of all the adults.' Seventy years later two-thirds of all Ngwato churchgoers were women.[58] That was the pattern throughout nineteenth-century southern Africa: positive response to missionary work came predominantly from women, owing to their subordination and the missionaries' inability to accommodate their teaching to heroic male honour.[59]

This gendered response to Christianity was especially clear among the southern Nguni-speaking groups nearest to the Cape Colony, the Xhosa and closely related Thembu and Mpondo. Like the Zulu they lived mainly from agriculture but attached great value to cattle, with a sharp sexual division of labour between the two activities. They too practised a dispersed and patriarchal residential pattern in which manhood was achieved 'by presiding justly, wisely and generously over a rural homestead.'[60] Although women were respected for their labour and fertility, they were, as Nelson Mandela later wrote, 'second-class citizens'. They were expected to practise nonpenetrative sex before marriage but were abused and punished if they became pregnant, when the man owed compensation to the parents. Marriage, following initiation, was by bridewealth in cattle. Women were consequently unevenly distributed; among the western Xhosa in 1848, 20 per cent of household (not homestead) heads were polygynous, 47 per cent monogamous, and 32 per cent unmarried. Poor women might work for wealthy families in return for food. Newly married brides probably suffered

---

[57] Paul Stuart Landau, *The realm of the word: language, gender, and Christianity in a Southern African Kingdom* (Portsmouth, N.H., 1995), p. xvii; Margaret Kinsman, '"Beasts of burden": the subordination of southern Tswana women, ca.1800–1840,' *JSAS*, 10 (1983–4), 39–54.

[58] Moffat to Tidman, 14 November 1855, CWM incoming letters, box 29 (3/A/17); Landau, *Realm*, p. 82.

[59] Norman Etherington, 'Gender issues in south-east African missions, 1835–85,' in Henry Bredekamp and Robert Ross (ed.), *Missions and Christianity in South African history* (Johannesburg, 1995), p. 147; Heidi Gangenbach, '"What my heart wanted": gendered stories of early colonial encounters in southern Mozambique,' in Allman and others, *Women*, pp. 19–27.

[60] Henry Lichtenstein, *Travels in Southern Africa in the years 1803, 1804, 1805 and 1806* (trans. A. Plumtre, reprinted, 2 vols., Cape Town, 1928), vol. 1, p. 328; Dunbar Moodie, 'Social existence and the practice of personal integrity,' in Andrew D. Spiegel and Patrick A. McAllister (eds.), *Tradition and transition in southern Africa* (New Brunswick, N.J. [1991]), p. 40.

much exploitation.[61] 'Even in the way that I walked, I showed deference,' a later woman recalled. 'I went about that homestead very carefully, taking the long way around, being very submissive to my in-laws. . . . I followed the custom of the young wife – walking behind, keeping to the rear, taking care not to be too forward.'[62] If a wife committed adultery, she was more likely to be beaten than divorced; her lover owed compensation but suffered no disgrace or further punishment unless the offended husband was his father or a chief.[63] It is not surprising, therefore, that many early Xhosa Christians were women escaping marital dilemmas. A number were widows, for whom a pioneer missionary erected 'three rows of small cottages' at his station. Others were younger women victimised by the loss of cattle to white colonists, for this prevented young men from marrying, exposed young women to sexual violence or adventure, and increased the number of women obliged to become junior wives in polygynous households. The missionaries, by contrast, advocated monogamous marriage, without initiation rites or bridewealth, between partners more equal in age. By the 1840s the number of women seeking refuge at the missions alarmed senior men.[64]

Male hostility to Christianity was fostered by its apparent incompatibility with the heroic ethos that Xhosa shared with Zulu. Xhosa were not organised into a single kingdom but preserved an older Nguni political pattern, with a large ruling house each of whose senior male members headed a chiefdom, the whole being loosely bound together by genealogical relationships among the rulers. A Xhosa chief 'governs only as long as they choose to obey,' wrote an early nineteenth-century traveller, for dissidents could easily transfer allegiance. Yet rank enjoyed great respect, which the chiefs jealously defended by exploiting privileged access to cattle and women, outlawing any personal violence against

---

[61] Nelson Mandela, *Long walk to freedom: the autobiography of Nelson Mandela* (London, 1994), p. 20; Natasha Erlank, 'Gendered reactions to social dislocation and missionary activity in Xhosaland 1836–1847,' *African Studies*, 59 (2000), 208–9; Jack Lewis, 'The rise and fall of the South African peasantry,' *JSAS*, 11 (1984–5), 5; Ludwig Alberti, *Ludwig Alberti's account of the tribal life and customs of the Xhosa in 1807* (trans. W. Fehr, Cape Town, 1968), p. 74; Monica Hunter, *Reaction to conquest: effects of contact with Europeans on the Pondo of South Africa* (2nd edn, London, 1961), pp. 35–6.

[62] Harold Scheub, 'And so I grew up: the autobiography of Nongenile Masthathu Zenani,' in Patricia W. Romero (ed.), *Life histories of African women* (London, 1988), p. 41.

[63] 'Mr Warner's notes,' in [John] Maclean, *A compendium of Kafir laws and customs* (Mount Coke, 1858), p. 70; Erlank, 'Gendered reactions,' p. 210.

[64] J. B. Peires, *The house of Phalo: a history of the Xhosa people in the days of their independence* (Berkeley, 1982), p. 77; Andrew Steedman, *Wanderings and adventures in the interior of southern Africa* (2 vols., London, 1835), vol 1, p. 34; Erlank, 'Gendered reactions,' pp. 211–23.

them even in warfare, and observing an aristocratic demeanour.[65] Similarly, although Xhosa did not experience militarisation on Zulu lines, instead gradually adding firearms and some horses to their spears, they nevertheless put great emphasis on physical prowess and military courage. Eighteenth-century warfare between Xhosa groups had much the character of a tournament fought at an agreed time in an open plain by two sides throwing spears from a distance of twenty or thirty metres. They might close and fight hand-to-hand, but more often one side retreated and the other sought to capture its cattle, women, and children. It then demanded recognition of superiority before returning the women and children – who were never harmed – and some of the cattle. Young men were trained for combat from early youth, when they competed in stick-fighting groups, undertook training at the chief's kraal, experienced a painful initiation into manhood, and then formed the front line of the chief's forces until marriage left them liable for service only in war.[66] In normal times, however, Xhosa country was neither especially violent nor anarchic. European sailors shipwrecked there in 1689 reported that '[r]evenge has little or no sway among them, as they are obliged to submit their disputes to the king,' who took any resulting fine – graduated according to the rank of the injured person – on the principle that 'no man can eat his own blood.'[67]

Honour was of central importance to Xhosa men. Some took a medicine alleged to guarantee fame. Warriors received names of honour and composed their own praises. Expert poets chronicled events affecting a chiefdom and delineated the characters of individual chiefs, but there is no historical study to show whether their poetry's tone changed during the nineteenth century. Perhaps, like Tswana poetry, it expressed rather the society's enduring norms, as did the women's folktales known as *ntsomi*, whose heroes were not merely men of valour but personifications of social values.[68] Xhosa men of rank, in particular, cultivated the arts of peace as well as war. 'The graceful air and gentlemanlike manner in which they thank you is really astonishing,' wrote a European officer. 'No French marquis of the *ancien régime* could exceed their bow and expression of countenance.'[69] Another officer offended one senior

[65] Peires, *House of Phalo*, pp. 19–22, 27–32, 40, 92–3; Jeff Opland, *Xhosa oral poetry: aspects of a black South African tradition* (Cambridge, 1983), p. 123.

[66] Alberti, *Xhosa*, pp. 39–41, 90–2; John Henderson Soga, *The Ama-Xosa: life and customs* (Lovedale [c.1932]), pp. 312–13; Peires, *House of Phalo*, ch. 9.

[67] Noel Mostert, *Frontiers: the epic of South Africa's creation and the tragedy of the Xhosa people* (London, 1992), p. 151; 'Rev H. H. Dugmore's papers,' in Maclean, *Compendium*, p. 35.

[68] Albert Kropf, *A Kaffir-English dictionary* (Lovedale, 1899), p. 86; Opland, *Poetry*, pp. 4, 32, 36, 51; Harold Scheub, *The Xhosa ntsomi* (Oxford, 1975), p. 86.

[69] Sir Harry Smith, quoted in Mostert, *Frontiers*, pp. 721–2.

chief by offering to be the first to fulfil his side of an agreement. He insulted another by implying that he was harbouring a stolen horse:

He then extended his hand to me and declared: that he was no robber, that he had exchanged that horse with a Hottentot, who had represented to him that it was his property, apart from which, had I, as his equal, discussed the matter with him, he would very willingly have accepted that there was no question of suspicion; but he did not want, as he expressed it, to be messed on by dogs, by which he meant those Colonists.[70]

These principles were tested and to some degree changed during the century of warfare from 1779 to 1878 in which Xhosa resisted with ever greater bitterness the seizure of their land and destruction of their society by the Europeans of the Cape Colony. In the initial encounters, Xhosa displayed 'unbelievable fearlessness' and observed their customary chivalry. In 1819 they gave the British advanced warning of a frontal assault on Grahamstown. 'Our fathers were *men*,' their spokesmen declared after its failure; 'they loved their cattle; their wives and children lived upon milk; they fought for their property.... Make peace with us.'[71] But as the succeeding wars grew longer and more brutal, Xhosa replaced spears by firearms, abandoned open battlefields for guerilla tactics and, like their adversaries, often tortured captives to death instead of exchanging them.[72] Two leaders of this resistance stood out. One was Maqoma, 'a gallant, bold fellow,' as a British officer described him, famed for both his courage and his drinking, who was the dominant war-leader of the western Xhosa in the front line of resistance. After mounting eighteen months of guerilla resistance in the Amatola Mountains during 1850–2, he spent most of his last sixteen years as a defiant prisoner on Robben Island, dying 'of old age and dejection, at being here alone.'[73] By then leadership had passed to Sarhili, the last great chief of the eastern Xhosa, 'in every sense a noble man,' as a British commander observed, a conservative who personified the traditional values of Xhosa chieftainship and was venerated by his people for his humanity and dignity. He avoided conflict with the Cape Colony until 1850, when his people were drawn into Maqoma's guerilla war, but Sarhili managed to negotiate peace terms that left him essentially independent. Seven years later, his attachment to Xhosa beliefs led him to support a prophet who urged the people to abandon cultivation and slaughter their cattle in readiness for the return of Xhosa ancestors to renew the world

---

[70] Alberti, *Xhosa*, pp. 72–3, 117.

[71] Ibid., p. 48; Ben Maclennan, *A proper degree of terror: John Graham and the Cape's eastern frontier* (Johannesburg, 1986), p. 190; Thomas Pringle, *Narrative of a residence in South Africa* (London, 1835), pp. 304–5.

[72] Peires, *House of Phalo*, ch. 9; Mostert, *Frontiers*, p. 900.

[73] Mostert, *Frontiers*, p. 613; Timothy J. Stapleton, *Maqoma: Xhosa resistance to colonial advance 1798–1873* (Johannesburg, 1994), pp. 153–66, 207.

and drive the whites into the sea. When the promise proved false, Sarhili tried to kill himself, declaring that 'He is no more a Chief, or even a man.'[74] Yet he preserved his chiefdom until 1878, when he was at last compelled to turn and fight. Abandoning guerilla tactics for frontal attack, Sarhili's people were slaughtered by artillery and the chief himself took to the bush. With £1,000 on his head, he spent his last fifteen years 'like a baboon in a hole,' as he put it, in a refuge 'accessible only by clambering in single file across a series of ridges bounded by abrupt precipices hundreds of metres deep.' He died there in 1893, still, in a sense, a free man.[75]

Maqoma personified the Xhosa notion of honour as *indumo*, connoting fame and renown. Sarhili, perhaps, personified honour as *imbeko*, connoting respect and decency.[76] The two notions were not incompatible, but they expressed the distinction between hero and householder. Householder honour left few traces in Africa's military and political records, but among the Xhosa and their neighbours it can for once be studied from the legal records commonly used as sources for the history of honour, especially by examining the grounds on which plaintiffs sought to defend their reputations through suits for slander or defamation. As the Cape Colony gradually conquered and administered Xhosa country during the second half of the nineteenth century, it established divisional magistrates' courts, conducted by white officials, to which Africans could bring civil cases of defamation. Between 1850, when the first case was recorded, and 1901, after which most case records have been destroyed, the records of twenty divisions contain 236 actions in which the nature of the alleged defamation can be identified.[77]

That Xhosa should have submitted their disputes to colonial courts so soon after conquest illustrated their preference for legal action over vengeance or feud. It also demonstrated the sensitivity to defamation that their honour culture shared with the Akan peoples of the Gold Coast, the Dinka and their neighbours in the southern Sudan, and probably other African peoples for whom research

---

[74] Mostert, *Frontiers*, pp. 1184, 1254; J. B. Peires, *The dead will arise: Nongqawuse and the great Xhosa cattle-killing movement of 1856–7* (Johannesburg, 1989), pp. 81–7, 148–59; *Wesleyan Missionary Notices*, 1859, p. 54.

[75] Soga, *Ama-Xosa*, pp. 118–23; Leo Switzer, *Power and resistance in an African society: the Ciskei Xhosa and the making of South Africa* (Madison, 1993), p. 74; Peires, *The dead*, p. 334.

[76] Kropf, *Kaffir-English dictionary*, pp. 27–8, 85–6.

[77] The divisions studied were Alice, Butterworth, Engcobo, Fort Beaufort, Herschel (Sterkspruit), Idutywa, Keiskamahoek, Kentani, Kingwilliamstown, Komgha, Mount Ayliff, Mount Frere, Nqamakwe, Peddie, Queenstown, Qumbu, Somerset East, Tsolo, Tsomo, and Umtata. They were chosen as those most likely to have entertained cases between Africans.

has not yet been undertaken.[78] Whether Xhosa and their neighbours regarded slander as a civil offence was, however, much disputed among the Cape Colony's officials. Until the mid 1870s their courts, operating only west of the Great Kei River, applied British law and accepted defamation actions brought by Africans. When courts were established east of the Kei during the later 1870s, however, legislation provided that civil suits between Africans who had not adopted Christianity and European culture might be heard under African law.[79] After a period of confusion, magistrates questioned whether Xhosa law recognised a civil offence of slander. There was a Xhosa word for it (*intlebo*) and the earliest compendium of Xhosa law had affirmed in 1856 that 'originators and spreaders of a public libel or scandal, render themselves liable to an action at law, and damages may be recovered,'[80] but by 1894 the white magistrates of the Native Appeal Court for Tembuland, Transkei, and Pondoland had ruled that 'under native law no action for damages for slander lies,'[81] because 'it is regarded purely as a Criminal Offence and any penalty awarded would be claimed by the Chief.'[82] When queried, the chief commissioner conceded only that this ruling should not apply to '[n]atives who have adopted Christianity and made advancement in civilization.'[83] African leaders disputed the ruling and the Native Appeal Court for Griqualand East rejected it, as did the Natal Native Code and the Laws of Lerotholi that governed Lesotho. Despite prolonged African pressure, however, it remained a principle of the Eastern Cape's official 'customary law' for the next hundred years that Africans had no civil action for defamation.[84]

Nevertheless, 236 identifiable actions reached twenty divisional courts between 1850 and 1901. Of these, 179 were brought by men and 57 by women (or by men acting on behalf of women). Table 1 shows the insults of which plaintiffs complained. Two points stand out. One is that not a single person complained of offence against the two main components of heroic honour: physical courage

---

[78] This volume, pp. 88–9; Deng, *Tradition*, pp. 217, 224–5.

[79] Cape of Good Hope, *Report on Native Laws*, p. 18.

[80] Kropf, *Kaffir-English dictionary*, p. 393; 'Mr Brownlee's notes,' in Maclean, *Compendium*, p. 120.

[81] Quoted in judgment, *J. Ntobongwana vs. J. Darama*, 8 June 1894, Qumbu civil case 166 of 1894, CA 1/QBU 2/1/1/17.

[82] Judgment, *Mzondo vs. Tati*, Butterworth civil appeal case 40 of 1896, CA 1/BUT Add. 1/1/2/1.

[83] Elliot, memorandum [1 March 1897?] Nqamakwe civil case 253 of 1896, CA 1/NKE 2/1/1/26.

[84] Statement of Ntantiso Nofolyo, Nqamakwe civil case 54 of 1896, CA 1/NKE 2/1/1/23; judgment of Griqualand East Native Appeal Court, *Charles Ntuli vs. Levi Somngesi*, 24 April 1899, in Tsolo civil case 157 of 1898, CA 1/TSO 2/1/21; Stafford, *Native law*, pp. 122, 124; Patrick Duncan, *Sotho laws and customs* (Cape Town, 1960), p. 142; R. B. Mqeke, 'The customary law of defamation of character with special reference to the law of Xhosa-speaking peoples of Transkei and Ciskei,' *Tydskrif vir Ledendaagse Romeins-Hollandse Reg*, 44 (1981), 425–8.

TABLE I. *Insults Provoking Actions for Slander or Defamation by Africans in Twenty Eastern Cape Divisions, 1850–1901*

Type of Insult	Actions by Men	Actions by Women	All Actions
Stock theft	61	0	61
Other theft	28	8	36
Theft (unspecified)	11	1	12
Sexual immorality	23	31	54
Witchcraft and sorcery	28	11	39
Other	28	6	34
Total	179	57	236

Note: Other includes five cases of dual classification.

Source: Civil case records for twenty divisions listed in note 77 for this chapter.

and male virility. The other is that at least 85 per cent of complaints concerned three accusations threatening householder honour: theft, witchcraft, and sexual immorality.

The most common cause of action, in 61 cases, was for men – and only men – to contest accusations of stock theft, long the most widespread offence in Xhosa society.[85] 'You are a thief, you stole my goat' was the charge against which men most often complained.[86] Many cases arose because Xhosa law assumed accused persons to be guilty until they proved innocence.[87] This was compounded by the Spoor Law imposed on the western Xhosa in 1817 in order to recover cattle stolen from white settlers. It empowered those following the trail of stolen stock to enter and search any homestead to which the trail appeared to lead, thus violating the sanctity of herd and homestead fundamental to householder honour.[88] 'It was as much as he could do to restrain both his people and himself from firing,' one headman declared, '... for ... it was an insult to a "man" to have his cattle interfered with by another man.'[89] In a typical case, the defendants had entered the plaintiff's homestead, found him eating a goat, insisted on searching, and declared him a thief unless he could produce the goat's head and skin. The magistrate dismissed his case without calling the defence evidence, finding that the defendants had acted reasonably.[90] Such actions left much

[85] 'Mr Warner's notes,' in Maclean, *Compendium*, p. 65.

[86] For example, Peddie civil case 86 of 1885, CA 1/PDE 2/1/1/22.

[87] 'Rev H. H. Dugmore's papers,' in Maclean, *Compendium*, p. 37.

[88] Hercules Tennant and Edgar Michael Jackson (eds.), *Statutes of the Cape of Good Hope, 1652–1895: volume 2* (Cape Town, 1895), pp. 2393–4; Mostert, *Frontiers*, p. 450.

[89] Quoted in Cape of Good Hope, *Blue-book on native affairs, 1880* (G.13–80: Cape Town, 1880), p. 82.

[90] Tsomo civil case 140 of 1885, CA 1/TSM 2/1/1/5.

offended honour. 'I did not steal his sheep,' one plaintiff protested. 'I never stole in my life and have never been accused of theft before.... My feelings have been injured, very much hurt by this accusation.'[91] Allegations of stock theft had serious social consequences. 'I am afraid to associate with the people on account of this charge,' one plaintiff explained. '... I am not hated but have suffered damages in my heart and people have made remarks about this case.'[92] Some plaintiffs also had material reasons to defend their reputations, as often in matters of honour. 'He blackened my name in order to do me harm,' one protested. '... Europeans will not trust me with their stock now.'[93]

Material considerations also bulked large in actions arising from the thirty-six accusations of theft of articles other than stock and the twelve cases where the articles were not specified. Nine of these actions were by or on behalf of women, especially women who had entered the colonial economy. 'This is the first time since I left school that I have gone into service,' a young housemaid explained when accused of stealing a blanket, 'and I feel hurt at my honour being tarnished.... I positively swear that Mrs Jackson turned me away from her service in consequence of this suspicion.'[94] Men made similar complaints: 'I have lost my good name in consequence of this charge. I might have got a situation in the police – and now my character is gone.'[95] A reputation for honesty was equally important within the African community. 'Before this accusation I had many friends at Trinity Mission now I have none as they do not want to associate with a thief, because Petros said I was a thief,' a plaintiff stated. A witness confirmed it: 'He does not associate with others and appears to be afraid. The people believe him to be a thief and I also believe it, as it has not been proved to the contrary.'[96]

Much as Xhosa execrated theft, they reserved their most terrible punishments for those suspected of witchcraft.[97] Some twenty-eight men and eleven women, both Christian and non-Christian, claimed defamation by accusations of witchcraft. Both men and women sued close neighbours, while women were more likely than men to bring actions against kinsfolk or agnates. Six men and four women had been accused of causing death by witchcraft. 'To be called a witch is the blackest epithet that can be addressed to a native,' an elderly widow

---

[91] Evidence of Lusizi, Mount Frere civil case 12 of 1896, CA 1/MFE 2/1/1/17.

[92] Evidence of Cuku, Tsomo civil case 13 of 1891, CA 1/TSM 2/1/1/11.

[93] Evidence of Langeni, Mount Frere civil case 32 of 1883, CA 1/MFE 2/1/1/2.

[94] Evidence of Lizzy Koyana, Alice civil case 19 of 1895, CA 1/ALC 2/1/1/28.

[95] Evidence of Botchane, Alice civil case 21 of 1881, CA 1/ALC 2/1/1/16.

[96] Evidence of Siko Malungaza and William Mhlaba, Fort Beaufort civil case 23 of 1901, CA 1/FBF 2/1/1/62.

[97] Alberti, *Xhosa*, pp. 49–51.

told the court. '. . . I have suffered in my heart through the imputation. I can't fix any material value.' Her son supported her, explaining, 'We come of the Headman's family. And in our position the words are very slanderous as all the people look on us as the children [of a] witch, and if true we would have to leave the district.'[98] Where an alleged witch was accused of a lesser crime than homicide, it might be bewitching crops (if a woman) or cattle (if a man).[99] The most common charge against men, however, was bewitching women, often, it appears, to seduce them. One defendant described behaviour exactly conforming to indigenous notions of love-magic (*ukuposela*): 'as soon as my sister saw him she cried out here is the man who has bewitched me. . . . She caught hold of him and held him, and said it is Major who made me like this.'[100]

Accusations of sexual immorality were the third grounds of action for slander, pursued by thirty-one women and twenty-three men. Both Christian and non-Christian women sued on this score, whereas all male plaintiffs appear to have been Christians or at least committed to colonial society, reinforcing the point that in indigenous Xhosa culture promiscuity did not damage a man's reputation, provided that he compensated a wronged husband or father, but was dishonourable in a woman, especially if it led to pregnancy.[101] Cases brought by Christians are considered later.[102] Those brought by apparently non-Christian women show how vital were their reputations and how brutal the attacks upon them. Nomampingi of Engcobo division, subjected to vulgar sexual abuse, declared indignantly, 'I am still a virgin. He said all this out of spite because he made love to me and I refused him.'[103] When Makakoli of Peddie division separated two girls quarrelling at a dance, the mother of one 'slapped me on the face and said you are an old girl who has had many children and buried them in ant-heaps. . . . Such words of course injure a young girl.' Her father shared her concern: 'My daughter is about sixteen years of age and is marriageable and of course I expect a dowry for her. If such words are used towards a young girl they spoil her chance of getting married well.'[104] Makakoli received damages, for magistrates sympathised with young rural women whose reputations

---

[98] Evidence of Mancubungashe and Mpesi, Sterkspruit (Herschel) civil case 35 of 1889, CA 1/SPT 2/1/1/7.

[99] Idutywa civil case 15 of 1883, CA 1/IDW 2/2/1/1/2; Peddie civil case 22 of 1891, CA 1/PDE 2/2/5.

[100] Evidence of Maclean, Nqamakwe civil case 96 of 1888, CA 1/NKE 2/1/1/5. For *ukuposela*, see H. W. Warner (ed.), *A digest of South African native civil case law 1894–1957* (Cape Town, 1961), p. 199.

[101] This volume, pp. 151–2.

[102] This volume, p. 257.

[103] Engcobo civil case 76 of 1901, CA 1/ECO 2/1/1/57.

[104] Evidence of Makakoli and Sazzotihanya [?] Peddie civil case 177 of 1883, CA 1/PDE 2/1/1/18.

had been impugned. One successfully sued a neighbour for saying, 'How is it that Georgina looks so handsome, is she still whole, come let us examine her,' and later adding, 'She is no longer a maiden, she is like me and I have born eight children.'[105] Another young woman won damages from those who had falsely said, 'You are light coloured even to the feet . . . and that means you are pregnant.'[106]

Accusations of theft, witchcraft, and female promiscuity appear as the chief slurs on the reputation of the Xhosa homestead. They marked out an indigenous notion of respectability complementing military heroism and pride of rank. This was probably the norm in sub-Saharan Africa. Here it can for once be demonstrated.

[105] Summons in Idutywa civil case 21 of 1897, CA 1/IDW 2/1/1/23.
[106] Plaint in Tsomo civil case 129 of 1893, CA 1/TSM 2/2/4.

10   *Ekitiibwa* and Martyrdom

This final chapter on notions of honour in precolonial Africa examines the Bantu-speaking kingdoms of the Great Lakes region of East Africa. It considers first the highly stratified kingdoms of Bunyoro, Nkore, Buhaya, Rwanda, and Burundi whose ruling minorities prided themselves on pastoral traditions, demanded honour in its vertical dimension from subordinate agriculturalists, competed among themselves for horizontal honour by their prowess in warfare and aristocratic culture, and enabled royal women to occupy important roles within the state. The second part of the chapter, by contrast, concentrates on the later nineteenth-century Buganda kingdom, where missionary and literate African sources describe unique circumstances in which a culture of honour (*ekitiibwa*) fused with Christian teaching.

The relatively well-watered region west of Lake Victoria was settled in the first millennium B.C. by Bantu-speaking agriculturalists who created small, largely ritual chiefdoms with related languages, a common culture, and a religious system venerating a heroic pantheon of gods.[1] By the second millennium A.D. specialised pastoralists also emerged. During the seventeenth and eighteenth centuries, an immigrant clan, the Bito, created a larger kingdom named Bunyoro in the north of the region. This started a chain-reaction of pastoral migration and defensive state-formation further south.[2] In the rich grasslands of Nkore, Hima pastoralists established a loose and predatory relationship with Iru cultivators. The smaller kingdoms of Buhaya on the western shore of

---

[1] David Lee Schoenbrun, *A green place, a good place: agrarian change, gender, and social identity in the Great Lakes region to the 15th century* (Portsmouth, N.H., 1998), chs. 2 and 5.
[2] Jan Vansina, *Le Rwanda ancien: le royaume nyiginya* (Paris, 2001), pp. 63–4.

Lake Victoria were more tightly integrated. Further west, powerful kingdoms took shape during the seventeenth and eighteenth centuries in Rwanda and Burundi, where cattle-ownership, military power, and state office became near-monopolies of a ruling stratum who by the late nineteenth century knew themselves as Tutsi and categorised the subordinated agricultural majority as Hutu or rustics.[3]

In all these states, honour was due firstly to the king, 'He who exceeds all men, and who relieves distress,' as the ruler of Bunyoro was entitled.[4] Royal ideology culminated in Rwanda's dynastic poetry, which celebrated kingship with an elegance and hyperbole unsurpassed in Africa:

> Royalty is the privilege of a single line,
> O Race of God! . . .
> The God who multiplied cattle
> Began by creating kings;
> Having invested them under the sign of the drums,
> He poured blessings on them.

Such rulers were more than human:

> The King is not a man . . .
> He is a man before his selection for the throne,
> But once nominated, he is separated from the ordinary nobility
> And acquires a place apart . . .
> The King is neither a common nobleman,
> Nor can he be a simple prince of the blood;
> He is the exalted and he dominates human beings.[5]

The latter poem, however, addressed King Mibambwe Sentabyo (died c.1801), whose brief reign was marked by civil war and extreme royal weakness against the aristocratic lineages that dominated nineteenth-century Rwanda.[6] Dynastic poetry was propaganda.

The nobility sought to appropriate honour to themselves. Burundi's earliest dictionary gave two words for it. One, *insoni*, also meaning shame, signified honour in the sense of decency and probity, but the other, *ubukuru*, meant honour in the sense of glory and was cognate with *abakuru*, meaning men of

---

[3] Martin R. Doornbos, 'Images and reality of stratification in pre-colonial Nkore,' *Canadian Journal of African Studies*, 7 (1973), 477–95; Roland Oliver, 'The East African interior,' in his *Cambridge history of Africa: volume 3* (Cambridge, 1977), p. 640; Vansina, *Le Rwanda*, ch. 5; idem, *La legende du passé: traditions orales du Burundi* (Tervuren, 1972), pp. 193–203.

[4] John Beattie, *The Nyoro state* (Oxford, 1971), p. 108.

[5] Alexis Kagame, *La poésie dynastique au Rwanda* (Brussels, 1951), pp. 78–9, 53–6.

[6] Vansina, *Le Rwanda*, p. 180.

nobility or power.[7] Rwandans learned the arts of nobility in an *itorero*, a cadet corps maintained by a major chief or royal, where Tutsi youths – the few Hutu entrants were segregated – were trained in military skills, athletics, dancing, music, poetry, genealogy, speech, etiquette, obedience, and command. As in other honour cultures, they learned the importance of appearances, the need to conceal feelings behind the stylised inscrutability essential to survival at a dangerous court.[8] Like their counterparts in Burundi, they admired *ubwenge*, intelligence employed in pursuit of personal advantage: 'The art of astutely disguising one's thought with consummate deception, of not seeing, not understanding, not reacting, is the sign of distinction. . . . To survive, all means are good. To avenge oneself, also. And equally, to enjoy security.'[9]

Aristocrats practised a heroic ethos. As part of their cadet training, the Hima pastoralists of Nkore learned to compose their own praises, declaimed spear in hand to celebrate their prowess in cattle-raiding:

> I Who Am Praised thus held out in battle among foreigners along with
>   The Overthrower;
> I Who Ravish Spear In Each Hand stood out resplendent in my cotton cloth.[10]

In Burundi, too, much oral poetry celebrated cattle-lifting:

> Who is the chief of the [cattle-] thiefs?
> It is He-who-shakes-the-house-in-passing, my dear,
> But who gets his fun from the cattle.
> I would rather let myself be impaled, my dear,
> I would rather let myself be impaled
> Than give up carving the cattle.[11]

Burundi's bards sang ballads to the *enanga* trough-zither, while in Buhaya they performed an epic poetry whose subjects ranged from the gods and rulers of the heroic pantheon to the royal ancestors and the warrior heroes of their own times. They told, for example, of the warrior Kilenzi who set out to discover the meaning of a dream of marriage and death. He found and married the woman of his dream, Nyakandalo, but was then summoned by his king to suppress a popular rebellion. Despite fearsome portents and Nyakandalo's pleas, Kilenzi obeyed the code of heroic honour, but after slaying nine hundred rebels,

---

[7] F. Ménard, *Dictionnaire Français-Kirundi et Kirundi-Français* (2 parts, Roulers, 1909), part 1, p. 122, and part 2, pp. 149–50, 238.

[8] Helen Codere, *The biography of an African society: Rwanda 1900–1960: based on forty-eight Rwandan autobiographies* (Tervuren, 1973), pp. 21–3, 53–6, 75.

[9] F. M. Rodegem (ed.), *Anthologie rundi* ([Paris], 1973), pp. 17–20.

[10] H. F. Morris, *The heroic recitations of the Bahima of Ankole* (Oxford, 1964), p. 42.

[11] Rodegem, *Anthologie*, pp. 107–9.

he – like heroes of the West African savanna – fell victim to the treacherous arrow of a mere peasant:

> A little diminutive fellow
> It was Lulyandibwa himself
> He was caked with dirt about the buttocks
> You know, it emitted such a stench.

Nyakandalo avenged her husband. By travelling the country, attracting suitors, and requiring them to recite their praise-poems, she identified Lulyandibwa, married him, drugged him and his kinsmen at the wedding, slaughtered all 2,070 of them, and carried their testicles home.[12]

The heroic ethos found most elaborate expression in Rwanda, where King Cyirima Rujugira created a uniquely elaborate military system during the later eighteenth century. Every man of whatever rank belonged to an army that had not only military but social and administrative functions, with its own cattle herds scattered throughout the kingdom. Membership was hereditary, but kings and great noblemen also created new regiments and drafted men to them. Members were differentiated between an elite of warriors, who received special military training and gradually became the Tutsi stratum, and their retainers, who provided and carried supplies, foraged for food, herded captured cattle, formed irregular bands known as 'the undisciplined', and became identified as Hutu.[13] Nkore, Burundi, and other kingdoms trained similar warrior elites, some of whom took service throughout the region as 'a single privileged and international class' of *condottiere*.[14] Battles usually developed into individual combat in which warriors competed to capture testicles to demonstrate valour:

Nkore gives the signal for war. The invasion is reported to the frontier camp.... Our hero stands forth before the enemy and drives him back. He slaughters a large number of warriors, who are mutilated.... Rwandans not inured to war, young recruits little skilled in the use of arms, remain in the camp, where the fearful join them. Thus the battle is won by a handful of elite warriors.[15]

The victorious army paraded before the king, vaunted their deeds, and received their rewards in cattle and fame. A Rwandan warrior with seven kills earned an

---

[12] M. Mulokozi, 'The nanga bards of Tanzania: are they epic artists?' *RAL*, 14 (1983), 283–311.

[13] Vansina, *Le Rwanda*, pp. 98–106, 173; Alexis Kagame, *Le code des institutions politiques du Rwanda précolonial* (Brussels, 1952), pp. 61–2.

[14] Samwiri Rubaraza Karugire, *A history of the kingdom of Nkore in western Uganda to 1896* (Oxford, 1971), pp. 162–4; Roger Botte, 'La guerre interne au Burundi,' in Jean Bazin and Emmanuel Terray (eds.), *Guerres de lignages et guerres d'Etats en Afrique* (Paris, 1982), pp. 280–1; Vansina, *Le Rwanda*, p. 116.

[15] Alexis Kagame, 'La poésie guerrière,' *Présence Africaine*, 11 (1956), 119–20.

iron necklace adorned with bells. Seven more entitled him to a bracelet of iron and brass. With another seven he was made a national hero at the ceremony of burning the javelin, performed on the highest mountain in his region.[16] Bunyoro, similarly, had a special rank of crown-wearers honoured for conspicuous public service such as a major military victory.[17]

Rwanda's armies fought mainly with spears and bows, finding relatively little value in the first old muskets they obtained late in the nineteenth century. Nkore's warriors are said to have despised firearms as 'weapons of the cowards'. The only kingdom to adopt muskets extensively before colonial rule was Bunyoro, where King Kabalega (1869–99) bought guns from Sudanese traders and created a professional army, eventually some three thousand strong, known as *Abarasura* (Ravagers). With these he strengthened royal authority, reconquered dissident provinces, and restored something of Bunyoro's regional status lost in earlier reigns. *Abarasura* were mercenaries, often not Nyoro, rather than the nobility in arms. Like the slave-soldiers of Segu or Ibadan, they practised a new style of military honour, although in East Africa this developed fully only under colonial rule.[18]

These were violent societies. By the nineteenth century, the small Haya states had partially suppressed blood feud, but private vengeance remained a possibility in Bunyoro and an obligation in Burundi and in Rwanda, where great noble families intrigued and fought against one another at every royal succession and kings could establish a degree of control only by employing even greater violence. Nkore's king might grant the right of blood revenge to one Hima lineage against another or one Iru lineage against another, but Hima claimed to execute it against Iru without seeking royal approval, while Iru had no right of revenge against Hima but could only appeal to the king.[19] Amidst this violence, Nyakandalo's bloody revenge expressed perhaps a male ideal of female aristocratic honour, but it was not out of character with the

---

[16] Kagame, *Le code*, pp. 75–6. Slightly different details are given in Peter Schumacher (trans.), 'Lebensgeschichte des Grossfürsten Kayijuka und seiner Ahnen seit Sultan Yuhi Mazimpaka, König von Ruanda,' *Mitteilungen der Ausland-Hochschule an der Universität Berlin, dritte Abteilung*, 41 (1938), 143.

[17] Beattie, *Nyoro state*, pp. 119–20.

[18] A. Pagès, *Un royaume hamite au centre de l'Afrique* (Brussels, 1933), p. 164; Karugire, *History of Nkore*, p. 196; G. N. Uzoigwe, 'Kabalega's Abarusura: the military factor in Bunyoro,' in University of East Africa Social Sciences Council Conference 1968/69, *History papers* (Kampala, n.d.), pp. 303–24.

[19] Peter Seitel, *The powers of genre: interpreting Haya oral literature* (New York, 1999), p. 23; Beattie, *Nyoro state*, pp. 133–4; Gaetan Sebudandi and Pierre-Olivier Richard, *Le drame burundais: hantise du pouvoir ou tentation suicidaire* (Paris, 1996), p. 131; Schumacher, 'Lebensgeschichte,' passim; K. Oberg, 'The kingdom of Ankole in Uganda,' in Fortes and Evans-Pritchard, *African political systems*, pp. 131, 134.

ruthlessness displayed by Rwanda's Queen Mothers, who shared power with their sons and often acted as regents, as did their counterparts in Nkore.[20] As in Asante, state power in this region gave unusual influence to aristocratic women, as did the more companionate form of marriage in societies where polygyny was relatively uncommon. Aristocratic women were raised strictly. In Nkore they were forbidden all manual tasks and veiled when outside their houses. They learned cultural as well as domestic skills and were required to preserve chastity before marriage and modesty within it. Tutsi women were intensely conscious of rank, controlled great households, and patronised Hutu women, whose eagerness to imitate Tutsi behaviour is well documented, along with resentment of Tutsi frivolity and idleness.[21] Ordinary women might find outlets in religious activities, for female mediums communicated with the gods of the heroic pantheon, the widespread cult of the hero Ryangombe concerned especially female fertility, and the dissident Nyabingi cult on Rwanda's borders spoke of a women's world of equality and local autonomy challenging the masculine dynastic order.[22]

For men the chief protection in this dangerous world was a powerful patron. As a Rwandan proverb said: 'A dog is not feared for his fangs, but for his lord.'[23] At one level, patronage created hierarchical ties among aristocrats, often sealed by loans of cattle in return for deference and service. The first missionaries to Rwanda found such relationships utterly inescapable. They were perhaps less pervasive elsewhere but existed almost throughout the region.[24] So did a second hierarchical relationship: the extraction of tributary food and labour from the peasantry by power-holders in return not so much for protection as for abstention from violence. Nkore chiefs levied such tribute on Iru cultivators and redistributed it to Hima pastoralists. Haya kings allocated their henchmen blocks of peasant holdings as *nyarubanja* estates from which to draw tribute.

---

[20] Vansina, *Le Rwanda*, pp. 191–3; Oberg in Fortes and Evans-Pritchard, *African political systems*, p. 138.

[21] Alexis Kagame, *Les organisations socio-familiales de l'ancien Rwanda* (Brussels, 1954), pp. 234–5; Joshua Muvumba, 'The politics of stratification and transformation in the kingdom of Ankole, Uganda,' PhD thesis, Harvard University, 1982, pp. 85–6; Codere, *Biography*, pp. 138–80, 247–8.

[22] Iris Berger, *Religion and resistance: East African kingdoms in the precolonial period* (Tervuren, 1981), pp. 22–3, 89; Steven Feierman, 'Colonizers, scholars, and the creation of invisible histories,' in Victoria E. Bonnell and Lynn Hunt (eds.), *Beyond the cultural turn* (Berkeley, 1999), pp. 189–200.

[23] Jacques J. Maquet, *The premise of inequality in Ruanda* (London, 1961), p. 134.

[24] Ian Linden, *Church and revolution in Rwanda* (Manchester, 1977), p. 98; Jacques Maquet, 'Institutionalisation féodale des relations de dépendance dans quatre cultures interlacustres,' *CEA*, 9 (1969), 402–14; Robert G. Carlson, 'Hierarchy and the Haya divine kingship,' *American Ethnologist*, 20 (1993), 316.

Access to land in Burundi's central provinces depended increasingly on gifts to chiefs and service on royal demesnes.[25] Yet this was far from the *uburetwa* labour service – notionally two days work in every four – which Tutsi chiefs imposed on Rwandan peasants during the late nineteenth century in return for access to land. Tutsi tradition described it as punishment for Hutu cowardice in war. *Uburetwa* did more than anything else to differentiate Hutu from Tutsi, provoking insurrection in several border regions, as did military exactions in Burundi. Yet occupation of land was vital to Hutu, preserving them from the dishonourable status of landless labourers. To secure a Tutsi patron's protection offered the best chance of escaping *uburetwa*.[26] Some Hutu clients claimed vicarious participation in the Tutsi world, much like the *horso* retainers of the Middle Niger. A historian of Nkore, similarly, found that whereas the Hima elite gave themselves laudatory names, those borne by Iru peasants often expressed antipathy to other people or even to themselves.[27]

Early mission Christianity was as unsuccessful in accommodating the heroic ethos among Rwanda's nobility as it was in western and southern Africa. The ritualised monarchy threatened to kill any Tutsi who converted and posted the missionaries to border provinces, where Hutu flocked to them as potential patrons. The response in Burundi was similar: 'only very poor or socially marginal elements' initially accepted Christianity. Yet elsewhere in the region the experience was different. By 1914 the rulers of Bunyoro and Nkore were Christians, as were many former *Abarusura*, and the new religion was winning converts among young Haya aristocrats.[28] Their evangelists came from Buganda.

Ideas of honour were unusually well defined and documented in Buganda. *Ekitiibwa* meant literally 'that which is feared'. It is commonly translated as honour, glory, prestige, dignity, respect, reverence, or pomp, but, as a modern dictionary adds, 'None of the preceding equivalents expresses the full meaning of *kitiibwa* which is perhaps the greatest ideal and the most sought after attribute of the

---

[25] Oberg in Fortes and Evans-Pritchard, *African political systems*, pp. 131–2; Priscilla Copeland Reining, 'The Haya: the agrarian system of a sedentary people,' PhD thesis, University of Chicago, 1967, pp. 250–61; Roger Botte, 'Burundi: de quoi vivait l'Etat,' *CEA*, 22 (1982), 301–11.

[26] Vansina, *Le Rwanda*, pp. 171–8, 243; Claudine Vidal, 'Economie de la société féodale rwandaise,' *CEA*, 14 (1974), 52–74; Joseph Rwabukumba and Vincent Mudandagizi, 'Les formes historiques de la dépendance personnelle dans l'Etat rwandais,' *CEA*, 14 (1974), 22; Botte in Bazin and Terray, *Guerres*, p. 273.

[27] Codere, *Biography*, p. 201; Muvumba, 'Politics of stratification,' pp. 82–3.

[28] Linden, *Church and revolution*, pp. 3, 32–4; Joseph Gahama, *Le Burundi sous administration belge: le période du mandat 1919–1939* (Paris, 1983), p. 228; M. Louise Pirouet, *Black evangelists: the spread of Christianity in Uganda 1891–1914* (London, 1978), pp. 89, 125; Ralph A. Austen, *Northwest Tanzania under German and British rule* (New Haven, 1968), p. 104.

Baganda. It has an importance comparable to that of "face" in the Orient.'[29]
In contrast to comparable notions in highly stratified societies like Rwanda,
moreover, *ekitiibwa* was not conferred by birth. It was a right to respect for
which Baganda openly competed.

The difference was rooted in the history and structure of the Buganda kingdom.[30] It shared the general Bantu culture and heroic religion of the region,
but its rulers, although claiming immigrant origin, had abandoned any pastoral
tradition in this lakeshore environment unsuited to cattle, becoming culturally
indistinguishable from their subjects and intricately intermarried with them.
Unlike Rwanda, Buganda had neither a royal lineage occupying senior chieftainships nor a hereditary aristocracy. Nor, by the mid nineteenth century, was
it dominated by clan loyalties, for the kingdom's growth from a small nucleus
had dispersed the clans and created many military and administrative offices
in the gift of the king (*Kabaka*). He conferred them in return for loyalty and
service so that Buganda's politics centred on competition for office and its associated *ekitiibwa*, a competition open in principle to any man of talent and
courage.

The Kabaka was the fount of honour. He had few ritual functions, for the
ancient religious system was tied more to the clans, but he was surrounded with
great ceremony, his court was the focus of national life, and his capital was
the most populous in the region. In the absence of a hereditary aristocracy, two
vertical ties of clientage dominated nineteenth-century Buganda's public life.
One was between king and chief, for the Kabaka personally appointed chiefs
at all levels, from the chief minister (*Katikkiro*) downwards. Every fifth man
may have been a chief.[31] The other four were chiefs' men, for the second major
relationship was between chief and follower, a relationship that the follower
could choose and (if he dared) change: 'As soon as the chiefs saw a stranger
come in, they asked me, "Where have you come from, and what do you want?
Have you come to look for a new master?" When I said yes, they all got up, and
each asked me if I wished to serve him.'[32] Chiefs competed for men to fight for
them, cultivate their official estates, staff their courts, support their ambitions,
and do them honour. The weapons of competition were generosity, affability,

[29] John D. Murphy, *Luganda-English dictionary* (Washington, D.C., 1972), p. 210.

[30] Excellent introductory accounts are John Allen Rowe, 'Revolution in Buganda, 1856–1900: part
one: the reign of Kabaka Mukabya Mutesa, 1856–1884,' PhD thesis, University of Wisconsin,
1966; L. A. Fallers (ed.), *The king's men: leadership and status in Buganda on the eve of
independence* (London, 1964).

[31] Fallers, *King's men*, p. 160.

[32] 'The early life of the Rev. Aloni Muyinda,' 1902, CMS UP/276/F4. See also Robert Pickering
Ashe, *Two kings of Uganda* (2nd edn, London, 1970), p. 95.

justice, and, above all, success. The conflict between a man's loyalty to his chief and to his king was to trouble many late nineteenth-century Ganda.

Although the existence of these loyalties, as in Asante, meant that Buganda was no longer a purely heroic society in which the egotism of the individual warrior was all, it nevertheless retained strongly heroic qualities. Every adult man was in principle a warrior. Chiefs were fighting men, each with his own war cry and boastful drumbeat. Warriors generally carried both throwing-spears and a stabbing-spear to use as the forces closed for hand-to-hand combat. A coward might be burned to death on the battlefield. If spared, a piece of banana stem might be bound behind him, in imitation of a woman giving birth, before he was put to women's work. A hero, by contrast, was rewarded by the king and fed by his father at a ceremonial meal.[33] Away from the battlefield there is no evidence of duelling or blood-feud, although quarrels might be settled by wrestling – the favourite chief of Kabaka Mutesa (1856–84) was his former wrestling trainer – and grudges were never forgotten: 'He who makes you shed tears, you make him shed blood,' said a proverb. Shedding blood, however, was a prerogative of the king and his senior chiefs, who practised it with a frequency and cruelty that both horrified and fascinated their subjects. A missionary was to write of 'the terrible Baganda grin of pleasure in cruelty.' By some accounts, a brave man was expected to go to execution with silent composure, just as everyone should endure pain with stoicism.[34]

The man of honour was not merely violent. Mutesa's favourite, Tebukoza Kyambalango, was not merely two metres tall, a great wrestler and warrior, who could crack *mpafu* nuts with his teeth, but he entertained the court with songs to his own accompaniment on the *enanga* zither and spoke a passable Arabic, for in the mid nineteenth century traders from Zanzibar had brought Islam, which Mutesa's young chiefs had eagerly absorbed in their competition for advancement.[35] Tebukoza was a formidable courtier, but no match for his rival, Mutesa's Katikkiro, Mukasa, who was not only a handsome and intelligent diplomat, soldier, and early Arabic scholar but the son of a great chief, an

---

[33] John A. Rowe, 'Eyewitness accounts of Buganda history: the memoirs of Ham Mukasa and his generation,' *Ethnohistory*, 36 (1989), 69; Richard J. Reid, *Political power in pre-colonial Buganda: economy, society and warfare in the nineteenth century* (Oxford, 2002), p. 218; Sir Apolo Kagwa, *The customs of the Baganda* (trans. E. B. Kalibala, New York, 1934), pp. 92–3.

[34] Ferdinand Walser, *Luganda proverbs* (Berlin, 1982), no. 0293; [J. W. Harrison,] *A. M. Mackay, pioneer missionary* (new edn, London, 1970), p. 183; John Roscoe, *Twenty-five years in East Africa* (Cambridge, 1921), p. 154; A. R. Cook, journal, 28 October 1897, in *Mercy and Truth*, 1898, p. 57.

[35] B. Musoke Zimbe, 'Buganda and the King,' typescript translation by F. Kamoga of *Buganda ne Kabaka* (Mengo, 1939), p. 249 (copy in CUL); Franz Stuhlmann (ed.), *Die Tagebücher von Dr Emin Pascha* (6 vols., Braunschweig, 1916–27), vol. 1, pp. 138, 142.

important asset where, despite the absence of an aristocracy, a man's ancestry was always scrutinised.[36] He was also renowned for his speech and manners, vital qualities in an oral culture that regarded the jawbone as the repository of the soul and could remember a Kabaka for the particular elegance with which he wore his barkcloth.[37] Tebukoza, however, was a famous hunter, a favourite pastime and proof of manliness. Sexual virility added further lustre: 'The Native code of Morality . . . consistently spares the daring sins,' a missionary observed. A man of honour could seduce, intrigue, plot, and deceive without loss of reputation. But he could not flinch.[38]

Notions of honour were not confined to courtiers. Crafts were highly specialised, and their leaders were honoured. Free peasants might kill themselves from shame if discovered in theft, cowardice, or inability to pay tribute. They looked down on the foreign-born slaves who became increasingly common during the nineteenth century. 'A person giving away his dignity' was likened proverbially to 'a woman eating with the slaves'.[39] Slave women could be married without bridewealth, but for free women both bridewealth and virginity were necessary to a fully honourable marriage, which women entered later than was common in Africa, rarely before twenty.[40] A married woman's status depended chiefly on her ancestry and her husband's rank. Royal women were categorised socially as men; the most senior enjoyed great deference, controlled estates and their own hierarchies of chiefs, and exercised considerable political influence. Other women gained respect by control of the household economy and by their fertility; loss of a baby was a woman's most common reason for suicide.[41]

At all social levels, the ambitious had to combine *okufugibwa*, the art of deference to superiors, with daring and resilience, for few political careers escaped a period of destitution. There were medicines to ensure that a boy would secure a chieftainship and medicines for protection when visiting the

[36] Rowe, 'Revolution,' pp. 139–45.

[37] Christopher Wrigley, *Kingship and state: the Buganda dynasty* (Cambridge, 1996), p. 25; Zimbe, 'Buganda,' p. 190.

[38] *Uganda Notes*, October 1915; Twaddle, *Kakungulu*, p. 81.

[39] Reid, *Political power*, pp. 83, 88; Albert R. Cook, 'Notes on the diseases met with in Uganda,' *Journal of Tropical Medicine*, 4 (1901), 177; Michael Twaddle, 'The ending of slavery in Buganda,' in Miers and Roberts, *End of slavery*, pp. 121–2; Walser, *Luganda proverbs*, no. 2079.

[40] L. P. Mair, *Native marriage in Buganda* (London, 1940), pp. 10, 17; *Chronique Trimestrielle de la Société des Missionnaires d'Afrique (Pères Blancs)*, 103 (February 1904), 35.

[41] Nakanyike B. Musisi, 'Women, "elite polygyny", and Buganda state formation,' *Signs*, 16 (1991), 773–82; Mair, *Native marriage*, pp. 13–14; Sir Albert R. Cook, *Uganda memories (1897–1940)* (Kampala, 1945), p. 299.

capital or court.[42] The intense competition for status, power, and security in a face-to-face society, generally characteristic of an honour culture, fostered suspicion, intrigue, and a personalised view of politics and history. Buganda's first major historian was content to write that the civil war that transformed the kingdom in the late nineteenth century began 'because Kabaka Mwanga decided to enlarge his lake.'[43]

In reality the first impetus towards that transformation came with the arrival of Zanzibari traders in the mid nineteenth century. Mutesa was attracted by their material novelties, unconstrained by ritual duties, and perhaps anxious for a state cult to balance the clan-based indigenous religion. He encouraged his young courtiers to study Islam and literacy, constructed a mosque, observed the annual Ramadan fast from 1867, and in 1875 executed chiefs who opposed the new faith. Competition among the young courtiers ensured an eager response. Several were circumcised. In 1876, however, a teacher from the more rigorous Islamic environment of the Sudan is said to have urged the courtiers to reject the heterodox religious leadership of the uncircumcised Mutesa: 'The power of the Kabaka is only in the rule of his land, but concerning religion, it is otherwise.' Some seventy were burned at Namugongo, and others were killed in the countryside.[44] The survivors adopted a lower profile, but their religion had gained a heroic quality.

Within a decade Christianity passed through almost the same experience. The first Anglican and Roman Catholic missionaries, arriving in 1877 and 1879, respectively, found Mutesa eager for material and political benefits but suspicious of religious teaching, which he now realised could divide his kingdom. The young courtiers, however, remained eager for skills, especially literacy, which might profit them in competing for office. Each mission quickly gained a following of young 'readers', aware that their covert attendance might cost their lives, but aware also that they could be killed at court for nothing.[45] Initially, however, Christians formed only tiny quietist cells. That their religion might

---

[42] Michael Twaddle, 'The "Bakungu" chiefs of Buganda under British colonial rule, 1900–1930,' *JAH*, 10 (1969), 313; 'The life of Ham Mukasa. Written by himself,' in J. D. Mullins, *The wonderful story of Uganda* (London, 1904), p. 174; John Roscoe, *The Baganda: an account of their native customs and beliefs* (2nd edn, London, 1965), p. 323.

[43] Apolo Kagwa, 'The reign of Mwanga,' unpublished translation by Simon Musoke of pp. 138–277 of *Ekitabo kya Basekabaka be Buganda* (Kampala, 1901), p. 143 (copy in CUL).

[44] Arye Oded, *Islam in Uganda* (New York, 1974), pp. 60–80, 152–62; Ham Mukasa, 'Do not retreat,' typescript translation by J. A. Rowe of *Simuda nyuma* (3 vols., only vol. 1 published: London, 1938), vol. 1, pp. 17–23. I am indebted to Dr Rowe for a copy of his translation.

[45] Mackay, journal, 25 December 1881, in *Church Missionary Intelligencer*, September 1883, p. 533. For a general account of responses to Christianity, see D. A. Low, *Religion and society in Buganda, 1875–1900* (Kampala, n.d.)

conflict with Buganda's heroic ethos, as it did elsewhere in Africa, became clear in 1880 when a reader begged the Kabaka for command of a plundering expedition and found to his astonishment that the Protestant missionaries disapproved such violence. He abandoned the reading classes, along with Tebukoza and other prominent chiefs, saying they would postpone conversion until they were no longer interested in becoming rich. The mission backed down but some did not return.[46]

The crisis that would reconcile Christianity and heroic honour was precipitated by Mutesa's death in 1884 and the succession of his young son Mwanga. Like every new Kabaka, Mwanga sought to assert his authority over his father's chiefs by promoting men of his own generation, some of them now Muslims or Christians. The old chiefs resisted. Amidst growing danger of European colonial invasion, they accused their Christian rivals of betraying state secrets to the missionaries. When Mwanga denounced the missionaries in November 1885 because 'double-tongued lads . . . tell you my secrets,' Katikkiro Mukasa seized the chance to execute the leading Christian, Joseph Mukasa Balikuddembe, who was tipped as his likely successor.[47] Shortly afterwards the crisis deepened when Buganda's army was defeated by the traditional enemy in Bunyoro.[48] In May 1886 Mwanga surprised a young page teaching Christianity to the king's current homosexual partner, who was also the Katikkiro's son. Mwanga summoned his pages and ordered those who prayed to stand on one side. They were taken to execution at Namugongo, where their leader, Charles Lwanga, was killed with special cruelty, and the others – an uncertain number, but possibly fourteen Protestants and eleven Catholics – were burned on a common pyre. Most were aged between fifteen and thirty. Including later executions, up to a hundred Christians may have died in a haphazard persecution aimed at control rather than extermination.[49]

The martyrs' motives cannot now be reconstructed with certainty. Many could have escaped death, either by fleeing the palace, hiding in the countryside, or denying their faith. The pages under Charles Lwanga's leadership, at least, made a collective decision to stand firm, while one or two Christians deliberately

---

[46] Rowe, 'Revolution,' pp. 170–1; Mukasa, 'Do not retreat,' vol. 1, p. 62; Mackay, journal, 26 November 1885, in *Church Missionary Intelligencer*, June 1886, p. 495.

[47] Mackay, journal, 28 October, 11 and 15 November 1885, in *Church Missionary Intelligencer*, June 1886, pp. 485–6, 489, 492; Rubaga journal, 11 and 15 November 1885, in *Chronique Trimestrielle*, 32 (October 1886), 367–9.

[48] This volume, p. 174.

[49] The chief eyewitness account is Lourdel's journal of 26 May 1886, incorporated in Livinhac to Lavigerie, 29 September 1886, published in *Les Missions Catholiques*, 18 (1886), 140–3. For later accounts, see J. P. Thoonen, *Black martyrs* (London, 1941); J. F. Faupel, *African holocaust* (London, 1962); J. A. Rowe, 'The purge of Christians at Mwanga's court,' *JAH*, 5 (1964), 55–71.

surrendered to the authorities.[50] A few denied their faith and were spared, although some were killed all the same.[51] Belief in eternal life was vital to many, as in the earliest days of Christianity. Denis Kamyuka, spared at the last moment, recalled that on the way to Namugongo they had said, 'In only a brief moment we shall see Jesus Christ.' Lwanga's parting words were, 'We shall meet again in heaven.'[52] The Roman Catholic missionaries had warned their converts of the risk of martyrdom. Now the converts had to live up to the courage they had then asserted. 'To offer oneself to do a fine deed and then omit it at the last moment is the action of a craven and a coward,' Denis Kamyuka remembered them saying on the way to Namugongo.[53] To die with silent courage was expected of young men of the ruling class[54] and especially important to them when tormented by their elders. As the slow fire ate into his body, Lwanga told his torturer and personal enemy, 'What you call fire is only fresh water. God will one day pour out on you the real fire.'[55]

If it was vital to be brave, it was vital also not to appear disloyal. Alexis Ssebowa, later a great Catholic chief, recalled that the pages refused to flee the court lest they be called rebels and disgrace the chiefs who had sent them.[56] Some younger pages did escape at the prompting of older colleagues, but they anxiously sought assurance from the missionaries that this was not apostasy and some quickly returned, for 'we felt rather ashamed of ourselves in running away and leaving our fellows to suffer death alone.'[57] Ssebowa himself surrendered to his chief, the Katikkiro, who – after failing to persuade him to renounce Christianity – begged Mwanga to spare him. Ham Mukasa hid for several months before returning to court to beg forgiveness with his chief's support. As so often in Buganda, the tie between chief and followers restrained royal despotism.[58]

By demonstrating to young people that Christianity could demand the highest courage, the martyrdom was an important stage in breaking the heroic culture's

---

[50] S. Lourdel, C. Denoit, and A. Delmas, 'Enquête relative au martyre des chrétiens: Ste Marie de Rubaga, Buganda, 1888,' WFA C/15; Rowe, 'Purge,' pp. 63–70.

[51] Livinhac to Lavigerie, 18 July 1887 and 20 February 1888, WFA C/13/86 and 94; James Kabazzi Miti, 'A history of Buganda' (typescript, 3 vols. [1938?] in SOAS Library), vol. 1, p. 281.

[52] 'Copia Publica Transumpti Processus Apostolica . . . super martyrio . . . vulgo de "Ouganda" . . . Anno 1916,' pp. 235–6, WFA manuscript Y.16.

[53] Ibid., p. 228.

[54] Roscoe, *Baganda*, pp. 334, 338; Michael Wright, *Buganda in the heroic age* (Nairobi, 1971), pp. 19–20.

[55] Lourdel to Lavigerie, 4 November 1886, WFA C/14/176.

[56] 'Copia Publica,' p. 110, WFA manuscript Y.16.

[57] Miti, 'History,' vol. 1, ch. 21.

[58] 'Copia Publica,' pp. 104–5, WFA manuscript Y.16; Mukasa in Mullins, *Wonderful story*, pp. 184–5; Wright, *Buganda*, pp. 19–24.

resistance to the new religion. Yet passive endurance was scarcely central to the heroic ethos. Rather, the next step in the reconciliation between Christianity and warrior virtues was the work of Mwanga, who late in 1886 armed the Christians he had recently persecuted.[59] His reasons were probably his personal position and the impact of firearms on regional power relations. When Zanzibar's traders introduced guns, Kabaka Mutesa created a royal bodyguard of musketeers. Some were captives, others 'the elect of Uganda'.[60] They provided the missionaries with many early converts. When Mwanga launched his army against Bunyoro in January 1886, however, it still consisted mainly of spearmen and at its departure the commander, Tebukoza, expressed a man of honour's disgust at the new warfare facing them:

Now we are no longer in the time of hand-to-hand fighting, where a man of courage could pride himself on the strength of his arm, on his bravery in combat, on his skill in handling a shield; we are entering a new kind of battle, where the hand of a coward hidden in the grass can end the days of the most courageous soldier. So we are going to fight with guns, for guns are the fashion.[61]

The outcome was even worse than he feared. Kabalega's *Abarusura* slaughtered Buganda's spearmen. 'If anyone has not seen guns, let him go to Bulega,' sang the retreating army.[62] The Christian martyrdom then intervened, but in October 1886 Buganda itself was raided. A few days later, Mwanga began to form his young courtiers into four additional regiments armed with guns – including Buganda's first breech-loaders – endowing them with estates that they were to seize from the old chiefs currently occupying them.[63] One regiment was given to Honorat Nyonyintono, who had succeeded Charles Lwanga as the leading Catholic after being castrated during the persecution. Apolo Kaggwa, a leading Protestant who had been severely beaten, gained command of another, while the two further regiments had Muslim commanders, although at this stage all regiments contained followers of all faiths, including the indigenous religion.[64] Mwanga may have felt that the unpopularity of Christians and Muslims would guarantee their loyalty to him, as the Christians' obedience during persecution

---

[59] For the dating, see Rubaga journal, 21 October 1886, in *Chronique Trimestrielle*, 36 (October 1887), 588; Mukasa in Mullins, *Wonderful story*, p. 186.

[60] Norman R. Bennett (ed.), *Stanley's despatches to the 'New York Herald'* (Boston, 1970), p. 221.

[61] Rubaga journal, 21 March 1887, in *Chronique Trimestrielle*, 38 (April 1888), 243–4.

[62] J. W. Nyakatura, *Anatomy of an African kingdom: a history of Bunyoro-Kitara* (trans. T. Muganwa, New York, 1973), p. 136; Rubaga journal, 21 March 1887, in *Chronique Trimestrielle*, 38 (April 1888), 244.

[63] Rubaga journal, 9–21 October 1886, in *Chronique Trimestrielle*, 36 (October 1887), 585–8; Mukasa in Mullins, *Wonderful story*, p. 186; Zimbe, 'Buganda,' pp. 157–62.

[64] Wright, *Buganda*, pp. 25–8.

suggested. Initially the strategy appeared successful. Mwanga used his *Abapere* – the 'crazy' or 'tarnished' – to plunder the old chiefs and supervise the excavation of a royal lake, work in which even great chiefs had to dig with their hands in the mud.[65] In May 1887 the Kabaka again launched his army against Bunyoro.[66] A year later soldiers asked their missionaries whether this warfare was compatible with their Christianity. Alert to Mwanga's accusations of Christian disloyalty, the missionaries told them to obey orders and fight better than anyone else for their king. Another psychological barrier was broken.[67]

The old chiefs retaliated. They told the readers, probably falsely, that the Kabaka planned to maroon them on an island in Lake Victoria. 'They were our fathers,' a reader recalled, 'and Mwanga had killed some of our friends at Namugongo, the memory of which was still fresh, we therefore readily believed what we were told.'[68] The readers refused Mwanga's orders, deposed him in September 1888 in favour of his elder brother Kiwewa, and shared the chieftainships between them.[69] At this time, the Roman Catholic mission claimed fewer than 2,000 readers in all Buganda. There were even fewer Protestants. The Muslims were more numerous and had clearer political goals. When the two parties quarrelled, the Muslims drove the Christians from the capital on 12 October 1888 and began to create an Islamic state.[70]

Sixteen months of civil war followed before the Christians finally captured the capital on 11 February 1890 and – for lack of another candidate – reinstalled Mwanga as their puppet. During this period of violence, Christianity became as fully integrated with heroic notions of honour as it did in Europe during the Crusades. 'Our chiefs are a curious mixture of Christian conscientiousness and heathen cruelty,' wrote a missionary:

> They believe that God will not give them the victory if they do anything wrong, and therefore they do not like to take any advantage of their enemy. They thought it necessary to write and tell the enemy that they were coming to attack them, lest they should be taken off their guard. Yet when they are victorious they have more than once speared the leader of the opposite side when he was taken prisoner. They complain of the unfair advantage the Mohammedans take by lying in wait in the long grass and attacking the Christians on the march. This is a sort of twilight Christianity.[71]

---

[65] Zimbe, 'Buganda,' pp. 148–56.

[66] Mackay to Ashe, 25 May 1887, CMS UP/72/F2.

[67] Walker to his mother, 3 June 1888, CMS UP/88; Rowe, 'Revolution,' p. 171.

[68] Zimbe, 'Buganda,' p. 163.

[69] Ibid., pp. 178–84.

[70] Livinhac to Lesmayoux, 23 June 1888, WFA C/15/17; *Church Missionary Intelligencer*, October 1891, p. 767; Michael Twaddle, 'The Muslim revolution in Buganda,' *African Affairs*, 71 (1972), 59–65.

[71] Walker, 3 February 1890, in *Church Missionary Intelligencer*, September 1890, p. 623.

In reality, of course, it was heroic warfare. Firearms had not yet changed that. Only the Christian and Muslim elites – perhaps two thousand or three thousand on each side – yet possessed even muskets, each named and valued more highly than its bearer. By contrast, the spearmen forming the bulk of the civil war armies took little part in the fighting but concentrated on foraging and on pursuing defeated adversaries.[72] As in Rwanda, this was heroic warfare by small elite forces. They deliberately courted danger by wearing the most conspicuous white cloth. They used their guns much like spears, firing from the hip. The leaders on each side formed the front rank and their men lined up behind them.[73] The two armies closed, drums beating, until the bravest broke ranks to charge: 'Their way is to run up with a loaded gun to within a few yards, fire, retire behind the cover of their own side, load and run up again.' 'If big men on the other side fall, then victory is assured to this party, and they carry all before them. I should say that the first ten minutes determine the day.' That was certainly true at the major Battle of Mawuki, where the Christians lost their revered commander Nyonyintono, 'were seized with fright,' and quit the field.[74] Smaller engagements were generally guerilla raids like the Christians capturing a dhow that was bringing munitions across Lake Victoria and massacring one hundred fifty Muslims with the brutality all participants displayed. Nicodemo Sebwato, the most senior Protestant leader and church councillor, was eager to execute a Zanzibari believed to have practised witchcraft against Christians.[75]

As Mawuki showed, leadership was crucial to heroic warfare. The Christian commanders were as egocentric and quarrelsome as Homeric heroes. When first expelled from Buganda, Protestants and Catholics built separate camps at Kabula, where denominational hostility crystallised as the two parties disputed strategy and taunted one another with cowardice.[76] Each party was also internally divided. Among the Protestants, the senior leader, Sebwato, was too cautious for younger men, who insulted him as 'you old man who is here afraid' and replaced him by the twenty-four-year-old Apolo Kaggwa, a fighting

---

[72] Lourdel to Superior-General, 25 January 1890, in *Chronique Trimestrielle*, 47 (July 1890), 531.

[73] Zimbe, 'Buganda,' p. 268; J. R. L. Macdonald, *Soldiering and surveying in British East Africa, 1891–1894* (London, 1897), pp. 141–2.

[74] Pilkington to Mrs. Pilkington, 17 March 1892, CMS G3/A5/O/1892/263; Walker to his father, 24 October 1889, in *Church Missionary Intelligencer*, June 1890, p. 370; Zimbe, 'Buganda,' p. 251.

[75] Abbé Nicq, *Le Père Siméon Lourdel* (3rd edn, Algiers, 1922), p. 480; Walker to his brother, 4 January 1890, CMS UP/88.

[76] John Mary Waliggo, 'The Catholic Church in the Buddu Province of Buganda, 1879–1925,' PhD thesis, University of Cambridge, 1976, pp. 59–60.

man of great strength and ambition who boasted his prowess while swinging his gun around his head and enjoyed the praise-song, 'Apolo's chest is solid gun-metal.'[77] As the war developed, however, Kaggwa's impulsiveness, authoritarianism, and military failures turned his men instead to Semei Kakungulu, a royal elephant hunter, relatively late convert to Christianity, and irregular commander of genius whose followers marched to the song, 'Whoever does not smoke marijuana is a frog.' Kakungulu restored Mwanga to his capital with the provocative words, 'I have conquered Kalema. Come in pomp and reascend the throne.'[78] A similar division between political chiefs and military freebooters emerged among Catholics, older leaders like Alexis Ssebowa and Stanislas Mugwanya being challenged by the dashing young Gabrieli Kintu, who became Mwanga's favoured commander as the restored Kabaka began once more to construct a royal party.[79]

Mwanga's restoration in February 1890 did not end the struggle. The Christians occupied the capital and divided the chieftainships among their fighting men, but a Muslim army survived in northern Buganda, as did a strong traditionalist resistance in the east. Moreover, the Christian chiefs soon quarrelled with one another and with the Kabaka, whose tactical preference for the Catholic party won it growing support. Protestant weakness persuaded Apolo Kaggwa (as Katikkiro) to ally with Captain Lugard of the Imperial British East Africa Company when he reached Buganda with a small military force in December 1890. Lugard found that the heroic culture made it impossible to arrange a compromise. 'Once Waganda quarrel,' he noted, 'they must fight to the death, for no reconciliation is possible since neither side can trust the other.'[80] Instead, he defeated the Muslims, recruited Sudanese troops left behind by the Egyptian army in northern Uganda, helped Protestants to defeat Catholics in February 1892, and laid foundations for the British protectorate declared over Buganda in 1894. Mwanga rebelled unsuccessfully in 1897 and was deposed. The Uganda Agreement of 1900 preserved the kingdom under the domination of the Christian chiefs.[81]

Throughout the conflicts of the 1890s, Buganda's indigenous notions of honour shaped the behaviour of Christians and non-Christians alike. All competed

---

[77] Zimbe, 'Buganda,' pp. 234, 239.

[78] Ibid., pp. 300–5; Twaddle, *Kakungulu*, pp. 50–6; idem, 'Muslim revolution,' p. 68.

[79] Waliggo, 'Catholic Church,' p. 71 n3; Wright, *Buganda*, p. 83. A similar division opened among Muslim leaders: Wright, *Buganda*, pp. 89–90, 137–40.

[80] Margery Perham and Mary Bull (eds.), *The diaries of Lord Lugard* (4 vols., London, 1959–63), vol. 3, p. 247 (entry for 18 May 1892).

[81] See John A. Rowe, *Lugard at Kampala* (Kampala, 1969); D. A. Low and R. C. Pratt, *Buganda and British overrule, 1900–1955: two studies* (Nairobi, 1970), part 1.

relentlessly for the predominance that *ekitiibwa* demanded. As the Protestant drums proclaimed:

> We ate Buganda, we ate it, we ate it,
> We ate it secretly, but we ate it.[82]

Mwanga, although profoundly unheroic, remained the fount of honour, capable of attracting support to the Catholic Party in 1890–1 and threatening Apolo Kaggwa's position as Katikkiro thereafter. 'You are no longer my ministers nor my subjects,' he is said to have told Kaggwa in 1894. 'You have deserted and offered your services to white foreigners.'[83] In reply, the chiefs exploited European support and their control of office, land, and wealth. The crisis came when Mwanga rebelled in 1897. 'If our men do not desert us to join the Kabaka we have a lot of men,' Kaggwa wrote from the battle-front. 'But most people in Budu love the Kabaka very much, many of them do and the chiefs' servants have deserted them for the Kabaka.' In the event, ties of clientage held, and enough men fought resolutely to defeat their king, although some preferred to kill themselves.[84]

It was also through ties of clientage that the Christians spread their militant religion so rapidly during the two decades after their victory. In 1911 a rough census showed that, of Buganda's 705,615 people, 181,141 were already Catholics, 140,144 were Protestants, and 58,401 were Muslims, against 325,929 followers of indigenous religion.[85] Not only did many chiefs conduct services and preach – in 1900 Ham Mukasa 'preached a capital sermon taking Ulysses as an illustration' – but they often compelled their subjects to listen, although the state council demurred at a proposal by Kaggwa and the Protestant clergy that all pagan children should be compulsorily baptised. The most authoritarian theocracy was the Catholic county of Buddu, where the chiefs made Catholic instruction compulsory for the young, employed catechists as resident chaplains, presented candidates for baptism, marched their people to church on Sundays, and persecuted adherents of indigenous religion.[86] Moreover, militant Christianity appropriated Buganda's competitive energy. Literacy and baptism became essential qualifications for an official career, generally launched as a teacher, perhaps in some remote and dangerous outpost where a patron was

---

[82] Waliggo, 'Catholic Church,' p. 85.

[83] Miti, 'History,' vol. 2, p. 467.

[84] Kaggwa to Kago, 18 July 1897, in Henri Médard, 'Croissance et crises de la royauté du Buganda au XIXe siècle,' Thèse de Docteur de l'Université Paris I, 2001, pp. 540 n6, 553.

[85] *CMS Gazette*, 1912, p. 144.

[86] A. R. Cook, diary, 9 September 1900, Wellcome Institute for the History of Medicine, London; Rubaga journal, 23 September 1898 and 1 March 1899, in *Chronique Trimestrielle*, 82 (April 1899), 199, and 84 (October 1899), 467; Waliggo, 'Catholic Church,' ch. 3.

seeking to expand his own and the kingdom's power. During 1902, when all but one of the nineteen Protestant teachers posted to Busoga contracted sleeping sickness and the Church Council resolved to replace them only with volunteers, it received twenty-seven offers.[87] Yet teaching was only a stage in a career either in chieftainship or the church. Broadly speaking, men of high birth, courtly training, and military qualities moved into chieftainship; those without those qualifications might find advancement through ordination, which became open to Ganda at an exceptionally early date because of the competition between the missions and because, as the Anglican bishop explained, 'There were those moving in and out daily amongst us whose faith in Christ had been tested and tried in times of fierce persecution.'[88] Chiefs and clergy, in turn, competed in propagating the enlightenment essential to a modern man of honour. Ever hungry for *ekitiibwa*, Apolo Kaggwa later claimed to have been the first Ganda to own a watch, ride a horse, eat at a table, drink tea, use a paraffin lamp, ride a bicycle, write a book, and build a two-storey brick house.[89] His close ally, Ham Mukasa, took as the title of his memoirs one of the old battle-cries, *Simuda nyuma*, 'Do not retreat'. Like their contemporaries, the Meiji reformers of Japan, the Christian reformers of Buganda had gone so far that they could only go further.[90]

Yet that was not true of all Ganda. The Christians had established a claim to honour but not a monopoly of it. The contest culminated in Mwanga's revolt of 1897. In his struggle to create a royal party, the Kabaka had courted those excluded from power in the new order: royalists, traditionalists, young men attracted by his dissolute court, and especially the military freebooters who had distinguished themselves in war but had been denied high office in peace. One of the most notable freebooters was Gabrieli Kintu, who maintained in Buddu the lifestyle of a traditional warrior, defying the authorities' attempt in January 1897 to punish him for torturing to death a man suspected of having stolen his gun. Rumours of planned revolt began to circulate, and Mwanga's own conflict with the authorities culminated in a traumatic contest of *ekitiibwa* with Kaggwa, which left the king with 'his face streaming with tears'.[91] On 6 July 1897, Mwanga abandoned the capital and raised his standard in Buddu.

[87] Papers of A. G. Fraser, folio 1/2/27, RH.

[88] Low, *Religion and society*, p. 14; Hastings, *Church*, pp. 392–3; Alfred R. Tucker, *Eighteen years in Uganda and East Africa* (new edn, London, 1911), p. 110.

[89] Manuscript translation by J. A. Rowe of extracts from Sir Apolo Kagwa, *Ekitabo kye kika kye Nsenene* (2nd edn, Mengo [1905?]), pp. 134–8. I owe this translation to Professor Rowe.

[90] Thomas C. Smith, *Political change and industrial development in Japan* (Stanford, 1955), p. 34.

[91] Kagwa, 'Reign of Mwanga,' pp. 194–203; John A. Rowe, 'Erieza Kintu's *Sulutani anatoloka*,' *History in Africa*, 20 (1993), 315.

'A gust of enthusiasm and delirious joy passed over the Catholic province and brought the great majority of the population to Mwanga's feet,' wrote the bishop. Gabrieli and the Buddu dissidents took command of Mwanga's forces. Many of the queen mother's clan, elephant-hunters and pagans from the forests, militant Muslim survivors from the civil wars, traditionally royalist canoemen, most of the capital's policemen, and the dissatisfied of all kinds rallied to the king. The Christian establishment mobilised against him.[92] The subsequent fighting displayed extreme confusion, conflicts of loyalty, and the continuing strength of the heroic ethos. The Battle of Nyendo became known as 'Get out of my gun' because friends and brothers found themselves on opposite sides. Seperiya Mutagwanya, once a Catholic military freebooter, sent retainers to join Mwanga but defended a Catholic mission against Muslim rebels. Lui Kibanyi, deputy county chief of Buddu, joined the king and died on the scaffold with crucifix and rosary in hand, denouncing Kaggwa as a traitor. Gabrieli's enemies sneered at his guerilla tactics: 'Coward that he was that he would make sudden attacks against his enemy usually by stealth and under cover of night, do whatever little mischief he could in his hurry and then run away with only a few head of cattle.' But Gabrieli himself insisted that he 'never stole anything belonging to the Church' nor fought on Sundays.[93] And the ruling Christian chiefs like Kaggwa used the war to demonstrate that they were still fighting men, that Apolo's chest was still solid gun-metal. Kaggwa's account of the decisive Battle of Kabuwoko on 20 July 1897 – the greatest battle of the civil wars, with an estimated fourteen thousand on each side[94] – captured the essence of heroic Christianity:

I, the author of this book and Stanislas Mugwanya attacked while riding our horses as we despised the strength of the enemy who had been converted Christians and had turned to fight for the support of vicious customs of olden times. When we felt that they had reconverted from God to paganism, we felt much stronger. The living God was plainly with us and although our enemies tried several times to aim at us as they could easily see us up on horses, but none of their aims ever touched us. We were then convinced that this was so through divine providence from God. This was the first time for any Muganda to engage in fighting while on a horse back.[95]

---

[92] Streicher to Livinhac, July 1897, WFA I/82/082; Wright, *Buganda*, ch. 6; A. R. Cook, journal, 7–13 July 1897, in *Church Missionary Intelligencer*, November 1897, pp. 814–15.

[93] Waliggo, 'Catholic Church,' pp. 150–2; Mukasa, 'Do not retreat,' vol. 3, p. 470; Hastings, *Church*, pp. 481–2; Miti, 'History,' vol. 2, p. 587.

[94] Trevor Ternan, *Some experiences of an Old Bromsgrovian* (Birmingham, 1930), p. 312.

[95] Kagwa, 'Reign of Mwanga,' p. 208.

Part Two

Fragmentation and Mutation

11 The Deaths of Heroes

The partial amalgamation of *ekitiibwa* with militant Christianity provides a paradigm for what happened to notions of honour elsewhere in twentieth-century Africa, which is the subject of the second half of this book. The relative smoothness of the process in Buganda was, however, exceptional. Normally the heroic code fragmented before accommodation with new ethics was possible.

That is the subject of this chapter. The European invasion in the late nineteenth century was a challenge to which many Africans responded in a heroic manner. Yet the invasion was facilitated by advances in military technology that made many old notions of honour redundant. Some Africans nevertheless clung to them and charged straight at the machine-guns; for them honour was, as so often, self-destructive. Others sacrificed honour to survival or personal advantage. Others again sought either new military tactics or more effective forms of social mobilisation, often at the expense of cherished notions of loyalty, rank, or courage. This chapter considers first those who clung to old tactics and then those who sought new ones. In either case, when the fighting ended, many Africans could console themselves in defeat with the knowledge that they had preserved their honour. Now they had to find new ways to express it.

During the three centuries before 1870, muzzle-loading muskets had made an uneven impact on African warfare. A few peoples had adopted tactics maximising the effectiveness of firearms, notably the mounted gunmen of Lesotho, the infantry armies of Asante and Dahomey, and the Yoruba warboys and East African warlords who constructed defensive fortifications. Many isolated peoples and some major states like Rwanda and Sokoto, by contrast, gave only a marginal role to firearms. Often, as in Buganda, muskets were adopted but scarcely altered military tactics.

During the last third of the nineteenth century, Europeans changed all this. In 1868 French forces in Senegal adopted breech-loading rifles with paper cartridges; in 1876, bolt-action rifles with metal cartridges; and in 1885, magazine rifles.[1] Breech-loading rifles were vastly superior to muskets in range, accuracy, speed of fire, and stopping-power, especially when firing soft-nosed bullets, as in Africa they usually did. 'You have no idea of the effect of the Gras rifle,' a French lieutenant told his brother in 1890: 'a bullet in the head takes off the whole skull, a bullet in the chest makes a hole in the back the size of a plate, the limbs are mangled and the bones broken in a horrible manner. . . . If these chaps were armed like us, we should be in a fine mess.'[2] Unlike muskets, moreover, breech-loading rifles could be fired from a prone position, an immense advantage, which ended the wielding of guns like spears. 'Each soldier must remember,' General Wolseley told the British troops invading Asante in 1873, 'that with his breech-loader he is equal to at least twenty Ashantis, wretchedly armed as they are with old flint-muskets, firing slugs or pieces of stone that do not hurt badly at more than 40 or 50 yards range.'[3] A Hausa poet agreed:

> The [Africans'] weapons could not reach the Christians,
> But *their* weapons could reach us
> Although they were aiming from afar off . . .
> They had a dreadful gun,
> There was the magazine rifle, hear what the Christians had . . .
> Quiver, bow, sword and even spears,
> Such weapons are objects of scorn to the Christians![4]

As will be seen, the European conquest was not the walk-over these accounts suggest, but it was easier than would have been possible either before the 1870s, when both sides had only muskets, or after 1918, when precision weapons became more widely available.

Moreover, the breech-loader was only one new weapon. The Asante expedition of 1873 also deployed the first machine-gun, which immediately jammed; the first fully effective model was the Maxim, patented in 1884 and firing eleven bullets a second. The British and Germans relied heavily on machine-guns. The French scarcely used them, favouring light field artillery to defend or destroy fortifications almost impregnable to local forces. In 1890 artillery drove Segu's

---

[1] Yves Person, *Samori: une révolution dyula* (3 vols., Dakar, 1968–75), vol. 3, p. 907.

[2] François Descostes, *Au Soudan (1890–1891): souvenirs d'un tirailleur sénégalais* (Paris, 1893), pp. 32, 35.

[3] Brackenbury, *Ashanti War*, vol. 1, p. 364.

[4] Imam Umar of Kete-Krachi, writing in the early 1900s, quoted in Mervyn Hiskett, *The development of Islam in West Africa* (London, 1984), p. 263.

defenders from their capital without a single French casualty.[5] Meanwhile the compact 'British square' of riflemen was virtually impenetrable for Africans because they lacked the artillery that had driven this technique from European battlefields half a century earlier.[6]

It would be wrong to attribute the European conquest purely to military technology. It owed much to superior logistics and organisation, the courage and training of European officers and their mainly African troops, the small scale and internal divisions of many African societies, and the fact that Africans had to feed themselves as well as fight. Yet most of these European advantages had long existed. What was *new* in the late nineteenth century was chiefly the military technology. That was what compelled Africans to rethink their notions of military honour.

The dilemma was especially acute for the proud horsemen who had long dominated the West African savanna. In 1897 the British invaded the Sokoto Caliphate, the largest and most impressive state in sub-Saharan Africa but so remote from the coast that it had been slow to adopt firearms. During the next six years, the British conquered its emirates one by one, with some local fighting but no coordinated resistance. Finally, in March 1903, a British force of some 750 largely African troops reached the walls of the capital.[7] Caliph Attahiru and his advisers hesitated. Some urged *hijra*, withdrawal before the overwhelming power of unbelievers. Others recommended defending the city walls with bows and muskets. Attahiru, however, obeyed the normal impulse of an honour culture in crisis: he decided to attack in traditional style. Yet as he drew up his 2,000 horsemen before the city walls, gunfire dispersed them before they could even charge. Individual zealots 'exhibited extraordinary bravery and charged right up to the Square in twos and threes only to be riddled with bullets':[8]

At the end of the slaughter, a slave boy aged 15 or 16 walked slowly up to the square with an axe on his shoulder, and paid no attention to orders to throw his axe down. When within 10 yards he suddenly dashed at an officer and was shot in the act of trying to cut him down. They found out afterwards that he had determined to die because his master had been killed.[9]

---

[5] Daniel R. Headrick, *The tools of empire* (New York, 1981), pp. 100–2; [Louis] Archinard, *Le Soudan Français en 1889–1890; rapport militaire* (Paris, 1891), pp. 18–20.

[6] Bruce Vandervort, *Wars of imperial conquest in Africa, 1830–1914* (London, 1998), p. 64.

[7] For descriptions of the campaign, see Richard H. Dusgate, *The conquest of Northern Nigeria* (London, 1985), ch. 16; Risto Marjomaa, *War on the savannah: the military collapse of the Sokoto Caliphate under the invasion of the British Empire, 1897–1903* (n.p., 1998), ch. 7.

[8] Abadie to his family, 21 March 1903, Abadie Papers, RH.

[9] Grier to Dorothy Grier, 25 February 1908, Grier Papers, box 1, RH.

'Sokoto occupied 15th March: feeble resistance,' the British commander cabled.[10]

Yet Sokoto's leaders were not animated purely by heroic honour. They were heirs to Usuman dan Fodio's jihad, to the disciplining of aristocratic honour by Islam. Those who returned to the capital and submitted were led by Muhammad al-Bukhari, the aged Wazir, who later explained that he had consulted Usuman dan Fodio's writings and found that when the power of unbelievers was overwhelming, a legitimate course for Muslims was 'having relation with unbelievers and befriending them (out of fear of them), with the tongue but not with the heart.' When he met the British, 'I heard from them a talk which did not bear on the prohibition of prayer. . . . I then stayed in Sokoto and worked with them.' Still uneasy, he consulted a scholar who assured him that there had been precedents for *taqiyya* (dissembling in defence of the faith) when the Qarmatians had sacked Mecca in 930 and the Mongols had taken Baghdad in 1258. 'I became filled with rejoicing and happiness,' the Wazir wrote, 'and gave thanks to God for it.' He had not dishonoured his religion or himself.[11]

The fighting at Sokoto demonstrated that European firepower ruled out the massed cavalry charges of savanna tradition. Instead, Sokoto's most effective resistance came when the equestrian nobility joined with Muslim zealots to defend their walled towns with bows and muskets. This happened later in 1903 at Burmi, a Mahdist stronghold where Caliph Attahiru took refuge. The first British attempt to take the town was repelled 'with desperate fanaticism' by repeated infantry charges in which the defenders lost two hundred fifty to three hundred dead 'lying in heaps behind, in, and in front of the gate.' The British then brought up artillery and the defenders took cover in trenches surrounding the town, some of them lashed together so that they could not retreat. Burmi was finally stormed and taken in hand-to-hand fighting in which seven hundred defenders were killed, including Attahiru and ninety of his men who died around him.[12]

Yet Sokoto's noblemen never attempted guerilla resistance, which in a region so vast and hostile to Christian control might have made British conquest unacceptably expensive. The Caliphate's open plains were poor country for guerilla warfare, but perhaps the chief obstacle was the distinction between the Fula aristocracy and their retainers, on the one hand, and the unarmed Hausa peasantry

[10] Lugard to Chamberlain, 19 March 1903, CO 446/30/724.

[11] R. A. Adeleye, 'The dilemma of the Wazir,' *JHSN*, 4 (1968), 306–11.

[12] Dusgate, *Conquest*, pp. 204–6, 218–21; Sword to Brigade Major, 24 May 1903, CO 445/17/31592; Barlow to Brigade Major, 1 August 1903, and Wallace to Chamberlain, 16 August and 18 September 1903, CO 446/32/527, 354, 518; D. J. M. Muffett, *Concerning brave captains* (London, 1964), p. 201.

and numerous slaves, on the other, for the noblemen feared popular insurrection as they feared Christian rule. This appeared vividly at Satiru, a village under Mahdist influence near Sokoto, where peasants and escaped slaves armed with 'some spears and bows and arrows, but mostly hoes, axes and such agricultural implements' ambushed and killed British officers in 1906. Sokoto's leaders, having submitted to the British, mobilised three thousand men to suppress the resistance. Initially, most refused to fight, to their leaders' intense shame. 'The native Chiefs are now begging to be given the chance of wiping out the former disgrace,' the Resident reported.[13] But the British also wanted revenge:

Early on the 10th March Major Goodwin attacked. The enemy twice charged the Infantry, and once the Mounted Infantry; but, being an almost unarmed rabble, they suffered terrible loss from the rifles and Maxim fire, and were almost exterminated. The force then advanced, and found the village held in force, and it was taken at the point of the bayonet, – the enemy persistently awaiting every charge. Driven from the place, they were pursued by the Mounted Infantry, who found a body of them collected in thick bush and attacked and routed them. The native horsemen continued the pursuit in every direction. The numbers opposed to our forces are estimated at about 2000, and they have been annihilated.[14]

Satiru was razed to the ground and Attahiru's successor cursed anyone building or farming there.[15]

Equestrian aristocracies found it especially difficult to adapt to the new technology. So also did those isolated and commonly stateless peoples who had little experience with firearms and saw warfare largely as an intervillage tournament. The Gishu of Mount Elgon in Uganda, renowned for the severity of their initiation rites, suffered a yet more brutal initiation in 1907. 'They at first displayed a great contempt for the rifles,' the British commander reported, 'even coming down the hill to attack the troops, who got within about 20 yds of the enemy; who then retired slowly up the slopes of the hills throwing wooden spears and rocks at close range.' Some 80 were killed, 966 huts burned, and 920 cattle captured before their chief submitted and said they had learned their lesson.[16] When Europeans occupied the Mount Kenya region, similarly, local girls taunted the young warriors, 'You dance shivering and the whiteman came yesterday; where will you go to fight?' In response, warriors 'on several

---

[13] Burdon to High Commissioner, 21 February 1906, CO 446/53/115.
[14] Lugard to Elgin, 16 March 1906, CO 446/53/219.
[15] R. A. Adeleye, 'Mahdist triumph and British revenge in Northern Nigeria: Satiru 1906,' *JHSN*, 6 (1972), 193–214.
[16] 'Uganda Protectorate: Intelligence Report No. 30,' April 1907, CO 536/13/115.

occasions ran up to within a few feet of our rifles before they were shot down.'[17] Neighbouring Kikuyu warriors, after their first experience with such firepower, dipped their hide shields in a river to harden them before attacking again.[18]

Yet colonial armies learned not to underestimate such lightly armed peoples. Their poisoned arrows were generally more feared than musket-balls. Their ability to exploit natural defences could make them very dangerous. The toughest fighting the British faced in Northern Nigeria was not against Sokoto's horsemen but against the Chibuk hillsmen of the Mandara Mountains. They took refuge in an extraordinary fastness of hilltops, caverns, and underground water sources defended with poisoned arrows fired at close range. The first British assault fired fifty-five thousand rounds, killed between two hundred fifty and three hundred Chibuk, and cost fifty-two casualties on the British side without evicting the defenders. The British commander then 'entered the lower caves and worked [his] way towards the summit of the hill under ground,' but 'found such a labyrinth of caves and passages occupied by pagans who shot arrows from black holes below, and on either side of the passages and caves that it was impossible to clear them.' He withdrew to blockade the mountains for several weeks until the defenders broke through his lines into open country. When he regrouped to pursue them, they reoccupied the mountains, and another expedition was needed to dislodge them.[19]

Chibuk defiance illustrates the general point that despite their technological weakness, stateless villagers often resisted colonial conquest with exceptional courage and success, owing to their local knowledge, experience of small-scale warfare, willingness to adopt guerilla tactics, hostility to government of any kind, and lack of any leadership whose defeat or capture could end the fighting. It took the British over twenty years to suppress Igbo resistance in south-eastern Nigeria, mounted chiefly by young warriors known as Ekumeku, 'the silent ones', who specialised in attacking government property, missions, and local collaborators. The French took almost as long, from 1893 to 1911, to subdue the Baoule people of the forest-savanna fringe in Côte d'Ivoire, whose uncoordinated resistance concentrated on ambushing French columns from trenches dug on either side of forest paths. The Nuer of the southern Sudan fought the British for the first time in 1902 and for the last time

---

[17] H. S. K. Mwaniki, *Embu historical texts* (Nairobi, 1974), p. 68; R. Meinertzhagen, 'Intelligence report on operations against some Kikuyu tribes living south of Kenya and north of the Tana River during February and March, 1904,' FOCP 8356/70.

[18] Henry Muoria, *I, the Gikuyu and the white fury* (Nairobi, 1994), p. 4.

[19] Chapman to Brigade Major, 12 December 1906, CO 446/62/148; Wolseley to Adjutant, 14 January and 19 February 1907, CO 446/63/187 and 180; Hasler to High Commissioner, 11 May 1907, CO 446/63/173.

in 1930.[20] They were pastoral warriors such as often defied European control, sometimes transforming their tactics in doing so. In 1902, for example, a Turkana leader in northern Kenya informed the local British official 'that he would shortly come down with his warriors and make short work of him and his station.' Turkana held off both British and Ethiopian control for the next twenty-two years, learning meanwhile to fight with modern rifles.[21] Further south, the Nandi pastoralists who resisted British conquest of Kenya most fiercely were quick to grasp that breech-loaders obliged them to adopt guerilla techniques.[22]

To confront precision weapons demanded either great courage or some belief in supernatural protection such as inspired two great rebellions against colonial control, the Maji Maji rising of 1905–7 in German East Africa (mainland Tanzania) and the Kongo-Wara rebellion of 1928–32 in French Equatorial Africa (especially the future Central African Republic). Both embraced numerous ethnic groups, mostly stateless peoples without strong military traditions, brought together by prophets who offered a ritual means – a water medicine in Maji Maji and a sacred hoe-shaft in Kongo-Wara – to render warriors invulnerable to European bullets. These promises inspired unmilitarised villagers to acts of reckless bravery. Kongo-Wara's devotees fought a mainly defensive guerilla war, but with moments of open defiance, as when a man danced before the French commander, threatening him with a spear and chanting, 'Fire, big gorilla; your gun will shoot only water.' The Maji Maji rebels, by contrast, launched massed attacks on German fortifications:

They advanced on the boma in close columns. There must have been over a thousand men. . . . Two machine-guns, Europeans, and soldiers rained death and destruction among the ranks of the advancing enemy. Although we saw the ranks thin, the survivors maintained order for about a quarter of an hour, marching closer amidst a hail of bullets. But then the ranks broke apart and took cover behind the numerous small rocks. . . . Then suddenly . . . a second column of at least 1,200 men was advancing towards us. . . . The first attackers were only three paces from the firing line when they sank to the ground.[23]

[20] Don C. Ohadike, *The Ekumeku movement* (Athens, Ohio, 1991); Timothy C. Weiskel, *French colonial rule and the Baule peoples* (Oxford, 1980), esp. pp. 201, 218–21; Douglas H. Johnson, *Nuer prophets* (Oxford, 1994), pp. 5–6, 164–203.

[21] 'Uganda Protectorate Intelligence Report, No. 15,' July 1902, FOCP 7954/190; John Lamphear, *The scattering time: Turkana responses to colonial rule* (Oxford, 1992), pp. 227–31, 263 (which expresses some scepticism about the 1902 report), 274.

[22] A. T. Matson, *The Nandi campaign against the British 1895–1906* (Nairobi, 1974), p. 14.

[23] Raphael Nzabakomada-Yakoma, *L'Afrique Centrale insurgée: la guerre du Kongo-Wara (1928–1930)* (Paris, 1986), p. 23; Kwiro Chronicle, 31 August 1905 (written November 1907), Kwiro Mission Archives, Tanzania: I owe access to this document, and information on the second assault, to Dr. L. E. Larson.

In a further assault two days later, rebels came close enough to throw flasks of magic water against the walls of the fort.

To abandon notions of military honour in order to face the new realities of warfare was especially traumatic for southern African peoples who inherited the heroic traditions of Shaka and his counterparts. The Sotho, relying on horses and firearms, found adaptation relatively simple, fighting successfully in 1880–1 to prevent the Cape Colony from depriving them of the guns considered essential to their survival and masculinity.[24] For the Zulu, by contrast, the success of massed assaults by disciplined spearmen had bred notions of heroic honour that became self-destructive in the face of precision weapons. It was not that Zulu leaders ignored the superiority of firearms, which they were incorporating into their tactics even before their terrible slaughter at the Battle of Blood River in 1838. Forty years later, as the British prepared to invade the Zulu state, King Cetshwayo ordered every man to obtain a gun and display it when parading before him.[25] In their initial victory at Isandhlwana in 1879, the Zulu advanced cautiously, using all available cover, and their losses probably equalled those of the British. But the subsequent unsuccessful assault on the British post at Rorke's Drift – the work of inexperienced Zulu reserves determined to blood their spears – had no strategic significance, cost some six hundred Zulu against seventeen British dead, and perfectly illustrated the self-destructive potential of heroic honour by weakening the army's enthusiasm for the war. Cetshwayo knew that he had no hope against modern weapons defending prepared positions, but when the British renewed their invasion, the Zulu army again forgot this and attacked a fortified position at Khambula, losing perhaps three thousand men against twenty-eight on the other side. During the cavalry pursuit that followed the Zulu withdrawal, 'some turned to expose their chests to their pursuers, while others just stood waiting to be shot.'[26] The king now wanted peace, but the young regiments opposed him, determined to prove themselves as brave as their fathers. 'Is the king afraid?' they asked. 'Does he think he will be defeated because those who sit round the eating-mat have been killed?' Cetshwayo replied, 'If you prod the ground with your stick, the earth will be hard.' When he sent oxen to the British as a peace-offering, the regiments

---

[24] Anthony Atmore and Peter Sanders, 'Sotho arms and ammunition in the nineteenth century,' *JAH*, 12 (1971), 543–4.

[25] Etherington, *Great treks*, pp. 275, 280; evidence of Mpatshana kaSodondo, 1912, in Webb and Wright, *James Stuart Archive*, vol. 3, p. 305.

[26] Laband, *Rise and fall*, pp. 224–9, 232–9, 253, 263–77 (quotation on pp. 275–6).

blocked their delivery.[27] In any case, the British wanted revenge. They had it next day at Ulundi, where the Zulu army advanced cautiously but bravely to less than 100 metres from the British square but made no impact on it, largely because their marksmanship was appalling. Cetshwayo always maintained that the British had fought behind iron shields. The Zulu lost some fifteen hundred men, and two taken prisoner. Thirteen British were killed.[28] The war was over, the kingdom was destroyed, but the heroic tradition retained its baleful fascination. When sections of the Zulu were forced into rebellion in 1906, they were condemned by traditionalists because their mode of fighting 'differed from that of Zulus by taking refuge in forests and fastnesses until hunted up by the Europeans. Zulus would have taken up a position in the open and come face to face with the foe. They waylaid Europeans wherever they could. We laughed at them for this.'[29]

Sokoto horsemen, stateless villagers, and Zulu regiments all faced colonial armies whose combination of technology and professionalism they could not match. In much of the West African savanna, however, it was different. There warfare was dominated by professionals like the *sebbe* of Senegal with long experience with firearms, jealous codes of honour, and often the support of relatively powerful kingdoms. There, moreover, the conquest took half a century and was commanded by French officers equally alert to considerations of honour. The European technological advantage ensured that it was not an equal contest, but it was perhaps more equal, harder-fought, and more prolific in ostentatious heroism than anywhere else in sub-Saharan Africa outside Ethiopia.

The *sebbe* themselves proved surprisingly ineffective when Governor Faidherbe initiated French conquest of the Senegal Valley in 1855. Although, as he reported, *sebbe* were 'susceptible of showing courage in certain circumstances,' their extortions and brutality had made them hated by the peasants and their Muslim leaders in a society fragmented by the slave trade and its abolition. This remained true during the best-known Wolof resistance to conquest, that of Lat Dior, ruler of Kajoor, a skilful warrior who personified many *ceddo* qualities and died gallantly in 1886 while fighting a guerilla war against the French occupation of his kingdom, but who had frequently cooperated with them in the past and had alienated Muslim reformers, peasant subjects, and

---

[27] Evidence of Mtshapi kaNoradu, 1918, and Ndukwana kaMbengwana, 1900, in Webb and Wright, *James Stuart Archive*, vol. 4, pp. 72–3, 288.

[28] Laband, *Rise and fall*, pp. 282, 297, 303, 316–23.

[29] Evidence of Mpatshana kaSodondo, 1912, in Webb and Wright, *James Stuart Archive*, vol. 3, p. 320.

many of his own *sebbe* by his selfish pursuit of royal power.[30] More formidable resistance was mounted by the Tukulor state in the upper Senegal and Niger valleys founded by a jihad launched in 1852 by al-Hajj Umar Tall. Although he failed to establish a stable polity to match the Sokoto Caliphate, Umar created a formidable army. Its core consisted of between four thousand and ten thousand *talibe*, Muslim zealots of Umar's own Tijaniyya brotherhood, bound to him by ties of discipleship as well as military discipline, exemplifying the fusion of heroic honour and Islamic earnestness taking place throughout Senegambia at that time. To these were added about twice as many *sofa*, lifelong military slaves, mainly of Bamana origin, held in some contempt by *talibe*. The army was especially strong in cavalry, generally armed with muskets, sabres, and lances. The infantry mostly carried flintlock muskets. The army's greatest assets were morale and tactical discipline.[31] 'The Tukulor,' Faidherbe reported after first meeting them,

show in this war a courage and composure of which one can have no conception in Senegal. They can be seen to march into fire as if to martyrdom with an evident desire to be killed.

It is only with difficulty that the natural sense of self-preservation regains the upper hand over their exaltation and they are obliged to retreat, and even then they retire slowly, never turning their backs.[32]

Later French officers were universal in their admiration. 'There were instances of magnificent madness,' one wrote, 'as when a horseman came to plant his banner some twenty paces from the French . . . dismounted, and continued to fire until he was killed, facing us alone.' The garrison of Ouossebougou defended the town house by house, hurling stones when their ammunition was exhausted, until their commander blew up his fortress and the women killed their children and themselves.[33] 'Not one fled; all died at their stations,' a French officer wrote of another incident. 'Many, having nothing more to fire, knelt and quietly said their rosary, awaiting the final blow. We learned that they were the

---

[30] Boubacar Barry, *Le royaume du Waalo* (Paris, 1972), p. 305; Diouf, *Kajoor*, pp. 251–61, 282–5.

[31] Madina Ly-Tall, *Un Islam militant en Afrique de l'ouest au XIXe siècle: le Tijaniyya de Saiku Umar Futiyu contre les pouvoirs traditionnels et la puissance coloniale* (Paris, 1991), pp. 274–7; A. S. Kanya-Forstner, 'Mali – Tukulor,' in Michael Crowder (ed.), *West African resistance* (London, 1971), pp. 57–61.

[32] Faidherbe, 23 July 1857, in Ly-Tall, *Un Islam militant*, p. 311. For first-hand accounts of Tukulor warfare, see John H. Hanson, 'Islam, ethnicity and Fulbe-Mande relations in the era of Umar Tal's *jihad*,' in Mirjam de Bruijn and Han van Dijk (eds.), *Peuls et Mandingues: dialectique des constructions identitaires* (Paris, 1997), ch. 3.

[33] Charles Mangin, quoted in Charles John Balesi, *From adversaries to comrades-in-arms: West Africans and the French military, 1885–1918* (Waltham, Mass., 1979), p. 13; Archinard, *Le Soudan Français*, pp. 38–52; [Albert] Baratier, *A travers l'Afrique* (Paris, 1912), ch. 7.

talibe.' Neither side took prisoners: 'they were led a few paces from the camp without even binding them: "Kneel, bend you neck." ... The indifference of all these people is really admirable: not a wince, not a shudder.' Umar's successor explained, 'They fell upon us from dawn to dusk and routed us because of the difference between our weapons and theirs, not because of [their bravery].'[34]

The Tukulor army, for all its disciplined courage, was transitional from the cavalry forces and walled towns of savanna tradition to the new tactics of mobility and disciplined firepower. That transition was carried further in the Mande-speaking military empire of Samori, established in the 1860s between the upper-middle Niger and the forest edge. Samori resisted the French until 1898. Operating in an environment less suited to horses, he virtually abandoned cavalry warfare, using horses only as officers' mounts and for scouting and harrying fleeing enemies. He also reduced his regular infantry to about twelve thousand men, largely military slaves, while arming half of them with breech-loaders, improving their marksmanship, supplying them with home-made cartridges, training them to manoeuvre by command, abandoning fixed positions, and emphasising mobility, all in the manner of his French adversaries and partly under the training of men who had served them.[35] 'Samori's troops fight exactly like Europeans,' a French commander reported, 'with less discipline perhaps, but with much greater determination.' Samori himself begged for death when captured and later tried to kill himself in order to escape deportation to Gabon.[36]

Other peoples who mounted fierce resistance to European firepower had similarly to rethink their tactics and sometimes to sacrifice their notions of military honour. Dahomey's rulers, for example, learned from their first clash with the French in 1890 that they could no longer rely on muskets, mobility, surprise, and raw courage. During the next two years they bought at least seventeen hundred (mostly outdated) breech-loaders, five machine-guns, six light field-guns, and appropriate ammunition. They also hired European and Senegalese instructors. When some two thousand French troops invaded Dahomey in 1892, it took them nearly two months to reach the capital, 120 kilometres inland, in the face

---

[34] Descostes, *Au Soudan*, pp. 38, 32; John Hanson and David Robinson, *After the jihad: the reign of Ahmad al-Kabir in the Western Sudan* (East Lansing, 1991), p. 255.

[35] Etienne Péroz, *Au Soudan Français* (Paris, 1891), pp. 409–12; Person, *Samori*, vol. 2, pp. 891–923, 951–67, 973–81; Martin Legassick, 'Firearms, horses and Samorian army organization 1870–1898,' *JAH*, 7 (1966), 95–115.

[36] Humbert, 12 January 1892, quoted in A. S. Kanya-Forstner, *The conquest of the Western Sudan* (Cambridge, 1969), p. 187; Bé Watara, 'Témoignage d'un Dyan de Diébougou incorporé dans les troupes coloniales africaines (1898–1901),' *Journal des Africanistes*, 68 (1998), 279.

of entrenched positions and artillery control of river crossings. King Gbehanzin burned his palace, exhumed his ancestors' remains, removed key royal regalia, and took to the bush, remaining at large for the next fourteen months until his people's exhaustion forced his surrender.[37]

The most striking adaptation to technological change in West Africa took place in Asante. The British expedition that destroyed Kumase in 1873–4 and then withdrew exposed the ineffectiveness of skirmishing tactics by musketeers against 'guns which hit five Ashantees at once'. It also released all the kingdom's fissiparous forces. When attempts to rebuild the state provoked a second invasion in 1896, Asante did not resist, Asantehene Prempe was exiled, and a British military regime was established.[38] Many Asante regretted this passivity and there was much talk of revolt, but probably little planning, until the governor visited Kumase in March 1900, announced that Prempe would never return, insisted on payment for the costs of conquest, and demanded the surrender of the Golden Stool symbolising the kingdom.[39] At a meeting of chiefs that night, the queen mother of the Edweso chiefdom, Yaw Asantewaa, is said to have seized a gun and declared, 'If you, the chiefs of Asante, are going to behave like cowards and not fight, you should exchange your loin-cloths for my undergarments.' After much indecision and skirmishing, troops searching for the Golden Stool blundered into Edweso, were driven back, and a widespread rising took place.[40]

Effective leadership appears to have been shared between warchiefs, Kumase chiefs, and younger warriors who emerged during the fighting, notably Kofi Kofia, the commander-in-chief for most of the rebellion, and Kobina Kyere, who supplanted him in the final stages after making a name for extreme cruelty and intransigence. Prempe's supporters generally joined the rebellion while his opponents backed the British, but many Asante suffered conflicting loyalties.[41]

Initially the rebels ignored the lessons of 1874 and launched two mass attacks on the British fort at Kumase which were repelled with heavy losses. Thereafter 'we determined not to attack Kumasi again, as too many men were killed, but stockades were to be built all round Kumasi and starve the whiteman out, without losing a lot of people.'[42] These stockades were tactical novelties, for

---

[37] David Ross, 'Dahomey,' in Crowder, *Resistance*, p. 158; Foà, *Le Dahomey*, pp. 392–407; Luc Garcia, *Le royaume du Dahomé face à la pénétration coloniale* (Paris, 1988), pp. 145, 185.

[38] Wilks, *Asante*, pp. 505–6, 654–62.

[39] 'Notes taken at a Palace Palaver of Native Kings and Chiefs,' 28 March 1900, CO 96/359/92.

[40] Aidoo, 'Political crisis,' p. 669; Armitage and Montanaro, *Ashanti campaign*, pp. 26–9.

[41] List enclosed in Nathan to Chamberlain, 19 March 1901, CO 96/378/307; Fell, notes on chiefdoms, 2 March 1914, CO 96/528/9916; Armitage and Montanaro, *Ashanti campaign*, pp. 199, 208; McCaskie, *Identities*, pp. 76–9.

[42] Evidence of Eben Boatin, in Stewart to CS, 25 January 1901, CO 96/378/293.

Asante had not previously fought from fixed positions. Eleven were constructed across or alongside roads leading into Kumase.[43] The Patassi stockade

> was a wonderful structure some six or seven feet high and three or four feet in thickness, built of gigantic forest trees laid lengthways, the interstices filled up with swish [mud] and twigs and brambles, and bound together with telegraph wire. In some of the stockades the Government iron telegraph poles had been used. The Patassi stockade had wings to it, which extended into the bush on either side, and were thus hidden from sight, but the front had been cleared so as to give the occupants of it a clear view forward. Like other stockades round Kumassi it had been carefully loopholed.[44]

Other stockades were built parallel to forest paths, some thirty metres from them and hence invisible, and as much as three hundred metres long, so that 'no one can tell them till a volley tells us where they are as they are built all from behind and never a footprint to show that a man has passed.'[45] Hitherto the British had followed Asante's paths in long columns, driving off ambushes by blind volleys. Stoockades made these tactics impossibly costly in ammunition. They could be taken only by desperate bayonet charges, the first of which won its author the Victoria Cross.[46] Asante, wedded for two centuries to firearms, found no answer. As one later put it, the British 'did not fight fair in using knives (he meant the bayonet and sword) when the Ashantis only had guns.'[47]

Consequently, after British forces relieved Kumase and sent out punitive expeditions, Asante again changed their tactics. At Obassa in September 1900, the British commander reported:

> The position was deliberately prepared; no stockades were erected, but the undergrowth was carefully thinned or entirely cut down according to [Kofi Kofia's] ideas of our methods of attack. . . . At 9 a.m. the advanced scouts were fired on from the front, and left flank, and almost before any deployment could take place, the enemy, who occupied a low crescent-shaped ridge poured in a heavy fire, freely using our .303 carbines of which they had a great number, captured near Kumasi.

When the British charged, the Asante retreated only a few metres to a second position and renewed their fire. Eventually, they were forced to abandon this position too, leaving one hundred fifty dead.[48] It was the last major battle of the rebellion. Hard-core rebels took refuge in the Ahafo Forest. Kofi Kofia, surrendered by his own people, insisted that 'I have not murdered anybody

---

[43] See the map in Lady Hodgson, *The siege of Kumassi* (London, 1901).
[44] Ibid., p. 208.
[45] Willcocks to ?, 28 July [1900], Lugard Papers 33/249, RH.
[46] Willcocks to Chamberlain, 14 August 1900, CO 96/375/30478.
[47] Armitage and Montanaro, *Ashanti campaign*, p. 207.
[48] Willcocks to Chamberlain, 25 December 1900, CO 96/376/3879.

except in fair fighting' and was deported.[49] Yaa Asantewaa, exiled with him, is said to have declared as he left, 'Asante women, I pity you. . . . The men died at the battle front.'[50] Kobina Kyere, surprised and captured, was hanged for murder: 'He marched to the scaffold with a firm step, his head erect, and his eyes glaring defiance at the white man.' He is said to have spat in the British commander's face.[51]

The most detailed evidence of the impact of military innovation on inherited notions of honour comes from Ethiopia. Its people had accepted firearms with remarkable alacrity from the sixteenth century, perhaps in part because they first arrived in numbers at a moment of desperate resistance to Muslim invasion. Nevertheless, muskets were so slow to reload that even in the mid nineteenth century cavalry still dominated the battlefield. Warriors continued to dress as conspicuously as possible and fight in open country, while only elite troops knelt to fire.[52] Defeat by an Egyptian army in 1848 led the future Emperor Tewodros to attempt more systematic training, but expatriate drill instructors met ridicule – 'we fight man for man, but you fight like a herd of slaves' – and the troops preserved the heroic emphasis on individual panache.[53] By the late nineteenth century, however, breech-loading rifles were compelling change. Emperor Menelik II (1889–1913) had an elite force of some five thousand cavalry recruited from 'men of certain position and property,' but the bulk of his central army – estimated in 1902 at thirty thousand men – consisted of mounted infantry armed with rifles, stiffened by some five hundred professional riflemen 'who form the one regiment which has some rudimentary notions of discipline,' as a British diplomat put it. The central army possessed an assortment of artillery and machine-guns and could be supplemented by provincial troops and peasant militia variously estimated at around three hundred thousand men, many of whom habitually carried a rifle as a point of honour.[54] This army gained victory over the Italians at Adwa in 1896 not only by skilful strategy, effective use of modern weapons, and realisation that massed frontal attacks without regard for

[49] Evidence of Kofi Kofia, in Stewart to CS, 25 January 1901, CO 96/378/282.
[50] Emmanuel Akyeampong and Pashington Obeng, 'Spirituality, gender, and power in Asante history,' *IJAHS*, 28 (1995), 506.
[51] Armitage and Montanaro, *Ashanti campaign*, p. 212; Fell, notes on chiefdoms, 2 March 1914, CO 96/528/9916.
[52] Pankhurst, *Economic history*, pp. 560–1; Plowden, *Travels*, pp. 64–8; Guidi, *Annales*, pp. 245–6.
[53] G. F.-H. Berkeley, *The campaign of Adowa and the rise of Menelik* (new edn, London, 1935), p. 12.
[54] Clark, 'General report on Abyssinia for the year 1906,' FOCP 9041/1; C. C. Bigham, *Military report on Abyssinia (provisional)* (London, 1902), pp. 93–101; Pankhurst, *Economic history*, pp. 603–5.

cover were seldom practicable, but also by traditional courage and panache, the new technology being superimposed on the old ethos.[55] Dejazmach Demisie's men were to taunt him for the rest of his life for hiding behind a rock at Adwa, where the Ethiopians rushed three positions defended by artillery and magazine rifles, actions accounting for many of their estimated seven thousand dead, a toll similar to that of the defeated Italians.[56]

How precision weapons slowly changed the traditional military ethos appeared during the crisis following Menelik's death in 1913, when his grandson and chosen successor, Lij Yasu, was deposed in 1916 by the Shoan military nobility. Lij Yasu's powerful father, Negus Mikael of Wollo, summoned his followers in traditional fashion:

People of Wello, Tigray, Gonder, Gojjam, youths and adults – all males: Follow me! I have lost my son, and help me to find him! Do not worry about provisions or food for the journey: I am your provision – go looting and eat and drink! Those who have guns, take up your guns! Those who have no guns, take up your shield and spear and help me![57]

As Mikael's army advanced on Addis Ababa, the Shoan vanguard commander, Ras Lulsegged, fought a delaying action described in heroic terms reminiscent of Amda Siyon:

The notables close to him said: 'We have lost many men and some have fled; let us retreat to the lowlands and wait until the Shewan army arrives to help us.' And when Ras Lulsegged heard of the matter, he thought it was the plan of cowardice and said: 'I, Abba Belay [his horse-name], the slave of Danyaw [i.e. Menelik], do not want to destroy my name; I will not be the laughing-stock of Wello. If you are afraid, flee! I shall fight as long as I can and I shall die here.' And those whose names are mentioned in the above lines, such fearless warriors as Asallafi Abbe, had grown up in the Palace of Emperor Menelik; and saying, 'As for us, what is the use to live after being separated from you?' they fought together, and felling soldiers from Wello like dry leaves, they died in the battle with Ras Lulsegged.[58]

The delaying action enabled the main Shoan army to defeat Mikael's forces at Sagale on 27 October 1916. Instead of following up this success, the Shoans returned in triumph to Addis Ababa, 'decked with the bloodstained clothes they

[55] Sven Rubenson, 'Adwa 1896: the resounding protest,' in R. I. Rotberg and A. A. Mazrui (eds.), *Protest and power in black Africa* (New York, 1970), pp. 122–7; Bigham, *Military report*, p. 97.

[56] Doughty-Wylie to Grey, 30 November 1911, FO 403/421/117; Berkeley, *Campaign*, pp. 345–6; Rubenson in Rotberg and Mazrui, *Protest*, p. 126.

[57] Reidulf K. Molvaer (ed.), *Prowess, piety and politics: the chronicle of* Abeto *Iyasu and Empress Zewditu of Ethiopia (1909–1930), recorded by* Aleqa *Gebre-Igziabiher Elyas* (Cologne, 1994), p. 367. In quoting from this book, I have omitted most of the distracting editorial interpolations.

[58] Ibid., p. 368.

had taken from the dead.'[59] Yet Sagale had been won by abandoning heroic tactics:

[T]he notables of Wello . . . drew their sabres, and both cavalry and infantry closed with the Shewan army courageously, without fear. But the soldiers of Shewa were trained to lie down and shoot while lying down in rows, so that the soldiers of Wello thought that they had been shot down; and when they approached while singing war-chants in order to take away [their weapons], they [the Shewans] fired in quick succession and felled [the soldiers of Wello] like leaves.[60]

Not everyone considered these tactics honourable. Fitawrari Adal Bezzabbih, for example, 'wanting to make himself famous by heroic deeds, went outside the fortifications and with drawn sabre he killed soldiers from Wello and died there.'[61]

Men of honour found it even more difficult to make the innovations needed to resist the Italian invasion of 1935. Mechanical transport, aeroplanes, and poison gas gave the Italians massive technological superiority over an army complacent from its victory at Adwa and still composed of a small professional force and a mass of peasant irregulars:

Soldiers are coming in from all parts of the country with their chiefs. They assemble in Addis Abeba and then march past the Emperor behind their (so-called) feudal chiefs shouting their valour. The Emperor watches these parades with a mournful eye. The men are enthusiastic but ill equipped and armed with rifles forty years old. . . . What is more many of the men are beginning to realise this. . . . In fact during some of these parades before the Emperor the men from the provinces have thrown their old rifles before him shouting that they will fight with their hands since they are to be sent to war unarmed.[62]

Through the winter of 1935–6, the army fought a brave, conventional retreat southwards towards Addis Ababa, suffering terrible losses. By May 1936, it was clearly defeated. Emperor Haile Selassie, having proclaimed, 'We are forever with you until Our life expires,' accepted his ministers' advice to go into exile and represent Ethiopia's case in Europe, after failing to negotiate a compromise with Mussolini. He never entirely lived down what many Ethiopians considered cowardice.[63]

---

[59] Thesiger, *Life*, p. 429.
[60] Molvaer, *Prowess*, pp. 370–1.
[61] Ibid., p. 387.
[62] De Halpert to Perham, 3 November 1935, de Halpert Papers, RH.
[63] Haile Sellassie, *My life and Ethiopia's progress 1892–1937* (trans. E. Ullendorff, London, 1976), pp. 245, 290; Alberto Sbacchi, *Ethiopia under Mussolini: fascism and the colonial experience* (London, 1985), pp. 27, 32.

Resistance passed to guerilla groups, estimated in 1937–8 at some twenty-five thousand fighters.[64] Guerilla tactics were as uncongenial as trench warfare to men of honour. 'We have learned to be cowards,' one guerilla chief told a journalist in 1939. 'Once upon a time we fought face to face with our enemies. Now we know the value of guerilla warfare – we call it coward's fighting. But that way we shall defeat the Italians.' By then the lessons of initial defeat were widely understood:

Do they think we are fools? Do they think we shall throw ourselves against these modern fortified works as we did during the campaign? No. We shall wait until the Italians are hard pressed in Europe or by guerilla warfare here. Then we shall surround their cities and camps; we shall harass them but never attack them direct; we shall cut their communications; we shall starve them.[65]

Guerilla warfare both contravened and exploited Ethiopian traditions. The average guerilla band was estimated in 1938 to be about four hundred to five hundred strong, fluctuating with the agricultural season. It normally included men without guns who picked up those of fallen members, plus numbers of women and children; the women not only provided services but sometimes fought, which was unprecedented, so that about one-third of the patriots later recommended for medals were women.[66] Some guerilla bands appear to have been regular troops who were joined by peasants defending their localities in traditional manner. Other bands were of purely local peasant origin with elected leaders. A few formed around men long in revolt, such as the brigand chief Balay Zalaqa in Gojjam, who initially sought to avenge his father killed in resisting tax collection but became a gifted and patriotic guerilla leader.[67] Italian brutality drove many localities into resistance. Guerillas themselves could be brutal and predatory, but generally they could rely on peasant support, while at their strongest – as in the Mänz area of Shoa – they established virtual governments in liberated areas.[68] Honour was one important motive driving young men to join the resistance. Stories tell of men who sang war-songs at weddings, were accused by their elders of having no right to claim such valour, and took to the *maquis*.[69] Guerilla culture drew on the heroic ethos. 'A soldier had the right over what he captured, whether a man or a weapon,' their

[64] Sbacchi, *Ethiopia under Mussolini*, p. 177.
[65] *New Times and Ethiopia News*, 29 April 1939.
[66] Ibid., 17 September 1938; Richard Pankhurst, 'The Ethiopian patriots: the lone struggle, 1936–1940,' *Ethiopia Observer*, 13 (1970), 51; Berhane-Selassie, 'Traditions,' pp. 377–89.
[67] Berhane-Selassie, 'Traditions,' pp. ii–iii, 366–7, 372, 403–8.
[68] *New Times and Ethiopia News*, 17 July 1937 and 29 July 1939.
[69] Salome Gabre Egziabher, 'The Ethiopian patriots, 1936–1941,' *Ethiopia Observer*, 12 (1969), 87.

historian has written. 'Sometimes they gave what they had captured to their leader to show their allegiance. This action was accompanied by the singing of warsongs.... The central theme of such songs was praise to the gallant and insult to the cowardly.'[70] Acts of special gallantry were rewarded by distinctive ornaments. Guerillas often fought barefoot and cultivated a wild, unwashed appearance with uncut hair and masses of cartridge belts. Many were strongly religious – the largest guerilla band in Shoa carried with it the *tabot* from St. George's cathedral in Addis Ababa – and one account tells of a contingent refusing to move until its soothsayer declared the time propitious.[71] Discipline remained hierarchical: 'The old forms of respect, such as bowing and not speaking directly to the chief, were ... rigidly maintained, as far as time and place allowed.'[72] A few individualistic guerilla leaders took titles for themselves and their followers. Balay Zalaqa called himself Prince, 'Avenger of the Blood of Ethiopia', or 'The Overlord' (his horse-name). One leader called himself Negus (King). Others, like Haile Mariam Manno, the first guerilla leader in Shoa, were ordinary farmers.[73] But many prominent guerilla leaders were junior officers from the lower nobility, often with a modern military training, men like Abebe Aregay of Shoa, the only major guerilla leader to survive throughout the war, 'a quiet, thoughtful and a well-loved man' who had been a captain in the royal bodyguard and Chief of Police in Addis Ababa.[74] Leadership retained many heroic features:

The Patriot leader would give the order for attack. He was the one who determined from which side they should advance and other matters of tactics. However, many a leader would refuse to order the retreat, and would die where he was fighting unless his men dragged him off the field. The soldiers always took into their own hands the order for retreat.

A British officer who marched with them at the end of the war wrote that 'the Patriots fought with open-eyed bravery.'[75]

They were, however, divided, occasionally fighting one another. Some remained loyal to Haile Selassie; others wanted to shoot him. In Gojjam, where guerillas were most numerous, the majority probably wanted provincial autonomy. A few groups championed Lij Yasu's heirs. Others sought a

[70] Ibid., p. 69.
[71] Berhane-Selassie, 'Traditions,' p. 368; Egziabher, 'Patriots,' p. 68; *New Times and Ethiopia News*, 15 April 1939.
[72] Egziabher, 'Patriots,' pp. 67–8.
[73] Berhane-Selassie, 'Traditions,' p. 405; Egziabher, 'Patriots,' pp. 68, 76.
[74] Egziabher, 'Patriots,' pp. 73–4; Sbacchi, *Ethiopia under Mussolini*, pp. 34, 204.
[75] Egziabher, 'Patriots,' p. 69; Richard Pankhurst, 'The Ethiopian patriots and the collapse of Italian rule in East Africa, 1940–41,' *Ethiopia Observer*, 12 (1969), 124.

republic.[76] By 1939 the war had reached stalemate and many patriot leaders
made local deals with Italian commanders. Even Abebe Aregay practised a passive stand-off while he waited for Italy to enter the Second World War.[77] Once it
did so, the British invaded Ethiopia and restored Haile Selassie. Many patriots
were disgusted. Abebe Aregay ostentatiously seized the Ministry of War. Some
former guerillas continued to display their weapons and wild appearances at
ceremonies celebrating valour. Many became conservative opponents of imperial modernisation.[78] The emperor himself began to construct a new heroic
myth:

> Holding his banner with his left hand,
> and with his right holding his drawn sword,
> see him begin the march to gain freedom . . .
> He had left the country in grief and lamentation;
> but see, when God's chosen time came,
> he returned home as conqueror.[79]

[76] Alberto Sbacchi, *Legacy of bitterness: Ethiopia and Fascist Italy, 1935–41* (Lawrenceville, N.J.,
1997), pp. 165–6, 181; idem, *Ethiopia under Mussolini*, p. 224.

[77] Sbacchi, *Legacy of bitterness*, pp. 137, 187–8, 193–4.

[78] Sbacchi, *Ethiopia under Mussolini*, pp. 219–20; Molvaer, *Tradition*, p. 41; Sbacchi, *Legacy of
bitterness*, p. 195.

[79] Murad Kamil, 'Amharische Kaiserlieder,' *Abhandlungen für die Kunde des Morgenlandes*, 32,
4 (1957), 48.

12 Honour in Defeat

European conquest and the eventual suppression of internal warfare destroyed much of the rationale for African notions of heroic honour, but colonial rulers were less successful – much less successful than the Tokugawa rulers of Japan – in channelling heroic notions in constructive directions. Rather, by threatening Africa's ruling elites, European conquest increased their sensitivity to issues of rank and vertical honour. Some hereditary rulers were destroyed; others were temporarily eclipsed by upstart collaborators. Some elites defended the old order with a conservatism that historians have neglected; others gained strength by allying with European power and exploiting colonial innovations. Yet not only rulers but entire privileged classes were threatened. The most immediate challenge was the abolition of slavery, enforced cautiously by colonial governments but more radically by the slaves themselves, for whom conquest was as much an opportunity to gain honour as for their masters to lose it. Yet in this area, too, elites defended their status with mixed success, as they did also against two other colonial innovations threatening inherited notions of honour: rural capitalism and Western education. Not all elite responses were conservative; literacy, for example, could be used to sustain or reformulate heroic ideals. Not all conservatism was confined to elites, for heroic values might gleam brightly amidst the gloom of colonial rule. Nor was assertion confined to slaves, for European control offered the enterprising new avenues to distinction and the young new opportunities for respect. The only certainty was that defeat brought great confusion in which the pursuit of honour remained a guiding principle.

'I am a woman at the feet of the white people,' Mbovu kaMtshumayeli lamented in 1904 to James Stuart, whose collection of oral testimonies from Zulu and related peoples is a unique record of the bitterness with which men of honour suffered defeat.[1] 'Europeans regard natives as they do flies which have fallen into their drink, as something to be taken out and thrown away,' Lazarus Mxaba had protested four years earlier.[2] 'We are your dogs,' the seventy-four-year-old Mkando kaDhlova complained:

... You make a law; we obey it. ... Over and over again you promulgate fresh laws and we abide by them cheerfully, and this sort of thing has continued until we have become old and grey-headed, and not even now, advanced in years as we are, do we know the meaning of your policy.

The ancestors, he added, 'have nowadays turned their backs on us,'[3] for, as another elder explained, 'When we kill a beast nowadays we do not praise the ancestors. We simply remain silent, for if we praise the ancestors our own children who have become Christians will not partake of it.'[4] Instead, as an elderly woman complained, 'The people are by degrees falling to pieces in every direction as a result of European government' and its accompanying 'indiscriminate and fearless way in which people go about *takataing* [bewitching] one another.'[5] 'Nowadays,' Mkando grumbled, 'there are never any pleasant dreams as before.'[6]

Two aspects of subjection most offended men of honour. One was loss of authority over the women and young people of their homesteads. 'Parents have practically lost control over their girls and women,' a headman protested.[7] 'Girls doing as they like,' elders added, 'destroys the rank existing between people, for it tends to bring about that equality which does not exist. Girls then go and marry those not of her rank,' defying their fathers' wishes.[8] Worse, a girl might prostitute herself in one of the new towns, 'induced to leave her kraal or home because she wishes to earn money to dress herself . . . this kind of woman . . . is in the habit of saying that they have control over themselves, that they enjoy "responsible government".'[9] Young men were as bad. 'Your own child can abuse you even as he helps himself to your food.'[10] Much blame lay with Christianity. 'The men in the neighbourhood come to me . . . and complain

---

[1] Evidence of Mbovu kaMtshumayeli, 1904, in Webb and Wright, *James Stuart Archive*, vol. 3, p. 34.

[2] Evidence of Lazarus Mxaba, 1900, in ibid., vol. 1, p. 243.

[3] Evidence of Mkando kaDhlova, 1902, in ibid., vol. 3, pp. 155, 172.

[4] Evidence of Mqaikana kaYenge, 1916, in ibid., vol. 4, p. 15.

[5] Evidence of Nombango, 1903, in ibid., vol. 5, p. 138.

[6] Evidence of Mkando kaDhlova, 1902, in ibid., vol. 3, p. 168.

[7] Evidence of John Kumalo, 1900, in ibid., vol. 1, p. 225.

[8] Evidence of Nungu kaMatshobana and others, 1903, in ibid., vol. 5, p. 212.

[9] Evidence of Qalizwe kaDhlozi, 1899, in ibid., vol. 5, pp. 229–30.

[10] Evidence of John Gama, 1898, in ibid., vol. 1, p. 137.

about their children becoming *amakolwa* [Christians] against their (the men's) inclination,' a headman reported. 'I reply, "That is the white people's affair. I suffer too."'[11]

More bitter yet to men of honour was loss of the respect due to rank. *Abatsha* (new ones) in European service lorded it over those of noble ancestry. 'They act with disrespect towards their former "fathers".... They do not show us respect because they think themselves chiefs.... They say to us, "What are they now? The old ways are gone. Let *us* be raised up."'[12] 'People only get 10 cattle for children' as *lobola* (bridewealth), Mbovu protested:

> Rank is not studied. Official witnesses and those who register *isibalo* [forced] workers are only allowed 15 cattle as *lobola*. The Government does not inquire into the rank of officials recommended by the chief. I am of rank and yet am obliged to get only 10 head. I am of rank; I am the offspring of a chief and therefore should get more cattle. The Government only increase *lobola* where the man is engaged in doing government duty....
>
> By not allowing me to have more cattle I am unable to maintain my authority and claim people's respect. They jeer at me by saying, 'We are all equal now. Who are you to speak in this way?'

'Why do you stir up these old graves?' he demanded in reply to Stuart's historical enquiries. 'When the tribe is still standing and flourishing it is something, but now we are broken and scattered.'[13]

Colonial rule had no place for embittered enemies wedded to the past. As the French conquered the Tukulor state, its ruler withdrew eastwards to die in the Sokoto Caliphate. His surviving followers helped to defend Burmi against the British in 1903. A few reached Mecca. Meanwhile nearly ten thousand followed a French column back towards their homeland in Senegal, warned that they could not be guaranteed protection if they remained in their former conquered territory.[14] Obsessed by security and contemptuous of kingship, French officers were especially destructive of hereditary authority. They destroyed Dahomey's monarchy and looted its smouldering palace, leaving the kingdom without its essential source of vitality. 'Only a few women faithful to the memory have remained around the tombs and thrones of the kings,' the Resident wrote in 1911. 'They are distinctly old and as shaky as the ruins amidst which they live.'[15] Some members of the enormous royal family became domestic

---

[11] Evidence of Ngabiyana kaBiji, 1899, in ibid., vol. 5, p. 21.

[12] Evidence of Madikane kaMlomowetole, 1903, in ibid., vol. 2, pp. 51–2.

[13] Evidence of Mbovu kaMtshumayeli, 1904, in ibid., vol. 3, pp. 28, 35, 38.

[14] Archinard, *Le Soudan Français*, pp. 26, 62; Hanson and Robinson, *After the jihad*, pp. 242 n2, 252.

[15] Le Herissé, *L'ancien royaume*, p. 32.

servants. Others tried to recoup their position by marrying daughters to French officials, serving in the French army, or gaining education. As a group they retained most of the kingdom's wealth and almost all its cantonal chieftainships, creating hereditary local dynasties, appropriating royal rituals, presiding over bowdlerised ceremonies, and ruling in the old authoritarian style. 'Tradition governs the life of Dahomey,' anthropologists were told in 1931, almost as often as they were told the history of the kings.[16]

British officials were more sensitive to rank, but they too subordinated it to security. After the hard-fought Asante rebellion of 1900, for example, they replaced many rebel chiefs with collaborators, often men of low rank who had taken refuge in the Gold Coast, made money in trade, and returned under British protection. With customary constraints removed, these parvenus greedily exploited their subjects and the opportunities for wealth through cocoa-growing and urban house-building brought by British rule. The first to experience popular anger was Yaw Berku, whom the British had imposed as chief of Offinsu. In 1904 his subjects accused him of having accumulated sixty wives, taken bribes, imposed heavy fines, and built a large house in Kumase with chiefdom funds. When they 'asked him to come down from his basket chair and close his state umbrella,' he threatened to advise the British to arrest and imprison them, at which 'the people became furious and had him bound at once (flogged him as reported) and sent him to the thick bush pending instructions.' Asked by the British whether he wished to be reinstated, he agreed provided he was given sufficient soldiers. Instead they deposed him.[17] Two years later, it was the turn of Kwame Tua, whose main qualification for the distinguished post of Gyaasewahene was that he had fraudulently undertaken to lead the governor to the Golden Stool. A notorious extortioner and womaniser, his subjects raided his house, seized his regalia, and, although initially punished, refused so absolutely to receive him back that he was obliged to resign.[18] His brother, Yaw Awua, was more fortunate. In 1901 he was given the chiefdom of Edweso for his services during the rebellion, after a career in which he had established himself in trade with gold melted down from purloined insignia, had prospered as an arms dealer, and had spent two periods in gaol. Edweso had been Yaw Asantewaa's chiefdom and Yaw Awua was soon in trouble. 'All my subjects refused to obey me,' he complained in 1903, 'and they know very well that I get

[16] Ibid., pp. 35–6; Bay, *Wives*, p. 310; Jacques Lombard, *Autorités traditionnelles et pouvoirs européens en Afrique noire: le déclin d'une aristocratie sous le régime colonial* (Paris, 1967), pp. 243, 269; Maurice Ahanhanzo Glélé, *Le Danxome* (Paris, 1974), pp. 233–45; Herskovits and Herskovits, *Narrative*, pp. 9, 20.

[17] *Gold Coast Leader*, 10 September 1904.

[18] Ibid., 14, 21, and 28 October and 9 December 1905; Rodger to Lyttelton, 22 December 1905, CO 96/433/2127; McCaskie, *Identities*, pp. 79–80.

no prison the same as Yah Asantewah. . . . Again your honour let me get prison for this my people.' Two years later he fled to Kumase before his people could depose him, but in this case his patrons restored him.[19]

The great survivor and personification of perverted Asante honour was Kwame Boakye, a member of Agona's royal family.[20] Defiance of the Asantehene had forced him into refuge in the Gold Coast, where he prospered in trade and cultivated the British, who placed him on the Agona stool in 1896. During the rebellion, he fought 'in the most gallant manner' on the British side. He carried a gun, a coiled whip, and a bandolier full of knives; wore a hereditary, charm-encrusted war-coat; and was attended by horn-blowers and well primed with alcohol. So much did the rebels hate him that they threatened to 'place him in a huge wooden trough in which he would be pounded to death by their women.'[21] Following British victory, he proclaimed himself 'a King like the Ashanti Kings of old,' victimised his enemies – at least two were killed – and exploited his subjects by building a 'palace' costing £2,800, indulging his obsessive love of gold ornaments and elaborate umbrellas, and amassing 150 wives but no child – an occasion for cruel insults and repeated adultery cases. After abortive attempts to depose him, his opponents pursued him to Kumase, 'armed with native swords and matchets marching . . . with drums and gong-gongs beating, in the direction of the quarter where Botchie and his adherents lived.' The British dispersed them, gaoled the leaders, and brokered an agreement confining Kwame Boakye to twenty wives, barring him from flogging his adult subjects or calling them slaves, and limiting the share of their property he could demand as death duties.[22] There were further crises in 1909 and 1911, but the British maintained Kwame Boakye in office until he died in 1915.

By then Asante was prosperous, politically more stable, and displaying wartime loyalty. Moreover, the British were anxious to strengthen chieftainship against increasingly assertive 'youngmen' (or commoners). In 1924 Asantehene Prempe was allowed back from exile as a private citizen, in 1926 he became Chief of Kumase, and in 1935 his successor was reinstated as Asantehene in a restored confederacy.[23] Rank now had its revenge for forty years of

---

[19] Wilks, *Asante*, pp. 713–14; Yaw Awuah to Chief Commissioner, 10 March 1903, CO 96/407/18349; *Gold Coast Leader*, 9 December 1905; Great Britain, *Ashanti: annual report for 1905*, PP, 1906, LXXIII, 249.

[20] This paragraph is based chiefly on McCaskie, 'Consuming passions,' pp. 43–62.

[21] Armitage to Resident, 9 September 1901, CO 96/383/146.

[22] Armitage to CS, 28 September 1906, and enclosure, CO 96/446/43120.

[23] William Tordoff, *Ashanti under the Prempehs, 1888–1935* (London, 1965), pp. 184–5, 219–23, 322–56.

dishonour. Chiefs who opposed the restoration were deposed and early colonial collaborators demoted. In 1936 the restored Confederacy Council abolished all youngmen's associations for their 'unwarranted militancy'. Rank was to dominate Asante to the end of colonial rule.[24]

Even where British authority was established with a minimum of violence, as in Yorubaland, the military leaders of the nineteenth century had great difficulty in subordinating their notions of honour to colonial control. Alanamu, leader of Ilorin's resistance to British conquest in 1897, refused for several years to emerge from his compound. Fabunmi of Okemesi and Ogedemgbe of Ilesha, the two heroes of the Kiriji War against Ibadan, struggled to reconcile their warboys to loss of occupation and independence, Ogedemgbe suffering imprisonment before he was tamed.[25] Ibadan experienced bitter mortification. Its warriors did not resist in 1894 when the British arrested their senior chief, the Baale. 'We are cowards, and afraid of the English Government,' his deputy declared a decade later. In 1907 and again in 1917, senior chiefs committed suicide to escape humiliation and ruin arising from conflict with the British authorities. Military titles atrophied, starting with the cavalry, and political intrigue intensified as it replaced military prowess as the main route to chieftainship and honour.[26] The town itself was humiliated by an administration whose notion of hereditary legitimacy was to strengthen the Alafin of Oyo against all rivals. Not until the 1930s did the Baale of Ibadan gain a respectable place in the colonial order, against the Alafin's violent opposition. 'You are shaming me,' the Alafin wrote to a new British official in 1932. 'Captain Ross did not use to treat me like this. . . . You are my Resident of Oyo and not Ibadan.'[27] Meanwhile the Oni of Ife was reduced to tears 'as he complained that the ancient authority and dignity of his crown were rapidly passing away under the British regime.'[28]

Attempts to restore the Oyo Empire and Asante Confederacy were applications of the indirect rule policy which the British first devised in the Sokoto Caliphate. The swift British victory in 1903 made it possible to preserve the

---

[24] Ibid., p. 227; Gold Coast, *Report on Ashanti for the year April, 1927 to March, 1928* (Accra, n.d.), p. 20; Hodson to Bottomley, 8 July 1937, CO 96/741/7/3; Agnes A. Aidoo, 'Order and conflict in the Asante Empire,' *African Studies Review*, 20, 1 (April 1977), 31; Arhin, 'Rank,' p. 2.

[25] Lethem to his mother, 29 April 1911, Lethem Papers 22/1/42, RH; Falola and Oguntomisin, *Warlords*, pp. 78, 106–7.

[26] Toyin Falola, *Politics and economy in Ibadan, 1893–1945* (Lagos, 1989), pp. 54, 61, 159, 170 n204; George Jenkins, 'Government and politics in Ibadan,' in Lloyd, Mabogunje, and Awe, *Ibadan*, p. 218; Ruth Watson, 'Murder and the political body in early colonial Ibadan,' *Africa*, 70 (2000), 29, 32.

[27] Quoted in Olufemi Vaughan, *Nigerian chiefs: traditional power in modern politics, 1890s–1990s* (Rochester, N.Y., 2000), p. 40.

[28] H. L. Ward Price, *Dark subjects* (London, 1939), p. 137.

Caliphate's rulers and institutions in order to administer the huge territory of Northern Nigeria relatively cheaply, replacing hostile emirs by more compliant relatives and abolishing only the Caliph's overarching authority. Most emirs were scholars and administrators rather than warriors and perhaps found submission easier than did Asante's military chiefs. Some were certainly hostile. Muhammad of Gwandu rejected armed resistance as folly in 1903 but observed three years later that he would kill both the British resident and himself if he suffered another unkind word. Sympathising with the Satiru rebels, he was deposed in 1906 along with the emir of Katsina, who had destroyed the British barracks after the troops left for Satiru. They were two of a dozen emirs removed between 1897 and 1906.[29] Others submitted only reluctantly. The emirs of Bauchi and Yola tried unsuccessfully to avoid swearing loyalty to the British in public. The shehu of Borno did so only after securing a public promise of freedom to practise Islam.[30] Emir Abbas of Kano (1903–19) practised *taqiyya*. So fearful of the Europeans that he commissioned scholars to pray for his survival, he was overtly compliant – sending the British governor an annual present of a horse – but covertly hostile, while using the British to assert his own independence of Sokoto and his family's domination of the emirate.[31] His distinguished contemporary in Katsina, Muhammadu Dikko, achieved a more harmonious and progressive relationship with his rulers without sacrificing Islamic principles. All, however, had to reckon with British ruthlessness when security was threatened.[32]

The emirs cultivated their rulers with great skill. They played upon a shared delight in horsemanship and ceremony, a shared taste for dignity and propriety, a shared enjoyment of deference and good manners. 'I find them all wonderfully charming to deal with,' Governor Lugard wrote, 'dignified and polished native gentlemen of high intelligence and apparently most loyal and I would almost say *grateful*.'[33] The emirs had reason to make a display of gratitude. 'Praise and thanks are due you,' one assured Lugard, 'because of what you have given me, that is to say a kingdom and honour. You have given me power over my

---

[29] Adeleye, 'Mahdist triumph,' p. 213; Alhaji Mahmood Yakubu, *An aristocracy in political crisis: the end of indirect rule and the emergence of party politics in the emirates of Northern Nigeria* (Aldershot, 1996), p. 22.

[30] Edward J. Lugard, 'Journal jottings: Northern Nigeria,' 9 and 31 October and 30 November 1904, Lugard Papers, RH.

[31] Christelow, *Thus ruled*, p. 16; Abbas to Lugard, 4 September 1913, Lugard Papers 48/75, RH; Tahir, 'Scholars,' p. 339.

[32] Kirk-Greene, *Mutumin Kirkii*, p. 15; Peter Kazenga Tibenderana, 'The making and unmaking of the Sultan of Sokoto, Muhammadu Tambari, 1922–31,' *JHSN*, 9, 1 (December 1977), 109.

[33] Lugard to Chamberlain [April 1905?] Lugard Papers 33/266, RH.

peasants in town and village.'[34] British officials were keen to protect those peasants, but without publicly criticising their rulers. 'Never let it be thought you are a friend of the people,' a young official was instructed in the early 1930s. Officials who forgot that principle were quickly transferred.[35] Moreover, the emirs learned to use colonial rule to reinforce the dominance of rank. Of the major district headships into which the first British resident divided Kano emirate, Emir Abbas gave almost half to family members, especially districts surrounding the capital. When the resident tried to demonstrate British control by appointing a slave official as wazir, Abbas secured the removal of both wazir and resident, obliging the former to wear his slave loincloth in public.[36] Generally, however, the British were even keener than the emirs to confine power to men of rank. As the governor declared in 1927, 'The descendants of the great men who have ruled Kano in the past, and the mallams and other people who have knowledge and are of distinguished birth should assist the Emir to govern the country.' From 1911 emirs and their officials were awarded salaries. Of the 588 people on the Zaria native administration's payroll in 1945, 120 belonged to the emir's lineage and 84 to its two leading rivals.[37]

Such contests for rank and honour took place throughout Africa during the first half century of colonial rule, but perhaps the best example comes from Buganda. Two men dominated the kingdom during this period. One was 'that new and model Dictator' Apolo Kaggwa, Katikkiro from 1889 to 1926.[38] No African of his time was more alert to his own *ekitiibwa* and that of his kingdom. Although no longer known for his gun-metal chest – rather, so his enemies claimed, for his overextended belly[39] – Kaggwa nevertheless associated himself with any military activity, holding an honorary commission during the First World War. He remained a passionate advocate of improvement – promoting education, establishing hospitals, building churches, supporting medical research, and even encouraging the training of Catholic priests – and an equally passionate enemy of everything he thought backward, arresting anyone he found practising indigenous medicine. Having taught himself to write while in his twenties, he wrote and printed Buganda's first books and was active in

---

[34] Ibrahim Sarikin Wushishi to Lugard [July 1918?] Lugard Papers, RH.

[35] A. T. Weatherhead, 'But always as friends,' typescript, Weatherhead Papers, RH; Tibenderana, 'Making,' pp. 93–8.

[36] C. N. Ubah, *Government and administration of Kano Emirate 1900–1930* (Nsukka, 1985), pp. 55–7, 101; Sean Stilwell, 'Power, honour and shame: the ideology of royal slavery in the Sokoto Caliphate,' *Africa*, 70 (2000), 412–13.

[37] *The Nigerian Pioneer*, 4 March 1927; Smith, 'Political corruption,' pp. 186, 190.

[38] The phrase was from A. B. Mukwaya, 'The heir,' *Makerere College Magazine*, 3, 1 (December 1940), 27.

[39] Rowe, 'Eyewitness accounts,' p. 67.

4. *Ham Mukasa and Apolo Kagwa in 1902.* From Ham Mukasa, *Sir Apolo Kagwa discovers Britain* (ed. Taban lo Liyong, London, 1975), plate 1. Reproduced by permission of the Syndics of Cambridge University Library.

launching its first newspaper.[40] He ruthlessly resisted attacks on his honour, mobilising seventy-nine witnesses to trounce a critic who accused him of stealing his land and being not a Ganda but a Soga; the accuser earned two years in gaol and the loss of his land.[41] Kaggwa sued journalists for accusing him, inter alia, of worshipping pagan fetishes, being a Soga, and keeping fifty-one wives. He denied improperly appropriating vast areas of land, infringing the rights of the young Kabaka Daudi Chwa, or even attempting to engineer his death.[42] Kaggwa's last and greatest battle was with the British. He had invited them into Buganda in 1890, regarded the Uganda Agreement as a 'Sacred Document' protecting the kingdom, and bitterly resented young British officials for whom Buganda's special status was merely a nuisance. In 1925 he publicly accused a new provincial commissioner of trying to bypass the Buganda government and administer directly. 'In future,' he wrote, 'the Buganda Government is not prepared to regard as right and to take into consideration matters conducted after this fashion.' The provincial commissioner demanded his apology and suggested his retirement. Kaggwa was mortally offended. 'This action,' he told the governor, 'clearly shows that the Protectorate Government does not in any way think of and consider the Africans.' The governor had to order him out of his office after the elderly Katikkiro, by one account, had prepared to fight him. 'Sir Apolo,' a witness noted, 'was pleased to have annoyed the Governor and said, "Now I have overcome the Governor, and he will be a better ruler that he has been annoyed".' Four months later Kaggwa resigned. Some one hundred thousand people reportedly attended his burial when he died in 1927, leaving his nineteen children over 25,000 hectares of land. Perhaps even Kaggwa's *ekitiibwa* was satisfied.[43]

Neither Kaggwa nor his Christian colleagues had a monopoly of honour. Kabaka Daudi Chwa (1898–1939) also saw *ekitiibwa* as a blend of rank, personal dignity, and patriotism, but the blend was entirely different. Thirty-fourth

---

[40] Waliggo, 'Catholic Church,' pp. 179–82; Diane Leinwand Zeller, 'The establishment of Western medicine in Buganda,' PhD thesis, Columbia University, 1971, p. 269; Apolo Kaggwa, *The kings of Buganda* (trans. M. S. M. Kiwanuka, Nairobi, 1971), pp. xxiv–xxx.

[41] Kagwa, *Kika kye Nsenene*, pp. 151–60; 'This is the charge of Ipuliti Kajubi against Apolo, Katikiro' [copy of Lukiiko judgment, n.d.] CO 536/27/571.

[42] J. A. Rowe, 'Myth, memoir and moral admonition: Luganda historical writing, 1893–1969,' *Uganda Journal*, 33, 1 (1969), 219; Kagwa to Kabaka, 8 November 1922, in [Apolo Kagwa], 'Select documents and letters from the collected Apolo Kagwa Papers at Makerere College Library,' microfilm, CUL; Kabaka [Mutesa II] of Buganda, *Desecration of my kingdom* (London, 1967), p. 73.

[43] Kabaka Daudi Chwa II, 'Why Sir Apolo Kagwa, Katikiro of Buganda, resigned' (typescript translation by S. Musoke of *Lwaki Sir Apolo Kagwa, Katikiro w'Ebuganda yawumula* [1928] in Kagwa, 'Select documents'), passim (quotations on pp. 19, 48, 51); Kabaka of Buganda, *Desecration*, p. 74; *Munno*, May 1927.

Kabaka of Buganda, by some counts,[44] he had been born in Apolo Kaggwa's house, placed on the throne as a baby, and brought up under Christian tutelage. Yet his instincts were those of his ancestors. On coming of age in 1914, he refused continued tuition, lest 'further learning might put him out of touch with the outlook of the Baganda.' Two years later, like his father, he clashed with his Christian ministers when they insisted on deporting his drinking companion. He was excommunicated in 1921 for infidelity to his Christian wife.[45] After Kaggwa's retirement the Kabaka became the spokesman for Buganda's fears of losing its special status and being incorporated into a British East African dominion. He also became increasingly hostile to the Christian establishment and its British patrons, complaining publicly that 'so-called education and civilization' were destroying Buganda's 'native and traditional customs, habits and good breedings.'[46] A formidable man, 'graceful and ceremonious in his manner,' he was massively polygynous, with forty-three children by women other than his Christian wife; was constantly short of money to support his innumerable dependants; and by the late 1930s was also alcoholic, gravely ill, and bitterly resentful of colonial officials who 'sent for him' like a petty chief.[47] To escape them, he retreated to a lakeside lodge where his cronies plotted against the establishment and his musicians sang:

> I laugh at them, I laugh at them
> Who give away their country to foreigners
> Through greed for wealth
> And land which destroyed truth in some of them.[48]

This unconcealed defiance made him a hero to the kingdom's growing popular forces. The British were preparing to depose him when he died in November 1939, leaving his personal property to his eldest but 'illegitimate' son Mawanda while the establishment enthroned his 'Christian' son Mutesa, thereby preparing another thirty years of conflict.[49]

---

[44] Kiwanuka in Kaggwa, *Kings*, p. 195.

[45] Jackson to S of S, 15 January 1914, CO 536/67/134; Jackson to S of S, 8 November 1916, CO 536/82/301; Bengt Sundkler and Christopher Steed, *A history of the Church in Africa* (Cambridge, 2000), p. 852.

[46] Daudi Chwa to Ormsby-Gore, 2 September 1927, CO 536/147/14342/1; D. A. Low (ed.), *The mind of Buganda* (London, 1971), pp. 104–8.

[47] Perham, diary, 17 January 1937, Perham Papers 49/3, RH; Stuart to Archbishop of Canterbury, 30 October 1943, Anti-Slavery Society Papers G.552, RH; Mitchell to Parkinson, 19 January 1938, CO 536/197/40080/5/6; Mitchell, diary, 7 June 1937, Mitchell Papers, RH.

[48] *Tulankunyonyole*, 10 March 1938, enclosed in Mitchell to Dawe, 24 August 1938, CO 536/197/40080/1/10.

[49] 'Commission of Inquiry into civil disturbances in Uganda – January 1945: supplementary secret report,' CO 536/215/40339/1/secret/encl; Mitchell, diary, 25 and 30 August 1939, Mitchell

In their different ways, Daudi Chwa and Apolo Kaggwa, Emir Abbas and Kwame Boakye all defended ideas of rank and honour inherited from an aristocratic world of violence and the show of power. European officials welcomed the show of power while seeking to tame the violence. In addition to arousing great resentment by disarming their subjects, they were especially anxious to repress feud and private vengeance among stateless peoples, thinking it the essence of anarchy. Early colonial governments generally executed any revenge-killers they caught, as an example to others.[50] With time and growing power, they devised more systematic controls. Among the Nuer, for example, men who killed in fair fight were imprisoned for one to six years and also paid a standard bloodwealth, part of which the government took as a fine, while premeditated homicide was punished by a death penalty normally commuted to life imprisonment plus the payment of bloodwealth. In either case, the gaol replaced the ritualist's homestead as sanctuary for the killer.[51] Organised states could be equally violent. In Rwanda, for example, the last known massacre of members of an opposing clan took place only just before the First World War.[52] That was an extreme case, for most colonial regimes were quicker to control state violence, outlawing torture and trial by ordeal, especially if it led to the death of supposed witches, and steadily asserting a monopoly of legitimate force. In 1895, for example, the German authorities publicly hanged one of East Africa's most powerful chiefs for killing one of his wives and her lover. By 1914 the major emirs of Northern Nigeria were almost the only rulers in British Africa with power to try capital cases, although their sentences required confirmation.[53]

Rulers often keenly resented their loss of jurisdiction, whether to European officials in French territories or to 'native courts' in British tropical Africa. Some rulers tried to preserve a parallel jurisdiction. When Kano's Judicial Council could not avoid implementing British enactments, it categorised them disdainfully as 'the rule of our time.' Yet power-holders like Kaggwa and his successors in Buganda did not hesitate to use their position to impose heavy penalties on those who challenged their dignity. 'It is very rare that a peasant

Papers, RH; Acting Resident, Buganda, 'An account of the death of His Highness Sir Daudi Chwa . . . November 1939,' CO 536/202/40080/9/14.

[50] For example, Sangster to Governor, 5 July 1902, CO 87/167/30150.

[51] Howell, *Manual*, pp. 39–41, 66–7, 235–7; Sharon Hutchinson, *Nuer dilemmas: coping with money, war, and the state* (Berkeley, 1996), pp. 126–9.

[52] Vansina, *Le Rwanda*, p. 236.

[53] 'Verfahren gegen den Jumben Kimeri (Mputa) von Wuga, Sohn Simboja's,' 30 April 1895, RKA 404/51; Steven Feierman, *Peasant intellectuals: anthropology and history in Tanzania* (Madison, 1990), p. 125; Yakubu, *Aristocracy*, p. 31.

wins a case against a Chief,' a Ugandan journalist complained in 1948.[54] Ethiopia's Criminal Code of 1930 decreed that 'Damages for abuse are to be decided according to the rank of the person abused and according to the degree of the abuse,' the penalty ranging from 30 dollars for insulting a commoner to 300 dollars for a *ras*. A study in part of the Lozi kingdom found that issues of rank and honour, such as the respect due to chiefs and elders, were especially likely to reach official courts because they involved accepted principles of behaviour by which judges could distinguish right from wrong, whereas complex quarrels among neighbours were reserved for informal conciliation.[55] Often, as in the Eastern Cape, actions for defamation were among the most common civil cases in colonial courts. In Asante, for example, they were outnumbered only by suits for recovery of debt. One-third of a small sample of cases heard by the Accra Native Tribunal in 1925 dealt with defamation, especially accusations of witchcraft or 'fetishism'. Some native courts awarded damages for 'spoiling the name' of those falsely accused of witchcraft. Elsewhere people so accused flocked to prove their innocence before the witchcraft eradicators who proliferated throughout colonial Africa.[56]

African leaders also had to contend with European notions of integrity. Officials were convinced that African societies were pervasively corrupt. 'There is probably no branch of mankind which is so little touched by the sense of honour,' one complained.[57] Perhaps the problem was more that Africans and their leaders were concerned with honour in its older forms, practising gift-exchange and rarely distinguishing between public and private wealth, at a time when rulers had lost many sources of revenue, numerous activities were for the first time monetised, and bureaucratisation multiplied opportunities for impersonal extortion. In the Gold Coast and Uganda, for example, many transactions regarded by Europeans as corrupt were either customary payments to office-holders for services or were uses of public wealth for political purposes.[58]

---

[54] E. A. Ayandele, *The Ijebu of Yorubaland, 1850–1950: politics, economy and society* (Ibadan, 1992), p. 55; Christelow, *Thus ruled*, p. 3; this volume, p. 211; editor of *Dobozi*, quoted in Uganda African affairs fortnightly review, 21 October 1948, CO 537/3601/24.

[55] 'Abyssinian criminal code 1930' (typescript translation), preface and para. 273, de Halpert Papers, RH; Wim M. J. van Binsbergen, 'Law in the context of Nkoya society,' in Simon Roberts (ed.), *Law and the family in Africa* (The Hague, 1977), pp. 51–2.

[56] K. A. Busia, *The position of the chief in the modern political system of Ashanti* (reprinted, London, 1968), pp. 153–4; Roger Gocking, 'British justice and the native tribunals of the southern Gold Coast Colony,' *JAH*, 34 (1993), 100; I. Schapera, 'Witchcraft beyond reasonable doubt,' *Man*, 55 (1955), 72; L. E. Larson, 'Problems in the study of witchcraft eradication movements in southern Tanzania,' *Ufahamu*, 6, 3 (1976), 88–100.

[57] W. R. Crocker, *Nigeria: a critique of British colonial administration* (London, 1936), p. 204.

[58] Victor T. Le Vine, *Political corruption: the Ghana case* (Stanford, 1975), pp. 82–5; Beattie, *Nyoro state*, p. 142.

Yet many Africans, too, felt that unacceptable corruption coexisted with customary practices. The Ashanti Confederacy Council tried during the later 1930s to distinguish bribes from the customary gifts that candidates for chieftainships offered electors. Others tried to separate a bribe paid to gain a specific favour from a gift or tribute made to a power-holder in return for general protection.[59] These issues were especially acute in the Sokoto Caliphate, where the funds controlled by Africans were unusually large and Usuman dan Fodio had attacked corruption with little success, leaving the incoming British regime to find the old practices still flourishing. Careful of the emirs' interests, the British declined to prohibit *gaisuwa*, the gift presented by those seeking appointment to office, although many emirs sold offices to meet their burdensome financial obligations. Accusations of extortion, nepotism, and corruption surrounded even successive rulers in Sokoto.[60] The reforming Emir Yahaya of Gwandu was so alarmed that he announced in 1938 'that he would receive no presents from anyone, great or small. Anything he accepted on tour or elsewhere would be paid for.'[61] Another earnest reformer, the future prime minister Abubakar Tafawa Balewa, created a sensation in 1950 by denouncing the 'twin curses of bribery and corruption which pervade every rank and department.'[62] His attack helped to stimulate Northern Nigeria's Customary Presents Order of 1955, which banned gifts to accompany appointments or promotions, secure preferential treatment, oblige superiors to make reciprocal presents, or sweeten messengers and officials, although it permitted gifts to notables at family celebrations. Barely half the emirates even enacted the order during the following decade.[63]

While European regimes sought to eradicate what they saw as violence, injustice, and corruption, they shared their predecessors' taste for the show of power to awe their subjects. Empire Day for the British, Bastille Day for the French, the Kaiser's Birthday for the Germans were annual occasions to display not only military might but the hierarchy of rank in which African leaders had their places. Many such leaders, especially during the earlier decades of colonial rule, were keen to be incorporated into imperial culture. The Lozi Paramount Chief – much offended, like Kabakas of Buganda, because he was not recognised as a king – nevertheless considered that 'nothing that mattered now remained to be done' once he had given the royal salute to King George VI

---

59 Busia, *Position*, pp. 212–13; Jingoes, *A chief*, pp. 172–3.

60 Smith, 'Political corruption,' p. 185; Tibenderana, 'Making,' pp. 93, 118.

61 Weatherhead, 'But always as friends,' p. 124, Weatherhead Papers, RH.

62 Trevor Clark, *A right honourable gentleman: Abubakar from the black rock* (London, 1991), p. 144.

63 Whitaker, *Politics of tradition*, pp. 102–3, 205, 498–502.

at his coronation.[64] Imperial honours were eagerly coveted. King Denis, who ceded the Gabon estuary to France in 1844, was perhaps the first African to receive the *Légion d'honneur*. Apolo Kaggwa was knighted in 1905, to his intense delight. A year later the emir of Sokoto became a Commander of the Order of St. Michael and St. George for helping to suppress the Satiru rebellion. Lesser figures received awards such as the King's Medal for Chiefs. 'At a recent meeting' in the Gambia in 1922, 'it was noticed that those Chiefs present who were not eligible were barely able to conceal their chagrin when their colleagues were decorated.'[65] Rulers quickly imitated these models. Emperor Tewodros of Ethiopia invented the Cross of Solomon, Menelik II added the Star of Ethiopia, and Haile Selassie outdid them with orders of the Queen of Sheba, Menelik II, and the Trinity. Buganda awarded the Order of the Shield and Spear, while Zanzibar distributed honours in embarrassing profusion.[66] Indigenous title systems, too, experienced an 'inflation of honours' as younger men of wealth bought them in a process later described as money-laundering. By the late 1920s officials were complaining that Luba *mulopwe* titles had become monopolised by wealthy men. Elsewhere, as among the Yoruba and their neighbours, old elites deliberately domesticated successful businessmen by incorporating them into – and thereby legitimating – title systems.[67] Just as indigenous honours flourished, so did indigenous display. Northern Nigeria's great equestrian durbars – Emir Abbas paraded over fifteen thousand horsemen to welcome the Governor in 1913 – dramatised the sharing of power between Sokoto's rulers and the British, as also, more subtly, did the annual Sallah prayer-meeting at the end of Ramadan, which white officials attended as tolerated guests.[68] Ceremony could convey many messages. Buganda's victorious Christians declared the anniversary of their capture of the capital a public holiday and composed a national anthem, *Kitibwa kya Buganda*. At Asantehene Prempe II's installation in 1935, the Golden Stool was placed before the altar of the Anglican

---

[64] Quoted in Terence Ranger, 'Making Northern Rhodesia imperial,' *African Affairs*, 79, (1980), 370.

[65] *Les Missions Catholiques*, 8 (1876), 413; Kagwa to Sadler, 1 July 1905, UNA A.8/6/196; Adeleye, 'Mahdist triumph,' p. 208; Great Britain, *Gambia: report for 1922*, Colonial No. 1160 (London, 1923), p. 9.

[66] Guèbrè Sellassié, *Chronique*, vol. 1, p. 101 n2; Haile Sellassie, *My life*, p. 69; *Uganda Herald*, 6 August 1941; Cave to Lansdowne, 17 June 1905, FOCP 8692/12.

[67] Peter Geschiere, *The modernity of witchcraft* (trans. P. Geschiere and J. Roitman, Charlottesville, 1997), p. 161; Jean-Luc Vellut, 'Rural poverty in western Shaba, c.1890–1930,' in Robin Palmer and Neil Parsons (ed.), *The roots of rural poverty in central and southern Africa* (London, 1977), p. 308; J. D. Y. Peel, *Ijeshas and Nigerians: the incorporation of a Yoruba kingdom, 1890s–1970s* (Cambridge, 1983), pp. 144–5; Nadel, *Black Byzantium*, p. 365.

[68] *The Times*, 27 February 1913.

Church.[69] King Sobhuza's revival of the *incwala* harvest ritual during the 1920s signalled the deliberate revitalisation of the Swazi monarchy.[70] And in 1930 Solomon kaDinuzulu, pretender to the vacant Zulu throne, was fined £250 for drunkenly declaring at a durbar that '[t]hings in this country will never be right until I am recognised as the head.'[71]

Not only former rulers but entire systems of rank and honour were threatened by the abolition of slavery. Warned by the expense and economic disruption caused during the 1830s by emancipation in the Americas (and, to a lesser extent, in the Cape Colony), early colonial regimes in tropical Africa seldom attacked slavery directly but banned slave-trading and new enslavement, abolished the legal status of slavery, and left the slaves to free themselves by finding new economic opportunities.[72] As revolts in the Cape Colony had shown, slaves never felt so dishonoured as at the moment when emancipation seemed possible. 'Formerly it was thought that to be a slave was merely a misfortune; now it is held to be a disgrace,' an official in Nyasaland wrote in 1896. At Saba in the Gambia in 1894, 'a fine, powerful body' of home-born slaves, 'saying that the English were governing the country, and there would be no more slaving,' mocked the warboys brought in to make them work, drove them from the town, and seized their masters' estates. In Dahomey and parts of Yorubaland and the Sokoto Caliphate, thousands of slaves fled their owners as European troops invaded. A mass desertion from Banamba on the middle Niger in 1905 set off a chain reaction that led nearly a million slaves in French West Africa to free themselves during the next eight years.[73] Elsewhere, however, self-emancipation was deterred by the need to find alternative livelihoods. First-generation slaves held relatively close to their homes might return to their villages, although there are few accounts of affectionate homecomings.[74] One common alternative was to seek land for a peasant holding, but landowners and

---

[69] 'The honour of Buganda.' See *CMS Gazette*, 1907, p. 14; Uganda African affairs fortnightly review, 18 May 1950, CO 537/5868/11; Sundkler and Steed, *History*, p. 726.

[70] Hilda Kuper, *Sobhuza II, Ngwenyama and King of Swaziland: the story of an hereditary ruler and his country* (London, 1978), p. 164.

[71] Shula Marks, *The ambiguities of dependence in South Africa* (Baltimore, 1986), p. 17.

[72] See Miers and Roberts, *End of slavery*, ch. 1.

[73] *British Central Africa Gazette*, 15 April 1896; Ozanne to Administrator, 28 June 1894, CO 87/146/12598; Juff and others to Administrator, 4 October 1894, CO 87/147/18671; Patrick Manning, *Slavery, colonialism and economic growth in Dahomey, 1640–1960* (Cambridge, 1982), pp. 190–1; Toyin Falola, 'The end of slavery among the Yoruba,' in Miers and Klein, *Slavery*, p. 236; Lovejoy and Hogendorn, *Slow death*, pp. 45–54; Richard Roberts and Martin A. Klein, 'The Banamba slave exodus of 1905 and the decline of slavery in the Western Sudan,' *JAH*, 21 (1980), 375–94.

[74] Carter to Chamberlain, 20 April 1896, CO 879/45/32.

colonial authorities might obstruct this. Some slaves sought refuge at mission stations. More moved to towns or entered the colonial economy as labourers. A majority probably remained with their masters,[75] especially women – more than half of Africa's slaves – who had little chance of alternative livelihood, were often tied by children, and were deterred from leaving by colonial regimes sensitive to the masculine honour of slave-owners. In Zanzibar, for example, the British decreed that 'Concubines shall be regarded as inmates of the harem in the same sense as wives, and shall remain in their present relations unless they should demand their dissolution on the ground of cruelty.'[76]

The slaves' assertions of freedom and honour were nevertheless sufficient to threaten their masters, who responded in equally diverse ways. One was simply to ignore emancipation. Hamman Yaji, emir of Madagali on the south-eastern frontier of the Sokoto Caliphate, kept a diary recording not only the capture of 2,016 slaves in raids between 1912 and 1920 but his brutality towards them. 'I fixed the penalty for every slave who leaves me without cause at four slave girls and if he is a poor man 200 lashes,' he noted in 1917. Some twenty years later, the director of Ethiopia's Interior Ministry expressed the common view of African slave-owners when insisting, against strong international pressure, 'that to free a large number of slaves would have the most unsatisfactory results in the country and cause much hardship and misery.'[77] A second response was open resistance. There were proslavery revolts in the Sudan in 1904 and 1906, while hostility to emancipation fed into the Sierra Leone Hut Tax War of 1898, the Asante rebellion of 1900, the long resistance to British conquest of Somaliland, and doubtless many other protests.[78] Some Gola slave-owners in Liberia are said to have killed themselves when emancipation was enforced. Dominant classes like the Arab sugar planters of the German East African coast and the Maraka entrepreneurs of Banamba were ruined.[79] But most slave-owners responded more positively. 'What must we do, we, the "former masters"?' an elderly chief in French West Africa asked: '. . . Work and make our sons work.

---

[75] Igor Kopytoff, 'The cultural context of African abolition,' in Miers and Klein, *Slavery*, p. 487.

[76] Armitage to Cave, 20 August 1902, FOCP 8040/5.

[77] James H. Vaughan and Anthony H. M. Kirk-Greene (ed.), *The diary of Hamman Yaji* (Bloomington, 1995), pp. 13, 63; Blatengueta Walde Mariam, 'Report on slavery,' n.d., de Halpert Papers, RH.

[78] Taj Hargey, *'Festina lente:* slavery policy and practice in the Anglo-Egyptian Sudan,' in Miers and Klein, *Slavery*, p. 253; Great Britain, *Report . . . on the . . . insurrection in the Sierra Leone Protectorate 1898: part I*, PP, 1899, LX, 24, 27, 61, 113; Hodgson to Chamberlain, 16 April 1900, CO 96/359/180; Cassanelli in Miers and Roberts, *End of slavery*, p. 319.

[79] Warren L. d'Azevedo, 'A tribal reaction to nationalism,' *Liberian Studies Journal*, 2, 2 (1970), 102; John Iliffe, *A modern history of Tanganyika* (Cambridge, 1979), p. 132; Roberts, *Warriors*, p. 200.

If not, we shall eventually become the servants of our former slaves.' As a Nigerian historian has put it, after emancipation slave-owners had literally to paddle their own canoes.[80] Yet many found others to do it. Much former slave work passed to young men and probably even more to women. Pawning of child labour in return for loans increased greatly.[81] And slave-owners often had other resources. One was power to bar slaves from access to land, which had ensured that most Cape Colony slaves remained agricultural labourers after emancipation and was equally effective in Zanzibar, where many former slaves became labour-tenants on clove estates, and in land-scarce Futa Jalon, where some two hundred thousand *rimdinabe* remained servile tenants, share-croppers, or wage-labourers even in the late 1950s.[82] The term had originally referred to freed slaves but now included their descendants, perpetuating a social superiority reinforced by encouraging *rimdinabe* to believe that adoption of Islam was essential to higher status while initially excluding them from Islamic worship – freedmen entered Futa Jalon's mosques only after 1945, and some were then beaten – and later from Islamic office. 'Whoever says a Fulbe and a serf are equal,' older *rimdinabe* explained in the late 1960s, 'it's true for the blood. But for the law, that which Allah has made, they are not equal.'[83] Marriage was another bastion of rank; Fula men generally prevented their women from marrying men of other social groups while themselves taking non-Fula wives and mistresses. Such discrimination against freedmen was especially strong in Islamic societies, which denied the authority of colonial emancipation laws. In some non-Islamic, mainly stateless societies discrimination disappeared during the twentieth century. Yet in the 1970s it still caused great offence among the Sherbro of Sierra Leone if a man even rested his hand on a hammock rope while another lay inside. Although slavery proper and the rank-ordering based upon it almost disappeared from sub-Saharan Africa during the colonial period,

---

[80] Félix de Kersaint-Gilly, 'Essai sur l'évolution de l'esclavage en Afrique Occidentale Française,' *Bulletin du Comité d'Etudes Historiques et Scientifiques de l'Afrique Occidentale Française*, 7 (1924), 476; Don C. Ohadike, '"When slaves left, owners wept": entrepreneurs and emancipation among the Igbo people,' in Miers and Klein, *Slavery*, p. 203.

[81] Martin A. Klein (ed.), *Peasants in Africa* (Beverly Hills, 1980), p. 27; Twaddle in Miers and Roberts, *End of slavery*, pp. 139–40; Toyin Falola and Paul Lovejoy (ed.), *Pawnship in Africa* (Boulder, 1994), passim.

[82] Robert Ross, '"Rather mental than physical": emancipations and the Cape economy,' in Worden and Crais, *Breaking the chains*, pp. 163–4; Frederick Cooper, *From slaves to squatters: plantation labor and agriculture in Zanzibar and coastal Kenya, 1890–1925* (New Haven, 1980), pp. 85–92; Klein, *Slavery and colonial rule*, p. 194.

[83] Quoted in William Derman, *Serfs, peasants, and socialists: a former serf village in the Republic of Guinea* (Berkeley, 1973), p. 247. See also Ver Eecke, 'Slave experience,' p. 29; Botte, 'Stigmates,' p. 131.

the legacy survived in many notions of honour, often in ways too sensitive for public discussion.[84]

By undermining slavery and command of violence, colonial rule weakened the sources of rank and vertical honour. But it also created alternative sources, notably wealth and education, for those with the wit to exploit them. European notions of property were especially important. Africans who lost land to European settlers also lost honour thereby, but Apolo Kaggwa bequeathed twenty-five thousand hectares of Buganda as private property because he had been quick to grasp that land might be purchased, rather than held precariously from the Kabaka in return for political loyalty, and had helped to entrench this in the Uganda Agreement of 1900, which divided all Ganda land among some four thousand 'chiefs and private landowners,' everyone else becoming their tenants. In selecting their land, the new owners observed inherited notions of *ekitiibwa*, for they chose not vacant land for entrepreneurial farming but the areas most densely populated with peasants to pay them rent and do them honour, extending the meaning of *okusenga* from serving a chief to renting land. Landowners automatically acted as chiefs over their tenants, even without official appointment.[85]

In the long term, freehold landownership undermined Buganda's system of rank because extravagant landowners sold plots to tenants. In the short term, however, it extended *ekitiibwa* into the capitalist economy, to the distaste of the Colonial Office, which insisted elsewhere that African land was communal property.[86] Yet this did not prevent commercial farming from entrenching rank. Major Yoruba rulers levied tribute on cocoa trees until the 1950s. Asante chiefs failed in their claim to one-third or one-quarter of the cocoa produced by their subjects, but they did secure such tribute from strangers growing cocoa in their chiefdoms, and they did use control of land and labour to establish official estates.[87] Moreover, commercial agriculture combined easily with notions of

---

[84] Botte, 'Stigmates,' pp. 122–3; Klein, *Slavery and colonial rule*, pp. 226, 251; Carol P. MacCormack, 'Wono: institutionalized dependency in Sherbro descent groups,' in Miers and Kopytoff, *Slavery*, p. 188.

[85] Viera E. Pawliková, 'The transformation of Buganda, 1894–1914,' *Asian and African Studies* (Bratislava), 6 (1976), 100 n22; Low and Pratt, *Buganda*, p. 144; *Church Missionary Intelligencer*, April 1901, p. 296; R. A. Snoxall, *Luganda-English dictionary* (Oxford, 1967), s.v. *kusenga*; L. P. Mair, *An African people in the twentieth century* (London, 1934), p. 200.

[86] Henry W. West, *Land policy in Buganda* (Cambridge, 1972), pp. 116, 195; S. K. B. Asante, *Property law and social goals in Ghana, 1844–1966* (Accra, 1975), pp. 33–45; Martin Chanock, 'Paradigms, policies and property: a review of the customary law of land tenure,' in Mann and Roberts, *Law*, pp. 65–6.

[87] Vaughan, *Nigerian chiefs*, p. 147; Gold Coast, *Report on Ashanti for 1920* (Accra, 1921), p. 23; Gareth Austin, 'The emergence of capitalist relations in south Asante cocoa-farming, c.1916–33,' *JAH*, 28 (1987), 262.

householder honour, especially in stateless societies. Beti and Fang Big Men adopted cocoa-farming with the competitive enthusiasm they had devoted to earlier forms of accumulation. By 1924 Charles Atangana, government chief of the Beti and quintessential Big Man, was said to own one hundred hectares of cocoa and five hundred hectares of oil palms.[88]

Colonial rule offered other means of entrenching rank. Belgian rulers of Rwanda and Burundi, believing they were reducing the *uburetwa* labour that Tutsi aristocrats exacted from Hutu peasants, in fact made it more burdensome.[89] Colonial chiefs in stateless societies, with new access to tribute and shares of taxation, became 'fabulously wealthy' when compared with previous local headmen. Some invested in wives, the Beti chief Fouda Ngono possessing 583 when he died in 1939. Others coveted horses: in 1906 the emir of Zaria was said to own some 500.[90] Seven years later his counterpart in Katsina bought a motor car, the essential status symbol of colonial rank:

> On the day when *Etsu* Bello bought a motor-car,
> The whole of Bida went out to build a road . . .
> *Etsu* Bello has the money to buy the car,
> But the car will benefit all the people of Bida, from the farms and from the city,
> The great man and the servant.
> They thank *Etsu* Bello because he bought the car.[91]

Admiration mingled with resentment. 'The chiefs tour round in big motor cars and have no association with the peasants,' a Sotho dissident complained in 1933. Nine years later the kingdom's 145,000 people supported 1,300 chiefs who 'ate' nearly £50,000 a year in fines alone. Yet even Sotho dissidents, influenced by pan-African and communist ideas, wanted chieftainship purified and strengthened rather than abolished.[92] Rank, as such, was seldom yet questioned.

Beneath the surface, however, two forces were eroding it. One was wage labour. Before colonial rule, it had sometimes been considered even more shameful than slavery, especially when undertaken for neighbours, because it was voluntarily chosen and usually lacked reciprocal claims to patronage.

---

[88] Jeanne Koopman Henn, 'Peasants, workers, and capital: the political economy of labor and incomes in Cameroon,' PhD thesis, Harvard University, 1978, p. 125.

[89] M. Catherine Newbury, '*Ubureetwa* and *thangata*: catalysts to peasant political consciousness in Rwanda and Malawi,' *Canadian Journal of African Studies*, 14 (1980), 101–3; Gahama, *Le Burundi*, pp. 324–8.

[90] Fortes in Fortes and Evans-Pritchard, *African political systems*, pp. 264–5; Jane I. Guyer, 'The value of Beti bridewealth,' in her *Money matters: instability, values and social payments in the modern history of West African communities* (Portsmouth, N.H., 1995), p. 125; Grier to Dorothy Grier, 21 November 1906, Grier Papers, box 1, RH.

[91] Nadel, *Black Byzantium*, p. 140.

[92] Robert Edgar, *Prophets with honour: a documentary history of Lekhotla la Bafo* (Johannesburg, n.d.), pp. 91, 113, 169; David Rooney, *Sir Charles Arden-Clarke* (London, 1982), p. 58.

This attitude survived into the colonial period as one of the most powerful legacies from the honour culture. Often those obliged to seek employment travelled long distances rather than shame themselves by working for neighbours, even on better terms.[93] Labour migration to centres of colonial development brought humiliating status reversals: Nyoro working for Ganda, savanna Muslims for forest 'pagans'. Migration might reinforce rank in receiving societies, but it challenged the hierarchy of age in exporting areas. In the contest for labour following the abolition of slavery and the emergence of colonial economic opportunities, many young men defied their elders by seeking 'accelerated seniority' through wage employment to earn the money needed for marriage. Elders struggled to maintain control by demanding that labour earnings be transferred to them, raising bridewealth demands, monopolising prestige goods payable as bridewealth, controlling the land without which marriage was impossible, excluding their juniors from public affairs, or simply brutalising them. It was a long-drawn contest in which the young gradually gained the advantage.[94]

The second and related force threatening rank was Western education. In many parts of the colonial world, notably India, indigenous elites maintained their status and claims to honour by securing privileged access to European schooling. This happened in parts of colonial Africa such as Buganda and Bulozi, but in others, including Yorubaland, rulers neglected the opportunity, while the greatest enthusiasm for education was displayed by competitive stateless peoples like Igbo, Beti, Tonga, and Kikuyu.[95] Even where men of rank initially gained an educational advantage, it was easily lost. Of 298 elite members surveyed in Buganda in 1957–8, 122 were sons of peasants and only one-third had fathers allocated land under the 1900 Agreement. In Futa Toro at that time,

[93] Iliffe, *Emergence*, pp. 6–17; G. Ancey, J. Chevassu, and J. Michotte, *L'économie de l'espace rural de la région de Bouake* (Paris, 1974), p. 23; Thomas Spear, *Mountain farmers: moral economies of land and agricultural development in Arusha and Meru* (Oxford, 1997), p. 13; Deng, *Dinka*, p. 161.

[94] J. D. Y. Peel, 'The changing family in modern Ijesha history,' duplicated conference paper, 1981, p. 6; William Beinart, *The political economy of Pondoland 1860–1930* (Cambridge, 1982), pp. 64–9; this volume, p. 269; Douglas, *Lele*, p. 63; Gérard Ancey, 'Variation Mossi sur le thème: reproduction des milieux ruraux mis en contact avec le système capitaliste extérieur,' in Ancey and others, *Essais sur le reproduction de formations sociales dominées* (Paris, 1977), pp. 9–11; *Muigwithania*, February 1929; Charles van Onselen, *The seed is mine: the life of Kas Maine, a South African sharecropper, 1894–1985* (New York, 1996), pp. 258, 422.

[95] Judith M. Brown, *Modern India* (Delhi, 1985), p. 77; Vaughan, *Nigerian chiefs*, pp. 32–3; G. P. McGregor, *King's College, Budo: the first sixty years* (Nairobi, 1967), ch. 1; Caplan, *Elites*, pp. 93–4; Isichei, *Igbo*, ch. 12; Laburthe-Tolra, *Vers la lumière*, pp. 164–74; J. K. Karanja, *Founding an African faith: Kikuyu Anglican Christianity, 1900–1945* (Nairobi, 1999), ch. 3.

the average income of Torodbe aristocrats was lower than those of all other strata, including their former slaves.[96]

With loss of rank often went loss of cultural distinction. On Ukerewe Island in Lake Victoria, where before colonial rule each status group had monopolised certain musical instruments, even young men came to sing to the *enanga* zither or dance to the drums hitherto reserved for royalty. The colonial chief Charles Atangana, an uninitiated Christian, abolished the Beti initiation ritual in 1907 and is said to have instructed men and women to tell one another their ritual secrets. Odwira, prohibited by the British when they occupied Asante in 1896, was not celebrated again until 1985. Colonial regimes banned hunting, censored dancing, deprecated drinking. 'What with no drumming and no brewing of beer we might as well be living in a prison,' a townsman from Northern Nigeria complained.[97]

To preserve indigenous culture was for some a matter of honour. Many West Africans continued to patronise griots long after they could afford it. Dahomeyan royals spent lavishly to maintain customary ceremonies. Rwanda's dynastic praise-poets became extinct during the 1940s, but by then a Catholic priest from a family of court historians, Alexis Kagame, had recorded their texts and begun to reshape them to fit European notions of historical truth. Yoruba *oriki* regained their emphasis on peaceful virtues after nineteenth-century violence was past,[98] but southern African praise-poetry retained its belligerent metaphors, not only to honour pacific living rulers but even to celebrate Christianity:

> I swear by Jehova of the heavens
> That Jesus accepts no cowards:
> He despatches Gabriel to keep them out![99]

The major change in praise-poetry was that warrior kings were now also national unifiers. The earliest praise emphasising that Shaka 'welded together the Zulu nation' was recorded in 1927, coinciding with a reassertion of Zulu

---

[96] Fallers, *King's men*, pp. 198–9; J.-L. Boutillier, P. Cantrelle, J. Cause, C. Lavrent, and T. Ndoye, *La moyenne vallée du Sénégal* (Paris, 1962), p. 202.

[97] Gerald W. Hartwig, 'The historical and social role of Kerebe music,' *Tanzania Notes and Records*, 70 (1969), 41–56; Philippe Laburthe-Tolra, *Initiations et sociétés secrètes au Cameroun* (Paris, 1985), p. 230; Vincent, *Traditions*, p. 80; McCaskie, *State and society*, p. 151; anonymous letter in Lugard Papers (Mss.Brit.Emp.s.77, folio 126), RH.

[98] This volume, pp. 281–2; Lombard, *Autorités traditionnelles*, p. 87; A. Coupez and Th. Kamanzi, *Littérature de cour au Rwanda* (Oxford, 1970), p. 1; Claudine Vidal, 'Alexis Kagame entre mémoire et histoire,' *History in Africa*, 15 (1988), 493–504; Barber, 'Documenting,' p. 51.

[99] Damane and Sanders, *Lithoko*, p. 255. See also Vail and White, *Power*, p. 191.

identity after half a century of disaster and earlier portrayals of the king as a savage tyrant.[100] Such rethinking was common between the wars as chiefs and intellectuals sought honourable antecedents. Historians of Buganda and Bunyoro vied for the longer king-list. Beti lineages attached themselves to Noah and his sons.[101] Literature began also to celebrate modern heroes. The epic form of Swahili *tenzi* was used, somewhat ambivalently, to dramatise resistance to German conquest.[102] A pioneer Hausa novel, Bello Kagara's *Gandoki*, set an epic equestrian hero into the context of resistance at Burmi. Paul Hazoume's *Doguicimi* depicted both the cruelty and the heroic ethos of nineteenth-century Dahomey. And survivors of Buganda's civil wars wrote memoirs like Ham Mukasa's 'Do not retreat' to urge the next generation not to forsake the course the Christian heroes had set.[103]

Yet others sought not to celebrate Christian victory but to preserve honour amidst defeat by defending their religious heritage. They kept a low profile and no records, but in the forest areas of western Africa and the more remote parts of the south and east, indigenous shrines generally survived. They had their martyrs, not only the prophetic leaders of Maji Maji and Kongo-Wara but also the less dramatic figures like the Jola ritual leader Sihalebe, who starved himself to death when imprisoned among followers before whom he might not eat or drink. In 1905 Oyo's Master of the Horse was one of several to poison himself at the Alafin's death, declaring, 'I care not what the District Commissioner says, I am not going to forsake my master.' Forty-one years later, when a successor was prevented from the same course, his son redeemed family honour by dying in his place.[104]

Muslims, too, could find consolation in their religion and its historical capacity to absorb notions of honour. A few, like the Tukulor hard-core, pursued their *hijra* as far as Mecca. More gained honour by making the Pilgrimage.[105]

---

[100] E. W. Grant, 'The izibongo of the Zulu chiefs,' *Bantu Studies*, 3 (1927–9), 205–44; Vail and White, *Power*, pp. 64–6; Malaba, 'Shaka,' pp. 90–1.

[101] David P. Henige, *The chronology of oral tradition* (Oxford, 1974), pp. 105–14; Laburthe-Tolra, *Les seigneurs*, p. 52.

[102] Hemedi bin Abdallah el Buhriy, *Utenzi wa vita vya Wadachi kutamalaki Mrima 1307 A.H.* (trans. J. W. T. Allen, 2nd edn, Dar es Salaam, 1960); Mwenyi Shomari bin Mwenyi Kambi, 'Kufa kwa Mkwawa,' in C. Velten (ed.), 'Suaheli Gedichte,' *Mitteilungen des Seminars für Orientalische Sprachen zu Berlin*, 21 (1918), 152–74; Abdul Karim bin Jamaliddini, *Utenzi wa vita vya Maji-Maji* (trans. W. H. Whiteley, Kampala, 1957).

[103] Graham Furniss, *Poetry, prose and popular culture in Hausa* (Edinburgh, 1996), pp. 26–9; Hazoume, *Doguicimi*; Mukasa, 'Do not retreat.' See also Rowe, 'Myth, memoir.'

[104] Christian Roche, *Histoire de la Casamance: conquête et résistance: 1850–1920* (reprinted, Paris, 1985), p. 281; *Church Missionary Intelligencer*, 56 (1905), 855; E. M. Birbalsingh, 'Soyinka's "Death and the King's Horseman",' *Présence Africaine*, 124 (1982), 202–3.

[105] This volume, p. 283.

Taqiyya offered a psychological escape; the British resident in Kano reported in 1904 that 'it was not unusual for the people to spit on the ground as a European passed.'[106] The most positive response to defeat, however, was that of Wolof military society, which was in some measure reintegrated in the early twentieth century by an Islamic brotherhood, the Mourides, who taught quasi-military obedience by the disciple to his sheikh and created a hierarchy of disciplined settlements dedicated to Islam and the cultivation of groundnuts. 'No more Holy War,' they declared, 'except against the bush.'[107] By 1912 they had seventy thousand members and had bridged the ancient divisions not only between *ceddo* and *marabout* but between slave and free, for many ex-slaves joined on equal terms and the founder, Amadou Bamba, discouraged caste or class differences. His lifestyle was austere, but Mourides generally had no ascetic ideal, regarding opulence as evidence of spiritual power. They included an eccentric wing, the Bay Fall, who refused to pray or fast but smoked, drank, practised magic, and worked intensively, associating virtue with the discipline, strength, and violence of the *ceddo* warrior class from which most were drawn.[108] Similar processes probably happened in Somalia, where former slaves and masters found refuge in Islamic brotherhoods, and among the Yao of Nyasaland and Mozambique, who, after three centuries of trade with the East African coast, became Muslims en masse during and immediately after their fierce resistance to European conquest.[109]

Christianity, too, could console defeated heroes. Humbled by war in 1879 and unsuccessful rebellion in 1906, the traditional Zulu values recorded by James Stuart found new expression from 1916 in Isaiah Shembe's Nazarite Church, described in his praise-poem as 'a perch for the birds of Zulu.' Shembe claimed a covenant with God to lead the Zulu people from white bondage. He 'pestered the royal line', as his praise-poem put it, appropriating the first-fruits ceremony and other royal rituals into Christian rites. His church celebrated the heroes and martyrs of Zulu history.[110] 'All the people in this church belong to the old

[106] Quoted in Yakubu, *Aristocracy*, p. 21.
[107] André Vanhaeverbeke, *Rémunération du travail et commerce extérieur: essor d'une économie paysanne exportatrice et termes de l'échange des producteurs d'arachides au Sénégal* (Louvain, 1970), p. 50.
[108] Donal B. Cruise O'Brien, *The Mourides of Senegal* (Oxford, 1971), pp. 15, 56, 141–58; idem, *Saints and politicians: essays in the organisation of a Senegalese peasant society* (Cambridge, 1975), pp. 21, 70, 79.
[109] Cassanelli in Miers and Roberts, *End of slavery*, p. 323; E. A. Alpers, 'Towards a history of the expansion of Islam in East Africa: the matrilineal peoples of the southern interior,' in T. O. Ranger and I. N. Kimambo (ed.), *The historical study of African religion* (London, 1972), pp. 172–201.
[110] Malaba, 'Shaka,' p. 112; Absolom Vilakazi with Bongani Mthethwa and Mthembeni Mpanza, *Shembe: the revitalization of African society* (Johannesburg, 1986), pp. 19, 40;

and dying Zulu cultural world,' a Zulu academic wrote in 1952. 'They find in the Shembe Church cultural sanctuary where the old values are still respected; respect for seniority; parental authority over children; the subordinate position of women; and the acceptance of polygamy as a form of marriage.'[111]

Elisabeth Gunner, 'New wine in old bottles: imagery in the Izibongo of the Zulu Zionist prophet, Isaiah Shembe,' *Journal of the Anthropological Society of Oxford*, 13 (1982), 100–2; Bengt G. M. Sundkler, *Bantu prophets in South Africa* (2nd edn, London, 1961), p. 313.

[111] Vilakazi, *Shembe*, p. 54

13　The Honour of the Mercenary

This book's central thesis is that African notions of honour survived vigorously until the colonial period and then fragmented, partly surviving, partly disappearing, but chiefly being transmuted and absorbed into other ethics, which themselves were most effective when drawing on traditions of honour. Although colonial regimes in Africa were not especially successful in channelling male honour in new directions, three ethics were relatively effective: the regimental ethos of colonial armies, Christian respectability, and working-class masculinity. This chapter considers the regimental ethos.

At first sight, colonial armies might seem particularly capable of attracting and absorbing heroic traditions. Colonial publicists thought so. 'Battle is in his blood,' it was said of France's *Tirailleurs Sénégalais* (Senegalese Sharpshooters).[1] Yet unlike the early British Indian army, African colonial armies did not generally recruit those with the strongest heroic traditions because, by the late nineteenth century, their methods of warfare had become archaic. Rather than savanna horsemen or Zulu spearmen, European rulers recruited either the mercenary musketeers already serving African rulers or robust but poor young men from 'tribes that are still uncivilized.'[2] Some recent writers have therefore seen African colonial soldiers as 'mercenaries protecting the interests of

---

[1] Werner Glinga, 'Le tirailleur sénégalais: a protagonist of African colonial society,' in P. F. de Moraes Farias and Karin Barber (eds.), *Self-assertion and brokerage: early cultural nationalism in West Africa* (Birmingham, 1990), p. 156.

[2] David Killingray, 'The mutiny of the West African Regiment in the Gold Coast, 1901,' *IJAHS*, 16 (1983), 444. For the Indian contrast, see David Omissi, *The sepoy and the raj: the Indian Army, 1860–1940* (Basingstoke, 1994), pp. 4, 52–3.

imperial Britain,' 'a class of unskilled, but privileged, labour migrants.'[3] Yet, as David Omissi has written of India, 'The duties of a coolie on a tea plantation did not include laying down his life.' Men from honour cultures angrily denied that they were mercenaries.[4] The Xhosa poet Samuel Mqhayi spoke for them during the First World War:

> Say it was not for just a bribe
> Or for meat you left the hunger of your tribe . . .
> It was not for the King by any loyal tie,
> It was not for Britain you went out to die.[5]

This chapter seeks to unravel the mixed motives of honour and profit for which African colonial soldiers went out to die, for which they fought to survive, and for which, on occasion, they mutinied.

The first documented African colonial troops were the Cape Mounted Rifles, a Khoi force with white officers that was raised in 1793 and later employed in frontier warfare. Disaffected and mutinous, they were replaced after 1850 by white troopers.[6] For a century thereafter black South Africans, with minor exceptions, served only as temporary auxiliaries or unarmed labourers. In tropical Africa, by contrast, colonial armies generally consisted of African infantrymen commanded by small numbers (usually only 6 or 7 per cent) of European officers and noncommissioned officers (NCOs).[7] The most famous force were the *Tirailleurs Sénégalais*, formed in 1857 and expanded into a French West African army. Initially they were recruited mainly from slaves and then from the professional armies of defeated adversaries like the Tukulor, whose military traditions they inherited. From 1914 to 1960, however, the French also employed short-term conscripts throughout their empire and in Europe during both world wars. 'The typical recruit was a physically fit peasant youth of low status, and without traditional skills,' preferably from a 'martial race' like the Bamana,

---

[3] C. N. Ubah, *Colonial army and society in Northern Nigeria* (Kaduna, 1998), p. 252; Timothy H. Parsons, *The African rank-and-file: social implications of colonial military service in the King's African Rifles, 1902–1964* (Portsmouth, N.H., 1999), p. 4.

[4] Omissi, *Sepoy*, p. 75; Uganda African affairs fortnightly review, 11 October 1945, CO 536/215/40342/15.

[5] S. E. K. Mqhayi, 'The sinking of the *Mendi*,' reprinted in Norman Clothier, *Black valour: the South African Native Labour Contingent, 1916–1918, and the sinking of the Mendi* (Pietermaritzburg, 1987), p. xv.

[6] An earlier Khoi force had been raised briefly in 1781. See Johannes de Villiers, 'Hottentot-Regimente aan die Kaap, 1781–1806,' *Argiefjaarboek vir Suid-Afrikaanse Geskiedenis*, 33, 2 (1977), 123–7; Richard Cannon, *History of the Cape Mounted Riflemen* (London, 1842).

[7] Marc Michel, *L'appel à l'Afrique: contributions et réactions à l'effort de guerre en A.O.F. (1914–1919)* (Paris, 1982), p. 289; Parsons, *Rank-and-file*, p. 3.

Wolof, Mossi, or Sara.[8] Similar thinking shaped the small forces recruited in British West African colonies during the nineteenth century and amalgamated in 1901 into the West African Frontier Force (W.A.F.F.). A volunteer force, its initial recruits were mainly 'Hausa' – mostly perhaps escaped slaves from the Sokoto Caliphate – or unemployed Yoruba warboys.[9] Early colonial armies in equatorial Africa drew on the musketeers employed by African and Arab warlords. The Force Publique in the Congo – after initially hiring Hausa, Zanzibaris, and 350 disappointingly unwarlike 'Zulu' – recruited numerous 'Tetela' from the defeated armies of local slave-raiders; they proved to be as mutinous as the Khoi and far more violent.[10] The archetypal mercenaries were Sudanese who had been impressed into the Egyptian army, marooned on the Upper Nile by the Mahdist rebellion of 1881, and recruited into British service as the nucleus of the Ugandan and Kenyan battalions of the King's African Rifles (K.A.R.). The German Defence Force that invaded East Africa in 1889 similarly hired 600 unemployed Sudanese.[11]

In 1914 the K.A.R. numbered 2,383 men; in 1918 it numbered 33,348 who were mainly engaged in conquering German East Africa, as were W.A.F.F. and Force Publique units. The *Tirailleurs Sénégalais* expanded even more dramatically: the 31,000 under arms in 1914 were supplemented by some 178,000 recruited during the war, plus 7,200 *originaires* from Senegalese coastal towns who joined the metropolitan army. About 180,000 served overseas and something over 30,000 died, a casualty rate similar to the French army's but concentrated into the second half of the war.[12] Conscription continued in French West Africa between the wars, generally taking about 12,000 men a year, or perhaps 7 per cent of each male age group.[13] During the Second World War, however, France recruited over 200,000 West Africans, of whom between eleven thousand and sixteen thousand were taken prisoner in 1940 – half of these died – and another 100,000 participated in the liberation of France.[14] This war

---

[8] Myron Echenberg, *Colonial conscripts: the* Tirailleurs Sénégalais *in French West Africa, 1857–1960* (Portsmouth, N.H., 1991), pp. 62–3.

[9] A. Haywood and F. A. S. Clarke, *The history of the Royal West African Frontier Force* (Aldershot, 1964), chs. 1 and 2.

[10] [F. Flament,] *La Force Publique de sa naissance à 1914: participation des militaires à l'histoire des premières années du Congo* (Brussels, 1952), pp. 10–13, 250.

[11] Parsons, *Rank-and-file*, pp. 14–16; Rochus Schmidt, *Geschichte des Araberaufstandes in Ost-Afrika* (Frankfurt am Oder, 1892), p. 46.

[12] Commandant to S of S, 14 February 1919, CO 534/30/315; Michel, *L'appel*, pp. 404, 407–8, 423, 472; Joe Lunn, *Memoirs of the maelstrom: a Senegalese oral history of the First World War* (Portsmouth, N.H., 1999), pp. 100, 140–7.

[13] Echenberg, *Conscripts*, pp. 50, 58–9.

[14] Ibid., p. 88; David Killingray, 'African voices from two world wars,' *Historical Research*, 74 (2001), 438.

had even greater impact on British colonies. Using conscription for the first time, the K.A.R. recruited 323,483 East Africans, employing them especially against Italian forces in Ethiopia and the Japanese in Burma, where they were joined by West African units. In May 1945 some 374,000 African troops were serving in British military units. Approximately 165,000 others had formed unarmed pioneer and labour battalions, especially in the Middle East and North Africa.[15] After 1945 smaller, more professional colonial armies served chiefly against liberation movements in Africa and South-East Asia.

The character of African colonial armies was determined chiefly by the European rulers. Many Africans, especially in French colonies and during world wars, had little choice whether they served or not. Yet other – perhaps most – African soldiers were volunteers. Their motives and the terms they would accept also shaped colonial armies. The most important motives were material. Although volunteers were not *merely* migrant labourers, they *were* migrant labourers: they had to be attracted by pay and conditions superior to those in their rural homes and in alternative employment. 'They joined for the money,' a Nyasaland veteran recalled: 'It is just like the way people go to the mines in South Africa.'[16] Eastern Africa's low wage levels enabled the peacetime K.A.R. to attract volunteers by paying three or four times the average unskilled wage. By contrast, one reason for French conscription was unwillingness to compete with West Africa's higher wages. The W.A.F.F. often faced the same difficulty, as did the recruitment of military labourers in South Africa.[17] Mercenary motives were most transparent when soldiers switched from one army to another. In 1918 the British recruited almost an entire battalion of prisoners and deserters from the German Defence Force, some of whom had joined the Germans before the war from a disbanded K.A.R. battalion.[18]

These early colonial soldiers were feared and resented. In Sokoto they were so unwelcome that they seldom entered the town. This owed much to their arrogance, brutality, and rapacity. 'They are intensely proud,' it was reported

---

[15] Parsons, *Rank-and-file*, p. 35; R. D. Pearce, *The turning point in Africa: British colonial policy 1938–48* (London, 1982), p. 22; Ashley Jackson, 'African soldiers and imperial authorities: tensions and unrest during the service of High Commission soldiers in the British Army, 1941–46,' *JSAS*, 25 (1999), 646 n2; Mirjana Roth, '"If you give us rights we will fight": black involvement in the Second World War,' *SAHJ*, 15 (1983), 94.

[16] Melvin E. Page, 'The war of *thangata*: Nyasaland and the East African campaign, 1914–1918,' *JAH*, 19 (1978), 89.

[17] Parsons, *Rank-and-file*, p. 62; Echenberg, *Conscripts*, p. 23; Dobell, 'Report of the Inspector-General, WAFF on the Gambia Company, WAFF,' 24 April 1914, CO 445/34/17726; Albert Grundlingh, *Fighting their own war: South African blacks and the First World War* (Johannesburg, 1987), p. 74.

[18] Critchley-Salmonson, 'K.A.R. recruiting: brief report on progress, situation and prospects 30/12/17 to 25/5/18,' CO 534/26/264.

of Uganda's Sudanese in 1906, 'looking down, and with justice too, on the other local tribes as being vastly inferior.'[19] Loot was a major incentive to recruitment. 'The *tirailleurs* and the *spahis*,' a French officer wrote in 1894, 'only enlist under our flag ... with but one goal: to get captives,' whom they sold to the slave traders accompanying French expeditions.[20] Even when that was banned, armies offered advancement to men of low status. 'I don't want to be discharged,' a Ugandan soldier wrote in 1945. 'I was poor before I joined the Army and it is war that has made me rich.'[21] Cynical officials welcomed the troops' unpopularity, as affording 'a great measure of military security,' and officers encouraged a sense of superiority considered good for morale.[22] Soldiers were intensely proud of their uniforms and appearance, as Sergeant-Major Robert Kakembo explained:

The soldiers go home on leave smartly dressed in His Majesty's uniform and with plenty of money. A man leaves his village and goes into the Army; he disappears for some eighteen months, and on his return home on leave he is 100 percent changed. He is fat and strong, clean and clever, with plenty to talk about and lots of money to spend. The young girls of the village worship him; the young men follow him about.[23]

A soldier might return 'clever' because many used the army to acquire education, especially during the later colonial period. 'My father had no money to send me to school,' a Ugandan soldier wrote in 1945, 'but I am lucky to get education free of charge in the army. I can beat the man educated in civil schools, I know four languages and have been in countries he has merely read about.' By then many recruits joined specialised units in order to acquire skills useful in civilian life, perhaps as drivers or mechanics.[24] Others sought promotion within the service. African NCOs had an especially important and ambiguous status, mediating between European notions of hierarchy and the more egalitarian instincts of fellow soldiers. Further promotion to commissioned rank was possible for *tirailleurs* – by 1921 at least thirty-eight had achieved this – but the British abandoned an early experiment with African officers in West Africa and phased out the category of *effendi* (native officer) among the Sudanese. Only during the Second World War did the first African gain a King's Commission. Even thereafter, and despite complaints, the K.A.R. refused until 1959 to award full

---

[19] John N. Paden, *Ahmadu Bello, Sardauna of Sokoto: values and leadership in Nigeria* (London, 1986), p. 69; 'Information regarding the Uganda Protectorate' [July 1906] CO 534/3/833.

[20] Quoted in Balesi, *Adversaries*, p. 42.

[21] Uganda African affairs fortnightly review, 2 August 1945, CO 536/215/40342/10.

[22] Temple to Harcourt, 29 April 1911, CO 445/31/17733; Parsons, *Rank-and-file*, p. 104.

[23] Robert Kakembo, *An African soldier speaks* (London, 1947), p. 9.

[24] Uganda African affairs fortnightly review, 6 December 1945, CO 536/215/40342/19; McDonald, 'Blantyre Administrative Unit: annual report, 1942,' MNA NSB 7/1/6.

commissions.[25] Whereas at independence in 1960 Senegal's army was commanded by a Senegalese general commissioned twenty-eight years earlier, the highest-ranking Nigerian officer was the newly promoted Colonel Ironsi.[26]

One perquisite that every soldier could expect was a woman. Not only did early French commanders and the British in Uganda distribute captured women to their troops, but colonial armies often advanced unmarried soldiers the money needed for bridewealth, believing that soldiers with wives and families were more contented and less likely to desert, assault local women, or contract venereal disease.[27] Soldiers were especially sensitive to issues of honour concerning their wives and families, bitterly resenting compulsory venereal inspections – as, of course, did the women – eagerly demanding news from home while on active service, absenting themselves without leave to resolve family problems, and reacting so violently to adultery between their wives and other soldiers that the K.A.R. routinely flogged adulterers.[28]

Comradeship became a treasured aspect of military experience for many soldiers. 'One thing that impressed me so much when I was in the battlefield was the degree of friendliness. . . . Each soldier would appear to be his brother's keeper,' one recalled.[29] Yet few mentioned comradeship as a motive for enlistment, perhaps because they could find it equally in village life. More important were travel and adventure. Several South African volunteers for military labour during the First World War saw it as a chance of 'learning about the world and becoming well informed men.' Soldiers from French West Africa delighted in the opportunity to explore France. The same was true during the Second World War, when soldiers based in India might absent themselves to travel as far as China.[30] Others explored their own continent. Ganda troops sang in 1918:

> We left with joy,
> But more so:
> Among the countries we saw
> Buganda was the best.[31]

[25] Balesi, *Adversaries*, p. 129; minute, L. G. C. to Strachey, 4 August 1906, CO 445/22/28481; Killingray, 'African voices,' p. 432; Parsons, *Rank-and-file*, pp. 109–10.

[26] Echenberg, *Conscripts*, pp. 68–9; Ubah, *Colonial army*, p. 293.

[27] J. Malcolm Thompson, 'Colonial policy and the family life of black troops in French West Africa, 1817–1904,' *IJAHS*, 23 (1990), 423–53; Parsons, *Rank-and-file*, pp. 148–51; [Flament], *Force Publique*, p. 81.

[28] Parsons, *Rank-and-file*, pp. 152, 154, 168; Slater to S of S, 28 April 1925, CO 445/67/21570.

[29] Isaac Fadoyebo, *A stroke of unbelievable luck* (ed. D. Killingray, Madison, 1999), p. 64.

[30] Grundlingh, *Fighting*, p. 77: Lieutenant N'Tchorère, 'Le tirailleur revenu de l'extérieur, tel que je l'ai vu,' *Revue des Troupes Coloniales*, 24 (1930), 149–62; Tadman to Rolleston, 29 October 1944, CO 820/55/3.

[31] *Ebifa mu Buganda*, 1917, pp. 234–6.

Others discovered rather their inadequacies: 'We have travelled throughout East Africa and find that Acholi is the most backward country in the whole area. We feel ashamed.' Many returning soldiers were glad to be 'thrown back into the old, traditional ways.'[32] In the words of the favourite K.A.R. marching song:

> When we have beaten the enemy we shall come home,
> And the children will be waiting and clapping their hands,
> We shall start digging our gardens,
> And we shall look after our cattle for ever.[33]

For the Nandi of Kenya, it has been claimed, the opportunity to preserve warrior status through military service made the army a conservative force. Other veterans, however, became active local innovators, led opposition to conservative chiefs, or were themselves given chieftainships by governments valuing their loyalty and leadership. In 1947 some thousands briefly seized partial control of the Kankan *cercle* of Guinea. At that time 58 per cent of Dahomey's African voters were former conscripts.[34] Yet apart from some involvement in trade union activity and violent movements such as Mau Mau, ex-soldiers seldom had sufficient education to take leading posts in national politics.[35] Rather, the mercenary dimension of military service survived demobilisation. The British did not pay military pensions, so their soldiers pressed for employment and opportunities to invest savings and gratuities in trade. Francophone veterans, by contrast, concentrated on securing their pension entitlements from the complex bureaucracy, caught between pride in their service and discontent with its rewards.[36]

---

[32] Uganda African affairs fortnightly review, 3 January 1946, CO 537/1508/1; Jingoes, *A chief*, p. 93.

[33] Anthony Clayton, *Communication for new loyalties: African soldiers' songs* (Athens, Ohio, 1978), p. 37.

[34] Lewis J. Greenstein, 'The Nandi experience in the First World War,' in Melvin E. Page (ed.), *Africa and the First World War* (Basingstoke, 1987), pp. 82–6, 92; Anne Summers and R. W. Johnson, 'World War I conscription and social change in Guinea,' *JAH*, 19 (1978), 28–37; Jean Suret-Canale, 'La fin de la chefferie en Guinée,' *JAH*, 7 (1966), 477–8; R. Grivot, *Réactions dahoméennes* (Paris, 1954), p. 80.

[35] Major exceptions would include Benedicto Kiwanuka of Uganda and Herman Toivo Ja Toivo of South-West Africa. See Albert Bade, *Benedicto Kiwanuka: the man and his politics* (Kampala, 1996); Peter H. Katjavivi, *A history of resistance in Namibia* (London, 1988), pp. 20–2. Generally, see G. O. Olusanya, *The Second World War and politics in Nigeria 1939–1953* (Lagos, 1973); Louis Grundlingh, 'Soldiers and politics: a study of the political consciousness of black South African soldiers during and after the Second World War,' *Historia* (Pretoria), 36, 2 (November 1991), 55–66.

[36] Parsons, *Rank-and-file*, pp. 231–60; Nancy Ellen Lawler, *Soldiers of misfortune: Ivoirien tirailleurs of World War II* (Athens, Ohio, 1992), ch. 9.

Although many soldiers were conscripts or enlisted for mercenary reasons, the fact that they came from honour cultures was important in leading them to volunteer and in shaping their conduct. Colonial officers recognised this. The K.A.R.'s newspaper was named *Heshima* (Honour) and its posters urged recruits to 'Join the K.A.R. and lead a man's life.' An 'appeal to the African sense of manliness far outweighed any appeal to his instinct for money,' an officer wrote in 1944.[37] Many volunteers explained their decisions in these terms. 'We joined the war because we were men,' one recalled of 1914. 'I wanted to test my manhood,' said another. 'The army was a suitable job for a warrior. . . . It showed that we were men,' a third explained.[38] Kande Kamara, a Susu aristocrat from Guinea, felt it incumbent on him 'to be a warrior like my father,' while anguishing over whether he would acquit himself honourably. 'I said to myself, I'm a pure coward! What am I waiting here for? My father fought against the Boers,' Jason Jingoes remembered of his decision to join the South African Native Labour Contingent. His comrade William Mathumetse, aged sixteen, was urged not to volunteer by his clergyman father but was strongly encouraged by his grandfather, a former warrior. That survival of a living warrior tradition was important in motivating volunteers and still existed almost everywhere in Africa in 1914 to motivate the first disarmed generation to display their manhood. Entire school classes in Buganda then sacrificed their educational future by volunteering for military service.[39] It was different three years later, when only mass conscription could replace losses on the Western Front or in the East African campaign. It was yet more different in the next war. 'Now that war is coming,' A Disgruntled Muganda wrote in September 1938, 'now that I must, or rather should – hold myself in readiness to take up arms again, I do not feel like fighting. After all what advantage did I reap from the 1914–1918 victory?'[40] Younger Ganda, especially educated men, did not volunteer in 1939 with the enthusiasm of 1914, for they were a generation further away from a living military tradition and more sensitive to discrimination. Joseph Conombo of Upper Volta, a medical trainee like many who had volunteered in 1914, was threatened with a firing squad in 1939 when his class refused to wear what they considered the humiliating uniform

[37] Parsons, *Rank-and-file*, p. 149; A. G. Dickson, quoted in Joanna Lewis, *Empire state-building: war and welfare in Kenya, 1925–52* (Oxford, 2000), p. 211.

[38] Page, 'War of *thangata*,' p. 88; idem, *Africa*, p. 4; Parsons, *Rank-and-file*, p. 150.

[39] Joe Harris Lunn, 'Kande Kamara speaks,' in Page, *Africa*, pp. 33–5; Jingoes, *A chief*, p. 73; Clothier, *Black valour*, pp. 24–5; McGregor, *Budo*, p. 42.

[40] *Uganda Herald*, 21 September 1938.

of *tirailleurs*. South Africans, similarly, showed markedly less enthusiasm in 1939.[41]

Given their superior firepower, colonial troops fighting African peoples did not always face the highest tests of courage. Most K.A.R. operations before 1914 have been called 'large-scale cattle raids.' There were exceptions, especially when storming walled towns like Burmi or stockades like those erected by Asante. Bush-fighting, too, was unnerving, while a massed cavalry charge, however ineffective, was a fearsome sight.[42] Yet these experiences did little to prepare troops for the courage needed during the First World War, when they met firepower equal to their own. 'Our native troops,' a British officer on the Nigeria-Cameroun front wrote after two months of fighting, 'are not doing well – with exceptions – some are bad, generally our officers fault. . . . The men know the deadliness of Maxims &c. and have never been accustomed to face fire of any importance in our native wars and never imagined they would have to.'[43] This comment followed an unsuccessful attack on a formidable German position at Garua, where 'the British native troops broke and fled' when counterattacked; 'all the efforts of their officers and non-commissioned officers failing to rally them until they reached camp.' Yet the Germans too found warfare between equals profoundly unsettling. Garua eventually fell in 1915 when shelling drove its African defenders to mutiny, loot the fortress, and seek to break through the encircling forces, mostly without success.[44] The mutiny illustrated the limits of a colonial army's loyalty. Similar limits appeared in the East African campaign, a war of exhausting pursuit in appalling terrain as German forces gradually retreated southwards, seeking to commit as many Allied troops as possible. During the battle for the mud of the Rufiji Valley late in 1916, for example, a newly trained K.A.R. company held an exposed hilltop for fifty-two hours under shellfire but refused to follow their NCOs in a bayonet charge to clear the hill of German troops.[45] The German forces, ill-supplied and fighting rearguard actions against vastly superior numbers, suffered piecemeal desertions that became a flood during the final retreat. Of their 13,430 African

[41] 'War diaries, No. 2 Uganda Field Ambulance Coy, November 1939 to January 1940,' WO 177/2589; Joseph Issoufou Conombo, *Souvenirs de guerre d'un 'tirailleur sénégalais'* (Paris, 1989), pp. 35–6; Roth, 'Rights,' p. 87.

[42] Parsons, *Rank-and-file*, p. 16; this volume, pp. 186, 194–5.

[43] Lethem to his mother, 28 October 1914, Lethem Papers 22/4/82, RH.

[44] F. J. Moberly, *Military operations: Togoland and the Cameroons, 1914–1916* (London, 1931), pp. 95, 298–9.

[45] Hardingham, 'Report on "C" Company's 52 hours on Picquet Hill,' 18 December 1916, WO 95/5340.

troops, 2,847 deserted, leaving 1,168 still in arms when the war ended. Only with great difficulty were the survivors persuaded to surrender their weapons.[46]

The supreme test of courage and honour came for the *tirailleurs* on the Western Front. On their first day of action, two hundred fifty men were killed and over six hundred were wounded. Demoralised by further terrible losses in mass attacks against machine-guns and artillery, one regiment mostly composed of recruits panicked. Despite gallantry elsewhere, African troops gained a reputation for unreliability under fire and, like British Indian regiments, were removed from the front line.[47] Gradually, the *tirailleurs* rebuilt their reputation, at enormous cost. At Verdun an entire battalion broke under artillery fire – and were shot in the back by French machine-guns as they fled – but this was compensated by a brilliantly successful assault on the position at Douaumont, which dominated the battlefield.[48] This won the *tirailleurs* a dangerous reputation as shock-troops. They were employed in that role during the disastrous Nivelle offensive of April 1917, during which Adjutant Seko Kone took a German post single-handedly, killing all its occupants with a machete. The *tirailleurs* formed 14 per cent of Allied troops in this offensive and suffered 33 per cent of casualties. 'I would much prefer to have ten blacks killed than a single Frenchman,' the prime minister observed. African troops were earmarked to spearhead yet another offensive when the Germans surrendered.[49] By then some *tirailleurs* bitterly resented their use as cannon-fodder. Others were exhausted and fatalistic, but most became more outspoken and demanding as the campaign progressed. All remembered most vividly the noise, the fear, the dead, the hardship, the cold and wet, and above all the combat.[50] One survivor compared it tellingly to initiation:

To be a soldier in those days was like being circumcised. [When you went into the] secret bushes, there were many things you never knew about before that they would tell you; and after you left the circumcision bush you'd be aware of a lot of things [that you never understood before]. And that's the same parallel as warfare, as being a soldier.[51]

---

[46] Ludwig Boell, *Die Operationen in Ost-Afrika: Weltkrieg, 1914–1918* (Hamburg, 1951), pp. 271, 296 n4, 404, 424–7.

[47] Balesi, *Adversaries*, p. 78; Michel, *L'appel*, pp. 289–93; Omissi, *Sepoy*, pp. 38, 114–18.

[48] Echenberg, *Conscripts*, p. 36; Michel, *L'appel*, pp. 301–4; Alphonse Séche, *Les noirs (d'après des documents officiels)* (Paris, 1919), pp. 176–87.

[49] Michel, *L'appel*, pp. 311–21; Séche, *Les noirs*, p. 209; Lunn, *Memoirs*, p. 140; Balesi, *Adversaries*, p. 122.

[50] Bakary Diallo, *Force-Bonté* (reprinted, Paris, 1985), p. 146; Michel, *L'appel*, pp. 337, 356–7, 385, 473; Lunn, *Memoirs*, pp. 127–47.

[51] Kande Kamara, quoted by Lunn in Page, *Africa*, pp. 39–40.

'His experience had made him really serious,' the missionary Albert Schweitzer wrote of another veteran; 'it weighed him down like a burdensome secret. "In the village (he said to me) they are always asking me to tell them about the war, but I can't do it. And they wouldn't understand if I did. It was all so horrible, so horrible!"'[52]

Fighting the Japanese in Burma during the Second World War was almost equally horrible but demanded qualities more akin to those of the East African campaign. This was bush warfare in dense rainforest and mountainous terrain against an exceptionally determined enemy, a test of endurance and individual courage in close combat. A sergeant-major was decorated for directing three assaults on a hilltop position when badly wounded, a sergeant for leading an attack on a Japanese bunker, a corporal for destroying a Japanese patrol and returning with the officer's sword and marked map. Each side learned to respect the other. 'Because of their belief,' a captured Japanese diary recorded of African troops, 'they are not afraid to die, so even if their comrades have fallen they keep on advancing as if nothing had happened. They have an excellent physique and are very brave, so fighting against these soldiers is somewhat troublesome.'[53] Unsympathetic British commanders, by contrast, concluded 'that the East Africans did not reach the standard of other troops engaged.' Inexperienced Somali and Ugandan units had broken under Japanese attacks and a battalion had refused to advance further after capturing Kalewa, believing it had been promised rest.[54]

Studies of warfare have suggested that men in battle fight primarily for survival, the respect of their comrades, and fear of punishment. The limited evidence available for African colonial soldiers appears to fit this model,[55] but perhaps with three qualifications. One was that the mercenary element in their character led them to weigh their commitment especially carefully against the dangers it entailed, as in the mutinies at Garua and Kalewa. Before the *tirailleurs* took part in the invasion of southern France in 1944, a sergeant from Upper Volta who had survived the defeat of 1940 warned his countrymen:

You know that everywhere we Voltaics are renowned for our bravery? I do not tell you not to be brave, but know that the best bravery consists in surviving the others [*consiste*

---

[52] Albert Schweitzer, *More from the primeval forest* (trans. C. T. Campion, London, 1931), p. 63.

[53] Parsons, *Rank-and-file*, p. 34; Haywood and Clarke, *History*, pp. 468, 470.

[54] 'Note on the war effort of East Africa' [1945?] WO 106/5863/17B; Duke of Devonshire, Report on visit to African troops, February–March 1945, CO 820/55/11; 'Report on the morale of British, Indian, and Colonial troops of Allied Land Forces, South-East Asia,' November 1944–January 1945, WO 203/2268; Parsons, *Rank-and-file*, pp. 32–3.

[55] See John Keegan, *The face of battle* (reprinted, London, 1991), pp. 52–3, 70–4; Omissi, *Sepoy*, pp. 83, 111; Echenberg, *Conscripts*, p. 38.

à descendre les autres] and returning to your village to tell of your exploits! It is useless to offer your chest foolishly to the enemy when you are not protected or when he is stronger than you.[56]

A second qualification, especially in the early colonial period, was that battlefield behaviour was influenced by vertical ties of loyalty between officers and men similar to the clientage relationships in many African societies. Many awards for gallantry made to Africans were for protecting white officers. 'I have never seen a braver man,' a British officer wrote of Sergeant-Major Belo Akure during the East African campaign:

His one idea is that his officers must on no account run into unnecessary danger; on no account will he let an officer go in front of him on a road. Any cover that is handy must be reserved to conceal his officers, even if he himself must lie down in the open. I have seen him deliberately get in front of a European so that if anyone should be hit it would be himself.[57]

Such accounts were coloured by self-serving white perspectives, as was the award of decorations. The interesting point is that although some similar accounts exist from the Second World War, recorded acts of gallantry in that campaign more often served the interests of African comrades or entire units.[58]

The nature of collective loyalties was a third distinctive feature of African military behaviour. Like Asante or Zulu commanders, European officers valued regimental discipline above egotistical heroism. Regimental loyalties in colonial armies were strong, perhaps as much in conflict with civilians or other regiments as with the enemy. 'These *tirailleurs* are excellent soldiers,' Colonel Gallieni wrote in 1887, 'but they have an extraordinary *esprit de corps*. As soon as one of them is touched, they instantly make common cause with their brother in arms.' Numerous fights confirmed this.[59] Officers also sought to inculcate loyalty to the colonial power. This was a more abstract concept and the willingness of troops to change sides during the East African campaign shows that it often had little purchase, but it was not always a European myth. 'We all had the same ambition, that is to say, to defeat the enemy. France's victory signified ours,' a

---

[56] Conombo, *Souvenirs*, p. 53.

[57] W. D. Downes, *With the Nigerians in German East Africa* (London, 1919), pp. 104–5. Among numerous other examples, see Baratier, *A travers l'Afrique*, pp. 82–3, 93; Haywood and Clarke, *History*, p. 109 n1; Ubah, *Colonial army*, p. 298; Séche, *Les noirs*, p. 175.

[58] See especially E. Marling Samson, *Beyond the call of duty: African deeds of bravery in wartime* (London, 1952). I owe this reference to Dr. Lonsdale.

[59] [J. S.] Gallieni, *Deux campagnes au Soudan Français, 1886–1888* (Paris, 1891), p. 434. Among examples, see Rodolphe Alexandre, *La révolte des Tirailleurs Sénégalais à Cayenne, 24–25 février 1946* (Paris, 1995); Charles-André Julien, *Le Maroc face aux impérialismes 1415–1956* (Paris, 1978), p. 199.

veteran of the Western Front explained.[60] Yet these imposed loyalties were less powerful than indigenous identities. Tribal honour was an important stimulus to military prowess. Young volunteers left Buganda in 1917 to the beat of the royal drums 'because the job we were going for was to honour Buganda . . . if we perform well, Buganda is also known.' Tukulor troops in Flanders sang the *ceddo*'s *gumbala* before battle. During the Cameroun campaign of 1915 'Hausa' troops fighting for one side occasionally allowed those on the other to escape.[61] In combat with non-Africans, moreover, racial honour became a major incentive to courage. 'The people who once called us African apes are finding out their mistake for we are beating him like a woman,' a soldier wrote of his Japanese adversaries in Burma in 1944.[62] Mqhayi's poetry, in particular, caught the widespread belief that world war was an opportunity to demonstrate the heroic qualities of Africans as a race:

> Win Africa's fame by your bravery,
> Win Africa's fame by your strength,
> Win Africa's fame by your comradeship,
> Win Africa's fame by your health,
> By the sharpness of eyes and of ears,
> And by courage of soul and of mind.[63]

The interplay between mercenary calculation and warrior honour appeared most clearly in forms of protest. The most common in early colonial armies was desertion, which, as in Ethiopia, some African military traditions saw as scarcely an offence. It was most common among new recruits serving close to their homes, but it later became widespread among men on leave from Burma or expecting service there. Late in 1943 over 15 per cent of the Gold Coast Regiment were posted as deserters, while in 1945 East Africa Command reported over 14,000. There are indications that one reason why the British refused home leave to most African troops serving in Burma was that many were expected to desert.[64] Others, however, would have been deeply ashamed. 'I considered

---

[60] Quoted in Michel, *L'appel*, p. 357 (a very sensitive discussion of this point).

[61] *Ebifa mu Buganda*, 1917, pp. 234–6; Lunn, *Memoirs*, p. 133; War diary, Sierra Leone Brigade, WAFF, 12 June 1915, WO 95/5388.

[62] 'Report on the morale of British, Indian, and Colonial troops of Allied Land Forces, South-East Asia,' August–October 1944, WO 203/2268.

[63] S. E. K. Mqhayi, 'The army of the dark-skinned,' in Perham Papers 366/5, RH.

[64] This volume, p. 63; Ubah, *Colonial army*, pp. 253–4; Anthony Clayton and David Killingray, *Khaki and blue: military and police in British colonial Africa* (Athens, Ohio, 1989), p. 182; Parsons, *Rank-and-file*, p. 198; Sabben-Clare, 'The colonial military forces in the Second World War,' para. 159 [November 1945] WO 106/5863/11A.

desertion to be disgraceful,' one wrote. 'Where would I hide my head in the event of desertion?'[65]

Whereas Indian troops on the Western Front frequently disabled themselves by self-inflicted wounds, there is little evidence of this among Africans, although some injured themselves to avoid conscription or feigned sickness to escape the trenches or the later Burma campaign. A few men committed suicide in camp or at sea rather than fight in France.[66] Others killed or wounded themselves over issues of honour, much like slaves in the past. A soldier in German East Africa attempted suicide in response to an NCO's harshness. In 1901 a Yoruba shot himself in the thigh because a colour-sergeant 'had a down on him'. Some East African troops during the Second World War hanged or shot themselves 'when subjected to racial taunts by British pesonnel.' One Somali killed himself after the humiliation of a flogging. A striking illustration of African soldiers' sensitivity to honour was their strong objection to being sworn at by NCOs in the manner habitual in European armies.[67]

Individual violence against officers and NCOs was rare in peacetime and was generally a response to humiliation (such as reduction in rank) or unjust punishment, although occasionally a soldier might 'run amok'.[68] Individual violence was more common on active service, where it could more easily be concealed. In 1917 a company of the Force Publique refused action against a comrade who killed his commanding officer after suffering punishment.[69] Incidents peaked in the Burma campaign, where thirty-eight East Africans were court-martialled for 'violence to a superior' between August 1944 and October 1945. One soldier sentenced to flogging held off his officers with a live grenade, two shot officers thought to have punished them unjustly, and another threw a grenade that killed or wounded most of his company officers.[70]

---

[65] Fadoyebo, *A stroke*, p. 33.

[66] Omissi, *Sepoy*, p. 119; Mouhamed Moustapha Kane, 'A history of Fuuta Tooro, 1890s–1920s: Senegal under colonial rule,' PhD thesis, Michigan State University, 1987, pp. 396–7; Lunn in Page, *Africa*, p. 40; Parsons, *Rank-and-file*, p. 198; Lunn, *Memoirs*, p. 44.

[67] 'General-Sanitäts-Bericht über die Kaiserliche Schutztruppe für Deutsch-Ostafrika für das Berichtsjahr 1894/95,' *Arbeiten aus dem Kaiserlichen Gesundheitsamte*, 13 (1897), 38; Wilkin to Rupert, 26 March 1901, Wilkin Papers, RH; Parsons, *Rank-and-file*, pp. 197, 188; 'A short account of relations between Bechuana and British in a H.A.A. troop,' 1945, DO 35/1183.

[68] Kane, 'History,' pp. 86–7; Parsons, *Rank-and-file*, p. 154; Uganda annual medical report 1900, FOCP 7867/93.

[69] F. A. Vandewalle, 'Deuxième note au sujet des mutineries au Congo Belge,' *Zaire*, 2 (1948), 905–6. For other instances during the First World War, see Lunn, *Memoirs*, p. 137; Parsons, *Rank-and-file*, p. 183.

[70] Parsons, *Rank-and-file*, pp. 201–2; John Nunneley, *Tales from the King's African Rifles* (Petersham, 1998), pp. 108–9, 170–2; morale reports, South-East Asia, 1944–6, in WO 203/2268; F. A. Vandewalle, 'Mutineries au Congo Belge,' *Zaire*, 1 (1947), 488.

More commonly, however, soldiers protested collectively and often – but not always – peacefully in the acts of insubordination that European armies called mutiny. Such actions had been common in precolonial armies, as also in early twentieth-century Ethiopia, whose modern imperial army threatened mutiny on three occasions between 1910 and 1928.[71] African colonial troops used mutiny both as collective bargaining and to defend their honour. Their most common motive was belief that their employers had broken the contract between them by excessive severity, overwork, underpayment, or withdrawal of some customary right. In 1895, for example, Tetela men of the Force Publique mutinied against the brutality of their commander, whom they killed, and his failure to meet obligations of pay and feeding. Two years later they mutinied again, with much greater bloodshed, when an ill-prepared expedition lost itself in the foodless Aruwimi Forest. 'We have rebelled because we were treated like slaves,' they protested.[72] It took three years to suppress them, an experience paralleled by a mutiny of some five hundred of the sixteen hundred Sudanese troops in Uganda who refused to march to the upper Nile in 1897, complaining of exhaustion, delayed and inadequate pay, and breach of their customary right to take their families with them to new stations.[73] Similar grievances animated a smaller mutiny at Kumase in 1901, when Sierra Leonean troops garrisoning Asante were retained longer than expected and feared to be defrauded of their pay.[74]

Once early colonial disorder ended, mutiny as collective bargaining was largely confined to the two world wars.[75] *Tirailleurs* did not participate in the widespread mutiny in France during May and June 1917, but one battalion mutinied during August, refusing to undertake another offensive after losing over two-thirds of its personnel. 'I am tired, you can kill me,' one soldier declared. Withdrawn temporarily, the battalion returned to the trenches six weeks later without incident.[76] The mutiny at Garua in Cameroun under artillery bombardment in 1915, already described, was the most important during the African campaigns of the First World War, but there was much discontent towards its end, when men believed that they were being held beyond their

[71] Smaldone, *Warfare*, pp. 143–6; Barth, *Travels*, vol. 2, pp. 360–1; Zewde in Hutchful and Bathily, *Military and militarism*, pp. 265–6, 277–8.

[72] [Flament], *Force Publique*, pp. 349–459 (quotation on p. 438); Marcel Storme, *La mutinerie militaire au Kasai en 1895: introduction* (Brussels, 1970); Pierre Salmon, *La révolte des Batetela de l'expédition du Haut-Ituri (1897): témoignages inédits* (Brussels, 1977).

[73] H. Moyse-Bartlett, *The King's African Rifles* (Aldershot, 1956), pp. 69–80.

[74] Correspondence in WO 32/4349; Killingray, 'Mutiny,' pp. 441–54.

[75] For an exception, see Jama Mohamed, 'The 1937 Somaliland Camel Corps mutiny,' *IJAHS*, 33 (2000), 613–34.

[76] Michel, *L'appel*, pp. 350–2.

contracts, denied their pay, or sent to new theatres rather than demobilised.[77] The same pattern took place during the Second World War. Unwillingness to fight was rare, except in the incident at Kalewa. There was more objection to posting to distant theatres; an entire K.A.R. infantry brigade in Eritrea refused embarkation for South-East Asia until granted leave. Insubordination was most common at the end of the war when troops and labour battalions in North Africa, the Middle East, and Asia protested against the long delay in their repatriation by violent incidents that cost several lives.[78] 'They had contracted to come and fight the war,' one spokesman complained, 'and they were told that when the war was over they would be taken home quickly. The war was over, they were very tired, so tired they could not work any more, and they wanted the authorities to send them home, or at least to get them under way. . . . Was it a crime to have won the war?'[79] This discontent peaked at the Thiaroye camp outside Dakar in November 1944, when thirty-five African soldiers repatriated from German prison camps were killed and several hundred injured while demanding back-pay and demobilisation.[80]

Yet mutinies were not merely strikes. Soldiers from honour cultures were intensely sensitive to insult and, when seeking to avenge it, might behave quite differently from mercenaries. This happened in 1893 in Cameroun, where the Germans had formed a small colonial army by buying slaves from the King of Dahomey and contracting them for five years without pay to work off their 'manumission fee'. This, plus overwork and brutality, laid a basis for discontent, but it flared into mutiny when the hated acting governor ordered the public stripping and flogging of soldiers' wives in their husbands' presence. Declaring 'That is too much. We wish rather to die than to see another,' the soldiers resolved to kill the governor, capture the armoury, and expel the whites. The governor escaped, but some forty-seven mutineers and forty-three women held Government House for a week before German marines dispersed them.[81] Control and protection of women were central to male honour. So was resentment

---

[77] This volume, p. 235; Clothier, *Black valour*, pp. 146–7; Anne Summers and R. W. Johnson, 'World War I conscription and social change in Guinea,' *JAH*, 19 (1978), pp. 32–3; Ubah, *Colonial army*, pp. 255–6.

[78] This volume, p. 237; Parsons, *Rank-and-file*, pp. 203–6; Jackson, 'African soldiers,' pp. 645–65; Cray to British Military Mission, Pretoria, 15 January 1946, DO 35/1183; Roth, 'Rights,' p. 101.

[79] Acutt, 'Report of visit to 57 Gp HQ,' November 1945, DO 35/1183.

[80] Myron J. Echenberg, 'Tragedy at Thiaroye,' in Peter C. W. Gutkind, Robin Cohen, and Jean Copans (eds.), *African labor history* (Beverly Hills, 1978), ch. 4.

[81] Adolf Rüger, 'Der Aufstand der Polizeisoldaten,' in Helmuth Stoecker (ed.), *Kamerun unter deutscher Kolonialherrschaft: Band I* (Berlin, 1960), pp. 97–147; Adjai Paulin Oloukpona-Yinnon, *La révolte des esclaves mercenaires: Douala 1893* (Bayreuth, 1987), passim (quotation on p. 35).

of the humiliation of flogging, common in all colonial armies before 1918 and practised illicitly in some until independence. Somali troops sentenced to flogging mutinied in the Jubaland region of north-eastern Kenya in 1920, shot their officer, fled across the border with a machine-gun, and remained at liberty for several years.[82] Another recurrent cause of insubordination was rivalry between combat troops and labour battalions. Often mocked by soldiers, East African labourers struck in Kenya in 1939 to demand combat pioneer status, mutinied during the retreat from Tobruk in 1942, and were court-martialled for beating their commanders in 1944.[83] West African labourers burned down a battalion headquarters in 1942. When a South African labour unit in Europe broke out of its fenced compound in 1917, the guards killed four and wounded eleven. Twenty-six years later, six members of a similar unit in Egypt were sentenced to death after a racial conflict in which three white South African soldiers were killed. Soldiers, in turn, might mutiny if ordered to undertake porters' or labourers' work.[84]

Mutiny less often had explicitly political objectives. They existed in Ethiopian mutinies and possibly among Sudanese and Tetela leaders who could dream of regaining former power. In 1939 the communist-inspired West African Youth League persuaded troops in strategically sensitive Freetown to refuse to parade unless issued with boots, also bringing the artillery battery out on strike and precipitating disaffection, which simmered throughout the war.[85] Two more serious incidents took place in 1944. In one the Somaliland Camel Corps was disbanded after a mass mutiny designed to prevent transfer to Kenya, where they expected to be treated as Africans rather than Arabs, a long-standing issue of ethnic honour and political status for Somali.[86] In the other, troops of the Force Publique in Katanga mutinied chiefly as a result of military grievances but in alliance with educated civilians and with some influence from millenarian beliefs.[87] Subsequently, there is no evidence that African troops hesitated to

---

[82] David Killingray, 'The "rod of empire": the debate over corporal punishment in the British African colonial forces, 1888–1946,' *JAH*, 35 (1994), 201–16; Parsons, *Rank-and-file*, pp. 186–9; 'Proceedings of a Court of Enquiry assembled at Serenli, northern Jubaland,' 5 April 1920, CO 534/39/644.

[83] Parsons, *Rank-and-file*, pp. 25–6, 92, 207–9; O. J. E. Shiroya, *Kenya and World War II: African soldiers in the European war* (Nairobi, 1985), pp. 35–6.

[84] Clayton and Killingray, *Khaki*, p. 165; Grundlingh, *Fighting*, p. 113; Killingray, 'African voices,' p. 434; Lamphear, *Scattering time*, p. 181.

[85] This volume, p. 241; Leo Spitzer, *The Creoles of Sierra Leone* (Madison, 1974), pp. 201–5.

[86] Correspondence in WO 32/10863; Jama Mohamed, 'The 1944 Somaliland Camel Corps mutiny and popular politics,' *History Workshop Journal*, 50 (Autumn 2000), 93–118.

[87] Vandewalle, 'Mutineries'; idem, 'Deuxième note'; Bruce Fetter, 'The Luluabourg revolt at Elisabethville,' *African Historical Studies*, 2 (1969), 269–77.

suppress nationalism in Africa or Asia, apart from some sale of weapons to Mau Mau rebels and an alleged refusal in 1950 to fire on demonstrators in Côte d'Ivoire.[88] Rather, the two most political mutinies had taken place in the nineteenth century among the Khoi troops of the Cape Mounted Rifles. Their context was the long resistance of Khoi and Xhosa to the expansion of white settlement. The mutiny of 1838 was the almost single-handed work of Acting Corporal Antony Meyers, a man partially of Khoi origin whose education by the London Missionary Society gave him remarkable ascendancy over soldiers whom he incited to shoot an officer in the false expectation of precipitating a wider uprising.[89] Meyers was executed, but disaffection erupted again in 1851 when soldiers of the Cape Mounted Rifles deserted to join Khoi and Xhosa rebels rather than fight against them.[90]

Although Meyers' role was exceptional, several mutinies were led by NCOs or African officers, especially when they had commanded the men before they entered European service, as with the Tetela and Sudanese. Yet in other cases, NCOs opposed mutiny. Those of the *tirailleurs* unit of August 1917 'marched to show that they did not identify with it.' The Somali mutineers of 1920 fired on their NCOs and took them prisoner, taking their lead rather from a man from the ranks who had made the Pilgrimage and acted as *imam*.[91] Similar popular leaders included Mamadu, an enslaved former trader who headed the Cameroun mutiny of 1893, and Private Morlai Mandingo, a thrice-wounded man of acknowledged courage who was elected 'colonel' by the Kumase mutineers of 1901.[92] Both were executed. To avoid such victimisation, other mutinies remained ostensibly leaderless. French military authorities planned to shoot the leaders of the *tirailleurs*' mutiny of 1917 but could find nobody to shoot, for the mutineers' spokesmen insisted that they were merely interpreters.[93]

Scarcely any mutiny was unanimous. Ethnic solidarity united the Tetela in 1895 but alienated their Hausa comrades, just as the small Wolof contingent

[88] Timothy H. Parsons, '"Wakamba warriors are soldiers of the Queen",' *Ethnohistory*, 46 (1999), 691; Parsons, *Rank-and-file*, pp. 211–14; Lawler, *Soldiers*, p. 222.

[89] The court martial proceedings are in WO 71/301. See also Stockenström to Napier, 25 February 1838, CO 48/188/no.12/encl; T. A. Anderson, *The story of Pacaltsdorp and some reminiscences* (Port Elizabeth [1957]), pp. 27–41 (I owe this reference to Dr. M. C. Bilbe).

[90] Smith to Grey, 17 March 1851, CA GH 23/20/58; correspondence in CO 48/314; Elizabeth Elbourne, '"Race", warfare, and religion in mid-nineteenth-century Southern Africa,' *JACS*, 13 (2000), 17–42.

[91] Michel, *L'appel*, p. 351; 'Proceedings of a Court of Enquiry,' 5 April 1920, and 'Findings of the Court,' CO 534/39/644 and 660.

[92] Oloukpona-Yinnon, 'La révolte,' p. 77; A. J. N. Tremearne, *The tailed head-hunters of Nigeria* (London, 1912), p. 218.

[93] Michel, *L'appel*, pp. 350–1.

in Kumase resisted the mutiny of 1901.[94] Men involved in that movement 'said . . . that they were soldiers and not afraid to die,' the governor reported. 'They were ready to take their chances with their fellow mutineers and seemed to look on it as a point of honour not to give up. This corroborated a statement I had heard that the deserters had drunk fetish together to stand by each other.'[95] The Camel Corps mutineers took two oaths of solidarity, one at a holy man's tomb. Bilal Amin, the senior Sudanese officer, personally shot two European officers early in the Uganda mutiny to discourage his men from hoping for clemency if they surrendered.[96]

Having called attention to their grievances, most mutineers made for their homes. All three groups in the Belgian Congo did so, as in a sense did the Sudanese mutineers, who headed for their former stronghold in northern Uganda. By contrast, the former slaves who mutinied in Cameroun in 1893, bent on revenge and possessing no accessible common home, captured and defended Government House. Such mutineers seeking vengeance might take the initiative in violence, as did Corporal Meyers' politically motivated action, but those protesting mercenary grievances generally turned to violence only if attacked or prevented from reaching home. Similarly, officers faced with mutiny over mercenary issues generally sought to negotiate and persuade the men to lay down their arms and disperse, recognising that most mutinies were appeals to authority rather than rejections of it. In these terms, several mutinies were successful. The Sudanese, for example, secured the quadrupling of their pay.[97] Their leaders, however, were executed. The Belgians were ruthless in suppressing mutiny, as were the French at Thiaroye. But the most remorseless reaction was that of the Germans in Cameroun, who hanged thirty-four mutineers (including three women), sentenced a roughly equal number (mainly women) to hard labour (mostly for life), and demonstrated their power by burning several African quarters of Duala that had taken no part in the disturbances.[98] It was striking that the most brutal response followed the mutiny arising most clearly from motives of honour.

---

[94] [Flament], *Force Publique*, p. 360; 'Proceedings of a Court of Enquiry assembled at Tower Hill Barracks, Sierra Leone on the 6 April 1901,' WO 32/4349.

[95] Nathan to Chamberlain, 5 May 1901, CO 96/379/520.

[96] Mohamed, '1944 mutiny,' p. 96; J. V. Wild, *The Uganda mutiny, 1897* (London, 1954), p. 38.

[97] W. Lloyd-Jones, *K.A.R.* (London, 1926), p. 67.

[98] Oloukpona-Yinnon, *La révolte*, pp. 40–1.

14   Respectability

Respectability, like other forms of honour, was a right to respect that individuals believed they possessed but could enjoy only if it was admitted by others. It had no necessary connection with Christianity or European lifestyle but had existed among earnest nineteenth-century Muslims and in African notions of householder honour as described, for example, by Kenyatta.[1] It was therefore not merely imposed on Africans by missionary imperialists. In early colonial Africa, however, respectability most commonly required the possession of sufficient freedom, resources, knowledge, and seriousness of mind to adopt the dominant European lifestyle.[2] It was, in principle, accessible to all men and women, although this chapter concentrates on the male dimension, leaving female experience to the next chapter. Respectability was the chief means by which Europeans tried to domesticate African notions of honour, replacing their emphasis on rank and prowess with stress on virtue and duty. Africans, equally, adopted respectability to liberate themselves from ideas of honour no longer in tune with reality. The main instruments of change were schools, especially secondary boarding schools. Like other attempts to tame African ideas of honour, however, respectability only partly succeeded. The *amarespectables*, as they were sometimes known among the Zulu,[3] enjoyed high status in most African societies at independence, but in achieving it they experienced much conflict with earlier honour codes and incorporated many

---

[1] This volume, pp. 66, 110–11.

[2] I have found the most useful definition in Geoffrey Crossick, *An artisan elite in Victorian society: Kentish London 1840–1880* (London, 1978), pp. 134–9, 156.

[3] Paul la Hausse de Lalouvière, *Restless identities: signatures of nationalism, Zulu ethnicity and history in the lives of Petros Lamula (c.1881–1948) and Lymon Maling (1889–c.1936)* (Pietermaritzburg, 2000), p. 14.

elements from them, especially in gender relations and an intense concern with appearances.

Historians have described the rise of respectability among white people in the Cape Colony during the earlier nineteenth century, when the Dutch regime of rank, slave-ownership, and exclusive Company rule gave way to a more open society in which any respectable white man might participate. By mid century this social pattern was spreading to the emerging Coloured community, an amalgam of former slaves and Khoisan people. It was crystallised in 1853 by the establishment of an elected legislature with low, nonracial franchise qualifications embracing the upper stratum of Coloured men. 'The 1853 constitution put a price on respectability,' Robert Ross has written. 'Men whose property was worth £25 were within the limits, as were their families. The rest were not.'[4] Meanwhile, the eastward expansion of white settlement and missionary work introduced these processes into Bantu-speaking societies. The first to accept them were the 'Mfengu', a miscellany of refugees and captives from western Xhosa country drawn into the Cape Colony especially after the frontier war of 1835. Initially labourers, they acquired cattle and land, served the British in frontier wars, frequently became Christians, and acted as pioneers of respectability. 'A most industrious people they are,' a missionary wrote of one group in 1863:

Most of them have been farm-servants in the Colony; and after many years of hard labour, having accumulated a little property, they have come to reside here. Two of them, not content to live in Caffre huts, within the last year set to work and erected European houses for themselves. . . . The school is well attended, and the children manifest a strong desire to receive instruction.[5]

As missionary work expanded further into South Africa, similar communities of *kholwa* (believers) took shape, often clustering around mission stations. By 1904 something approaching two thousand Africans in Natal held the certificates exempting them from native law that manifested respectable status.[6] In tropical Africa the same role was played by freed slaves settled on the coast during the nineteenth century, generally under mission auspices. From Freetown, Monrovia, Ouidah, Libreville, Zanzibar, Bagamoyo, and Mombasa, they spread

[4] McKenzie, 'Gender,' chs. 1 and 2; Ross, *Status and respectability*, p. 173.

[5] J. A. Chalmers, 4 July 1863, in Donovan Williams (ed.), *The journal and selected writings of the Reverend Tiyo Soga* (Cape Town, 1983), p. 94. Generally, see Richard A. Moyer, 'A history of the Mfengu of the Eastern Cape 1815–1865,' PhD thesis, University of London, 1976.

[6] Etherington, *Preachers*, chs. 5 and 6; Shula Marks, *Reluctant rebellion: the 1906–8 disturbances in Natal* (Oxford, 1970), p. 58.

along the coast and carried into the hinterland a Christian, Westernised lifestyle as a model for other groups. The standard dictionary of the language spoken by the Creole people of Freetown contains a word *respektebul* but no word for honour.[7]

These pioneer Christians were commonly called 'readers' (in East Africa and the Gold Coast) or 'people of the book' (in Yorubaland). The knowledge, resources, seriousness, ambition, and cultural dependence characteristic of respectability all came principally from their education in mission boarding schools like Lovedale, established in the Eastern Cape in 1841 to inculcate godliness, cleanliness, industry, and discipline. During its first forty-five years, Lovedale trained, among others, 369 teachers, 299 farmers, and 100 storekeepers, both black and white.[8] The initial models were frankly European. 'We have left the race of our forefathers,' a leading *kholwa* said in 1863, 'we have left the black race and clung to the white. We imitate them in anything we can. We feel we are in the midst of a civilised people, and that when we became converts to their faith we belonged to them.'[9] Mission schooling aimed to tame the 'love of dignity' inculcated at institutions like Rwanda's *intore* and channel it into the pursuit of public duty rather than personal fame. Young men were no longer trained for war but for service, 'so to subjugate ourselves that we may rule,' in the words of the school song at Achimota in the Gold Coast. 'I promise to do my duty,' prefects vowed at King's College Budo in Buganda, 'seeking not my own comfort, glory or popularity, but sacrificing myself for the good of Budo.'[10]

Respectability demanded, first, sufficient economic independence to allow the individual to reshape his lifestyle. 'One's occupation is one's honour [*ekitiibwa*],' said a motto on a Kampala wall.[11] For most Africans that occupation was farming. Evangelical missionaries in southern Africa were especially keen to create a 'class of native yeomen,' owning their land, employing family labour, using ox-drawn ploughs and wagons, producing for the market, and creating well-housed, well-dressed, literate, educated, and God-fearing

[7] Clifford N. Fyle and Eldred D. Jones, *A Krio-English dictionary* (Oxford, 1980), p. 313.

[8] Robert H. W. Shepherd, *Lovedale, South Africa: the story of a century, 1841–1941* (Lovedale, n.d.), pp. 212, 484.

[9] Johannes Kumalo, quoted in La Hausse, *Identities*, p. 260.

[10] Caldwell to ?, 8 November 1925, Mengo Papers 12, Albert Cook Library, Mulago, Kampala; C. Kingsley Williams, *Achimota: the early years, 1924–1948* (Accra, 1962), p. 25; McGregor, *Budo*, p. 108.

[11] A. W. Southall and P. C. W. Gutkind, *Townsmen in the making: Kampala and its suburbs* (Kampala, 1957), p. 124.

communities – an ideal closely matching traditional notions of householder honour. Mfengu pioneers began to use ploughs in the 1830s. By 1890 there were probably between one thousand and two thousand African commercial farmers in the Cape Province, plus many smaller peasants.[12] 'Mahonga is one of the best specimens of a thoroughly civilized and Christianized Tambookie [Thembu] Kaffir,' a missionary reported from Glen Grey in 1870:

Some twenty-five years ago he was a red-clayed and barbarous heathen; but now he lives in a large and beautiful house, which he has built, at a cost of £400, on a splendid farm of two thousand five hundred acres, with flocks and herds, &c., all his own, and surrounded by a loving family, all on their way to the better land.[13]

By then the first Christian commercial farmers had appeared in tropical Africa, initially in Liberia in mid century, then the cocoa-growers of the Gold Coast and Yorubaland, and in the early twentieth century the first cotton- and coffee-growers of East Africa.[14] Almost everywhere farming provided the essential economic foundation for respectability. The exception was the West African coast, where freed slaves found greater opportunities in trade. Mid-century merchants like Charles Heddle of Freetown, James Bannerman of Cape Coast, and H. Lafayette Crusoe of Monrovia traded directly with Europe on a large scale. In 1880 some 57 per cent of elite African men in Lagos were merchants.[15]

Schooling opened other routes to respectability. Many young men began as clerks. 'He started early in life in a humble situation,' one explained, 'toiling slowly but steadily up life's steep ladder, plodding his way through the interstices of the world's jungle, from one Department to another, each in its turn yielding its own improvements, either pecuniarily or intellectual, till in the year 1907, he entered the Government Service as a Postman.'[16] However humble his duties, a clerk was a man of power and status in his own eyes and in those of the illiterate. When Daniel Anirare failed to find clercial employment in Lagos and took manual work instead, 'In order not to arouse the suspicion of gossiping housewives in my residence I had to dress up like a clerk going to a large office

---

[12] Colin Bundy, *The rise and fall of the South African peasantry* (London, 1979), pp. 45–6, 94.

[13] *Wesleyan Missionary Notices*, 1870, p. 133.

[14] Tom W. Shick, *Behold the promised land: a history of Afro-American settler society in nineteenth-century Liberia* (Baltimore, 1977), pp. 112–16; Iliffe, *Africans*, pp. 203, 206.

[15] Christopher Fyfe, 'Charles Heddle: an African "merchant prince",' duplicated conference paper, 1981; Edward Reynolds, *Trade and economic change on the Gold Coast, 1807–1874* (Harlow, 1974), p. 80; M. B. Akpan, 'The Liberian economy in the nineteenth century: the state of agriculture and commerce,' *Liberian Studies Journal*, 6, 1 (1975), 12; Kristin Mann, *Marrying well: marriage, status and social change among the educated elite in colonial Lagos* (Cambridge, 1985), p. 25.

[16] Asatu to Lugard, n.d., Lugard Papers 48, RH.

when leaving home in the morning, and that included putting on a tie to match my outfit. As soon as I got to the site I changed to my labour garment. At the end of the day's work I returned home a neat worker with the appearance of a clerk.'[17] Yet many hoped to rise further, especially in West Africa. By 1880 Africans had held posts in the Lagos Administration as treasurer, superintendent of police, and acting colonial secretary. Twelve years later they held eighteen of the forty senior official posts in Sierra Leone.[18]

The other major career path to respectability began with schoolteaching:

> Mr Joseph Fondini . . . was a man of many talents, and also people admired his manner of doing things. This man had been working at East London before, and he came with the town fashions. He belonged to the Wesleyan Church. . . . Even his music seemed to have been different from the music of other teachers. In his general appearance, he was smart and lively and with it went self-respect, and consciousness of his being an educated man.[19]

Like clerks, however, teachers contrasted their prestige with their routine tasks and low pay. In Southern Rhodesia 'only the most dedicated individuals remained in the profession any longer than they had to.'[20] In the early days of mission work, many aspired to ordination, then the pinnacle of respectability. Lovedale's first African students included five future clergymen, notably Tiyo Soga, ordained as South Africa's first black minister in 1856 after two periods of training in Scotland. The recaptive slave Samuel Crowther, consecrated Bishop of the Niger in 1864, was the unchallenged leader of respectable African society on the west coast. Yet clergymen not only faced African opposition and European criticism, but their salaries from cash-strapped missions quickly fell behind other elite occupations. By the late nineteenth century, they had been overtaken by African lawyers and doctors. The model among lawyers was Sir Samuel Lewis, the son of a Yoruba freed slave, who qualified in England and practised in Freetown from 1872 to 1903, specialising profitably in property transactions. In 1882 he joined the Legislative Council as a Creole spokesman. He twice acted as chief justice and was knighted in 1896, the first African so honoured. No other West African lawyer quite equalled this success, but men of the next generation like John Mensah Sarbah and Joseph Casely Hayford of the Gold Coast were the most prominent elite figures of their

---

[17] Quoted in Philip S. Zachernuk, *Colonial subjects: an African intelligentsia and Atlantic ideas* (Charlottesville, 2000), p. 84.

[18] Iliffe, *Africans*, p. 156; Christopher Fyfe, *A history of Sierra Leone* (London, 1962), p. 615.

[19] 'A short autobiography of Samuel Krune Mqhayi,' in Patricia E. Scott (ed.), *Mqhayi in translation* (Grahamstown, 1976), p. 13.

[20] Michael Oliver West, 'African middle-class formation in colonial Zimbabwe, 1890–1965,' PhD thesis, Harvard University, 1990, p. 43.

time, while Kobina Sekyi of Cape Coast earned more than £2,500 a year between 1918 and 1924, only slightly less than the governor.[21] South Africa's first African lawyers entered practice in 1910, too late to share in the opportunities of Victorian liberalism; instead, they took the initiative in founding the African National Congress. East Africa's colonial governments deliberately obstructed legal education.[22] Medical training was more widely available. The pioneer was John Macaulay Wilson, who served as an assistant colonial surgeon in Sierra Leone during the 1820s. Other West Africans followed from the 1850s, either practising privately in coastal towns or joining government service. The pioneer in South Africa was Tiyo Soga's son, William Anderson Soga, who returned from Scotland as a medical missionary in 1885. Most of his successors practised privately, finding little scope in government service.[23] East Africa's first African doctors, by contrast, were mostly trained locally at Makerere College, entered government employment, but did not gain full recognition until 1957.

Medicine illustrates how inherited notions of honour were transformed into new ethics, in this case professionalism.[24] In East Africa, most Africans employed in modern medicine during the nineteenth and early twentieth centuries were of low status and performed menial tasks, which they found disgusting and dishonourable. After work-patterns were established, however, they were taught by educated people through rigorous hospital training, often reinforced by Christian notions of service. Medical assistants became model modern elites, dedicated to science, respectability, and modernity. Yet they were ambitious for still greater *ekitiibwa*, demanding a fully professional training recognised by Britain's General Medical Council. Once granted professional status, they defended it ruthlessly against the rival aspirations of nurses and paramedics. At independence, doctors were the recognised apex of the African elite, the 'cream of the cream,' as they liked to say. That their status depended on education, technical skill, and professional organisation showed how greatly respectability

---

[21] J. D. Hargreaves, *A life of Sir Samuel Lewis* (London, 1958); H. Lynch, introduction to Sarbah, *Fanti customary laws*, pp. v–xiii; Roger Stephen Gocking, 'The historic Akoto: a social history of Cape Coast Ghana, 1848–1948,' PhD thesis, Stanford University, 1981, p. 262 n91.

[22] Leo Kuper, *An African bourgeoisie: race, class, and politics in South Africa* (New Haven, 1965), p. 75; Peter Walshe, *The rise of African nationalism in South Africa: the African National Congress, 1912–1952* (London, 1970), p. 31; Coryndon to S of S, 17 September 1920, CO 536/103/17.

[23] M. C. F. Easmon, 'Sierra Leone doctors,' *Sierra Leone Studies*, NS, 6 (June 1956), 81–96; Adelola Adeloye, *African pioneers of modern medicine: Nigerian doctors of the nineteenth century* (Ibadan, 1985); *Imvo Zabantsundu*, 15 July 1885.

[24] This paragraph is based on John Iliffe, *East African doctors: a history of the modern profession* (Cambridge, 1998).

differed from heroic honour. That they defended their status so jealously showed how much it remained the same.

'The African who believes that Jesus is preparing for him a glorious mansion in Heaven,' an aspiring missionary wrote in 1858, 'will endeavour to build for himself a decent house on earth.'[25] Better housing was part of the cultural package that Africans had to adopt if others were to acknowledge their respectability. It also became a means by which they displayed their distinction. A better house meant a square house – in 1931 a Nigerian congregation insisted that 'they want a church with four corners' – because, so it was claimed, only a square house could be divided into rooms permitting 'refinement and delicacy' and only a square house could accommodate European furniture. 'I believe a great step upward is made,' a missionary claimed, 'when people are taught to get up from the floor and live in a well-lighted room with windows and doors and with some simple furniture.'[26] Respectable Africans shared this concern for housing, investing almost as heavily in cement and corrugated iron as in education, especially in towns where the option was often a sordid shanty. Yet respectable Africans insisted also that the house must be their own, not the property of a landlord or municipality.[27] And, as people from honour cultures, they used their houses to display their status. The eight-room bungalow of ANC President Dr. Xuma was the cynosure of the Sophiatown freehold settlement in Johannesburg, with 'separate bedrooms, a room for sitting, another for eating, and a room to be alone, for reading or thinking, to shut out South Africa and not be black,' as an envious observer described. Xuma's medical colleague in Lagos, Dr. Obadiah Johnson, named his residence Marble Hall, although it lacked the ballroom and 'electric orchestrion' gracing the merchant Samuel Pearse's Elephant House. In the 1950s, whether in Johannesburg or Lagos, the car outside the house was as much a symbol of respectability as the furniture within it. Xuma's house had *two* garages.[28]

Dress also illustrated the ambivalence between respectability and display. 'One's first endeavour is to get into his mind that he must wear clothes,' a pioneer missionary to the Kikuyu of Kenya explained. 'That is the first step to self-respect.' Governments agreed. Sierra Leone required all freed slaves

---

[25] Anthony J. Dachs (ed.), *Papers of John Mackenzie* (Johannesburg, 1975), p. 72.

[26] J. C. Bull, diary, 14 December 1931, Bull Papers, RH; Jane Waterston, 1883, quoted in Shepherd, *Lovedale*, p. 436; Archdeacon Johnson in *The Mission Field*, 65 (1920), 167.

[27] For example, Ezekiel Mphahlele, *Down Second Avenue* (reprinted, London, 1990), pp. 152–3.

[28] Bloke Modisane, *Blame me on history* (reprinted, Parklands, 1990), p. 34; 0. Johnson to Baylis, 2 December 1899, CMS G3/A2/O/1899/169; Allister Macmillan, *The red book of West Africa* (London, 1920), p. 97; Kuper, *African bourgeoisie*, p. 112.

to wear European clothes and the Cape Colony threatened anyone indecently clad with three months hard labour.[29] Again many Africans agreed, but saw clothing in terms of display as well as decency. European wedding costume was so widely admired that even Cape Muslims adopted it. Frock-coats and kid gloves were conspicuous on the West African coast. The cult of male fashion (*sape*) in the French Congo dates to the early colonial period when domestic servants strove to imitate their employers. In 1934 Phillip Lebotsa successfully defended his title as South Africa's dressing champion for the tenth time.[30]

For the missionaries, the cultural package of respectability included moral as well as material elements. Lovedale was the location of South Africa's first black 'temple' of the temperance movement, which from the 1870s won much support in West and Southern Africa not only among respectable people who saw it partly as an attack on the use of alcohol in pagan ceremonies, but also among elders anxious to protect their privileges from usurpation by the young and among those who saw liquor as a means by which Europeans undermined African autonomy and self-respect.[31] Thrift, by contrast, probably had more appeal to Mfengu smallholders than to West African traditions of largess. A work-ethic was widely distributed. Most widespread of all was the belief in education and the profitability of investment in it. 'You can have all the education you want, I am prepared to suffer for your sake,' the Reverend Thompson Samkange of Southern Rhodesia assured his son. The future South African communist leader, Moses Kotane, was told by his father, 'The only thing you can steal is a book.' Nor was it only parents who invested in education: three-quarters of those taking post-primary courses in Southern Rhodesia in the early 1960s did so through correspondence colleges.[32] Educational benevolence was especially admired. Kibedi Zirabamuzale, interpreter and chief in Busoga, Uganda, reportedly paid the school fees for ninety-eight young people who reached university. Successful Mfengu financed two major schools at Healdtown and Blythswood and took

[29] J. W. Arthur in *Kikuyu News*, 1 (March 1908), 6; Arthur T. Porter, *Creoledom* (London, 1963), p. 101; Cape of Good Hope, *Report on Native Laws*, appendix, p. 4.

[30] Robert C.-H. Shell, 'Rites and rebellion: Islamic conversion at the Cape, 1808 to 1915,' in Christopher Saunders and others (ed.), *Studies in the history of Cape Town: volume 5* (Cape Town, 1983), p. 31; Shick, *Behold*, p. 43; Ch. Didier Gondola, 'Dream and drama: the search for elegance among Congolese youth,' *African Studies Review*, 42, 1 (April 1999), 26; *Bantu World*, 4 August 1934.

[31] Wallace G. Mills, 'The roots of African nationalism in the Cape Colony: temperance, 1866–1898,' *IJAHS*, 13 (1980), 197–213; Emmanuel Kwaku Akyeampong, *Drink, power, and cultural change: a social history of alcohol in Ghana, c. 1800 to recent times* (Portsmouth, N.H., 1996), pp. 16–17, 21–5, 71–4.

[32] Terence Ranger, *Are we not also men? The Samkange family and African politics in Zimbabwe, 1920–64* (London, 1995), p. 52; Brian Bunting, *Moses Kotane: South African revolutionary* (London, 1975), p. 12; West, 'African middle-class formation,' p. 57.

a large part in the foundation in 1916 of sub-Saharan Africa's first university college for Africans at Fort Hare.[33]

'With education,' wrote the *abbé* Boilat of Senegal, '. . . you will see the fall of all those gross, if not dishonourable, ways known as *the custom of the country*.' One of the first was generally indigenous dancing, 'notoriously the cause of many vices.' In its place, Creoles patronised Dignity Balls in which European styles of ballroom dancing became occasions for competitive display. The *ahyiko* dance introduced from Monrovia into the Gold Coast during the 1920s required expensive clothes, handbags, and hats. 'Only people with money, *gentlemanfoo* (gentlemen), took part in the dance, people who had travelled and came back,' a participant remembered. 'It was not a small thing, it was very beautiful for those with money.'[34] In music, similarly, respectable South African taste adapted traditional choral singing to Christian hymns and Afro-American spirituals. South Africa's first Eisteddfod took place in 1931, although by then the young elite of Johannesburg were flocking rather to the New Inchcape Palais de Dance and the Bantu Men's Social Centre to dance to the American styles of Japanese Express or the Jazz Maniacs.[35] Respectability did not damage sociability; it demanded peer recognition in a public sphere of associations, meetings, and the literary clubs 'springing up around us like mushrooms' in early twentieth-century Gold Coast towns.[36] Respectable people were serious, reading people. After the Bible, their favourite material was commonly *Pilgrim's progress*, but they were also avid readers of the newspapers that flourished in West and South Africa from the 1880s. Dahomey alone produced more than forty newspapers during the colonial period, mostly edited by dedicated Westernisers from the 'Brazilian' returned-slave community of Ouidah.[37]

Serious as they were, respectable people retained that serious concern with appearances characteristic of honour cultures. Nowhere did they display this more clearly than in death. In southern Africa, death had not generally been

---

[33] David William Cohen (ed.), *Towards a reconstructed past: historical texts from Busoga* (Oxford, 1986), p. 304; Moyer, 'Mfengu,' p. 556; D. D. T. Jabavu, *The life of John Tengo Jabavu* (Lovedale [1922]), pp. 93–8.

[34] Quoted in Robert W. July, *The origins of modern African thought* (London, 1968), p. 160; Spitzer, *Creoles*, p. 23; Stephan Felix Miescher, 'Becoming a man in Kwawu: gender, law, personhood, and the construction of masculinities in colonial Ghana, 1875–1957,' PhD thesis, Northwestern University, 1997, p. 239.

[35] Coplan, *In township tonight*, pp. 28–33, 38–9, 116, 130–2.

[36] *Gold Coast Leader*, 2 August 1902; Stephanie Newell, *Ghanaian popular fiction* (Oxford, 2002), ch. 4.

[37] Fred I. A. Omu, *Press and politics in Nigeria, 1880–1937* (London, 1978), chs. 1 and 2; Switzer, *Power*, pp. 121–2, 147–50; Dov Ronen, 'The colonial elite in Dahomey,' *African Studies Review*, 17, 1 (April 1974), 55–9.

attended with much ceremony, but Christians sought to give it greater solemnity, emphasising Victorian notions of a good death and a fitting funeral. Missionaries rejoiced when 'a very decent coffin had been brought by the parents, and the family followed in suitable mourning-apparel.' The message found a rapid response. Burial societies guaranteeing Africans respectable funerals existed by the late nineteenth century; by 1944 some 65 per cent of households in the Western Native Township of Johannesburg belonged to them and the style of funeral offered became increasingly elaborate as time passed.[38] In West Africa, by contrast, early evangelists were shocked by the lavish celebrations attending the funerals of prominent men. 'Funeral ceremonies here are altogether ruinous and demoralizing,' Archdeacon James Johnson wrote from Abeokuta in 1879. Instead, they advocated a sober Victorian ceremony, with black crepe and mourning clothes. Africans were delighted by the new fashion. 'This was the first of its kind in Abeokuta for grandeur and popularity,' one wrote. By the 1870s several companies in Freetown were advertising hearses 'of the most modern pattern . . . with rich plumes.' When John Mensah Sarbah died in 1910, 'The procession to the Wesleyan Cemetery . . . was the longest and the most numerously attended within living memory. It was a record funeral.'[39] During the following century Christian funerals in West Africa were to reach astonishing levels of ostentation, and the fashion spread also to the east. The culture of honour had captured the challenge of respectability.[40]

The first respectable generation saw themselves as sharing with their missionaries and colonial rulers the task of enlightening a people whom Bishop Crowther described as 'still in the darkness of superstition, ignorance, and vice, in a most servile and abject degradation and slavery, and in a state of spiritual death.' To achieve this they deliberately distinguished themselves from 'the outside Natives,' as *kholwa* described them. The distinction was embodied in their early political organisations – 'no member eligible unless educated,' as the rules of the West Nyasa Native Association put it – and above all in the right to vote for

---

[38] Williams, *Journal of Soga*, pp. 20–1, 29; Ayliff, journal, 23 June 1849, in *Wesleyan Missionary Notices*, 8 (1850), 76; *Bantu World*, 6 May 1933; Hilda Kuper and Selma Kaplan, 'Voluntary associations in an urban township,' *African Studies*, 3 (1944), 178.

[39] J. Johnson to Wright, January 1879, CMS C.A2/O. 56/54; Doherty, journal, 9 September 1882, CMS G3/A2/O/1883/73; Fyfe, *History*, p. 379; Akyeampong, *Drink*, p. 38; *Gold Coast Leader*, 10 December 1910.

[40] Vivian Burns, 'Travel to heaven: fantasy coffins,' *African Arts*, 7, 2 (Winter 1974), 24–5; Claudine Vidal, *Sociologie des passions (Rwanda, Côte d'Ivoire)* (Paris, 1991), ch. 4; Sjaak van der Geest, 'Funerals for the living,' *African Studies Review*, 43, 3 (December 2000), 103–29; *Sunday Vision*, 22 September 1996.

members of legislatures.[41] The Cape franchise of 1853, although non-racial, was not intended to include Africans because few had then been born within the Cape Colony, but by 1876 some were becoming eligible and from 1884 systematic registration took place. Two years later Africans were reckoned to form 43 per cent of voters in the six constituencies where they were most numerous. Some 2 per cent of African men in the Colony were enfranchised, mainly skilled artisans, teachers, clerks, clergymen, and the most prosperous smallholders. They valued it 'not merely because it gives potential influence, but because . . . it is a symbol of manhood.'[42] In Liberia, where male citizens could vote from 1839, the right was similarly a mark of status, as it became when introduced into the coastal towns of British West Africa during the 1920s. So, yet more clearly, was candidacy for election. Of fifty-six candidates for Nigeria's Legislative Council between 1923 and 1947, twenty-four were lawyers and ten doctors.[43]

The respectable had to defend their status against attacks from many directions. Other Africans often despised them as 'children of slaves' or 'black Europeans'. Touring the Ijebu kingdom of Yorubaland in 1892, James Johnson was treated 'as if I had been a slave, a criminal, a fugitive slave or one suspected of having committed a serious crime in his own country.'[44] Europeans, by contrast, frequently resented African pretensions to culture and equality. The earliest recorded defamation action by an African in an Eastern Cape court was launched by Constable Jacob Bokwe, one of Lovedale's first students and founder of a dynasty of distinguished professional men, who in 1850 unsuccessfully sued a European for publicly calling him 'a gross liar'. Sixty years later, a Nigerian barrister pursued a successful action against a European official who arrested him for refusing to remove his hat.[45] Other educated men struggled to defend themselves against the widespread European view 'that an

[41] Quoted in Zachernuk, *Colonial subjects*, p. 36; Heather Hughes, 'Doubly elite: exploring the life of John Langalibalele Dube,' *JSAS*, 27 (2001), 448; McCracken, *Politics and Christianity*, p. 267.

[42] Stanley Trapido, 'White conflict and non-white participation in the politics of the Cape of Good Hope, 1853–1910,' PhD thesis, University of London, 1970, pp. 225–31, 247; Robert Ross, *A concise history of South Africa* (Cambridge, 1999), p. 81; *The Christian Express*, 1 October 1921; D. D. T. Jabavu (1933) in Thomas Karis and others (eds.), *From protest to challenge: a documentary history of African politics in South Africa* (5 vols., Stanford, 1972–97), vol. 1, p. 250.

[43] Shick, *Behold*, p. 39; G.Wesley Johnson, Jr., *The emergence of black politics in Senegal: the struggle for power in the four communes* (Stanford, 1971), p. 49; Zachernuk, *Colonial subjects*, p. 85.

[44] Spitzer, *Creoles*, p. 84; Ayandele, *Ijebu*, p. 16.

[45] Alice (Victoria) civil case 55 of 1850, CA 1/ALC 2/2/1/1; *Gold Coast Leader*, 30 April 1910.

African cannot be trusted with a sixpence of Government money.'[46] Corruption probably was common among African officials, for their respectable lifestyle was expensive, their wages were low, their families were demanding, their opportunities were great, and their notions of gift-exchange came from honour cultures. Yet some bitterly resented the charge. In 1908 a gaoler in the Gold Coast cut his throat when accused of freeing a prisoner with whose wife he was cohabiting, leaving a note: 'DC, I am not guilty of this charge and yet people dont believe me I must perish. I have served the Government for 25 years.' Several respectable men in the Eastern Cape sued for slander when accused of corruption. A constable took action when alleged to have accepted money to hush up a theft. A local preacher contested an allegation of attempted bribery that had led to his excommunication.

Other respectable men faced the novel dilemma of defending their sexual reputations. As will be seen later, neither they nor their African counterparts necessarily regarded monogamy as essential to respectability, but Europeans did so regard it, while respectable Africans certainly condemned philandering. During 1893, for example, two schoolteachers in the Eastern Cape secured damages from men who, by accusing them of having impregnated women not their wives, had lost them employment.[47] But colonial life was often too novel and confused to allow a young man to clear his name. When Daniel Mali was publicly accused of having impreganted Napo while both were working in Kingwilliamstown, he sued his detractors, claiming that she had forged a letter supposedly written by him, that she had been his sweetheart (*imetsha*) but he had 'sacked her in town,' and that although they had shared a room there with other young people, 'I have never had a woman to sleep with under the blankets.' The court refused to apportion blame.[48]

The tension between respectability and older notions of rank and honour was especially acute in Ethiopia, where innovators did not enjoy European protection. A few young Ethiopians were educated in Europe during the early nineteenth century, chiefly by Christian missions. The first three students were sent officially in 1864. Such men, generally of quite humble birth, found roles in the technological and administrative innovations that Emperor Menelik introduced from the 1890s, culminating in the ministerial system of 1907. After Ras Tafari (Haile Selassie) became regent in 1916, he took the process further.

---

[46] Crocker, *Nigeria*, p. 204.

[47] *Gold Coast Leader*, 13 June 1908; Peddie civil case 175 of 1881, CA 1/PDE 2/1/1/14; Tsolo civil case 57 of 1893, CA 1/TSO 2/1/11; Tsomo civil cases 43 and 76 of 1893, CA 1/TSM 2/1/1/13.

[48] Kingwilliamstown civil case 127 of 1892, CA 1/KWT 2/1/1/1/325.

Because he had been educated by missionaries, he believed in modernisation provided it did not threaten his power and so inserted men with Western training into key administrative posts, leaving political positions to the traditional aristocracy. The officials enjoyed his backing – the Criminal Code of 1930 decreed a special penalty for 'a man who abuses educated men who are doing intellectual work' – provided they did not irreparably alienate traditionalists.[49] Their common experience was shame at Ethiopia's backwardness, which they determined to eradicate and blamed on aristocratic exploitation. 'The authorities of the country eat, drink, sleep, and grow fat like Easter lambs at the expense of the property of the poor people,' said the Ethiopian speaker in a dialogue published in 1908 by the Italian-educated Afäwärq Gäbra Iyyäsus. Others agreed: Ethiopia's first modern play, performed in the mid 1910s, satirised the aristocracy so fiercely that no further play was permitted before 1930.[50] Blame also fell on the military – 'the whole army of the empire which knows no work other than to pillage and oppress,' as Afäwärq wrote – and its underlying ethos: 'We are suspicious of one another and believe, wrongly, in internecine wars as heroism.'[51] The church, similarly, was seen as parasitic and obscurantist. In 1932 Blatten Geta Heruy Wäldä-Sellase, a man of modest birth and ecclesiastical education who was Haile Selassie's most trusted agent as minister of foreign affairs, published a novel, *The new world*, whose hero, a church reformer, clashed with the authorities on returning from Europe by choosing his own wife and refusing to finance an expensive wedding or *tezkar* feast for his father, insisting instead on giving the money to charity.[52]

Conservative Ethiopians found reform profoundly dishonourable. Villagers petitioned provincial governors to end it. Churchmen blamed it for the influenza epidemic of 1918. Men with a 'heavy, noble parentage that cannot be lifted with two hands' doubted the patriotism of *parvenus* like Heruy and persuaded the emperor not to appoint the Swiss-educated Käntiba Gäbra Dästa to a ministry in 1907 because he lacked a fief or retainers. Blatta Gäbra-Egziabher, another moderniser, was once imprisoned for stating publicly that the earth revolved

---

[49] Richard Pankhurst, 'Misoneism and innovation in Ethiopian history,' *Ethiopia Observer*, 7 (1964), 305; John Markakis, *Ethiopia: anatomy of a traditional polity* (Oxford, 1974), pp. 144–6; Haile Sellassie, *My life*, pp. 65–76; de Halpert report, 22 May 1934, and 'Abyssinian Criminal Code 1930' (para. 284), de Halpert Papers, RH; Bahru Zewde, *Pioneers of change in Ethiopia: the reformist intellectuals of the early twentieth century* (Oxford, 2002), pp. 171, 177–8.

[50] G. J. Afevork, *Guide du voyageur en Abyssinie* (Rome, 1908), p. 182; Albert X. Gerard, 'Amharic creative literature: the early phase,' *JES*, 6, 2 (1968), 46; Zewde, *Pioneers*, pp. 120–2.

[51] Afevork, *Guide*, p. 214; Gebrehiwot Baikedagn (early 1920s), quoted by Shiferaw Jammo, 'An overview of the economy 1941–74,' in Shiferaw Bekele (ed.), *An economic history of modern Ethiopia* (Dakar, 1995), p. 55.

[52] Gerard, 'Amharic creative literature,' pp. 50–1; Zewde, *Pioneers*, pp. 70–3.

around the sun.[53] 'Abyssinians in general, and especially the well-to-do and the "officer" classes,' a diplomat reported in 1906,

are intensely jealous of those educated Abyssinians who may from time to time find their way back to their country; and while inwardly envying their superior knowledge of general subjects, of which they themselves are entirely ignorant, they outwardly display an open contempt for them. . . . There are several Abyssinians in the country who were formerly well-considered and fairly prosperous, but who have been deliberately ruined by their fellow-countrymen – including Menelek himself – for acting as interpreters to Europeans.[54]

Yet despite this hostility, the new men in reality absorbed many traditional Ethiopian notions of honour, just as they were themselves absorbed by marriage into the ruling class. When ministers were first appointed in 1907, Habtä Giyorgis (an Oromo captive) celebrated his elevation to the War Ministry with a massive feast for soldiers, priests, and paupers, while the first minister of foreign affairs, Näggadras Haylä-Giyorgis, appeared 'with his usual escort of some hundred or so retainers,' and even the austere Heruy displayed himself in public after his appointment as director general of foreign affairs, 'his genial face beaming under his shiny top hat in response to the plaudits of the multitude.'[55] But it was in their writings that the new men best displayed their inherited sense of honour. Afäwärq's dialogue, however critical of the old order, described the Ethiopian spokesman giving an exquisite lesson in good manners to his brash European interlocutor, enabling its hypersensitive author to revenge himself not only for insults by Ethiopian aristocrats but for slights suffered in Europe. 'Why, sir, do you show yourself astonished by my punctuality at the rendez-vous?' the Ethiopian enquired. 'Unless it be for a serious and unexpected accident, it is a lack of courtesy to keep anyone waiting at a rendez-vous. It is so not only in Europe; among us too it is shameful.' While accepting that European civilisation was more advanced, Afäwärq also insisted that Ethiopia was more civilised than its African neighbours. His novel of 1908 (roughly *A tale of the imagination*) was both a story of romantic love in an alien vein and an allegory in which the heroine, Ethiopia, brought Christianity and civilisation to a war-ravaged region. Like other writers of his generation, he accepted seemingly

---

[53] James McCann, *From poverty to famine in northeast Ethiopia* (Philadelphia, 1987), p. 142; Campbell to Balfour, 11 December 1918, FO 403/450/11640/12; Molvaer, *Tradition*, p. 25; Zewde, *Pioneers*, pp. 45, 67.

[54] Clerk, 'General report on Abyssinia for the year 1906,' FOCP 9041/1.

[55] Markakis, *Ethiopia*, p. 186; Peter Phillips Garretson, 'A history of Addis Ababa from its foundation in 1886 to 1910,' PhD thesis, University of London, 1974, p. 150; Borg G. Steffanson and Ronald K. Starrett (eds.), *Documents on Ethiopian politics* (3 vols., Salisbury, N.C., 1976–7), vol. 1, p. 1, and vol. 2, p. 70.

without question the empire's monarchical structure and social stratification, drawing his heroes from the nobility or the church and insisting only on moral reform of the established leadership.[56]

This view was widely shared in other regions. 'All intelligent Africans would desire that the Native Potentates should continue to maintain their ancestral position and status under the light and influence of civilized government,' the leading Lagos newspaper declared in 1894.[57] One reason for this was that the respectable needed protection. Some hundreds of Freetown Creoles were murdered by upcountry people during the Sierra Leone Hut Tax War of 1898. 'They will kill everyone they find with European clothes,' a mission teacher reported of the Maji Maji rebels.[58] Beyond this, however, respectable men also recognised that alliance with hereditary authority was necessary both to resist European domination and to achieve reform. The respectable merchants of the Gold Coast involved their 'natural rulers' in modernising political experiments like the Fante Confederation of 1868–73 and the Aborigines Rights Protection Society of 1897. The lawyers who founded the African National Congress of South Africa in 1912 appealed to 'chiefs of royal blood and gentlemen of our race.' 'In the Gold Coast the tribal connection is the chief insurance of respectability,' the pioneer nationalist leader J. B. Danquah explained in 1942. 'Once cut a Gold Coast man off from that connection, and he feels like a fish out of water, a man without a background – no tradition – the inferior of a slave, never mind his high and modern education.'[59]

Towards the end of the nineteenth century, many respectable men became more critical of Westernisation. One reason was a realisation that, however respectable Africans might become, Europeans would not accept them as equals, as was demonstrated by the growing segregation of institutions and residential areas in both South and West Africa.[60] In the south, the African commercial farmers of the mid nineteenth century were gradually impoverished by land alienation, population growth, and competition from European and overseas producers. In the west, steam-shipping and the economic depression of 1880–92 drove many African merchants out of business. The proportion of elite African men in Lagos who were merchants fell between 1880 and 1902 from

---

[56] Afevork, *Guide*, p. 91; Alain Rouaud, *Afä-Wârq, 1868–1947: un intellectuel éthiopien témoin de son temps* (Paris, 1991), pp. 236, 244, 268–75.

[57] *Lagos Weekly Record*, 8 September 1894, quoted in Zachernuk, *Colonial subjects*, pp. 61–2.

[58] Spitzer, *Creoles*, p. 96; Yosefu Sihaba to Wehrmeister, 16 November 1905, in Cyrillus Wehrmeister, *Vor dem Sturm* (St Ottilien, 1906), p. 186.

[59] David Kimble, *A political history of Ghana* (Oxford, 1963), pp. 247–9, 341–3; Walshe, *Rise*, p. 34; Danquah to Perham, 9 February 1942, Perham Papers 389/2/1, RH.

[60] Vivian Bickford-Smith, *Ethnic pride and racial prejudice in Victorian Cape Town* (Cambridge, 1995), esp. pp. 8–9; Spitzer, *Creoles*, pp. 52–62.

57 to 38 per cent.[61] Instead they became increasingly dependent on government employment, but at the same time the racialism of expanding colonial administrations reserved many higher posts for Europeans. Whereas in 1892 Africans held eighteen of the forty top positions in Sierra Leone, by 1912 they held only fifteen of ninety-two. In 1902 African doctors were refused admission on equal terms to the newly formed West African Medical Service. Much the same happened in religious institutions, where several frustrated African clergymen in both West and South Africa broke away from mission control during the 1880s and 1890s to form independent churches.[62]

As uncritical Westernisation came to seem a cul-de-sac, educated West Africans searched their indigenous cultures and values for elements to strengthen their claims to respect in African, if not European, eyes. Even the most acculturated Creoles already venerated their ancestors at anniversary ceremonies and life-cycle rituals. Now African names, dress, and dance became respectable. A Dress Reform Society opened in Freetown in 1887; nine years later a daring Lagos lawyer even sponsored an Egungun masquerade representing ancestral spirits.[63] The South African elite, more dominated by white culture, was less adventurous, but there too a concert programme of the 1890s might include a 'Matabili War Song' or a 'Bushman Chorus'.[64] With these cultural adaptations went concessions to earlier notions of honour. One was a growing pride of race, in reaction to the European racialism that cast doubt on the ideal of respectability. Another was anxiety to preserve inherited gender relationships, notions of masculinity, kinship systems such as matriliny, and extended family ties, all of which are considered in the next chapter. Respectable people rejoiced also in display, seen above all in their new death rituals but encouraged also by their hunger for academic qualifications and professional status, educational success being distinctively a personal achievement that fostered ostentatious elitism.[65] In all these ways, respectability absorbed elements, but only some elements, of older notions of honour.

---

[61] Bundy, *Rise and fall*, ch. 4; Martin Lynn, *Commerce and economic change in West Africa* (Cambridge, 1997), pp. 154–6, 170; Mann, *Marrying well*, p. 25.

[62] Fyfe, *History*, p. 615; Ralph Schram, *A history of the Nigerian health services* (Ibadan, 1971), p. 130; Hastings, *Church*, pp. 493–9.

[63] Spitzer, *Creoles*, pp. 27, 36; E. A. Ayandele, *The missionary impact on modern Nigeria 1842–1914* (London, 1966), ch. 8; Mac Dixon-Fyle, *A Saro community in the Niger Delta, 1912–1984* (Rochester, N.Y., 1999), pp. 34–7; Patrick Cole, *Modern and traditional elites in the politics of Lagos* (Cambridge, 1975), p. 83.

[64] Coplan, *In township tonight*, p. 41.

[65] Zachernuk, *Colonial subjects*, pp. 66–7; this volume, pp. 251–2, 254–5; Rémy Bazenguissa-Ganga, *Les voies du politique au Congo: essai de sociologie historique* (Paris, 1997), p. 26.

15   Honour and Gender

Earlier chapters have argued that although virginity before marriage and chastity within it were important, especially in eastern and southern Africa, female honour in sub-Saharan Africa before colonial rule was not so obsessively focussed on these as is commonly said to have been the case in Mediterranean societies. Women had to reckon with the male dominance expressed in polygyny, the double standards of sexual behaviour, and the sexual division of labour. Yet in some (but not all) West African societies, women enjoyed unusual freedom in marriage, especially where inheritance was matrilineal or bilateral. In centralised states, elite women could exercise political influence, but elsewhere their public role was generally limited to the religious sphere and purely female institutions. Nineteenth-century Islamic reform secluded elite women in Hausaland, although it also left, in the writings of Nana Asma'u, the first good evidence of what women honoured in themselves and one another. By her account, they set high value on a respectable married life in accordance with the norms of their society. In particular, they valued fertility, modesty, piety, neighbourliness, an active contribution to household economy, and the care of children. Female honour was closer to that of the householder than that of the hero.[1]

This chapter examines what happened to these notions during the twentieth century. Because the notions were so different from the issues of status, purity, and prowess commonly associated with honour, the chapter deals with matters of marital organisation and economic activity not normally discussed in this context. The most drastic change was the loss of vertical honour by women

[1] This volume, p. 47.

who had held high status in African states but were deprived of it during the early colonial period by either the destruction of kingdoms or the colonial rulers' prejudice against female political activity.[2] With that exception, however, the most striking point is that notions of female honour – especially those held by women themselves – proved especially resistant to change, despite the fact that both women themselves and European officials and missionaries desired it. One reason why they achieved little was that they wanted different things. European notions of female honour led them to seek to make African marriage more domesticated and confining. African women, by contrast, saw honour more in terms of providing for their families and consequently sought greater freedom of action and economic opportunity. Both, moreover, faced the second reason why little change occurred: that African men defended their own notions of female honour, centring on fertility and industry under protective male dominance. A century of contention between these three notions brought a bewildering confusion of small-scale changes but no radical alteration of status except for the most highly educated women, who regained something of the position lost by the precolonial elite. Others generally held to notions of the 'proper woman' embodied in respectable marriage as understood by the community, fertility, economic activity, neighbourliness, and child-care.

Although European reformers held African marriage patterns in low esteem, they had little success in changing them. Because they believed that chastity was the core of female honour, Europeans gave it first place in schemes to elevate African womanhood. Yet the importance that African women themselves attached to chastity varied greatly.[3] In the forest regions of West Africa, they often enjoyed unusual freedom, viewing marriage – as did the Asante – as a flexible process for the procreation of children with a man's care and financial support, but without otherwise merging individual identities. Many Asante thought it foolish to marry without first living experimentally with the intended partner. Such views probably became more common in non-Islamic areas of West Africa during the twentieth century. By contrast, in eastern and southern Africa, where women were exchanged in marriage for bridewealth in cattle, virginity and especially the avoidance of premarital pregnancy had often been vital to a bride's honour and remained so in many areas even in the 1990s. 'I had

---

[2] For example, Beverly Mack, 'Royal wives in Kano,' in Catherine Coles and Beverly Mack (eds.), *Hausa women in the twentieth century* (Madison, 1991), p. 114; Allman and Tashjian, *'I will not eat stone'*, p. 18.

[3] Caldwell, Caldwell, and Orubuloye, 'Family,' pp. 385–410.

hopes for a happy life,' a young South African nurse wrote, probably in 1951. '...I wish now I had not known a man....My father [a Methodist teacher] would have nothing to do with me. He wept very bitterly. I do not know how I am going to pay for those tears.' Twenty years later a researcher in Durban was surprised at the number of young African women who killed themselves on account of premarital pregnancy, although other observers found that parents were more tolerant in practice than in theory.[4] European concern with this issue in southern Africa focused on 'illegitimacy'. During the 1930s, about half the registered African births in South African towns took place outside legal marriage. The proportion in the rural reserves in 1980 was 43 per cent. In Botswana, of women with children in 1971, 66 per cent of those between the ages of 15 and 19 and 49 per cent of those between the ages of 20 and 24 had never married. Although European observers often blamed this on immorality, the main reasons were poverty, labour migration, the complexity of marriage laws and customary practices, and the fact that women were marrying later for economic and educational reasons. In the rural Keiskamahoek area of the Eastern Cape, for example, women's average age at first marriage rose between 1890 and the 1940s from 19.3 to 23.6 years. Young women were being condemned for fertility which in the past would have won honour.[5]

Whereas Europeans emphasised illegitimacy, Africans were more alarmed by infertility. Childbearing had always been the main source of a woman's respect. Infertility almost certainly increased during the early colonial period, especially in Equatorial Africa as a result of epidemic gonorrhoea. Of women in Gabon studied in the 1960s, 20 per cent of those born before 1890 and 36 per cent of those born between 1915 and 1919 had never borne a living child. Barren women in the equatorial region were commonly blamed – and blamed themselves – for their condition. They could expect contempt, divorce, and perhaps abandonment as families with children withdrew from villages dominated by childless women. A study in Uganda as late as the early 1970s found that 'strong negative attitudes toward female infertility' were the main surviving

---

[4] Allman and Tashjian, 'I will not eat stone', pp. 50–60; Renne, 'Changes,' esp. p. 123; Bernard Taverne, 'Valeurs morales et messages de prévention: la "fidélité" contre le sida au Burkina Faso,' in Charles Becker, Jean-Pierre Dozon, Christine Obbo, and Moriba Toure (eds.), *Vivre et penser le sida en Afrique* (Paris, 1999), p. 513; Ranger, *Are we not also men?* p. 61; Fatima Meer, *Race and suicide in South Africa* (London, 1976), p. 148; Cherryl Walker, 'Conceptualising motherhood in twentieth century South Africa,' *JSAS*, 21 (1995), 431.

[5] Iliffe, *Poor*, pp. 133, 270–1; Monica Wilson, Selma Kaplan, Theresa Maki, and Edith M. Walton, *Keiskammahoek rural survey: volume 3: social structure* (Pietermaritzburg, 1952), p. 90; Deborah Potts and Shula Marks, 'Fertility in southern Africa: the quiet revolution,' *JSAS*, 27 (2001), 198.

vestiges of traditional sexual attitudes.[6] By then, however, rising birthrates and falling deathrates had given Africa as a whole the most rapid population growth the world had seen. Child-rearing and food-production became enormous burdens for women in the late twentieth century, although many must have felt them outweighed by the joy and prestige of motherhood. 'It is a woman's major battle,' Nkore women said in the late 1960s; 'if she dies in labour she dies bravely.'[7]

European reformers also targeted polygyny, seeing it as merely an expression of male lust. They recognised, however, that this was an especially delicate question, for although they were not often sensitive to African notions of honour, they made the exception that men, especially Muslim men, might react violently to interference with their women. One of the best-known stories in British Africa told how a warrior chief in Northern Nigeria, the Magajin Keffi, had killed a British resident to avenge an accidental violation of the harem.[8] Most governments therefore attacked polygyny indirectly, often by taxing plural wives, although Buganda's zealous Christian reformers banned new polygynous marriages early in the twentieth century, as did the Belgian government of the Congo in 1951.[9] Some early Protestant missions accepted polygynous members, thinking it wrong to dissolve existing marriages, but most eventually abandoned this position and insisted on monogamy. Much-subordinated Beti women greeted Christian monogamy with delight; the men, with consternation.[10] In most of southern Africa, polygyny virtually disappeared during the twentieth century owing to land scarcity, labour migration, urban living conditions, education, and Christianity. Parallel changes took place more slowly and unevenly in eastern Africa, where in the late twentieth century some 20

---

[6] Rita Headrick, 'Studying the population of French Equatorial Africa,' in Bruce Fetter (ed.), *Demography from scanty evidence* (Boulder, 1990), p. 282; Anne Retel-Laurentin, *Un pays à la dérive: une société en régression démographique: les Nzakara de l'est centrafricain* (Paris, 1979), pp. 81–2, 105–7, 119, 136, 207–13; Mere Nakateregga Kisekka, 'Heterosexual relationships in Uganda,' PhD thesis, University of Missouri, 1973, p. 222.

[7] Iliffe, *Africans*, pp. 243–6; Ann Whitehead, 'Rural women and food production in sub-Saharan Africa,' in Jean Drèze and Amartya Sen (eds.), *The political economy of hunger* (3 vols., Oxford, 1990–1), vol. 1, ch. 11; K. W. Masters, 'Custom, tradition and maternity care in the Ankole District of Uganda,' *Afya*, 3, 10 (October 1969), 4.

[8] Great Britain, *Colonial reports – annual: Northern Nigeria, 1902*, p. 70; 'Account of the war of the Magaji of Keffi and Captain Moloney, Resident Keffi, by Sergeant Major Usuman Umaisha, Chief Warder of Keffi,' 12 September 1937, Usuman Umaisha Papers, RH.

[9] Hunter, *Reaction to conquest*, p. 202; Christine Obbo, *African women: their struggle for economic independence* (London, 1980), pp. 37, 77; Etienne van de Walle, 'Marriage in African censuses and inquiries,' in William Brass and others, *The demography of tropical Africa* (Princeton, 1968), p. 194.

[10] Hastings, *Church*, pp. 319–20; Vincent, *Traditions*, p. 40.

or 30 per cent of married women were normally in polygynous marriages. By contrast, the typical proportion in West Africa then was about 40 per cent.[11] The chief defenders of polygyny in tropical areas were, of course, African men. In the early colonial period, when the abolition of slavery and growth of commercial farming made labour especially valuable, many chiefs and notables maintained or expanded great households,[12] but these later gave way to 'middle-class polygyny', the acquisition of two or three wives by successful farmers, traders, or urban employees. Many Christian men in tropical Africa remained polygynous, although they might describe their plural wives as girlfriends or 'outside wives'.[13] Women often resented polygyny, especially perhaps those with modern education, but not all took that view, for polygynous wives often enjoyed more freedom and less labour.[14] Moreover, many wives of polygynists would otherwise have lacked male support; one study in Senegambia showed that 50 per cent of second wives had been widows and 33 per cent divorcees. Burundi, with high levels of Christian monogamy, had equally large numbers of unmarried women.[15]

Nevertheless, the resilience of polygyny was chiefly the work of senior men. That was equally true of the survival of large patriarchal households, although, as with polygyny in southern Africa, even the most determined patriarch could not resist economic forces forever. In the more remote savanna regions, large, complex households survived colonial rule virtually unchanged. Among the Gbaya on the border between Cameroun and the Central African Republic – the people chiefly responsible for the Kongo-Wara rebellion – the average household in 1968–70 still contained twenty-three people.[16] Moreover, many modern entrepreneurial farmers clustered dependents around them because they needed labour, could provide support, and offered their sons education, bridewealth, and

---

[11]   Colin Murray, *Families divided: the impact of migrant labour in Lesotho* (Cambridge, 1981), p. 127; John C. Caldwell, I. O. Orubuloye, and Pat Caldwell, 'The destabilization of the traditional Yoruba sexual system,' *Population and Development Review*, 17 (1991), 249; idem, 'Family,' p. 386.

[12]   This volume, p. 221. See also Fortes, *Web of kinship*, pp. 83–4; Wilson, *For men*, p. 117.

[13]   Vernon R. Dorjahn, 'Fertility, polygyny and their interrelations in Temne society,' *American Anthropologist*, 60 (1958), 844–5; Gilles Sautter, *De l'Atlantique au fleuve Congo: une géographie du sous-peuplement* (2 vols., Paris, 1966), vol. 2, p. 954; Kisekka, 'Heterosexual relationships,' p. 73.

[14]   J. D. Y. Peel, *Aladura: a religious movement among the Yoruba* (London, 1968), p. 183; Obbo, *African women*, p. 39; Bledsoe, *Women*, p. 85.

[15]   David P. Gamble, *The Wolof of Senegambia* (London, 1957), p. 54; Van de Walle in Brass, *Demography*, p. 199.

[16]   Philip Burnham, *Opportunity and constraint in a savanna society* (London, 1980), p. 90. See also Fortes, *Web of kinship*, pp. 64, 72.

inheritance.[17] Alternatively, where land was very scarce, as around Northern Nigerian cities or in South African resettlement sites where 'surplus' Africans were dumped during the 1960 and 1970s, family members clung together in shared poverty.[18] Nevertheless, more clearly than with polygyny, the general trend was for patriarchal households to fragment. Yorubaland's large urban compounds began to break up after 1920 and continued to do so throughout the century.[19] Alongside residential fragmentation went the dissolution of many corporate kinship obligations. In 1895, for example, Buganda's legislators made it 'an offence to arrest or to threaten to arrest sons, women, slaves or peasants for the satisfaction of debts due by their fathers, husbands, masters or anybody else.'[20]

Patriarchs defending their domestic domination found that their most powerful weapon was control of marriage and bridewealth. Europeans commonly despised bridewealth along with polygyny but were even less effective in ending it. Early Protestant missionaries often attempted abolition, as in Yorubaland and in Botswana, where they encouraged Khama to ban it in 1875 with eventual success.[21] The Cape Colony officially ignored the custom until the 1880s, although for a decade before that its courts recognised bridewealth among non-Christians, indicating a growing belief that the custom was best left to die naturally. That became South African policy until the 1920s, by which time the authorities had come to see bridewealth as a buttress to tribal stability.[22] Several Protestant missions similarly reversed their early policies, while some colonial governments came to encourage marriage by bridewealth as preferable to other practices such as brideservice in Northern Rhodesia or exchange marriage in Equatorial Africa. Ironically, therefore, bridewealth became more common during the colonial period. Most South African townsmen

[17] A. K. H. Weinrich, *African farmers in Rhodesia* (London, 1975), p. 88; Mary Tiffen, *The enterprising peasant: economic development in Gombe Emirate* (London, 1976), p. 102.

[18] Polly Hill, *Population, prosperity and poverty: rural Kano, 1900 and 1970* (Cambridge, 1977), pp. 83, 99, 101, 180–8; Iliffe, *Poor*, p. 277.

[19] Peel, *Ijeshas*, p. 141; Peter Marris, *Family and social change in an African city: a study of rehousing in Lagos* (London, 1961), pp. 17–24. See also Beinart, *Political economy*, p. 97.

[20] Kagwa, 'Reign of Mwanga,' p. 183.

[21] Tugwell, 'Regarding burials, heathen and Christian' [September 1898] CMS G3/A2/O/1898/149; 'Minutes of the meetings of the Bechwana District Committee held at Kuruman, October 1875,' CWM 38/1/B; I. Schapera, *Tribal innovators* (London, 1970), p. 138; idem, *Migrant labour and tribal life: a study of conditions in the Bechuanaland Protectorate* (London, 1947), p. 143.

[22] S. M. Seymour, *Bantu law in South Africa* (3rd edn, Cape Town, 1970), p. 2; Peddie civil case 7 of 1870, CA 1/PDE 2/2/1; Cape of Good Hope, *South African Native Affairs Commission 1903–5* (5 vols., Cape Town, 1905), vol. 1, p. 60; Saul Dubow, *Racial segregation and the origins of Apartheid in South Africa, 1919–36* (Basingstoke, 1989), pp. 111–17.

still paid it late in the twentieth century.[23] Nineteenth-century chiefs had justified it in blatantly chauvinistic terms: 'You sell your children the same as you buy this jacket.' Later intellectuals, by contrast, called it 'the Bantu woman's charter of liberty.'[24] Many women wished to preserve the institution because it strengthened their security, although they generally wished to keep bridewealth low lest they should need to repay it in seeking divorce. Change in the means of payment from cattle to cash, on the other hand, might disadvantage brides, robbing them of a share in the property and of kinship ties to provide security.[25]

The main objection to bridewealth came from young men. Kenyan soldiers returning from the Second World War formed a short-lived Anti-Dowry Association to boycott girls whose parents demanded payment. Gakaara wa Wanjau's *Marriage procedures*, published in Kikuyu at that time and turning on conflict over brideprice between the mission-educated young and the prospective bride's father, long remained Kenya's most popular vernacular novel.[26] Some critics denounced the practice as merely a sale, others objected not to the principle but the scale of payment. There is virtually no evidence of bridewealth levels declining during the colonial period as a whole. Some remained low throughout, as in Buganda where young people had long had the decisive voice in choosing marriage partners. Other levels may have kept pace with inflation, as possibly among the Fang of Gabon, or remained stable when expressed in cattle, as in many parts of southern Africa.[27] Generally, however, bridewealth rose in real terms in response to the growing value of female labour and increasing access to cash. The highest absolute levels were among pastoralists, but the steepest increases seem to have been in stateless agricultural areas, perhaps because conjugal labour was so valuable there and no authority existed

---

[23] I. Schapera, *Married life in an African tribe* (London, 1940), pp. 24, 85–6; Richards, *Land*, p. xv; Eric de Dampierre, *Un ancien royaume bandia du Haut-Oubangui* (Paris, 1967), pp. 299–300; S. B. Burman and J. Barry, 'Divorce and deprivation in South Africa,' Carnegie Conference Paper 87 (Cape Town, 1984), p. 20.

[24] Evidence of Chief Gangelizwe, 28 October 1881, in Cape of Good Hope, *Report on Native Laws*, p. 439; Soga, *Ama-Xosa*, p. 275.

[25] Sylvia Leith-Ross, *African women: a study of the Ibo of Nigeria* (London, 1939), p. 202; Barbara M. Cooper, *Marriage in Maradi: gender and culture in a Hausa society in Niger, 1900–1989* (Portsmouth, N.H., 1997), p. 17; Harriet Ngubane, 'The consequences for women of marriage payments in a society with patrilineal descent,' in David Parkin and David Nyamwaya (eds.), *Transformations of African marriage* (Manchester, 1987), p. 173.

[26] John Lonsdale, 'KAU's cultures: imaginations of community and constructions of leadership in Kenya after the Second World War,' *JACS*, 13 (2000), 113–14.

[27] Kisekka, 'Heterosexual relationships,' p. 41; James W. Fernandez, *Bwiti* (Princeton, 1982), p. 136 (questioned in Guyer, *Money matters*, p. 114); Kuper, *Wives for cattle*, p. 167. See also Hutchinson, *Nuer dilemmas*, pp. 81–2.

to impose controls.[28] In 1920 Igbo were already protesting inflated demands of up to £50. By the 1930s figures had topped £100. Then returning soldiers' gratuities launched a runaway inflation so that four-figure levels were quoted in the 1960s.[29] Similar increases occurred among stateless peoples in Kenya, Côte d'Ivoire, and French Equatorial Africa, where the Second World War appears to have detached bridewealth from customary payments and tied it to cash incomes.[30] Attempts by missionaries, native authorities, and territorial governments to limit bridewealth payments were undermined by inflation and evaded by supplementary payments or more extravagant weddings.

Bridewealth was the core of patriarchy. 'A son-in-law is the food of his wife's parents,' said a Tswana proverb.[31] Not only could elders extract the earnings of young labourers, but they could demand payment in cattle or traditional prestige goods that only other elders possessed, while European suppression of violence deprived young men of their most effective countervailing power and alternative means of gaining wives. Among the Mossi of Burkina, forced by remoteness into labour migration, the elders' refusal to monetise either bridewealth or scarce land enabled them to retain control of adult sons late into the twentieth century, breeding great generational tension.[32] Yet young men did break free from their fathers' authority, first as schoolboys, then as migrant labourers, and finally as married householders. In the Ilesha kingdom of Yorubaland only 24 per cent of a small sample of men born in the 1880s married before they were 30, as against 72 per cent of those born in the 1910s. Evidence elsewhere is less specific but generally points in the same direction.[33]

The early colonial period saw intense generational conflict over women, with implications for male virility and the honour of both sexes. Elopement

[28] B. W. Andrzejewski and I. M. Lewis, *Somali poetry: an introduction* (Oxford, 1964), p. 23; P. H. Gulliver, *The family herds* (London, 1955), p. 197; Pierre-Philippe Rey, *Colonialisme, néo-colonialisme et transition au capitalisme: exemple de la 'Comilog' au Congo-Brazzaville* (Paris, 1971), p. 65 n29.

[29] G. T. Basden, *Among the Ibos of Nigeria* (reprinted, London, 1966), pp. 70, 101; idem, *Niger Ibos*, p. 216; Emmanuel Obiechina, *An African popular literature: a study of Onitsha market pamphlets* (Cambridge, 1973), p. 52.

[30] Gavin Kitching, *Class and economic change in Kenya: the making of an African petite bourgeoisie 1905–1970* (New Haven, 1980), pp. 206–7, 224–33; A. J. F. Köbben, 'Le planteur noir,' *Etudes Eburnéennes*, 5 (1956), ch. 6; Jane I. Guyer, 'The value of Beti bridewealth,' in her *Money matters*, ch. 5.

[31] Schapera, *Married life*, p. 65.

[32] Claude Meillassoux, *Anthropologie économique des Gouro de Côte d'Ivoire* (3rd edn, Paris, 1974), pp. 214–24; Wilson, *For men*, p. 27; Ancey and others, *Essais*, pp. 1–13.

[33] Peel, *Ijeshas*, p. 119; Henri A. Junod, *The life of a South African tribe* (2nd edn, 2 vols., reprinted, New York, 1962), vol. 1, p. 99; Emmanuel Terray, *L'organisation sociale des Dida de Côte d'Ivoire* (Abidjan, 1969), p. 326.

had long been a recognised, if inferior, form of marriage in many societies. Now it became increasingly common in some areas as a way of escaping rising bridewealth costs and wedding expenses. In the Burnshill (Keiskamahoek) area, some 15 per cent of marriages took this form in the 1920s, 30 per cent in the 1940s, and 56 per cent between 1950 and 1977.[34] Adultery, too, reached allegedly epidemic proportions in many areas as migrant labourers with money threatened the large polygynous households that powerful men still maintained but could no longer defend by extreme violence. In Southern Rhodesia, for example, chiefs pressed the state to criminalise adultery, as it did in 1916, at the same time as Northern Rhodesia and two years earlier than Buganda.[35] 'Great satisfaction was expressed by the Chiefs and Headmen' in Southern Rhodesia, ' . . . they appear to appreciate more than anything the fact that their women were liable to punishment when proved to be a consenting party, but regretted that corporal punishment could not be inflicted on the guilty woman.' The chiefs were less satisfied, however, that the penalty for an adulterous man was now a fine rather than the damages hitherto demanded by offended husbands but vetoed by European legislators as degrading to marriage.[36]

The dual standard implicit in the chiefs' view of adultery remained strongly entrenched in African sexual attitudes, not only among men: both in Buganda and among the Creoles of Freetown faithful husbands might be derided as lacking sexual vigour, while Ghanaian women were chiefly concerned with how their husbands spent their money rather than their time.[37] What little is known of sexual behaviour suggests a pervasive male egotism, although levels of male aggression varied enormously between individuals, as investigations of sexual networking showed.[38] The most traditional form of untamed masculinity was personified by the Dinka chief Deng Majok (1942–69), who treated his

---

[34] C. W. Manona, 'Marriage, family life, and migrancy in a Ciskei village,' in Philip Mayer (ed.), *Black villagers in an industrial society; anthropological perspectives on labour migration in South Africa* (Cape Town, 1980), p. 190.

[35] Diana Jeater, *Marriage, perversion, and power: the construction of moral discourse in Southern Rhodesia, 1894–1930* (Oxford, 1993), ch. 5; Martin Chanock, 'Making customary laws: men, women, and courts in colonial Northern Rhodesia,' in Hay and Wright, *African women*, p. 62; 'Adultery and Fornication Law,' 17 September 1917, CO 536/86/261.

[36] 'Report of the Native Commissioner, Salisbury for the year ended 31st December 1916,' ZNA N9/1/19/85; Chanock in Hay and Wright, *African women*, p. 64.

[37] Kisekka, 'Heterosexual relations,' p. 50; Barbara Harrell-Bond, 'Some influential attitudes about family limitation and the use of contraceptives among the professional group in Sierra Leone,' in John C. Caldwell (ed.), *Population growth and socioeconomic change in West Africa* (New York, 1975), p. 487; Newell, *Ghanaian popular fiction*, p. 139.

[38] Schapera, *Married life*, ch. 7; Kisekka, 'Heterosexual relations,' pp. 50–1; Helen Pickering, Martin Okongo, Kenneth Bwanika, Betty Nnalusiba, and James Whitworth, 'Sexual mixing patterns in Uganda: small-time urban/rural traders,' *AIDS*, 10 (1996), 535.

two hundred wives like breeding stock, beating and abusing them.[39] Alongside this went the cavalier irresponsibility of young men in areas like Asante for whom marriage was often a regrettable and ephemeral last resort:

You take a girlfriend and get her pregnant – then she will be asked by the parents who is responsible – then you have to answer and perform the customary rites – but if you do not want to marry the girl, you don't send any booze to the parents, but the child is still yours. Alternatively, rather than taking her as a girlfriend first, you can go straight to the parents and ask for her. Not many people do this these days. There are plenty of girls so there is no need to bother yourself with formalities.[40]

Such male chauvinism was especially strong in white-dominated areas of southern and eastern Africa where men compensated for their own humiliations by dominating women. In the Ciskei area of the Eastern Cape after the Second World War, for example, the scarcity of land on which to establish viable households led women to stress motherhood above marriage and caused men to value women less for their fertility than as objects for sexual gratification and even rape – attitudes even more prevalent amidst the violence and poverty of South African townships.[41]

A less violent assertion of male domination was the increasing seclusion of Muslim women among the Hausa people of Nigeria and Niger. By the end of the nineteenth century only women of the political, commercial, and clerical elite in the Sokoto Caliphate were normally secluded. Thereafter it gradually spread among commoners as a triumph of honour over interest, given the enhanced value of female labour following the emancipation of slaves. By the 1980s women in towns and large villages and the wives of teachers and wealthy merchants and farmers in rural areas were likely to be secluded; for peasant women, however, seclusion was minimal, while poor urban women found it difficult if not impossible to maintain, although it did restrain them from undertaking factory work and other formal employment. Secluded women were seldom alone, and many contributed to the household by cooking food for sale by their children, an occupation so fundamental to Hausa women's identity that even the emir of Kano's wives engaged in it. Most women appear to have been glad to escape agricultural drudgery and to have accepted seclusion as necessary to respectability, but it could be severely constraining: Hajiya Husaina, married to a Kano tailor at the age of twelve, had never seen the city's palace

---

[39] Deng, *Deng Majok*, ch. 10.

[40] Quoted by Katherine Abu, 'The separateness of spouses: conjugal resources in an Ashanti town,' in Oppong, *Female and male*, p. 158.

[41] Anne Kelk Mager, *Gender and the making of a South African Bantustan: a social history of the Ciskei, 1945–1959* (Portsmouth, N.H., 1999), chs. 6 and 7; this volume, pp. 304, 364.

or central mosque when interviewed thirty-three years later. At the end of the twentieth century, Hausa feminists attacked seclusion as no longer necessary to its Koranic purpose of protecting chastity, while many women in major cities began to attend adult education classes and other sanctioned public activities, often wearing the all-concealing *chador* popularised by Islamic fundamentalists. Hausaland faced the possibility of replacing seclusion by veiling, thereby, perhaps, adopting more distinctively Mediterranean notions of female honour.[42]

Christianity, too, sought to impose its principles of respectability on African gender relations. Missionaries believed that African women must be relieved of work outside the household in order to perform their proper duties of homemaking and child-care. The missionaries had their first success with the Cape Colony's former slaves, for when emancipated in 1838 slave women generally left the employed workforce, at least in the first generation, to concentrate on building the family life hitherto denied them.[43] Elsewhere, however, although the respectable welcomed aspects of marital domesticity, women were generally unwilling to abandon the active economic role that was part of their notion of female honour. 'What a pleasure it is,' a missionary in Natal rejoiced in 1873, 'to think that men and boys now eagerly do the work that once fell heavily upon the poor women, and that the swift plough has superseded the clumsy hoe!' The women were less sure. When Tswana men took up the plough, their women complained that they would lose control of the household's food.[44] The missionaries, however, pressed forward with domestication. At Basel mission settlements in the Gold Coast, for example,

Contrary to local practice, a husband and wife were expected to live together in a monogamous marriage under one roof in the Christian Quarters. They should be emotionally committed to each other. Husband and wife were supposed to eat together in order to share a prayer before every meal, and to walk next to each other, not behind each other.[45]

There was much resistance to these innovations. Kristin Mann has shown that elite Yoruba men in late nineteenth-century Lagos, pressed by their churches and

---

[42] This volume, p. 47; Coles and Mack, *Hausa women*, pp. 8–9, 47, 93, 119, 168–9, 188, 202; Enid Schildkrout, 'Dependence and autonomy: the economic activities of secluded Hausa women in Kano,' in Oppong, *Female and male*, ch. 7; Cooper, *Marriage*, pp. 138–9; Enid Schildkrout, 'Hajiya Husaina,' in Romero, *Life histories*, pp. 80–1, 87; Novian Whitsitt, 'Islamic-Hausa feminism and Kano market literature: Qur'anic reinterpretation in the novels of Balaraba Yakubu,' *RAL*, 33 (2002), 119–36.

[43] Scully, *Liberating*, pp. 93–7.

[44] T. B. Jenkinson in *Mission Field*, 19 (1874), 98; Jean Comaroff and John L. Comaroff, 'Homemade hegemony: modernity, domesticity, and colonialism in South Africa,' in Karen Tranberg Hansen (ed.), *African encounters with domesticity* (New Brunswick, N.J., 1992), p. 46.

[45] Miescher, 'Becoming a man,' p. 104.

their concern for respectability to contract monogamous marriages under British law, found that monogamy brought them neither the children nor the sexual satisfaction they desired where women customarily practised a two- or three-year postpartum taboo on sexual intercourse. Unable to resort to polygyny, 54 of the 113 men studied took concubines, known as 'outside wives'. Respectable women, although generally more attracted by monogamy, also suffered from its operation under British law in African circumstances. If childless, they might forgive their husbands their outside wives, but those with children were likely to resent their husbands' expenditure on illegitimate unions where a wife could not sue for divorce on grounds of adultery, could not therefore hope for a better marriage, rarely enjoyed the companionship that was supposed to accompany monogamy, and was generally barred by the conventions of respectability from the economic activities (especially trading) by which Yoruba women customarily provided for their children.[46] By the 1950s only 25 per cent of Anglican church members in Buganda had been married in church. Against this, however, must be set genuinely companionate Christian marriages in which both partners were active in creating progressive households, a relationship epitomised by Thompson and Grace Samkange of Southern Rhodesia.[47] With the growth of higher education after the Second World War and the entry of many Africans into managerial and administrative jobs, members of the elite increasingly chose their own marriage partners and aspired to this more companionate relationship, although male authority remained dominant, so that Akan women in such marriages, although pursuing their own careers, nevertheless found themselves more dependent upon their husbands than in more traditional unions. Some ambitious West African women preferred the greater freedom of outside wives or mistresses.[48] The reshaping of Christian respectability to male advantage was perhaps the best illustration of the resilience of inherited gender relations.

While Europeans tried to contain African women within reformed domestic relations, the women themselves sought to expand their opportunities outside the household in order to support their families. Their different approach can be seen in their response to the attempts by early colonial officials to give them greater legal freedom. 'Our courts looked benevolently on every rebellion by the weak against the strong,' a French official in Futa Jalon recalled: 'wives against husband, young against old, sons and daughters against father.' During the 1930s

[46] Mann, *Marrying well*, pp. 55, 62, 77–91, 118.
[47] John V. Taylor, *The growth of the Church in Buganda* (London, 1958), p. 176; Ranger, *Are we not also men?*
[48] Christine Oppong, *Marriage among a matrilineal elite* (Cambridge, 1974), pp. 116–18; Bledsoe, *Women*, pp. 120–1; Vidal, *Sociologie*, p. 151.

Asante women ventured to sue other women for adultery, men for defaming their characters, and husbands for compensation for infidelity.[49] Courts in many parts of the continent were flooded with divorce cases. In the Ekiti region of Yorubaland, these undermined not only parentally arranged marriage but belief in the virtue of premarital virginity. 'To secure a divorce in the native court today,' a judge in the Benin kingdom declared in 1943, 'is almost as simple a matter as buying a railway ticket.'[50] Indignant elders thought that the two were indeed connected: that it was railways (and later motor transport) that enabled women to seek independence. Khama forbade women to travel by train. Apolo Kaggwa blamed 'the emancipation of the women' for the spread of venereal disease. Swazi elders blamed it for a supposed wave of sorcery against husbands.[51] As Teresa Barnes has written: 'The most important interpersonal gender dynamic of the colonial era was the hostility of the African male – and the overall community – toward women who responded (or tried to respond) independently to the new political economy.'[52]

These conflicts arising from female assertion first surfaced in later nineteenth-century Natal, where the authorities, fearing male discontent and a breakdown of authority, responded by codifying customary law in a form favouring senior men, placing all women under male guardianship and empowering homestead heads to flog them. As male protests mounted in tropical Africa between the wars, officials similarly established 'patriarchal coalitions' with African elders who provided them with versions of unwritten customary law that entrenched the authority of senior men. In Northern Rhodesia, for example, the African courts established during the late 1930s discouraged divorce and insisted on parental permission and high bridewealth payments in towns to which women had hitherto flocked in pursuit of independence.[53] Such anxiety to prevent

---

[49] Gilbert Vieillard, 'Notes sur les Peuls du Fouta-Djallon,' *BIFAN*, 2 (1940), 125; Akyeampong, *Drink*, pp. 65–6; Allman and Tashjian, *'I will not eat stone'*, pp. 175–7.

[50] Quoted in Philip Aigbona Igbafe, *Benin under British administration* (London, 1979), p. 241; Renne, 'Changes,' pp. 122–3; Jane L. Parpart, 'Sexuality and power on the Zambian Copperbelt: 1926–1964,' in Sharon B. Stichter and Jane L. Parpart (eds.), *Patriarchy and class: African women in the home and the workforce* (Boulder, 1988), p. 117; Hutchinson, *Nuer dilemmas*, pp. 223–4.

[51] Southern Rhodesia, *Report of the Chief Native Commissioner for the year 1932*, p. 2; Bessie Head, *Serowe, village of the rainwind* (London, 1981), p. 176; 'Col. F. J. Lambkin's mission to the Uganda Protectorate on the prevalence of venereal diseases: summary of evidence' [1907] CO 536/15/268; Evidence of Mnkonkoni, 1898, in Webb and Wright, *James Stuart Archive*, vol. 3, pp. 287–8.

[52] Teresa A. Barnes, *'We women worked so hard': gender, urbanization, and social reproduction in colonial Harare, Zimbabwe, 1930–1956* (Portsmouth, N.H., 1999), p. 97.

[53] John Lambert, *Betrayed trust: Africans and the state in colonial Natal* (Scottsville, 1995), pp. 135–6; Parpart in Stichter and Parpart, *Patriarchy*, pp. 115, 121.

women leaving their homes for towns – and supposedly for prostitution – was a central element in the moral panic of the mid-colonial period and an issue on which gendered notions of honour clashed fundamentally. Women seeking to provide for households were eager to market produce, earn wages, or sell beer and other domestic comforts to miners or industrial workers. Men, by contrast, saw female urbanisation as a threat to their *ekitiibwa*: 'Many of our old and young women are living on mines and Town locations as prostitutes.... They have brought disgrace to our nation. The white people are despising us.'[54] Extraordinary measures were taken in eastern and southern Africa to assuage masculine pride. Ovambo women in northern Namibia were legally forbidden to leave their region. Chiefs posted guards on the roads to prevent women from trading in Nairobi. Buganda's Lukiiko (state council) decreed in 1901 that 'every married woman will visit only the home indicated by her husband.' The Luo Union deported 'prostitutes' from Kampala 'wearing a jute sack with holes in the lower sections of the back and front.' In Southern Rhodesia a campaign culminated in 1936 in the introduction of passes for women going to towns.[55]

Passes introduced further gendered questions of honour. The first South African territory to require African townswomen to carry them was the Orange Free State. Men there complained that 'native women ... under pretext of this requirement are examined (sometimes indecently) by the police in the streets.' Women complained of rape and the impact of arrest upon their children. In 1913 respectable women in several Free State towns mounted South Africa's first anti-pass protest, for which over two hundred were imprisoned. The passes were abolished in 1923, but during following years there were repeated attempts to subject black South African townswomen to curfew, much to the offence of male dignity.[56] 'Rightly or wrongly,' an African newspaper proclaimed in 1931, 'we consider this action of the Government as a challenge to our manhood.... As men we can submit to injustice as long as we must; but we cannot tolerate the subjection of our womenfolk to the indignities and

---

[54] Amandebele Patriotic Society, 15 December 1915, quoted in West, 'African middle-class formation,' p. 467.

[55] Meredith McKittrick, 'The "burden" of young men: property and generational conflict in Namibia,' *African Economic History*, 24 (1996), 125; *Muigwithania*, November 1928; Nakanyike B. Musisi, 'Morality as identity: the missionary moral agenda in Buganda, 1877–1945,' *Journal of Religious History*, 23 (1999), 61; Obbo, *African women*, p. 110; Jeater, *Marriage*, p. 259 (although Barnes, *'We women'*, p. 72, says this was seldom enforced).

[56] Petition from the Orange River Colony Native Congress, June 1906, in Karis and others, *From protest*, vol. 1, p. 49; Cherryl Walker, *Women and resistance in South Africa* (London, 1982), p. 28; Julia Wells, 'Passes and bypasses: freedom of movement for African women under the Urban Areas Act of South Africa,' in Hay and Wright, *African women*, pp. 130–2, 138.

barbarities of the pass laws.'[57] The authorities again backed off. They renewed the attack in 1952, when legislation required African women to carry reference books. Both women and men resisted this throughout the 1950s. Women complained that under influx control regulations they might have to enter marriage or permanent employment in order to reside in town, which might separate them from their rural homes and children. Men saw rather an issue of male honour. 'The government cannot give your women pass if you do not want to,' a speaker told an anti-pass meeting, 'because the woman she is under the control of a man.'[58] The resistance was finally defeated in 1963.

Women's attempts to provide for their families by their labour were severely threatened by economic changes of the early colonial period that imposed new burdens on that labour, notably the abolition of slavery, the absence of husbands as migrant labourers and of children as pupils, the cultivation of cash crops like cocoa, coffee, and cotton on which women often did much of the work while men took the profits, and even the introduction of ploughs, which reduced the burden of breaking land but increased the effort of weeding and harvesting larger areas. Most Gold Coast cocoa farms, for example, were owned by men who relied heavily on their wives' labour, to which, in the Akan matrilineal system, men had previously made less claim. Moreover, neither wives nor their children could inherit the cocoa farms on which they worked. Women responded between the wars by establishing their own cocoa farms, pressing their husbands to transfer farms to them during their lifetime, and divorcing husbands once the essential rearing of children was ended.[59] The even more independent Baoule women of Côte d'Ivoire, whose labour was demanded for their husbands' cocoa farms at the same time as their own weaving industry was undermined by imported cloth, responded in many cases by quitting the countryside entirely to live as urban 'free women'.[60] These women could at least own land; that this was barred to women in most patrilineal areas was a major reason for subordination and dependence. Where land was especially scarce, as in the Kikuyu area of Kenya or the South African reserves, the tendency in the twentieth century was for women to lose even the limited rights they possessed.[61]

[57] ANC statement in *Umteteli*, 27 June 1931, reprinted in Karis and others, *From protest*, vol. 1, p. 311.

[58] Walker, *Women and resistance*, chs. 10, 15–18, 22 (quotation on p. 196).

[59] Allman and Tashjian, *'I will not eat stone'*, esp. ch. 4.

[60] Mona Etienne, 'Gender relations and conjugality among the Baule,' in Oppong, *Female and male*, ch. 22.

[61] H. W. O. Okoth-Ogendo, 'African land tenure reform,' in Judith Heyer, J. K. Maitha, and W. M. Senga (eds.), *Agricultural development in Kenya* (Nairobi, 1976), p. 177; Wilson and others, *Keiskammahoek survey*, vol. 3, pp. 107–8.

Male labour migration from the countryside presented women with further dilemmas, delaying marriages, encouraging 'illegitimacy', increasing their burden of labour, and possibly leaving them destitute if ill-paid migrants withheld remittances or never returned. During the later twentieth century, roughly half the rural households in South African reserves and about one-third in Botswana and Lesotho were headed by women. These households were not homogeneous, but a disproportionate number were poor. Migration also disrupted families, alienating fathers from children they seldom saw and creating tensions between spouses over the upbringing of children and the operation of homesteads. Men often responded with a domineering machismo. Yet women adapted to this situation. In the absence of husbands, many took their children to live with their parents, who often cared for the children while the mother worked. During the 1970s half of Lesotho's households contained three generations, normally with a woman as the middle generation.[62]

Moreover, women, too, could migrate to towns, despite the obstacles often placed in their way. In the early colonial period, relatively small numbers moved permanently to towns to exploit income-earning opportunities. Others went less permanently to join migrant husbands.[63] From the 1940s the trickle became a flood, first in South Africa, owing to the impoverishment of the rural reserves, and then in tropical Africa, as wealth and opportunity increasingly concentrated in cities. The position of women in new colonial towns was especially difficult. The mining industries of the Belgian Congo, Northern Rhodesia, and South Africa, for example, wanted only male workers; if they allowed women to join these workers, it was only as dependents. In 1954 only 8 per cent of women on the Northern Rhodesian Copperbelt lived alone; many of the others were 'town wives' in what Copperbelt men called piece-work marriages. Moreover, because men held virtually all jobs in the mining industry and enjoyed almost all income, women could contribute to their households or enjoy some economic independence only through informal activities like petty trade, brewing, or prostitution which fostered the stereotype of urban women as corrupt and vicious. The alternative was complete financial dependence on men, who in turn saw women as grasping, demanded a degree of freedom for themselves and subservience for their wives which women resented, and often – in the absence

---

[62] Iliffe, *Poor*, pp. 220–1; Pamela F. Reynolds, 'Men without children,' Carnegie Conference Paper 5 (Cape Town, 1984), pp. 12–28.

[63] Phillip Bonner, 'African urbanization on the Rand between the 1930s and 1960s,' *JSAS*, 21 (1995), 115–18; Emmanuel Akyeampong, 'Urbanization, individualism and gender relations in colonial Ghana,' in Anderson and Rathbone, *Africa's urban past*, p. 230; James Ferguson, 'Mobile workers, modernist narratives: a critique of the historiography of transition on the Zambian Copperbelt,' *JSAS*, 16 (1990), 385–412.

of restraining kin groups – tried to enforce control by the domestic violence for which these towns were notorious. Copperbelt women of the 1950s *expected* to be beaten by their husbands. Matrimonial cases choked the courts and sexual antagonism in mining towns was marked by 'ubiquity and terrible intensity.'[64]

In many other towns the problem was not male dominance of earnings but general poverty, which prevented men from supporting families. The priority that women gave to that task in their scheme of honour often led them to respond more effectively, sacrificing themselves to create and support independent households. In Soweto, for example, some 14 per cent of households were female-headed in 1960, while females headed 22 per cent of all households in 1970. In the early 1990s, in a small South African town like Bathurst in the Eastern Cape, two-thirds of adult women were single, often distrusting all men, establishing strong all-female networks, and concentrating on educating their daughters, whereas earlier generations of African women had educated their sons.[65] Similar social patterns existed in some of the poorest informal settlements in tropical cities, such as Mathare Valley in Nairobi.[66]

The possibility of owning property denied them in the countryside was one attraction drawing women to towns and keeping them there. By the mid 1920s half of Nairobi's African property-owners were women, often elderly people who had made careers in the urban informal sector, usually as traders, sex-workers, or brewers.[67] Their dependence on informal activities resulted from the scarcity of formal jobs for women in early colonial economies. Many agricultural workers were women – about one-third of South Africa's farm labour force in the 1970s – but in towns, as will be seen, even domestic service was predominantly a male occupation or left to much-exploited adolescent girls, except in South Africa where men could find better-paying jobs.[68] Factory work was

---

[64] Parpart in Stichter and Parpart, *Patriarchy*, pp. 123–34; Godfrey Wilson, *An essay of the economics of detribalization in Northern Rhodesia* (2 parts, Livingstone, 1941–2), part 2, p. 72; James Ferguson, *Expectations of modernity: myths and meanings of urban life on the Zambian Copperbelt* (Berkeley, 1999), ch. 5; Jeater, *Marriage*, p. 182; A. L. Epstein, *Urbanization and kinship: the domestic domain on the Copperbelt of Zambia, 1950–1956* (London, 1981), pp. 35, 58–9, 112, 119–21 (quotation on p. 119).

[65] Eleanor Preston-Whyte, 'Families without marriage: a Zulu case study,' in John Argyle and Eleanor Preston-Whyte (eds.), *Social system and tradition in southern Africa* (Cape Town, 1978), p. 56; Sean Jonathan Wilshire Jones, 'The matrifilial family: single motherhood, domestic organisation and kinship among Xhosa in a country township, South Africa,' PhD thesis, University of Cambridge, 1996, pp. 53, 67–8.

[66] Nici Nelson, 'Female-centred families: changing patterns of marriage and family among *buzaa* brewers of Mathare Valley,' *African Urban Studies*, NS, 3 (Winter 1978–9), 85–103.

[67] Luise White, *Speaking with vampires: rumour and history in colonial Africa* (Berkeley, 2000), p. 153.

[68] J. B. Knight, 'Is South Africa running out of unskilled labour?' in Francis Wilson, Alide Kooy, and Delia Hendrie (eds.), *Farm labour in South Africa* (Cape Town, 1977), p. 47; Deborah

long considered unsuitable for African women; the suggestion that Uganda's cigarette factory should employ them was denounced by men as an attempt to create prostitution and reduce the birthrate. Women factory workers became numerous in South Africa only from the 1960s and were still rare in much of tropical Africa at the end of the twentieth century. By then, however, women's informal earnings were shifting the gender balance in their favour, and increasing numbers of women were also securing formal urban jobs – in Dar es Salaam their share rose between 1961 and 1980 from 4 to 20 per cent – mainly owing to the expansion of female education following political independence.[69]

Education was crucial to the changing status and self-image of women. In 1965 only about 30 per cent of primary-age girls in sub-Saharan Africa were at school in contrast to 52 per cent of boys; the proportions for secondary-age children were 2 per cent for girls and 6 per cent for boys. By 1993 the figures for girls had risen to 65 per cent at primary age and 22 per cent at secondary age.[70] The early schooling for girls, especially by missionaries, was intended to be domesticating, 'to produce Christian womanhood, to make our girls good wives and mothers.' Yet students seldom used their education as their teachers intended. Many independent Yoruba women of Lagos who studied needlework and domestic science used them to set up as dressmakers, bakers, caterers, and restaurant-owners.[71] Others went on to become the women schoolteachers, nurses, and eventually lawyers, doctors, and other professionals who gained a new kind of equality, respect, and freedom for African women. Schoolmistresses often enjoyed special respect within their communities.[72] Nurses began as menials but first received professional training at Lovedale in 1903; by 1990 South Africa had some 100,000 black nurses, outnumbering the entire black male elite.[73] It was mainly through these professions – these

Gaitskell, Judy Kimble, Moira Maconachie, and Elaine Unterhalter, 'Class, race and gender: domestic workers in South Africa,' *Review of African Political Economy*, 27 (1984), 86–108; this volume, p. 287.

[69] Uganda African affairs fortnightly review, 23 February and 27 July 1950, CO 537/5868/5 and 16; Iris Berger, *Threads of solidarity: women in South African industry, 1900–1980* (Bloomington, 1992), pp. 250–3; Aili Mari Tripp, *Changing the rules: the politics of liberalization and the urban informal economy in Tanzania* (Berkeley, 1997), p. 119; International Labour Office, *Basic needs in danger: a basic needs oriented development strategy for Tanzania* (Addis Ababa, 1982), p. xxxii.

[70] World Bank, *World development reports*, 1990, p. 235, and 1997, p. 227.

[71] The aim of the Hope Fountain Girls' Boarding School, Southern Rhodesia (founded 1915) in West, 'African middle-class formation,' p. 91; LaRay Denzer, 'Domestic science training in colonial Yorubaland,' in Hansen, *African encouters*, p. 135.

[72] Augustine S. O. Okwu, 'The mission of the Irish Holy Ghost Fathers among the Igbo of south-eastern Nigeria, 1905–1956,' PhD thesis, Columbia University, 1977, pp. 410–11.

[73] Shula Marks, *Divided sisterhood: race, class and gender in the South African nursing profession* (Basingstoke, 1994), pp. 2, 10.

modern codes of honour – that African women regained a place in the public sphere. And it was such professional women who enjoyed the highest female status in independent states.

Most ordinary women, however, preserved notions of honour more modest than those of the professionals and more conventional than those of Baoule 'free women'. They had no single ideal, but one that probably expressed many attitudes was the notion current in Kampala during the 1990s of a 'proper woman' (*omukyala omutufu*). Because single women there were still despised as likely prostitutes, a stable relationship recognised by neighbours as marriage was essential for a proper woman. So were neighbourliness, modesty, good conduct, and self-respect. A proper woman had an income-earning activity (but not brewing or prostitution) by which she both maintained a degree of economic independence and helped to provide for her family, for her final and defining characteristic was to bear and support children. '*Omukyala omutufu*,' one explained, 'is that one who is married, has children and looks after them very well. She looks after her home, welcomes visitors, and is well mannered.'[74] As a notion of female honour it was less spectacular than the chastity obsessing Mediterranean men. But it provided the underlying continuity of modern African social history.

[74] Jessica A. Ogden, '"Producing" respect: the "proper woman" in postcolonial Kampala,' in Richard Werbner and Terence Ranger (eds.), *Postcolonial identities in Africa* (London, 1996), ch. 6. See also Jessica Ann Ogden, 'Reproductive identity and the proper woman: the response of urban women to AIDS in Uganda,' PhD thesis, University of Hull, 1995 (quotation on p. 201).

16   Urbanisation and Masculinity

When defeat and colonial rule fragmented African notions of honour, elements were absorbed not only into the ethics of colonial armies and respectable Christians but also into a working-class ethic designed to ensure survival and dignity in towns and workplaces. That towns threatened honour was a cliché of twentieth-century African thought and literature. The aristocrat ruined by outmoded pride, the young countryman threatened in his manhood, and the woman dragged down into urban vice peopled a hundred novels. This chapter investigates these dilemmas. It examines also how the perspectives of honour cultures continued to shape African views of wage labour, how feminine principles of endurance and family care underwrote urban survival, how heroic notions of masculinity were transferred from the battlefield to the mine, and how rural youth cultures were transformed into the assertive machismo of urban gangs whose behaviour – honourable to themselves, dishonourable to others – illustrates most clearly that honour remained a contested category.

Men of rank struggled to maintain dignity amid urban growth and change. Dahomey's royal palace fell into ruin, but its counterpart in Kano still housed over a thousand people in the late twentieth century,[1] and Hausa emirs, like Yoruba, Ganda, and Asante kings, still enjoyed great respect within their capitals. Should they visit a new colonial city elsewhere, however, they might receive little reverence, as the Zulu king found when 'joyously howled down by an irresponsible group of young hoodlums' in Johannesburg.[2] Notables trod cautiously

---

[1] Heidi J. Nast, 'The impact of British imperialism on the landscape of female slavery in the Kano palace, Northern Nigeria,' *Africa*, 64 (1994), 36.

[2] Ray E. Phillips, *The Bantu in the city* (Lovedale, n.d.), p. 50.

in such shameless agglomerations. Mombasa's *waungwana* (free gentlemen) carefully distinguished themselves from those with slave or pagan ancestry and cultivated honour (*fakhri*) through 'notable accomplishments in religion, education, politics, or the professions,' 'personal character and demeanour,' and wealth if properly acquired. Futa Toro's sensitive but impoverished noblemen might accept such degrading work as domestic service, factory labour, or even road-sweeping, but only at a safe distance in Dakar and only for alien employers. Former *sebbe* warriors sought honourable posts as estate-guards or motor-drivers.[3] The surviving power of heroic tradition was captured in Ousmane Soce Diop's novel *Karim* (1935), whose protagonist, a clerk from Saint-Louis, wooed the beautiful Marième by posing as a dashing *samba-linguère*, ruined himself by paying griots to sing of Sunjata, courage, and love, matched himself unsuccessfully against a richer rival in a formal contest of generosity, instantly resigned his job when affronted by his European employer, and ended with his honour but not his illusions intact.[4]

For others, by contrast, towns were opportunities to seek honour hitherto denied them. Many townspeople were freed or fugitive slaves. Some, like the 'Bella' from the Sahara and Sahel who did much heavy labour in West African towns, remained stigmatised, but others, like the 'Manyema' from the eastern Congo who formed the core population of central Tanzanian towns, asserted their *ustaarabu*, their urban and Islamic civilisation.[5] The stigma attached to occupational groups in West Africa sometimes survived in private and marital relationships, but by the 1960s it was losing salience in public life and had not prevented stigmatised individuals from succeeding in business and Islamic leadership.[6] Griots, threatened when their aristocratic patrons lost status, either moved into other occupations or found new urban patrons among politicians, businessmen, wrestlers, or anyone like Karim moved by vanity or fearful of abuse, while some won wealth and fame through the media.[7] Southern African

---

[3] Swartz, *The way*, pp. 158–9; Wane, *Les Toucouleurs*, pp. 37–8, 41.

[4] Ousmane Soce [Diop], *Karim: roman sénégalais* (3rd edn., Paris, 1948). For an interesting, nonfictional parallel, see Alioune Diop, 'History of a black schoolboy (by himself),' *RAL*, 28 (1997), 215–19.

[5] Klein, *Slavery and colonial rule*, p. 251; Suzanne Bernus, *Particularismes ethniques en milieu urbain: l'exemple de Niamey* (Paris, 1969), pp. 139, 177; J. A. K. Leslie, *A survey of Dar es Salaam* (London, 1963), p. 49.

[6] Tamari, *Les castes*, pp. 70–2; Wane, *Les Toucouleurs*, pp. 80–1; Ousmane Silla, 'Persistance des castes dans la société wolof contemporaine,' *BIFAN*, 28B (1966), esp. pp. 736, 745; Johnson, *Emergence*, p. 15.

[7] Cornelia Panzacchi, 'The livelihoods of traditional griots in modern Senegal,' *Africa*, 64 (1994), 190–210; Thomas A. Hale, *Griots and griottes* (Bloomington, 1998), ch. 6 and pp. 184–7, 221–42.

praise-singers similarly adapted their skills to written media and political or trade union functions.[8]

Among the most prominent new townsmen were entrepreneurs. In Yorubaland it was mainly successful businessmen who challenged traditional urban authorities during the early twentieth century. Many Hausa merchants, similarly, prospered during the colonial period, although success required a modest personal lifestyle, a deferential relationship with Fula aristocrats, and significant social investment. Until the last decades of the century, studies of urban public opinion showed that inequality was frankly accepted, patrons were eagerly sought, and wealth was not resented provided it was distributed generously for the public good.[9] The Pilgrimage, in particular, provided many opportunities to convert wealth into honour, especially when air transport became available during the 1950s. To undertake it at one's own expense – the ideal procedure – was proof of commercial respectability and almost a *rite de passage* into local leadership throughout Islamic West Africa. To finance others – as Hausaland's wealthiest merchant, Alhassan Dantata, did on a lavish scale – was the ultimate in benevolence. During 1977 Nigeria sent a peak of 106,000 pilgrims to Mecca. By the 1990s the distinction was so widespread that some demonstrated piety rather through zealous fundamentalism.[10]

The Pilgrimage conferred the respectability much coveted in crowded, impoverished, underserviced, and unpoliced townships. Respectability separated the Ooscuse-me from the Oomac, as the strata were known in Cape Town, but it was not confined to an elite and was widely sought by urban workers.[11] Although family life adapted to urban conditions rather than disintegrated, many Africans, like the newly urbanised elsewhere, saw towns as degenerate. The most sweeping denunciation was the mine clerk Rolfes Dhlomo's novel *An African tragedy* (1928?), in which Robert Zulu left his village for Johannesburg

[8] J. Opland, 'Nontsizi Mgqwetho: stranger in town,' in Graham Furniss and Liz Gunner (eds.), *Power, marginality and African oral literature* (Cambridge, 1995), ch. 13; Alfred Temba Qabula, Mi S'Dumo Hlatshwayo, and Nise Malange, *Black mamba rising: South African worker poets in struggle* (ed. A. Sitas, Durban, 1986).

[9] Peel, *Ijeshas*, p. 130; Whitaker, *Politics of tradition*, pp. 332–5; P. C. Lloyd, *Power and independence: urban Africans' perception of social inequality* (London, 1974), esp. ch. 6.

[10] Christian Coulon, 'Les itinéraires politiques de l'islam au Nord-Nigeria,' in Jean-François Bayart (ed.), *Religion et modernité politique en Afrique noire* (Paris, 1993), p. 44; Tahir, 'Scholars,' p. 386; Toyin Falola, *Violence in Nigeria: the crisis of religious politics and secular ideologies* (Rochester, N.Y., 1998), p. 173; Cooper, *Marriage*, p. 132.

[11] Monica Wilson and Archie Mafeje, *Langa* (Cape Town, 1963), ch. 7; David Goodhew, 'Working-class respectability: the example of the Western Areas of Johannesburg, 1930–55,' *JAH*, 41 (2000), 241–66.

to earn the 'silly huge sum of money' needed for bridewealth. Evil companions led him to the notorious Prospect Township,

a revolting immoral place; where the black sons and daughters of Africa are kicked about by their unbridled passions as a football is on the playfields.... The room in which they found themselves was already half full with people of both sexes. The air was reeking with the evil smell of drinks and perspirations. As they entered, Robert shivered involuntarily. He had not bargained for such a scene of pleasure.

At one end of the room an organ was being hammered by a drunken youth. Couples – literally fastened to each other – were swaying giddily wildly, to this barbaric tune. In this mood young girls are deflowered in their youth.

Pressed to drink the notorious *skokiaan*, 'Robert Zulu was now lost.' He became a drunkard, mixed with loose women, frequented dance halls, tangled with the police, witnessed a murder, fled to the countryside, infected his wife with venereal disease, fathered a blind baby, and died of poison.[12] This emphasis on urban dishonour survived throughout Africa to the end of the century.[13] It was challenged most effectively during the 1950s by the South African journalists of *Drum* magazine, for whom 'the sprawling, cacophonous, strutting, brawling, vibrating life' of the townships represented rather a new kind of honour, 'the strength and the will to survive by ordinary masses of the African people.' *Drum*'s blatant sexism and romanticisation of violence and illegality created an image as partial as Dhlomo's, but it captured the thinking of an urban-born generation that emerged in the 1930s and incorporated the adventurous young rural immigrants who thereafter flocked into the cities throughout sub-Saharan Africa. They included Nelson Mandela, who in the 1940s found the African freehold township of Alexandra, bordering Johannesburg, 'exhilarating and precarious . . . a kind of heaven . . . an urban Promised Land.'[14]

Southern Africa's first labour migrants adopted the style and language of heroic warfare. Many were sent by their chiefs in contingents to raid the white economy for guns and cattle and blankets. Tswana, it was reported in 1887, regarded the Kimberley diamond mines as part of their hunting field. By then economic motives were forcing men to seek employment: the need to pay tax or bridewealth, to support a household during scarcity, and eventually to support a household during normal times as population growth on the scarce land of the labour

---

[12] R. R. R. Dhlomo, *An African tragedy* (Lovedale [1928?]), quotations on pp. 5–6, 11.

[13] John Lonsdale, 'Town life in colonial Kenya,' in Andrew Burton (ed.), *The urban experience in eastern Africa, c. 1750–2000* (Nairobi, 2002), pp. 207–22; Stephanie Newell (ed.), *Readings in African popular fiction* (Bloomington, 2002), pp. 6–8.

[14] Lewis Nkosi, 'obituary,' in Can Themba, *The will to die* (Cape Town, 1972), p. viii; Mandela, *Long walk*, p. 71.

reserves made whole societies dependent on urban earnings. Of 297 Tswana workers questioned during the late 1930s, only six gave anything but economic reasons for their migration.[15] As elsewhere in Africa, 'The men who go away are not considered brave but poor.'[16]

Young men prepared well for their adventure. In Lesotho – where men in the 1970s averaged about fifteen years of their lives working in South Africa – it became customary to present initiation candidates with the gumboots and other equipment needed in the mines.[17] Novices generally joined a party led by an experienced worker. As they crossed the River Caledon into South Africa, Sotho sang, 'This side I have to be tough and assume manhood.' Along the well-trodden paths men carved signs into tree-trunks and constructed shelters in the branches for protection at night against lions. Lorries and even aeroplanes eventually became available, although Sotho always pictured themselves travelling by train, 'Owner-of-Gunsmoke Hundred-Footed Trudger.' The return journey might be easier, for the migrant now had money, but also more dangerous; not only might he be sick or injured, but he was burdened with presents, and in the early days there were highwaymen to relieve him of them.[18] Estimates of the proportion of their earnings that migrants took or sent to the countryside varied from 15 to 50 per cent. To 'build the homestead' in this way was a twentieth-century expression of householder honour. To return without gifts was as shameful as to return defeated from the battlefield. 'I resolved to stay abroad until I had at least 500 francs to show my wife,' a Rwandan migrant recalled, only to find, when he returned after nine years, that his wife was dead and his land confiscated. Determination to arrive in triumph was probably an important reason why a proportion – perhaps 5 per cent of Tswana migrants during the 1930s – never returned.[19]

Arrival at the workplace might also be stage-managed. 'About 200 Zulus marched into town from the Natal direction on Wednesday,' a Johannesburg

---

[15] Peter Delius, *The land belongs to us: the Pedi polity, the Boers and the British in the nineteenth-century Transvaal* (London, 1984), ch. 3; Price to Shippard, 28 September 1887, CO 417/16/445; Schapera, *Migrant labour*, p. 121.

[16] Hunter, *Reaction to conquest*, p. 143.

[17] Murray, *Families divided*, p. 41; John and Cassandra Perry in Jingoes, *A chief*, p. 241.

[18] Strange, 'Report of the Assistant Native Commissioner, Rusambo for the year ended 31st December 1926,' ZNA S.235/504; Belinda Bozzoli, 'History, experience and culture,' in her *Town and countryside in the Transvaal: capitalist penetration and popular response* (Johannesburg, 1983), p. 9; Helen Bradford, 'Getting away with murder,' in Philip Bonner, Peter Delius, and Deborah Posel (eds.), *Apartheid's genesis 1935–1962* (Braamfontein, 1993), p. 99; Coplan, *Cannibals*, p. 126; *Diggers' News and Witwatersrand Advertiser*, 3 November, 1888.

[19] Wilson, *Essay*, vol. 1, p. 45; Schapera, *Migrant labour*, p. 211; Codere, *Biography*, p. 220; Schapera, *Married life*, p. 147.

newspaper reported in 1889. Not all arrived so triumphantly. Men reaching Durban in the early twentieth century were dipped in disinfectant before entering the town, while women migrants to Southern Rhodesian towns underwent compulsory examination for venereal disease.[20] Most men, moreover, had no job to go to. The first step was often to locate a kinsman, beg a sleeping-place on his floor, and hope he could find one a job. If not, the immigrant might tramp the streets for months. Competition for work was brutal. 'In the city it is like this: all the time you are fighting.... And you look only after yourself. If you do not you are finished. If you are soft everyone will spit in your face,' the Shebeen Queen (woman bar-owner) told the newly arrived countryman in Peter Abrahams' *Mine boy* (1946).[21] The first jobs generally lasted only a few months and were those nobody wanted. Jason Jingoes, crossing the Caledon for the first time, earned his first pay-packet as a police informer trapping illegal beer-sellers and his second as a domestic servant.[22] Eventually he found what he wanted:

Underground workers are the heroes of the mines.... They despise the surface workers, who usually work on top because they cannot manage heavier duties for reasons of health or because they are lazy. So I did not want to work anywhere but underground, not wanting to be called a weakling. Besides, my uncle Maphuphuta was in that compound, and he would have thrashed me had I taken a surface job.[23]

Such discrimination among jobs ruled throughout the colonial economy. Dockworkers, for example, cultivated a carefree arrogance, for their work was hard, dangerous, well-paid, and sporadic. Not only was it well known 'that a docker never lacks for a girl or a drink,' but dockers refused to handle 'dirty' cargoes like coal or timber, leaving them to women, youths, or casuals.[24] Such manual labour in West African coastal towns was commonly undertaken by the Kru labourers particularly despised by the respectable. South African townsmen took the same view of the *Amaoveralls* living in bachelor hostels. In 1952, 81 per cent of Salisbury's municipal workers came from outside Southern Rhodesia. They doubtless included the sanitary labourers who formed the lowest stratum in

[20] *Diggers' News and Witwatersrand Advertiser*, 28 September 1889; Clements Kadalie, *My life and the ICU* (ed. S. Trapido, London, 1970), p. 96; Lynette A. Jackson, '"When in the white man's town": Zimbabwean women remember *Chibeura*,' in Allman and others, *Women*, ch. 8.

[21] Peter Abrahams, *Mine boy* (reprinted, London, 1989), p. 50.

[22] Sheila T. van der Horst, 'Native urban employment: a study of Johannesburg employment records, 1936–1944,' *South African Journal of Economics*, 16 (1948), 254–5; Jingoes, *A chief*, pp. 56–8.

[23] Jingoes, *A chief*, p. 69.

[24] Leslie, *Survey*, p. 105; Jeanne Marie Penvenne, *African workers and colonial racism* (Portsmouth, N.H., 1995), pp. 79–82.

colonial towns and were usually drawn from latecomers to the labour market. So despised were they in Nigeria that they veiled their faces to avoid recognition.[25]

Given that choice of employment was shaped by notions of honour, and given the centrality of the sexual division of labour to those notions, it is surprising that domestic service – a major sector of employment often considered quintessentially feminine – should have been virtually monopolised by men almost everywhere in tropical Africa.[26] The pattern probably originated in the employment of African men as clients and henchmen by the first generation of mobile European bachelors. Once established, it survived, despite denunciation by African women's leaders, because almost all those involved saw major objections to feminisation: male servants defended an occupation that gave reasonable pay and status; white officials urged African women to concentrate on their families; African women wanted to avoid employment that damaged their family life; white women wanted to keep their husbands away from black women; and African men wanted to control their women and protect them from white men.[27] Considerations of honour weighed on both sides, but domestic service was nevertheless demeaning. It was humiliating to take orders from any woman. 'I lasted a month,' Jason Jingoes recalled, 'because I wanted the money and because when she scolded me I paid no attention whatever to her.' To assert their dignity, servants dressed especially well, associated themselves with the clerks and other new men of the colonial world, or found outlets for their masculinity in violent youth groups.[28]

Nothing, however, could disguise the fact that the urban environment within which heroic culture survived most strongly was the mining industry. 'Manhood is hard,' said a Sotho proverb; 'it is dug out from the rocks.' Underground mining was a terrible job – 'hell mechanized', as a missionary described it – often carried out in a squatting posture, great heat (the legal maximum was 33 degrees centigrade), appalling noise, and, by the 1990s, up to 3.6 kilometres below the surface. Andreas Shipanga found the conditions so terrible that he deserted after a single day. Moreover, the work was immensely dangerous. Between 1905 and 1989, 66,000 miners died in accidents in South African

[25] *Gold Coast Aborigines*, 13 January 1900; *Work in Progress*, August 1993; Southern Rhodesia, *Report of the Secretary of Native Affairs . . . for the year 1952*, p. 8; Andrew G. Onokerhoraye, *Social services in Nigeria* (London, 1984), pp. 282–3.

[26] Many West African families employed young African girls as housemaids. See Mary H. Moran 'Civilized servants: child fosterage and training for status among the Glebo of Liberia,' in Hansen, *African encounters*, ch. 3.

[27] See the essays in Hansen, *African encounters*; Charles van Onselen, *Studies in the social and economic history of the Witwatersrand, 1886–1914* (2 vols., Harlow, 1982), vol. 2, p. 17.

[28] Jingoes, *A chief*, p. 58; Van Onselen, *Studies*, vol. 2, pp. 54–60.

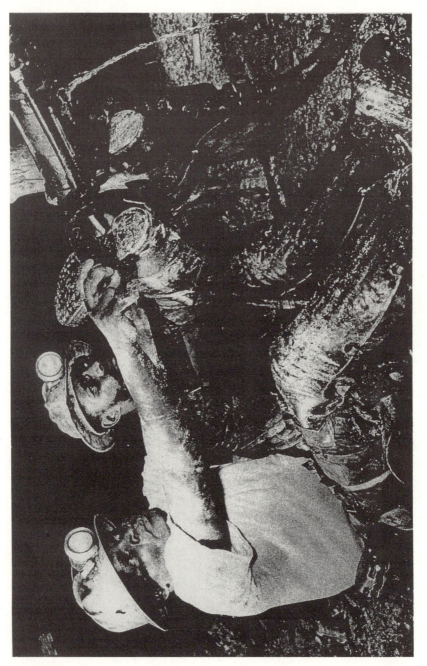

5. *Drilling at the Stope Face.* From Francis Wilson, *Labour in the South African Gold Mines* (Cambridge, 1972), plate 3.

goldmines.[29] 'I witnessed a horrible accident underground in which six people died,' one miner recalled. 'Their limbs were cut off and some were buried alive. I could not eat nor sleep that night. . . . You are never sure if you will make it safely back (to the) surface each day you descend.' 'All the time we are down there we pray silently,' a colleague added. Miners took great care, used much magic, and developed a sixth sense of danger. 'Workers think of seismic movements as an animal or monster that moves from shaft to shaft causing accidents. Tales about the "creature" are common at Western Deep Levels.'[30] They protected themselves by fierce camaraderie, aggressive pride in 'men's work,' and insistence on special pay:

Underground workers . . . assert that they like working underground. 'We get much money there. Only one or two tickets then you already feel that you have something in your pocket. It is dangerous, but we are interested in money.' . . .
    Underground workers emphasize that they are good people who treat everyone equally. . . . More than at any other work-place on the Mine, the stress is on teamwork. . . . Underground workers, particularly those at the workface, see themselves as the epitome of manliness and courage. This camaraderie is so strong that workers who have been promoted or who, because of accidents have been given better paying jobs on the surface, often try to get back to underground work.[31]

The elite among underground miners, in their own eyes, were the shaft-sinkers, an especially skilled and dangerous task that in the gold mines became virtually a Sotho ethnic monopoly. 'Every "shaft" is dug by Basotho,' one veteran claimed in 1983. 'When they have dug it, and it is completely finished, then other kinds of people arrive.' 'We opened the mines' became a claim for Sotho to set against the military reputation of Zulu, who commonly eschewed underground mining.[32]

Mineworkers entered an industrial structure of companies, recruits, squads, and deserters, which was as militarised as their own march to work. Recruits to the gold mines underwent a harsh initiatory training to prepare them for the

[29] Coplan, *Cannibals*, pp. 102, 130; *C.R. – The Chronicle of the Community of the Resurrection*, 103 (1928), 24; Matsheliso Palesa Molapo, 'Job stress, health and perceptions of migrant mineworkers,' in Jonathan Crush and Wilmot James (eds.), *Crossing boundaries: mine migrancy in a democratic South Africa* (Cape Town, 1995), p. 89; Sue Armstrong, *In search of freedom: the Andreas Shipanga story* (Gibraltar, 1989), p. 28; Wilmot G. James, *Our precious metal: African labour in South Africa's gold industry, 1970–1990* (Cape Town, 1992), p. 27.

[30] Molapo in Crush and James, *Crossing boundaries*, pp. 89–90; Dunbar Moodie, 'Mine culture and miners' identity on the South African gold mines,' in Bozzoli, *Town and countryside*, p. 181.

[31] Robert J. Gordon, *Mines, masters and migrants: life in a Namibian mine compound* (Johannesburg, 1977), pp. 162–3.

[32] Jeff Guy and Motlatsi Thabane, 'Technology, ethnicity and ideology: Basotho miners and shaft-sinking on the South African gold mines,' *JSAS*, 14 (1987–8), p. 260; British South Africa Company, *Reports on the administration of Rhodesia, 1897–1898*, p. 216.

brutal underground discipline. They were joshed by older miners and compelled to learn the unwritten laws of the compounds:

When novices arrive at the mine [the Coprock mine in Namibia] one of the first and most vital tasks which they set themselves is to enquire what the *Weta Zomina*, the 'Law' of the Mine, is. This 'Law' . . . provides the migrant with explanatory information as to the behavior of the Whites, how to stay out of trouble with them and with fellow-workers, what 'the money is like,' how to 'make money' in the 'informal sector', and conditions in general.[33]

It was fundamental to southern African mining that any white man could tell any black man to do anything. Africans therefore had to devise means to protect themselves against white caprice. One was to seek a white patron, a response natural to young men from patriarchal societies.[34] 'I have always worked at Mufulira and I have always worked well. I and others are always afraid,' a Copperbelt miner said in 1935, to which his interpreter added: 'I think he means always respectful and loyal.' Until the late twentieth century, miners normally accepted and even welcomed paternalistic management.[35] Another protection against capricious brutality was the patronage of a senior miner, perhaps one of the elected dormitory heads who were the effective workers' leaders. This patronage took extreme form on the Witwatersrand in 'mine marriage', in which the senior man offered favouritism and payment in return for domestic and possibly sexual services, so that both could make some advance towards the homestead-head ideal of masculinity they had brought from the countryside, while avoiding expensive entanglements with local women.[36] More commonly, miners found protection among 'home boys' from their locality, among mates from their own language group befriended at the mine – so that ethnic loyalties remained strong – or more generally in the brotherhood of blacks against whites. The culture of brotherhood blended mutual aid and respect with insistent sociability, reliance on alcohol and drugs as a release from underground dangers, and an aggressive machismo. Although theft from a fellow miner was

---

[33] Gordon, *Mines*, p. 88. See also Charles van Onselen, *Chibaro: African mine labour in Southern Rhodesia, 1900–1933* (London, 1976), p. 136; Moodie in Bozzoli, *Town and countryside*, pp. 190–1; Jingoes, *A chief*, p. 64.

[34] Gordon, *Mines*, pp. 82, 98, 138.

[35] Evidence of James Mutali, in Northern Rhodesia, *Evidence taken by Commission appointed to enquire into the disturbances in the Copperbelt* (2 vols., Lusaka, 1935), vol. 1, p. 232; Alan H. Jeeves, 'Identity, culture and consciousness: industrial work and rural migration in southern Africa, 1860–1987,' *SAHJ*, 33 (1995), 202–3.

[36] Patrick Harries, *Work, culture, and identity: migrant laborers in Mozambique and South Africa, c.1860–1910* (Portsmouth, N.H., 1994), pp. 200–8; T. Dunbar Moodie with Vivienne Ndatshe, *Going for gold: men, mines, and migration* (Berkeley, 1994), pp. 119–40.

deplored, 'taking' from whites enjoyed the same admiration as raiding an enemy's cattle.[37]

From the late nineteenth century, southern Africans created a working class masculinity that had parallels in many tough jobs elsewhere in the continent. At its core was an angry resentment of insult. 'By calling me a "Kaffir"... they mean I do not deserve respect and that they can behave any way they want with me,' a Namibian miner complained during the 1970s. Like African colonial soldiers, workers particularly resented being sworn at 'because it impinges dramatically on their sense of manliness.' They also complained that they received lower accident compensation payments than Europeans: 'Does it mean that I am less of a person than the White?' To be addressed by numbers – *manamba*, the generic term for migrant labourers in East Africa – was equally resented.[38] But the chief complaint of underground miners was the brutality of white supervisors and African 'bossboys', which was fostered by the occupation's stress on physical strength, the danger created by lapses of discipline, and the dependence of earnings on output. 'The first day I arrived here under contract I was hammered, and I went to the shift boss and he went for me... then I went to the Mine Captain and he hammered me too,' a miner told an inquiry in 1913. 'We are not children, we are men,' another witness added, 'and yet they catch us by the neck and throw us into the [lift] cage and kick us when we are going in, and we dare not do anything as we can't fight the white man.'[39] To attack an African bossboy was dangerous enough. 'If you hit the induna you lose your job,' one worker observed. 'It's possible though that you can hit him in the night.' Yet even those willing to assault bossboys might fear to raise their hands against whites, 'otherwise we could be jailed.'[40] Some did nevertheless retaliate when provoked beyond endurance, especially where mining offered concealment:

The nature of underground work enforces an equality between Black and White not witnessed at any other work-place on the Mine. Accidents do not discriminate: 'Today it is a White, tomorrow it is a Black. They both go out of the Mine on the same stretcher.' Equally important is the general acceptance of the fact that while accidents do happen indiscriminately, they can also be made to happen to certain unpopular people.[41]

[37] Gordon, *Mines*, pp. 102–9, 116–17, 183; J. K. McNamara, 'Brothers and work mates,' in Mayer, *Black villagers*, pp. 305–40; Moodie, *Going*, chs. 5 and 6.

[38] Gordon, *Mines*, pp. 90, 94–5, 164–5; this volume, p. 240.

[39] Quoted in Keith Breckenridge, 'The allure of violence: men, race and masculinity on the South African goldmines, 1900–1950,' *JSAS*, 24 (1998), 682–3.

[40] Mandlenkosi Makhoba, *The sun shall rise for the workers* (Braamfontein, 1984), p. 20; Breckenridge, 'Allure,' p. 687.

[41] Gordon, *Mines*, p. 164.

Individual defiance was a dangerous luxury. One early migrant to the Kimberley diamond mines stoutly refused to work for less than the customary wage and starved to death on the way to the hospital.[42] Other workers learned to defend their honour and interests by collective organisation. Normally their first associations were not specifically workers' bodies but traditional organisations brought from the countryside to provide mutual aid, care in sickness or death, entertainment, and magical protection. In Elisabethville (Lubumbashi) the first copper production in 1911 coincided roughly with the introduction of the Butwa society by Luba and Bemba townsmen and the Bambudye society by Lunda from Kazembe's kingdom. In Salisbury, similarly, one of the earliest welfare organisations was the ancient Nyau dance society of the Chewa people from Nyasaland.[43] Gradually more specifically industrial organisations emerged, generally first among craftsmen anxious to demonstrate respectability. In 1883, for example, workmen in Lagos established a Mechanic's Mutual Aid Provident and Mutual Improvement Association, soon followed by a Carpenters' Union and other craft societies. Commercial clerks there organised in 1911; civil servants, in 1912; and railway workers, in 1919.[44] Early labour organisation was dangerous. Not until the 1930s did African trade unions generally enjoy legal protection; they remained illegal well after 1950 in settler colonies like Southern Rhodesia, which regularly deported or imprisoned 'industrial agitators'. Employers, both black and white, also victimised union organisers. One South African mine 'retrenched' 93 of its 95 shop stewards as late as 1992.[45]

The dangerous character of their work and their financial dependence on subscriptions from ill-paid workers who admired courage led many trade union leaders to adopt a heroic style that fostered authoritarianism, clientelism, corruption, sporadic militancy, and institutional fragility. In South Africa, Clements Kadalie, General Secretary of the Industrial and Commercial Workers' Union during the 1920s, personified this style of leadership. Claiming to have become a union organiser when kicked off a Cape Town pavement by a policeman,

---

[42] Louis Cohen, *Reminiscences of Kimberley* (London, 1911), pp. 292–3.

[43] Bruce Fetter, 'African associations in Elisabethville, 1910–1935,' *Etudes d'Histoire Africaine*, 6 (1974), 208–10; John Higginson, *A working class in the making* (Madison, 1989), p. 80; Tsuneo Yoshikuni, 'Black migrants in a white city: a social history of African Harare, 1890–1925,' PhD thesis, University of Zimbabwe, 1989, p. 239.

[44] *Lagos Times and Gold Coast Advertiser*, 8 August 1883; *Lagos Weekly Record*, 17 October 1896; Arnold Hughes and Robin Cohen, 'An emerging working class: the Lagos experience, 1897–1939,' in Gutkind and others, *African labor history*, pp. 36–43.

[45] Nyasaland, *Report on the administration of the Police Department*, 1927 and 1928, MNA S1/776/28 and SI/773/29; Gay W. Seidman, 'Shafted: the social impact of down-scaling in the OFS goldfields,' in Crush and James, *Crossing boundaries*, p. 186.

he affected a slight American accent, delighted in the symbols of bureaucratic power, and excelled at defiant speeches. His notion of organisation consisted largely of touring the country recruiting new members and spending the entrance fees extracted by millenarian promises. His equally flamboyant colleague and rival in Durban, A. W. G. Champion, infused the ICU with Zulu heroic traditions of dancing, marching, and praise-singing.[46] As urban workers gathered experience, however, they learned to distrust the leadership of flamboyant heroes, literate clerks, and union officials with transparent political ambitions. 'The only leader to be trusted is the leader working at your side,' Nigerian factory workers declared in the early 1970s.[47] Experience of industrial strikes taught the same lesson. Although strike leaders like Ibrahim Sarr of the Senegalese railway workers and Chege Kibachia of the Mombasa dockworkers, both in the late 1940s, demonstrated courage and commitment,[48] many strikes, like military mutinies, were deliberately leaderless in order to avoid victimisation. 'We said, "No we don't want to elect anybody to come and speak to you because we fear you are going to victimise that person. You'll say he's our leader,"' a South African trade unionist remembered of his first dispute in 1958.[49] It was at this level of collective workforce commitment that traditional means were employed to strengthen solidarity. Those who planned Dar es Salaam's dock strike in 1947, for example, first took an Islamic oath.[50] It was also at this level that appeals to notions of honour were most compelling. Strikers on the Copperbelt in 1935 were said to have been stirred into action partly – although some denied this – by warnings that otherwise 'our brothers . . . will laugh at us and will call us women' and partly by the provocative behaviour of the police: 'They said, "These people have come to beat us." The Awemba [Bemba] do not like to be frightened like children.'[51]

Work might bring many humiliations to a man of honour, but few were so great as the humiliation of long remaining unemployed. In early colonial Africa,

---

[46] Kadalie, *My life*, pp. 39–40, 66, 135; Helen Bradford, *A taste of freedom: the ICU in rural South Africa 1924–1930* (New Haven, 1987), pp. 85, 107; P. L. Wickins, *The Industrial and Commercial Workers' Union of Africa* (Cape Town, 1978), pp. 90, 116, 147, 168–70; Paul la Hausse, 'The message of the warriors,' in Philip Bonner, Isabel Hofmeyr, Deborah James, and Tom Lodge (eds.), *Holding their ground* (Johannesburg, 1989), pp. 34–5, 37, 44–5.

[47] Adrian J. Peace, *Choice, class and conflict: a study of southern Nigerian factory workers* (Brighton, 1979), p. 129.

[48] Frederick Cooper, '"Our strike": equality, anticolonial politics and the 1947–48 railway strike in French West Africa,' *JAH*, 37 (1996), 86–103; idem, *On the African waterfront* (New Haven, 1987), pp. 84–108.

[49] Petrus Tom, *My life struggle* (Braamfontein, 1985), p. 15.

[50] Mohamed Said, *The life and times of Abdulwahid Sykes* (London, 1998), p. 63.

[51] Northern Rhodesia, *Evidence*, vol. 1, p. 485, and vol. 2, pp. 769, 779.

labour was scarce and unemployment rare. It appeared among Africans in South African towns before the First World War and became acute during the depression of the early 1930s. 'They go from gate to gate in the Johannesburg suburbs,' it was written in 1934, 'touching their aged hats and saying – what is often their one word of English – "job".' Some joined violent protests under communist leadership. Others relied on the generosity of fellow tribesmen. 'It would be a point of honour for a Wemba to feed another who had no food,' a Bemba elder told the Copperbelt enquiry of 1935.[52] Thereafter economic activity and war absorbed labour once more, but from the 1950s the rapid growth of population and primary education created a continental problem of youth unemployment. In Pretoria in 1951, some 80 per cent of youths between the ages of fifteen and twenty were unemployed; fifteen years later, 69 per cent of the unemployed in Kampala and Jinja were aged twenty-four or less.[53] Unemployed youths 'hang on the lean pay roll of their relatives and friends' for months or even years, provoking growing irritation. One such youth poisoned himself from shame. Another, a distinguished footballer, killed himself 'because, as he said, he could not find a job commensurate with his skills.' A third threatened to denounce an uncle who refused him hospitality, for many townspeople had to dishonour themselves by turning away needy relatives or acquaintances.[54] The most desperate unemployment resulted from the economic decline of the late twentieth century. By the mid 1990s retrenchment in South Africa's gold mines had left some 40 per cent of Lesotho's labour force without work, many of them career miners with dependent families:

It's a terrible situation. When you look at people and they look back at you and you think that they know you're unemployed. People think you're worthless. Any real man can support his family. I used to be a real man now I am worth less than a loaf of bread. Bread is more use to them than me. . . . My wife she's just bitter. She takes it out on me and accuses me of not wanting to support her and the children. She says I'm a hopeless person.[55]

---

[52] Van Onselen, *Studies*, vol. 2, pp. 18–19; S. G. Millin, quoted in Baruch Hirson, *Yours for the union* (London, 1989), p. 18; evidence of Councillor Muruka, in Northern Rhodesia, *Evidence*, vol. 1, p. 131.

[53] Deborah Posel, *The making of Apartheid, 1948–1961* (Oxford, 1991), p. 86; Caroline Hutton, *Reluctant farmers? a study of unemployment and planned rural development in Uganda* (Nairobi, 1973), p. 302.

[54] *Uganda Pilot*, quoted in Uganda African affairs fortnightly review, 7 October 1948, CO 537/3601/23; K. A. Busia, *Report on a social survey of Sekondi-Takoradi* (London, 1950), p. 63; Samuel Ekpe Akpabot, *Football in Nigeria* (London, 1985), p. 21; Peter C. W. Gutkind, 'The energy of despair,' *Civilisations*, 17 (1967), 197–8.

[55] Bruce Irvine, 'The psychological effects of unemployment – an exploratory study,' Carnegie Conference Paper 126 (Cape Town, 1984), pp. 19, 23. See also *Mail and Guardian*, 11 July 1997.

As an alternative to unemployment people of all ages scraped a living in the informal sector embracing almost any unregulated occupation from backstreet engineering to scrap-collecting. In 1978 Nigeria's informal sector employed an estimated 72 per cent of its urban labour force, while even in South Africa, where white authorities had long repressed unregulated enterprise, some 18 per cent of the potential labour force practised informal occupations in 2001.[56] Informal activities shaded imperceptibly into crime, which had an ambiguous standing in the calculus of honour. On the one hand, the strong precolonial antipathy to crime within the community remained a powerful constraint. A study of suicide in Durban between 1940 and 1970 found that Africans were more likely than people of other races to kill themselves when accused of some shameful crime such as rape or theft. Community action against criminals – beating, killing, or public humiliation – was common where police were few. Yet a period in gaol often carried little stigma, for much low-level crime, especially theft, grew out of common poverty and, if directed against whites, was often seen as akin to redistribution.[57] Criminal gangs, especially of the young, attracted widespread loathing, but there was much fascination with notorious criminals who defied alien authorities, such as the Nigerian robber Aeroplane, who was believed to turn himself into a crow; Four-Toe Jim, eventually convicted of ten burglaries of European property in Nyasaland; Yaadikkoon, who specialised in leading gangs of adolescents into Dakar shops and distributing the merchandise to them; or the Sotho gang leader Tseule Tsilo (Big King) whose reputation for violence, generosity, and protective medicine deterred anyone from testifying against him until, like an epic hero, he was betrayed by a beautiful woman and stabbed by a rival gangster.[58] Disrespect for the law was especially widespread in South Africa, where influx control criminalised much of the population, a survey found that police raids were the most frequent motifs in African dreams, and any policeman who entered an urban location did so at risk of his life. 'I killed him, he insulted me and everyone who carries my blood in their veins,' one policeman's murderer told a court.[59]

---

[56] International Labour Office, *First things first: meeting the basic needs of the people of Nigeria* (Addis Ababa, 1981), p. 217; SAIRR, *Fast Facts*, February 2002.

[57] Meer, *Race and suicide*, p. 139; Thokozani Xaba, 'Masculinity and its malcontents,' in Robert Morrell (ed.), *Changing men in southern Africa* (London, 2001), pp. 113–19; Gordon, *Mines*, p. 183.

[58] Smith, *Baba*, p. 184; Anson to Commissioner, 1 June 1945, MNA POL.5/2/11; Ibrahima Thioub, 'Banditisme social et ordre colonial: Yaadikkoon (1922–1984),' *Annales de la Faculté des Lettres et Sciences Humaines* (Dakar), 22 (1992), 170; Gary Kynoch, '"A man among men": gender, identity and power in South Africa's Marashea gangs,' *Gender and History*, 13 (2001), 260–9.

[59] Hunter, *Reaction to conquest*, p. 470; Mphahlele, *Down Second Avenue*, pp. 122, 142.

For women, in particular, the most profitable urban occupations were often illegal. This was less true in the forest areas of West Africa, where the traditional female role in market trade expanded during the colonial period as men entered other occupations. By 1960 some 83 per cent of Ghana's 323,900 traders were women. In East Africa, however, there was strong competition from Indian merchants, and trade was sometimes thought disreputable for women, as in Kampala, while in the south municipal authorities discouraged informal trade until their power weakened at the end of the century.[60] Consequently many urban women relied on two illegal and widely despised activities whose defiance of authority nevertheless bred its own sense of honour. One was prostitution, the epitome of urban degradation in respectable eyes and the target of much hypocritical persecution by men, but in fact a highly stratified occupation, ranging from the street-walker or mine prostitute who offered intercourse to any passing client, through the entrepreneurial women who provided a range of domestic services and the good-time girls for whom a lover's gifts were normal accompaniments of a sexual relationship, to the fashionable *vedettes* of Kinshasa and *karuwai* of Northern Nigeria whose independent lifestyles excited both jealousy and admiration. The striking feature of African prostitution was that women moulded it to their notions of female enterprise: highly individualistic, with few brothels (except in Ethiopia), strong networks of mutual aid (especially to care for children), the goal of investment in home-ownership, and simultaneous engagement in other income-earning and domestic activities by women for whom sex often carried less moral weight than it bore in Mediterranean cultures.[61] Much the same was true of women's other major illegal activity, brewing or distilling, a squalid and dangerous occupation that many respectable women eschewed but others practised as a means of meeting what they considered to be the true criterion of respectability: the upbringing and education of children. 'I started selling liquor in 1965,' one explained. 'This is when my husband left to stay

---

[60] Rowena M. Lawson, 'The supply response of retail trading services to urban population growth in Ghana,' in Claude Meillassoux (ed.), *The development of indigenous trade and markets in West Africa* (London, 1971), p. 380; Elizabeth Mandeville, 'Poverty, work and the financing of single women in Kampala,' *Africa*, 49 (1979), 49; Christopher Myles Rogerson, 'The casual poor of Johannesburg, South Africa: the rise and fall of coffee-cart trading,' PhD thesis, Queen's University, Kingston, Ontario, 1983, ch. 5.

[61] See Luise White, *The comforts of home: prostitution in colonial Nairobi* (Chicago, 1990); Christopher J. Bakwesegha, *Profiles of urban prostitution: a case study from Uganda* (Nairobi, 1982), pp. 42–50; Jean S. la Fontaine, 'The free women of Kinshasa,' in J. Davis (ed.), *Choice and change* (London, 1974), ch. 6; Jerome H. Barkow, 'The institution of courtesanship in the northern states of Nigeria,' *Genève-Afrique*, 10 (1971), 58–73; Laketch Dirasse, 'The socio-economic position of women in Addis Ababa: the case of prostitution,' PhD thesis, Boston University, 1978.

with another woman. He left me with five kids. I had to feed, clothe, and educate them. Mind, these are only the kids. You must still pay rent and do other things. Where are you supposed to get that money? . . . If you want to survive, you must make a plan.'[62]

Women adapted better than men to urban working-class life. European or elite African domination of civic affairs and workplaces blocked male aspirations to compete, display, control, and distribute, leaving men ashamed of their poverty, frustrated by conflict, and seeking release in drink, leisure, or violence. Feminine ideals of endurance and provision for the family, by contrast, gave them greater resolution in the struggle for survival. Women recognised this. 'Men's dignity has gone into a bottle of wine,' domestic servants in the Eastern Cape explained.[63] African literature also recognised it in the strong women and inadequate men who peopled the urban novels of Peter Abrahams, Sembene Ousmane, and Cyprien Ekwensi.[64] Female resilience was the chief reason why working-class quarters seldom bred feckless 'cultures of poverty' but were rather 'slums of hope', places of energetic striving to live with dignity.[65] 'In spite of the hard conditions of life we find no spirit of hopeless resignation, such as one finds among the rural poor,' an anthropologist wrote of Pretoria's African locations in 1934. 'On the contrary, a study of the sources of income in family budgets reveals feverish activity on the part of almost every member of the family to make what money he can, and every possible avenue of increasing their earnings is exploited.'[66] Similar energy went into housing. Men generally concentrated on building themselves better houses. Women focused on improving what they had. 'We polished in order to keep some self-respect,'one remembered. '. . . We believed in cleaning those houses. They were our pride. What else did we have to show pride in? Only our little rooms were our pride.'[67]

Alongside these mundane claims to dignity went more flamboyant forms of self-assertion. One was dress, the emphasis on appearance crucial to honour cultures in which dress not merely expressed identity but was a means of creating

---

[62] Dinga Sikwebu, 'Area study of Cape Town: profile of Nyanga,' Carnegie Conference Paper 10a (Cape Town, 1984), p. 16. See also Ellen Hellmann, *Rooiyard: a sociological survey of an urban native slum yard* (Cape Town, 1948); Akyeampong, *Drink*, ch. 5.

[63] Jacklyn Cock, *Maids and madams* (Johannesburg, 1980), p. 114.

[64] Abrahams, *Mine boy*; Ousmane Sembene, *God's bits of wood* (trans. F. Price, London, 1970); Cyprien Ekwensi, *Jagua Nana* (London, 1961).

[65] Alejandro Portes, 'Rationality in the slum: an essay on interpretive sociology,' *CSSH*, 14 (1971–2), 268–86.

[66] Eileen Jensen Krige, 'Some social and economic facts revealed in native family budgets,' *Race Relations*, 1 (1933–4), 95.

[67] Emma Mashinini, *Strikes have followed me all my life: a South African autobiography* (London, 1989), pp. 10, 17.

it, of inventing oneself. Costume had been vital in precolonial societies, whether in the elaborate hairstyles of Beti youths or the sober attire of Black Victorians. It remained vital in twentieth-century towns, as an anthropologist observed in Northern Rhodesia in 1942:

The desire for clothes is the normal conscious motive that brings men to town, and 'naked-ness' is the usual answer to the question 'what made you leave the country?' ... Every African man of whatever social group tries to dress smartly for strolling round the town, or for visiting in his spare time, and loves to astonish the world with a new jacket, or a new pair of trousers of distinguished appearance. Women behave in the same way; and they judge husbands and lovers largely according to the amounts of money which they are given by them to spend on clothes. Clothes are discussed unceasingly, in much the same way that I have heard primitive villagers discuss their cattle.... The Africans of Broken Hill are not a cattle people ... they are a dressed people.[68]

'Our men in those days, especially the uneducated ones ... would spend all their money on clothes imported from the U.S.A.,' Emma Mashinini recalled. 'Perhaps they were trying to maintain their dignity, which they felt was stripped from them in the terrible oppression we suffered, and they needed to look smart in those imported clothes, as if to say, Look, I'm so smart, I am human after all.'[69] Townspeople also used dress to express particular claims to distinction. Poor young men defied adult conventions. Sophiatown's wide guys challenged one another to estimate the cost of their clothes. Clerks adopted a neat European style, which their employers rightly recognised as a challenge to their superior-ity.[70] The obsession culminated in Brazzaville during the 1940s and 1950s in the cult of *sape* (from Société des Ambianceurs et de Personnes Elégantes) in which often unemployed young men vied to *frimer* (show off) by wearing with style the most expensive Parisian modes, not in protest against social conventions but as demonstrable mastery of them.[71]

A second route to fame, if not honour, was musical skill. During the twentieth century urban sub-elites of young clerks, artisans, drivers, and other employees took the Westernised musical styles favoured by the respectable and blended them with African rhythms, melodies, and instruments. Geographical mobility, the recording industry, and broadcasting then enabled certain styles and per-formers, both men and women, to gain territorial and international audiences,

---

[68] Wilson, *Essay*, vol. 2, p. 18.

[69] Mashinini, *Strikes*, p. 11.

[70] Michael Dingake, *My fight against apartheid* (London, 1987), p. 36; Justin-Daniel Gandoulou, *Dandies à Bacongo: le culte de l'élégance dans la société congolaise contemporaine* (Paris, 1989), p. 30.

[71] Gandoulou, *Dandies*, passim; Jonathan Friedman, 'The political economy of elegance: an African cult of beauty,' *Culture and History*, 7 (1990), 101–25.

which surmounted class divisions and created an entirely new kind of fame. This began in South Africa before 1914, when the Witwatersrand's shebeens bred the syncretic *marabi* dance music which horrified Robert Zulu but dominated urban popular taste until the 1930s, when fashion shifted to larger bands playing in township dance halls.[72] Ballroom dancing now became popular throughout sub-Saharan Africa at all levels of urban society. Imported modes fused with local traditions to create regional styles – Highlife, Juju, Congo Jazz – which were exported to international audiences during the 1950s.[73] In South Africa, the radio, recording industry, and popular press converted the respectable dance-band vocalists of the 1930s into the sensationalised stars of the 1950s, notably female vocalists like the domestic servant's daughter Dolly Rathebe – diva, sex-symbol, gangster's moll, and mother – whose emergence was the most striking example of women's success in the urban environment.[74]

Sporting prowess offered a third route to fame. Wrestling remained the national sport of Senegal, practised in marketplaces by gorgeously attired champions using magic and ritual challenges taken from *sebbe* heroes, but also commercialised between the wars by city entrepreneurs.[75] In southern Africa, by contrast, wrestling gave way to boxing. Contests in Salisbury during the 1930s attracted 2,000 spectators but puzzled European observers because they seemed occasions for display more than serious violence. By the 1950s, however, Africa was producing boxers of championship quality, including Ezekiel 'King Kong' Dhlamini, who ran out of opponents, murdered his girlfriend, and drowned himself in gaol from boredom.[76]

The new craze was football, which outpaced rivals as a way for youths to display manliness and for social groups to seek prestige. It inherited the teamwork of group dancing, the language of warfare, and the *cachet* of modernity. The

---

[72] This volume, p. 284; Christopher Ballantine, *Marabi nights: early South African jazz and vaudeville* (Johannesburg, 1993); Coplan, *In township tonight*, pp. 94–110, 129–33, 137–9.

[73] John Collins, *E. T. Mensah: the king of highlife* (London, [1986]); Christopher Alan Waterman, *Juju: a social history and ethnography of an African popular music* (Chicago, 1990); Sylvain Bemba, *Cinquante ans de musique du Congo-Zaïre (1920–1970)* (Paris, 1984).

[74] Can Themba, 'The life and love of Dolly Rathebe,' in Essop Patel (ed.), *The world of Can Themba* (Braamfontein, 1985), pp. 175–205; Lora Victoria Allen, 'Representation, gender and women in black South African popular music, 1948–1960,' PhD thesis, University of Cambridge, 2000.

[75] Ousseynou Faye, 'Sport, argent et politique: la lutte libre à Dakar (1800–2000),' in Momar-Coumba Diop (ed.), *Le Sénégal contemporain* (Paris, 2002), pp. 309–24.

[76] Terence Ranger, 'Pugilism and pathology: African boxing and the black urban experience in Southern Rhodesia,' in Baker and Mangan, *Sport*, pp. 203–6; Nat Nakasa, 'The life and death of King Kong,' in Essop Patel (ed.), *The world of Nat Nakasa* (Johannesburg, 1975), pp. 119–25.

British army introduced football into South Africa during the mid nineteenth century. In the 1890s it became popular at mission schools, whose alumni formed many prominent early teams.[77] British mission schools were also the pioneers in tropical Africa. In 1884 two mission stations drew East Africa's first recorded match, although the major popularisers there were Kiungani School in Zanzibar and King's College Budo in Uganda. In West Africa, similarly, the chief pioneers were Cape Coast Excelsior (based on the Government School) and King's College, Lagos, although French missionaries were less enthusiastic and football in French colonies was learned in streets rather than schools.[78] In some territories the elite teams long remained dominant. United Budonians headed Uganda's football league as late as 1949. Generally, however, such teams were marginalised as football became a key expression of working-class masculinity. Some clubs, such as Young Africans in Dar es Salaam, were founded by educated men but were gradually taken over by blue-collar workers. More were based from the start on particular workplaces, like Sekondi Eleven Wise, founded in 1919 among Gold Coast railway workers, the Christian Industrial Breadmakers of Abidjan, and almost all southern Africa's major clubs after 1945. Other forms of solidarity also found expression. Asante Kotoko – formally gifted to the Asantehene at his restoration in 1935 – represented ethnic competition, as did Abaluhya F. C. and Jaluo (later Gor Mahia) who dominated Kenyan football for decades.[79] Several prominent footballers of the 1940s, such as Emmanuel Dadet in the French Congo, built political careers on sporting reputations. More often, however, football was a political asset for the innumerable club officials and sponsors. The pioneer, as in many fields, was the Nigerian nationalist Nnamdi Azikiwe, whose ZAC Bombers won Nigeria's Challenge Cup in 1942. Although subsequently constrained by professionalisation, which began in South Africa in 1959, ostentatious patronage remained a feature of African football.[80] So did a particular style of play. 'The aim,' a journalist explained, 'is not only to score goals, but to score them with style and elan.' The

---

[77] Nigel Worden, Elizabeth van Heyningen, and Vivian Bickford-Smith, *Cape Town* (2 vols., Cape Town, 1998–9), vol. 1, pp. 196–7; Tim Couzens, 'An introduction to the history of football in South Africa,' in Bozzoli, *Town and countryside*, pp. 199–200, 208.

[78] Magila Mission Diary, 17 September 1884, TNA; Iliffe, *Modern history*, p. 393; McGregor, *Budo*, p. 18; Anver Versi, *Football in Africa* (London, 1986), p. 71; Akpabot, *Football in Nigeria*, p. 1; Phyllis M. Martin, *Leisure and society in colonial Brazzaville* (Cambridge, 1995), pp. 100–4.

[79] *Matalisi*, 24 June 1949; Iliffe, *Modern history*, p. 393; Versi, *Football*, pp. 77, 80, 85, 118.

[80] Martin, *Leisure*, p. 119; Kuper, *African bourgeoisie*, ch. 22; Ian Jeffrey, 'Street rivalry and patron-managers: football in Sharpeville, 1945–1985,' *African Studies*, 51 (1992), 68–94; Akpabot, *Football in Nigeria*, pp. 2–4.

Kenyan star, Kadenge, was known to wait for his beaten opponents to recover before putting the ball past them, explaining 'it was no *fun* scoring into an empty net.' 'When Africans are on top,' said Roger Milla of Cameroun, 'they resort to individual display.'[81]

The clearest example of the process by which indigenous notions of honour were incorporated and transformed into urban lifestyles concerned youth gangs. They had roots in the competitive aggression which many precolonial societies deliberately fostered in young men, as in stick-fighting between Xhosa neighbourhoods:

These fights are often very serious affairs, and it is quite a common occurrence for one or more boys to be killed in the course of them, or to die later of wounds. Serious wounds are the order of the day, but these are regarded with pride by the sufferer, much as German students regard the sabre cuts received in their college duels.... Boys in the prime of health and strength of body, who are nearing the stage of circumcision are usually the class involved in this amusement.[82]

Southern Africans commonly regarded these rural traditions as the progenitors of urban youth violence, but there were profound differences between the two. Rural youth groups functioned under the oversight of elders who could admit the young into adulthood, whereas urban youth groups generally had no adult patrons and could achieve maturity only by self-assertion. Moreover, stick-fighting was for uncircumcised youths; circumcision, marriage and adult warriorhood were expected to replace the aggression of boys by the restrained respect for law demanded of men. This transition was often frustrated in the twentieth century even in the countryside, where men could no longer prove their manhood as warriors or, where land was scarce, as homestead heads.[83] It was frustrated more clearly in towns, where adults were often too poor to support families or transfer inheritance and where many Christian townspeople rejected the whole tradition of youthful violence, for one reason why youth culture became deviant was that adult culture became respectable. Moreover, the violence of rural youth was not *necessarily* transposed

[81] Versi, *Football*, pp. 4–5; *West Africa*, 25 July 1994, p. 1296.

[82] Soga, *Ama-Xosa*, pp. 312–13. See also Philip and Iona Mayer, 'Socialization peers: the youth organization of the Red Xhosa,' in Philip Mayer (ed.), *Socialization: the approach from social anthropology* (London, 1970), pp. 159–89.

[83] Don Pinnock with Dudu Douglas-Hamilton, *Gangs, rituals and rites of passage* (Cape Town, 1997), p. 28; Mager, *Gender*, pp. 75, 129; Moodie, *Going*, pp. 37–41.

to urban life. Many West African savanna peoples, including the Hausa, had traditions of fighting between nondeviant youth groups, but these did not in the twentieth century breed deviant urban gangs.[84] The tradition was transmuted into gang culture only in those urban contexts where it was functional to the young, specifically in South African cities from the early twentieth century and in certain tropical African towns during and after the last years of colonial rule.

In Cape Town a tradition of youth gangs survived from the days of runaway slaves – one gang of young thieves is recorded in 1826 – and extended with substantial continuity to the *skollies* (from *schoelje*, scavenger) who fought turf wars in the city centre during the 1940s and to the scores of late twentieth-century gangs terrorising the bleak housing estates created by apartheid.[85] In other South African cities, the first violent youth groups were probably the Amalaita, bands of young immigrants from the countryside who in the early twentieth century transformed the stick-fighting tradition into bare-fisted boxing contests. Often organised in ethnic groups with a hierarchy of ranks and smart European clothing, Amalaita were in part 'the "houseboys" liberation army fighting to reassert its decolonised manhood,' although some deviated into criminal violence so that, by the 1930s, they were generally loathed.[86] Perhaps partly in opposition to them, a different type of gang emerged at that time, especially on the Witwatersrand, composed of town-born youths little concerned with ethnic origins or rural stick-fighting but motivated rather by the needs of urban survival amidst poverty, unemployment, family breakdown, lack of educational opportunities, and state oppression. Street-wise and contemptuous of country-born yokels, their 'ranches' affected American cinema culture, favoured the knife, and greatly increased township violence. As mass urbanisation intensified social problems during the 1940s, the most urbanised gang members became known as *tsotsis* (supposedly from the zoot-suits they wore), their numbers and depredations escalated, and many gangs adopted defiant names like Spoilers, Gestapo, or Black Swines. Some fought with rival white gangs called Ducktails. Others feuded with the Mareshea (Russians), a self-defence organisation of adult Sotho immigrants formed in 1947, which

---

[84] Raynaut, *Structures normatives*, pp. 124–5.

[85] Bank, 'Slavery,' p. 160; Robin Hallett, 'The Hooligan Riots, Cape Town: August 1906,' in Christopher Saunders (ed.), *Studies in the history of Cape Town, volume 1* (Cape Town, 1979), pp. 51, 70, 83; Don Pinnock, *The brotherhoods: street gangs and state control in Cape Town* (Cape Town, 1984).

[86] Van Onselen, *Studies*, vol. 2, pp. 54–60 (quotation on p. 59); Mphahlele, *Down Second Avenue*, pp. 100–1.

dominated several Rand townships and ran protection rackets in mine compounds.[87]

Although occasional youth gangs existed in tropical African towns from the late nineteenth century,[88] the social conditions that made youth violence functional in South African cities did not generally exist elsewhere until the 1940s, when population growth and primary education brought young people to towns more quickly than jobs and facilities became available. Juvenile gangs became a 'problem' in West African ports during the Second World War, in Kinshasa and several inland towns of West Africa during the 1950s, and at the same period on the Copperbelt, although several regions, including the Great Lakes area, scarcely experienced this phenomenon. Initially most gangs were formed by frightened and homeless boys seeking mutual protection and subsistence, but that easily led into violence, crime, and deviance, expressed in a defiant gang culture often shaped by the cinema or by prison or reformatory experience.[89]

The core of gang culture was an aggressive masculinity inherited from warrior traditions. Mareshea members called themselves fighters or soldiers and conducted military funerals for those killed in conflict. 'We never thought of death; only of making a name for ourselves,' a gang-leader recalled. Cape Town gangs initiated new members with tattoos often expressing masculinity or defiance: 'Death before dishonour', 'You can only kick back', 'Bruin kaffir'.[90] 'A fight is like football,' a Mareshea member commented: it had rules, a code of honour, and sometimes a high degree of organisation, as when gangs travelled to neighbouring Rand townships to take on the local competition.[91] The honour of a *tsotsi* could be as prickly as that of a Spanish nobleman. It required defence of territory and silence in the face of authority, sometimes

---

[87] Clive Glaser, *Bo-Tsotsi: the youth gangs of Soweto, 1935–1976* (Portsmouth, N.H., 2000), ch. 3; Katie Mooney, '"Ducktails, flick-knives and pugnacity": subcultural and hegemonic masculinities in South Africa, 1948–1960,' *JSAS*, 24 (1998), 753–74; Philip Bonner, 'The Russians on the Reef, 1947–1957,' in Bonner and others, *Apartheid's genesis*, pp. 160–94; Kynoch, '"A man among men",' pp. 249–72.

[88] For example, Spitzer, *Creoles*, p. 87; *Mambo Leo*, November 1924 and January 1926; Simon Heap, '"Jaguda boys": pickpocketing in Ibadan, 1930–1960,' *Urban History*, 24 (1997), 324–43.

[89] Iliffe, *Poor*, pp. 186–9.

[90] Kynoch, '"A man among men",' p. 259; Don Mattera, *Gone with the twilight: a story of Sophiatown* (London, 1987), p. 107; Don Pinnock, 'From argie boys to skolly gangsters,' in Christopher Saunders and Howard Phillips (ed.), *Studies in the history of Cape Town: volume 3* (Cape Town, 1980), pp. 154–5.

[91] Jeff Guy and Motlatsi Thabane, 'The Ma-Reshea: a participant's perspective,' in Belinda Bozzoli (ed.), *Class, community and conflict: South African perspectives* (Johannesburg, 1987), p. 441; *Drum*, May 1961, p. 52.

enforced on those who broke it. The prestigious Americans gang in Alexandra made it a point of honour not to submit to the homosexual rape threatening almost any youth committed to an adult prison. Gaol experience often carried high prestige.[92]

Although some gangs, like the Americans, specialised in large-scale crimes against white targets, most preyed on other Africans. Their criminal activities were sometimes deliberately conspicuous to the point of reducing their profitability, as a footballer might make scoring unnecessarily difficult.[93] Much gang activity centred on control of women. Mareshea commonly integrated Sotho women into their gangs and allocated them to male members, requiring nonmembers to pay for access to them. Some gangs, as in Kinshasa, practised indiscriminate kidnapping and rape. Most sought rather to monopolise the young women of their territory as largely passive trophies – 'cherries', in Sophiatown usage – to be enjoyed, defended, and flaunted. Women were seldom active in gang conflict, although they had been in the early Amalaita gangs. Rather, domination over women was the only sphere in which young, black, working-class males could assert supremacy, as they did in the most brutally sexist manner. 'A tsotsi was a man but his masculinity was unconvincing if he did not have a woman to dominate.'[94]

Deviant and criminal gangs generally expressed defiance also in dress, which was as important to them as to *sapeurs*. In South Africa the cowboy styles of the interwar period gave way to *tsotsi* fashions – narrow-bottomed trousers and broad-brimmed hats – although Kinshasa's youth gangs clung to the earlier patterns and spoke an argot, known as Kindoubil (Ki + Indian + [Buffalo] Bill), of the kind frequently invented by first-generation town-born youths. All shared concerns with football, music, alcohol, and drugs (mainly cannabis).[95] It would be wrong to see youth culture as wholly deviant. In tropical Africa, especially, the gangs of the 1950s were often led by educated youths, known in Ouagadougou as *Docteurs en droit*. Moreover, except in Cape Town, it would

---

[92] Joan Wardrop, '"Simply the best": the Soweto Flying Squad, professional masculinities and the rejection of *machismo*,' in Morrell, *Changing men*, p. 261; Glaser, *Bo-Tsotsi*, pp. 63, 136–7; Mattera, *Gone with the twilight*, p. 99; Pinnock, *Gangs*, p. 39.

[93] Glaser, *Bo-Tsotsi*, p. 62.

[94] Kynoch, '"A man among men",' pp. 251–7; Paul Raymaekers, 'Pre-delinquency and juvenile delinquency in Leopoldville,' *Inter-African Labour Institute Bulletin*, 10 (1963), 344–6; Dingake, *My fight*, p. 30; Berger, *Threads*, p. 41; Clive Glaser, 'Anti-social bandits: juvenile delinquency and the tsotsi youth gang subculture on the Witwatersrand 1935–1960,' MA thesis, University of the Witwatersrand, 1990, p. 193.

[95] Glaser, *Bo-Tsotsi*, pp. 50–1, 68–71; J. S. la Fontaine, 'Two types of youth groups in Kinshasa,' in Mayer, *Socialization*, pp. 199–200; Paul Raymaekers, *L'organisation des zones de squatting* (Paris, 1964), pp. 112–13.

appear, marriage generally ended a man's gang activity so that youthful gang-sters might mature into respectable elders.[96] Yet senior townsmen in South Africa organised themselves into vigilante groups, sometimes known as 'fathers of the homesteads,' which handled deviant youths very roughly, much as adult householders had in the past sought to impose control over young warriors.[97] It was ironic that the urban category most sensitive of their honour should have been regarded by most townspeople as the epitome of dishonour. But honour is always a contested notion.

[96] Jean Hochet, *Inadaptation sociale et délinquance juvénile en Haute-Volta* (Paris, 1967), p. 159; Danièle Poitou, *La délinquance juvénile au Niger* (Niamey, 1978), pp. 67, 152; Glaser, 'Anti-social bandits,' p. 10.

[97] David Goodhew, 'The people's police-force: communal policing initiatives in the Western Areas of Johannesburg, circa 1930–62,' *JSAS*, 19 (1993), 447–70; Glaser, *Bo-Tsotsi*, pp. 147–53.

17   Honour, Race, and Nation

In Europe and Japan, notions of honour inherited from heroic warfare and aristocratic culture found modern expression especially in nationalism.[1] This chapter suggests that in Africa, similarly, elements of the honour culture fragmented by colonial conquest were absorbed into the movements of racial and national assertion which regained independence. This does not mean that African nationalism was simply an outgrowth of honour culture, for nationalism had complex origins in which grievances, interests, ambitions, and political ideas were at least equally important. Yet the remarkable speed and success of nationalist movements – the most effective political organisations that modern Africa has seen – probably owed a good deal to their resonance with notions of honour. In particular, these notions underlay sensitivity to the racial contempt that nationalists strove to eradicate by securing political freedom. To achieve that, in turn, they appealed directly to their followers' honour and drew on heroic models for their rhetoric, symbolism, and style of leadership. Constitutional nationalism gave scope for the notions of honour held by householders, townspeople, women, and the respectable. Heroic honour found expression especially in armed liberation movements, although, as in epic literature, the warrior's valour coexisted uneasily with society's desire to restrain him.

Resentment of racial contempt was a primary source of nationalist thought and action. It inspired intellectuals like Edward Blyden and Léopold Senghor who took European racial ideas, inverted them, and prided themselves on the unique qualities of the black race. It stimulated those in multiracial societies

---

[1] Geoffrey Best, *Honour among men and nations: transformation of an idea* (Toronto, 1982), esp. pp. 12, 57; Ikegami, *Taming*, p. 361.

who, like the first president of the African National Congress of South Africa, professed a pride of race as strong as any Indian's or European's. It mobilised ethnic groups such as the Igbo, denigrated by their neighbours as primitive but reassured by their leaders that they were 'specially created ... to lead the children of Africa from the bondage of the ages.'[2] For individuals, too, racial insult was a formative experience. The Igbo leader, Azikiwe, like many others educated abroad, worked his way through college by a series of menial jobs and was obliged to defend himself against humiliation, even with his fists. Within Africa, likewise, many nationalists experienced insult. Agostinho Neto of Angola was flogged in front of his family. Dr Alfred Xuma, ANC President during the 1940s, was assaulted by a European constable who 'told me not to forget that I was black, called me a damn liar ... and slapped my face.' Henry Chipembere, struck by a Rhodesian official for not removing his hat, 'resolved that I was going to dedicate my life to the destruction of white domination.' Patrice Lumumba of the Congo never forgot the European woman who called him a monkey.[3]

Nationalists who had suffered humiliation held that only independence could free them from it. 'It is only when people are politically free,' wrote Kwame Nkrumah of the Gold Coast, 'that other races can give them the respect that is due to them.' To achieve this, they drew on Africa's traditions of heroic leadership. 'Human nature is such that it needs a hero to be hero-worshipped if the political struggle is to succeed,' the young Chipembere assured Hastings Banda when inviting him to lead Nyasaland's nationalist movement. Nkrumah, perhaps, most completely filled the heroic role, symbolising for his people the assertion of African racial pride. This came partly from his heroic reading of history, his conviction that he – *Osagyefo*, the Redeemer – was a man of destiny, and his appropriation for his movement of a heroic ancestry stretching back through the elite politics of the early colonial period and the military traditions of Asante to the ancient kingdom of Ghana.[4] Other leaders claimed

---

[2] Hollis Lynch, *Edward Wilmot Blyden, pan-Negro patriot, 1832–1912* (London, 1967); Abiola Irele, 'Négritude or black cultural nationalism,' *JMAS*, 3 (1965), 321–48; Hughes, 'Doubly elite,' p. 458; Azikiwe, quoted in 'Nigeria political summary (June–July, 1949),' CO 537/4727/4.

[3] Nnamdi Azikiwe, *My odyssey: an autobiography* (London, 1970), p. 214; John Marcum, *The Angolan revolution* (2 vols., Cambridge, Mass., 1969–78), vol. 1, p. 39; *Bantu World*, 8 March 1941; H. B. M. Chipembere, *Hero of the nation* (ed. R. I. Rotberg, Blantyre, 2001), p. 105; Jean-Claude Willame, *Patrice Lumumba: la crise congolaise revisitée* (Paris, 1990), p. 29.

[4] Kwame Nkrumah, *The autobiography of Kwame Nkrumah* (Edinburgh, 1957), pp. viii–ix, 197–201; David Birmingham and Terence Ranger, 'Settlers and liberators in the south,' in Birmingham and Martin, *History*, vol. 2, p. 367.

similar inheritances. Nelson Mandela, at his Rivonia trial, captured the heroic culture that had borne and shaped him:

In my youth in the Transkei I listened to the elders of my tribe telling . . . of wars fought by our ancestors in defence of the fatherland. The names of Dingane and Bambata, Hintsa and Makana, Squngthi and Dalasile, Moshoeshoe and Sekhukhuni, were praised as the glory of the entire African nation. I hoped then that life might offer me the opportunity to serve my people and make my own humble contribution to their freedom struggle. This is what has motivated me in all that I have done.[5]

To the indigenous traditions were added heroic models garnered from Western schooling. For Ndabaningi Sithole of Southern Rhodesia, they were Gandhi and Luther, Churchill and Livingstone, Lincoln and Martin Luther King. South African prisoners on Robben Island cheered one another by declaiming Macaulay's *Horatius*.[6]

To appropriate the heroic tradition, a leader had to display defiance. He dared to do and say what others felt but feared to express. The founders of the Tanganyika African National Union (TANU) in 1954 chiefly remembered not the business their meeting had discussed but the statement by their leader, Julius Nyerere, that the queen of England was not legally queen of Tanganyika. 'I knew in my heart,' one recalled, 'that Mr Julius K. Nyerere was really a man.' When Nyerere later visited the Usambara Mountains, peasant activists, schoolteachers, and other organic intellectuals, long at odds with local power-holders, were amazed 'that he said openly what many common people knew, but what others feared to say: that British rule needed to end so that Tanzanians could govern themselves. The power of Nyerere's message lay in its audacity.' In their defiance, many leaders accepted arrest and imprisonment, knowing that a prison graduate gained prestige. Nor were their risks merely nominal. Between 1959 and 1979 Maurice Nyagumbo of Southern Rhodesia spent less than three years out of prison.[7]

To crowds hearing the nationalist message for the first time, the impact could be electric:

The meeting slowly broke up, the crowd remaining for a long time in small groups debating all the marvellous things he had spoken and discussing the great future he would bring us. This was the year that Kenyatta first began to teach our people how to love their country . . .

[5] Karis and others, *From protest*, vol. 3, p. 771.

[6] Ndabaningi Sithole, *African nationalism* (Cape Town, 1959), pp. 86–91; Benjamin Pogrund, *How can man die better . . . Sobukwe and Apartheid* (London, 1990), p. 91.

[7] Saadani Abdul Kandoro, *Mwito wa uhuru* (Dar es Salaam, 1961), p. 73; Feierman, *Peasant intellectuals*, pp. 179, 212; Maurice Nyagumbo, *With the people: an autobiography from the Zimbabwe struggle* (London, 1980), p. 11.

I myself was fundamentally changed by his statesmanlike words and his burning personality. I vowed there and then that I would struggle with him for justice and freedom for our country and I dedicated myself to follow him in his crusade to remove the sufferings and humiliations of our people.[8]

To the leaders, too, what Mandela called 'the intensity of the experience of addressing a crowd' gave strength and inspiration. 'The sight of a crowd before me was all I needed to encourage the words to flow,' Nkrumah recalled. The leader's function was not to awaken the desire for freedom but to convince his audience that it was possible. 'Everyone wants to be free,' Nyerere reflected, 'and the task of a nationalist is simply to rouse the people to a confidence in their own power of protest.'[9] To do so, leaders played on many emotions, one of which was the sense of honour. Guinea's nationalist party named its newspaper *Horoya*, dignity. 'How easy it is to inflame an insulted people!' Nyerere warned. His speeches repeatedly returned to the themes of honour – 'To be ruled by another nation is an indelible disgrace' – and of slavery, for slave emancipation was within living memory and 'the slavery of being ruled' had great resonance among Tanganyikan audiences.[10] Tanganyikan politics were thoroughly peaceful, but TANU's language was often that of war. Conditions of great danger, as in South Africa, evoked the full warrior rhetoric: 'Cry day and night for Afrika. Go to gaols for the sake of Afrika. Be expelled from places where you stay for the sake of Afrika. Die in gaols and be hanged for the sake of Afrika. This is the time of heroes. We appeal to you our heroes.'[11] Praise-singing amplified the effect, as Mandela recalled:

Suddenly there were no Xhosas or Zulus, no Indians or Africans, no rightists or leftists, no religious or political leaders; we were all nationalists and patriots bound together by a love of our common history, our culture, our country and our people. In that moment, something stirred deep inside all of us, something strong and intimate, that bound us to one another. In that moment we felt the hand of the great past that made us what we were and the power of the great cause that linked us all together.[12]

The appeal to honour had much resonance among people from poor but ancient societies. 'Mali was poor,' a perceptive observer wrote, 'and politics

[8] Josiah Mwangi Kariuki, *'Mau Mau' detainee* (Harmondsworth, 1964), p. 38.

[9] Mandela, *Long walk*, p. 245; Nkrumah, *Autobiography*, p. 183; Julius K. Nyerere, *Freedom and socialism* (Dar es Salaam, 1968), p. 29.

[10] Julius K. Nyerere, *Freedom and unity* (Dar es Salaam, 1966), p. 28; Public Relations Officer to District Commissioner, Ukerewe, 29 November 1958, TNA 158/A/6/7/I/186; S. S. Chamshama, 'Taarifa ya Mkuu wa Kiti wa Jimbo kwa mwaka 1958,' 4 April 1959, TANU 27/14/encl (for the reference, see Iliffe, *Modern history*, p. 578); Feierman, *Peasant intellectuals*, p. 213.

[11] Skei Gwentshe (1952), quoted in Mager, *Gender*, p. 155.

[12] Mandela, *Long walk*, p. 188.

6. *Nkrumah addressing a party rally*. From Kwame Nkrumah, *I Speak of Freedom* (London, 1961), plate 1. Reproduced by permission of the Syndics of Cambridge University Library.

often turned around questions of deportment, propriety, and prestige rather than property.' Party declarations there showed intense concern with issues of honour, morality, and dignity. Competition for *ekitiibwa* in local arenas was commonly more important than grand issues of policy in determining nationalist affiliations.[13] Africa's hard-headed countrymen were scarcely eager to march to their deaths for nationalist principles. When Tonga peasants in Northern Rhodesia were urged 'to die in defence of their party's cause,' they replied, 'If you want to be killed, that is your affair. We want to live.' Their notion of householder honour stressed endurance. Yet they were nevertheless the core of Northern Rhodesia's African National Congress, which championed their agrarian interests.[14] Householder honour could inspire support for nationalism, but in its own idiom. Meru peasants in northern Tanganyika, evicted from their land, 'took an oath that they will endure the sufferings until they have been given their lands back':

We will bear anything that you do to us, but we will not retaliate. We will not do what you want us to do; we will not disinherit our own children by helping government officers take away our food and animals. We will not use our own legs to leave the place our fathers gave us for our homes. If you want to take away our Meru land by shooting us all with guns, go ahead. It is better for you to finish off the WaMeru and then stand upon our blood.[15]

Nationalists strove to preserve respectability, for respectable elites had generally created their organisations, but expansion of the franchise and the growth of mass politics made this increasingly difficult. That Eastern Nigeria's ruling party included in its election budget for 1959 a sum of £8,360 to pay 'Thugs – 12 to a Division' helps to explain why many respectable people in the region had abandoned electoral politics.[16] 'The time of politics', as it was often known, was widely remembered as a period of conflict and insecurity. The Creoles of Sierra Leone saw their leadership overthrown by hinterland peoples whose political style, in the words of a Creole newspaper, 'boils down to savagery and slavery.' 'I hate all that Nkrumah and the other C.P.P. leaders stand for in our political history – the dangling of false paradises before the trusting masses,

---

[13] Ruth Schachter Morgenthau, *Political parties in French-speaking West Africa* (Oxford, 1964), pp. 296, 263; Nicholas S. Hopkins, *Popular government in an African town: Kita, Mali* (Chicago, 1972), p. 115; Peel, *Ijeshas*, pp. 225–8.

[14] Colson in Beidelman, *Translation*, p. 25; Mac Dixon-Fyle, 'Agricultural improvement and political protest on the Tonga Plateau,' *JAH*, 18 (1977), 590–5.

[15] Sablak, Lengoroi, and Japhet to Bunche, 19 March 1952, Japhet Papers, TNA; Anton Nelson, *The freemen of Meru* (Nairobi, 1967), p. 41.

[16] Rankine to S of S, 15 January 1959, CO 554/2127/101; Vile to Yeldham, minute, 17 May 1950, CO 537/5808.

and stirring up of stupid and illegal hatred in the masses,' wrote J. B. Danquah, doyen of Gold Coast elite politicians.[17] The most socially subversive nationalist movement was the Parti Démocratique de Guinée. Its leader, Sekou Toure, the son of a poor Malinke peasant, had been expelled from school at fifteen and based his political career on trade union support. From this radical urban base, the PDG mobilised rural commoners against chiefs in a manner repeated by radical parties in Ghana, Tanganyika, Mali, Dahomey, and especially Rwanda. The PDG incited the *rimdinabe* serfs of Futa Jalon against their Fula masters. Mobs insulted chiefs. Merchants were paraded in old sacks and mocked by streetboys. Among stateless peoples, too, the PDG evoked radical responses, especially by its 'demystification campaign' of 1959, which incited village youths to abolish initiation rites and destroy the cult objects and secret societies embodying the power of elders.[18] 'Sekou understands the power of humiliation among this proud people,' one of his many enemies later observed. 'He made use of it during his political struggles and still uses it because he knows that the Guinean of every ethnic group, as moreover every proud and worthy man, prefers the bayonet rather than submission to an enemy who has humiliation as a weapon against him.'[19] The PDG also appealed with great success to women, scandalising their husbands by urging their wives to refuse them sex unless they joined the nationalist movement.[20] In Tanganyika, similarly, Muslim women found new opportunities for dignity and equality within TANU and were the majority of its members during the first eighteen months, although their role was primarily supportive within a women's wing, as was the normal experience of women within nationalist movements that distrusted autonomous women's organisations.[21]

Inkatha, the Zulu ethnic movement that drew more than half its members from women, found that what most appealed to them were promises of modernisation and development. It approached men, by contrast, 'through the language

[17] Yakubu, *Aristocracy*, p. 4; *Evening Despatch*, quoted in 'Sierra Leone political intelligence report, March–April, 1951,' CO 537/7234/6; Danquah to *Daily Graphic*, 1 June 1951, in H. K. Akyeampong (ed.), *Journey to independence and after (J. B. Danquah's letters)* (3 vols., Accra, 1970–2), vol. 2, p. 137.

[18] Morgenthau, *Political parties*, ch. 6; Claude Rivière, *Guinea: the mobilization of a people* (trans. V. Thompson and R. Adloff, Ithaca, 1977), pp. 85–6, 232–4; Klein, *Slavery and colonial rule*, pp. 238–9.

[19] Kaba Camara, *Dans la Guinée de Sékou Touré* (Paris, 1998), p. 73. (This was written in the early 1980s.)

[20] Elizabeth Schmidt, '"Emancipate your husbands!" Women and nationalism in Guinea, 1953–1958,' in Allman and others, *Women*, p. 295.

[21] Susan Geiger, *TANU women: gender and culture in the making of Tanganyikan nationalism, 1955–1965* (Portsmouth, N.H., 1997), pp. 1, 45–61, 90–1; Iliffe, *Modern history*, pp. 530–2; Nina Emma Mba, *Nigerian women mobilized* (Berkeley, 1982), ch. 8.

of cultural history and tradition, through appeals to their duties as breadwinners and obedient industrial workers, and through definitions of an ideal manhood.'[22] Its leader, Gatsha Buthelezi, was especially skilful in appealing to both the heroic and the householder versions of Zulu masculinity. He exploited resentment of disarmament by encouraging his followers to carry 'cultural weapons'. He taunted his ANC rivals with cowardice in deserting their country for the safety of exile. During the bloody struggle between the two parties for control of Kwazulu-Natal, which cost over fifteen thousand lives, masculinity was contested in its most violent form. 'We are a proud people,' Buthelezi told his assembled followers in 1979:

It is important for us to walk tall – to be men amongst men. We Zulus are a courteous and gentle people. We would live in peace with every man and be men amongst men. [But] when our manhood is subverted, when our dignity is sullied, when our courtesy is despised, mistakes were made which are costly. . . . We have shown our bravery in the past. We can show it again.[23]

Yet, as this speech emphasised, honour also embraced the peaceful virtues of the householder. Inkatha won much support by championing adult male control over women and the young against the threats of labour migration and mass education:

As workers, men were entreated to be a regiment of disciplined labourers and responsible breadwinners. As warriors, they were offered the privileges of Zulu patriarchal tradition through invocations of the valour, pride, and glory of their renowned forebears. . . . Paired within the framework of Buthelezi's mobilisation discourse, the identities of worker and warrior were constructed as complementary and essential aspects of Zulu masculinity.[24]

Nationalist movements incorporated not only generalised notions of dignity but the diverse traditions of indigenous honour cultures. This diversity was personified in the four main leaders of Nigeria's competing regions and parties: Ahmadu Bello and Abubakar Tafawa Balewa from the north, Obafemi Awolowo from the west, and Nnamdi Azikiwe from the east.

Alhaji Sir Ahmadu Bello, the Sardauna (captain of the bodyguard) of Sokoto, was a Fula aristocrat and descendant of Usuman dan Fodio who inherited the ostentatious traditions of West Africa's equestrian nobility, as well as a pious

---

[22] Roger Southall, 'Buthelezi, Inkatha and the politics of compromise,' *African Affairs*, 80 (1981), 457; Thembisa Waetjen and Gerhard Maré, '"Men amongst men": masculinity and Zulu nationalism in the 1980s,' in Morrell, *Changing men*, p. 196.

[23] South Africa: Truth and Reconciliation Commission, *Report* (5 vols., Cape Town, 1998), vol. 3, p. 173; Waetjen and Maré in Morrell, *Changing men*, pp. 195, 201.

[24] Waetjen and Maré in Morrell, *Changing men*, pp. 200–1.

Muslim and an educated and effective modern administrator. Ambitious above all to become sultan of Sokoto, he displayed extreme pride of rank and ancestry. 'I'd rather be dead than a Hausa – I am a Fulani,' he once declared. Accepting with regret the need to participate in party politics, he nevertheless considered democratic competition beneath his dignity, outlawing it in his constituency and leaving interparty bargaining to 'young kids'. He saw politics rather as patronage, appointing ministers without consulting them and treating close civil servants as junior members of his family.[25] Yet qualities deemed 'vain and pompous' by the British won admiration in the north. 'He was always superbly dressed,' it was recalled, 'and the sight of him, and the glittering cortege of large American cars that accompanied him, never failed to please a people that loved display for its own sake.' The crowds delighted in his ostentatious and reckless munificence, which thronged his house with supplicants and threw him into debt, which his bank discreetly cancelled.[26] Northerners admired, too, his determination to remedy their region's backwardness and his defiant contempt for southern critics. 'As regards slaves,' he once declared, 'it is only because the Moslem power is not strong here that we have not got the slaves to sell, and they are there.'[27] His loathing of southern politics was sharpened in 1953 when northern legislators who vetoed a resolution demanding self-government in 1956 were subjected to 'the screams and insults of the large crowds of Lagos thugs.' 'Next time I come, I'll have a sword in my hand!' he warned as he boarded his train.[28] Ahmadu Bello thereafter concentrated on exercising power as premier of the north and left Abubakar Tafawa Balewa to represent northern interests as chief minister of the Nigerian federation; nevertheless, the Sardauna remained jealous of him, taking offence at any precedence given to him, treating him on occasion with studied discourtesy, and privately calling him 'my deputy'.[29]

Sir Abubakar Tafawa Balewa personified the West African savanna's alternative notion of honour as reshaped by Islam. The son of a district chief's retainer, his training as a schoolteacher and his rise to become Nigeria's first

[25] Clark, *Abubakar*, pp. 211, 243, 651; Maddocks to Williamson, 11 October 1956, CO 554/1277/24; Shehu Shagari, *Beckoned to serve: an autobiography* (Ibadan, 2001), p. 77; Paden, *Ahmadu Bello*, pp. 158, 491–2.

[26] 'Nigeria': British Cabinet paper, July 1958, CO 554/1548/18; Sir Bryan Sharwood Smith, *'But always as friends': Northern Nigeria and the Cameroons, 1921–1957* (London, 1969), p. 375; Governor, North, to S of S, 4 December 1958, CO 554/1916/2.

[27] Northern Nigeria political intelligence notes, 19 March 1955, CO 554/1183/4.

[28] Alhaji Sir Ahmadu Bello, *My life* (Cambridge, 1962), p. 134; Clark, *Abubakar*, p. 196.

[29] Sharwood Smith to Williamson, 26 April 1957, CO 554/1583/56; 'Proceedings of the Resumed Nigeria Constitutional Conference,' 39th session, 25 October 1958, p. 667, CO 554/2595; Awolowo, statement at press conference, 15 September 1958, CO 554/1761/2.

prime minister never erased his humble rank within the Caliphate. Instead he
made modesty a political asset:

Abubakar knew that the traditional attitudes would always prevail over the ephemeral
popularity of an individual. . . . Greatness was still for royalty . . . when it was a matter
of caste, he knew his place. It hurt, but his lack of ambition for empty fame did not let
it rankle for long. Nor indeed did he ever seek any office that was not pressed upon him
by circumstance or by active encouragement.[30]

A moral and political reformer in the tradition of Usuman dan Fodio, Abubakar
began his career as a critic of the authoritarianism and corruption of native authorities, but he was always a gradualist, fond of observing that nothing in the
Koran had changed for fourteen hundred years. Austere, incorruptible, prudent,
quietly eloquent, self-doubting, and repeatedly tempted to return to teaching,
he had few friends but many respectful admirers among Nigerian politicians.
He was driven by a blend of religious duty and honour which came straight
from the moral teachings of northern reformers.[31] The ostentatious style of
southern politics disgusted him, especially as practised by Nkrumah and by
Azikiwe – 'Shiny', as he called him – whom he regarded as 'a menace to the
Eastern Region and to Nigeria.'[32] Initially, this distaste led Abubakar to defend
northern autonomy and resist Nigerian self-government, but as independence
approached he became more concerned to bring together a stable federal government representing all regions and parties. When this eluded him, he grew
increasingly pessimistic. 'I myself do not believe that the present type of federation can exist without the British Administration,' he confided in 1957.[33] Yet
he also grew more determined:

He said, 'Quite frankly I know that we are going to have trouble after independence.
Personally, in my own heart, I know that this country is not ready for it. But we will have
to be ready to deal with the trouble.' . . . He was quiet and even cheerful but he said, 'I
am committed to it now and I must work for it.'[34]

Abubakar held to his duty until 1966, then died for it, personifying the distinctive
blend of honour and piety that he had inherited. 'We politicians,' he said, 'we
are all butterflies in a thunderstorm.'[35]

[30] Clark, *Abubakar*, p. 239.
[31] This volume, p. 215; Clark, *Abubakar*, pp. 206, 256, 324, 380, 476, 633; Robertson, 'Note on
    conversation,' 20 April 1957, CO 554/1583/51; Robertson to S of S, 15 September 1960, CO
    554/2479/8.
[32] Clark, *Abubakar*, pp. 387, 417; Robertson to Eastwood, 31 July 1958, CO 554/2129/129.
[33] *Daily Times*, 1 May 1947, enclosed in Richards to S of S, 5 June 1947, CO 583/292/2/19; Clark,
    Abubakar, p. 652; Sharwood Smith, *'But always'*, p. 363.
[34] Grey to Eastwood, 9 July 1958, CO 554/1548/13.
[35] Clark, *Abubakar*, p. 270.

That thought would not have occurred to Obafemi Awolowo. A self-made man, ascetic and dedicated, he had 'a supreme confidence in his own ability' and a conviction that he was called to lead Nigeria and his Yoruba people, once declaring that God had revealed this to him in dreams. His autobiography, peppered with self-praise – 'I wrestled as brilliantly as ever' – and a score of allusions to courage, displayed both the competitive hunger for reputation found in nineteenth-century *oriki* and the faith in enlightenment that had animated Yoruba responses to colonial rule.[36] Lacking the oratory and charisma of Azikiwe – of whom he was obsessively jealous – Awolowo dominated the Western Region's Action Group by a ruthless administrative ability, which made its government the most effective in tropical Africa during the 1950s. '"Face" is all important to them,' the region's British governor observed. 'They desire, with a passionate intensity almost beyond our means to comprehend, to show that they can govern themselves.'[37] To this racial sensitivity was added the insecurity resulting from Yorubaland's intensely competitive politics, where every town and faction had an ancient rival. Insecurity and ambition made Awolowo as ruthless in his use of power as any nineteenth-century warlord, ostentatiously displaying his wealth, transfering public money lavishly to party funds, victimising his opponents – even the Alafin of Oyo was driven into exile – and displaying such arrogance towards other regional parties as to unite them against him.[38] 'An African to the backbone, Awo rarely disguised his feelings and diplomatic niceties were a humbug to him,' wrote a Yoruba admirer.[39] As a description of Abubakar Tafawa Balewa, the comment would have been absurd.

The most elusive of the four Nigerian leaders, Nnamdi Azikiwe, came appropriately from the fluid, stateless, immensely complex society of the Igbo. Azikiwe fascinated and perplexed his contemporaries. 'He is very bad,' Abubakar mused, 'but he is the only man the Ibos will follow.'[40] That relationship was the key to Azikiwe's political personality. Sent to the United States by

[36] Character sketch, 1957, in CO 554/2025/35; Peel, *Aladura*, p. 123; Obafemi Awolowo, *Awo: the autobiography of Chief Obafemi Awolowo* (Cambridge, 1960), p. 42; O. Lawuyi, 'Mirror of an identity,' in Olasope O. Oyelaran, Toyin Falola, Mokwugo Okoye, and Adewale Thompson (eds.), *Obafemi Awolowo: the end of an era?* (Ile-Ife, 1988), pp. 130–2.

[37] Williamson, 'Basic brief for the Secretary of State for his visit to Nigeria, January 1955,' CO 554/840/76; Rankine to Lennox-Boyd, 19 January 1955, 15 July 1959, and 4 January 1958, Rankine Papers, RH.

[38] Laitin, *Hegemony*, p. 67; Richard L. Sklar, *Nigerian political parties: power in an emergent African nation* (Princeton, 1963), pp. 235–7, 458; Rankine to S of S, 29 February 1960, CO 554/2392/1.

[39] M. Okoye, 'Awolowo and his contemporaries,' in Oyelaran and others, *Obafemi Awolowo*, p. 151.

[40] Grey, note, 7 July 1958, CO 554/2129/117/E.

his father to 'bring back the Golden Fleece' of learning, he returned in 1934 as the first Igbo graduate and was received as the redeemer of their honour. 'By your achievements,' an address of welcome declared, 'the Ibo tribe has been reassured that given equal opportunities with her sister tribes she can cut her niche in the African temple.'[41] His welcome excited Azikiwe as much as his lectures excited his audiences:

In a manner which was both charming and disarming, he subtly and implicitly laid claims to fields of learning which were truly catholic and almost limitless. 'Now let us run through the pages of history,' he proclaimed . . . and there was thunderous applause which lasted some two minutes. It was the first time in Nigeria, so we his hearers believed, that any Nigerian was academically competent and self-confident enough . . . to run through the pages of *all* history.[42]

Azikiwe was genuinely learned, but he was also dazzled by his own eloquence and his audiences' response. 'Blessed are the youth,' he proclaimed in 1937, 'for theirs is the earth and all therein.' The youth responded. 'We were completely overwhelmed by his simplicity and candour,' recalled Kolawole Balogun, who remained devoted to his 'political father' despite public humiliation by him.[43] Balogun was one of many gifted young men whom Azikiwe launched into politics through employment on his newspapers and then supported through education at American universities. He taught them to challenge the domination of Lagos and southern Nigeria by its Yoruba Protestant elite – later personified by Awolowo – against whom he fought a lifelong struggle for Igbo equality. In leading his aggressively acephalous people, Azikiwe supplemented his charisma and oratorical gifts by great political skill and ruthlessness. He destroyed the political career of his closest lieutenant, Mbonu Ojike, at the first sign of independence and responded to a women's educational protest in 1958 by observing 'that Ibos are a lawless lot, and that the crack of a rifle is the only thing they will listen to.'[44] Yet his megalomania and paranoid fear of assassination were responses to the extreme insecurity of a leader whose position had no traditional or institutional basis. As he explained in 1948, 'he, contrary to what was believed, was not in the position of a dictator but had inevitably to bow to the majority view and on many occasions agree to action which, if he

[41] K. A. B. Jones-Quartey, *A life of Azikiwe* (Harmondsworth, 1965), p. 61; Azikiwe, *My odyssey*, p. 244.

[42] Awolowo, *Awo*, p. 87.

[43] Nnamdi Azikiwe, *Renascent Africa* (reprinted, London, 1968), p. 47; Kolawole Balogun, *Village boy: my own story* (Ibadan, 1969), pp. 35, 96–8, 135.

[44] Guise to Smith, 11 November 1955, Azikiwe Papers, RH; Balogun, *Village boy*, pp. 76–9; Stapledon to Eastwood, 15 March 1958, CO 554/2129/74.

had been responsible for the decision, he would not have taken.'[45] At that time he was struggling to retain the support of the radical Zikist movement without allowing it to implicate him in subversion. Later he repeated the balancing act with trade unionism and the ethnic chauvinism of the Igbo State Union. Like Kenyatta – who attempted the same feat for the same reason but with less success – the resulting ambiguity earned Azikiwe a reputation for unscrupulousness and even cowardice. Certainly it reinforced his mercurial personality and eclectic mind, capable of espousing simultaneously both liberalism and authoritarianism, socialism and ostentatious philanthropy, tribalism, nationalism, and pan-Africanism.[46] Only a man of such complexity could have personified the range of Igbo aspirations. Azikiwe's pursuit of fame was as self-dramatising and vulnerable as that of a hero among any stateless people of the past.

Nationalism posed a particular threat to rank, but the example of Ahmadu Bello shows that the threat could be contained. Even radical parties were initially keen to win the support of chiefs. Sometimes they shared common interests, as in Nyasaland, where a commission of enquiry in 1959 found not a single chief who supported the Central African Federation, the chief target of nationalist attack. Privileged access to education and influence sometimes gave members of chiefly families a dominant political role. Six of Lesotho's first nine cabinet ministers were descendants of Moshoeshoe, while in 1957 some 84 per cent of Sierra Leone's parliamentarians had kinship ties to chiefs.[47] Moreover, aristocrats might be quick to see that they must lead nationalism or lose to it. Burundi's crown prince founded his country's successful party. Chief Seretse Khama led Bechuanaland to independence. In the extreme case of Swaziland, King Sobhuza first launched his own national movement and then, having regained independence, abolished all political parties.[48]

Yet not all men of rank succeeded in harnessing nationalism to their interests. Many, as in the French Soudan (Mali), committed themselves to pioneering parties overtaken by more radical rivals. There chieftainship was abolished at independence and the first national cabinet contained no aristocratic member.

---

[45] Azikiwe, *My odyssey*, pp. 359–67; 'Report on police investigations into allegations of a plot to assassinate the Premier, Eastern Region,' 4 December 1958, CO 554/2130/1; Savage, note, [December 1948], CO 537/3557/12.

[46] Ehiedu E. G. Iweriebor, *Radical politics in Nigeria, 1945–1950: the significance of the Zikist movement* (Zaria, 1996), pp. 200–6; Balogun, *Village boy*, p. 47; Sklar, *Nigerian parties*, pp. 70–1, 230; Anthony Enahoro, *Fugitive offender* (London, 1965), pp. 96–7.

[47] Nkrumah, *Autobiography*, p. 72; Great Britain, *Report of the Nyasaland Commission of Inquiry* (Cmd 814), PP, 1958–9, X, 796; Thompson, *Survival*, p. 325; Martin Kilson, *Political change in a West African state* (Cambridge, Mass., 1966), p. 233.

[48] Sebudandi and Richard, *Le drame burundais*, p. 171; Kuper, *Sobhuza*, pp. 249–54, 335–6.

Other chiefs, as in Southern Rhodesia, might be so vulnerable to white control that they had little choice but to oppose the politicians. Some totally misjudged the new situation, as did the Mossi paramount in 1958 when he ordered his horsemen to besiege Upper Volta's territorial assembly, permanently alienating himself from the nationalist regime.[49] A particularly bitter contest took place in Ghana, where the Asantehene and his chiefs took control of the National Liberation Movement's (NLM) attempt to resist domination of Asante by Nkrumah's CPP. Committed 'to honour, respect and be loyal to our traditional rulers,' the NLM presented its campaign as a defence of Asante's honour and interests, drawing on the kingdom's military culture and at times on West African motifs dating back to heroic epic. One CPP stalwart, it claimed, was invulnerable until a NLM woman seduced him and learned the secret of the magic bullet needed to kill him.[50]

The role of honour in shaping responses to nationalism and decolonisation was most vividly displayed in Buganda. In 1953 Kabaka Mutesa II used an indiscreet speech by the British Colonial Secretary as an opportunity to resist Buganda's absorption into an independent Uganda. The British deported him but had to allow him back two years later because their action had irreparably offended the honour of the Ganda people and the Kabaka himself. The British had underrated the sentiment, for which the Ganda were willing to sacrifice other interests and elevate to a heroic and dominating status a Kabaka whom many had hitherto despised. The deportation crisis is one of the most striking illustrations of the role of honour in modern African history.

The central thread of Mutesa's inglorious life was the defence of his prerogatives as a king in a distinguished line, identifying himself especially with his brilliant, fickle, self-indulgent great-grandfather Mutesa I, whose 'actions were beyond judgment or question.'[51] Yet the second Mutesa was of uncertain legitimacy, owed his throne to the British, and was morbidly anxious to demonstrate virility both as ruler and man. Surrounded by rivals for the throne, his unpopularity was accentuated by the humiliating manner in which the British used him to suppress dissidence and implement reform of Buganda's institutions. Like all young Kabakas, Mutesa craved independence from older statesmen, which now meant breaking free from the brilliant, modernising governor, Sir Andrew

[49] Morgenthau, *Political parties*, pp. 257, 289–90; Jocelyn Alexander, JoAnn McGregor, and Terence Ranger, *Violence and memory: one hundred years in the 'dark forests' of Matabeleland* (Oxford, 2000), pp. 91–3; Claudette Savonnet-Guyot, 'Le prince et le Naaba,' *Politique Africaine*, 20 (December 1985), 29–43.

[50] Jean Marie Allman, *The quills of the porcupine: Asante nationalism in an emergent Ghana* (Madison, 1993), esp. pp. 17, 68; Akyeampong, *Drink*, p. 137; this volume, p. 23.

[51] Kabaka of Buganda, *Desecration*, ch. 2 (quotation on p. 31).

Cohen. The colonial secretary's gaffe in July 1953 offered the opportunity, especially as Mutesa was rumoured to have been paid to agree to it.[52] Challenging Cohen's determination to develop Uganda as a unitary state, the Kabaka demanded 'a plan designed to achieve our [i.e., Buganda's] independence.' When, after lengthy argument, Cohen finally required 'loyal cooperation' according to the Uganda Agreement of 1900, Mutesa refused – 'If I am to choose between loyalty to you and loyalty to my people I will be loyal to my people' – and Cohen ordered his deportation on 30 November 1953.[53]

As the meaning of Cohen's action sank home, it became, he reported, 'a tremendous shock to the pride of the Baganda,' far beyond his expectation. Ganda confessed that 'they now realize that they are a conquered people.' A moderate vernacular newspaper declared that the Kabaka's honour was the honour of every Ganda and of the nation; a nation that did not uphold its honour would cease to exist.[54] Not only were royalists outraged – Mutesa's official sister died of shock – but even 'Baganda with strong personal grievances against the Kabaka instantly rallied to his support.' Only a few stern Christian moralists, modernising chiefs committed to the British regime, and dissident royals opposed demands for his return. 'Never before has the Baganda people been so united as they are today,' an official delegation accurately declared a fortnight after the deportation. Cohen watched events with growing alarm: 'The Baganda have every appearance of having a fixation. Mutesa has been idealised and represents the national pride of the Baganda deeply wounded and personified.'[55] Moreover Ganda, as their saying went, were 'experts at being ruled'. Gradually they mobilised irresistible pressure for Mutesa's return. The Lukiiko refused to elect another Kabaka while Mutesa lived. Deputations lobbied influential sympathisers in Britain, especially through the Anglican mission, which was alarmed by a reversion to paganism. Individuals boycotted European contacts. 'The women,' according to Cohen, 'seem to have been

---

[52] Whitley, 'Commission of Inquiry into Civil Disturbances in Uganda – January, 1945: supplementary secret report,' 11 July 1945, CO 536/215/40339/1/secret/encl; Uganda, *Report of the Commission of Inquiry into the Disturbances in Uganda during April, 1949* (Entebbe, 1950), pp. 45, 50; Uganda African affairs fortnightly review, 26 March 1953 (CO 822/425/49), 30 July 1953 (CO 822/426/58), and 10 September 1953 (CO 822/426/61).

[53] Mutesa to Cohen, 6 August 1953, CO 822/341/20; 'Record of a meeting held at Government House on the 6th November 1953,' CO 822/567/5/encl; 'Record of a meeting held at Government House on the 30th November 1953,' CO 822/568/63.

[54] Cohen to Gorell Barnes, 4 December 1953, CO 822/568/91; *The Times*, 18 June 1954; *Uganda Empya*, 25 March 1954, translated in Uganda press summaries, Perham Papers 529/3, RH.

[55] Kabaka of Buganda, *Desecration*, p. 122; *The Times*, 18 June 1954; Cohen, 'The Uganda situation,' 29 September 1954, CO 822/751/41A; 'Statement by the official Buganda delegation,' 15 December 1953, CO 822/569/124.

even more emotionally affected than the men' and collected funds for the Kabaka's support, led by the young queen whom he had maltreated.[56] Most importantly, when Cohen took advantage of the crisis to negotiate a new relationship between Buganda and Uganda, the Lukiiko refused to implement it until Mutesa returned. This overcame the governor's resistance, while the British Cabinet was forced into concession by a court ruling that the deportation had not been strictly legal.[57] For them it was as much an issue of prestige as for the Ganda.

The Kabaka returned to an ecstatic welcome in November 1955, theoretically as a constitutional monarch but much increased in power. With the vindictive personalism of an honour culture, he took special pleasure in Cohen's humiliation. Mutesa failed to have the governor and his advisers removed, but they could not prevent him from purging Ganda suspected of inadequate loyalty during his exile.[58] The Katikkiro and other ministers were replaced by conspicuous loyalists, at least five senior chiefs were removed in favour of royal favourites, several traditional officers were dismissed, and crowds incited by politicians and the vernacular press beat up at least two chiefs and humiliated several others. When the British protested, Mutesa observed blandly, but with justification, that he was glad nothing worse had happened.[59] In the longer term, however, Buganda's revitalised sensitivity was to destabilise Uganda for the remainder of the century.

Where nationalists were compelled to use violence in pursuit of independence – principally in southern Africa, but also in Kenya, Cameroun, and Portuguese Guinea – they had special occasion to appeal to heroic traditions. They chose violence reluctantly. They knew that suggestion of it would deter potential supporters. In the area of southern Tanganyika where the Maji Maji rebellion had taken place, for example, Nyerere struggled to convince audiences 'that peaceful methods of struggle for independence were possible and could succeed.'[60] Moreover, violence offended the principles of respectable nationalists. 'I have embraced the non-violent Passive Resistance technique in fighting

---

[56] 'Report of the Buganda Kingdom Lukiiko delegation to England,' 23 March 1954, CO 822/894/8; Brown to Cohen, 25 July 1954, CO 822/751/4; Cohen to Lennox-Boyd, 8 August 1954, CO 822/751/4.

[57] Cohen, 'The Uganda situation,' 29 September 1954, CO 822/751/41A; Lennox-Boyd, 'Uganda Protectorate,' 9 November 1954, C(54)336, CAB 129/71.

[58] Kabaka of Buganda, *Desecration*, pp. 137, 140–1; Gorell Barnes, 'Note for record,' 29 August 1955, and Lloyd to Lennox-Boyd, 30 August 1955, CO 822/756/1 and 3.

[59] Mutesa to Lennox-Boyd, 15 December 1955, CO 822/815/69, and other papers in this file; Paulo Kavuma, *Crisis in Buganda 1953–55* (London, 1979), pp. 102–7.

[60] Nyerere, *Freedom and unity*, p. 2.

for freedom,' the president of the African National Congress of South Africa explained, 'because I am convinced it is the only non-revolutionary, legitimate and humane way that could be used by people denied, as we are, effective constitutional means to further aspirations. . . . The Road to Freedom Is Via The Cross.'[61] Even parties less committed to Christian principles, such as the Pan-African Congress, often shared this view. 'We are ready to die for our cause but we are not ready to kill,' their leader Robert Sobukwe declared shortly before the Sharpeville massacre of 1960.[62] One reason for rejecting violence was a widespread confidence, as Ruben Um Nyobe of Cameroun put it in 1952, that postwar colonial reform made it unnecessary.[63] Only repression destroyed that confidence. Deliberate French repression drove Um Nyobe's Union des Populations du Cameroun to take refuge in the forest. The British declaration of an emergency in Kenya in 1952 converted low-level Kikuyu violence into the armed Mau Mau rebellion. Only the suppression of peaceful protest at and after Sharpeville forced South Africa's nationalists, most unwillingly, to adopt armed struggle.[64]

It was not a romantic route to heroism, but heroism there was. As in resisting European invasion, the weapons available to liberation forces were vastly unequal to those of their adversaries. UPC militants, entirely surrounded by colonial territory, were virtually unarmed. Mau Mau, dependent on stolen weapons, valued guns as highly as their users. Frelimo launched its war in Mozambique with 'about 250 fighters, equipped with old repeater weapons, pistols and a few individual automatic weapons.' The relatively well-armed guerillas in Angola lived in fear of helicopter gunships, while inexperienced Kenyan guerillas were terrified by their first experience of bombing: 'In the fainting breath, each said his own prayers, asking God to save his life and to avenge against the injustices of our strong enemies.'[65] Casualties were correspondingly disproportionate. By the end of 1956, according to official figures, Mau Mau had caused 167 deaths among the security forces, against 11,503 'terrorists' killed,

[61] Albert Luthuli [November 1952?] in Karis and others, *From protest*, vol. 2, pp. 488–9.

[62] South Africa: TRC, *Report*, vol. 3, p. 533.

[63] Achille Mbembe, *La naissance du maquis dans le Sud-Cameroun (1920–1960)* (Paris, 1996), p. 327.

[64] Ibid., pp. 319–23, 328, 343; Carl G. Rosberg and John Nottingham, *The myth of 'Mau Mau'* (New York, 1966), pp. 277–8; Mandela, *Long walk*, pp. 258–61.

[65] Ruben Um Nyobe, *Le problème national Kamerunais* (ed. J. A. Mbembe, Paris, 1984), p. 437; Gucu G. Gikoyo, *We fought for freedom* (Nairobi, 1979), p. 130; Samora Machel, quoted in *West Africa*, 5 August 1985, p. 1595; Marcum, *Angolan revolution*, vol. 2, p. 213; Donald L. Barnett and Karari Njama, *Mau Mau from within: autobiography and analysis of Kenya's peasant revolt* (London, 1966), p. 203.

including over 1,000 hanged.[66] Heroism, in these circumstances, often meant a determination to survive, so that the evasive tactics of guerilla warfare – now legitimated by success in China and elsewhere – no longer carried the stigma of cowardice, which had disturbed Ethiopian patriots. The guerilla hero was pictured by Stanley Mathenge, himself an illiterate former soldier who refused the high ranks assumed by other Mau Mau commanders and insisted on leading from the front:

He told a story of a people who were engaged in a similar fight as ours. . . . As the years passed by, the enemy's bombs and foot soldiers killed the forest fighters and only one of them survived. This brave warrior refused to surrender and fought as if he was the whole army. . . . When his people were released from prisons and detention camps and formed the first Government, they then called their fighters who were living in the forest to march from the forest to the national flag where they would receive their honor for bravery and perseverance. . . . [T]hey were very much surprised to see only one warrior carrying many different kinds of weapons . . . but . . . the brave courageous and persevering fighter received the greatest honor that was to be granted to all the country's fighters.[67]

Mathenge himself did not live to enjoy this modern heroic apotheosis; he was killed in action shortly after telling the story, after three years in the forest.

Young men found the heroic appeal most compelling. The Mau Mau oath was known as circumcision. Guerilla accounts of the Rhodesian War 'are often told as a series of ordeals or rites of passage which served to turn boys into men, and men into professional soldiers able to combat such an awesome enemy.' There, in 1979, some 78 per cent of the Zimbabwe African National Union's combatants who were trained or in training were between the ages of nineteen and twenty-four. The first had often been peasants or labourers living outside Rhodesia or their children, but subsequently whole secondary school classes left the country for military training.[68] The secondary school students who broke the impasse of South African politics in the Soweto riots of 1976 not only supplied many of the country's first trained guerillas but were models for the 'comrades' who made African townships ungovernable during the mid 1980s.

---

[66] Great Britain, *Historical survey of the origins and growth of Mau Mau* (Cmd. 1030, London, 1960), p. 316.

[67] Barnett and Karari Njama, *Mau Mau*, pp. 423–4.

[68] John Lonsdale, 'Authority, gender and violence,' in E. S. Atieno Odhiambo and John Lonsdale (eds.), *Mau Mau and nationhood* (Oxford, 2003), p. 69; Alexander and others, *Violence*, p. 146; Josiah Tungamirai, 'Recruitment to ZANLA,' in Ngwabi Bhebe and Terence Ranger (eds.), *Soldiers in Zimbabwe's liberation war* (London, 1995), p. 43; Fay Chung, 'Education and the liberation struggle,' in Ngwabi Bhebe and Terence Ranger (eds.), *Society in Zimbabwe's liberation war* (Oxford, 1996), pp. 139–40.

Many Kenyan forest fighters were young, illiterate men seeking, as one said, 'to regain the stolen lands and to become an adult.'[69]

Although often feared by their elders as a 'lost generation' perverted by mindless violence, 'comrades' and their counterparts elsewhere, while capable of great cruelty, were not anarchic. Mau Mau leaders condemned undisciplined fighters by a word, *komerera*, which implied idleness and cowardice. South Africa's comrades believed themselves to be distinctively disciplined and moral, in contrast to other township groups. They 'displayed an inordinate respect for an older generation of leadership in exile and in prison, offering their homage to these heroes in praise-songs, calling for them to come home, dedicating their lives to releasing them from prison.' 'I am not afraid to die now,' one declared, 'but when Mandela's released, *then* I'll be afraid to die.'[70] They saw themselves as freedom fighters temporarily committed to the harsh necessities of war, which made their parents' law-abiding respectability a form of cowardice. 'We are not carbon copies of our fathers. Where they failed, we will succeed,' Soweto students proclaimed in 1976.[71] Such emancipation came at high cost. Later psychiatric studies showed that many comrades lived in fear of adult violence, especially by the police or vigilantes, and depended heavily on family and group support. 'Bravado? . . . sure, maybe, but it helps us beat fear,' one activist explained. Many feared betrayal, which often accounted for the terrible 'necklacing' of suspected informers. 'Sisiology (to be a sissy) was not accommodated during that period,' one comrade recalled, 'you would leave your mother's heart at home.'[72] Other militants feared rival youths equally committed to war. Goodman Muswakhe Ngcobo, an Inkatha youth leader who later sought amnesty for fifteen murders, insisted that he had killed as a soldier: 'Youngsters, they were all politically involved and I was not killing old people. I was trying to crush these heads before they crushed me. . . . They killed us and we killed them, and this developed to a competition. . . . War was going

---

[69] John D. Brewer, *After Soweto* (Oxford, 1986), p. 133; Sam Thebere, quoted in Berman and Lonsdale, *Unhappy valley*, vol. 2, p. 326.

[70] Lonsdale in Atieno Odhiambo and Lonsdale, *Mau Mau*, p. 61; Monique Marks, *Young warriors: youth politics, identity and violence in South Africa* (Johannesburg, 2001), p. 59; David Hemson, '"For sure you are going to die!": political participation and the comrade movement in Inanda, KwaZulu-Natal,' *Social dynamics*, 22, 2 (Summer 1996), 79; Mashinini, *Strikes*, p. 135.

[71] Gill Straker, *Faces in the revolution: the psychological effects of violence on township youth in South Africa* (Cape Town, 1992), pp. 3, 135; Baruch Hirson, *Year of fire, year of ash: the Soweto revolt* (London, 1979), p. 250.

[72] Straker, *Faces*, pp. 85, 103; Matthew Kentridge, *An unofficial war: inside the conflict in Pietermaritzburg* (Cape Town, 1990), p. 24; Ntuthu Nomoyi and Willem Schurink, 'An exploratory study of insider accounts of necklacing in three Port Elizabeth townships,' in Elirea Bornman, René van Eeden, and Marie Wentzel (eds.), *Violence in South Africa* (Pretoria, 1998), pp. 155–6, 168.

on. . . . I was doing this to protect myself and the community I was living in.'
He described himself as 'the son of liberation'.[73]

The violence of politicised youth compelled other groups to respond. South
Africa's criminal youth gangs, for example, had taken only a sporadic and
largely destructive part in politics before the late 1970s, when the previous
distinction between gangs and students in some townships narrowed as the
school system collapsed, educated unemployment increased, student politics
grew more violent, and the distinction between political and criminal activity
blurred. The comrades who powered the township revolt of the mid 1980s
sometimes embraced both categories, blending the students' political awareness
with the gangs' machismo. 'They all used a similar rhetoric, adhered to the
same dress code . . . and clustered in predominantly male groups.' It was neither
universal nor permanent, however, breaking up during the 1990s into a renewed
contest to control the streets and define masculinity.[74]

Other South African urban groups fiercely contested youth violence. Immigrant workers from the countryside, often clustered into hostels and sometimes affiliated with Inkatha, resented 'uncircumcised boys' coercing them into
stay-at-home strikes and liquor boycotts that damaged their earnings and their
working-class culture. The result was bloody fighting, often fostered by the
police and sometimes merging with attempts by township bosses or elders
to regain control, often through adult vigilante gangs.[75] Outside South Africa,
too, youthful dominance of liberation movements threatened patriarchal power.
Rhodesian guerillas fearful of betrayal might assert an authority over villagers
that clashed with that of local elders, while poorer villagers, women, and especially the young might use the guerillas' presence to attempt 'a revolution
within the revolution'. Mau Mau met open resistance from the Kikuyu elite,
especially those with strong Christian beliefs.[76] The contest between heroic and
householder honour was played out once more.

The heroes themselves faced conflicts of loyalty and honour. Given the inferiority of their weapons, the likelihood of interrogation or death if captured,
and the risk of disclosure by noncombatants coerced by the authorities, all liberation movements were racked by suspicions of betrayal, while some – as in

---

[73] South Africa: TRC, *Report*, vol. 3, p. 310; South Africa: TRC, 'Proceedings,' application
5632/97, pp. 11, 13, 28, 32, 23 (typescript, CUL).

[74] Glaser, *Bo-Tsotsi*, chs. 4, 7, and pp. 189–90; Marks, *Young warriors*, pp. 44–5, 52, 62; Xaba in
Morrell, *Changing men*, pp. 112–20.

[75] South Africa, *Report of the Commission of Inquiry into the riots at Soweto and elsewhere* (2
vols., Pretoria, 1980), vol. 1, pp. 310–24; Nicholas Haysom, *Apartheid's private army: the rise
of right-wing vigilantes in South Africa* (London, 1986).

[76] Norma Kriger, 'The Zimbabwean war of liberation: struggle within the struggle,' *JSAS*, 14
(1987–8), 306–7; Greet Kershaw, *Mau Mau from below* (Oxford, 1997), pp. 237–41.

Namibia and South Africa – conducted brutal internal purges. The most powerful fictional reconstruction of guerilla warfare (based on personal experience), Artur Carlos Mauricio dos Santos' *Mayombe*, highlighted the ethnic tensions and distrust within the liberation forces, especially the *mestizo* intellectual's 'fear of feeling fear,' lest his comrades 'remember that I am not the same as the others.'[77] Such tensions could reach paranoia as security forces closed in. Ruben Um Nyobe, refusing guards for fear of betrayal, was instead given away by defectors. Dedan Kimathi, who tried to assert leadership over Mau Mau's forest bands and prevent piecemeal surrender, was betrayed by a fighter he had flogged for sleeping with a woman.[78] Many Mau Mau detainees long refused to cooperate with their captors, despite physical brutality and denial of release. Most eventually acquiesced, although a hard core at the Hola Prison Camp in 1959 held out while eleven were beaten to death, the survivors refusing even to identify the corpses.[79]

Courage and honour were tested most terribly by police torture in South Africa, where it was used not only to secure information but to intimidate. The subsequent Truth and Reconciliation Commission recorded 5,002 instances of torture.[80] Many were effective. 'The police ended up arresting me,' a nineteen-year-old former student activist explained before he was necklaced, 'they took me to the cells and they assaulted me and after assaulting us we spent a week in jail and at the end of that the police gave us uniforms and they gave us guns. . . . I thought that they would leave me alone.'[81] Others resisted. Mamagotla Paulina Mohale was arrested when trying to join the ANC in Swaziland. Beaten, subjected to electric shocks, drugged, threatened with being thrown from a tenth-floor window, and told that her arrested mother would be killed, she refused to identify photographs of students who had left the country for guerilla training. 'When I just heard the key unlocking the prison cell I just used to be so petrified,' she recalled. Tried and acquitted, she nevertheless suffered mental breakdown.[82] Several were driven insane. Some drew strength from a long history of defiance. Nobuhle Mohapi's husband, a Black Consciousness activist, died in police custody in 1976. As Steve Biko's secretary, she was herself arrested, held for six months in solitary confinement, beaten, and falsely

[77] 'Pepetela', *Mayombe* (trans. M. Wolfers, Oxford, 1996), pp. 201, 9.

[78] Um Nyobe, *Le problème*, pp. 428–9, 437; Lonsdale in Atieno Odhiambo and Lonsdale, *Mau Mau*, p. 65.

[79] Lennox-Boyd, 'Hola Detention Camp,' 2 June 1959, C(59)92, CAB 129/97; Gakaara wa Wanjau, *Mau Mau author in detention* (trans. P. N. Njoroge, Nairobi, 1988), pp. 35–49, 58, 74–85, 200–1.

[80] South Africa: TRC, *Report*, vol. 3, pp. 7, 597–8.

[81] Ibid., p. 668.

[82] Ibid., pp. 571–2.

told that her child was dead in an unsuccessful attempt to make her incriminate Biko. She recalled her husband's warning:

You must be strong, you must never show the police, especially the Boers that you are weak. They shouldn't see you crying because what they want every time, they want to see a person crying. They want to see that this pain that is inflicted on a person really has an effect. Every time show them your strong face.[83]

---

[83] South Africa: TRC, 'Proceedings,' vol. 2, p. 346; South Africa: TRC, *Report*, vol. 3, pp. 64–5.

18   Political Honour

The political behaviour of postcolonial African rulers continued to be influenced by inherited notions of honour, especially honour in its prideful aspect. Influence is all that is suggested. Survival, security, and interest were all more important political motives than honour, but rulers were nevertheless influenced by their ideas of what would entitle them to respect. These ideas were not necessarily honourable by contemporary Western criteria, making African political behaviour difficult for foreign observers to understand. This chapter considers the attitudes of the rulers; the next will deal with the ruled.

Whereas in earlier periods elements of heroic honour were absorbed into new ethics – militant Islam, Buganda's Christianity, mining culture, nationalism – when those elements were functional to new situations, the heroic legacy was essentially inimical to the stable democracy that most African states professed to seek at independence. Heroic notions encouraged excessive concern with appearances, unrestrained competition for personal supremacy, inflated importance of individuals as against institutions, display of wealth and power, refusal to compromise or accept defeat, intolerance of criticism, and willingness to employ violence. Democracy required the antitheses to all those qualities. To a limited degree, it found them in the alternative notions of householder honour and respectability. Yet democracy in postcolonial Africa failed to identify itself with the mainstream tradition of honour, much as it failed in interwar Japan, where the heirs to the samurai tradition found liberal democracy so shameful that they overthrew it. There was, however, a crucial difference between Japanese and African responses. In Japan the samurai tradition had been tamed and disciplined, so that its heirs criticised liberal democracy for its selfish and anarchic individualism.[1] In Africa, by contrast, colonial rule had failed to tame the heroic ethos, whose egotism found democratic principles confining rather than anarchic.

The chapter first describes the assertion of honour in international relations and national institutions. It then considers the influence of heroic legacies on political behaviour and attempts to counter that influence. After discussing corruption and changes in status ranking during the first generation of independence, the chapter examines military honour in African armies.

Victorious nationalists sought to assert their claim to racial respect in international affairs. 'For too long have we been kicked around; for too long have been treated like adolescents who cannot discern their interests and act accordingly,' Nigeria's military leader told the Organisation of African Unity in 1976 when successfully persuading it to unite against South African intervention in Angola. 'We were fully in the arena of Super Power confrontations on the issue of Angola,' a senior officer wrote with satisfaction.[2] Other assertions brought disillusionment. Simon Kapwepwe, Zambia's foreign minister during the mid 1960s, recorded his frustration in his diary. 'The Europeans still feel strongly that the Africans are subhuman and thus inferior to them,' he wrote during one Commonwealth Conference. More bitter still were setbacks like Nkrumah's deposition: 'I saw Africa going back politically where we started. In short this means Africa would be ruled by the West through the army.'[3] Yet Africa also had its triumphs. Julius Nyerere's ambition to liberate the entire continent from foreign rule within his lifetime was achieved.

Racial sensitivity and the concern for appearances characteristic of honour cultures might lead rulers to sacrifice their people's interests to national pride. Some refused to admit the existence of famine, 'a sign of self-respect vis-à-vis the international community,' as President Lamizana of Upper Volta described it in 1973. 'If we have to describe the situation the way you have in your report in order to generate international assistance,' an Ethiopian official told relief workers, 'then we don't want that assistance. The embarrassment to the government isn't worth it.'[4] A decade later, Ethiopia's military dictator, Mengistu

---

[1] See Japan Ministry of Education, 'The unique national polity' (1937) in Ivan Morris (ed.), *Japan, 1931–1945: militarism, fascism, Japanism* (Boston, 1963), pp. 46–52.

[2] Murtala Mohammed, 11 January 1976, in Olusegun Obasanjo, *Not my will* (Ibadan, 1990), p. 250; James J. Oluleye, *Military leadership in Nigeria, 1966–1979* (Ibadan, 1985), p. 177.

[3] Goodwin Mwangilwa (ed.), *The Kapwepwe diaries* (Lusaka, 1986), pp. 80, 66.

[4] Jonathan Derrick, 'The great West African drought, 1972–1974,' *African Affairs*, 76 (1977), 554; Jack Shepherd, *The politics of starvation* (New York, 1975), p. 33.

Haile Mariam, issued similar instructions during the worst famine of the late twentieth century:

He said that imperialist elements would do everything possible to thwart our efforts, to embarrass us, to destroy the gains of the revolution. One way of trying to embarrass us, he said, was by exploiting the drought. The menace in his voice was unmistakable. He told me that I had to be careful not to fall into their trap. My statement to the UN was inaccurate, exaggerated, he said; it showed Ethiopia in a bad light because it told only of disaster and nothing of governmental achievements or efforts to overcome the crisis. I had not emphasized that it was a natural disaster – a drought, not a famine.[5]

Mengistu's successor took the opposite course and sacrificed his pride to his people's welfare. There was similar diversity in responses to the AIDS epidemic. President Museveni of Uganda decided that a preventative campaign demanded maximum publicity, but leaders in Kenya, Botswana, Congo-Brazzaville, and elsewhere long remained silent, fearing for their own or their countries' dignity, while in South Africa President Mbeki's pride in the face of white criticism led him to prevaricate in much the same manner as his white predecessors.[6] Necessary devaluation of national currencies, similarly, might be resisted because, as a Nigerian leader explained, 'It does not give any prestige to the country.' Desire to impress foreign visitors bred ruthlessness towards the poor of capital cities.[7] Most damaging of all, but fortunately rare, was warfare to satisfy national prestige, notably that between Ethiopia and Eritrea in 1998–2000 in which between fifty thousand and one hundred thousand soldiers died over a strip of arid borderland left uncertain on colonial maps.[8]

Within their countries, too, victorious nationalists hastened to set their triumphs in stone – generally an independence monument in the capital's main square or, if liberation had required violence, a Heroes' Acre, where political leaders assembled for anniversary ceremonies. Schoolchildren were prominent at these occasions, for expanded education was the chief means by which governments sought to inculcate a national consciousness and a national (generally colonial) language. Together with party youth wings and national service corps for adolescents, the schools also sought to channel heroic traditions into public

[5] Dawit Wolde Giorgis, *Red tears: war, famine and revolution in Ethiopia* (Trenton, N.J., 1989), pp. 155–6.

[6] Iliffe, *Doctors*, pp. 223, 231; Didier Fassin, 'Le domaine privé de la santé publique: pouvoir, politique et sida au Congo,' *Annales E.S.C.*, 49 (1994), 759–62; Louis Grundlingh, 'Government responses to HIV/AIDS in South Africa as reported in the media, 1983–1994,' *SAHJ*, 45 (November 2001), 124–53; Anthony Brink, *Debating AZT: Mbeki and the AIDS drug controversy* (Pietermaritzburg, 2000), pp. 70–5.

[7] Kingsley Ozuomba Mbadiwe, *Rebirth of a nation (autobiography)* (Enugu, 1991), p. 254; Iliffe, *Poor*, pp. 248–9.

[8] Tekeste Negash and Kjetil Tronvoll, *Brothers at war* (Oxford, 2000), pp. 23–4, 53.

service. Little is known about the impact of this indoctrination, but national languages spread very widely, and by the 1990s there were indications of strong if elemental popular nationalism, expressed in the idolisation of national football teams and, more cruelly, in the xenophobia that peaked in Kinshasa in 1998 when townspeople helped to repel advancing Rwandan troops and then took a terrible revenge on available Tutsi.[9] Liberation heroes themselves, by contrast, often felt forgotten, not least because their actions had frequently been divisive. Kenyatta's Independence Day speech did not mention Mau Mau. Cameroun's conservative regime virtually outlawed mention of the UPC. Even Zimbabwe's freedom fighters, whose leaders had taken power, received little help in adjusting to peace. Eight years after independence some thirty thousand were thought to be unemployed, and they regained official favour only when mobilised to cow a yet younger generation.[10]

Most independent regimes devised Western-style honours systems: Nigeria's Order of the Federal Republic and Order of the Niger, Gabon's Equatorial Star, Malawi's Order of the Lion, the Congo Democratic Republic's Order of the Leopard. Conservatives preferred older distinctions. Ahmadu Bello presented each member of his first cabinet with a horse. Chieftaincy titles in West Africa were never in greater demand, Moshood Abiola reputedly amassing over one hundred fifty before he won Nigeria's abortive presidential election of 1993.[11] The best way to legitimise any project in the years after independence was to claim that it revived an African tradition, as Nyerere demonstrated when advocating socialism to Tanzanians.[12] The projects themselves, however, gained prestige by displaying modernity. Almost every regime had its prestige projects: the Volta Dam in Ghana, the Yamoussoukro basilica in Côte d'Ivoire, the Trans-Gabon railway to President Bongo's natal village. 'Build beautiful, big, and forever!' an Ivoirian minister decreed in 1963. Many regimes spent massively on display. Jean-Bedel Bokassa's coronation as emperor of Central Africa cost some $22 million. Sierra Leone's budget for an OAU summit meeting was nearly ten times as much. 'I endeavoured to boost the image of Nigeria in New York,' Kingsley Mbadiwe recalled, 'by throwing a dinner party for distinguished members of the world body at the Waldorf Astoria

[9] Gauthier de Villers and Jean Omasombo Tshonda, 'La bataille de Kinshasa,' *Politique Africaine*, 84 (December 2001), 17–20, 26.

[10] Norma J. Kriger, 'The politics of creating national heroes,' in Bhebe and Ranger, *Soldiers*, p. 156.

[11] Whitaker, *Politics of tradition*, p. 350; Ebere Nwaubani, 'Chieftaincy among the Igbo: a guest on the center-stage,' *IJAHS*, 27 (1994), 347, 364–70; Karl Maier, *This house has fallen: Nigeria in crisis* (London, 2000), p. 27.

[12] Nyerere, *'Ujamaa* – the basis of African socialism' (1962) in his *Freedom and unity*, pp. 162–71.

during the sitting of the United Nations Assembly. That was how to achieve greatness.'[13]

Respectability probably aided stable democracy, if as only a secondary factor. In Botswana, the continent's most successful democracy, the political elite possessed traditions of public debate and accountable civilian chieftainship further domesticated by Victorian Protestantism, although Botswana's political success owed more to its ethnic homogeneity and diamond wealth.[14] Senegal, another stable and relatively democratic state, also had the advantage of homogeneity, while against its tradition of aristocratic honour and its widespread corruption it could set an Islamic legacy of dignified sobriety captured by the presidential praise-singers:

> Yes, you went the [right] way, Diouf . . .
> What makes a man is courage and seriousness . . .
> They are shouting, but you keep your dignity.
> They are shouting, but you keep your calmness.
> It is by calmness that you can rule a country.[15]

By contrast with these traditions of respectability, however, Côte d'Ivoire, a one-party state under Houphouet-Boigny until 1993 but a stable and open society, had precolonial notions of honour either of the vertical kind found in Asante or of the horizontal variety common in competitive stateless societies. Its stability and liberalism came instead from Houphouet-Boigny's political style, which was that of the wise elder, dissipating conflict by astute mediation, creating manifold outlets for individual ambition, and dispensing both generous patronage and humane paternalism. Houphouet was a singularly unheroic figure, 'a little man at the head of a little state,' as he once described himself.[16]

Elsewhere the heroic style of leadership was a major obstacle to stable democracy. The style had emerged from the needs of nationalist movements and survived as a response to the frailty of the new states. Nkrumah, as ever, led the way. Having survived with difficulty the challenge of Asante's regionalism, he took steps immediately after independence to politicise the provincial

---

[13] Michael A. Cohen, *Urban policy and political conflict in Africa* (Chicago, 1974), p. 34; Brian Titley, *Dark age: the political odyssey of Emperor Bokassa* ([Liverpool], 1997), p. 91; William Reno, *Corruption and state politics in Sierra Leone* (Cambridge, 1995), p. 137; Mbadiwe, *Rebirth*, p. 177.

[14] See Patrick P. Molutsi and John D. Holm, 'Developing democracy when civil society is weak: the case of Botswana,' *African Affairs*, 89 (1990), 323–40.

[15] Panzacchi, 'Livelihoods,' p. 205.

[16] *West Africa*, 21 October 1985, p. 2191.

administration, expand the intelligence services, destroy the autonomy of chiefs, and create a one-party state. His deposition by the army in 1966 checked his career well short of tyranny, but Sekou Toure of Guinea, a more brutal man in a less sophisticated country, survived another eighteen years and over twenty supposed conspiracies to create what his successors accurately called a 'bloody and ruthless dictatorship.'[17] Perhaps the most enduring and typical of the new authoritarian regimes was created not by a nationalist politician but by a former sergeant in the French colonial army, Gnassingbe Eyadema, who claimed to have shot Togo's first president in 1963, seized power himself in 1967, and still held it thirty-seven years later. Like most rulers of military origin, Eyadema quickly adopted a civilian, more paternal image, but his power rested on an army recruited largely from his fellow Kabre people, a single party that long monopolised political expression, a network of informers, and the liberal use of torture. He also elaborated an extravagantly heroic personality cult. The assassination of 1963, unplanned and probably carried out when the assassin was inebriated, was converted into a liberation from tyranny. His escape from an aeroplane accident became a divine deliverance from imperialist conspiracy. (Pilgrims to the plane's carefully preserved wreckage declared, 'Eyadema the brave, the Great God is with you.') Eyademaism – the veneration of his patriotism and the codification of his ideas – was taught as national ideology. The hero himself, depicted in statues in all important towns, required even his ministers to display abject servility. While living modestly and maintaining ties with Kabre village society, he dispensed lavish largess.[18]

The accumulation, display, and distribution of wealth – 'the quest for aristocratic effect'[19] – remained central elements of heroic style. Wealth was widely believed to demonstrate both probity and the power to ward off envy. 'I have billions abroad, in Switzerland, but I also have billions in the Ivory Coast, which proves I have confidence in my country,' Houphouet-Boigny assured his followers. Poverty, by contrast, commonly suggested not integrity but indolence. 'Kaggia, what have you done for yourself?' Kenyatta rounded on a former comrade turned radical critic. Many did well for themselves. President Siaka Stevens of Sierra Leone – 'Fountain Head of Unity, Honour, Freedom and Justice,' as his title proclaimed – built himself an ostentatious hilltop palace which he sold to the government and then received back as a present from

---

[17] Richard Rathbone, *Nkrumah and the chiefs: the politics of chieftaincy in Ghana, 1951–60* (Oxford, 2000), ch. 8; Robert H. Jackson and Carl G. Rosberg, *Personal rule in black Africa* (Berkeley, 1982), pp. 208–19; *West Africa*, 9 April 1984, p. 756.

[18] This account is based on Comi M. Toulabor, *Le Togo sous Eyadéma* (Paris, 1986).

[19] Ali Mazrui, quoted in Le Vine, *Political corruption*, p. 88.

a grateful public.[20] Wealth in itself attracted honour, but doubly so if generously distributed. Nkrumah accumulated perhaps half a million pounds by illicit means but was remembered by the poor of Accra for his generosity in dispensing jobs and favours, invariably at public expense. Mengistu celebrated his occupation of Ethiopia's royal palace by a feast for the poor in the manner of past emperors. His instinct was accurate: critics of Congo-Brazzaville's austere President Massamba-Débat complained that he did not dress well enough for a president, whereas his predecessor, the Abbé Fulbert Youlou, had supposedly bought his *soutanes* from Christian Dior.[21] Youlou had lived with an official mistress, a statement of virility of the kind that earned kudos for other autocrats like Eyadema and Bokassa. By contrast, a later ruler of Congo-Brazzaville, Denis Sassou-Nguesso, was widely considered effeminate and lacking in courage to seize and exercise power. His long tenure was attributed instead to command of sorcery, a reputation especially common among leaders in western Equatorial Africa.[22] And behind all these attributes lay the violence that was an integral element of the hero's power, whether in the hands of cold manipulators like Mobutu of the Congo and Mugabe of Zimbabwe or crude militarists like Bokassa or Amin of Uganda.

Nevertheless, heroic autocracy was not the only alternative to political frailty. Genuine heroes like Mandela did not resort to it. Nor did Julius Nyerere of Tanzania, whose distaste for heroic honour owed something to the householder values of his stateless society but perhaps more to mission Christianity, secular Western socialism, and the Swahili ideal of *heshima*.[23] Personally modest and austere, he ridiculed the emerging heroic style:

Whenever I have questioned the value of all this very undemocratic pomposity, I have been assured that 'the people like it.' But this is highly doubtful. . . . Do they really love being shouted at to get off the road because the President, or a Minister, or a Regional Commissioner, is taking an afternoon drive? . . .

We should stop deceiving ourselves. This sort of pomposity has nothing to do with the people, for it is the very reverse of democratic. We must stop it. We must begin to

---

[20] Patrick Chabal, *Power in Africa* (Basingstoke, 1992), p. 215; *West Africa*, 9 May 1983, p. 1142; M. Tamarkin, 'The roots of political stability in Kenya,' *African Affairs*, 77 (1978), 312; Reno, *Corruption*, p. 143.

[21] Ghana, *Report of the Commission appointed . . . to enquire into the properties of Kwame Nkrumah* (Accra-Tema, [1967]), pp. 3–12, 17–22, 68; Richard Sandbrook and Jack Arn, *The labouring poor and urban class formation: the case of Greater Accra* (Montreal, 1977), p. 62; René Lefort, *Ethiopie: la révolution hérétique* (Paris, 1981), p. 382; Rémy Bazenguissa-Ganga, *Les voies du politique au Congo: essai de sociologie historique* (Paris, 1997), pp. 71, 103.

[22] Bazenguissa, *Les voies*, pp. 68, 268, 324; Toulabor, *Le Togo*, p. 304; Titley, *Dark age*, p. 51; Marc-Eric Gruénais, Florent Mouanda Mbambi, and Joseph Tonda, 'Messies, fétiches et lutte de pouvoirs entre les "grands hommes" du Congo démocratique,' *CEA*, 35 (1995), 163–93.

[23] This volume, pp. 33, 110.

7. *Mobutu*, as seen by P. Moke in 1975. Reproduced by permission of the Syndics of Cambridge University Library.

treat pomposity with the scorn it deserves. Dignity does not need pomposity to uphold it; and pomposity in all its forms is a wrong. Even if it were proved that the people really did enjoy it – which I very much doubt – it would still be a wrong; and as such it would still be our duty to put a stop to it, and to tell the people that what they had learned to enjoy was wrong.[24]

---

[24] Nyerere, 'Pomposity' (1963) in his *Freedom and unity*, p. 226.

Tanzania's leadership code of 1967 sought to prevent the accumulation of private wealth that was taking place elsewhere. Nyerere's dislike of violence and corruption, discussed later in this chapter, belonged to the same critique. His *ujamaa* programme of rural socialism attacked the emergence of local Big Men.[25] In international affairs, likewise, Nyerere despised display and empty bravado, insisting in 1965 on complying with a grandiloquent OAU resolution calling on African states to sever relations with Britain if it failed to end white Rhodesia's unilateral declaration of independence. 'Do African states meet in solemn conclave to make a noise? Or do they mean what they say?' Nyerere demanded:

If we ignore our own resolution, neither our suffering brethren in Rhodesia, in Mozambique, in Angola, in South Africa, in South West Africa, nor the broad masses of the people of Africa, or for that matter the non-African members of the United Nations Organization could ever trust Africa to honour a pledge solemnly undertaken by Africa's leaders. Smith will rejoice; Verwoerd will rejoice; Salazar will rejoice. Where can we hide ourselves for shame?

We are not proposing to break diplomatic relations with Britain because we wish to do so; we shall do it only if it becomes necessary for our own honour, for the honour of Africa.[26]

The decision cost Tanzania £7.5 million in British aid. Only four other countries severed relations and Africa lost credibility.[27] The radicalism of Nyerere's critique of the honour culture was often overlooked because he concealed it beneath legitimising appeals to 'tradition'. But it was clear enough to his uninhibited Ugandan neighbour, General Amin, who offered to marry him.

The impact of heroic ideas on post-independence politics extended beyond presidential pomposity. Given the weakness of new institutions, these regimes were governments of men and not of laws, polities in which personal rivalries and ambitions were pursued with a full-blooded panache which explained the African taste for Shakespeare. Vanity and pique, especially in generational relationships, were common motives for political action, in which the winner invariably took all. To survive defeat was almost as difficult for a modern politician as for an Asante general. Defeat was therefore seldom admitted. Parties anticipating it commonly boycotted elections. If they contested and lost, they denounced the poll as rigged, challenged the results, or refused to take their seats. 'My people must not be humiliated,' Jonas Savimbi declared when rejecting defeat in Angola's 1992 election.[28] After Shehu Shagari's installation

---

[25] Nyerere, *Freedom and socialism*, pp. 249, 342–5; this volume, p. 337.

[26] Nyerere, 'The honour of Africa' (1965) in his *Freedom and socialism*, pp. 128–30.

[27] Andrew Coulson, *Tanzania: a political economy* (Oxford, 1982), p. 143.

[28] *West Africa*, 28 December 1992, p. 2237.

as president of Nigeria in 1979, opposition parties used their regional power to frustrate even those central government policies beneficial to their regions. His presidency repeatedly demonstrated the incompatibility between democracy and an honour culture with strong heroic traditions, but he had been elected only because his opponents refused to give way to one another in order to mount united opposition.[29] Politics, as an Ethiopian explained, 'is not the art of compromise but of victory.' It was also the art of humiliation. 'In Nigeria, once you fail, you are beaten by your successful opponent until you can get up no more,' a journalist reflected. Mockery, scatological abuse, and violence were common weapons. Only when further resistance was plainly impossible could reconciliation take place, as it did when the Nigerian Civil War ended in 1970.[30]

Where personal ambition was unconstrained, the problem was to harness it to state service. Asante had done so by encouraging the pursuit of wealth in gold, which the state could reward or confiscate. Postcolonial Big Men similarly combined political office and personal accumulation, not simply to acquire wealth – this was not just 'the politics of the belly'[31] – but to gain social honour. As a Kenyan novelist put it, 'The rich yearn for respect and popularity just like the poor yearn for riches.' Successful businessmen sought political office, married their daughters into notable families, and bought chieftaincy titles. Politicians and civil servants used their offices to launch private enterprises, often with official encouragement.[32] Both legitimised their wealth and power by philanthropy and patronage. Moshood Abiola, newspaper tycoon become Nigerian presidential candidate, granted over 1,000 scholarships, made donations to all federal and state universities, and financed the successful Abiola Babes football club. Kenneth Matiba, former permanent secretary and brewing magnate become Kenyan presidential candidate, patronised the equally successful Kenya Breweries team.[33] Their clientelist style was best illustrated by the Kenyan *harambee* (let us pull together), the fund-raising meeting for some local development project to which notables and ordinary citizens were expected to

[29] Shagari, *Beckoned*, ch. 8.

[30] Andargachew Tiruneh, *The Ethiopian revolution, 1974–1987* (Cambridge, 1993), p. 155; *Newswatch*, 25 February 2002, p. 13; Achille Mbembe, 'Provisional notes on the postcolony,' *Africa*, 62 (1992), 3–37; John de St. Jorre, *The Nigerian Civil War* (London, 1972), p. 407.

[31] Jean-François Bayart, *The state in Africa: the politics of the belly* (trans. M. Harper, C. Harrison, and E. Harrison, London, 1993).

[32] John Kiriamiti, *Son of fate* (Nairobi, 1994), p. 166; Bayart, *State*, ch. 6; Jean-François Médard, 'Le "Big Man" en Afrique: esquisse d'analyse du politicien entrepreneur,' *L'Année Sociologique*, 42 (1992), 167–92.

[33] *West Africa*, 12 April 1993, p. 590; Akpabot, *Football in Nigeria*, pp. 56–7; David W. Throup and Charles Hornsby, *Multi-party politics in Kenya: the kenyatta and Moi states and the triumph of the system in the 1992 election* (Oxford, 1998), p. 34; Versi, *Football*, p. 124.

contribute in proportion to wealth and rank, much as Asante chiefs had contributed to the funeral customs of their subjects. *Harambee* was in fact the modern equivalent of Asante's gold in binding private ambition to public welfare. At one *harambee* in aid of Nairobi schools in 1980, for example, President Moi donated Shs.145,100 'from himself and friends,' the local M.P. contributed Shs.245,530 'from himself and friends,' another local politician supplied five hectares of land, the mayor gave Shs.10,440, and the attorney-general added Shs.10,000. The total collected was Shs.4,738,200.[34] A newspaper estimated that, during the exceptionally extravagant election year of 1992, Moi gave £40 million to various causes. Côte d'Ivoire's urban elite invested similarly in their natal villages because it 'touches on their honour.'[35]

Such clientelist relationships were the core of politics during the first generation of independence. For most ordinary people the locality was the important political unit. It needed a patron, a representative at the centre with the skills and contacts to secure its share of the national cake. 'You must have a Cabinet Minister so that when the meat is being cut you are seen. . . . Otherwise you will chew bones,' a Kenyan parliamentarian (and archbishop) warned his followers.[36] So long as the patron fulfilled his side of the bargain, he was not grudged wealth, deference, or votes, but this was not simply manipulation of the poor by the rich. It was a reciprocal relationship between elites and vigorous peasant societies that judged their representatives by harsh standards of performance. 'The electorate torment you with demands because they voted for you,' grumbled a Nigerian minister who claimed to see seven hundred people a day.[37] Peasant communities often welcomed the one-party states predominant until the 1990s because party competition divided communities and was widely seen as vulgar, especially in hierarchical societies like Hausaland or Buganda.[38] But when the urban-based democratisation movements of the 1990s took multiparty politics to the countryside, candidates and constituents adapted effortlessly:

Under a large mango tree a crowd waits. Suddenly a 4-by-4 draws up amidst the applause of the villagers. In a stentorian voice a young man intones a song to the glory of the illustrious guest, man of property, son of good family, worthy representative of the region in the National Assembly. The man descends from his vehicle, essays a few dance steps. Acclamation! Women run up. Some spread out their cloths in his path, others cover him

[34] *Sunday Standard*, 28 September 1980. See also François Grignon and Hervé Maupeu, 'Les aléas du contrat social kényan,' *Politique Africaine*, 70 (June 1998), 4–5.

[35] Throup and Hornsby, *Multi-party politics*, p. 358; Vidal, *Sociologie*, p. 118.

[36] Archbishop Stephen Ondiek, in *The People* (Nairobi), 11 December 1994.

[37] Tom Forrest, *Politics and economic development in Nigeria* (Boulder, 1995), p. 75.

[38] William Miles, *Elections in Nigeria* (Boulder, 1988), pp. 64–75; Mikael Karlström, 'Imagining democracy: political culture and democratisation in Buganda,' *Africa*, 66 (1996), 494–8.

with them. 'The honourable deputy' takes out a wad of banknotes. 500 franc CFA notes 'salute' foreheads. The man is retrieved by the village chief who leads him into a house before returning to take their seats amidst the cheers of the audience. Visibly satisfied, the chief announces that the guest has just given 100,000 francs CFA and something 'to moisten the throat'. Hurrah! People sing, drink, thank. Leaflets bearing the party symbol are distributed to all present, who promise to vote for this deputy, worthy of his glorious ancestors.

That very day the village has received five delegations from different political parties. Four have been 'polite'. Hands on their hearts, the villagers have promised to vote for each of the four parties. The fifth delegation was found a little mean.[39]

Corruption raised many issues of honour. Originating in the generalised gift-exchange of personalised societies, it had survived with them into the twentieth century but had been denounced as bribery by Muslim reformers and colonial governments when the gift had sought a specific reciprocal favour. After the Second World War, greater bureaucracy, monetisation, and social scale exacerbated the problem. A commission reported in 1948 that every African interviewed in the Gold Coast had said that corruption was common. In Nigeria, especially, party competition demanded funds that politicians could acquire only by mis-using office.[40] Independence vastly reinforced these tendencies. In the extreme case of the Democratic Republic of the Congo in 1971, an estimated 60 per cent of the annual budget was not spent on its official purpose. Uganda's auditor-general reckoned the proportion misused in the late 1990s at between 10 and 20 per cent.[41] Yet these figures were only tips of icebergs, for the corruption most affecting ordinary people was routine extortion by low-level personnel. A Kenyan survey during the early 1990s showed that the lower a person's education, the greater his expectation of having to pay a bribe in order to obtain employment. Two-thirds of users questioned in Uganda in 1998 said they had paid bribes to the police, and one-half had paid bribes to the judiciary. Kinshasa had professional bribe-payers.[42]

[39] Jérôme-Adjakou Badou, describing an election meeting in Bénin in 1995, quoted in Richard Banégas, 'Marchandisation du vote, citoyenneté et consolidation démocratique au Bénin,' *Politique Africaine*, 69 (March 1998), 77.

[40] Le Vine, *Political corruption*, p. 12; S. O. Osoba, 'Corruption in Nigeria: historical perspectives,' *Review of African Political Economy*, 69 (1996), 371–4.

[41] J. P. Peemans, 'The social and economic development of Zaire since independence,' *African Affairs*, 74 (1975), 162; David Watt, Richard Flanary, and Robin Theobald, 'Democratisation or the democratisation of corruption? The case of Uganda,' *Journal of Commonwealth and Comparative Politics*, 37 (1999), 37.

[42] Kivutha Kibwana, Smokin Wanjala, and Okech-Owiti (eds.), *The anatomy of corruption in Kenya* (Nairobi, 1996), p. 84; Watt and others, 'Democratisation,' p. 46; Kempe Ronald Hope, Sr., and Bornwell C. Chikulo (eds.), *Corruption and development in Africa: lessons from country case-studies* (Basingstoke, 2000), p. 27.

At the higher levels, one reason for greater corruption after 1950 was that the scale of funds available to African power-holders was beyond previous imagination. 'It was ... quite a shattering revelation to me,' Siaka Stevens recalled of his ministerial apprenticeship,

to find that many foreigners who visited me practised our 'shake-hand' with a vengeance, offering what to my mind represented a positive fortune. ... When I was finally left alone to collect my thoughts and decide what action I had to take, all I could think about was how on earth anybody could afford to give away so much money.

Stevens hesitated only briefly before taking the money, repeatedly.[43] Foreign investment and aid both encouraged peculation. Nkrumah instructed his cabinet in 1956 to levy between a 5 and 10 per cent commission on all government contracts to finance the CPP, a task handled routinely by the National Development Corporation. Marketing Board funds were also channelled to the CPP and, as 'loans', to some fifteen thousand supporters. Western Nigeria's Action Group appropriated nearly £4 million from this source. Politicians awarded contracts to their own companies, allocated themselves import or distribution licences for scarce goods, used their political influence to 'borrow' from commercial banks, or voted themselves extravagant 'expenses'. During the 1970s Sierra Leone collected less than 2 per cent of assessed income tax.[44]

'Harambee is at the root of the vicious cycle of corruption which bedevils the country,' a Kenyan wrote in 1998. The sums expected at such meetings could indeed be raised only by illegal means. Yet open electoral competition was equally expensive, especially where parties were not divided by principle or interest. Whereas in the late 1950s a Nigerian parliamentary contest might cost a candidate between £2,000 and £4,000, an arms-dealer with presidential aspirations told a London court, no doubt with exaggeration, that the Senate seat he won in 1983 cost £8,500,000.[45] He held it for about four months before the army intervened. Others invested more wisely but still heavily. Kenya's ruling party is thought to have inflated the national money supply by about 30 per cent in order to win the vital 1992 election. Ghana's two annual government deficits during the 1990s coincided with election years.[46]

---

[43] Siaka Stevens, *What life has taught me* (Bourne End, 1984), p. 162; Governor's Deputy to S of S, 27 March 1960, CO 554/2232/1.

[44] Ghana, *Report ... Kwame Nkrumah*, pp. 13–15; Le Vine, *Political corruption*, pp. 31–2; Björn Beckman, *Organising the farmers* (Uppsala, 1976), p. 62; Sklar, *Nigerian parties*, p. 458; *Africa*, October 1980, p. 43.

[45] T. M. Mboya in *EastAfrican*, 30 November 1998; Sklar, *Nigerian parties*, p. 29; *West Africa*, 23 February 1987, p. 354.

[46] Throup and Hornsby, *Multi-party politics*, p. 353; Ernest Aryeetey, Jane Harrigan, and Machiko Nissanke (eds.), *Economic reforms in Ghana* (Oxford, 2000), pp. 13, 15.

If the cost of politics stimulated high-level corruption, the cost of living imposed it at the lower level. The real salary of a senior civil servant in Zambia fell by 78 per cent during the decade after 1976, while the highest pay earned by any Congolese official early in 1997 was worth six American dollars a month.[47] Public servants had little option but to exploit opportunities for corruption. These multiplied, for not only did state regulation and bureaucratic staffing expand massively, but the expansion also bred administrative confusion, which facilitated corruption and made it especially difficult to remedy, because honest officials might be victimised by colleagues or superiors. 'Everybody started to chop money, chop cars, chop stores, and those who didn't chop and said it was unlawful were soon sacked,' a senior Ghanaian explained. 'So I learned my lessons and chopped without worry, for myself and my brothers.' In extreme cases like Sierra Leone, as debt repayment drained wealth from the bureaucratic state, an illicit 'shadow state' of personal relationships emerged to serve the interests of power-holders.[48]

Behind corruption lay attitudes and relationships appropriate to small-scale societies with honour cultures but surviving into larger, richer, less personalised, independent states. The principles of clientage were widely seen to legitimise the misappropriation of money and jobs for distribution amongst dependents. When seven tax-collectors embezzled 3.5 billion francs CFA from the Senegalese treasury in 1999, scandal dissipated 'as soon as they distinguished themselves by their generosity and largess.' Not to reward dependents might be seen as folly or selfishness, just as refusal to 'give kola' when seeking a service might appear to be bad manners.[49] As in politics, therefore, much of the impetus towards corruption came from below. The incorruptible President Shagari 'found the pressures from job-seekers, their advocates, ethnic interests, and groups within the [ruling parties] indescribably oppressive.' So did a young magistrate in Niger:

The temptation is not only with regard to the magistrates, it is first in the mind of the accused. In my nine or ten months of experience I have made the bitter discovery that, in the minds of the people, justice is to be bought. . . . Thus nobody is imprisoned whose family does not come to offer you something.[50]

[47] Hope and Chikulo, *Corruption*, p. 21; *AIDS Analysis Africa*, August 1997.

[48] Le Vine, *Political corruption*, p. 45; Reno, *Corruption*, pp. 1–4.

[49] Margaret Peil, *Nigerian politics: the people's view* (London, 1976), pp. 49, 58, 64; Giorgio Blundo and Jean-Pierre Olivier de Sardan, 'Le corruption quotidienne en Afrique de l'ouest,' *Politique Africaine*, 83 (October 2001), 19; J. P. Olivier de Sardan, 'A moral economy of corruption in Africa?' *JMAS*, 37 (1999), 39.

[50] Shagari, *Beckoned*, p. 239; Mahaman Tidjani Alou, 'La justice au plus offrant,' *Politique Africaine*, 83 (October 2001), 64–5.

Poverty strengthened the compulsion. 'We have to bribe because we are poor,' a South African migrant labourer said of his illicit liquor business: '. . . The blackjacks [policemen] understand when you diza [bribe] them.' In oppressive societies, corruption could become defiance, as in General Amin's Uganda. More generally it was dignified by euphemisms implying cunning – to 'eat' or 'win' or 'fix' – and justified in the language of the old honour code: to recover one's due, enjoy the privileges of rank, confer favour, redistribute wealth, or benefit one's friends.[51]

Yet this legitimising ethos coexisted with moral condemnation by world religions and European notions of propriety. The result was much ambivalence and hypocrisy. During the last years of colonial rule, for example, nationalist ministers with vast opportunities for peculation had to observe, at least outwardly, an alien code of official behaviour. The *cause célèbre* of the period, the Foster-Sutton Tribunal of 1956, found Nnamdi Azikiwe, pioneer nationalist and premier of Eastern Nigeria, 'guilty of misconduct as a Minister' in failing to relinquish his financial interest in a bank into which his government channelled public money, although the enquiry also revealed that Azikiwe and his colleagues had gone to considerable lengths to appear to follow British rules of ministerial behaviour.[52] Azikiwe responded to the verdict by appealing to the electorate, winning a resounding victory, and, when opportunity presented itself, launching another enquiry, which found that the rival Action Group had acted even more improperly. European notions of probity were most commonly used in this way to criticise opponents. Nkrumah's successors appointed over forty commissions to discredit his regime. Hypocrisy surrounded the whole issue. 'The sooner we take firm and decisive steps to eradicate this scourge the healthier will our society become,' proclaimed Siaka Stevens, who created Sierra Leone's shadow state and died owning at least seventeen houses.[53]

Yet, as with the heroic style of political behaviour, there were also serious critics. Among individuals, Martin Shikuku of Kenya condemned corruption throughout his political career at the cost of poverty and exclusion from office, while Maurice Nyagumbo killed himself when implicated in a Harare housing

---

[51] Makhoba, *The sun shall rise*, p. 6; Rachel Flanary and David Watt, 'The state of corruption: a case study of Uganda,' *Third World Quarterly*, 20 (1999), 521; Giorgio Blundo and Jean-Pierre Olivier de Sardan, 'Sémiologie populaire de la corruption,' *Politique Africaine*, 83 (October 2001), 98–114.

[52] Great Britain, *Report of the Tribunal . . . on the official conduct of the Premier of . . . the Eastern Region of Nigeria* (Cmd. 51), PP, 1956–7, X, 682; 'Tribunal of Inquiry, Lagos: evidence, day XVI,' 5 October 1956, pp. 106–8, CO 554/1455.

[53] Robert L. Tignor, 'Political corruption in Nigeria before independence,' *JMAS*, 31 (1993), 196; Le Vine, *Political corruption*, p. xi; Stevens, *What life*, p. 164; Reno, *Corruption*, p. 4; *West Africa*, 6 September 1993, p. 1591.

scandal.[54] At the official level, the most determined opponent of corruption was, predictably, Nyerere, who believed that it 'should be treated in almost the same way as you treat treason' and had considerable success in restraining it by propaganda and legal penalties during his first twenty years in office.[55] In Nigeria both Abubakar Tafawa Balewa and Shehu Shagari, although dedicated Muslims and personally incorrupt, totally failed to contain the problem. Hastings Banda, uniquely, restrained corruption at the popular level while practising it massively himself.[56] The most effective anticorruption programme was in Botswana, which established a Directorate on Corruption and Economic Crime modelled on Hong Kong's draconian procedures, with some one hundred staff and extensive legal powers.[57] Although several countries created institutions with similar objectives, none had remotely comparable resources or impact. Instead, economic crises and waning state power sapped the moral impetus even of reforming regimes. By the late 1970s, corruption was spreading rapidly in Tanzania. 'The whole nation is stinking,' Nyerere fumed in 1995. Banda's fall in 1994 made corruption 'a way of life' in Malawi. Museveni's regime in Uganda, which seized power in 1986 promising revolutionary probity, sank within a decade into generalised corruption, not least because international agencies demanded a privatisation programme creating irresistible opportunities for fraud. This was the general experience: in African circumstances the economic liberalisation of the 1990s, like political pluralism, only intensified the problem.[58]

The corruption of the liberalising 1990s was only one aspect of a harsher materialism that reordered the honour ranking of social categories. Those least affected were traditional rulers. Radical governments had abolished their offices, while those who survived elsewhere had often clashed with centralising nationalist or military regimes. Kingdoms had fallen in Uganda and Burundi. Yet rulers proved remarkably resilient in retaining the respect of their subjects. In 1981 a mob murdered a state official who had the effrontery to issue an ultimatum to

---

[54] Médard, 'Le "Big Man",' p. 185; *Weekly Review*, 28 April 1989.

[55] Nyerere, 'Corruption as an enemy of the people' (1960) in his *Freedom and unity*, p. 82.

[56] Jonathan Kydd, 'Malawi in the 1970s: development policies and economic change,' in K. J. McCracken (ed.), *Malawi: an alternative pattern of development* (Edinburgh, 1985), pp. 308–10, 320–8.

[57] Robin Theobald and Robert Williams, 'Combating corruption in Botswana,' *Journal of Commonwealth and Comparative Politics*, 37 (1999), 117–34.

[58] *Daily News*, 12 July 1995; Martin Ott, Kings M. Phiri, and Nandini Patel (eds.), *Malawi's second democratic elections* (Blantyre, 2000), pp. 17, 105–6; Watt and others, 'Democratisation,' pp. 49–58; Bornwell C. Chikulo, 'Corruption and accumulation in Zambia,' in Hope and Chikulo, *Corruption*, ch. 8.

the emir of Kano. Where central power disintegrated, as in the Democratic Republic of Congo, chiefs frequently regained local power, while other regimes, which could no longer claim credit for political liberation or economic success, were eager to ally with influential notables. Ghana's 1992 constitution restored chiefs' rights to hold public office and removed the government's power to veto their election. A year later Museveni's regime, grateful for Ganda support in its civil war, restored the Kabakaship. Even among the hitherto stateless Igbo the Nigerian government's desire for local allies and the communities' desire for effective representatives gave unprecedented influence to newly created 'traditional rulers' who constructed palaces, accumulated harems, invented festivals, and made red exclusively the colour of royalty.[59]

By contrast, the main victims of harsher materialism were the educated professionals who had enjoyed the highest status among commoners at independence. 'The myth of the intellectual', incarnated in Senegal's academician-president Senghor, was undermined by soldiers and street politicians before it was destroyed by inflation and the collapse of professional monopolies. None suffered more than the Western-trained doctors, the 'cream of the cream' among the late colonial elite but now demonised in public eyes by deteriorating health systems, reduced to striking for living wages in defiance of professional honour, and marginalised by competing paramedics and commercial medicine-sellers. By 1996 the entrance requirements for the Makerere Medical School in Uganda were lower than those for the more profitable course in pharmacy.[60] Schoolteachers suffered similar loss of status and allegedly revenged themselves physically upon their pupils. By 2000 a police constable in Cameroun earned as much as a university professor. The democratisation movements of the 1990s were in part attempts by professionals to regain their lost leadership.[61] The prominent role in them taken by clergymen from historic churches – every francophone national conference was chaired by a Catholic prelate – witnessed another declining status-group seeking to recover its position. Traditional Islamic teachers, partly marginalised by state education systems, similarly

[59] Vaughan, *Nigerian chiefs*, pp. 172, 174, 195–200, 210; Filip De Boeck, 'Postcolonialism, power and identity: local and global perspectives from Zaire,' in Werbner and Ranger, *Postcolonial identities*, pp. 82–8; Rathbone, *Nkrumah*, pp. 163–4; Karlström, 'Imagining democracy,' p. 487; Nwaubani, 'Chieftaincy,' pp. 366–71.

[60] Jean-François Havard, 'Ethos "bul faale" et nouvelles figures de la réussite au Sénégal,' *Politique Africaine*, 82 (June 2001), 63–4; Iliffe, *Doctors*, chs. 7–9 (esp. p. 165); S. Ogoh Alubo, 'The political economy of doctors' strikes in Nigeria,' *Social Science and Medicine*, 22 (1986), 467–77.

[61] *EastAfrican*, 3 July 1995; Charles M. Fornbad, 'Endemic corruption in Cameroon,' in Hope and Chikulo, *Corruption*, p. 255; Richard Banégas and Jean-Pierre Warnier, 'Nouvelles figures de la réussite et du pouvoir,' *Politique Africaine*, 82 (June 2001), 5–6.

sought to rehabilitate themselves through fundamentalism. By contrast, the rising religious group were the entrepreneurial leaders of the pentecostal churches whose extraordinary success in African cities from the 1970s converted many of their founders from austere critics of materialism to eager participants in it. In 1998 some thirty thousand followers saw Archbishop Benson Idahosa of the Church of God Mission International Incorporated buried in a $12,000 coffin and $120,000 marble mausoleum at his Miracle Centre in Benin State, Nigeria, where church property included a stadium, hospital, bank, and private university.[62]

Similar changes took place in commerce. Community-orientated urban businessmen were challenged by egotistical younger entrepreneurs, often of rural origin, who had grown rich by corrupt or criminal means: the *moodu-moodu* of Senegal or *feymen* of Cameroun, men whose hand-made (*fait main*) styles proclaimed their success.

From Nouakchott to Pretoria, and passing through Lagos, Kinshasa, or Nairobi, can be seen a redistribution of roles. The leading figures of the period of postcolonial authoritarianism are becoming minor actors in a scene where the sportsman, musician, businessman, religious operator, man of the diaspora, *feyman* . . . henceforth take over important roles as models to imitate and indeed as opinion-makers or popular leaders. . . . In particular, malice, astuteness, the right of the strongest – which have always formed important moral bearings for African societies – assert themselves more and more openly as central values of what one may call a moral economy of guile and strategem (*débrouille*).[63]

A Senegalese sociologist described this as a revival of the *ceddo* ethic.[64]

Notions of male honour, so strongly rooted in warfare, were of special importance to postcolonial African soldiers, who saw honour less as a general ideal of behaviour than as a code peculiar to the military which underlay their claims to superiority over politicians and other civilians, a code likened by Robin Luckham to that of German officers but equally akin to that of Songhai horsemen or Yoruba *eso*.[65] Soldiers asserted their notions of honour in their frequent acts

---

[62] Paul Gifford, 'Some recent developments in African Christianity,' *African Affairs*, 93 (1994), 513; Ruth Marshall-Fratani, 'Prospérité miraculeux: les pasteurs pentecôtistes et l'argent de dieu au Nigeria,' *Politique Africaine*, 82 (June 2001), 24–32.

[63] Banégas and Warnier, 'Nouvelles figures,' pp. 7–8. See also Dominique Malaquais, 'Arts de feyre au Cameroun,' *Politique Africaine*, 82 (June 2001), 101–18.

[64] Malick Ndiaye, *L'éthique ceddo et la société d'accaparement ou les conduites culturelles des sénégalais d'aujourd'hui* (2 vols., Dakar, 1996), cited by Jean Copans, 'Les noms du *géer*: essai de sociologie de la connaissance du Sénégal par lui-même,' in Diop, *Le Sénégal*, pp. 169–76. I have not found a copy of Ndiaye's book.

[65] Robin Luckham, *The Nigerian military* (Cambridge, 1971), pp. 127–8; this volume, pp. 17–18, 70–1.

of insubordination as well as on the battlefield. By 1998 independent Africa had experienced seventy-five military coups d'état and numerous mutinies that stopped short of overturning governments.[66] Many had almost entirely mercenary aims, notably the earliest mutiny that fatally weakened the Congolese government shortly after independence. Some were driven by personal fear or ambition, as was Amin's seizure of power in Uganda. Others were motivated by offended honour. In 1965 General Soglo overthrew the government of Benin one day after being openly insulted by the vice-president, his lifelong enemy. Ten years later, Chad's commanders deposed a president who had described them as 'cattle in uniform'. 'We were humiliated publicly,' Lieutenant Yaya Jammeh explained after taking power in the Gambia in 1994; '. . . the politicians accused us of plotting to overthrow the government, and we were searched in public. All soldiers were searched, weapons seized. And that was the last straw. . . . We are not here for praises, we are not here to enrich ourselves. We are here to set up a just system that is not corruptible.'[67] That was the proclaimed goal of most coups by junior officers, whose motives showed that combination of grievance, ambition, and concern for honour previously seen in colonial mutinies. Major Nzeogwu, who assassinated Ahmadu Bello during the coup of 1966 that led to the Nigerian Civil War, acted 'in the name of national honour', describing his targets as 'the political profiteers, the swindlers . . . the tribalists, the nepotists'. 'Even if I die tonight, it will be glorious', he told a fellow-officer. A spokesman for the coup proclaimed, 'My compatriots, you will no longer be ashamed to be Nigerians.' Thomas Sankara, parachute captain and son of a serf, renamed his country 'The Land of Honest Men' after seizing power in 1983 and erected a poster outside the airport proclaiming, 'Burkina Faso is not for sale.'[68] His style of leadership appealed especially to the NCOs and enlisted men who played an unusually prominant part in African coups d'état, echoing perhaps the history of mutiny in colonial armies. 'In the military the junior ranks don't like officers who are cowards,' explained an admirer of Sankara's Ghanaian counterpart, Flight-Lieutenant Jerry Rawlings. 'These "old-fashioned values" of courage and loyalty were ones that Rawlings understood all too well,' a commentator added. 'His own model was that of the heroic officer in comradeship with

---

[66] *West Africa*, 19 October 1998, p. 769.

[67] Samuel Decalo, *Coups and army rule in Africa* (New Haven, 1976), pp. 8–9; Thierno Bah, 'Soldiers and "combatants": the conquest of political power in Chad 1965–1990,' in Hutchful and Bathily, *Military and militarism*, p. 450; *West Africa*, 1 August 1994, pp. 1347–8.

[68] Luckham, *Nigerian military*, p. 286; Adewale Ademoyega, *Why we struck: the story of the first Nigerian coup* (Ibadan, 1981), p. 89; D. J. M. Muffett, *Let truth be told: volume I* (Zaria, 1982), p. 35; N. J. Miners, *The Nigerian army, 1956–1966* (London, 1971), p. 177; Michael Wilkins, 'The death of Thomas Sankara and the rectification of the people's revolution in Burkina Faso,' *African Affairs*, 88 (1989), 388.

his men, accepting (self-)sacrifice in return for the privilege of leadership. His theatricals ... were ... carefully calculated to maximise this charisma.'[69] Although their regimes often fell back into corruption and violence, such young officers remained jealous of their personal honour. Mathieu Kerekou refused to resign when pressed by Benin's national conference in 1990 but insisted on facing his critics while acknowledging their right to depose him. And some knew how to die if their bids for power failed. 'Tewodros has taught me something,' one member of Ethiopia's military nobility declared before killing himself after failing to overthrow Haile Selassie.[70]

The battlefield remained the supreme test of military honour. Some one hundred sixty Ethiopian troops were executed in 1977 for cowardice and other offences when routed by Somali invaders.[71] Eleven years later, concern for reputation appears to have been a major reason driving both Ethiopia and Eritrea into a full-scale war of massed assaults against fortified positions and automatic weapons. 'To die on the battlefield is one thing, there is honour,' an Eritrean general fulminated after an early skirmish, 'but to be killed in cold blood is completely unacceptable. They must be punished.' Ethiopia's leader replied with similar indignation: 'The whole thing was meant to bring us to our knees at gunpoint.' Aghast at the escalation, an Eritrean diplomat lamented 'that in our continent everything is a matter of prestige. You can't go back from what you said. ... But you go on to commit more and more errors.'[72] The Nigerian Civil War of 1967–70 had more substantial causes, but they included the Igbo desire to avenge a massacre of their kinsmen and the federalists' conviction that duty compelled them to resist secession.[73]

Notions of honour pervaded the Nigerian officer corps at the time of the Civil War. '"An officer and a gentleman" ... is one of the most frequently heard expressions in the Nigerian Army,' Luckham reported.

Officers are extremely sensitive to questions of honour, and there is a very strong reaction to any suggestion that they may not have acted as gentlemen in any given set of circumstances, to a point where it is not unknown for an officer to have threatened action against a superior under the [Military Forces] act if he felt dishonoured by the latter.[74]

---

[69] Eboe Hutchful, 'Internal decomposition and junior ranks' political action in Ghana,' in Hutchful and Bathily, *Military and militarism*, p. 249.

[70] F. Eboussi Boulega, *Les conférences nationales en Afrique noire* (Paris, 1993), pp. 74–5, 80–1; Richard Greenfield, *Ethiopia: a new political history* (London, 1965), p. 83.

[71] Gebru Tareke, 'The Ethiopia-Somali War of 1977 revisited,' *IJAHS*, 33 (2000), 647–50, 664.

[72] Patrick Gilkes and Martin Plant, *War in the Horn* (London, 1999), pp. 23, 25; *EastAfrican*, 15 June 1998; *Mail and Guardian*, 7 May 1999.

[73] Ntieyong U. Akpan, *The struggle for secession, 1966–1970* (2nd edn, London, 1976), pp. xiii, 89.

[74] Luckham, *Nigerian military*, pp. 160, 127.

Officers on both sides condemned in strongly emotional terms the conspirators who had killed comrades-in-arms during the two coups that precipitated the war.[75] Commanders on both sides struck heroic poses. Among the federal forces, the 'Black Scorpion', Benjamin Adekunle, cultivated a ferocious image and deployed his commandos with reckless disregard for losses, while the victorious field commander, Olusegun Obasanjo, depicted himself in a manner worthy of a nineteenth-century Bashorun.[76] On the Igbo (Biafran) side, similarly, the militia leader Joe Achuzia fostered a reputation for extreme ruthlessness, while Odumegwu Ojukwu, the military governor, 'took special delight in the hero's songs composed for him,' insisted that his forces would fight in the bush to the last man, and threatened to kill himself rather than retreat from his headquarters. He did, however, earn his enemies' contempt by fleeing the country at the end of the war rather than 'committing suicide . . . the usual course of action for a defeated commander-in-chief.'[77] Officers on both sides squabbled over issues of *ekitiibwa* in the true heroic manner, while accounts of the war by Biafran women stressed endurance and survival amidst strident jingoism.[78]

Nevertheless the Nigerian crisis evoked real heroism. When the commander-in-chief, Ironsi, was arrested during the July 1966 coup, his host, Colonel Fajuyi, insisted on accompanying his guest and died with him. The dashing Nzeogwu died bravely on a dangerous Biafran mission.[79] While federal forces generally advanced cautiously, Biafra's lack of resources compelled reliance on the raw courage of barely trained militia. When an officer signalled, 'Not a single round of ammunition held. . . . We who are about to die, salute you,' all Biafra's Army Commander could offer was more rattles to simulate machine-guns. 'Determination will not make a soldier bullet-proof,' he added, but his judgment of the hopelessness of Biafra's situation, shared by most of its professional officers, was condemned as defeatism by militia commanders like Achuzia, who nevertheless had to take precautions 'to minimize the risk of our own troops shooting their officers from behind.'[80] Although there was no major mutiny, there were several smaller ones on the Biafran side, much malingering on both

[75] Ibid., p. 127.

[76] Oluleye, *Military leadership*, pp. 121, 131, 134–6, 144; Olusegun Obasanjo, *My command: an account of the Nigerian civil war, 1967–1970* (reprinted, London, 1981), esp. pp. xii–xiii.

[77] Joe O. G. Achuzia, *Requiem Biafra* (Enugu, 1986), pp. 138–9, 256–7, 294; Ademoyega, *Why we struck*, p. 170; Akpan, *Struggle*, p. 23; Bernard Odogwu, *No place to hide (crises and conflicts inside Biafra)* (Enugu, 1985), pp. 99, 168; Oluleye, *Military leadership*, p. 141.

[78] Rose Njoku, *Withstand the storm* (Ibadan, 1986); Jane Bryce, 'Conflict and contradiction in women's writing on the Nigerian Civil War,' *African Languages and Cultures*, 4 (1991), 29–42.

[79] Muffett, *Let truth be told*, p. 109; Obasanjo, *My command*, p. 17.

[80] Alexander A. Madiebo, *The Nigerian revolution and the Biafran War* (Enugu, 1980), pp. 195–6, 94, 188; Achuzia, *Requiem Biafra*, pp. 65, 128–9, 313–14.

sides – Obasanjo shot a dozen men for self-inflicted wounds – and 'intensive and universal fraternisation,' including football matches, between the front lines in the later stages of the war.[81]

After Biafra collapsed, the positive aspects of military honour asserted themselves. Obasanjo, who commanded the final thrust, kept his troops under control and made surrender as easy as possible. Gowon, the federal supreme commander, was determined from the start 'to win the respect of the outside world for ourselves and for the African and his capacity to order his own affairs.' Refusing to demonise the Igbo, he ordered that '[w]e must all welcome, with open arms, the people now freed from the tyranny and deceit of Ojukwu and his gang.' Although there were some reprisals and atrocities, his orders were generally obeyed and what had been dreaded as genocide became for the most part magnanimity.[82]

---

[81] St. Jorre, *Nigerian Civil War*, p. 377; Achuzia, *Requiem Biafra*, pp. 81–2, 294; Madiebo, *Nigerian revolution*, pp. 211, 327; Obasanjo, *My command*, p. 89.

[82] Odogwu, *No place to hide*, pp. 161–4, 181; Verkijika G. Fanso, 'Leadership and national crisis in Africa: Gowon and the Nigerian Civil War,' *Présence Africaine*, 109 (1979), 42; Oluleye, *Military leadership*, pp. 154–7; St. Jorre, *Nigerian Civil War*, p. 407.

19   To Live in Dignity

While leaders of postcolonial states strove to assert a right to the respect of their citizens, the citizens too sought to defend their dignity. Indeed, inherited notions of honour – male or female, heroic or householder, respectable or proletarian – endured most strongly among them, illustrating once more that all social groups and not just an elite claimed a right to respect. The inherited notions endured, like the machismo of South African youth gangs, because people found them functional in postcolonial circumstances, whether in resisting oppression, asserting civil and political rights, defending property and livelihood, surviving amidst economic decay, protecting a family, achieving manhood, or preserving honour in the time of AIDS.

'To hold one's head high in the face of government repression' has historically been one manifestation of honour.[1] It was so in postcolonial Africa, where the courage with which citizens defied oppressors has seldom been recognised. Some defiance could be only endurance. At the terrible Camp Boiro in Guinea, where Sekou Toure's torturers extracted bogus confessions of subversion, prisoners measured courage by the number of torture sessions endured before submitting and by refusal to beg for relief when sentenced to 'black diet', death by denial of food and liquid. 'The condemned struggled at least to die without losing honour before the guards,' an inmate recalled.[2] Uganda's National Resistance Army named a unit after Edidian Luttamaguzi, a villager who with eight of his relatives was tortured to death without revealing the whereabouts of a nearby guerilla band. Benedicto Kiwanuka, Uganda's

---

[1] Herzfeld, *Poetics*, p. 23.
[2] Ardo Ousmane Ba, *Camp Boiro: sinistre geôle de Sékou Touré* (Paris, 1986), p. 208.

Chief Justice, suffered torture and death in defending the rule of law against General Amin. Muhammad Dikko Yusufu, Nigeria's much-respected former inspector-general of police, decided to risk contesting a presidential election against the dictator General Abacha because he believed that someone should do so.[3]

Other defiance was covert, especially the ridicule with which Africans delighted to mock their rulers' heroic pretensions. Much was obscene or scatological, as in distorting party slogans to comment on the presidential phallus, a genre that worked because so much power-play centred on sex and consumption. The ancient Nyau dance societies of Malawian villages depicted President Banda, with deadly accuracy, as a white man of unusual ferocity who attacked spectators and could be bought off only with money. Luanda's carnival, traditional since the early seventeenth century, evaded political control and celebrated instead the ingenuity of survival amid an apparently endless war, although, as always with carnival, mockery was also collusion, shading into the plaintive discontent of popular song and the widespread increase in alcoholism.[4]

Not all protest was covert. Students, although too dependent and vulnerable to sustain defiance, bravely challenged several dictatorial regimes. In Uganda they denounced Amin's anti-Asian campaign as racist, publicly condemned his army's pay increases, marched through the capital to protest the shooting of a student, and suffered a brutal military invasion of their campus. In 1963 a combination of youth and trade union demonstrations overthrew Fulbert Youlou's regime in Brazzaville, although within the next few years organised labour was emasculated almost everywhere except Zambia.[5] Women market traders conducted a brave and effective demonstration against Sekou Toure's government in 1977, but major urban protest generally needed the stimulus either of radical religious leadership, as in the Yan Tatsine disturbances, which cost up to ten thousand lives in Northern Nigerian cities during the early 1980s, of increased food prices, as in the demonstrations that destabilised regimes in Liberia in

---

[3] Ondoga Ori Amaza, *Museveni's long march* (Kampala, 1998), p. 58; *EastAfrican*, 3 May 1999; Bade, *Kiwanuka*, pp. 156–60; *Africa Today*, August 2001, p. 19.

[4] Mbembe, 'Provisional notes,' pp. 3–37; Comi Toulabor, 'Jeu de mots, jeu de vilains: lexique de la dérision politique au Togo,' *Politique Africaine*, 3 (September 1981), 55–71; Deborah Kaspin, 'Chewa visions and revisions of power,' in Jean Comaroff and John Comaroff (eds.), *Modernity and its malcontents* (Chicago, 1993), p. 48; David Birmingham, 'Carnival at Luanda,' *JAH*, 29 (1988), 102; Carlos Moore, *Fela, Fela: this bitch of a life* (London, 1982); Akyeampong, *Drink*, pp. 153–7; Bazenguissa-Ganga, *Les voies*, pp. 302–10.

[5] Bryan Langlands, 'Students and politics in Uganda,' seminar paper, Institute of Commonwealth Studies, London, 1976; Pierre Bonnafé, 'Une classe d'âge politique: la JMNR de la République du Congo-Brazzaville,' *CEA*, 8 (1969), 327–68.

1979 and Zambia in 1986, or of mutiny by the forces of repression, as in the Kinshasa riots of 1991.[6]

Although authoritarian regimes chiefly feared the urban crowd, the most effective assertions of collective dignity often came from rural people conscious of a separate identity. One of the most articulate and enduring of these protests involved the stateless and culturally distinctive Jola people of the Casamance region of southern Senegal. Their Atiika (Warrior) movement, led by retired *tirailleurs*, dated its origins to 1645, when Jola first resisted the Atlantic slave trade, and accused the politically dominant Wolof people of neglect, internal colonisation, and destruction of Jola culture and environment.[7] Other armed resistance movements drew on indigenous traditions of heroic honour, especially the duty of revenge. Nuer and Dinka peoples of the southern Sudan often regarded their war against the northern government as a feud and attributed it to specific insults: 'The Arabs called us dogs and slaves and said that we were no better than the dirt under their feet.' Nuer preserved their warrior traditions, even though Christians sought to check internecine warfare and the interminable fighting with northern troops wrought major changes in the military code. Adopting firearms extensively for the first time, Nuer developed an elaborate gun culture in which rifles became key symbols of masculinity. By the 1980s '[t]he ability of a boy to hold and aim a rifle was . . . one of the principal prerequisites for initiation.' No longer did every homicide demand purification; that was still necessary if the person killed was a kinsman, but otherwise it was enough to drink water from an empty cartridge case: 'No one stood up during the war and said "I killed someone" – death was everywhere!'[8] Personal vengeance remained an important motive for fighting, as it was in the Liberian civil war of the 1990s, where an observer 'was struck that most of the irregulars said they were fighting to avenge dead relatives.' Similarly, many leaders of the Ethiopian Peoples Revolutionary Democratic Front (EPRDF), which overthrew Mengistu's regime in 1991, had lost friends in his Red Terror of 1977. 'In our tradition,' one said, 'if you avenge, you are honored. . . . If you don't, if someone kills your brother, it is a shame if you take no action. . . . The EPRDF is our avenger. So, we have decided to fight.' Later enemies of the

---

[6] Falola, *Violence*, p. 137; *Africa*, May 1979, p. 28; Matthew Martin, 'Neither phoenix nor Icarus: negotiating economic reform in Ghana and Zambia,' in Thomas M. Callaghy and John Ravenhill (eds.), *Hemmed in: responses to Africa's economic decline* (New York, 1993), pp. 140, 150; René Devisch, 'Frenzy, violence and ethical renewal in Kinshasa,' *Public Culture*, 7, 3 (Spring 1995), 606.

[7] Dominique Darbon (ed.), '"La voix de la Casamance" . . . une parole diola,' *Politique Africaine*, 18 (June 1985), 125–38.

[8] Hutchinson, *Nuer dilemmas*, pp. 105, 110, 133, 136–44, 150, 155.

EPRDF cultivated similar traditions. The poet Jaarso Waaqo Qoot'o, for example, developed Oromo heroic song into a nationalist verse distributed on radio casettes. The Tutsi exiles of the Rwanda Patriotic Front who seized power in 1994 made similar use of their kingdom's heroic poetry and ideology.[9]

The Rwandan tragedy mobilised not only the warrior tradition but the honour of the respectable householder. Many Rwandans died in 1994 for refusing to participate in genocide. Edouard Sebushumbe, mayor of Giti, north of Kigali, refused to initiate slaughter for ten days after it had begun in the capital, long enough for the Rwanda Patriotic Front forces to arrive and prevent it. Sosthene Niyitegeka, Hutu shopkeeper and Adventist preacher, protected over a hundred Tutsi neighbours. 'Peasants, at peril of their lives, saved not only neighbours but also hunted people whom they had never previously seen. It is not easy to know from what forces, from what certainties they drew this heroism.' Christianity, no doubt, was one. Another, perhaps, may have been defiance of authority acting so plainly in conflict with law and common humanity.[10] Such open defiance, of course, was exceptional. The householder's normal response to unwelcome state demands was evasion. Occasionally, the demands became intolerable. In 1968 the peasants of Ouolossebougou, south of Bamako, were so exasperated by the attempts of Mali's socialist government to collectivise agriculture and monopolise trade that they boycotted political meetings, defied state orders, sent delegations to the capital, and marched on the gaol to release imprisoned neighbours, a sequence of protests contributing to the regime's overthrow in the coup d'état of that year. Opposition to agricultural collectivisation was almost universal. Northern Mozambican peasants built token socialist villages which they occupied only during official visits.[11] Their Tanzanian counterparts bitterly resented forced communalisation. 'We were treated like animals,' some remembered there in Iringa district, where one villager became a folk hero for shooting a regional commissioner who called him a dog in front of his

---

[9] Stephen Ellis, *The mask of anarchy: the destruction of Liberia and the religious dimension of an African civil war* (London, 1999), p. 113; Jenny Hammond, *Fire from the ashes* (Lawrenceville, N.J., 1999), p. 380; Abdullahi A. Shongolo, 'The poetics of nationalism,' in P. T. W. Baxter, Jan Hultin, and Alessandro Triulzi (eds.), *Being and becoming Oromo* (Uppsala, 1996), pp. 265–90; Warren Weinstein, 'Military continuities in the Rwanda state,' in Ali A. Mazrui (ed.), *The warrior tradition in modern Africa* (Leiden, 1977), pp. 48–66.

[10] John M. Janzen, 'Historical consciousness and a "prise de conscience" in genocidal Rwanda,' *JACS*, 13 (2000), 153–4, 164–5, 167; Claudine Vidal, 'Questions sur le rôle des paysans durant le génocide des Rwandais tutsi,' *CEA*, 38 (1998), 343; *Mail and Guardian*, 9 April 1999.

[11] Jean-Loup Amselle, 'La conscience paysanne: la révolte de Ouolossébougou,' *Canadian Journal of African Studies*, 12 (1978), 339–55; Christian Geffray, *La cause des armes au Mozambique* (Paris, 1990), pp. 178–86.

wife.[12] Conflict between rural householders and young 'revolutionaries' was widespread. 'These children wanted to make us eat shame,' village elders in Benin complained, 'but God will never leave an elder in shame before the young.... It was possible to save face.' Traditionalists in the Kefa region of southwestern Ethiopia burned alive the students sent from Addis Ababa in 1975 to enforce the Marxist regime's land reform programme.[13]

Defence of the land was the core of householder honour. 'There is no *rist* [right of land use] without liberty and no honour without *rist*,' Ethiopian elders told Haile Selassie, whose reign was punctuated by peasant rebellions to preserve those rights. A study in Burkina during the 1990s found that, along with courage and generosity, it was willingness and ability to defend land rights that attracted honour. To that end, 'farmers often pay more in bribes and in greasing the palms of the powerful in the legal system than the piece of land is worth. "It's a question of honour," people say.'[14] Possession of land might free the householder from dishonouring himself by seeking wage employment. It might enable him and his wife to meet their fundamental obligation to provide for their dependants. By contrast, the return of widespread famine to tropical Africa during the 1960s dishonoured many male householders. 'The region abounds in tales of suicide by men unable to support their families,' a journalist reported from the West African Sahel in 1974. Others were said to have killed their dependants. In Northern Nigeria 'men departed overnight without making arrangements for who was to cater for their families, or to pay their taxes, and without informing their elders.' It was the same in Ethiopia, where men killed themselves when unable to support their families during the terrible famines of the 1970s and 1980s, although few would exchange land or plough-oxen for food, arguing that 'it is better to die with one's honour without giving cause to the future generation to curse.'[15] Women, however, were led by their distinct notion of honour to a different response, protecting their children at all costs, clinging for

[12] James De Vries and Louise P. Fortmann, 'Large-scale villagization: Operation Sogeza in Iringa Region,' in Andrew Coulson (ed.), *African socialism in practice: the Tanzanian experience* (Nottingham, 1979), p. 130; *The Nationalist*, 27 December 1971; Philip Raikes, 'Agrarian crisis and economic liberalisation in Tanzania,' *JMAS*, 17 (1979), 316.

[13] Nassirou Bako-Arifari, 'La démocratie à Founongo,' in Thomas Bierschenk and Jean-Pierre Olivier de Sardan (eds.), *Les pouvoirs au village* (Paris, 1998), p. 84; Donald L. Donham, *Marxist modern: an ethnographic history of the Ethiopian Revolution* (Berkeley, 1999), p. 59.

[14] Gebru Tareke, *Ethiopia: power and protest* (Cambridge, 1991), p. 167; Christian Lund, 'A question of honour: property disputes and brokerage in Burkina Faso,' *Africa*, 69 (1999), 575.

[15] Richard W. Franke and Barbara H. Chasin, *Seeds of famine* (Montclair, 1980), p. 9; Thierry Brun, 'Manifestations nutritionnelles et médicales de la famine,' in Jean Copans (ed.), *Sécheresses et famines du Sahel* (2 vols., Paris, 1975), vol. 1, p. 89; G. Jan van Apeldoorn, *Perspectives on drought and famine in Nigeria* (London, 1981), p. 62; *Oxfam News*, October 1973; Mesfin Wolde Mariam, *Rural vulnerability to famine in Ethiopia* (London, 1986), pp. 62–5.

as long as possible to their homes, foraging in the bush, undertaking the most humiliating work, even prostituting themselves, and as a last resort taking their children to relief camps, where over 75 per cent of Somali refugee families in the early 1980s were headed by women.[16]

'I am no longer a man – no wife, no home, no family,' a victim of political violence told South Africa's Truth and Reconciliation Commission. To head a well-regulated family remained essential to a respectable householder. Nelson Mandela ended his autobiography by regretting he had sacrificed his family to his patriotic duty.[17] One essential aspect of respectability, the education of children, was increasingly expensive as narrowing employment opportunities intensified educational competition. Another, the care of the elderly, also became more burdensome as geographical mobility increased, although it remained a feature of their society in which Africans took particular pride. These financial burdens came at a time when inflation was eating into earnings and even, as in the extreme case of the Congo Democratic Republic, reducing all but an elite to common poverty. Postcolonial Africa was a bewildering and embittering place for the respectable. Many responded by advocating return to idealised traditional ways, others found refuge in the Pentecostal churches, which reinforced traditional moral teachings but inculcated a modern lifestyle and pictured the continent as a battleground between the godly and the satanic.[18]

Issues of honour were especially sensitive for the young African men of the late twentieth century. In the countryside many still proved their manhood by traditional means. Young Fula still held whipping contests and cultivated *pulaaku*, consulting the Guardian of the Fulbe Way, based in Adamawa, on the niceties of their code. Both elders and young people were often eager to preserve initiation rites – in 1994 a Kikuyu boy killed himself when denied them – although some educated parents and youths rejected them as barbaric, shameful, and divisive, winning their point even among the Nuer.[19] During the third quarter

---

[16] Suzanne Lallemand, 'La sécheresse dans un village mossi de Haute-Volta,' in Copans, *Sécheresses*, vol. 2, p. 54; J.-L. Amselle, 'Famine, prolétarisation et création de nouveaux liens de dépendance au Sahel,' *Politique Africaine*, 1 (1981), 15–17; Poitou, *La délinquance*, p. 56; Aderanti Adepoju, 'The dimension of the refugee problem in Africa,' *African Affairs*, 81 (1982), 31.

[17] Robert Morrell, 'The times of change,' in his *Changing men*, p. 30; Mandela, *Long walk*, pp. 615–16.

[18] Iliffe, *Poor*, pp. 245–7; Devisch, 'Frenzy,' p. 625; Ruth Marshall, 'Power in the Name of Jesus,' *Review of African Political Economy*, 52 (1991), 21–37.

[19] Ver Eecke, 'Pulaaku,' pp. 48, 340; Beth M. Ahlberg V. N. Kimani, L. W. Kirumbi, M. W. Kaara, and I. Krantz, 'Male circumcision,' in Becker and others, *Vivre et penser*, p. 609; *Daily Nation*, 5 December 1994; Hutchinson, *Nuer dilemmas*, pp. 270–1, 292–3, 296–7.

of the century, nationalism, guerilla movements, and the achievement of independence provided many opportunities for the young to achieve adulthood and enjoy social mobility. By the later 1970s, however, those opportunities were vanishing almost everywhere. The independence generation, still for the most part only middle-aged, was entrenched in power. Massive population growth from the 1950s swelled the numbers reaching working age. Mass primary schooling reduced the economic value of education. Declining economies from the later 1970s were unable to create employment, especially in the cities. Between 1977 and 1998, Kenya's official unemployment rate rose from 11 to 25 per cent. South Africa's rate in 2001 was 37 per cent, and the proportion was far higher among the young. Even those with work suffered a rapid decline of real earnings, by 84 per cent between 1974 and 1982 among Ghanaian industrial workers. Many young men had to scrape a living in the informal sector, which employed half of Senegal's urban labour force in 1975.[20] Informalisation was indeed a general process of the time, in shanty-town housing, unregulated minibus transport, widespread corruption, domestic groupings, and sexual relationships. By the mid 1980s, 35 per cent of men between the ages of twenty-five and twenty-nine in Dakar were unmarried, and the proportion was growing. In South Africa the Xhosa word *ubudoda*, which had meant the management of a homestead, had come for young people to refer only to the penis.[21] Unable to achieve adulthood as householders, young men sought other ways to assert a right to respect.

Many showed great enterprise. One of Africa's major growth sectors of the 1980s and 1990s was small-scale, open-cast mining for gold, diamonds, other precious stones, and a host of rare minerals used in advanced industrial economies. The sites, characteristically, were remote and lawless frontiers beyond the greedy hands of state authorities, such as eastern Sierra Leone and Angola or the Orientale and Lunda regions of the Congo Democratic Republic. The thousands of young men and women seeking fortunes in these rugged conditions often travelled in parties like the hunters and migrant labourers of the past, well protected by magic. They saw their experience as an initiation into adulthood, a training in courage, endurance, and self-control. Their earnings – which, on the diamond fields, could be substantial – were spent quickly, generously,

---

[20] *EastAfrican*, 17 August 1998; SAIRR, *Fast Facts*, February 2002, p. 9; M. M. Huq, *The economy of Ghana* (Basingstoke, 1989), p. 231; Richard Sandbrook, *The politics of basic needs* (London, 1982), p. 59.

[21] Bill Freund, 'The city of Durban,' in Anderson and Rathbone, *Africa's urban past*, pp. 155–6; Tshikala Kayembe Biaya, 'Les plaisirs de la ville: masculinité, sexualité et feminité à Dakar (1997–2000),' *African Studies Review*, 44, 2 (September 2001), 77; T. Dunbar Moodie, 'Black migrant mineworkers and the vicissitudes of male desire,' in Morrell, *Changing men*, pp. 302, 310.

and ostentatiously to claim status or establish some new enterprise.[22] Since some 80 per cent of Sierra Leone's diamonds were thought to be smuggled out of the country, mining was inseparable from the crime that was another growth sector of the time for the young. By the late 1990s Nigerians were major suppliers of cocaine and heroin to the United States and were alleged to control the similar trade in South Africa.[23] Other young people sought their fortunes through small-scale trade, sometimes travelling thousands of kilometres in search of opportunity. On the bottom rung were the parking-boys, but not with any intention of staying there: two interviewed in Nairobi in the late 1980s planned to become doctors. 'Today in Africa,' wrote Massa Makan Diabate, 'the true heroes, the true princes, are those who take up arms courageously against poverty.'[24]

As the conditions of physical danger and poverty that had long existed in South Africa spread widely through the continent's cities, so did the street gangs that appropriated traditions of rural violence to urban life. The most powerful gangs were still South African, especially the two major Coloured brotherhoods contesting Cape Town's drug trade (the Americans and the Hard Livings) and the Jackroller gangs of Durban and Soweto notorious for rape.[25] But violent gangs like the Ninjas of Lusaka also appeared in many tropical cities.[26] More numerous, especially as AIDS orphans proliferated, were the street-children who clustered together for mutual protection, roamed the streets collecting waste, and stole to survive. By 1996 Kenya had an estimated forty thousand street-children, some affiliated with adult criminal gangs through initiation by some display of bravado.[27]

---

[22] Jean Omasombo Tshonda ('Les diamants de Kisangani'), Sabakina Kivilu ('A la recherche du paradis terrestre'), and Filip De Boeck ('Comment dompter diamants et dollars') in Laurent Monnier, Bogumil Jewsiewicki, and Gauthier de Villers (eds.), *Chasse au diamant au Congo/Zaire* (Paris, 2001), pp. 93–101, 134, 163, 172–3, 187–91.

[23] Bayart, *State*, p. 101; Jean-François Bayart, Stephen Ellis, and Béatrice Hibou, *The criminalization of the state in Africa* (Oxford, 1999), pp. 9–13.

[24] E. P. Mihanjo and N. N. Luanda, 'The south-east economic backwater and the urban floating *Wamachinga*,' in Pekka Seppälä and Bertha Koda (eds.), *The making of a periphery* (Uppsala, 1998), pp. 222–3; Dorothy Munyakko, 'Kenya: the parking boys of Nairobi,' in Donatus de Silva (ed.), *Against all odds: breaking the poverty trap* (London, 1989), pp. 64–86; James R. McGuire, 'Narrating Mande heroism in the Malian novel,' *RAL*, 24, 3 (1993), 42.

[25] Wilfried Schärf and Clare Vale, 'The Firm – organised crime comes of age during the transition to democracy,' *Social Dynamics*, 22, 2 (1996), 30–6; Suzanne Leclerc-Madlala, 'Infect one, infect all: Zulu youth response to the AIDS epidemic in South Africa,' *Medical Anthropology*, 17 (1996–7), 373; Steve Mokwena, 'Living on the wrong side of the law,' in David Everatt and Elinor Sisulu (eds.), *Black youth in crisis* (Braamfontein, 1992), pp. 41, 44.

[26] *Moto*, February 1988, p. 15.

[27] *EastAfrican*, 12 August 1996; D. Rodriguez-Torres, 'Le gang Serena,' *Politique Africaine*, 63 (October 1996), 63–4.

Largely distinct from gangsters and street-children were the much greater number of young townspeople, unmarried and often unemployed or with only casual jobs, who asserted a distinct identity through youth cultures blending indigenous traditions with global fashions displaying the modernity which for the young was now an essential component of honour. The *bul faale* (play it cool) culture, which emerged in Dakar during the 1990s, was one example. Unlike gang culture, the *bul faale* ethos valorised hard work and self-creation. Some devotees were politically active, advocating *sopi* (change), the slogan of opposition to Senegal's entrenched nationalist party. Their Franco-Wolof argot also incorporated much English, and their music was an iconoclastic rap. Their physical appearance blended Afro-American/Caribbean styles with elements from the Mouride brotherhood tradition, especially its dissident Bay Fall off-shoot, which provided models for their use of alcohol and cannabis and their stress on physicality, including body-building, which acted as a partial surrogate for adult sexuality. These *boys Dakar*, as they called themselves, found a modern and materialistic hero in Mohammed Ndao, known as Tyson, an unemployed school drop-out who in 1995 broke into the closed world of professional wrestling by flooring an established champion for a prize of 30 million francs CFA (some $45,000). Tyson trained alone in the popular Pikine township, entered the ring wrapped in an American flag, and mocked his opponents as they made the lengthy traditional preparations for the contest. His triumphs became those of his generation.[28]

Other cities bred equally hybrid youth cultures, each with distinctive elements. The *shifta* culture of Addis Ababa – named from the term for a traditional bandit – made much use of alcohol, *khat* (an indigenous narcotic), and the *fukara* boast and wild dancing of Ethiopian military tradition but was predictably more insular than *bul faale*. The *shege* of Kinshasa focused their street culture around alcohol, sex, and especially popular music, which the city exported throughout the continent.[29] Across the river, Brazzaville remained the home of *sape* and high male fashion, now an expression of political defiance. The defiance was a response to defeat in the murderous civil war among Brazzaville's youth, which reached at least a temporary climax late in 1998 when the Cobras, the youth militia drawn from Congo's northern peoples and loyal to Denis Sassou-Nguesso, defeated (with the aid of the Angolan army) their two southern-based rivals, the Zulus and Ninjas. Although this conflict

---

[28] Havard, 'Ethos "bul faale",' pp. 63–77; Biaya, 'Les plaisirs,' pp. 76–84; Ndibuga Adrien Benga, 'Dakar et ses tempos,' and Faye, 'Sport,' in Diop, *Le Sénégal*, pp. 298–305, 333–6.

[29] Biaya, 'Les plaisirs,' pp. 15–17, 20–1, 24; Zewde in Hutchful and Bathily, *Military and militarism*, p. 274. *Shege* derived from Schengen, where the European Community's convention on internal migration was negotiated.

was rooted in regional and ethnic rivalries, long competition for control of the city, and the personal ambitions of leaders, it also had a dynamic in the young combatants' determination to achieve adulthood by the only means open to them: violence and pillage. At one point in the fighting, the rival militias came together to plunder the city centre. Pillage, in their view, was distinct from theft: it was the right to 'their share' enjoyed by victors who had been denied education and whose work for 'whites' – by whom they meant the ruling class of any race – had long gone unrewarded.[30]

Similar attitudes and aspirations animated many young men who formed the bulk of Africa's rebel armies of the 1980s and 1990s, the most dramatic means by which they expressed their masculinity. The guerilla armies of Uganda, Angola, Mozambique, Somalia, Liberia, Sierra Leone, and the Democratic Republic of the Congo incorporated many adolescents into a hybrid military culture of traditional and modern elements. It generally included some form of initiation, a traumatic act of brutality, and exposure to violence in some modern form such as the diet of Rambo films fed to young Sierra Leonean rebels. Brutalised and often drugged, these adolescent fighters could be horrifyingly careless of life: 'One young man shot his friend in front of a United Nations official who asked him why he had done it. "He pissed me off," was the reply.' They were especially violent to 'shining', visibly prosperous people.[31] A small minority may have had clearer political goals, notably the young Muslim fundamentalists who joined rebel forces in Somalia and Uganda, but the primary concern was survival: 'If I surrender my gun, who then will assure that I may eat?' sang the adolescent Somali warriors of Mogadishu. Most probably lived in fear. 'My brother and I were in the same camp,' a former Angolan fighter recalled. 'My brother was captured when he tried to flee. He was tied to a tree and killed. I watched it all, but I was obliged to hold myself back so as not to cry. They would have killed me if they had discovered that we were brothers.' The fear worked both ways. A war-weary Liberian guerilla observed that 'he must maintain a warrior's attitude lest the adolescents . . . suspect him of weakness.'[32] Yet these youthful rebels were not merely nihilistic. Like their counterparts at the

---

[30] Bazenguissa-Ganga, *Les voies*, pp. 185–7, 330; Rémy Bazenguissa-Ganga and Patrice Yengo, 'La popularisation de la violence politique au Congo,' *Politique Africaine*, 73 (March 1999), 186–92; Joseph Tonda, 'La guerre dans le "Camp Nord" au Congo-Brazzaville,' *Politique Africaine*, 72 (December 1998), 50–67.

[31] Paul Richards, *Fighting for the rain forest: war, youth and resources in Sierra Leone* (Oxford, 1996), pp. 57–9, 90–5, 109–11; Ellis, *Mask of anarchy*, pp. 117, 127.

[32] Crawford Young, 'In search of civil society,' in John W. Harbeson, Donald Rothchild, and Naomi Chazan (eds.), *Civil society and the state in Africa* (Boulder, 1994), p. 47; Alcinda Honwana, 'Innocents et coupables: les enfants-soldats comme acteurs tactiques,' *Politique Africaine*, 80 (December 2000), 70; *West Africa*, 15 April 1991, p. 560.

diamond fields or in the Brazzaville streets, they wanted a share of the modernity denied them by poverty and the disintegration of states and education systems. They listened avidly to international news broadcasts. Their guns were often the first modern equipment they had handled. Warfare offered unique access to possessions through looting. It also offered 'that rarest of all commodities, young women,' and through them access to adulthood. It might even offer what they coveted most: education and the opportunities it alone seemed to open. Guerillas often held this out as a bait to recruits. In 2000 Sierra Leone's West Side Boys were reported to have offered to barter a party of kidnapped British soldiers for a degree course at a British university.[33]

It is within this history of honour that the African AIDS epidemic must be understood. Its origins and development, of course, were shaped by many aspects of African history, but notions of male and female honour influenced both the sexual system within which the epidemic took place and, more particularly, the manner in which Africans reacted to the disease. In responding, their chief concern was to behave with dignity, as they understood it. The tragedy of AIDS was that, in the absence of a medical preventative or cure, the most effective responses were behavioural changes in flat conflict with heroic traditions of masculinity and in partial conflict with female concerns with fertility and endurance. One reason why sub-Saharan Africa suffered the first terrible AIDS epidemic was that honour cultures survived most vigorously there and displayed their self-destructive character in its most damaging form. As this book has shown, however, those cultures were themselves diverse so that they responded differently to the epidemic.

Analysts have argued that sub-Saharan Africa's traditional sexual systems, shaped by abundance of land, scarcity of people, and emphasis on fertility, aided the process by which AIDS became a heterosexual epidemic.[34] Although Africans were not especially promiscuous by international standards, sexual freedom was probably greater than was normal in other rural communities, where land scarcity fostered stricter control over access to women and property.[35] Yet the fact that AIDS first became epidemic in eastern and southern

---

[33] Richards, *Fighting*, pp. 28–9, 111–13; Ellis, *Mask of anarchy*, pp. 113, 122–3; Bayart, Ellis, and Hibou, *Criminalization*, p. 41; *Cape Times*, 12 September 2000.

[34] Caldwell and others, 'Social context,' pp. 186–8.

[35] John Cleland and Benoît Ferry (eds.), *Sexual behaviour and AIDS in the developing world* (London, 1995), p. 211; John C. Caldwell, 'Reasons for limited sexual behavioural change in the sub-Saharan African AIDS epidemic,' in Caldwell and others (eds.), *Resistances to behavioural change to reduce HIV/AIDS infection in predominantly heterosexual epidemics in Third World countries* (Canberra, 1999), p. 250.

Africa, where controls on sexual behaviour were commonly more rigid than in West Africa, suggests that there were more important reasons for the spread of the disease, as does the fact that epidemics soon followed in the different sexual systems of Thailand and India.[36] Among these reasons was the prevalence of 'bachelor' labour migration to the towns of eastern and southern Africa, with associated prostitution, low female status, poverty, and sexually transmitted diseases facilitating the transmission of HIV.[37] Yet perhaps the most important difference between the African epidemic and experience in Thailand or in Western countries was the failure to check transmission, which was not the result of popular ignorance of how HIV was spread – by the late 1990s awareness levels were commonly over 90 per cent – but of widespread African reluctance to change sexual behaviour in high-risk situations.[38] Reluctance was not total. Senegal limited adult HIV prevalence to 1–2 per cent by regulating prostitution, promoting safer sex, and drawing on patterns of restraint dating from the triumph of Islam.[39] In Uganda, more dramatically, experience of the epidemic, together with open discussion and widespread propaganda in highly integrated societies, induced people to reduce their sexual partners so severely as to cut prevalence rates among pregnant women between 1991 and 1998 from 21.1 to 9.7 per cent.[40] This pattern extended into north-western Tanzania, while less dramatic evidence of reduced prevalence appeared during the late 1990s in Lusaka, central Addis Ababa, and among teenage women in South Africa.[41] Generally, however, Africans showed a reluctance to change behaviour that was connected at many points to their notions of honour.

[36] Christine Obbo, 'Social science research: understanding and action,' in Becker and others, *Vivre et penser*, p. 69 n1. See also Caldwell and others, 'Family,' pp. 408–9.

[37] Joseph K. Konde-Lule, 'The effects of urbanization on the spread of AIDS in Africa,' *African Urban Quarterly*, 6 (1991), 13–18.

[38] Caldwell in Caldwell and others, *Resistances*, pp. 241–2. That biological as well as behavioural factors were important was argued in B. Auvert and others, 'Ecological and individual level analysis of risk factors for HIV infection in four urban populations in sub-Saharan Africa with different levels of HIV infection,' *AIDS*, 15 (2001), supplement 4, p. S.15.

[39] Nicolas Meda and others, 'Low and stable HIV infection rates in Senegal: natural course of the epidemic or evidence for success of prevention?' *AIDS*, 13 (1999), 1397–1405; this volume, p. 52.

[40] D. Low-Beer and R. Stoneburner, 'Uganda and the challenge of AIDS,' in A. Whiteside and N. Poku (eds.), *AIDS in Africa: context and challenges* (forthcoming).

[41] G. Kwesigabo and others, 'Decline in the prevalence of HIV-1 infection in young women in the Kagera region of Tanzania,' *Journal of AIDS*, 17 (1998), 262–8; Sohail Agha, 'Declines in casual sex in Lusaka, Zambia, 1996–1999,' *AIDS*, 16 (2002), 291–3; Aster Tsegaye and others, 'Decline in prevalence of HIV-1 infection and syphilis among young women attending antenatal care clinics in Addis Ababa, Ethiopia: results from sentinel surveillance, 1995–2001,' *Journal of AIDS*, 30 (2002), 359; UNAIDS/WHO, 'AIDS epidemic update: December 2002,' http.//www.unaids.org.

One connection was stoicism in the face of death. By the mid 1990s, for example, sixteen-year-olds in KwaZulu-Natal had so great a chance of contracting HIV that many regarded the disease as virtually inescapable, almost like childhood measles. 'We thought that with the new government we could relax, study, plan a future,' a man of twenty said at that time. 'Now AIDS is here to give us no future. Well, we'll all just get it and that's life. We're cursed; we really are the lost generation.' The only guarantee of safety was sexual abstinence, which both natural desire and peer pressure made impossible for most.[42] Resistance to behavioural change was especially strong in South Africa, where heroic notions of masculinity had been perpetuated by urban experience and opposition to apartheid. Many men believed that they were naturally polygynous and that male success was demonstrated by multiple sexual partners. They often regarded the use of condoms to prevent transmission as unmanly. 'A man must have flesh-to-flesh,' mineworkers explained, insisting that infection was a secondary risk to men in their perilous occupation. 'The truth is that I do not think anything when I am having sex,' one confessed. 'It is only when I am finished – that is when I start to think about AIDS.' 'Using a condom . . . breaks your dignity,' a young Zulu man added, 'because a girl feels that a condom during sex is nicer than your penis.'[43]

Most important of all, research in many parts of the continent showed that condoms had come to be identified with illicit sex. They were used almost exclusively with casual partners, especially sex-workers, who themselves adopted them quite eagerly to reduce the appalling risks of their profession – Senegalese sex-workers might collectively force a client to wear a condom – but seldom used them with their own regular partners.[44] A study in Cotonou (Benin) in 1998–9 found that whereas 81 per cent of sex-workers had used condoms during the previous week, over 80 per cent never used them with their own

---

[42] Brian Williams and Catherine Campbell, 'Understanding the epidemic of HIV in South Africa,' *South African Medical Journal*, 88 (1998), 249; Leclerc-Madlala, 'Infect one,' p. 363; Christine A. Varga, 'South African young people's sexual dynamics,' in Caldwell and others, *Resistances*, pp. 25–6.

[43] This volume, Chapters 9 and 16; Varga in Caldwell and others, *Resistances*, pp. 18–19; Terry-Ann Selikow, Bheki Zulu, and Eugene Cedras, 'The *ingagara*, the *regte* and the *cherry*: HIV/AIDS and youth culture in contemporary urban townships,' *Agenda*, 53 (2002), 24–5; Catherine Campbell, '"Going underground and going after women",' in Morrell, *Changing men*, p. 282; Catherine Campbell and Brian Williams, 'Beyond the biomedical and behavioural: towards an integrated approach to HIV prevention in the southern African mining industry,' *Social Science and Medicine*, 48 (1999), 1633.

[44] Ogden in Werbner and Ranger, *Postcolonial identities*, p. 185; C. A. Varga, 'Coping with HIV/AIDS in Durban's commercial sex industry,' *AIDS Care*, 13 (2001), 358–9; Michelle Lewis Renaud, *Women at the crossroads: a prostitute community's response to AIDS in urban Senegal* (Amsterdam, 1997), p. 3.

boyfriends, although HIV prevalence among the boyfriends was twice as high as among casual clients.[45] In Bamako, similarly, condoms were associated especially with sexual misbehaviour – 'the prostitute's identity card' – and were consequently rejected by the respectable: 'as much a matter of honour as a question of health.' 'No man used condoms to have sex with me,' a Ghanaian woman declared proudly. To suggest the use of a condom with a regular partner, much less a spouse, was either an insult or an admission of infection. At the least, it displayed lack of confidence in the relationship. 'I would be heartbroken. It means he does not trust me,' a young South African woman explained.[46] In Kampala a woman would commonly use a condom in intercourse with a friend, possibly with a lover (provided she did not hope to marry him), but never with a husband (whether formally married or not). Yet probably a majority – perhaps a large majority – of African women with HIV had been infected by their husbands.[47]

However recklessly people risked contracting HIV, the disease was inherently dishonourable, not only to the individual but the entire household. Studies suggested that those knowingly infected were thirty-five to forty times more likely to attempt suicide than the general population.[48] Silence was the rule almost everywhere, the silence of personal and family honour. Sufferers were concealed when living and concealed when dead. At least half the funerals in southern Zambia in the late 1990s were probably the result of AIDS, but only 3 per cent were so admitted by the family. Gugu Dlamini, an activist who publicly announced that she had the disease, was stoned to death in Durban for degrading her neighbourhood.[49] Modern doctors generally told their patients their diagnosis only when pressed, which in some countries was not often. 'I asked my nurse if we should inform Solomon of his disease,' one wrote. '"No way," she replied, "He could commit suicide."'[50] It was widely believed that those who knew they had HIV would respond violently, perhaps seeking to infect as many people as possible, although there was no

[45] Fred Eboko, 'L'état camerounais et les cadets sociaux face à la pandémie du sida,' *Politique Africaine*, 64 (December 1996), 139–40.

[46] Robert Vuarin, '"Le chapeau utile n'est pas dans le vestibule",' in Becker and others, *Vivre et penser*, pp. 441–2; Judy E. Mill and John K. Anarfi, 'HIV risk environment for Ghanaian women,' *Social Science and Medicine*, 54 (2002), 332; Varga in Caldwell and others, *Resistances*, p. 20.

[47] Ogden, 'Reproductive identity,' pp. 204–7; Obbo in Becker and others, *Vivre et penser*, p. 76.

[48] Judith Hassoun, *Femmes d'Abidjan face au sida* (Paris, 1997), p. 134; N. K. Ndosi and M. C. Waziri, 'The nature of parasuicide in Dar es Salaam,' *Social Science and Medicine*, 44 (1997), 59; *Mail and Guardian*, 31 October 2003.

[49] Caldwell in Caldwell and others, *Resistances*, p. 245; *South African Medical Journal*, 89 (1999), 218.

[50] Richard Hodes, 'Visiting Solomon: AIDS in Ethiopia,' *AIDS*, 16 (2002), 2.

evidence of this. 'For young women' in Durban 'the fear that young men could respond to an HIV positive diagnosis by raping women was cited as *the* major reason why medical authorities should desist in disclosing one's HIV status.'[51] The silence of patients and doctors was matched, as has been seen, by the silence of governments, with the notable exception of Museveni's Uganda.[52]

The measures most likely to contain the AIDS epidemic offended African male honour at almost every point. Their interaction with female honour was more complicated. One reason for the intensity of the African epidemic was precisely the low status of many women, which led them to be blamed for an infection most commonly transmitted by men. Women's economic dependence often prevented their leaving an infected partner or informing husbands of their own infection lest they be rejected. Economic autonomy, long a goal of women in West Africa and increasingly so elsewhere, was never so valuable as in the time of AIDS, nor so difficult as in a time of economic decline.[53] Within sexual relationships, moreover, male dominance often left women little chance to protect themselves against infection. One study in KwaZulu-Natal found that 71 per cent of women who had recently tried to refuse sex to a partner had failed. 'Once you have kissed each other that means you are preparing for sex. If she refuses at that point you must just force her,' a young townsman explained.[54] Moreover, although AIDS commonly reduced sexual desire and fertility, it could paradoxically stimulate women's wish for marriage and children. Single women, especially young widows, were particularly liable to stigma. For a 'proper woman' marriage and childbearing were essential almost everywhere. 'The fact that a woman's husband may have been diagnosed HIV-positive will weigh little against the expectation that she should bear children,' one investigator concluded. 'Furthermore, should she wish to use condoms if she suspects her husband to be HIV-positive, it is unlikely that he will concur.'[55] Moreover, safer sex militated against women's own intense desire for children, a desire encouraged by the possibility of early death and even in some women by knowledge of HIV infection, although then it might be countered by fear of

---

[51] Leclerc-Madlala, 'Infect one,' p. 372. See also Iliffe, *Doctors*, p. 239.

[52] This volume, pp. 329–30.

[53] Annie Le Palec, '"Le sida, une maladie des femmes",' in Becker and others, *Vivre et penser*, pp. 343–60; Ogden, 'Reproductive identity,' p. 256; Hassoun, *Femmes d'Abidjan*, p. 106.

[54] Varga in Caldwell and others, *Resistances*, pp. 18, 23.

[55] Basia Zaba and Simon Gregson, 'Measuring the impact of HIV on fertility in Africa,' *AIDS*, 12 (1998), supplement 1, pp. S.44–7; Hassoun, *Femmes d'Abidjan*, pp. 79, 87, 117; Ogden, 'Reproductive identities,' p. 217; Eleanor Preston-Whyte, 'Reproductive health and the condom dilemma,' in Caldwell and others, *Resistances*, p. 149.

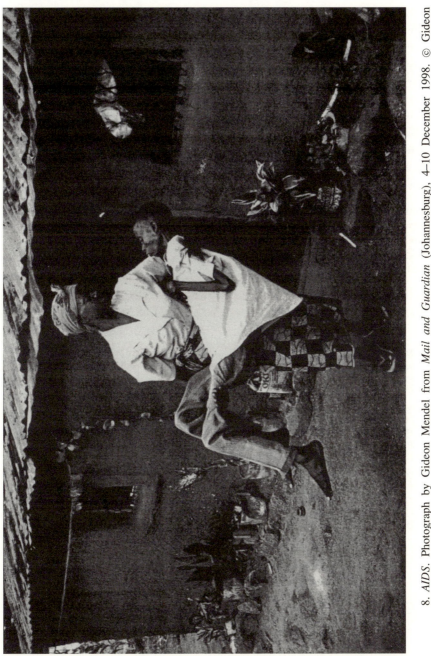

8. *AIDS*. Photograph by Gideon Mendel from *Mail and Guardian* (Johannesburg), 4–10 December 1998. © Gideon Mendel/CORBIS.

bearing infected babies or leaving them to be orphaned.[56] For women in Durban or Kampala, the first priority was fertility, preferably with safety but if necessary without.[57] Fertility was at the heart of African female honour. So was the care of children: 'When I inform a person tested that she is carrying HIV,' a doctor wrote, 'she cries immediately: "My children, Oh, my children!"'[58] Central also was endurance, for the burden of caring for AIDS sufferers throughout Africa fell overwhelmingly on wives or mothers. 'If a mother is the first member of a family to become ill,' an investigator in Uganda observed, 'she is likely to be regarded with some bitterness by both her husband and his family. On the other hand, if the husband falls ill first the wife usually stays by his side to the end.'[59] In West Africa, by contrast, marriages were more easily broken and the mother or sister might bear the burden of care, but it was almost always a woman:[60]

I washed him at all times. It was I who washed him, who did everything. And then, moreover, he was tuberculous. I had myself vaccinated for that because I attended him. . . . I don't know why, but truly it needed courage to endure all this. Because he spat, he vomited, and I cleaned it up. He defecated. . . . Because it is necessary to live for better and for worse. The worse had come, so I endured it.[61]

If the AIDS epidemic displayed heroic masculine honour at its most self-destructive, it also displayed female honour at its most heroic.

---

[56] Mira Grieser and others, 'Reproductive decision making and the HIV/AIDS epidemic in Zimbabwe,' *JSAS*, 27 (2001), 225–43; Madeleine Boumpoto, 'Sida, sexualité et procréation au Congo,' in Becker and others, *Vivre et penser*, p. 373; Ogden, 'Reproductive identities,' pp. 166, 270–1; C. Bungener, N. Marchand-Gonod, and R. Jouvent, 'African and European HIV-positive women: psychological and psychosocial differences,' *AIDS Care*, 12 (2000), 541, 545.

[57] Preston-Whyte in Caldwell and others, *Resistances*, p. 143; Ogden in Werbner and Ranger, *Postcolonial identities*, p. 186.

[58] Bernard Joinet and Theodore Mugolola, *Survivre face au sida en Afrique* (Paris, 1994), p. 147.

[59] Marble Gillianne Magezi, 'Against a sea of troubles: AIDS control in Uganda,' *World Health Forum*, 12 (1991), 306.

[60] John Kwasi Anarfi, 'The condition and care of AIDS victims in Ghana,' *Health Transition Review*, 5 (1995), supplement, p. 260; James P. M. Ntozi, 'AIDS morbidity and the role of the family in patient care in Uganda,' ibid., 7 (1997), supplement, pp. 11, 16–17.

[61] Quoted in Hassoun, *Femmes d'Abidjan*, p. 96.

20   Concluding Questions

This book has sought to demonstrate that honour, in its many forms, is a theme running through African history at all its recoverable stages and is still an important motive for African behaviour. Yet perhaps what the book has chiefly demonstrated is the great areas of ignorance where further research is needed. The areas are of two kinds.

First, a history of ideas of honour is needed for each of the major African peoples, especially those with written sources extending back to the nineteenth century and beyond. These histories might well be based on the two approaches most productive in other continents. One would be a study of the changing vocabulary of honour over time, using literary and other sources. Only scattered suggestions along these lines have been possible here, although they may have indicated the rich potential of this method.[1] The other approach would be to investigate the defence of honour in litigation, using court records of the kind employed here for the Eastern Cape.[2] A recent reference to 'the 600 bound volumes of customary court records housed at Manhyia Record Office in Kumasi' suggests the material that might be available in favoured areas.[3] Such studies could contribute immensely to Africa's social and intellectual history.

Second, the book has revealed many individual points at which skilled research might be especially rewarding. For the precolonial period they include the interaction between indigenous notions of honour and Islamic teaching, as might be revealed, perhaps, by the unpublished writings of Muslim reformers in

---

[1] This volume, pp. 32, 43–4, 57.
[2] This volume, pp. 155–60.
[3] Allman and Tashjian, *'I will not eat stone'*, p. xxvi.

Hausaland and other parts of the West African savanna, although the work needs to be pursued also into the twentieth century and into eastern Africa. Ethiopia's rich sources could similarly illuminate the interplay between its heroic traditions and Christianity. There and in all parts of the continent this book has sadly ignored family honour, partly because family history itself has been remarkably neglected in Africa.[4] The subject might perhaps be approached through oral sources. Also missing from this book is adequate consideration of folktale, insult, gift-exchange, and the relationships between honour cultures and Africa's indigenous religions. The transition from heroic egotism to military discipline might repay study in Asante, Dahomey, and other major kingdoms. The attempt made here to investigate what women honoured in one another, rather than what men honoured in women, deserves to be pressed further and given a dimension of historical change, although sources as illuminating as Nana Asma'u's poetry must sadly be rare. Perhaps it would also be possible to examine what women honoured in men.

The history of twentieth-century Africa needs studies of conservatism and the defence of vertical honour, which might be best documented in the records of ruling houses and native administrations. The colonial disarmament of Africans, the establishment of a monopoly of violence, and the ending of private vengeance have seldom been adequately studied; here the records of criminal cases might be especially valuable. Control of violence was one aspect of the larger process of taming heroic traditions, a task involving officials, military officers, missionaries, and schoolteachers which deserves further attention and needs to be seen also from the African side, in terms, perhaps, of the alternative means devised to display honour within colonial societies. Much material on this subject must exist in contemporary newspapers. One untouched question is whether legacies from honour cultures have impeded African entrepreneurship. Recent studies of labour migration, work experience, and masculinity among southern African mineworkers need to be paralleled for other occupational groups and regions. The history of urban youth has also been neglected outside South Africa. Remarkably little is known of the evolution of African racial attitudes, the impact of nation-building propaganda on the citizens of independent countries, or, most notably, decision making by the governments of those countries. Perhaps the largest gap in the recent history of honour in tropical Africa is the lack of studies of resistance to oppression and

---

[4] For rare exceptions, see Schumacher, 'Lebensgeschichte'; Margaret Priestley, *West African trade and coast society: a family study* (London, 1969); Ranger, *Are we not also men?* I have not seen Maximilien Quénum, *Les ancêtres de la famille Quénum* (Langres, 1981).

dictatorship in independent states, a subject pioneered chiefly in Zimbabwe.[5] The relationship between inherited notions of honour and behavioural responses to AIDS in different regions deserves greater consideration than it has received here. If this book has suggested these and other questions, it will have served a purpose.

[5] Alexander and others, *Violence*.

Bibliography

I. Newspapers and Journals

Africa (London)
Africa Today (London)
AIDS Analysis Africa (London)
Bantu World (Johannesburg)
British Central Africa Gazette (Zomba)
Cape Times (Cape Town)
Christian Express (Lovedale)
Chronique Trimestrielle de la Société des Missionnaires d'Afrique (Pères Blancs) (Lille)
Church Missionary Intelligencer (London)
CMS Gazette (London)
C.R. – The Chronicle of the Community of the Resurrection (Mirfield)
Daily Nation (Nairobi)
Daily News (Dar es Salaam)
Diggers' News and Witwatersrand Advertiser (Johannesburg)
Drum (Johannesburg)
EastAfrican (Nairobi)
Ebifa mu Buganda (Mengo, Budo, Namirembe)
Gold Coast Aborigines (Cape Coast)
Gold Coast Leader (Cape Coast)
Imvo Zabantsundu (Kingwilliamstown)
Kikuyu News (Edinburgh)
Lagos Times and Gold Coast Advertiser (Lagos)
Lagos Weekly Record (Lagos)
Mail and Guardian (Johannesburg)
Mambo Leo (Dar es Salaam)
Matalisi (Kampala)
Mercy and Truth (London)
Mission Field (London)
Les Missions Catholiques (Lyon)

Moto (Gweru)
Muigwithania (Nairobi)
Munno (Kampala)
The Nationalist (Dar es Salaam)
New Times and Ethiopia News (London)
New Vision (Kampala)
Newswatch (Lagos)
Nigerian Pioneer (Lagos)
The Observer (Monrovia)
Oxfam News (Oxford)
The People (Nairobi)
South African Commercial Advertiser (Cape Town)
Sunday Standard (Nairobi)
Sunday Vision (Kampala)
The Times (London)
Uganda Argus (Kampala)
Uganda Empya (Kampala)
Uganda Herald (Kampala)
Uganda Notes (Namirembe)
Weekly Review (Nairobi)
Wesleyan Missionary Notices (London)
West Africa (London)
Work in Progress (Johannesburg)

II. Works Cited More Than Once

Abdulaziz, Mohamed H. *Muyaka: 19th century Swahili popular poetry.* Nairobi, 1979.
Abrahams, Peter. *Mine boy.* London, 1989.
Abubakar, A. Y. 'The establishment and development of emirate government in Bauchi, 1805–1903,' PhD thesis, Ahmadu Bello University, Zaria, 1974.
Achuzia, Joe O. G. *Requiem Biafra.* Enugu, 1986.
Adeleye, R. A. 'Mahdist triumph and British revenge in Northern Nigeria: Satiru 1906,' *JHSN*, 6 (1972), 193–214.
Ademoyega, Adewale. *Why we struck: the story of the first Nigerian coup.* Ibadan, 1981.
Afevork, G. J. *Guide du voyageur en Abyssinie.* Rome, 1908.
Aidoo, Agnes Akosua. 'Political crisis and social change in the Asante kingdom, 1867–1901,' PhD thesis, University of California at Los Angeles, 1975.
Ajayi, J. F. A., and Michael Crowder (eds.) *History of West Africa.* 2 vols., Harlow: vol. 1, 3rd edn, 1985; vol. 2, 2nd edn, 1987.
Ajayi, J. F. Ade, and Robert Smith. *Yoruba warfare in the nineteenth century.* Cambridge, 1964.
Akinjogbin, Adeagbo (ed.) *War and peace in Yorubaland, 1793–1893.* Ibadan, 1998.
Akintoye, S. A. *Revolution and power politics in Yorubaland 1840–1893: Ibadan expansion and the rise of the Ekitiparapo.* London, 1971.
Akpabot, Samuel Ekpe. *Football in Nigeria.* London, 1985.
Akpan, Ntieyong U. *The struggle for secession, 1966–1970: a personal account of the Nigerian Civil War.* 2nd edn, London, 1976.

Akyeampong, Emmanuel Kwaku. *Drink, power, and cultural change: a social history of alcohol in Ghana, c.1800 to recent times*. Portsmouth, N.H., 1996.

Alberti, Ludwig. *Ludwig Alberti's account of the tribal life and customs of the Xhosa in 1807*. Trans. W. Fehr, Cape Town, 1968.

Alexander, Jocelyn, JoAnn McGregor, and Terence Ranger. *Violence and memory: one hundred years in the 'dark forests' of Matabeleland*. Oxford, 2000.

Allman, Jean, and Victoria Tashjian. *'I will not eat stone': a women's history of colonial Asante*. Portsmouth, N.H., 2000.

Allman, Jean, Susan Geiger, and Nakanyike Musisi (eds.) *Women in African colonial histories*. Bloomington, 2002.

Ancey, G., and others. *Essais sur la reproduction de formations sociales dominées*. Paris, 1977.

Anderson, David M., and Richard Rathbone (eds.) *Africa's urban past*. Oxford, 2000.

Archinard, [Louis]. *Le Soudan Français en 1889–1890: rapport militaire*. Paris, 1891.

Arhin, Kwame. 'Rank and class among the Asante and Fante in the nineteenth century,' *Africa*, 53 (1983), 2–22.

Armitage, C. H., and A. F. Montanaro. *The Ashanti campaign of 1900*. London, 1901.

Arnett, E. J. *The rise of the Sokoto Fulani being a paraphrase and in some parts a translation of the Infaku'l Maisuri of Sultan Mohammed Bello*. Kano, 1922.

Ashton, Hugh. *The Basuto: a social study of traditional and modern Lesotho*. 2nd edn, London, 1967.

Atieno Odhiambo, E. S., and John Lonsdale (eds.) *Mau Mau and nationhood*. Oxford, 2003.

Austen, Ralph A. (ed.) *In search of Sunjata: the Mande oral epic as history, literature and performance*. Bloomington, 1999.

Awe, Bolanle. 'Praise poems as historical data: the example of the Yoruba *oriki*,' *Africa*, 44 (1974), 331–49.

Awolowo, Obafemi. *Awo: the autobiography of Chief Obafemi Awolowo*. Cambridge, 1960.

Ayandele, E. A. *The Ijebu of Yorubaland, 1850–1950: politics, economy and society*. Ibadan, 1992.

Azikiwe, Nnamdi. *My odyssey: an autobiography*. London, 1970.

Bacuez, Pascal. 'Honneur et pudeur dans la société swahili de Zanzibar,' *Journal des Africanistes*, 67, 2 (1997), 25–48.

Bade, Albert. *Benedicto Kiwanuka: the man and his politics*. Kampala, 1996.

Bairu Tafla (ed.) *A chronicle of Emperor Yohannes IV (1872–89)*. Wiesbaden, 1977.

Baker, William J., and James A. Mangan (eds.) *Sport in Africa: essays in social history*. New York, 1987.

Balesi, Charles John. *From adversaries to comrades-in-arms: West Africans and the French military, 1885–1918*. Waltham, Mass., 1979.

Balogun, Kolawole. *Village boy: my own story*. Ibadan, 1969.

Banégas, Richard, and Jean-Pierre Warnier. 'Nouvelles figures de la réussite et du pouvoir,' *Politique Africaine*, 82 (June 2001), 5–21.

Bank, Andrew. 'Slavery in Cape Town, 1806 to 1834,' MA thesis, University of Cape Town, 1991.

Baratier, [Albert]. *A travers l'Afrique*. Paris, 1912.

Barber, Charles. *The theme of honour's tongue: a study of social attitudes in the English drama from Shakespeare to Dryden.* Göteborg, 1985.

Barber, Karin. 'Documenting social and ideological change through Yoruba oriki: a stylistic analysis,' *JHSN*, 10, 4 (June 1981), 39–52.

Barber, Karin. *I could speak until tomorrow: oriki, women, and the past in a Yoruba town.* Edinburgh, 1991.

Barnes, Teresa A. *'We women worked so hard': gender, urbanization, and social reproduction in colonial Harare, Zimbabwe, 1930–1956.* Portsmouth, N.H., 1999.

Barnett, Donald L., and Karari Njama. *Mau Mau from within: autobiography and analysis of Kenya's peasant revolt.* London, 1966.

Barth, Heinrich. *Travels and discoveries in North and Central Africa . . . in the years 1849–1855.* Reprinted, 3 vols., London, 1965.

Basden, G. T. *Niger Ibos.* Reprinted, London, 1966.

Bay, Edna G. *Wives of the leopard: gender, politics, and culture in the kingdom of Dahomey.* Charlottesville, 1998.

Bayart, Jean-François. *The state in Africa: the politics of the belly.* Trans. M. Harper, C. Harrison, and E. Harrison, London, 1993.

Bayart, Jean-François, Stephen Ellis, and Béatrice Hibou. *The criminalization of the state in Africa.* Oxford, 1999.

Bazenguissa-Ganga, Rémy. *Les voies du politique au Congo: essai de sociologie historique.* Paris, 1997.

Bazin, Jean, and Emmanuel Terray (eds.) *Guerres de lignages et guerres d'Etats en Afrique.* Paris, 1982.

Beattie, John. *The Nyoro state.* Oxford, 1971.

Becker, Charles, Jean-Pierre Dozon, Christine Obbo, and Moriba Touré (eds.) *Vivre et penser le sida en Afrique.* Paris, 1999.

Beckingham, C. F., and G. W. B. Huntingford (eds.) *The Prester John of the Indies . . . being the narrative of the Portuguese Embassy to Ethiopia in 1520 written by Father Francisco Alvares.* Trans. Lord Stanley of Alderley, 2 vols., Cambridge, 1961.

Beckingham, C. F., and G. W. B. Huntingford (eds.) *Some records of Ethiopia, 1593–1646.* London, 1954.

Beidelman, T. O. (ed.) *The translation of culture: essays to E. E. Evans-Pritchard.* London, 1971.

Beinart, William. *The political economy of Pondoland, 1860–1930.* Cambridge, 1982.

Belcher, Stephen. *Epic traditions of Africa.* Bloomington, 1999.

Berger, Iris. *Threads of solidarity: women in South African industry, 1900–1980.* Bloomington, 1992.

Berhane-Selassie, Tsehai. 'The political and military traditions of the Ethiopian peasantry (1800–1941),' DPhil thesis, University of Oxford, 1980.

Berkeley, G. F.-H. *The campaign of Adowa and the rise of Menelik.* New edn, London, 1935.

Berman, Bruce, and John Lonsdale. *Unhappy valley: conflict in Kenya and Africa.* 2 vols., London, 1992.

Bhebe, Ngwabi, and Terence Ranger (eds.) *Soldiers in Zimbabwe's liberation war.* London, 1995.

Biaya, Tshikala Kayembe. 'Les plaisirs de la ville: masculinité, sexualité et féminité à Dakar (1997–2000),' *African Studies Review*, 44, 2 (September 2001), 71–85.

Bigham, C. C. *Military report on Abyssinia (provisional)*. London, 1902.

Birmingham, David, and Phyllis M. Martin (eds.) *History of Central Africa*. 3 vols., London, 1983–98.

Bitima, Tamene. 'On some Oromo historical poems,' *Paideuma*, 29 (1983), 317–25.

Blackburn, Robin. *The overthrow of colonial slavery, 1776–1848*. London, 1988.

Bledsoe, Caroline H. *Women and marriage in Kpelle society*. Stanford, 1980.

Bohannan, Paul. *Justice and judgment among the Tiv*. London, 1957.

Boilat, P.-D. *Esquisses sénégalaises*. Reprinted, Paris, 1984.

Bonner, Philip, Peter Delius, and Deborah Posel (eds.) *Apartheid's genesis 1935–1962*. Braamfontein, 1993.

Botte, Roger. 'Stigmates sociaux et discriminations religieuses: l'ancienne classe servile au Fuuta Jaloo,' *CEA*, 34 (1994), 109–36.

Bowdich, T. Edward. *Mission from Cape Coast Castle to Ashantee*. 3rd edn, London, 1966.

Boyd, Jean. *The Caliph's sister: Nana Asma'u (1793–1865), teacher, poet and Islamic leader*. London, 1989.

Boyd, Jean, and Beverly B. Mack (eds.) *Collected works of Nana Asma'u, daughter of Usman dan Fodiyo (1793–1864)*. East Lansing, 1997.

Bozzoli, Belinda (ed.) *Town and countryside in the Transvaal: capitalist penetration and popular response*. Johannesburg, 1983.

Brackenbury, Henry. *The Ashanti War: a narrative*. Reprinted, 2 vols., London, 1968.

Brass, William, and others. *The demography of tropical Africa*. Princeton, 1968.

Breckenridge, Keith. 'The allure of violence: men, race and masculinity on the South African goldmines, 1900–1950', *JSAS*, 24 (1998), 669–93.

Budge, E. A. Wallis (ed.) *The life of Takla Haymanot*. 2 vols., London, 1906.

Bulman, Stephen Paul Dušan. 'Interpreting Sunjata: a comparative analysis and exegesis of the Malinke epic,' PhD thesis, University of Birmingham, 1990.

Bundy, Colin. *The rise and fall of the South African peasantry*. London, 1979.

Burton, Richard F. *Zanzibar; city, island, and coast*. 2 vols., London, 1872.

Busia, K. A. *The position of the chief in the modern political system of Ashanti*. Reprinted, London, 1968.

Caldwell, John C., Pat Caldwell, and I. O. Orubuloye. 'The family and sexual networking in sub-Saharan Africa: historical regional differences and present-day implications,' *Population Studies*, 46 (1992), 385–410.

Caldwell, John C., Pat Caldwell, and Pat Quiggin. 'The social context of AIDS in sub-Saharan Africa,' *Population and Development Review*, 15 (1989), 185–234.

Caldwell, John C., and others (eds.) *Resistances to behavioural change to reduce HIV/AIDS infection in predominantly heterosexual epidemics in Third World countries*. Canberra, 1999.

Cape of Good Hope. *Report and proceedings, with appendices, of the Government Commission on Native Laws and Customs*. G.4–83: Cape Town, 1883.

Caplan, Gerald L. *The elites of Barotseland, 1878–1969: a political history of Zambia's Western Province*. London, 1970.

Christelow, Allen (ed.) *Thus ruled Emir Abbas: selected cases from the records of the Emir of Kano's Judicial Council*. East Lansing, 1994.

Clapperton, Hugh. *Journal of a second expedition into the interior of Africa.* Reprinted, London, 1966.

Clark, Trevor. *A right honourable gentleman: Abubakar from the black rock.* London, 1991.

Clayton, Anthony, and David Killingray. *Khaki and blue: military and police in British colonial Africa.* Athens, Ohio, 1989.

Clothier, Norman. *Black valour: the South African Native Labour Contingent, 1916–1918, and the sinking of the Mendi.* Pietermaritzburg, 1987.

Codere, Helen. *The biography of an African society: Rwanda, 1900–1960: based on forty-eight Rwandan autobiographies.* Tervuren, 1973.

Coles, Catherine, and Beverly Mack (eds.) *Hausa women in the twentieth century.* Madison, 1991.

Colson, Elizabeth, and Max Gluckman (eds.) *Seven tribes of British Central Africa.* London, 1951.

Conombo, Joseph Issoufou. *Souvenirs de guerre d'un 'tirailleur sénégalais'.* Paris, 1989.

Conrad, David C. (ed.) *A state of intrigue: the epic of Bamana Segu according to Tayiru Banbera.* Oxford, 1990.

Cooper, Barbara M. *Marriage in Maradi: gender and culture in a Hausa society in Niger, 1900–1989.* Portsmouth, N.H., 1997.

Cooper, Frederick. *Plantation slavery on the east coast of Africa.* New Haven, 1977.

Copans, Jean (ed.) *Sécheresses et famines du Sahel.* 2 vols., Paris, 1975.

Cope, Trevor (ed.) *Izibongo: Zulu praise-poems.* Oxford, 1968.

Coplan, David. *In township tonight! South Africa's black city music and theatre.* London, 1985.

Coplan, David B. *In the time of cannibals: the word music of South Africa's Basotho migrants.* Johannesburg, 1994.

Crocker, W. R. *Nigeria: a critique of British colonial administration.* London, 1936.

Crowder, Michael (ed.) *West African resistance.* London, 1971.

Crummey, Donald. *Land and society in the Christian kingdom of Ethiopia from the thirteenth to the twentieth century.* Oxford, 2000.

Crush, Jonathan, and Wilmot James (eds.) *Crossing boundaries: mine migrancy in a democratic South Africa.* Cape Town, 1995.

da Caltanisetta, Luca. *Diaire congolais (1690–1701).* Trans. F. Bontinck, Louvain, 1970.

Damane, M., and P. B. Sanders (eds.) *Lithoko: Sotho praise poems.* Oxford, 1974.

Davis, Natalie Zemon. *The gift in sixteenth-century France.* Oxford, 2000.

Deng, Francis Mading. *The Dinka of the Sudan.* New York, 1972.

Deng, Francis Mading. *The man called Deng Majok: a biography of power, polygyny, and change.* New Haven, 1986.

Deng, Francis Mading. *Tradition and modernization: a challenge for law among the Dinka of the Sudan.* New Haven, 1971.

Denham, Dixon, and Hugh Clapperton. *Narrative of travels and discoveries in Northern and Central Africa in the years 1822, 1823, and 1824.* London, 1826.

Descostes, François. *Au Soudan (1890–1891): souvenirs d'un tirailleur sénégalais.* Paris, 1893.

Devisch, René. 'Frenzy, violence, and ethical renewal in Kinshasa,' *Public Culture*, 7, 3 (Spring 1995), 593–629.

Diawara, Mamadou. *La graine de la parole: dimension sociale et politique des traditions orales du royaume de Jaara (Mali) du XVe au milieu du XIXe siècle*. Stuttgart, 1990.

Dingake, Michael. *My fight against apartheid*. London, 1987.

Diop, Momar-Coumba (ed.) *Le Sénégal contemporain*. Paris, 2002.

Diouf, Mamadou. *Le Kajoor au XIXe siècle: pouvoir ceddo et conquête coloniale*. Paris, 1990.

Döhne, J. L. *A Zulu-Kafir dictionary*. Cape Town, 1857; reprinted Farnborough, 1967.

Donnan, Elizabeth (ed.) *Documents illustrative of the history of the slave trade to America*. 4 vols., Washington, D.C., 1930–5.

Dooling, Wayne. *Law and community in a slave society: Stellenbosch District, South Africa, c.1760–1820*. Cape Town, 1992.

Douglas, Mary. *The Lele of the Kasai*. London, 1963.

Dumestre, Gérard (ed.) *La geste de Ségou*. Paris, 1979.

Dunglas, Edouard. 'La première attaque des Dahoméens contre Abéokuta (3 mars 1851),' *Etudes Dahoméennes*, 1 (1948), 7–19.

Dusgate, Richard H. *The conquest of Northern Nigeria*. London, 1985.

Echenberg, Myron. *Colonial conscripts: the Tirailleurs Sénégalais in French West Africa, 1857–1960*. Portsmouth, N.H., 1991.

Egziabher, Salome Gabre. 'The Ethiopian patriots, 1936–1941,' *Ethiopia Observer*, 12 (1969), 63–91.

Ellis, Stephen. *The mask of anarchy: the destruction of Liberia and the religious dimension of an African civil war*. London, 1999.

El Zein, Abdul Hamid M. *The sacred meadows: a structural analysis of religious symbolism in an East African town*. [Evanston], 1974.

Erlank, Natasha. 'Gendered reactions to social dislocation and missionary activity in Xhosaland 1836–1847,' *African Studies*, 59 (2000), 205–27.

Etherington, Norman. *The great treks: the transformation of southern Africa, 1815–1854*. Harlow, 2001.

Etherington, Norman. *Preachers, peasants, and politics in southeast Africa, 1835–1880: African Christian communities in Natal, Pondoland, and Zululand*. London, 1978.

Evans-Pritchard, E. E. *The Nuer: a description of the modes of livelihood and political institutions of a Nilotic people*. Oxford, 1940.

Fadiman, Jeffrey A. *An oral history of tribal warfare: the Meru of Mt. Kenya*. Athens, Ohio, 1982.

Fadipe, N. A. *The sociology of the Yoruba*. Ibadan, 1970.

Fadoyebo, Isaac. *A stroke of unbelievable luck*. Ed. David Killingray, Madison, 1999.

Fallers, L. A. (ed.) *The king's men: leadership and status in Buganda on the eve of independence*. London, 1964.

Falola, Toyin. *The political economy of a pre-colonial African state: Ibadan, 1830–1900*. Ile-Ife, 1984.

Falola, Toyin. *Violence in Nigeria: the crisis of religious politics and secular ideologies*. Rochester, N.Y., 1998.

Falola, Toyin, and Dare Oguntomisin. *The military in nineteenth-century Yoruba politics*. Ife, 1984.

Falola, Toyin, and G. O. Oguntomisin. *Yoruba warlords of the nineteenth century*. Trenton, N.J., 2001.

Farès, Bichr. *L'honneur chez les Arabes avant l'Islam: étude de sociologie*. Paris, 1932.

Feierman, Steven. *Peasant intellectuals: anthropology and history in Tanzania.* Madison, 1990.

Ferguson, Douglas Edwin. 'Nineteenth-century Hausaland, being a description by Imam Imoru of the land, economy, and society of his people,' PhD thesis, University of California at Los Angeles, 1973.

Ferguson, R. Brian, and Neil L. Whitehead (eds.) *War in the tribal zone: expanding states and indigenous warfare.* 2nd edn, Santa Fe, 2000.

Finley, M. I. *The world of Odysseus.* 2nd edn, London, 1977.

Fisher, Humphrey J. *Slavery in the history of Muslim black Africa.* London, 2001.

[Flament, F.] *La Force Publique de sa naissance à 1914: participation des militaires à l'histoire des premières années du Congo.* Brussels, 1952.

Foà, Edouard. *Le Dahomey.* Paris, 1895.

Fortes, Meyer. *The web of kinship among the Tallensi.* London, 1949.

Fortes, M., and E. E. Evans-Pritchard (eds.) *African political systems.* London, 1940.

Fyfe, Christopher. *A history of Sierra Leone.* London, 1962.

Gaden, Henri. *Proverbes et maximes peuls et toucouleurs.* Paris, 1931.

Gahama, Joseph. *Le Burundi sous administration belge: la période du mandat, 1919–1939.* Paris, 1983.

Gandoulou, Justin-Daniel. *Dandies à Bacongo: le culte de l'élégance dans la société congolaise contemporaine.* Paris, 1989.

Gerard, Albert X. 'Amharic creative literature: the early phase,' *JES*, 6, 2 (1968), 39–59.

Ghana. *Report of the Commission appointed . . . to enquire into the properties of Kwame Nkrumah.* Accra-Tema [1967].

Gilmore, David D. (ed.) *Honor and shame and the unity of the Mediterranean.* Washington, D.C., 1987.

Glaser, Clive. 'Anti-social bandits: juvenile delinquency and the tsotsi youth gang subculture on the Witwatersrand 1935–1960,' MA thesis, University of the Witwatersrand, 1990.

Glaser, Clive. *Bo-Tsotsi: the youth gangs of Soweto, 1935–1976.* Portsmouth, N.H., 2000.

Glassman, Jonathon. *Feasts and riot: revelry, rebellion, and popular consciousness on the Swahili Coast, 1856–1888.* Portsmouth, N.H., 1995.

Gluckman, Max. *The ideas in Barotse jurisprudence.* Reprinted, Manchester, 1972.

Gluckman, Max. *The judicial process among the Barotse of Northern Rhodesia.* 2nd edn, Manchester, 1967.

Gobat, Samuel. *Journal of a three years' residence in Abyssinia.* London, 2nd edn, 1847.

Gordon, Robert J. *Mines, masters and migrants: life in a Namibian mine compound.* Johannesburg, 1977.

Greenberg, Kenneth S. *Honor and slavery.* Princeton, 1996.

Grundlingh, Albert. *Fighting their own war: South African blacks and the First World War.* Johannesburg, 1987.

Guèbrè Sellassié. *Chronique du règne de Ménélik II, Roi des Rois d'Ethiopie.* Trans. Tèsfa Sellassié, 2 vols., Paris, 1930–1.

Guidi, I. (ed.) *Annales Regum Iyasu II et Iyo'as.* Rome, 1912.

Gutkind, Peter C. W., Robin Cohen, and Jean Copans (eds.) *African labor history.* Beverly Hills, 1978.

Guyer, Jane I. (ed.) *Money matters: instability, values and social payments in the modern history of West African communities*. Portsmouth, N.H., 1995.

Haile Sellassie. *My life and Ethiopia's progress, 1892–1937*. Trans. E. Ullendorff, London, 1976.

Hallpike, C. R. *The Konso of Ethiopia: a study of the values of a Cushitic people*. Oxford, 1972.

Hampate Ba, Amadou, and Jacques Daget. *L'empire peul du Macina (1818–1853)*. Reprinted, Abidjan, 1984.

Hampate Ba, Amadou, and Lilyan Kesteloot (eds.) 'Une épopée peule: "Silamaka",' *L'homme*, 8 (1968), 1–36.

Hansen, Karen Tranberg (ed.) *African encounters with domesticity*. New Brunswick, N.J., 1992.

Hanson, John, and David Robinson. *After the jihad: the reign of Ahmad al-Kabir in the Western Sudan*. East Lansing, 1991.

Harries, Lyndon. *Swahili poetry*. Oxford, 1962.

Harris, W. Cornwallis. *The highlands of Aethiopia*. 3 vols., London, 1844.

Hassoun, Judith. *Femmes d'Abidjan face au sida*. Paris, 1997.

Hastings, Adrian. *The Church in Africa, 1450–1950*. Oxford, 1994.

Havard, Jean-François. 'Ethos "bul faale" et nouvelles figures de la réussite au Sénégal,' *Politique Africaine*, 82 (June 2001), 63–77.

Hay, Margaret Jean, and Marcia Wright (eds.) *African women and the law: historical perspectives*. Boston, 1982.

Haywood, A., and F. A. S. Clarke. *The history of the Royal West African Frontier Force*. Aldershot, 1964.

Hazoume, Paul. *Doguicimi*. Trans. R. Bjornson, Washington, D.C., 1990.

Heald, Suzette. *Manhood and morality: sex, violence and ritual in Gisu society*. London, 1999.

Herskovits, Melville J. *Dahomey: an ancient West African kingdom*. 2 vols., New York, 1938.

Herskovits, Melville J., and Frances S. Herskovits. *Dahomean narrative: a cross-cultural analysis*. Evanston, 1958.

Herzfeld, Michael. *The poetics of manhood: contest and identity in a Cretan mountain village*. Princeton, 1985.

Hilton, Anne. *The kingdom of Kongo*. Oxford, 1985.

Hinderer, Anna. *Seventeen years in the Yoruba country*. London, 1872.

Hiskett, Mervyn. *A history of Hausa Islamic verse*. London, 1975.

Hodgson, Lady. *The siege of Kumassi*. London, 1901.

Honwana, Alcinda. 'Innocents et coupables: les enfants-soldats comme acteurs tactiques,' *Politique Africaine*, 80 (December 2000), 58–78.

Hooton, E. A., and Natica I. Bates (eds.) *Varia Africana III*. Harvard African Studies, vol. 3. Cambridge, Mass., 1922.

Hope, Kempe Ronald, Sr., and Bornwell C. Chikulo (eds.) *Corruption and development in Africa: lessons from country case-studies*. Basingstoke, 2000.

Howell, P. P. *A manual of Nuer law, being an account of customary law, its evolution and development in the courts established by the Sudan Government*. London, 1954.

Hsien Chin Hu. 'The Chinese concepts of "face",' *American Anthropologist*, NS, 46 (1944), 45–64.

Hughes, Heather. 'Doubly elite: exploring the life of John Langalibalele Dube,' *JSAS*, 27 (2001), 445–58.

Hunter, Monica. *Reaction to conquest: effects of contact with Europeans on the Pondo of South Africa*. 2nd edn, London, 1961.

Huntingford, G. W. B. (ed.) *The glorious victories of Amda Seyon*. Oxford, 1965.

Hunwick, John O. *Timbuktu and the Songhay Empire: Al-Sadi's Tarikh al-sudan down to 1613 and other contemporary documents*. Leiden, 1999.

Hutchful, Eboe, and Abdoulaye Bathily (eds.) *The military and militarism in Africa*. Dakar, 1998.

Hutchinson, Sharon E. *Nuer dilemmas: coping with money, war, and the state*. Berkeley, 1996.

Ikegami, Eiko. *The taming of the samurai: honorific individualism and the making of modern Japan*. Cambridge, Mass., 1995.

Iliffe, John. *The African poor: a history*. Cambridge, 1987.

Iliffe, John. *Africans: the history of a continent*. Cambridge, 1995.

Iliffe, John. *East African doctors: a history of the modern profession*. Cambridge, 1998.

Iliffe, John. *The emergence of African capitalism*. London, 1983.

Iliffe, John. *A modern history of Tanganyika*. Cambridge, 1979.

Isichei, Elizabeth. *A history of the Igbo people*. London, 1976.

Isichei, Elizabeth. *A history of Nigeria*. London, 1983.

Jackson, Ashley. 'African soldiers and imperial authorities: tensions and unrest during the service of High Commission Territories soldiers in the British Army, 1941–46,' *JSAS*, 25 (1999), 645–65.

Jamous, Raymond. *Honneur et baraka: les structures sociales traditionnelles dans le Rif*. Cambridge, 1981.

Jeater, Diana. *Marriage, perversion, and power: the construction of moral discourse in Southern Rhodesia, 1894–1930*. Oxford, 1993.

Jingoes, Stimela Jason. *A chief is a chief by the people*. London, 1975.

Johnson, G. Wesley, Jr. *The emergence of black politics in Senegal: the struggle for power in the four communes, 1900–1920*. Stanford, 1971.

Johnson, John William, Thomas A. Hale, and Stephen Belcher (eds.) *Oral epics from Africa*. Bloomington, 1997.

Johnson, Samuel. *The history of the Yorubas, from the earliest times to the beginning of the British protectorate*. Reprinted, London, 1973.

Kabaka [Mutesa II] of Buganda. *Desecration of my kingdom*. London, 1967.

Kadalie, Clements. *My life and the ICU*. Ed. S. Trapido, London, 1970.

Kagame, Alexis. *Le code des institutions politiques du Rwanda précolonial*. Brussels, 1952.

Kaggwa, Sir Apolo. *The kings of Buganda*. Trans. M. S. M. Kiwanuka, Nairobi, 1971.

Kagwa, Sir Apolo. *Ekitabo kye kika kye Nsenene*. 2nd edn, Mengo [1905?]. [Manuscript translation of extracts, by J. A. Rowe.]

Kagwa, Apolo. 'The reign of Mwanga.' [Unpublished translation by Simon Musoke of pp. 138–277 of *Ekitabo kya Basekabaka be Buganda* (Kampala, 1901): copy in CUL.]

[Kagwa, Sir Apolo. Select documents and letters from the collected Apolo Kagwa Papers at Makerere College Library: microfilm copy in CUL.]

Kane, Mouhamed Moustapha. 'A history of Fuuta Tooro, 1890s–1920s: Senegal under colonial rule,' PhD thesis, Michigan State University, 1987.

Karis, Thomas, and others (eds.) *From protest to challenge: a documentary history of African politics in South Africa.* 5 vols., Stanford, 1972–97.

Karlström, Mikael. 'Imagining democracy: political culture and democratisation in Buganda,' *Africa*, 66 (1996), 485–505.

Karugire, Samwiri Rubaraza. *A history of the kingdom of Nkore in western Uganda to 1896.* Oxford, 1971.

Kenyatta, Jomo. *Facing Mount Kenya: the tribal life of the Gikuyu.* Reprinted, London, 1961.

Kershaw, Greet. *Mau Mau from below.* Oxford, 1997.

Killingray, David. 'African voices from two world wars,' *Historical Research*, 74 (2001), 425–43.

Killingray, David. 'The mutiny of the West African Regiment in the Gold Coast, 1901,' *IJAHS*, 16 (1983), 441–54.

Kirk-Greene, Anthony H. M. *Mutumin Kirkii: the concept of the good man in Hausa.* Bloomington, 1974.

Kisekka, Mere Nakateregga. 'Heterosexual relationships in Uganda,' PhD thesis, University of Missouri, 1973.

Kitching, Gavin. *Class and economic change in Kenya: the making of an African petite bourgeoisie 1905–1970.* New Haven, 1980.

Ki-Zerbo, Joseph. *Alfred Diban: premier chrétien de Haute-Volta.* Paris, 1983.

Klein, Martin A. *Slavery and colonial rule in French West Africa.* Cambridge, 1998.

Krapf, [J.] L. *A dictionary of the Suahili language*, London, 1882: reprinted, Ridgewood, N.J., n.d.

Kriel, T. J. *The new English-Sesotho dictionary.* N.p., 1958.

Krige, Eileen Jensen. *The social system of the Zulus.* 2nd edn, reprinted, Pietermaritzburg, 1950.

Kropf, Albert. *A Kaffir-English dictionary.* Lovedale, 1899.

Kunene, Daniel P. *Heroic poetry of the Basotho.* Oxford, 1971.

Kuper, Adam. *Wives for cattle: bridewealth and marriage in southern Africa.* London, 1982.

Kuper, Hilda. *Sobhuza II, Ngwenyama and King of Swaziland: the story of an hereditary ruler and his country.* London, 1978.

Kuper, Hilda, and Leo Kuper (eds.) *African law: adaptation and development.* Berkeley, 1965.

Kuper, Leo. *An African bourgeoisie: race, class, and politics in South Africa.* New Haven, 1965.

Kynoch, Gary. '"A man among men": gender, identity and power in South Africa's Marashea gangs,' *Gender and History*, 13 (2001), 249–72.

Laband, John. *The rise and fall of the Zulu nation.* London, 1997.

Laburthe-Tolra, Philippe. *Les seigneurs de la forêt: essai sur le passé historique, l'organisation sociale et les normes éthiques des anciens Beti du Cameroun.* Paris, 1981.

Laburthe-Tolra, Philippe. *Vers la lumière? ou la désir d'Ariel: à propos des Beti du Cameroun: sociologie de la conversion.* Paris, 1999.

la Fontaine, J. S. *Initiation.* Manchester, 1986.

la Hausse de Lalouvière, Paul. *Restless identities: signatures of nationalism, Zulu ethnicity and history in the lives of Petros Lamula (c.1881–1948) and Lymon Maling (1889–c.1936)*. Pietermaritzburg, 2000.

Laitin, David D. *Hegemony and culture: politics and religious change among the Yoruba*. Chicago, 1986.

Lamphear, John. *The scattering time: Turkana responses to colonial rule*. Oxford, 1992.

Landau, Paul Stuart. *The realm of the word: language, gender, and Christianity in a southern African kingdom*. Portsmouth, N.H., 1995.

Lander, Richard. *Records of Captain Clapperton's last expedition to Africa*. Reprinted, 2 vols., London, 1967.

Lange, Dierk. *Le Diwan des Sultans du [Kanem-]Bornu: chronologie et histoire d'un royaume africain (de la fin du Xe siècle jusqu'à 1808)*. Wiesbaden, 1977.

Lange, Dierk (ed.) *A Sudanic chronicle: the Borno expeditions of Idris Alauma (1564–1576)*. Stuttgart, 1987.

Last, Murray. *The Sokoto Caliphate*. London, 1967.

Law, Robin. *The Oyo Empire c.1600–c.1836: a West African imperialism in the era of the Atlantic slave trade*. Oxford, 1977.

Law, Robin. *The Slave Coast of West Africa, 1550–1750: the impact of the Atlantic slave trade on an African society*. Oxford, 1991.

Lawler, Nancy Ellen. *Soldiers of misfortune: Ivoirien tirailleurs of World War II*. Athens, Ohio, 1992.

Leclerc-Madlala, Suzanne. 'Infect one, infect all: Zulu youth response to the AIDS epidemic in South Africa,' *Medical Anthropology*, 17 (1996–7), 363–80.

Le Herissé, A. *L'ancien royaume du Dahomey*. Paris, 1911.

Leith-Ross, Sylvia. *African women: a study of the Ibo of Nigeria*. London, 1939.

Leslie, J. A. K. *A survey of Dar es Salaam*. London, 1963.

Lever, Alison. 'Honor as a red herring,' *Critique of Anthropology*, 6, 3 (Winter 1986), 83–106.

Levine, Donald N. 'The concept of masculinity in Ethiopian culture,' *International Journal of Social Psychiatry*, 12 (1966), 17–23.

Levine, Donald N. *Wax and gold: tradition and innovation in Ethiopian culture*. Reprinted, Chicago, 1972.

Le Vine, Victor T. *Political corruption: the Ghana case*. Stanford, 1975.

Levtzion, N., and J. F. P. Hopkins (eds.) *Corpus of early Arabic sources for West African history*. Cambridge, 1981.

Levtzion, Nehemia, and Randall L. Pouwels (eds.) *The history of Islam in Africa*. Athens, Ohio, 2000.

Linden, Ian. *Church and revolution in Rwanda*. Manchester, 1977.

Lindholm, Charles. *Generosity and jealousy: the Swat Pukhtun of northern Pakistan*. New York, 1982.

Littmann, Enno. *Die altamharischen Kaiserlieder*. Strassburg, 1914.

Lloyd, P. C., A. L. Mabogunje, and B. Awe (eds.) *The city of Ibadan*. Cambridge, 1967.

Lombard, Jacques. *Autorités traditionnelles et pouvoirs européens en Afrique noire: le déclin d'une aristocratie sous le régime colonial*. Paris, 1967.

Lovejoy, Paul E. *Transformations in slavery: a history of slavery in Africa*. Cambridge, 1983.

Lovejoy, Paul E., and Jan S. Hogendorn. *Slow death for slavery: the course of abolition in Northern Nigeria, 1897–1936*. Cambridge, 1993.

Low, D. A. *Religion and society in Buganda, 1875–1900*. Kampala, n.d.

Low, D. A., and R. C. Pratt. *Buganda and British overrule, 1900–1955: two studies*. Nairobi, 1970.

Luckham, Robin. *The Nigerian military*. Cambridge, 1971.

Lunn, Joe. *Memoirs of the maelstrom: a Senegalese oral history of the First World War*. Portsmouth, N.H., 1999.

Ly, Amadou (ed.) *L'épopée de Samba Gueladiegui*. n.p., 1991.

Ly, Boubakar. 'L'honneur dans les sociétés ouolof et toucouleur du Sénégal,' *Présence Africaine*, 61 (1967), 32–67.

Ly, Boubakar. 'L'honneur et les valeurs morales dans les sociétés ouolof et toucouleur du Sénégal,' Thèse pour le Doctorat de Troisième Cycle de Sociologie, Université de Paris (Faculté des Lettres et Sciences Humaines), 2 vols, 1966.

Ly-Tall, Madina. *Un Islam militant en Afrique de l'ouest au XIXe siècle: le Tijaniyya de Saiku Umar Futiyu contre les pouvoirs traditionnels et la puissance coloniale*. Paris, 1991.

Mack, Beverly B., and Jean Boyd. *One woman's jihad: Nana Asma'u, scholar and scribe*. Bloomington, 2000.

Maclean, [John]. *A compendium of Kafir laws and customs*. Mount Coke, 1858.

Madiebo, Alexander A. *The Nigerian revolution and the Biafran War*. Enugu, 1980.

Magel, Emil A. 'Hare and hyena: symbols of honor and shame in the oral narratives of the Wolof of the Senegambia,' PhD thesis, University of Wisconsin–Madison, 1977.

Mager, Anne Kelk. *Gender and the making of a South African Bantustan: a social history of the Ciskei, 1945–1959*. Portsmouth, N.H., 1999.

Mahmoud Kati. *Tarikh el-fettach*. Trans. O. Houdas and M. Delafosse, Paris, 1913.

Mair, L. P. *Native marriage in Buganda*. London, 1940.

Makhoba, Mandlenkosi. *The sun shall rise for the workers*. Braamfontein, 1984.

Malaba, Mbongeni Zikhethele. 'Shaka as a literary theme,' PhD thesis, University of York, 1986.

Mandela, Nelson. *Long walk to freedom: the autobiography of Nelson Mandela*. London, 1994.

Mann, Kristin. *Marrying well: marriage, status and social change among the educated elite in colonial Lagos*. Cambridge, 1985.

Mann, Kristin, and Richard Roberts (eds.) *Law in colonial Africa*. Portsmouth, N.H., 1991.

Marcum, John. *The Angolan revolution*. 2 vols., Cambridge, Mass., 1969–78.

Markakis, John. *Ethiopia: anatomy of a traditional polity*. Oxford, 1974.

Marks, Monique. *Young warriors: youth politics, identity and violence in South Africa*. Johannesburg, 2001.

Martin, Phyllis M. *Leisure and society in colonial Brazzaville*. Cambridge, 1995.

Mashinini, Emma. *Strikes have followed me all my life: a South African autobiography*. London, 1989.

Mason, John Edwin, Jr. ' "Fit for freedom": the slaves, slavery, and emancipation in the Cape Colony, South Africa, 1806 to 1842,' PhD thesis, Yale University, 1992.

Mason, John Edwin. 'Hendrik Albertus and his ex-slave Mey: a drama in three acts,' *JAH*, 31 (1990), 423–45.

Mattera, Don. *Gone with the twilight: a story of Sophiatown*. London, 1987.

Mayer, Philip (ed.) *Black villagers in an industrial society: anthropological perspectives on labour migration in South Africa*. Cape Town, 1980.

Mayer, Philip (ed.). *Socialization: the approach from social anthropology*. London, 1970.

Mbadiwe, Kingsley Ozuomba. *Rebirth of a nation (autobiography)*. Enugu, 1991.

Mbembe, Achille. *La naissance du maquis dans le Sud-Cameroun (1920–1960): histoire des usages de la raison en colonie*. Paris, 1996.

Mbembe, Achille. 'Provisional notes on the postcolony,' *Africa*, 62 (1992), 3–37.

McCaskie, T. C. *Asante identities: history and modernity in an African village, 1850–1950*. Edinburgh, 2000.

McCaskie, T. C. 'The consuming passions of Kwame Boakye: an essay on agency and identity in Asante history,' *JACS*, 13 (2000), 43–62.

McCaskie, T. C. *State and society in pre-colonial Asante*. Cambridge, 1995.

McCracken, John. *Politics and Christianity in Malawi, 1875–1940: the impact of the Livingstonia Mission in the Northern Province*. Cambridge, 1977.

McGowan, Winston. 'African resistance to the Atlantic slave trade in West Africa,' *Slavery and Abolition*, 11 (1990), 5–29.

McGregor, G. P. *King's College, Budo: the first sixty years*. Nairobi, 1967.

McKenzie, Kirsten Elizabeth. 'Gender and honour in middle-class Cape Town: the making of colonial identities 1828–1850,' DPhil thesis, University of Oxford, 1997.

Médard, Jean-François. 'Le "Big Man" en Afrique: esquisse d'analyse du politicien entrepreneur,' *L'Année Sociologique*, 42 (1992), 167–92.

Meer, Fatima. *Race and suicide in South Africa*. London, 1976.

Meinhof, C. 'Das Lied des Liongo,' *Zeitschrift für Eingeborenen-Sprachen*, 15 (1924–5), 241–65.

Michel, Marc. *L'appel à l'Afrique: contributions et réactions à l'effort de guerre en A.O.F. (1914–1919)*. Paris, 1982.

Middleton, John. *The world of the Swahili*. New Haven, 1992.

Middleton, John, and David Tait (eds.) *Tribes without rulers: studies in African segmentary systems*. London, 1958.

Miers, Suzanne, and Martin Klein (eds.) *Slavery and colonial rule in Africa*. London, 1999.

Miers, Suzanne, and Igor Kopytoff (eds.) *Slavery in Africa: historical and anthropological perspectives*. Madison, 1977.

Miers, Suzanne, and Richard Roberts (eds.) *The end of slavery in Africa*. Madison, 1988.

Miescher, Stephan Felix. 'Becoming a man in Kwawu: gender, law, personhood, and the construction of masculinities in colonial Ghana, 1875–1957,' PhD thesis, Northwestern University, 1997.

Miller, Joseph C. *Way of death: merchant capitalism and the Angolan slave trade 1730–1830*. London, 1988.

Miners, N. J. *The Nigerian army, 1956–1966*. London, 1971.

Miti, James Kabazzi. 'A history of Buganda.' Typescript, 3 vols., [1938?], SOAS Library.

Mohamed, Jama. 'The 1944 Somaliland Camel Corps mutiny and popular politics,' *History Workshop Journal*, 50 (Autumn 2000), 93–113.

Molvaer, Reidulf K. (ed.) *Prowess, piety and politics: the chronicle of* Abeto *Iyasu and Empress Zewditu of Ethiopia (1909–1930), recorded by* Aleqa *Gebre-Igziabiher Elyas*. Cologne, 1994.

Molvaer, Reidulf K. *Socialization and social control in Ethiopia*. Wiesbaden, 1995.

Molvaer, Reidulf Knut. *Tradition and change in Ethiopia: social and cultural life as reflected in Amharic fictional literature ca.1930–1974*. Leiden, 1980.

Moodie, T. Dunbar, with Vivienne Ndatshe. *Going for gold: men, mines, and migration*. Berkeley, 1994.

Morgan, Kemi. *Akinyele's outline history of Ibadan: part one*. Ibadan, n.d.

Morgenthau, Ruth Schachter. *Political parties in French-speaking West Africa*. Oxford, 1964.

Morrell, Robert (ed.) *Changing men in southern Africa*. Pietermaritzburg, 2001.

Mostert, Noel. *Frontiers: the epic of South Africa's creation and the tragedy of the Xhosa people*. London, 1992.

Moyer, Richard A. 'A history of the Mfengu of the Eastern Cape, 1815–1865,' PhD thesis, University of London, 1976.

Mphahlele, Ezekiel. *Down Second Avenue*. Reprinted, London, 1990.

Muffett, D. J. M. *Let truth be told: volume 1*. Zaria, 1982.

Mufuta, Patrice (ed.) *Le chant* kasala *des Luba*. Paris, 1968.

Mukasa, Ham. 'Do not retreat.' Typescript translation by J. A. Rowe of *Simuda nyuma*. 3 vols: only vol. 1 published, London, 1938.

Mullins, J. D. *The wonderful story of Uganda*. London, 1904.

Murray, Colin. *Families divided: the impact of migrant labour in Lesotho*. Cambridge, 1981.

Muvumba, Joshua. 'The politics of stratification and transformation in the kingdom of Ankole, Uganda,' PhD thesis, Harvard University, 1982.

Nadel, S. F. *A black Byzantium: the kingdom of Nupe in Nigeria*. Reprinted, London, 1969.

Newell, Stephanie. *Ghanaian popular fiction*. Oxford, 2000.

Niane, Djibril Tamsir. *Histoire des Mandingues de l'ouest: le royaume du Gabou*. Paris, 1989.

Niane, D. T. *Sundiata: an epic of old Mali*. Trans. G. D. Pickett, London, 1965.

Nkrumah, Kwame. *The autobiography of Kwame Nkrumah*. Edinburgh, 1957.

Norris, Edward Graham. *Wirtschaft und Wirtschaftspolitik in Abeokuta, 1830–1867: Aspekte der Ethnographie und Geschichte eines Yoruba-Staates im neunzehnten Jahrhundert*. Wiesbaden, 1978.

Northern Rhodesia. *Evidence taken by Commission appointed to enquire into the disturbances in the Copperbelt*. 2 vols., Lusaka, 1935.

Nwaubani, Ebere. 'Chieftaincy among the Igbo: a guest on the center-stage,' *IJAHS*, 27 (1994), 347–71.

Nyerere, Julius K. *Freedom and socialism*. Dar es Salaam, 1968.

Nyerere, Julius K. *Freedom and unity*. Dar es Salaam, 1966.

Obasanjo, Olusegun. *My command: an account of the Nigerian Civil War, 1967–1970*. Reprinted, London, 1981.

Obbo, Christine. *African women: their struggle for economic independence*. London, 1980.

Odogwu, Bernard. *No place to hide (crises and conflicts inside Biafra)*. Enugu, 1985.

Ogden, Jessica Ann. 'Reproductive identity and the proper woman: the response of urban women to AIDS in Uganda,' PhD thesis, University of Hull, 1995.

Ogot, B. A. (ed.) *UNESCO general history of Africa: volume V*. Oxford, 1992.

Okihiro, Gary Y. (ed.) *In resistance: studies in African, Caribbean, and Afro-American history*. Amherst, 1986.

Olivier de Sardan, Jean-Pierre. *Les sociétés Songhay-Zarma*. Paris, 1984.

Olivier de Sardan, J. P. (ed.) *Quand nos pères étaient captifs . . . : récits paysans du Niger*. Paris, 1976.

Oloukpona-Yinnon, Adjai Paulin. *La révolte des esclaves mercenaires: Douala 1893*. Bayreuth, 1987.

Oluleye, James J. *Military leadership in Nigeria, 1966–1979*. Ibadan, 1985.

Omissi, David. *The sepoy and the raj: the Indian Army, 1860–1940*. Basingstoke, 1994.

Opland, Jeff. *Xhosa oral poetry: aspects of a black South African tradition*. Cambridge, 1983.

Oppong, Christine (ed.) *Female and male in West Africa*. London, 1983.

Oyelaran, Olasope O., Toyin Falola, Mokwugo Okoye, and Adewale Thompson (eds.) *Obafemi Awolowo: the end of an era?* Ile-Ife, 1988.

Paden, John N. *Ahmadu Bello, Sardauna of Sokoto: values and leadership in Nigeria*. London, 1986.

Page, Melvin E. 'The war of *thangata*: Nyasaland and the East African campaign, 1914–1918,' *JAH*, 19 (1978), 87–100.

Page, Melvin E. (ed.) *Africa and the First World War*. Basingstoke, 1987.

Palmer, H. R. *Sudanese memoirs: being mainly translations of a number of Arabic manuscripts relating to the Central and Western Sudan*. 3 vols in 1, reprinted, London, 1967.

Pankhurst, Richard. *Economic history of Ethiopia, 1800–1935*. Addis Ababa, 1968.

Panzacchi, Cornelia. 'The livelihoods of traditional griots in modern Senegal,' *Africa*, 64 (1994), 190–210.

Parkyns, Mansfield. *Life in Abyssinia*. 2nd edn, reprinted, London, 1966.

Parsons, Timothy H. *The African rank-and-file: social implications of colonial military service in the King's African Rifles, 1902–1964*. Portsmouth, N.H., 1999.

Patterson, J. R. *Kanuri songs*. N.p., n.d.

Patterson, Orlando. *Slavery and social death: a comparative study*. Cambridge, Mass., 1982.

Pearce, Nathaniel. *The life and adventures of Nathaniel Pearce, written by himself*. 2 vols., London, 1831.

Peel, J. D. Y. *Aladura: a religious movement among the Yoruba*. London, 1968.

Peel, J. D. Y. *Ijeshas and Nigerians: the incorporation of a Yoruba kingdom, 1890s–1970s*. Cambridge, 1983.

Peel, J. D. Y. *Religious encounter and the making of the Yoruba*. Bloomington, 2000.

Peires, J. B. *The dead will arise: Nongqawuse and the great Xhosa cattle-killing movement of 1856–7*. Johannesburg, 1989.

Peires, J. B. *The house of Phalo: a history of the Xhosa people in the days of their independence*. Berkeley, 1982.

Peristiany, J. G. (ed.) *Honour and shame: the values of Mediterranean society*. London, 1965.

Peristiany, J. G., and Julian Pitt-Rivers (eds.) *Honor and grace in anthropology*. Cambridge, 1992.

Person, Yves. *Samori: une révolution dyula*. 3 vols., Dakar, 1968–75.

Pinnock, Don, with Dudu Douglas-Hamilton. *Gangs, rituals and rites of passage*. Cape Town, 1997.

Pitt-Rivers, Julian. 'Honor,' in *International encyclopaedia of the social sciences: volume VI*, pp. 503–11. New York, 1968.

Plowden, Walter Chichele. *Travels in Abyssinia and the Galla country*. London, 1868.

Poitou, Danièle. *La délinquance juvénile au Niger*. Niamey, 1978.

Ranger, Terence. *Are we not also men? The Samkange family and African politics in Zimbabwe 1920–64*. London, 1995.

Rathbone, Richard. *Nkrumah and the chiefs: the politics of chieftaincy in Ghana, 1951–60*. Oxford, 2000.

Rattray, R. S. *Ashanti law and constitution*. Oxford, 1929.

Rattray, R. S. *Religion and art in Ashanti*. Oxford, 1927.

Raynaut, Claude. *Structures normatives et relations électives: étude d'une communauté villageoise haoussa*. Paris, 1972.

Reefe, Thomas Q. *The rainbow and the kings: a history of the Luba empire to 1891*. Berkeley, 1981.

Reid, Richard J. *Political power in pre-colonial Buganda: economy, society and warfare in the nineteenth century*. Oxford, 2002.

Renne, Elisha P. 'Changes in adolescent sexuality and the perception of virginity in a southwestern Nigerian village,' *Health Transition Review*, 3 (1993), 121–33.

Reno, William. *Corruption and state politics in Sierra Leone*. Cambridge, 1995.

Richards, Audrey I. *Land, labour and diet in Northern Rhodesia: an economic study of the Bemba tribe*. 2nd edn, London, 1961.

Richards, Paul. *Fighting for the rain forest: war, youth and resources in Sierra Leone*. Oxford, 1996.

Riesman, Paul. *Freedom in Fulani social life: an introspective ethnography*. Trans. M. Fuller, Chicago, 1977.

Roberts, Richard L. *Warriors, merchants, and slaves: the state and the economy in the middle Niger valley, 1700–1914*. Stanford, 1987.

Robertson, Claire C., and Martin A. Klein (eds.) *Women and slavery in Africa*. Madison, 1983.

Rodegem, F. M. (ed.) *Anthologie rundi*. [Paris] 1973.

Romero, Patricia W. (ed.) *Life histories of African women*. London, 1988.

Roscoe, John. *The Baganda: an account of their native customs and beliefs*. 2nd edn, London, 1965.

Ross, Robert. *Cape of torments: slavery and resistance in South Africa*. London, 1983.

Ross, Robert. *Status and respectability in the Cape Colony, 1750–1870: a tragedy of manners*. Cambridge, 1999.

Rotberg, R. I., and A. A. Mazrui (eds.) *Protest and power in black Africa*. New York, 1970.

Roth, Mirjana. '"If you give us rights we will fight": black involvement in the Second World War,' *SAHJ*, 15 (1983), 85–104.

Rowe, John A. 'Eyewitness accounts of Buganda history: the memoirs of Ham Mukasa and his generation,' *Ethnohistory*, 36 (1989), 61–71.

Rowe, J. A. 'Myth, memoir and moral admonition: Luganda historical writing 1893–1969,' *Uganda Journal*, 33, 1 (1969), 17–40, and 33, 2 (1969), 217–19.

Rowe, J. A. 'The purge of Christians at Mwanga's court,' *JAH*, 5 (1964), 55–71.

Rowe, John Allen. 'Revolution in Buganda 1856–1900: part one: the reign of Kabaka Mukabya Mutesa 1856–1884,' PhD thesis, University of Wisconsin, 1966.

Samatar, Said S. *Oral poetry and Somali nationalism: the case of Sayyid Mohammad Abdille Hasan*. Cambridge, 1982.

Sanankoua, Bintou. *Un empire peul au XIXe siècle: le Diina du Maasina*. Paris, 1990.

Sarbah, John Mensah. *Fanti customary laws*. 3rd edn, London, 1968.

Sbacchi, Alberto. *Ethiopia under Mussolini: fascism and the colonial experience*. London, 1985.

Sbacchi, Alberto. *Legacy of bitterness: Ethiopia and Fascist Italy, 1935–41*. Lawrenceville, N.J., 1997.

Schapera, I. *Married life in an African tribe*. London, 1940.

Schapera, I. *Migrant labour and tribal life: a study of conditions in the Bechuanaland Protectorate*. London, 1947.

Schapera, I. (ed.) *Praise-poems of Tswana chiefs*. Oxford, 1965.

Schumacher, Peter (trans.) 'Lebensgeschichte des Grossfürsten Kayijuka und seiner Ahnen seit Sultan Yuhi Mazimpaka, König von Ruanda,' *Mitteilungen der Ausland-Hochschule an der Universität Berlin, dritte Abteilung*, 41 (1938), 103–70.

Scully, Pamela. *Liberating the family? Gender and British slave emancipation in the rural Western Cape, South Africa, 1823–1853*. Portsmouth, N.H., 1997.

Sebudandi, Gaetan, and Pierre-Olivier Richard. *Le drame burundais: hantise du pouvoir ou tentation suicidaire*. Paris, 1996.

Séche, Alphonse. *Les noirs (d'après des documents officiels)*. Paris, 1919.

Seydou, Christiane (ed.) *La geste de Ham-Bodêdio ou Hama le Rouge*. Paris, 1976.

Seydou, Christiane (ed.) *Silâmaka et Poullôri: récit épique peul raconté par Tinguidji*. Paris, 1972.

Shagari, Shehu. *Beckoned to serve: an autobiography*. Ibadan, 2001.

Sharwood Smith, Sir Bryan. *'But always as friends': Northern Nigeria and the Cameroons, 1921–1957*. London, 1969.

Shell, Robert C.-H. *Children of bondage: a social history of the slave society at the Cape of Good Hope, 1652–1838*. Johannesburg, 1994.

Shepherd, Robert H. W. *Lovedale, South Africa: the story of a century, 1841–1941*. Lovedale, n.d.

Shick, Tom W. *Behold the promised land: a history of Afro-American settler society in nineteenth-century Liberia*. Baltimore, 1977.

Silla, Ousmane. 'Persistance des castes dans la société wolof contemporaine,' *BIFAN*, 28B (1966), 731–70.

Sklar, Richard L. *Nigerian political parties: power in an emergent African nation*. Princeton, 1963.

Smaldone, Joseph P. *Warfare in the Sokoto Caliphate: historical and sociological perspectives*. Cambridge, 1977.

Smith, M. F. *Baba of Karo: a woman of the Muslim Hausa*. London, 1954.

Smith, M. G. *The affairs of Daura*. Berkeley, 1978.

Smith, M. G. *Government in Kano, 1350–1950*. Boulder, 1997.

Smith, M. G. 'Historical and cultural conditions of political corruption among the Hausa,' *CSSH*, 6 (1963–4), 164–94.

Soce [Diop], Ousmane. *Karim: roman sénégalais*. 3rd edn, Paris, 1948.

Soga, John Henderson. *The Ama-Xosa: life and customs*. Lovedale [1931?].

South Africa: Truth and Reconciliation Commission. 'Proceedings,' typescript, CUL.

South Africa: Truth and Reconciliation Commission. *Report*. 5 vols., Cape Town, 1998.

Sow, Abdoul Aziz. 'Fulani poetic genres,' *RAL*, 24 (1993), 61–77.

Spaulding, Jay. *The heroic age in Sinnar*. East Lansing, 1985.

Spear, Thomas. 'Early Swahili history reconsidered,' *IJAHS*, 33 (2000), 257–90.

Spencer, Paul. *The Samburu: a study of gerontocracy in a nomadic tribe*. London, 1965.

Spitzer, Leo. *The Creoles of Sierra Leone: responses to colonialism, 1870–1945*. Madison, 1974.

Stafford, W. G. *Native law as practised in Natal*. Johannesburg [c.1935].

Staudinger, Paul. *In the heart of the Hausa states*. Trans. J. Moody, 2 vols., Athens, Ohio, 1990.

Steffanson, Borg G., and Ronald K. Starrett (eds.) *Documents on Ethiopian politics*. 3 vols., Salisbury, N.C., 1976–7.

Stevens, Siaka. *What life has taught me*. Bourne End, 1984.

Stewart, Frank Henderson. *Honor*. Chicago, 1994.

Stichter, Sharon B., and Jane L. Parpart (eds.) *Patriarchy and class: African women in the home and the workforce*. Boulder, 1988.

St. Jorre, John de. *The Nigerian Civil War*. London, 1972.

Stone, R. H. *In Afric's forest and jungle or six years among the Yorubans*. Edinburgh, 1900.

Straker, Gill. *Faces in the revolution: the psychological effects of violence on township youth in South Africa*. Cape Town, 1992.

Summers, Anne, and R. W. Johnson. 'World War I conscription and social change in Guinea,' *JAH*, 19 (1978), 25–38.

Sundkler, Bengt, and Christopher Steed. *A history of the Church in Africa*. Cambridge, 2000.

Swa-Kabamba, Joseph N'Soko. *Le panégyrique mbiimbi: étude d'un genre littéraire poétique oral yaka (République Démocratique du Congo)*. Leiden, 1997.

Swartz, Marc J. *The way the world is: cultural processes and social relations among the Mombasa Swahili*. Berkeley, 1991.

Switzer, Leo. *Power and resistance in an African society: the Ciskei Xhosa and the making of South Africa*. Madison, 1993.

Sylla, Assane. *La philosophie morale des Wolof*. Lille, 1980.

Tahir, Ibrahim A. 'Scholars, sufis, saints and capitalists in Kano, 1904–1974: the pattern of bourgeois revolution in an Islamic society,' PhD thesis, University of Cambridge, 1975.

Tamari, Tal. *Les castes de l'Afrique occidentale: artisans et musiciens endogames*. Nanterre, 1997.

Temple, C. L. *Native races and their rulers: sketches and studies of official life and administrative problems in Nigeria*. 2nd edn, London, 1968.

Terray, Emmanuel. 'Contribution à une étude de l'armée asante,' *CEA*, 16 (1976), 297–356.

Theal, George McCall (ed.) *Records of the Cape Colony*. 36 vols., London, 1897–1905.

Thesiger, Wilfred. *The life of my choice*. London, 1987.

Thom, H. B. (ed.) *Journal of Jan van Riebeeck*. 3 vols., Cape Town, 1952–8.

Thompson, Leonard. *Survival in two worlds: Moshoeshoe of Lesotho, 1786–1870*. Oxford, 1975.

Thornton, John K. *Warfare in Atlantic Africa, 1500–1800*. London, 1999.

Throup, David W., and Charles Hornsby. *Multi-party politics in Kenya: the Kenyatta and Moi states and the triumph of the system in the 1992 election*. Oxford, 1998.

Tibenderana, Peter Kazenga. 'The making and unmaking of the Sultan of Sokoto, Muhammadu Tambari, 1922–31,' *JHSN*, 9, 1 (December 1977), 91–134.

Titley, Brian. *Dark age: the political odyssey of Emperor Bokassa*. [Liverpool], 1997.

Toulabor, Comi M. *Le Togo sous Eyadéma*. Paris, 1986.

Twaddle, Michael. *Kakungulu and the creation of Uganda, 1868–1928*. London, 1993.

Twaddle, Michael. 'The Muslim revolution in Buganda,' *African Affairs*, 71 (1972), 54–72.

Ubah, C. N. *Colonial army and society in Northern Nigeria*. Kaduna, 1998.

Um Nyobe, Ruben. *Le problème national Kamerunais*. Ed. J. A. Mbembe, Paris, 1984.

Usman, Yusufu Bala. *The transformation of Katsina (1400–1883): the emergence and overthrow of the* sarauta *system and the establishment of the emirate*. Zaria, 1981.

Uthman ibn Fudi. *Bayan wujub al-hijra ala 'l-ibad*. Trans. F. H. el Masri, Khartoum, 1978.

Vail, Leroy, and Landeg White. *Power and the praise poem: southern African voices in history*. Charlottesville, 1991.

Vandewalle, F. A. 'Deuxième note au sujet des mutineries au Congo Belge,' *Zaire*, 2 (1948), 903–7.

Vandewalle, F. A. 'Mutineries au Congo Belge,' *Zaire*, 1 (1947), 487–514.

Van Onselen, Charles. *Studies in the social and economic history of the Witwatersrand, 1886–1914*. 2 vols., Harlow, 1982.

Vansina, Jan. *The children of Woot: a history of the Kuba peoples*. Madison, 1978.

Vansina, Jan. *Paths in the rainforests: toward a history of political tradition in equatorial Africa*. London, 1990.

Vansina, Jan. *Le Rwanda ancien: le royaume nyiginya*. Paris, 2001.

Vansina, Jan. *The Tio kingdom of the middle Congo 1880–1892*. London, 1973.

Vansina, J. 'Les valeurs culturelles des Bushong,' *Zaire*, 8 (1954), 899–910.

Vaughan, Olufemi. *Nigerian chiefs: traditional power in modern politics, 1890s–1990s*. Rochester, N.Y., 2000.

Verdier, Raymond (ed.) *La vengeance: études d'ethnologie, d'histoire et de philosophie*. 4 vols., Paris, 1980.

Ver Eecke, Catherine. 'Pulaaku: Adamawa Fulbe identity and its transformations,' PhD thesis, University of Pennsylvania, 1988.

Ver Eecke, Catherine. 'The slave experience in Adamawa: past and present perspectives from Yola (Nigeria),' *CEA*, 34 (1994), 23–53.

Versi, Anver. *Football in Africa*. London, 1986.

Vidal, Claudine. *Sociologie des passions (Rwanda, Côte d'Ivoire)*. Paris, 1991.

Vilakazi, Absolom, with Bongani Mthethwa and Mthembeni Mpanza. *Shembe: the revitalization of African society*. Johannesburg, 1986.

Vincent, Jeanne-Françoise. *Traditions et transition: entretiens avec des femmes Beti du Sud-Cameroun*. Paris, 1976.

Waddell, Hope Masterton. *Twenty-nine years in the West Indies and Central Africa, 1829–1858*. 2nd edn, London, 1970.

Wali, Yusuf. 'The translation of the Nur-al-Albab (of Usuman ibn Fudi),' *Kano Studies*, NS, 2, 1 (1980), 10–36.

Waliggo, John Mary. 'The Catholic Church in the Buddu Province of Buganda, 1879–1925,' PhD thesis, University of Cambridge, 1976.

Walker, Cherryl. *Women and resistance in South Africa*. London, 1982.

Walser, Ferdinand. *Luganda proverbs*. Berlin, 1982.

Walshe, Peter. *The rise of African nationalism in South Africa: the African National Congress 1912–1952*. London, 1970.

Wamitila, Kyallo Wadi. *Archetypal criticism of Kiswahili poetry, with special reference to Fumo Liyongo*. Bayreuth, 2001.

Wane, Yaya. *Les Toucouleurs du Fouta Tooro (Sénégal): stratification sociale et structure familiale*. Dakar, 1969.

Watt, David, Rachel Flanary, and Robin Theobald. 'Democratisation or the democratisation of corruption? The case of Uganda,' *Journal of Commonwealth and Comparative Politics*, 37 (1999), 37–64.

Webb, C. de B., and J. B. Wright (eds.) *The James Stuart Archive of recorded oral evidence relating to the history of the Zulu and neighbouring peoples*. 5 vols., Pietermaritzburg, 1976–2001.

Werbner, Richard, and Terence Ranger (eds.) *Postcolonial identities in Africa*. London, 1996.

West, Michael Oliver. 'African middle-class formation in colonial Zimbabwe, 1890–1965,' PhD thesis, Harvard University, 1990.

Whitaker, C. S., Jr. *The politics of tradition: continuity and change in Northern Nigeria, 1946–1966*. Princeton, 1970.

Wikan, Unni. 'Shame and honour: a contestable pair,' *Man*, NS, 19 (1984), 635–52.

Wilks, Ivor. *Asante in the nineteenth century: the structure and evolution of a political order*. Cambridge, 1975.

Wilks, Ivor. 'The Golden Stool and the Elephant Tail: an essay on wealth in Asante,' *Research in Economic Anthropology*, 2 (1979), 1–36.

Williams, Donovan (ed.) *The journal and selected writings of the Reverend Tiyo Soga*. Cape Town, 1983.

Wilson, Godfrey. *An essay on the economics of detribalization in Northern Rhodesia*. 2 parts, Livingstone, 1941–2.

Wilson, Monica. *For men and elders: change in the relations of generations and of men and women among the Nyakyusa-Ngonde people 1875–1971*. London, 1977.

Wilson, Monica, Selma Kaplan, Theresa Maki, and Edith M. Walton. *Keiskammahoek rural survey: volume III: social structure*. Pietermaritzburg, 1952.

Worden, Nigel. *Slavery in Dutch South Africa*. Cambridge, 1985.

Worden, Nigel, and Clifton Crais (eds.) *Breaking the chains: slavery and its legacy in the nineteenth-century Cape Colony*. Johannesburg, 1994.

Wright, Michael. *Buganda in the heroic age*. Nairobi, 1971.

Wrigley, Christopher. *Kingship and state: the Buganda dynasty*. Cambridge, 1996.

Wyatt-Brown, Bertram. *The shaping of Southern culture: honor, grace, and war, 1760s–1890s*. Chapel Hill, 2001.

Wylde, Augustus B. *Modern Abyssinia*. London, 1901.

Yakubu, Alhaji Mahmood. *An aristocracy in political crisis: the end of indirect rule and the emergence of party politics in the emirates of Northern Nigeria*. Aldershot, 1996.

Yoder, John C. *The Kanyok of Zaire: an institutional and ideological history to 1895*. Cambridge, 1992.

Zachernuk, Philip S. *Colonial subjects: an African intelligentsia and Atlantic ideas*. Charlottesville, 2000.

Zartman, I. William (ed.) *Collapsed states: the disintegration and restoration of legitimate authority*. Boulder, 1995.

Zewde, Bahru. *Pioneers of change in Ethiopia: the reformist intellectuals of the early twentieth century*. Oxford, 2002.

Zimbe, B. Musoke. 'Buganda and the King.' Typescript translation by F. Kamoga of *Buganda ne Kabaka* (Mengo, 1939): copy in CUL.

Index

Abacha, S., 351
Abbas, emir, 208, 209, 216
Abebe Aregay, 200–201
Abeokuta, 74, 75, 76, 80, 81, 93, 131, 255
Abidjan, 300
Abiola, M., 331, 337
Aborigines Rights Protection Society, 260
Abrahams, P., 286, 297
Abubakar Tafawa Balewa, 215, 313–316, 343
Accra, 214
Achimota, 163, 248
Acholi, 233
Achuzia, J., 348
Action Group, 316, 340, 342
Adal, 54
Adal Bezzabbih, 198
Adamawa, 42, 45, 135, 355
Addis Ababa, 358, 361
Adekunle, B., 348
Adwa, Battle of, 196, 198
Afäwärq Gäbra Iyyäsus, 258–260
Afonso I of Kongo, 97
Africa, North, 2–3
African National Congress (of South Africa), 251, 260, 307, 313, 322
Afrikaners, 147, 149, 150, 327
Agyeman Kofi, 89

Ahmadu Bello, 313–314, 331, 346
AIDS, 4, 7, 329–330, 357, 360–366, 369, plate 8
Aijenku, 76
Akure, Belo, 238
alamari, 49
Alanamu, 207
Ali Abu Huneik, 30
Alula, Ras, 60
Amadou Bamba, 225
Amadu Lobbo, 35–37
Amalaita, 302, 304
Amda Siyon, 54–55, 59, 66, 197
Amin, I., 334, 336, 346, 351
ancestry, *see* genealogy
Angola, 322, 329, 356, 359
Anirare, D., 249
Ankole, *see* Nkore
Anoba, 76
Areya, Ras, 63
Arhin, K., 91
Asamoa Nkwanta, 87
Asante, 83–91, 97, 127, 134, 169, 183, 184, 194–196, 205–207, 214, 215, 218, 220, 223, 263, 271, 274, 307, 319, 337–338, 368
Asante Agyei, 89
Asante Kotoko, 300
Atangana, C., 103, 221, 223
Attahiru, Caliph, 185–186

393